Economics of
Labor Relations

Economics of
Labor Relations

GORDON F. BLOOM, Ph.D., LL.B.
Senior Lecturer, Sloan School of Management
Massachusetts Institute of Technology

HERBERT R. NORTHRUP, Ph.D.
Professor of Industry and
Chairman, Labor Relations Council
Wharton School of Finance and Commerce
University of Pennsylvania

1973   Seventh Edition
RICHARD D. IRWIN, INC.
Homewood, Illinois 60430
IRWIN-DORSEY LIMITED, Georgetown, Ontario

Seventh Edition

First printing, March 1973

ISBN 0–256–01388–8

Library of Congress Catalog Card No. 72–83993

Printed in the United States of America

SUMNER H. SLICHTER (1892–1959)
Teacher and Inspiring Friend

PREFACE

Labor relations and economics in the 1970s have been dominated by the interrelated key issues of unemployment, poverty, race relations, inflation, environmental matters, and public employee bargaining. These issues are not only integrated into each chapter of our completely rewritten Seventh Edition, but in addition special chapters are devoted to unemployment, civil rights legislation, the impact of union policies on inflation, and for the first time, manpower planning and collective bargaining in the public sector.

Because a complete revision was undertaken, current labor problems have been given great emphasis: wage controls and the Pay Board, early retirement, union policies in regard to black workers, and the latest developments in wage theory are among the many issues discussed in detail. All materials dealing with labor relations, race relations in industry, inflation and wage controls, labor force matters, and all figures, tables, and suggested readings have been brought up to date. In addition, at the suggestion of many kind adopters of the book and several reviewers, the writing has been tightened and the pages considerably reduced. In short, the authors have striven to make the Seventh Edition as new and fresh as the latest issue of the morning newspaper.

A feature of this Seventh Edition is the inclusion of mathematical appendixes in several chapters of Parts IV and V. The mathematical rendering of the relevant economic theory is not essential for understanding any aspect of the text, but will be of assistance to some teachers and to more advanced students, or to those desirous of probing deeply into the theory underlying the discussion of labor relations theory and practice. The authors are grateful to Messrs. Marti G. Subrohmanyam, Lester Rubin, and Stephen Schneider for assistance in the development of the appendixes in Part IV, and to Drs. Martin Kosters and Finis Welch and to the editors of the *American Economic Review* for permission to reproduce in Part V the contributions of these authors.

As in earlier editions, a major objective has been the integration of economic facts and economic analysis so that the student may acquire not only an awareness of labor problems, but also an understanding of conflicting views concerning their causes and possible solutions. Wherever possible the authors have incorporated in their discussion the latest views and approaches to various labor problems which have appeared in recent articles in professional journals. Considerable effort has been made to spell out clearly economic principles and the techniques of economic analysis.

The authors have not attempted to write a text with a general theme or a particular slant. Their main interest has been in making available to the teacher and student a text which discusses the field of labor problems in a clear, comprehensive, and interesting fashion. The material contained in the text has been organized in a manner which it was felt would make the study of labor problems both enjoyable and understandable to the beginning student. Part I, which contains a general introduction to the field of labor problems, is intended to orient the student to the subject matter. Parts II and III give a picture of labor history, union structure and government, and collective bargaining techniques and issues. Part IV uses the tools of economic analysis to illuminate a variety of labor problems. Part V discusses the economics of minimum wages and shorter hours, including the four-day week, and government programs to protect employees against the insecurities of old age, premature death, unemployment, accident, and illness. The collective bargaining impact of the Occupational Safety and Health Act of 1970 is also considered herein.

Part VI deals with the increasingly important role of the government in labor relations. As in previous editions, it contains detailed, up-to-date analysis of all major labor laws, including the Taft-Hartley Act and the Landrum-Griffin Act. In addition, Part VI contains the chapters dealing with the federal equal opportunity law and similar state laws, and the chapter on public employee bargaining and legislation. Part VII is devoted to concluding remarks of the authors; and, as has already been indicated, important questions are raised as to the future role of unions in our economy.

As in early editions, many persons have been most helpful. Mr. Ronald M. Cowin did some of the research, as did Miss Elsa Klemp. Mrs. Margaret E. Doyle and Mrs. Veronica M. Kent typed parts of the manuscript, and Mrs. Doyle took care of numerous administrative problems and did some proofreading as well.

Over the years, many professors who have used the book have aided the authors by constructive suggestions. These include Professors Frank T. deVyver, Duke University; Charles Killingsworth, Michigan State University; Emanuel Stein, New York University; John P. Troxell, Stanford University; John B. Ferguson, University of Hawaii; Russell S. Bauder, University of Missouri; Myles Hoffman, Temple University; Darrell S. Spriggs, University of Arkansas; John Burton, University of Chicago; Walter Galenson and George Hildebrand, Cornell University; and Edwin Young, University of Wisconsin; and Dr. Jack Ellenbogen. Many helpful suggestions have been received from colleagues at the Wharton School, including Professors George W. Taylor, William Gomberg, Edward B. Shils, Charles R. Perry, Marten S. Estey, Bernard Anderson, James Jordan, and especially Richard L. Rowan. The staffs of the U.S. Bureau of Labor Statistics, the Wage and Hour and Public Contracts Division, and the Office of Labor Management and Pension Welfare

Reports, all of the Department of Labor; the National Labor Relations Board; the Chamber of Commerce of the United States; and The Conference Board were all most helpful in supplying materials and data.

The authors are grateful to the following organizations, publishers, and journals for permission to quote copyrighted material: The Conference Board, the Chamber of Commerce of the United States, McGraw-Hill Book Co., University of Chicago Press, Brookings Institution, American Economic Association, *Antioch Review, Southern Economic Journal,* Harper and Row, Houghton Mifflin Co., Twentieth Century Fund, W. W. Norton and Company, Inc., *Quarterly Journal of Economics,* The Macmillan Company, *Harvard Business Review,* the Bureau of National Affairs, Inc., *U.S. News and World Report, Industrial and Labor Relations Review, Industrial Relations, Fortune,* Yale University Press, and many others cited in the text.

This book represents a joint undertaking for which joint responsibility is shared. The authors hope that their combination of academic background and practical experience in the field of labor relations has enabled them to introduce into this text a viewpoint and ideas which will make the field of labor as vital and interesting to the student as it always has been to them.

The opinions expressed herein are the responsibilities solely of the authors and are not to be attributed to any company or organization with which either author is now, or has been in the past, associated.

The first six editions of this book were dedicated to the late Sumner H. Slichter, who not only profoundly influenced both authors as well as the whole field of labor economics during our generation, but also gave to the undersigned his wise counsel and friendship. This edition is dedicated to his memory as a person, a teacher, and a friend.

February 1973   GORDON F. BLOOM
                                                             HERBERT R. NORTHRUP

CONTENTS

the Individual Firm: *Significance of Monopolistic Competition. Geometry versus Reality.* The Laws of Production: *The Law of Diminishing Returns. The Law of Scale.* Marginal Productivity Calculations: *Nature of Marginal Productivity Calculations. Value of the Marginal Physical Product of Labor. The Marginal Revenue Product of Labor.* Conditions of Profit Maximization in the Individual Firm: *Determination of Optimum Employment.* Exploitation of Labor: *Rising Supply Curve of Labor. Consequences of Exploitation.* Unions and Marginal Productivity Theory: *Effect of Union Rules.* Demand for Labor in the Economy. Critique of the Marginal Productivity Theory. The Bargaining Theory of Wages. Appendix.

Relative Share in National Income. Effect of Union Organization upon Income Shares. Wage Policy and Productivity Changes. Governmental Wage Stabilization: *World War II Stabilization. Dispute Cases versus Stabilization. Effects of World War II Stabilization.* Wage Stabilization during the Korean War: *The Wage Stabilization Board.* Analysis of Wage Controls of World War II and of the Korean War: *Different Economic and Psychological Conditions. The Changing Character of Labor and Management. "Stabilization" by Big Bargains.* The Nixon Administration Wage and Price Controls: *Organized Labor and Phase II Stabilization. Appraisal of the Phase II Wage Stabilization.* The Labor Dilemma: *The Concept of the Phillips Curve.* Unions and Wage Inflation: *Do Unions Accelerate the Rise in Wage Levels? Negative View. Wage Gains among Unorganized Workers. Do Unions Accelerate the Rise in Wage Levels? Affirmative View. The Effect of Cost-of-Living Provisions in Union Contracts.* Appraisal of the Dilemma. Appendix: Inflation, Unemployment, and the Phillips Curve.

The Extent of Unemployment. Measurement of Unemployment. The Changing Incidence of Unemployment: *Unemployment amid Labor Shortages.* Who Are the Unemployed? *Unskilled Workers. Youth. The Uneducated. Older Workers. Black Workers.* Occupational Characteristics of the Unemployed. The Location of Unemployment: *Unemployment in the Cities.* Poverty and Unemployment: *The Profile of Poverty. Programs to Eliminate Poverty.* Types of Unemployment: *Unemployment from the Worker's Point of View. Economic Classifications of Unemployment.* Cyclical Unemployment: *Characteristics of Cyclical Unemployment.* Secular Trends in Employment. Technological Unemployment: *Possibility of Permanent Technological Unemployment. Technological Progress and Employment Opportunities.* Seasonal Unemployment. Frictional Unemployment: *Demand versus Structural Unemployment.* The Challenge of a High-Employment Economy.

Manpower Planning at the Firm: *The New Emphasis.* Firm Manpower Planning and Unemployment. Federal Manpower Programs: *Manpower Programs: Enrollment and Costs. Scope and Purpose of Manpower Programs. The Parade of Programs. Appraisal of Federal Manpower Programs. The Emerging Role of Federal Manpower Policy. Manpower Policy and Public Employment. The Problem of Aspirations.*

Part V.   MINIMUM WAGES, MAXIMUM HOURS,
AND GOVERNMENTAL SECURITY PROGRAMS

The Federal Fair Labor Standards Act: *Superminimum and Prevailing Wages. State Minimum Wage Laws. Minimum Wages and Employ-*

PART I

Introduction

Chapter 1 THE NATURE OF LABOR PROBLEMS

Unemployment, wage demands, strikes—these are issues of vital concern today. Hard-core unemployment of minority groups in our urban centers poses one of our most explosive current domestic problems. Continuing union wage pressure adds fuel to the mounting forces of inflation in our economy. And strikes—by teachers, municipal employees, and hospital workers, as well as industrial workers—raise perplexing problems of the extent to which a free society should attempt to curtail the individual's right to withdraw his labor from essential occupations. Through radio, television, and the daily newspaper, all of us have become increasingly aware of these and other labor problems which confront our economy. Labor problems have become everyone's problems. They affect every man, woman, and child—every consumer, employer, and employee.

WHO IS LABOR?

The term *labor* is used in many different ways. Sometimes, it is used as synonymous with "the civilian labor force." This group, as we shall see, includes all persons who work for a living. Such a definition, therefore, lumps together in the same category the banker and the ditch-digger, the independent storekeeper and the president of the United States Steel Corporation. This heterogeneous group has one common characteristic, namely, that its members work for a living. In this respect, they are distinct from other groups in the population, such as the housewives, students, pensioners, those too young or too old to work, the incapacitated, and those who, for one reason or another, find it impossible to seek work.

On the other hand, the term *labor* is sometimes used to refer to much more limited groups. For example, when we refer to "skilled labor," we normally mean skilled craftsmen who work for hire for others and who are neither white-collar workers nor professional personnel. This definition excludes both the typist in the office and the doctor in the hospital, although both may work for hire and have highly developed skills. Similarly, if one reads that "labor" opposes the use of the injunction

3

as a strikebreaking weapon, it is likely that the term is intended to apply to a limited group of men and women, skilled and unskilled, white-collar and nonwhite-collar, who either are members of unions or are in groups which lend themselves to union organization. The term *labor*, therefore, may have various meanings and scope, depending upon the context in which it is used.

WHO ARE EMPLOYERS?

In order to understand the nature of the labor market in our economy and the factors which contributed to the development of trade-unions, one must understand who provides the jobs for our labor force. Today, most people work for someone else, whether it be a large farm operator, a giant industrial corporation, a governmental agency, or the corner drugstore. Self-employment has continually declined as a source of work. Today only about 7% of nonagricultural workers are self-employed.[1]

Nonfarm Business

There are about 8 million operating nonfarm businesses in the United States, most of them small proprietorships.[2] If employment in the entire economy were evenly distributed among a great many such small firms, our labor market would be quite different from what it actually is, and it is conceivable that workers would never have felt the need for unions to protect their interests. Averages, however, are deceptive. While small business enterprises are abundant in wholesale and retail trade and in various service occupations, a relatively small number of giant companies employ a substantial part of the entire nonfarm labor force. For example, in 1969 companies employing 100 or more workers accounted for slightly more than 2% of reporting companies under the Social Security Act but employed over 50% of all employees.[3] Manufacturing, in particular, is characterized by bigness, and generally bigness in corporate form. Approximately 3 out of every 4 workers in manufacturing are employed by corporations employing 100 or more persons.[4]

Most employees in nonagricultural business establishments are employed by corporations. This means that they are employed by a legal entity, which in turn is owned by stockholders, frequently numbering in the hundreds of thousands. In 1969, the 100 largest corporations accounted for almost 50% of all corporate assets.[5] Large corporations control the

---

[1] U.S. Bureau of Census, *Statistical Abstract of the United States, 1971*, (92nd ed.; Washington, D.C.: U.S. Government Printing Office, 1971), p. 223, Table 349.

[2] *Ibid.*, p. 459.

[3] *Ibid.*, p. 463, Table 720.

[4] *Ibid.*, p. 698, Table 1143.

[5] *Ibid.*, p. 467, Table 728.

bulk of our wealth and production; they set the tempo for wage adjustments; they establish the general framework of attitudes and policies which condition union-management relations in the country as a whole.

Because of the wide holdings of stock in this country, it might be argued that the ultimate employer of labor in the United States is the stockholding public. They own the assets which provide employment and, moreover, as stockholders they normally have the right to elect directors and so influence corporate policies. As a practical matter, however, corporate decisions tend to be made by a class of persons known as management, who are employed by stockholders to manage the day-to-day business of corporations. Management includes executives such as the officers and directors of corporations, as well as personnel directors, department heads, and foremen. To the average workman in a large corporation, it is this group—and not the remote stockholder-owners—which constitutes the employer. We shall discuss at a later point how the separation of the management function from ownership in American industry and the growth in size of corporations has exercised a profound effect upon the nature of collective bargaining.

It is important to recognize, however, that if we look not simply at the business sector of the economy but at the entire sphere of employment of labor—business, nonprofit institutions, and government—the majority of persons in the labor force do not work for business corporations. They work for government, unincorporated business or nonprofit institutions, or are self-employed. In 1969, less than half the total labor force was employed in the corporate sector.[6] This surprising result reflects the growing importance of government as a major employer of labor in the American economy.

Government

We are accustomed to thinking of the automobile industry, the steel industry, and other durable goods producers as the major source of employment in our economy. Yet today in the United States there are more persons employed by government—federal, state, and local—than by all durable goods manufacturing industries combined. Government employment has more than doubled since the end of World War II from 5,474,000 in 1947 to 12,853,000 in 1971.[7] Although the federal government is the largest single employer in the nation, with a total of 2,665,000 civilian employees in 1971, the bulk of governmental employees are found on the payrolls of state and local governments. In 1971, state and

---

[6] Neil H. Jacoby, "The Myth of the Corporate Economy," *The Conference Board Record* (June 1971), p. 49.

[7] U.S. Department of Labor, *Manpower Report of the President, 1972* (Washington, D.C.: U.S. Government Printing Office, 1972), p. 215.

local governments accounted for 10,188,000 employees.[8] If we add to the foregoing figures about 2.8 million members in the Armed Services and about 6.7 million persons employed in private industry supplying goods and services purchased by various governmental agencies,[9] we find that roughly 3 out of every 10 workers in the nonagricultural sector of the economy owe their jobs either directly or indirectly to governmental action. Since we tend to pride ourselves on the achievements of our private enterprise economy, it is sobering to consider the extent to which government expenditures and government decision making affect the level of employment.

Agriculture

Agriculture is the only major industry in which the majority of workers are self-employed or unpaid members of families. In 1971, hired workers accounted for less than 900,000 out of total farm employment of about 4 million.[10] The number of farms has dropped from over 6 million in 1940 to less than 3 million in 1970,[11] with the decrease concentrated among smaller farm units.

Although the size of the average farm has risen substantially over the years, employment per unit is not following the same trend, primarily because the rapid application of new technology has resulted in spectacular accomplishments in saving of labor in farm work. Employment in large numbers per farm unit seldom occurs except during seasonal harvest periods. Farms having five or more year-round hired men—usually dairies, stock ranches, or poultry farms—are few and exceptional.

THE LABOR FORCE

Suppose we want to find out how many people are in the "labor force" of the United States? How would we go about obtaining this information? Obviously we need two things: first, a definition of what we are seeking, and, second, the statistics to fill our classifications.

Definitions

The classification of the labor force and its components most commonly used is that adopted by the Bureau of Census, which compiles statistics for the U.S. Bureau of Labor Statistics. These definitions have been changed from time to time, but at this writing the following criteria are

---

[8] *Ibid.*

[9] *Ibid.*, p. 284.

[10] *Statistical Abstract, 1971*, p. 232, Table 365.

[11] *Ibid.*, p. 573, Table 924.

applied in classifying persons on the basis of activity during the survey week studied.[12]

Labor Force: The sum of persons in the Armed Forces plus persons in the civilian labor force, whether employed or unemployed.

Civilian Labor Force (limited to noninstitutional population 16 years of age or more).

Employed persons include:

1. All civilians who during the specified week did any work at all as paid employees or in their own business or profession, or on their own farm, or who worked 15 hours or more as unpaid workers on a farm or in a business operated by a member of the family;
2. All those who were not working but who had jobs or businesses from which they were temporarily absent because of illness, bad weather, vacation, or labor-management dispute, or because they were taking time off for personal reasons.

Unemployed persons include those civilians who had no employment during the survey week, were available for work, and:

1. Had engaged in any specific job-seeking activity within the past four weeks, such as registering with employment offices, checking with friends and relatives, meeting with prospective employers, etc.;
2. Were waiting to be called back to a job from which they had been laid off; or
3. Were waiting to report to a new wage or salary job scheduled to start within the following 30 days.

Persons Not in Labor Force: This category includes all persons not classified as employed, unemployed, or in the Armed Forces who are 16 years of age or over and are not inmates of institutions. These persons are further classified as follows:

1. Engaged in own homework;
2. In school;
3. Unable to work because of long-term physical or mental illness;
4. Other—this category includes persons who are retired, voluntarily idle, too old or temporarily unable to work, seasonal workers in off season who are not looking for work, and persons who did not look for work because they believed that no jobs were available in the area, or that no jobs were available for which they could qualify.

Data with respect to employment, unemployment, and labor force participation, as so defined, are obtained through monthly surveys of the population based upon a scientifically selected sample of households designed to represent the civilian noninstitutional population 16 years and over. Each month 47,000 occupied units are designated for interview. Members of households are questioned concerning activity or status during the calendar week Sunday through Saturday which includes

---

[12] For a discussion of current techniques and concepts, see U.S. Department of Labor, Bureau of Labor Statistics, *Employment and Earnings,* Vol. 18 (March 1972), pp. 128–31.

the 12th of the month. This week is known as the "survey week."

The statistics based upon these definitions are widely used and enter into formulation of major governmental policy decisions affecting the economy in general and the labor market in particular. Unfortunately, many people who use these figures are unaware of the restrictive definitions upon which they are based. Much careful thought and research has gone into the establishment of the criteria listed above; yet for certain purposes the definitions may produce misleading results. For example, any study of Negro unemployment must take account of the fact that the Bureau of Census definitions tend to understate the true amount of such unemployment by categorizing persons as being "not in labor force" if they have given up looking for a job because of a belief that they do not have the necessary skills.

Characteristics of the Labor Force

The civilian labor force is not a fixed group. It grows with the long-term growth of the population; it responds to the influence of economic forces; and it changes with the seasons. In July there are usually 3 or 4 million more job seekers than in January, as students look for summer jobs and housewives seek jobs in seasonal farm industries. December is another peak month, for it is the time when many persons take part-time jobs in department stores and other firms which do a heavy Christmas business.

Because of the movement in and out of the labor force during a given year, many more persons are employed (and unemployed) during the course of a year than is indicated by the annual averages in Table 1–1. For example, in 1970, about 94 million persons are estimated to have worked at some time during the year,[13] yet Table 1–1 shows civilian employment averaged only a little more than 79 million. On the other hand, only 52 million actually worked full-time, 50–52 weeks out of the year.[14] A total of 14.6 million persons were unemployed at some time during the year, representing 15.3% of all those who worked or looked for work at some time during the year.[15]

As can be seen from Table 1–1, the overall rate of participation[16] in the civilian labor force appears to have been remarkably stable since 1947. However, this apparent stability masks some striking changes in the participation rates of various component groups within the labor force. For example, from 1947 to 1971, the participation rate for males dropped

---

[13] *Manpower Report, 1972,* Table B–14, p. 210.

[14] *Ibid.*

[15] Anne M. Young and Kopp Michelotti, "Work Experience of the Population in 1970," *Monthly Labor Review,* Vol. 94 (December 1971), p. 35.

[16] The rate of participation is the percentage of persons of working age (16 years and over) in the population actually in the labor force.

TABLE 1-1

Employment Status of the Noninstitutional Population 16 Years and Over: Annual Averages, 1947-71 (numbers in thousands)

Year	Total noninstitutional population	Total labor force, including Armed Forces		Civilian labor force						Not in labor force
		Number	Percent of noninstitutional population	Total	Employed			Unemployed		
					Total	Agriculture	Nonagricultural industries	Number	Percent of labor force	
1947	103,418	60,941	58.9	59,350	57,039	7,891	49,148	2,311	3.9	42,477
1948	104,527	62,080	59.4	60,621	58,344	7,629	50,711	2,276	3.8	42,447
1949	105,611	62,903	59.6	61,286	57,649	7,656	49,990	3,637	5.9	42,708
1950	106,645	63,858	59.9	62,208	58,920	7,160	51,752	3,288	5.3	42,787
1951	107,721	65,117	60.4	62,017	59,962	6,726	53,230	2,055	3.3	42,604
1952	108,823	65,730	60.4	62,138	60,254	6,501	53,748	1,883	3.0	43,093
1953	110,601	66,560	60.2	63,015	61,181	6,261	54,915	1,834	2.9	44,041
1954	111,671	66,993	60.0	63,643	60,110	6,206	53,898	3,532	5.5	44,678
1955	112,732	68,072	60.4	65,023	62,171	6,449	55,718	2,852	4.4	44,660
1956	113,811	69,409	61.0	66,552	63,802	6,283	57,506	2,750	4.1	44,402
1957	115,065	69,729	60.6	66,929	64,071	5,947	58,123	2,859	4.3	45,336
1958	116,363	70,275	60.4	67,639	63,036	5,586	57,450	4,602	6.8	46,088
1959	117,881	70,921	60.2	68,369	64,630	5,565	59,065	3,740	5.5	46,960
1960	119,759	72,142	60.2	69,628	65,778	5,458	60,318	3,852	5.5	47,617
1961	121,343	73,031	60.2	70,459	65,746	5,200	60,546	4,714	6.7	48,312
1962	122,981	73,442	59.7	70,614	66,702	4,944	61,759	3,911	5.5	49,539
1963	125,154	74,571	59.6	71,833	67,762	4,687	63,076	4,070	5.7	50,583
1964	127,224	75,830	59.6	73,091	69,305	4,523	64,782	3,786	5.2	51,394
1965	129,236	77,178	59.7	74,455	71,088	4,361	66,726	3,366	4.5	52,058
1966	131,180	78,893	60.1	75,770	72,895	3,979	68,915	2,875	3.8	52,288
1967	133,319	80,793	60.6	77,347	74,372	3,844	70,527	2,975	3.8	52,527
1968	135,562	82,272	60.7	78,737	75,920	3,817	72,103	2,817	3.6	53,291
1969	137,841	84,239	61.1	80,733	77,902	3,606	74,296	2,831	3.5	53,602
1970	140,182	85,903	61.3	82,715	78,627	3,462	75,165	4,088	4.9	54,280
1971	142,596	86,929	61.0	84,113	79,120	3,387	75,732	4,993	5.9	55,666

Source: U.S. Department of Labor, *Manpower Report of the President, 1972* (Washington, D.C.: U.S. Government Printing Office, 1972), Table A-1, p. 157.

from 86.8% to 80.0%, while the rate for females rose from 31.8% to 43.4%.[17] The decline in the male participation rate has been concentrated among the youngest and oldest members of the labor force. Participation by young men has been reduced largely as a result of the increased term of education and the increase in school attendance. Participation by males over 65 fell precipitously over the past two decades, from 44.9% in 1951 to 25.8% in 1971,[18] reflecting the spread of public and private retirement programs, business policy aimed at compulsory retirement at age 65, and the diminishing importance of agriculture which historically had enabled older men to work, even if part-time, to an older age than industry now permits. For women, the rise in participation rates has been particularly marked among married women. In 1970, one half of all married women had jobs at some time during the year.[19] Changing social attitudes toward work by women and the increased utilization of laborsaving devices in the home have undoubtedly contributed to this change.

The relative stability in the ratio of the labor force to population is all the more remarkable when account is taken of the large number of men

---

[17] *Employment and Earnings,* Table A-2, p. 22.
[18] *Manpower Report, 1972,* Table A-2, p. 158.
[19] Young and Michelotti, "Work Experience," p. 35.

of working age who choose to remain outside the labor force at any given time. For example, in 1971, there were about 5.5 million men between the ages of 18 and 64 who were neither employed nor looking for work.[20] This group of men outside the labor force has increased both in absolute size and as a proportion of the population during the last decade. The proportion of men outside the labor force is greater among nonwhite than white men in all groups except those under age 24.[21]

Why do men and women stay out of the labor force? The reasons are varied: school attendance, physical or mental disability, family obligations, discouragement with job prospects, and other temporary circumstances. Prolonged inability to obtain jobs may cause men and women to drop out of the labor force. It is not surprising, then, that empirical research[22] suggests that the size of the civilian labor force may be inversely related to the level of unemployment. This implies that although some secondary workers enter the labor market when unemployment affects family earnings, more depart or delay their entrance until a more favorable labor market situation develops.

Projected Growth of the Labor Force

The rate of population growth in the United States is slackening; in fact the birthrate has plunged to levels below that registered in the depths of the Great Depression.[23] Despite this fact, the labor force will continue to grow at a rapid pace during the decade of the 1970s, reflecting the high birthrates of the postwar years. The labor force is expected to grow at an annual rate of 1.7% until 1980, and thereafter the rate will slow somewhat to 1.2% per annum.[24] Based upon these rates, the labor force will reach 100 million in 1980 and about 107 million in 1985. This means that there will be an average annual net increase in the labor force during the balance of the decade of 1.5 million persons.[25] About 94% of the increase in the labor force will be attributable to a larger population, with the remaining 6% accounted for by an expected increase in participation rate.[26]

Not only will the labor force be growing rapidly during the seventies,

---

[20] *Manpower Report, 1972*, Table A–7, p. 166.

[21] *Manpower Report, 1967*, pp. 131, 133.

[22] See Herbert S. Parnes, "Labor Force Participation and Labor Mobility," *A Review of Industrial Relations Research* (Madison, Wis.: Industrial Relations Research Association, 1970), Vol. I, pp. 1–33.

[23] The significance of the change in rate of population growth will be more fully discussed in Chapter 9.

[24] Sophia C. Travis, "The U.S. Labor Force: Projections to 1985," *Monthly Labor Review*, Vol. 93 (May 1970), p. 3.

[25] *Ibid.*

[26] U.S. Department of Labor, *The U.S. Economy in 1980* (Bulletin 1673 [Washington, D.C., 1970]), p. 4.

but also its composition will be changing due to the shifting importance of relative age groups in the working population. The teen-age labor force with all its special problems will grow much more slowly in the seventies than previously. Instead of year-to-year increases of about 250,000 in this age group, the average increases yearly will be closer to 100,000.[27] By contrast, the number of persons in the age group 25 to 34 will increase at a dramatic rate, growing by 800,000 a year, compared with an average of 175,000 per year in the previous decade.[28] Another marked change will occur in the age group 45 to 54, where the rapid growth of the previous decade will disappear and the number of workers

FIGURE 1–1

Labor Force Developments

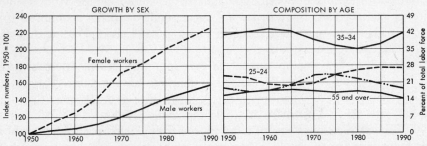

Source: Data, Departments of Commerce; Labor; and Health, Education, and Welfare; chart, *The U.S. Economy in 1990* (New York: The Conference Board, 1972), p. 9.

may even decline slightly in absolute numbers.[29] The changing significance of various age groups in the labor force is shown in Figure 1–1. Let us turn our attention now to some of the major components of the labor force and consider the special problems facing each of them in the years ahead.

Youth

During the past decade, the number of young people in the labor force increased at a spectacular rate. In 1970, there were 56% more workers under the age of 25 than at the beginning of the decade.[30] These were the wartime babies coming to maturity. However, as has already been mentioned, the growth rate for teen-agers as a group will slacken during the seventies. The number of white teen-agers in the labor force is expected

---

[27] Travis, "Labor Force: Projections," p. 3.

[28] *Ibid.*

[29] *Ibid.*

[30] *Manpower Report, 1972*, Table E–5, p. 255.

to rise by only 5% between 1970 and 1980, compared with 46% over the preceding decade. In contrast, a 44% growth in the number of black youth in the labor force is expected from 1970 to 1980, nearly as rapid as the 49% increase which occurred during the 1960s.[31] In view of the fact that black teen-agers in 1971 had an unemployment rate of 31.7%— about double[32] that for white teen-agers—the changing racial composition of the teen-age labor force poses a major challenge to the nation in providing adequate job opportunities for unemployed youth.

The increase in the number of young workers has been occurring despite increased school enrollment which normally would postpone entrance into the labor market. A remarkable phenomenon of the past decade has been the increase in the number of young people who work while attending school. Students in the teen-age labor force more than doubled in number between 1960 and 1970, whereas young workers not in school increased by only 13%[33] As a result, students accounted for 56% of the teen-age labor force in October 1971, compared with 41% in 1960.[34]

High teen-age unemployment is certainly one of the most critical problems which we face in the labor market. Young workers aged 16 to 19 have for years had an unemployment rate 4 or 5 times that for adults aged 25 and over. In 1971, the applicable ratios were 16.9% versus 4%.[35] These high rates are loaded with social dynamite, particularly when account is taken of the fact that many of the young jobless live under substandard conditions in our central city slums. However, in appraising the need for action to solve this problem, it is important to bear in mind that most teen-agers are not looking for full-time employment. In 1971, for example, students primarily interested in part-time jobs accounted for 56% of the teen-age labor force and 54% of the teen-age unemployed.[36] Thus, a particular kind of job must be found to meet the needs of these student-workers, many of whom require the funds from such part-time employment to maintain themselves in school.

Out-of-school youth, including both high school graduates and drop-outs, now constitute less than half of the teen-agers in the labor force. Nevertheless, they numbered over 3 million in 1971, and their unemployment rate was over 17%.[37] As might be expected, job-finding difficulties are compounded for those out-of-school youth who failed to complete high school. The unemployment rate for dropouts was 23% in 1971

---

[31] *Ibid.*, p. 80.

[32] *Ibid.*

[33] *Manpower Report, 1972*, p. 81.

[34] *Ibid.*

[35] *Manpower Report, 1972*, p. 77.

[36] *Ibid.*

[37] *Manpower Report, 1972*, p. 82.

compared with 14% for graduates.[38] In Chapter 15, we shall discuss various programs which seek to improve the school-to-work transition.

The Older Worker

At the other end of the age spectrum is the "older worker," who for labor market purposes is defined as a person 45 years of age or over. It is rather ironic that a society which has achieved such marked success in prolonging the average life-span should relegate workers in their productive middle years to the category of "older workers."

In 1970, there were about 31.5 million older workers in the labor force. The rate of growth of this age group in the labor force will slacken during the seventies, with an expected increase of only 1 million by 1980, compared with an increase of 4 million during the previous decade. The decline in growth of the older worker group is attributable to factors that include a smaller increase in the older population and a continued decline in the labor force participation rates of persons 65 years of age and over.[39]

Our concern with this group of workers rises out of the difficulty they experience in obtaining employment once they lose their current jobs. The rate of joblessness among workers over 45 is actually less than the average rate for the labor force as a whole. However, once unemployment strikes, the older worker tends to remain unemployed longer, because of hiring discrimination by employers, lack of mobility and specialized skills, and inability to adapt to a changing economic environment. In 1970, the average duration of unemployment for men 45 years of age and over was nearly double that of young men under 25 years of age.[40]

Although the U.S. Congress passed the Age Discrimination in Employment Act (ADEA) in 1967[41] for the specific purpose of promoting employment of older workers, discrimination in hiring against older workers is still practiced by many employers. In a survey of employed persons in 1969, over 500,000 workers 45 years of age and older indicated that they had experienced discrimination on the job.[42] However, caution must be exercised in making judgments about discrimination based upon employee opinions. Many of the problems of older workers are attributable to lack of skills required by new technology or decline in requisite physical abilities, but older workers may be reluctant to recognize these realities.

---

[38] *Ibid.*

[39] U.S. Department of Labor, *The Employment Problems of Older Workers* (Bulletin 1721 [Washington, D.C., 1971]), p. 3.

[40] *Ibid.,* p. 7.

[41] Public Law 90–202, effective June 1968. See Chapter 23 for detailed analysis.

[42] *Employment Problems of Older Workers,* p. 21.

Women at Work

In recent years, women have been entering the labor force at a rate more than double that of males. In 1940, one out of four persons in the labor force was a woman. By 1960, the ratio had risen to one out of three.

In 1970, women represented 36% of the labor force,[43] and 42% of all women in the population 16 years and over were in the labor force.[44] The extent to which the growth rate in female participation in the labor force has outstripped that of males is shown in Figure 1–1.

A marked change has occurred in the profile of the typical female worker over the years. In 1920, the typical working girl was 28 years old, single, and most likely worked in a factory. Only one in five of such workers had finished high school. Today the typical female worker is 39 years old and married. She is most likely employed in a clerical, service, or sales job. She has a high school diploma or some college education.[45]

The most dramatic trend in the labor market has been the movement of married women into paid employment. Forty-one percent of all married women, husband present, were in the labor force in March 1970, compared to only 31% 10 years before.[46] Until about 1967, the most rapid increases were taking place among women 45 to 64 years of age. In the last few years, labor force participation rates have been increasing sharply among women 20 to 44, and even among those who are mothers of preschool children.[47]

The movement of women into gainful employment represents a long-run trend of great significance for our economy. This trend has been closely associated with a number of changes, such as the reduction in the size of families, the transfer to the factory of much productive work formerly done in the home, the increased utilization of laborsaving equipment and conveniences in the home, and the increasing desire of women for economic independence. Furthermore, the shift of population from rural areas to towns and cities has placed more women in geographic locations where job opportunities are expanding in manufacturing and in clerical, sales, and service jobs. The opportunities for women to secure work outside the home have also been greatly augmented by the increasing acceptance of women in the professions and in clerical, sales, and similar fields of employment.

Despite the progress which women have made in recent years in gainful employment, they are still faced by major handicaps in the labor market. The range of jobs open to women is still limited; three out of

---

[43] *Statistical Abstract, 1971*, pp. 210, 213.

[44] *Ibid.*, p. 212, Table 331.

[45] *Morgan Guaranty Survey*, November 1970, p. 4.

[46] E. Waldman and A. M. Young, "Marital and Family Characteristics of Workers," *Monthly Labor Review*, Vol 94 (March 1971), pp. 4–6.

[47] Travis, "Labor Force: Projections," p. 11.

every five women workers end up with jobs classified as clerical, operative, or service. About one third of all women workers are found in just seven occupations: secretary, saleswoman, private household worker, elementary schoolteacher, bookkeeper, waitress, and professional nurse. Women still represent only a small proportion of professional jobs. For example, in the United States only 7% of all physicians are women. By contrast about 34% of all physicians are women in Finland, Israel, and the Philippines; 20% in West Germany; and 16% in England.[48]

Although the federal government, 33 states, and the District of Columbia have enacted laws requiring equal pay for equal work, women generally have lower earnings than men, even when employed in comparable occupations. In sales work they earn about two fifths as much as men; in clerical and professional occupations, where the income gap is smallest, they earn about two thirds as much as men.[49] If we lump together all types of jobs, we find that the median salary income for men in 1969 was $8,668. For women, the median income was $5,077, about 57% of that for males. In 1959, women workers earned about 61% of what male workers were being paid.[50] These gross figures suggest that despite efforts of "women's lib" advocates and various antidiscrimination laws, women seem to be falling behind men in levels of annual income earned. However, gross data of this nature can be misleading and fail to reveal changes in the job structure of men and women which can have an obvious effect upon median earnings. We shall examine the nature, extent, and causes of the male-female differential in more detail in Chapter 8.

The disadvantages women experience in the labor market are the result of interrupted job experience, emphasis on traditional occupational choices, limitations on education and training, limited physical strength, and socially accepted stereotypes about "women's jobs" and "men's jobs." These conditions are slow to change, and therefore it is likely to be some time before women actually achieve equality in the labor market.

Part-Time Workers

Part-time employment is generally defined as employment for fewer than 35 hours a week. Part-time employment has been growing at a considerably faster rate than the total volume of employment. Part-time employees represented 6.8% of the total employed labor force in 1956, 11.1% in 1968,[51] and 15% in 1971.[52] By 1980, the proportion is expected to be even larger. A substantial part of the increase in part-time schedules

---

[48] *Morgan Guaranty Survey*, p. 5.

[49] *Manpower Report, 1967*, pp. 134–39.

[50] *Morgan Guaranty Survey*, p. 6.

[51] *U.S. Economy in 1980*, pp. 4–5.

[52] G. P. Green and J. F. Stinson, "Employment and Unemployment in 1971," *Monthly Labor Review*, Vol. 95 (February 1972), p. 21.

in the last two years reflects reduced work schedules as a result of the slackening of business activity. Nevertheless, it is clear that there has been a long-run upward trend in voluntary part-time work in the American economy (see Figure 1–2).

As Figure 1–2 indicates, there are two general categories of part-time employees—those who voluntarily choose to work less than full-time schedules and those who would like full-time work but are on part-time

FIGURE 1–2

Employees on Part-Time Schedules, Voluntary and Involuntary, 1953–71

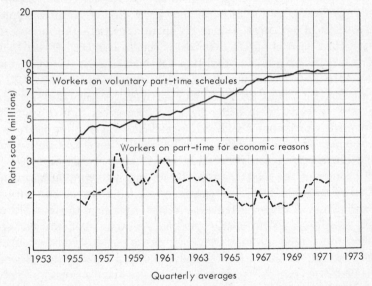

Quarterly averages

Source: U.S. Department of Labor, *Employment and Earnings*, Vol. 18 (March 1972), p. 10.

involuntarily for economic reasons. The former group is by far the most important. In February 1972, there were 3.1 million persons 16 years and over at work on part-time schedules for economic reasons, while 14.7 million were on voluntary part-time.[53] Part-time unemployment of the economic type represents a failure by our economy to utilize its human resources fully; it is a type of hidden unemployment. As can be seen from Figure 1–2, part-time employment of this kind fluctuates with the business cycle, rising in periods of recession and falling when business conditions improve.

Part-time employment—both voluntary and involuntary—is particularly common among the very young (under age 18) and those over the age of 65. Likewise, in almost every age class, women are more likely

---

[53] *Employment and Earnings*, March 1972, Table A–25, p. 40.

to be employed part-time than men. Part-time employment is prevalent among nonwhite workers and, as might be expected, involuntary part-time employment bears heavily upon this group.

The Changing Status of the Negro

Approximately 11% of the civilian labor force is classified as non-white—i.e., Negro, Oriental, or American Indian. Over 90% of this group is Negro. We shall therefore use the terms Negro, or black, and nonwhite interchangeably in the discussion in this text.

In recent years, there has been a gradual breaking down of some of the age-old barriers between white and nonwhite in terms of education, occupation, and social status. Nevertheless, important differences remain in the characteristics of the white and nonwhite components of the labor force. Thus, nonwhite persons go to work at an earlier age and remain in the labor force to a greater extent after 65 years of age; nonwhite women have a greater tendency to remain in the labor force after marriage; and because of high mortality and heavy toll of disability on the job, nonwhite workers have a considerably shorter average working life.

A majority of Negro families still live in the South, but there has been a heavy migration of Negroes to the metropolitan areas of the North. Over three fourths of the Negroes in the North and two thirds of the Negroes in the West reside in central cities. In the South, about 41% of Negroes live in central cities.[54] Negroes are increasing as a percent of the total population in almost all large cities, and today represent 28% of the population of central cities in the very largest metropolitan areas (2 million or more population) compared with only 20% in 1960.[55] This heavy migration of blacks to the central cities has occurred at the same time that many businesses have fled the high taxes, congestion, and other ills of the big city for the country. The geographical location of the supply of labor represented by the Negro population, therefore, poses difficult problems for the economy in bringing jobs and labor supply into balance.

The exodus of blacks from the South to the North is in part a reflection of the movement of black workers from a sharecropping existence on the farm to the industrial life of the big cities. It also represents a movement of people seeking better economic opportunities in an environment where they hoped the barriers of discrimination would be less rigid than in the society they left. The move from agriculture, where underemployment is chronic but total unemployment is comparatively rare, has brought new problems to blacks, for every recession falls with special force upon them. Moreover, the occupational stratification which has developed as a

---

[54] U.S. Department of Labor, *The Social and Economic Status of Negroes in the United States, 1970* (Special Studies, BLS Report No. 394 [Washington, D.C., July 1971]), p. 14.

[55] *Ibid.*, p. 16.

result of their lack of skills, on the one hand, and discriminatory practices by both employers and unions, on the other, has made them particularly vulnerable to unemployment.

Throughout the postwar period, unemployment has consistently fallen most heavily on the Negro worker. Unemployment rates for blacks were about double those for whites throughout the 1960s and were about 80% higher than the rate for whites in 1970.[56] Likewise, the teen-age unemployment rate of 29.1% for black youth is approximately double that for white youth.[57] Although the unemployment rate for black teen-agers is alarming, the problem could probably be dealt with if adequate programs and funding were applied, because the actual numbers of persons involved are within manageable limits. It has been estimated that the total number of male and female black teen-agers unemployed in central cities in 1971 amounted to only about 134,000.[58]

Black members of the labor force not only bear the heaviest burden of unemployment but also when employed their earnings tend to be less than that of whites in the same occupation. This comes about from two circumstances. In the first place, in any particular occupational grouping, Negro workers tend to have the jobs at the bottom of the ladder—the most menial and least skilled. In the second place, even on the same jobs, blacks may earn less because of lesser seniority.

Nevertheless, over the past decade, nonwhite workers have made important strides in entering occupational fields formerly unavailable to them. For example, between 1960 and 1970, the number of Negroes and other minority races employed in white-collar, craftsmen, and operative occupations—the better paying jobs in the occupational structure—increased by about 72%, while the increase among white workers was only 24%.[59] Likewise, nonwhites made major gains in clerical, professional, and technical occupations. Despite such gains, however, in 1970 about two fifths of all male workers of Negro and other minority races remained in service, labor, or farm occupations, a much higher proportion than was true for white males. Table 1–2 shows the high concentration of Negroes and other minority groups in the lower echelons of the job market structure.

Because of the changing structure of the job market, employment in the occupations in which Negroes are now concentrated will be growing more slowly than in other fields. As a consequence, if Negroes are to continue to improve their employment situation in the future, they will have to gain a larger proportion of the jobs in the white-collar and skilled occupations even faster than heretofore.

---

[56] *Social and Economic Status of Negroes*, p. 48.

[57] *Ibid.*, p. 49.

[58] *Manpower Report, 1972*, p. 85.

[59] *Ibid.*, p. 58.

There must be an acceleration in the rate of transfer of Negroes from blue-collar jobs to growth-oriented white-collar occupations if any substantial improvement is to be effected in reducing the already high Negro unemployment rate. The need for opening up additional job opportunities for Negroes is made even more pressing by the fact that the black work force will be growing at a faster rate in the decade of the seventies than the white labor force. Between 1968 and 1980, the black labor force is expected to grow by 33% compared with 21% for white workers. The difference in growth rates is primarily a consequence of a more rapid in-

TABLE 1–2

Percent Distribution of Employment by Occupation and Sex: 1970 (annual averages)

Occupation	Negro and Other Races		White	
	Male	*Female*	*Male*	*Female*
Total, employed (thousands).........	4,803	3,642	44,157	26,025
Percent........................	100	100	100	100
Professional, technical, and managerial.......	13	13	30	20
Clerical and sales.........................	9	23	13	44
Craftsmen and foremen....................	14	1	21	1
Operatives...............................	28	18	19	14
Service workers, excluding household........	13	26	6	15
Private household workers.................	—	18	—	3
Nonfarm laborers.........................	18	1	6	—
Farmers and farm workers.................	6	2	5	2

— Represents zero or rounds to zero.
Source: U.S. Department of Labor, *The Social and Economic Status of Negroes in the United States, 1970* (Special Studies, BLS Report No. 394 [Washington, D.C., July 1971]), p. 60.

crease in the black population of working age, particularly in ages under 35.[60]

The foregoing statistics highlight the problem faced by the black worker in the American economy. Black leaders believe that at the root of such problems is the persistence of discriminatory employment practices in American industry. Beginning with New York and New Jersey in 1945, 34 states have passed laws prohibiting discrimination based on race, religion, or national origin, and a federal law became effective in July 1965. A detailed discussion of these state and federal laws is found in Chapter 24.

The future of the black worker is tied inextricably with the fate of our central cities. We have already mentioned that the black population

---

[60] Travis, "Labor Force: Projections," p. 5.

is tending to concentrate in core city areas. These are also areas where poverty, substandard housing, and unemployment rates two or three times the national rate are commonplace. Negroes represent almost 40% of the persons living in poverty neighborhoods of the nation's largest metropolitan areas, although they constitute only 11% of the population.[61] The jobless rate for men in poverty areas was 2.3 times as high as the comparable rate in other urban areas.[62] An understanding of Negro unemployment can be obtained only after an examination of the problems of poverty, unemployment, and substandard employment which confront the residents of the nation's slum and depressed areas. We shall consider this problem in detail in Chapter 14.

Quality of the Labor Force

A nation's labor force is the source of its strength and wealth. These attributes cannot be measured in terms of numbers alone. More important are the educational attainments and skills of the people who compose the labor force and their adaptability to the needs of an ever-changing technology.

Measured by a number of criteria, the quality of the U.S. labor force will continue to improve during the decade of the seventies. As the median age of the population rises as a result of the decline in the birthrate, the average maturity and experience of the work force should increase. Likewise, with the substantially lessened flow of new job entrants, the problems of training unskilled youth should be somewhat eased. The upgrading of educational attainment of the labor force will continue. By 1980, four out of five young adult workers (25 to 34 years old) will be high school graduates or better and one in five will have completed four years of college or more. By contrast, in the 1968 work force, three out of four workers in this age group were high school graduates and one in six were college graduates.[63]

The increasing quality of the labor force is not, however, an assurance of full employment. The question is: Will the swelling rolls of better educated workers meet the job requirements of the marketplace? Between 1968 and 1980, it is estimated that over 10 million college-educated men and women will enter the labor force.[64] The U.S. Bureau of Labor Statistics has estimated that between 1968 and 1980, over 10 million new college graduates will be needed by industry to take care of occupational growth and rising entry requirements and to replace other workers who retire or die.[65] However, these aggregate figures which match so well

---

[61] P. M. Ryscavage and H. M. Willacy, "Employment of the Nation's Urban Poor," *Monthly Labor Review*, Vol. 91 (August 1968), p. 15.

[62] *Ibid.*, p. 16.

[63] *U.S. Economy in 1980*, p. 30.

[64] *Ibid.*, p. 35.

[65] *Ibid.*

mask the fact that many college graduates will find they have acquired the wrong skills. For example, the dramatic change in birthrates has suddenly produced a downturn in school enrollments, with the result that the teaching profession now has a large surplus of teachers who are unable to find employment. The financial bind in which universities find themselves has closed the market for many Ph.D's. The curtailment of federal defense and aerospace programs has produced a serious unemployment problem for engineers. Thus, a critical problem of matching skills to jobs is developing even among highly trained college graduates.

This matching problem is apparent throughout the labor market regardless of the level of skill involved. The fact is that the American labor force may become too highly educated to cope with the kinds of routine jobs that characterize much of American industry. The U.S. Department of Labor has cautioned:

> The job mix and the education mix are already out of balance. New kinds of jobs will be needed in order to provide employment for the growing number of high school graduates that will fully use their skills and education.[66]

There is some evidence to suggest that, beyond a certain point, increasing educational attainment may be associated with declining, rather than increasing, productivity on the job.[67] Indeed, education may be a factor accounting for dissatisfaction, poor employee morale, absenteeism, and frequent "quickie" strikes. Some observers point to the production problems encountered by General Motors Corporation at its Vega plant as evidence of the basic conflict which is developing in our society as a highly educated, intelligent work force is asked to perform repetitive monotonous job operations.[68]

It is obvious from the foregoing discussion that despite the rising level of educational achievement of the labor force, training and guidance services will be needed more than ever before. The problem of obsolescent skills which used to be associated with textile workers in mill towns is now a pressing problem for engineers in aerospace industries. Indeed, a recent study of 2,500 design and development engineers suggests that the problem of obsolescence is becoming more severe and that there is a trend toward earlier obsolescence of specialized skills.[69]

---

[66] William Deutermann, "Educational Attainment of Workers, March 1969 and 1970," *Monthly Labor Review*, Vol. 93 (October 1970), p. 15.

[67] Ivar Berg, *Education and Jobs: The Great Training Robbery* (New York: Praeger Publishers, Inc., 1970), pp. 85–94.

[68] In the Vega plant, the average age of workers is only 24. Workers are expected to take about 40 seconds to complete a task. Employees have struck against the speed of the line and have demanded the right to have a voice in the scheduling of work. See *New York Times*, January 23, 1972, Sec. 1, p. 1.

[69] Gene W. Dalton and Paul H. Thompson, "Accelerating Obsolescence of Older Engineers," *Harvard Business Review*, Vol. 49 (September–October 1971), pp. 57–67.

OCCUPATION AND SOCIOECONOMIC STATUS IN THE LABOR FORCE

In today's growing and complex society, it is not enough simply to know that there will be 100 million jobs for 100 million workers in 1980. It is important to know where those jobs will be. What skills will be required? What industries and occupations will grow at the most rapid rate? In the following section, we shall examine some of the basic trends which are shaping the nature of our economy and which will determine the job needs of the future.

The Decline in Agricultural Employment

As laborsaving machinery has taken over the backbreaking work which used to be required on the farm, the surplus population from our large farm families has gravitated to the cities to work in industry. Thus, as industrial employment has risen, agricultural employment has fallen drastically. In 1900, about one out of every three persons gainfully employed was engaged in farming or other agricultural pursuit. In 1971, by contrast, agriculture accounted for only 3,387,000 employees out of a total of 79,120,000 employed in both agriculture and nonagricultural industries, or about 4% of employment (see Table 1–1). Agricultural employment has been declining at the rate of about 200,000 workers per year over most of the past decade. The reduction from 1970 to 1971 of only 75,000 employees was one of the smallest in a decade and undoubtedly reflected the lack of job opportunities in nonagricultural industries.

The agricultural labor force is expected to continue to decline at a rate of about 4% per year. Most of the decline in employment is projected to occur among the self-employed and family workers. The number of hired workers will remain relatively stable. As the work force declines further and even more sophisticated machines are used on the farm, workers with training and skills will be much in demand. It is significant to observe, therefore, that in agriculture, as in industry, future developments will place a premium upon workers with proper skills and training.

The Shift from Goods-Producing to Service Industries

A surprising aspect of our machine-oriented industrial economy is the decline in importance of the goods-producing sector as a source of employment opportunities. Table 1–3 shows how employment was divided between the goods-producing and service sectors of the economy in 1947, 1960, and 1970, and also projects the changes expected for 1980. Whereas in 1947 about 42% of workers in nonagricultural industries were employed in the production of goods, by 1970 the proportion had fallen to 33%. Although the percentage of the labor force employed in goods-producing industries will show a further decline during the decade of the seventies, there will be some small growth in actual employment in this sector. However, the bulk of the new job opportunities will fall in the service sector. Figure 1–3 illustrates the diverging employment trends in these two sectors.

By 1980, almost 7 out of every 10 workers in nonagricultural industries—or 68 million persons—are expected to be employed in the service

TABLE 1–3

Percent Distribution of Actual and Projected Employment in Nonagricultural Establishments by Industry Division, 1947, 1960, 1970, and 1980

Industry Division	1947	1960	1970	1980*
Total	100.0	100.0	100.0	100.0
Goods-producing industries	42.1	37.6	33.0	31.3
Manufacturing	35.4	31.0	27.4	25.3
Durable goods	19.1	17.4	15.9	15.0
Nondurable goods	16.3	13.5	11.6	10.3
Mining	2.2	1.3	.9	.6
Construction	4.5	5.3	4.7	5.3
Service-producing industries	57.9	62.4	67.0	68.7
Transportation and other utilities	9.5	7.4	6.4	5.5
Trade	20.4	21.0	21.1	20.4
Finance, insurance, and real estate	4.0	4.9	5.2	4.9
Services and miscellaneous	11.5	13.7	16.5	18.6
Government	12.5	15.4	17.8	19.4
Federal	4.3	4.2	3.8	3.5
State and local	8.2	11.2	13.9	15.9

* Projected.
Source: U.S. Department of Labor, *Manpower Report of the President, 1972* (Washington, D.C.: U.S. Government Printing Office, 1972), Table C–1, p. 215; Table E–11, p. 259.

sector of the economy.[70] The fastest rates of growth will occur in the "government" and "services and miscellaneous" categories. Employment has been growing faster in government than in any other sector of the economy. For example, from 1960 to 1968, employment in government grew at a rate of 4.5% per annum, nearly 2½ times the rate for total employment.[71] During the seventies, employment by the federal government will rise only slightly, but state and local employment will continue to expand rapidly. However, the rate of growth will be somewhat less rapid than during the sixties, primarily because of an easing in the rate of growth for educational services which accounts for roughly half of total employment in state and local governments.[72]

[70] *U.S. Economy in 1980*, p. 17.
[71] *Ibid.*, p. 19.
[72] *Ibid.*

FIGURE 1–3

Employment* trends in goods-producing and services-producing industries, 1947–68 (actual) and 1968–80 (projected for a services economy with 3-percent unemployment)

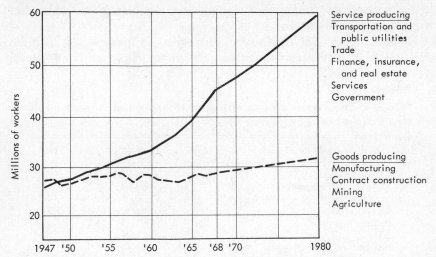

* Wage and salary workers only, except in agriculture, which includes self-employed and unpaid family workers.

Source: U.S. Department of Labor, *The U.S. Economy in 1980: A Summary of BLS Projections* (Washington, D.C.: U.S. Government Printing Office, 1970), Chart 4, p. 18.

Government employment is one area in which the changing composition of labor force will tend to favor union organization. The militancy demonstrated by unions which have become entrenched among key groups of government employees portends major problems of public policy in the years ahead. We shall explore some of these questions in depth in Chapter 22.

Within the services group, which includes personal, business, health and educational services, there will be continued rapid expansion in employment. Growth in business services is expected to be particularly rapid as firms rely increasingly on advertising, accounting, computer, maintenance, and other types of contract service. It is significant to note that while consumer services typically have a high concentration of female employment, these so-called "producer services" rendered to business firms have a greater percentage of male employment and higher average earnings than are shown for the labor force as a whole.[73]

The fastest growing industries during the period to 1980 will include such glamorous areas as office computing and accounting machines; optical, ophthalmic, and photographic equipment; electronic components

---

[73] Harry I. Greenfield, *Manpower and the Growth of Producer Services* (New York: Columbia University Press, 1966), p. 1.

and accessories; communications; and plastics and synthetic materials.[74] However, although the rate of growth of *output* in these industries will exceed that of industry in general, this does not necessarily imply that these industries will be major sources of job opportunities. Unemployed workers need jobs, not rates of growth, and in terms of total numbers of vacancies created, this group is not very significant in the entire economy. One reason is that rapidly growing industries frequently exhibit a high level of productivity improvement and this tends to limit employment opportunities.[75]

Despite the changing job structure in the decade ahead, manufacturing will account for about the same proportion of overall employment in 1980 as it did in 1950. However, as has already been indicated in Figure 1–3, significant growth in employment opportunities will occur in the service-producing industries listed in the figure. These industries, by and large, represent areas which in the past have been characterized by rather low levels or productivity change. The significance of this shift in structure of employment will be discussed in Chapter 13.

The Growth in White-Collar Employment

A characteristic trend in the development of American industry has been the shift in employment toward white-collar occupations, such as professional, managerial, clerical, and sales work, and away from the blue-collar occupations of craftsmen, operatives, and laborers. This change in the nature of the occupational content of jobs has been associated with the shift from goods-producing to service-producing industries and with the rapid growth of employment in the governmental sector of the economy, which creates jobs primarily for white-collar workers.

This trend toward more white-collar employment has been evident in our economy since the turn of the century and is part of the normal evolution of economic development which shifts labor resources from agriculture to manufacturing and then to services. The increasing importance of white-collar jobs is not, however, just another manifestation of the shift from goods-producing to service industries; for even within manufacturing industry itself, nonproduction white-collar employment has grown faster than production employment.

By the middle of the 1950s, white-collar workers began to outnumber blue-collar workers; by 1980, more workers will be in white-collar jobs than in the blue-collar and service groups combined.[76] White-collar jobs

---

[74] U.S. Department of Labor, *Patterns of U.S. Economic Growth* (Bulletin 1672 [Washington D.C.: U.S. Government Printing Office, 1970]), p. 33.

[75] U.S. Department of Labor, Bureau of Labor Statistics, *Productivity and the Economy* (Bulletin 1710 [Washington, D.C.: U.S. Government Printing Office, 1971]), p. 34.

[76] *U.S. Economy in 1980*, p. 34.

TABLE 1–4

Employment by Occupation Group, 1960, 1970, and Projected 1980 Requirements (numbers in thousands)

Occupation group	Actual				Projected 1980 [1] requirements		Number change		Annual rate of change	
	1960		1970							
	Number	Percent distribution	Number	Percent distribution	Number	Percent distribution	1960–70	1970–80	1960–70	1970–80
Total employment [2]	65,778	100.0	78,627	100.0	95,100	100.0	12,849	16,473	1.8	1.9
Professional and technical workers	7,469	11.4	11,140	14.2	15,500	16.3	3,671	4,360	4.1	3.4
Managers, officials, and proprietors	7,067	10.7	8,289	10.5	9,500	10.0	1,222	1,211	1.6	1.4
Clerical workers	9,762	14.8	13,714	17.4	17,300	18.2	3,952	3,586	3.5	2.4
Sales workers	4,224	6.4	4,854	6.2	6,000	6.3	630	1,146	1.4	2.1
Craftsmen and foremen	8,554	13.0	10,158	12.9	12,200	12.8	1,604	2,042	1.7	1.8
Operatives	11,950	18.2	13,909	17.7	15,400	16.2	1,959	1,491	1.5	1.0
Service workers	8,023	12.2	9,712	12.4	13,100	13.8	1,689	3,388	1.9	3.0
Nonfarm laborers	3,553	5.4	3,724	4.7	3,500	3.7	171	−224	.5	−.6
Farmers and farm laborers	5,176	7.9	3,126	4.0	2,600	2.7	−2,050	−526	−5.2	−1.8

[1] These projections assume 3% unemployment and a services economy in 1980, as described in Department of Labor, Bureau of Labor Statistics, *The U.S. Economy in 1980* (Bulletin 1673 [Washington, D.C., 1970]).

[2] Represents total employment as covered by the Current Population Survey.

Source: U.S. Department of Labor, *Manpower Report of the President, 1972* (Washington, D.C.: U.S. Government Printing Office, 1972), Table E–10; p. 259.

are not necessarily available only for highly educated workers. Actually, the category encompasses a wide range of educational qualifications. Managerial jobs range from presidents of large corporations to operators of hamburger stands; clerical jobs cover both executive secretaries and file clerks; sales work includes peddlers as well as stockbrokers.

Table 1–4 indicates projected changes between 1970 and 1980 in various occupational groupings. As can be seen, the most significant increase, will occur in the category of professional and technical workers. The change which has developed in this occupational classification mirrors the spectacular transformation which has occurred over the years in the labor market. In 1947, the proportion of the labor force in the skilled crafts was double that of professional and technical personnel. By 1975, professional and technical personnel will have surpassed skilled craftsmen in numerical representation in the labor force.[77] Whereas in both 1960 and in 1970 operatives were the most numerous occupational members in the labor force, by 1980 they will be surpassed in number by both clerical workers and professional and technical employees (see Table 1–4).

The foregoing statistics make one point abundantly clear: Although technological progress has been changing our economy into a nation of employees, it has not been building a proletariat of production workers bound to the machine. Scientists, supervisors, artists, teachers, professional workers, and other white-collar workers have been increasing at a much

---

[77] Chamber of Commerce of the United States, *The Emerging Labor Force* (Washington, D.C., undated), p. 7.

faster rate than the working population as a whole. The increasing importance of middle-class occupations has tended to strengthen the forces of conservatism and to some extent has made more difficult the task of union organization. White-collar workers often ally themselves with management groups in their thinking on economic matters; by and large, they have looked upon union organization as a blue-collar movement. Unions have found white-collar workers difficult to organize. Union members are a minority of the 19 million clerical and sales workers. Recent successful organizing drives among teachers and other government employees have made some inroads in the white-collar group, but most white-collar workers still remain outside the union fold. Union leaders, faced by the changing composition of the labor force, must find some way of attracting white-collar workers as members.

WHAT IS A LABOR PROBLEM?

We have reviewed briefly the composition, characteristics, and projected growth of the labor force. That term, as most commonly used, refers to the civilian labor force and therefore includes all of the gainfully employed persons in the country, whether they be bank presidents or common laborers. "Labor problems" typically involve only a certain segment of the civilian labor force. A simple illustration will serve to indicate the criterion which separates the group with which we are concerned from other members of the labor force. Consider the case of John Jones, the independent grocer, who owns his own store and is self-employed. His income depends upon the margin between his sales receipts and the cost of his wares, after covering expenses of operation. Suppose competition from other grocers compels him to reduce prices so that, as a consequence, his income is cut in half. John Jones may now complain that his labor is not being adequately compensated; yet ordinarily, this circumstance would not be considered a labor problem.

Now change the facts slightly. John Jones employs 10 clerks in his store. Competition forces him to cut their wages in half. Here, we have a labor problem. What is the essential difference between the two cases? The difference lies in the fact that John Jones is self-employed, while his clerks work for wages and are therefore dependent upon their employer for their livelihood. Labor problems grow out of the economic activity of that part of the working population which offers its services for hire to *others* and receives its compensation in the form of wages or salaries. Because they are dependent upon others to offer them employment, wage and salary earners are subject to the risk of unemployment. Because they are dependent upon employers for their daily income, their interests frequently clash with those of the latter group. The result is strikes, lockouts, slowdowns, and other manifestations of labor strife. Finally, because they have this common bond of dependence upon others for their employment and income, a certain feeling of solidarity tends to exist among members of this group, despite the diversity of their occupations. This sense of a common status has led many of them to join together in unions to present a common front to their employers and to the owners of the means of production.

Organized Labor and Labor Problems

While much of the theoretical discussion in later chapters of this book concerning the labor market, supply and demand, and related considerations is applicable to all persons who work for hire, our major emphasis will be upon organized labor and the problems which arise between unions and management in the collective bargaining process. The reason for this emphasis is clear. While only one out of every four workers is a union member, nevertheless union actions and union policies affect the working of the entire labor market. We have already noted that large corporations control the bulk of our industrial assets and employ the majority of our workers in manufacturing. For the most part, these giants of industry are unionized. As a consequence, agreements reached by management and union representatives in these companies profoundly affect production, income, prices, and employment throughout the economy.

In the manufacturing field, practically all our key industries are strongly unionized. The same is true for the railroads, air transport, and in many parts of the trucking, construction, electric light and power, and paper industries. While the growing importance of white-collar employment and the diminishing importance of production workers in our economy may in the long run weaken the position of organized labor, at the present time and for the foreseeable future organized labor exercises—and will continue to exercise—a major influence on trends in the labor market.

There would undoubtedly be labor problems without unions. For example, we experienced strikes, large wage increases, and a wage-price inflation in 1919 when unions were weak and industry was largely unorganized. But the fact remains that in our economy today the labor problems that make the headlines and require our study are primarily problems in which unions play a key role. We shall, therefore, begin our study of labor problems by reviewing the history and development of organized labor in this country so as to understand better the motivation, objectives, and policies of organized labor.

QUESTIONS FOR DISCUSSION

1. Discuss the various meanings which can be attached to the phrase "labor force." Consider how the following factors might affect the size of the

labor force: war mobilization; massive unemployment; increased social security benefits; elimination of discrimination in employment.

2. How does the changing occupational structure of employment affect the problem of providing jobs for Negroes in our economy?

3. Karl Marx predicted that the growth of capitalism would produce an industrial proletariat, squeeze out the small businessman and shopkeeper, and therefore set the stage for Communist revolution. To what extent has the development of capitalism in the United States differed from this prediction?

SUGGESTIONS FOR FURTHER READING

Economic Report of the President (Annual Reports). Washington, D.C.: U.S. Government Printing Office.

These annual reports constitute an invaluable source of current information on labor, population, business, and other economic trends and statistics.

PARNES, HERBERT S. "Labor Force Participation and Labor Mobility," *A Review of Industrial Relations Research,* Vol. I, pp. 1–33. Madison, Wis.: Industrial Relations Research Association, 1970.

An excellent summary of recent research on the determinants of labor force participation.

U.S. DEPARTMENT OF COMMERCE, BUREAU OF THE CENSUS. *The Social and Economic Status of the Black Population in the United States, 1971.* Current Population Reports, Series P–23, No. 24. Washington, D.C.: U.S. Government Printing Office, 1972.

A compendium of statistical data relating to Negro population distribution, income, unemployment, housing, education, and other significant economic and social conditions. Such reports are issued at regular intervals.

U.S. DEPARTMENT OF LABOR. *Manpower Report of the President* (Annual Reports). Washington, D.C.: U.S. Government Printing Office.

These annual reports contain concise explanations, supported by up-to-date statistics, of changes which have occurred and are occurring in population, labor force, employment, and other variables in the labor market.

PART II

Union History and Government

Chapter 2 HISTORY OF THE AMERICAN LABOR MOVEMENT

Unions today have a profound effect on the American economic system. The allocation of economic resource, the sharing of the product of industry, political attitudes and alignments, employment and unemployment, legal rights and duties, business stability, technical progress and the rate of innovation in industry, and the policies and attitudes of government of all levels—all are influenced by union policies and programs. Despite the failure of union membership growth to keep pace with the growth in the labor force, union membership today remains high (see Figure 2–1), and union power remains strong. Obviously, economic analysis must concern itself with union policy and practice if such analysis is to present a realistic contemporary picture.

THE CONDITIONS OF ORGANIZATION

Despite differences, all labor movements have certain characteristics in common. Labor movements arise initially out of the separation of the worker from his tools. When a man becomes an employee instead of a self-employed person, he loses control over the terms and conditions of his employment. With the development of a factory system of labor and a concentration of ownership employing large numbers of workers, the individual finds his influence over working conditions steadily lessened. Workers tend to show interest in organizing unions when they feel that their immediate opportunities for advancement in the organizational hierarchy to the employer class are limited. The acceptance of unionism by a worker in a society like ours, with its relatively fluid class lines, does not mean that the worker will reject future opportunities to rise above the working group. It merely means that the worker believes that his present economic situation will be best served by union activity.

Workers also join unions to obtain a voice in their wages, hours, and working conditions. Even those satisfied with what they are paid, often join unions in order to participate in the determination of the conditions under which they work.

A fundamental condition for the existence of trade-unionism every-

FIGURE 2–1

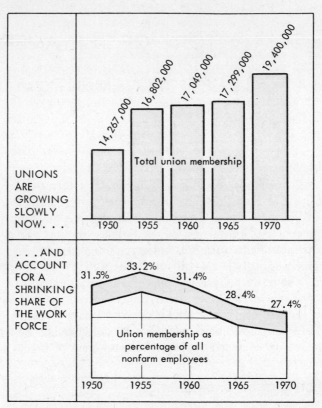

UNIONS
ARE
GROWING
SLOWLY
NOW. . .

Total union membership

14,267,000   16,802,000   17,049,000   17,299,000   19,400,000

1950   1955   1960   1965   1970

. . .AND
ACCOUNT
FOR A
SHRINKING
SHARE OF
THE WORK
FORCE

31.5%   33.2%   31.4%   28.4%   27.4%

Union membership as
percentage of all
nonfarm employees

1950   1955   1960   1965   1970

Source: Data, U.S. Department of Labor; chart copyright © 1972,
U.S. News & World Report, Inc. Reproduced from the issue of February
21, 1972.

where is the existence of freedom of speech, press, and assembly. The
so-called "unions" which operate in dictatorial or totalitarian countries
are, in fact, organs of the state, controlled and operated by the state, and
lacking in power to act except to transmit state orders. We shall be
concerned with unions in the traditional sense: organizations of workers
which function primarily as the agent of employees in collective bargaining with employers or management over the terms and conditions of
employment. Such unions may engage in a variety of supplementary
activities, but their primary interest is in collective bargaining, and they
are free, subject to some legal limitations, to act, unrestricted by state
control or domination.

Once the initial conditions are met, labor organizations emerge
among employees who have bargaining power which the employer must
respect. They are workers possessing a hard-to-replace skill, for example,
toolmakers; or those located at critical spots, for example, teamsters or

longshoremen. They may form a union solely of their own, or they may find it necessary or wise to bring in their less strategically located fellow employees. The skilled are the essentials of unionization.

The speed with which a labor movement organizes is a product of economic and political conditions. American labor unions have made their greatest gains in periods of rising prices and labor shortages (1863–72, 1896–1904, 1917–20, 1941–45, and 1965–68), and in periods of political unrest (1827–36, 1881–86, and 1933–37). When prices are rising and labor is in short demand, union growth occurs as employer resistance to large wage increases is tempered by high profits and difficulties of obtaining sufficient employees. In recent years, expansion of industries with compulsory union agreements has also spurred union growth.

THE AMERICAN ENVIRONMENT

If, however, the conditions of union organization and growth are similar in various lands, the environment is not. Five fundamental characteristics have contributed to the uniqueness of the American scene, and in turn that of American unions.

Class Fluidity

Penniless immigrants arriving in the United States have seen their sons become business executives, labor leaders, statesmen. In America, one is not born in a status. Since class lines are not hard and fast, workers have been able to advance as individuals. American workers have, therefore, been less interested in trade-union organization. Indeed, it was not until the Great Depression of the 1930s that large numbers of workers decided that they needed unions at all.

America's loose class lines have not only hindered union development but have shaped unionism as well. In being interested primarily in improving labor's conditions within the capitalistic system, American unions reflect their members' basic belief that this is still the land of opportunity.

Resources and Land

The rich resources of America have, of course, aided in preventing the rise of hard class barriers by providing the opportunities for advancement. Moreover, the traditional "rugged individualism" of American employers stems from the same sources. In labor relations, employer "individualism" has featured opposition to government or union "interference" in the operation of business and the refusal to recognize unions of employees or collective bargaining until compelled by law.

One of America's great resources has been abundance of land. The westward migrations drained off potential city proletariat. Many workers went West to seek individual fortunes instead of remaining in the East and joining unions to seek group advancement. The movement of industry from urban areas to suburban and rural environments in recent years has further hindered unionization by decentralizing plants and work forces.

Wide Markets

The size of the American market has been an important factor contributing to the growth of American unions. To protect the workers under its jurisdiction, a union cannot raise the price of labor too far beyond that which competitors of the company are paying. A union must organize the length and breadth of the market. Otherwise, nonunion plants, by paying lower wages, may take business away from the union plants and thus imperil the jobs of the union workers. In the 1830s, a union did not have to organize much more than a citywide market. Poor transportation made the city relatively immune from competition of other areas. Today, however, the market is more likely to cover a far greater area, or even be national in scope. A union, therefore, must often become a national union of tremendous size in order to be a successful union in a national market.

The development of the national market not only stimulated national labor organization but paradoxically made that organization more difficult. With a continental market, nonunion competitors can be a thousand miles apart. The resources which American unions require in order to organize an industry are thus very great.

Moreover, the large American market permitted the breaking down of jobs into small specialized units of the mass-production process. Thousands of workers are employed in unskilled or semiskilled jobs, their efforts combining to perform a task done in smaller countries by a single skilled worker. Since the semiskilled and unskilled are easier to replace than the skilled, the bargaining power of labor was correspondingly reduced, and the ability of unions to compel a reluctant management to recognize their existence was considerably lessened.

Heterogeneous Population

Another factor hindering the development of labor organization is the existence of many races and nationalities without common heritage, with rivalries, suspicions, and often without obvious mutuality of interests. Such heterogeneity presents a labor force which is difficult to weld into a labor movement. The policy of many factories in employing a "judicious mixture" of ethnic groups, or the practice of substituting a new wave of immigrants when an older wave showed signs of becoming restive with the status quo, kept racial and ethnic rivalries alive and made the task of the union organizer all the more difficult. Current animosities among white and black workers attest to the continued existence of the racial problem in union organization.

Social and Legal Background

The legal and social system in the United States, itself a result of the environmental factors of the American scene, has strongly conditioned American labor. The strong support of private property among the masses, the high esteem of businessmen in the population as a whole, and the consequent unpopularity among the dominant middle class of trade-unionism, which is often pictured as "antibusiness," have all helped to make the American labor movement difficult to build and to shape its policies as well. In recent years, however, favorable government laws and judicial rulings have aided unions.

THE BEGINNINGS, 1790–1825[1]

Records of local labor unions and of strikes antedate the Revolutionary War, but labor organizations in colonial times were very short-lived. Commencing in the 1790s, however, came the first known unions which survived for a number of years—shoemakers, carpenters, printers, bakers, tailors, longshoremen, and teamsters formed organizations of their crafts and groups. Sometimes organization was defensive against the merchant-capitalist, a new functionary who bought and sold in large quantities over wide areas and therefore broadened the scope of competition. This often either compelled master craftsmen to discontinue independent work and hire out as journeymen or else forced the master to reduce the wages of his journeymen. On other occasions, organization was spurred by the shortage of skilled labor and the desires of craftsmen to take advantage of the demand for their services.

These early unions were composed entirely of skilled or strategically located (teamsters, longshoremen) workers. In fact, throughout history, this group has always been the first to organize. Those who, by reason of skill or strategic location, can exert pressure or inflict a loss by withdrawing their services possess the ability to secure employer recognition long before their less favorably placed fellow workers.

Early unions did not engage in collective bargaining as we know it

[1] Although the authors accept full responsibility for interpretations, they have frankly based the pre-1950 section on secondary sources, including the pioneer works of John R. Commons and his associates, R. F. Hoxie, and Norman J. Ware, but especially on the admirable synthesis of Professor Royal E. Montgomery in H. A. Millis and R. E. Montgomery, *Organized Labor* (New York: McGraw-Hill Book Co., 1945), pp. 1–242. The lack of detailed documentation is for reader convenience and is not intended to understress our great debt to these authors.

today. Customarily, the union "posted its prices," i.e., announced the wages and working conditions for which its members would work. If the employer refused to agree, a strike would ensue, and perhaps a compromise would be worked out. Only slowly did the custom develop of joint employer-employee conferences at which bargaining occurred prior to direct union action. Even in the later part of the 19th century, when collective bargaining as we know it today was well under way, unilateral union posting of wage schedules was not uncommon.

The Conspiracy Doctrine

Early unions were not received with complacency by employers. The latter found a firm ally in the judiciary, which throughout the 19th century stood firmly with the well-to-do class from which its members were recruited. The ancient doctrine of conspiracy was brought out and applied to "labor combinations in restraint of trade." Although "there was nothing unlawful in combination itself, nothing unlawful in an individual's refusal to work, and nothing unlawful in a workman's desire to obtain better standards of employment,"[2] the early judges found it all added up to a conspiracy. Thus, in the famous *Philadelphia Cordwainers* case,[3] the learned judge declared: "A combination of workmen to raise their wages may be considered in a two-fold point of view: one is to benefit themselves . . . the other is to injure those who do not join the [combination]. . . The rule of law condemns both. . . ." Hence the workers were jailed and fined.

The judges were reasoning from their socioeconomic point of view. As time wore on, however, more reasoned justice asserted itself. In 1842, the Massachusetts Supreme Court dealt the criminal conspiracy doctrine a mortal blow by ruling in effect that the legality of a strike depended upon the end sought, and that the mere purpose of requiring all workers to join a union (closed shop) was not per se illegal.[4]

CITYWIDE MOVEMENTS AND POLITICS, 1825–37

Andrew Jackson rode into the presidency on a wave of agrarian and urban revolt against that era's prevailing economic and political inequalities between different classes. Most rankling to the urban wage earner was the length of the workday (sunup to sundown), imprisonment for debt, compulsory militia service from which the rich could buy excuse, absence of mechanics' lien laws to protect workers in case of employer

---

[2] Charles O. Gregory, *Labor and the Law* (2d rev. ed.; New York: W. W. Norton & Co., Inc., 1961), p. 19.

[3] An 1806 case. Cordwainers were shoemakers, originally those who worked on cordovan leather.

[4] *Commonwealth* v. *Hunt*, 4 Metcalf 111 (1842).

bankruptcy, property qualifications for voting, and lack of a free educational system. Workers in New York, Philadelphia, and other seaboard centers attempted to cope with these problems through their unions. The battle was fought both by direct economic action and by political action. The former technique was utilized to improve wages and working conditions, especially by reducing hours to a straight 10 per day.

It was in the political field, however, that the unions of this period made their most spectacular efforts. Workingmen's parties were formed and, particularly in New York and Philadelphia, held the balance of power between the Federalists and the Democrats for several years. Anxious to secure the workers' votes, New York's Tammany Hall adopted the basic workers' program—free public education, universal suffrage, and mechanics' lien laws were adopted or strengthened, and compulsory militia service commenced to disappear. By 1834, the workingmen's parties had folded, but their imprint remained.

The local unions in the cities formed central trades organizations to coordinate their activities, and a National Trades Union was formed in 1834. It lasted less than five years but did successfully agitate for the establishment of the 10-hour day in government employment. The workers' problems were primarily local, however, and they were unwilling to cede authority to a national body. The same factor hindered the estabment of national craft unions.

REFORMISM AND COOPERATION TO NATIONAL ORGANIZATION, 1840–67

The depression which began in 1837 was one of the severest in American history. The ranks of unions thinned out and disappeared in the face of mass unemployment. As new unions were formed, their interests were diverted toward reformist programs which were often more well-meaning than practical. Adherents of cooperation were especially prominent. The thesis that labor's problems can be solved by placing the ownership of the means of production into the hands of the worker and then having the worker take his share in profits has always had a great appeal to reformers of every era. But in the 1840s, as before and later, attempts at cooperation ran into difficulties. Workers found that it takes more than manual work to run a business.

The cooperative often could also not supply better conditions of employment than the capitalist, and all too often the cooperative could not even produce the goods as cheaply. Consequently, it was the practical trade-unionist who won out. He alone could deliver something more substantial than the promised milliennium to cope with the problems of wage earners—problems made more severe by the commencement of the "American Industrial Revolution." For it was about 1840 that the use of anthracite coal stimulated the rise of the steel industry, that railroad development began, and that increased industrialization and urbanization went forward rapidly. This decade also saw rapid increases in population, wealth, and prices, and a consequent increased demarcation between the property holders and the propertyless.

Unionism of this time was confined to the skilled, but it was vigorous and firmly rooted. Beginning in 1852 with the founding of the International Typographical Union,[5] during the following two decades at least a dozen organizations were formed which survive to this day. The Civil War, separating North from South, and dislocating industry and the economy, at first seriously set back the new unions; later, however, by creating a shortage of labor and stimulating industry, it fed union growth. By 1867, the union movement was ready for a serious attempt at national federation. The result was the National Labor Union, founded in that year.

Knowing nothing of the early struggles of labor, and beset by the problems of rapid post–Civil War industrialization, the union founders of the National Labor Union permitted political as well as labor organizations to affiliate. When, moreover, the organization's propaganda led to the adoption of the eight-hour day in federal employment, a näive faith in political action, often since reiterated, developed. Other panaceas or reform objectives, however, failed of attainment. States did not, as hoped, pass eight-hour laws; producer cooperation or worker ownership of industry failed to materialize; and "cheap money" or the Greenback movement brought no success to worker aspirations. Slowly, the unions dropped out, and the National Labor Union grew purely political, until in 1872 it became defunct.

THE KNIGHTS OF LABOR

Even before the National Labor Union was engulfed by politics, seven tailors met in Philadelphia determined to found an organization which would transcend the narrow limits of craft unionism and unite all workers under one banner, regardless of race, sex, nationality, or creed. Thus was created the Noble Order of the Knights of Labor, which as a secret society spread slowly through industralized Pennsylvania.

Gradually, the secrecy became a liability. Secret organizations were in ill-repute in Pennsylvania as a result of the activities of the Molly Maguires, a terroristic group which attempted to achieve social justice by murdering company officials. The Mollies were uncovered by a Pinkerton detective, who managed to become a Molly official and thus achieve fame as the first in a long line of labor spies. Several Molly officials were hanged for murder, but a question remains as to whether the real culprits were punished.

---

[5] Unions are called "international" in the United States because they have locals in Canada.

The Knights' secrecy was formally abolished in 1879, when Terence V. Powderly became the "Grand Master Workman." He insisted that this be done so that the official approval of the Catholic Church could be secured for the new organization. Thereafter the Knights grew rapidly.

The Knights of Labor attempted to weld together all elements of the working classes; and to do so, it permitted craft unions to affiliate directly with its "general assembly" (national organization) and also organized "mixed assemblies," i.e., local organizations composed of a variety of workers organized on either an industrial or a heterogeneous basis.[6] Its program stressed political reform and was closely allied with the agrarian revolt of this period which is known as the "Great Upheaval." T. V. Powderly, for many years leader of the Knights, was a kindly, friendly Irishman who had a keen sense of social justice, a yearning for a better life, a firm belief in the common virtues and the American system of private property. Some of his allies, however, were more radical, and they gave the Knights its tone, as local assemblies were autonomous.

The Knights of Labor reached its apex in 1886 after a strike on the Wabash, Missouri-Kansas-Texas, and Missouri Pacific railroads had forced Jay Gould, the financier who controlled these railroads, to grant recognition. From 100,000 the previous year, the Knights' membership rose to 700,000. Members came in so fast that it was necessary for the central office to suspend organizing to assure that no lawyers, bankers, gamblers, liquor dealers, or Pinkerton detectives—the only barred groups—would join the Knights.

The decline of the Knights was as rapid as its ascent. Losses in a number of strikes, including defeat in a second Missouri Pacific walkout, and the separation of the skilled men into a rival organization, later known as the American Federation of Labor, turned the tide. In 1888, the Knights claimed only 222,000 members; in 1890, 100,000; and in 1893, but 75,000. From then till the official dissolution 20 years later, their central office was engaged primarily in reform propaganda.

The structure and program of the Knights was ill-suited to the job of running a labor organization. Local organizations, known as "assemblies," often took in all comers, regardless of job or place of employment. The assumption was that all workers had the same interests and needs. The leadership of the Knights spent much of its energy, enthusiasm, and financial resources promoting producer cooperation and various monetary proposals such as Greenbackism and Bryan's "free silver" program. Meanwhile, day-to-day needs of wages and working conditions, and especially organization building, were neglected.

The membership of the Knights was very unstable, composed mainly

---

[6] An industrial union includes all workers in a plant, an industry, or industries, regardless of craft or trade, whereas a craft union includes workers of one craft or trade, regardless of the plant or industry in which they are employed. Heterogeneous unions are those which take membership on any basis.

of unskilled workers who flocked in and out so fast that it was once described as a "procession instead of an organization." These workers, being totally inexperienced in unionism, were great strikers but poor union members, disappearing from the organization as soon as a conflict was finished. At first, the skilled craftsmen and their unions were attracted to the Knights; but the ineffectiveness of the Knights in the day-to-day bread-and-butter unionism led the craftsmen to bow out and seek an organization suited to their special needs and ambitions.

THE RISE OF THE AMERICAN FEDERATION OF LABOR

While the Knights of Labor was achieving its great boom, a group of trade-union leaders met in 1881 and formed what was first called the Federation of Organized Trades and Labor Unions and then, after 1886, the American Federation of Labor (AFL). Led by Samuel Gompers and Adolph Strasser of the Cigarmakers' International Union, this group was composed primarily of representatives of the skilled trades who feared that the result of the Knights' activities would be the destruction of trade-unionism as they conceived it. They believed that trade-unionism could best succeed if confined to those who were able to organize themselves—in other words, to skilled or strategically located groups; and that trade-unionism should limit itself to the immediate issues of improving workers' wages and working conditions rather than work for a socialist Utopia or become entangled with other political movements or "uplift" campaigns.

The program of the AFL leaders was thus a pragmatic one, grounded firmly in the principles of American capitalism. They were out to improve the conditions of those whom they represented, and they represented the skilled workers or workers who, because of their strategic location, had bargaining power sufficient to command employer recognition. To the great mass of workers, they said, in effect: "Organizing will help you, but until you are ready for organization, we can best aid you by pulling up our wages and thus indirectly influencing yours to rise also."

Samuel Gompers

Samuel Gompers and his fellow founders of the AFL did not come to their conclusions concerning the type of labor movement that could prosper in America without patient study and experience. Early in his working career, he became acquainted with the German Socialists, mainly refugees from the unsuccessful European revolution of 1848. Through them, he became familiar with the writings of Marx and the other literature of socialism. At the same time, Gompers took an active role in the developing Cigarmakers' Union, and thus he acquired the practical experience of a trade-unionist. Although sympathetic with the aims of socialism, Gompers saw clearly that any organization which made a frontal attack on private property would alienate the dominant American middle classes and would find little support even among employees, who were less class-conscious and more interested in getting ahead as individuals than any of the European Socialist had been able to comprehend.

During the first year of the AFL, growth was slow but steady. As the Knights of Labor declined, the Federation forged ahead. In one year, 1894, the Socialists succeeded in defeating Gompers for the presidency. They were unable, however, to place their man at the helm for more than one year, and Gompers was returned to the office, which he held every year thereafter until he died in 1924. Later the Socialists attempted to form a rival organization known as the Socialist Trade and Labor Alliance. This organization failed, however, to gain a mass following.

In order to insure control of the AFL by national unions, Gompers was careful to reject affiliation offers by political groups. The constitution of the AFL maintained the national unions as autonomous organizations, each with exclusive jurisdictional rights in its territory. An executive committee, composed at various times of 5 to 15 persons, elected from affiliated national unions, plus a full-time president and secretary, governed the Federation between annual conventions. Representation in the AFL conventions was based on dues-paying membership. A combination of a few larger unions could thus control the AFL. The president's office had little authority. By leadership, force of personality, and an astute sense of politics, Gompers gave the AFL presidency vitality and power until his later and less vigorous years.

AFL Philosophy

The American Federation of Labor, as the true counterpart of American capitalism, traditionally opposed government intervention in industrial relations matters. Samuel Gompers and business exponents of laissez-faire were one in their belief that the government should confine its role in labor relations to policing and the maintenance of order and should not interfere in industrial relations matters or in the internal affairs of labor or business. Thus, Gompers opposed government intervention in labor disputes even to the extent of opposing government facilities for mediation and voluntary arbitration,[7] foreseeing that such intervention might lead to compulsory arbitration. Moreover, he wanted no part of government assistance in union organization. He did not think the government should outlaw discrimination against workers because of union

---

[7] Mediation or conciliation is the process whereby a third party attempts to secure settlement of persuasion and compromise. Arbitration involves the use of a third party to decide a dispute.

membership, believing that such government aid would lead to government control.[8]

In social welfare matters, Gompers likewise stood for "voluntarism." No less than businessmen, he was against a government minimum wage for men, and against government unemployment insurance and other forms of government social security. He believed that such welfare programs would weaken democracy by making citizens too dependent upon the state; that a minimum wage could tend to become a maximum and thus limit union action; and that minimum wages, unemployment insurance, and other social security measures could best be provided by the workers themselves through trade-unions. The only exception to this rule was maximum hours and minimum wage legislation for women and children, and for government employees, whom he felt were in need of special government protection.

The Injunction and the "Yellow-Dog" Contract

Of all the forms of government intervention, few have been resented by labor as bitterly as the "injunction." It became prominent in labor disputes in the latter half of the 1800s and was a carry-over from the common law, where it was devised to grant continuing relief where damages would not suffice to remedy a continuing harm. For example, if a farmer who depended upon a brook for water observed his neighbor upstream damming up that brook, he might, under certain conditions, go to court, petition a judge, and, without prior notice to the neighbor, secure a temporary injunction requiring him to cease work on the dam, to maintain the status quo, and to appear in court in a given period, usually a week or 10 days, to show cause why the injunction should not be made permanent. At the hearing, both parties had the right to plead before the judge as to what his course of action should be. The judge would then render an opinion, either dissolving the injunction or making it permanent. In any case, any party who fails to comply with an injunction, whether temporary or permanent, is in contempt of court and subject to penalties which the judge may impose without trial by jury.

Employers soon saw in the injunction an ideal weapon to curb the activities of labor unions. An employer who felt that a strike was impending could scurry to a judge with a complaint and rather easily secure an injunction requiring the union to stay any action on the ground that grave damages would befall the employer. Then the employer could discharge union members and otherwise undermine the organization so that by the time the hearing was held, the question whether the injunction was to be made permanent or to be dissolved was irrelevant.

---

[8] This was no idle fear. Twelve years after the prounion Wagner Act was passed, Congress enacted the Taft-Hartley law, which has definite union control features, and then 12 years later came more union control—the Landrum-Griffin Act.

To supplement the injunction, a legal technique was developed which was soon termed by organized labor, and is now known generally, as the "yellow-dog" contract. This is an agreement between an employer and a worker whereby, as a condition of employment, the worker agrees not to join the union. Unionists maintained that this was not a legal contract, since the worker was coerced into signing it. The courts of New York State upheld this contention by refusing to enforce it, but the federal courts and those in most states maintained that the mere fact of inequality of bargaining power did not necessarily render a contract unenforceable. Thus, if an employer had signed up his workers to yellow-dog contracts, he might get an injunction requiring the union organizer to cease attempting to induce employees to break their legal contracts!

The climax of government by judiciary came when the Supreme Court ruled that the Sherman Antitrust law, enacted in 1890 to curb cases of business combination, was applicable also to labor combinations and that employees who had instituted a nationwide boycott against a hat manufacturer could be successfully sued for the treble damages provided in the law.

This was the background which led to the 40-year AFL campaign to end "government by judiciary" and to "neutralize" the courts. In 1914, when Congress passed the Clayton Act, which Gompers thought removed unions from the jurisdiction of antitrust laws, he believed that he had won his aim; but the courts interpreted this act differently. Not until 1932, with the passage of the Norris–La Guardia Act, did this AFL legislative drive achieve fruition.

Industrial Relations, 1880–1914

The years of the great upheaval were also years which saw the first attempts at modern collective bargaining. National agreements negotiated in the stove, glass, and pottery industries, the beginning of regional collective bargaining in the bituminous coal industry, a large number of agreements in the building and printing trades, all showed promise of a conciliatory tone in industrial relations between labor and management. Under the leadership of John Mitchell, president of the United Mine Workers and one-time Gompers "heir apparent," the anthracite coal industry was organized and a working agreement achieved after two long strikes and federal intervention in the form of a fact-finding commission had forced the "hard-boiled" operators to negotiate.[9]

---

[9] Among them was George M. Baer, president of the Philadelphia and Reading Company, who immortalized himself with this statement: "The rights and interests of the laboring man will be protected and cared for not by labor agitators but by Christian men to whom God in his infinite wisdom has given control of the property interests of the country."

In the 1890s also, industrialists and bankers under the leadership of Mark Hanna, President William McKinley's campaign manager and later a senator from Ohio, joined with Gompers and other AFL leaders in founding the National Civic Federation. This body sought agreement between labor and industry on broad principles, promoted collective bargaining contracts, and maintained voluntary machinery for mediation and arbitration of labor disputes. By promoting collective bargaining, the Civic Federation aided the immediate interests of the AFL. It frowned, however, on aggressive unionism. Since the latter was needed to organize the unorganized, unskilled masses, the Civic Federation's influence was more friendly to established unions than to union growth.

If, however, the AFL had established a beachhead in industry it found no warm welcome in the new mass-production industries. Andrew Carnegie, rising genius of the steel industry, had at one time been anxious to deal with the Amalgamated Association of Iron, Steel and Tin Workers. He reasoned that by encouraging the union, he would encourage stability of prices; and since he figured he could outsell his competitors if he held them to equal costs, he promoted unionism to promote sales.

As Carnegie grew in the industry, however, his love for unionism declined. In 1892, he dealt the Amalgamated Association a terrific blow when he ousted it from his Homestead plant (near Pittsburgh, Pennsylvania) in a bloody strike. The course of unionism in steel from then on was downward; and as steel went, so went unionism in mass production. The United States Steel Corporation, which was formed in 1901, principally by Carnegie and Morgan interests under the latter's domination, refused to recognize the steel union, defeated it in its attempt to force recognition by a strike, and then gradually eliminated it from the plants where it had already been recognized. Mass-production industries which grew up between 1900 and 1933 followed the lead of the steel corporation. Detroit, the automobile capital; Akron, the center of rubber products; the Pittsburgh–Ohio Valley steel center; Chicago, the heart of the meat-packing combines—all kept unionism from their gates except for the briefest of periods during World War I, and other industries followed their lead.

As their spokesman, the antiunion interests found the National Association of Manufacturers an excellent crusader, with its campaign for the "open shop," which, to the NAM, meant the elimination of trade-unionism. Between 1900 and 1914, the American Federation of Labor was on the defensive. Its membership increased to 2 million by 1914, although it failed to keep pace with our growing industrial economy. Even in those industries such as glass, where it had a firm foothold, the AFL unions were confined largely to the skilled employees. Coal mining was one of the few union strongholds among semiskilled and unskilled employees.

The antiunion drive of the NAM and its allies served to give most of the new large corporations formed at the turn of the century the opportunity to utilize labor without restraint from unions. The worker who did not like his treatment, or who rebelled, could look elsewhere for a job; that was his only recourse against the power of the giant corporation. Of course, many employers had good cause to reject unionism around 1900. The history of industrial relations provides many examples of unions during 1880–1900 refusing to sign written agreements, adhering to "quickie" strikes, and placing restrictive rules on expanding industries. Industry, however, had the opportunity to work out an understanding with the AFL, but the "fight unionism" program of the National Association of Manufacturers prevailed over the cooperative program of the National Civic Federation.

The IWW

To American radicals at the turn of the century, the success of the antiunion crusade and the support which it elicited from the general public were evidence that "narrow" dollars-and-cents unionism of the AFL type could not succeed in working out a compromise with the capitalistic system. At the same time, the failure of the AFL to interest itself in the needs of the unskilled workers and the workers in such frontier industries as metal mining and logging and lumber drove these groups to seek a solution of their problems outside the AFL's orbit. The metal miners, who for a time had affiliated with the AFL, took their union, the Western Federation of Miners, out of the AFL in 1897. Lack of success in their own fierce labor struggles and an increased radical bent within the organization and among its leaders led the Western Federation of Miners and its allies from the West to make common cause with the Socialist Trade and Labor Alliance and with various dissident AFL locals. In June 1905, these groups launched the Industrial Workers of the World.

The IWW was the champion of the unskilled, but it never built an organization for them. It would not sign agreements, which it regarded as a form of capitalistic enslavement. The IWW depended on mass action used directly and without restraint. It hid nothing and apologized to no one for its anticapitalistic views. The press built up the "wobblies" as a tremendous organization. Their strength was more carefully appraised by a scholarly observer of the labor movement after he had witnessed their 1913 convention:

The first significant fact revealed by this convention, and by the whole history of the IWW as well, is that this body, which claims as its mission the organization of the whole working class for the overthrow of capitalism, is pathetically weak in effective membership and has failed utterly in its efforts to attach to itself permanently a considerable body of men representative of any section of American workers.[10]

---

[10] R. F. Hoxie, *Trade Unionism in the United States* (New York: D. Appleton-Century Co., 1924), p. 139.

WORLD WAR I TO THE GREAT DEPRESSION

As World War I approached, the Wilson administration sought labor support. Gompers, who at first had demonstrated a vigorous antiwar philosophy, soon was preaching for Wilson preparedness. A threatened strike by the four railroad brotherhoods for an eight-hour day was averted when President Wilson secured the passage of the Adamson Act, guaranteeing the eight-hour day without loss of pay from the previous 10 hours to all operating employees of railroads (hence, not extending the benefits to the still unorganized nonoperating group). As war neared, tripartite, public-labor-industry labor relations boards were established in critical industries, and the AFL was given official recognition as a representative of labor. In return, the Federation put aside voluntarism and cooperated thoroughly with the government.

When war finally broke out, President Wilson called together representatives of labor and industry; and they hammered out an agreement providing, among other things, for the establishment of a tripartite National War Labor Board, an agreement guaranteeing the right of organization, and a freeze on the closed-shop issue which stated that open shops were to remain open and closed shops closed for the duration. Aided by the shortage of labor, the official recognition by government, and a truce with industry, organized labor's ranks shot up to 5.5 million, which proved to be the highest membership figure prior to 1935.

World War I was followed by serious industrial strife. The nation had a coal strike in 1919 and an industrywide steel strike (which was mainly a demand for the end of the 12-hour day in blast furnaces and for recognition of the union). The strike failed after being portrayed as a "red menace." Serious stoppages also occurred in other industries such as meat-packing, with the result that, similar to another postwar year, 1946, the year 1919 was one of the costliest in terms of per capita days lost from work because of strikes.

The year 1919 was also an inflationary year with prices soaring, which, of course, was one of the serious reasons for labor discontent. High prices continued into 1920 and then fell sharply as the country experienced a short but serious depression. Labor's gains of the war evaporated as war industries closed and unemployment set in. Industry took the offensive with the "American plan," a version of the open shop dressed up by the first ingredients of personnel administration.

Company Unions

During the war, American industry had realized the high cost of hit-or-miss personnel policies. Industry became concerned for the first time over high labor turnover, foreman training, scientific salary administration, and other personnel policies which Frederick Taylor had been preaching for 20 years. Moreover, the public was demanding more democracy in industry, and the more forward-looking industrialists saw that they must have something to meet the trade-union challenge besides the famous remark attributed to the chairman of the United States Steel Corporation: "We do not deal with unions as such."

Out of this developed many elaborate schemes of employer representation and company unions. They were deficient in many ways. Certainly, the company union cannot give the worker the bargaining power to stand up and fight for an enlargement of his share, since it ultimately owes its strength to company toleration. Nevertheless, during the 1920s, it was the forward-looking, liberal employer who sponsored the company unions and the employee representation plans. The rest of the employers did not permit even such organization of their workers. Company unions also played a role in training future union leaders, in teaching employees to discuss their rights, to learn about business, and eventually to realize the impotence of company unions as bargaining agents.

The AFL Decays

American trade-unionism was in a state of decadence during the 1920s, despite the fact that 30 years later the AFL was still led by some of the leaders who were prominent during the 1920s. Some of them were old in spirit and unreceptive to new ideas by 1920. As technological and mass-production methods reduced skills and converted jobs into semiskilled operations, the AFL continued to hold on merely to the craft unions and made no serious attempt to organize the great body of workers. Membership slowly fell from the wartime peak to less than 3 million in 1932. The coal miners' union, which had been the largest in the AFL, not only failed to organize southern West Virginia and Kentucky, but it was eliminated from most of the northern mines as well. Even the building-trades unions, which were the bulwark of the AFL, lost their grip on San Francisco and failed to penetrate such new industrial areas as Detroit. Charges of corruption within its leadership, attacks by liberals and left-wing groups, and the effective antiunionism of employers all took their toll.

To succeed Samuel Gompers, who died in 1924, the Federation elected the United Mine Workers' secretary-treasurer, William Green. A compromise candidate, he remained in office till 1952 but never had the stature or power of Gompers.

Labor under the New Deal

The Roosevelt administration, which came to power in 1933, brought gains to labor which were unprecedented in American history. In the wake of such legislation as the National Recovery Act, the National Labor Relations (Wagner) Act, and the amendments to the Railway

Labor Act, trade-union organization increased to an all-time high, which, with the final impetus of war, continued prosperity, and shortage of labor, drove union membership to a figure of 18 million.[11]

Under the first great New Deal law, the National Industrial Recovery Act, business and agriculture were encouraged to plan scarcity in order to raise prices, and labor was given the right to organize without management interference. Labor's right was not enforceable to a very important extent, but energetic unionism took immediate advantage of it. Gambling the last $75,000 in the miners' union treasury, John L. Lewis sent expert organizers throughout the country's coal fields, and within three months he had enrolled 400,000 coal miners, including those in the previously impregnable antiunion strongholds of Kentucky and southern West Virginia. The International Ladies' Garment Workers' Union resurrected and expanded itself, as did the Amalgamated Clothing Workers in the men's clothing industry. Unionism sprang up in the mass-production industries, unaided, unguided, and confused; but if some organizations sprang into action under the magic of NRA, most of the AFL lay quiet and asleep. Not until after considerable prodding did AFL organizers appear on the scene to help unionization in previously unorganized industries. Then, in industries such as rubber and automobiles, where no AFL affiliate had general jurisdiction, the Federation chartered directly AFL-affiliated or "federal" locals.

Without a central organization, however, these new locals were often inept in bargaining. Moreover, craft unions of carpenters, electrical workers, machinists, etc., claimed the right to, and often did, demand that craftsmen in newly organized federal locals be turned over to them. The effect was usually to destroy the federal local and to estrange the transferred craftsmen from the labor movement until organizations suited to their purposes were founded.

In the steel and meat-packing industries, AFL unions did exist. The Amalgamated Association of Iron, Steel and Tin Workers, however, had had an unbroken record of failures since the Homestead strike in 1892, and its leadership had neither the resources nor the capacity to undertake a large-scale organizing drive. Except for a short World War I interval, the Amalgamated Meat Cutters and Butcher Workmen never had penetrated the major meat-packing centers. Until revitalized in the late 1930s, it appeared content to confine its organization to the small packing establishments and to retail butchers.

The Founding of the CIO

The AFL's failure to organize mass-production industries gave impetus to a movement led by John L. Lewis to issue industrial union

---

[11] Discussion of legislation on collective bargaining is reserved for Part VI.

charters to organizations in the mass-production industries. Both Lewis and the craft union adherents realized, of course, that if thousands of new recruits came into the AFL, the power balance within labor's rank would change, and Lewis, with a revitalized miners' union and the recognized champion of the industrial unionists, would be in a strong position. In 1935, for the third time, the craft unionists refused to permit the issuance of industrial union charters. The issue was fought in terms of union structure, but the basic issue was power in the AFL.

Lewis went ahead anyway. The industrial union group, under his leadership and that of David Dubinsky of the Ladies' Garment Workers' Union, Sidney Hillman of Amalgamated Clothing Workers, and including unions in the oil, textile, and metal mines industries, met and formed the Committee for Industrial Organization for the avowed purpose of organizing unorganized workers. The original unions were soon joined by others, such as the rubber, flat glass, automobile, shipbuilding, and electrical appliance workers' unions, who had pleaded in vain with the AFL for industrial union charters. The CIO immediately offered the AFL $500,000 to organize the steel industry. When the latter's Executive Council turned it down, Lewis succeeded in inducing the leadership of the virtually dormant Amalgamated Association of Iron, Steel and Tin Workers to put itself in a receivership to a newly organized Steel Workers Organizing Committee headed by Philip Murray, then vice president of the United Mine Workers.

The AFL viewed these developments with alarm. Its Executive Council ordered the CIO to disband. When the latter refused and Lewis resigned as a vice president of the AFL, the AFL Executive Council suspended the CIO affiliates for "promoting dual unionism." The haste with which the Executive Council acted and the probable lack of constitutionality in its suspension were not seriously challenged by the CIO unions, except the Ladies' Garment Workers' Union.[12] The CIO group had given up the possibility that mass-production industries could be organized within the framework of the AFL. Hence, when the AFL convention met in 1936, the CIO unions were not represented, and the action of the Executive Council was sustained. Two years later the CIO unions were formally expelled.

---

[12] In 1935, the AFL constitution said nothing about Executive Council jurisdiction to suspend an affiliate. Unions could be expelled only by a two-thirds convention vote. If the CIO unions had been represented at the 1936 convention, no two-thirds vote would have been possible. The 1936 convention was reminded by several delegates that the Executive Council was "in such a hurry" to suspend the CIO that the procedure was questionable. Matthew Woll, leading exponent of the Executive Council viewpoint, later defended the suspension as follows: "The fact is that if the Council had not acted there would have been possible disintegration within the American Federation of Labor which would have been disastrous. The Council acted not so much to punish those who had formed the CIO, but rather to prevent disintegration from within." (*The Hat Worker*, June 15, 1939, p. 11.)

The CIO Organizes Steel

The CIO challenge to the antiunion policies of the steel industry was met vigorously by the steel companies. Once more, men were spied on and fired for union activity; the rights of assembly and free speech in company-dominated towns were curtailed; and violence, bloodshed, and death erupted on the industrial scene.

The steel companies also used more refined tactics in trying to overcome the new union threat to their traditional methods of controlling labor relations. Large sums were spent on a nationwide advertising campaign condemning unionism as a threat to the country. And considerable effort and money were expended to form and to maintain company unions.

This time, however, the steel companies met more than their match. The money, effort, and above all, the activities of union organizers who had already penetrated antiunion citadels made the CIO drive as tough and effective as the companies' counter campaigns. The tactics and flair for showmanship demonstrated by Philip Murray and his aides were superior to those put on in any previous organizing campaign.

For example, the CIO realized that the nationwide advertisements sponsored by the companies gave the organizing campaign widespread publicity which it could not otherwise have obtained. Hence, in its rejoinder to the company publicity, which was often so extreme as to alienate the public, the union replied softly. Moreover the CIO allied itself fully with President Roosevelt's 1936 reelection campaign. His overwhelming reelection was followed by a large influx of steelworkers into the CIO.

Toward company unions, Philip Murray, leader of the CIO drive, also adopted a new tactic. Instead of regarding them as archenemies, he saw company unions as a training ground. The CIO people attacked them by trying to get control and succeeded in a large measure. The United States Steel Corporation's money spent for company union agitation frequently served to promote the CIO. By January 1937, it was apparent that the new steel union could close down Carnegie-Illinois, U.S. Steel's biggest subsidiary, if it so chose.

At this point, probably through the friendly offices of President Roosevelt and Senator Joseph Guffey of Pennsylvania, Myron Taylor, chairman of the board of U.S. Steel, and John L. Lewis were brought together. The result was an agreement recognizing the CIO as bargaining agent for its members in all U.S. Steel subsidiaries in the iron and steel industry. The arch-opponent of unionism thus came to an agreement with a new CIO union, a triumph for the latter that insured its existence.

The CIO drive in steel was temporarily slowed down by the defeat of its recognition strikes against several of the major "Little Steel" companies.[13] Four years later, in 1941, however, the steel union came back to win bargaining rights in all these concerns. Today, under the name of the United Steelworkers of America, this union has a membership of over one million and contracts covering nearly all major steel concerns, as well as numerous companies in related industries.

Rubber, Automobiles, and Other CIO Drives

While the steel drive was getting under way, labor erupted in the rubber and automobile industries. These unions were not started from the top down, as in steel, but grew straight from the rank and file. Using a new technique, the "sit-down" strike, workers in the rubber and automobile industries took possession of plants of such giant corporations as Goodyear, Chrysler, and General Motors. This unorthodox and undoubtedly illegal procedure won recognition from these corporations because of general public sympathy with the objective of union recognition. (There never was any attempt by the unionists to seize permanent control of the plants.) The lawlessness involved in the sit-down, however, soon became sufficiently apparent to react against unionism. It was shortly abandoned as an approved tactic, so that by early 1938, sit-downs virtually disappeared from the American scene—until revived as a tactic by college students and some radical groups in the mid-1960s!

In the rubber industry the CIO won bargaining rights at United States Rubber, Firestone, and Goodrich in the 1930s, but the status of the union at Goodyear was not officially recognized until 1941. Today the CIO Rubber Workers' Union is not only dominant in this industry but has spread out in the cork, linoleum, floor tile, and plastic industries as well.

Although sit-down strikes won the CIO recognition at Chrysler and General Motors, Ford did not yield until 1941, when a strike closed down the great plant at River Rouge. Today the Automobile Workers, after expanding into the aerospace and agricultural implement industries, boast a membership approaching 1.5 million.

CIO unions also organized the packinghouses and stockyards in the large centers, as well as the bulk of the electrical manufacturing industry. The old Western Federation of Miners, now known as the International Union of Mine, Mill and Smelter Workers, near extinction in 1935, became a CIO charter member and gained over 20,000 workers 10 years later, principally in the western silver and copper mines and smelters. A new union, the National Maritime Union, started from remnants of the then decadent International Seamen's Union, AFL, brought unionism to the East Coast seamen for the first time since World War I.

---

[13] Bethlehem, Republic, Youngstown, and Inland, all giant corporations.

The revolt of the East Coast seamen also did something else. It forced the AFL to reorganize its seamen's union, in effect dissolving the International Seamen's Union and forming in its stead the Seafarers' International Union. To a lesser degree, the CIO had the same general effect on the AFL as the formation of the National Maritime Union had on the AFL seamen's organization. Forced to meet an energetic rival for the first time since it outdistanced the Knights of Labor (the IWW of pre–World War I was no great threat organizationally), the AFL and its constituent unions got out of their easy chairs and really went to work. Although the CIO surpassed the AFL in membership in 1937 and 1938 when it established a permanent federation, the Congress of Industrial Organizations, it never did after that. For the first time, AFL unions such as the Machinists and the Teamsters really made an effort to take in the thousands of workers within their jurisdictions. By 1953, membership in the AFL included almost half of the 16.9 million unionized. By then the CIO, having lost the Ladies' Garment Workers and the United Mine Workers, and having expelled the Communist-led unions, as will be narrated below, could claim but 4.5 million, with the remaining unionized found in nonaffiliated unions.

Once the CIO was firmly established in the mass-production industries, the AFL leaders made no more pretense of opposition to industrial organization. Indeed, if only as a defensive measure, the AFL accepted industrial organization wherever the alternative might be loss of jurisdiction to the CIO. For example, the Machinists were granted exclusive AFL jurisdiction in aircraft manufacturing to counteract the CIO Automobile Workers' drive in the same industry. But although acceptance of industrial unionism was admittedly eliminated as a basic thorn in the side of labor unity, it was replaced by concurrent jurisdictional claims as both the AFL and the CIO lost little time in chartering rival unions in jurisdictions dominated by affiliates of the other and opening their doors to dissident groups of the other. The CIO chartered groups in such AFL-dominated areas as building construction, railway shop crafts, and pulp and paper. The AFL, in turn, welcomed rump groups from the CIO-dominated automobile and rubber industries, and tried mightily to gain a foothold in the CIO industrial union stronghold of steel. Thus each federation built up vested interests in the form of jobholders dependent upon disunity, and each side encroached upon the jurisdictional claims of the other.

WORLD WAR II TO THE KOREAN WAR

World War II was a period of expanding union membership. Soon after our entrance into the war, a National War Labor Board was established with union and management as well as public representation, the

SAMUEL GOMPERS
President, AFL, 1886–94 and
1895–1924

Photograph by Rogers Studio, Seattle

WILLIAM GREEN
President, AFL, 1924–52

Photograph by Maurice Seymour, Chicago

JOHN L. LEWIS
President, UMW, 1920–60
Chairman and President, CIO,
1935–40

Photograph by Chase-Statler

PHILIP MURRAY
President, CIO, 1940–52

Photograph by Chase, Washington, D.C.

Photograph by Chase, Washington, D.C.

WALTER P. REUTHER
President, UAW, 1946– 70
and CIO, 1952–55

GEORGE MEANY
President, AFL, 1952–55
and AFL–CIO, 1955–

union groups being divided equally between the AFL and the CIO. Despite the strains, the NWLB maintained a high record for peaceful settlement; and apart from numerous "quickie" strikes, labor generally observed its no-strike pledge. The tight labor market and expanding industry aided union membership to grow steadily. But the large number of small stoppages, combined with the few large ones, particularly the miners' strikes under John L. Lewis, saw public opinion turn against unions.

The end of war and the lifting of economic controls resulted in a psychological outburst on many fronts. Labor's response was strikes—1946 was the greatest strike year in American history in terms of man-days lost. Wherever the responsibility may have belonged, the public blamed labor; the result contributed to the congressional election sweep of the Republicans in 1946 and to the passage of the Taft-Hartley Act in the following spring.

The severity of the postwar strike wave came as a surprise to both union and management leaders. During the war a strike was a signal for a flurry of government and management activity to get the men back to work. As a result, wartime strikes were of short duration. When the postwar strike wave started, management did not think that unions could hold out for a long period, and the unions did not think that the strikes would last long. Neither could have been more wrong. The General Motors employees were out on strike for nearly three months in the coldest part of the year, from December 1945 to March 1946; Westinghouse employees stayed out almost four months; strikes in steel, coal, and other industries were also of long duration. Yet the workers did not seem to give serious consideration to returning to work without their union approval. Managements, fortified by the knowledge that economic losses resulting from strikes could be partially made up by offsets on previous years' excess profits taxes, were in no hurry to settle until certain that the government would not continue its short-lived attempt to hold the price line after the war as it had done during the war.

Despite the fact that most large postwar strikes resulted in substantial wage increases for the strikers, unions did not gain in favor or significantly in membership during the period between the end of World War II and the beginning of the Korean War. Much-publicized CIO and AFL drives to organize the South were almost completely unsuccessful. Gains in membership which the CIO and AFL recorded during this period resulted mainly from the expansion of employment in plants already unionized. Price increases which generally followed large wage increases were blamed often by press and public upon the unions. State legislatures, dominated by rural interests, appeared eager to pass legislation designed to curb unions. And the most popular of these laws echoed the NAM's 50-year-old campaign to maintain the "worker's right to work" by outlawing the union shop or any variation thereof which requires union membership as a condition of employment. Such laws now exist in 19 states, all in the South and Midwest.

COMMUNIST UNIONISM

Following the Russian Revolution, the American Communist party was organized in 1919 and secured the adherence of William Z. Foster, a brilliant organizer who had led the great, unsuccessful steel strike in 1919. Foster first attempted to capture the unions in the needle trades, but after almost succeeding, lost out completely to the anti-Communist leadership of David Dubinsky in the Ladies' Garment Workers' Union.

In the 1930s, however, the new CIO was in need of organizers, and John L. Lewis, against the advice of David Dubinsky, hired Communists to fill hundreds of CIO jobs. They organized well, but they also used their positions to seize power and to convent some of the new unions into propaganda transmission agencies for their communist views.

When the Nazi-Soviet Russia pact of 1939 opened the way for the Nazi attack on Poland, the Communists opposed the defense program and fomented strikes to interfere with it. Here again, they found common cause with John L. Lewis. He was a confirmed isolationist, with a gradually growing hatred of President Roosevelt, which began in 1937 when the President declined to support the Little Steel strike as strongly as Lewis wished him to. Lewis thus opposed Roosevelt in 1940 for reasons very different from those of the Communists. Lewis resigned from the presidency of the CIO following the 1940 national elections, and Philip Murray succeeded him.

At first, the Communists obstructed Murray at every turn because he supported the war effort, and agitated for Lewis' return to power. Then, after the German invasion of Russia in 1941, the Communists deserted Lewis. Murray, who in his own words, "was in the estimation of some people in 1940 down in the bottomless pits of hell" because he had supported the defense program, suddenly found that "there came a day, the 23rd of June [when Germany invaded Russia] and I was still supporting my country. I was dragged by these same citizens from the bottomless pits of hell and lifted to a veritable sainthood."[14]

Henceforth, Murray effectively assumed the helm of the CIO and remained also president of its strongest affiliate, the United Steelworkers. Lewis gradually dropped into the background of CIO affairs; and then, in 1943, he took the United Mine Workers out of the organization which it had done so much to create. With Lewis went "District 50," a nationwide branch of the Mine Workers which was set up originally for coke

---

[14] *Steel Labor*, March 1948.

and by-product workers but was later expanded to take in any industrial group it could organize. (In 1968, District 50 was expelled from the UMW for supporting atomic energy power plants as competitors of coal. In 1972, it affiliated with the United Steelworkers.)

Reasonable cooperation between the AFL and the CIO in an all-out war effort featured the war years 1942 to 1946, with the Communists preaching full cooperation with industry and government. Then the left and the right in the CIO grew steadily worse as the right wing backed the Marshall plan for European reconstruction and opposed the third, "Progressive," party of Henry Wallace, while the left opposed the former and promoted the latter. Aided no little by the anti-Communist requirements of the Taft-Hartley Act and the leadership by Walter P. Reuther of the United Automobile Workers, the right wing of the CIO administered a series of drubbings to the Communists.

Reuther ousted the Communists from the automobile union. Joseph Curran, president of the National Maritime Union (CIO), and Michael Quill, president of the Transport Workers' Union (CIO), both at one time fellow travelers of the Communists, broke with the party and wrested control of their unions from it. At the CIO's 1949 convention, the Farm Equipment Workers were expelled for not merging with the UAW. Instead, this union merged with another Communist-led union, the United Electrical, Radio and Machine Workers, which also left and merged. The CIO promptly set up a rival union for the electrical product jurisdiction, the International Union of Electrical, Radio and Machine Workers, which soon established itself as the major union in this jurisdiction. Later the UAW took over the farm equipment group.

At the 1950 convention, action was begun which led to the expulsion of nine other Communist-controlled unions.[15] Since then, only two of these unions have not disbanded or been absorbed by other unions: the United Electrical, Radio and Machine Workers and the International Longshoremen's and Warehousemen's Union. The former has shrunk from 600,000 to 167,000 members; the latter, still under the leadership of Harry Bridges, has a membership of 60,000 as compared with a high of 65,000, and it retains its grip on waterfronts of the West Coast and Hawaii, and on the plantations of Hawaii as well.

Today, the Communists are not a significant factor in the American labor movement. They never had a mass following, but their strength was concentrated in a few unions. They lost out when they chose to subvert trade-union objectives to Communist party policy.

---

[15] Mine, Mill and Smelter Workers; United Office and Professional Workers; United Public Workers; International Fur and Leather Workers; Food, Tobacco and Allied Workers; Marine Cooks' and Stewards' Association; Fishermen's Union; International Longshoremen's and Warehousemen's Union; and American Communications Association.

RELIGIOUS LEADERSHIP IN UNIONS

An important factor in many unions has been the Association of Catholic Trade Unionists, which was founded in 1937. The ACTU has not aimed at building a Catholic trade-union movement, such as exists in many European countries. Rather, it has devoted its energies to the direction and support of workers seeking aid to unseat unsatisfactory leadership or needing help in organization. Thus, ACTU aided the New York City subway workers, a predominantly Catholic group, rid themselves of Communistic leaders and was for many years the only effective opposition to the mobsters who prey on longshoremen.

The Protestant and Jewish churches maintain no group similar to the ACTU, but they have been active in the labor field. A special section of the National Council of Churches of the Protestant churches is devoted to the task of bringing the church and labor together. Labor institutes, interpretation of labor's aims to the churches, and the church's to labor, and various acts of assistance to labor union problems have been among the functions performed by the Protestant group.[16]

Jewish groups were once active in the labor field to an even greater extent than that ACTU, but the Jewish organization, the United Hebrew Trades, was not developed under the leadership of Jewish synagogues. Rather, the UHT served as an organization and communications vehicle between the Jewish immigrants working primarily in the New York City needle trades and the AFL. UHT leadership was an important factor in saving the Ladies' Garment Workers' Union from Communist domination in the 1920's.

When Samuel Gompers assisted in organization of the United Hebrew Trades in 1888, he had serious qualms about the propriety of organizing a separate Jewish group because he did not believe in organizing workers along religious lines. Gompers, however, supported the United Hebrew Trades on the ground that "to organize Hebrew Trade Unions was the first step in getting these immigrants into the American Labor movement." Gompers was proved right in believing that the UHT would draw Jewish immigrants into AFL unions rather than separate them from such unions. The ACTU has apparently had the same impact.

UNITY AND DISUNITY

In November 1952, within two weeks of each other, Philip Murray, president of the CIO, and William Green, president of the AFL, passed

---

[16] See Phillip Taft, "The Association of Catholic Trade Unionists," *Industrial and Labor Relations Review*, Vol. 2 (January 1949), pp. 210–18; Will Herberg, "Jewish Labor Movement in America," *Industrial and Labor Relations Review*, Vol. 5 (July 1952), pp. 501–23, and October 1952, pp. 44–66; and James Meyers, *Do You Know Labor?* (New York: John Day Co., Inc., 1940), chap. xviii, for backgrounds of religious organizations.

away. Walter Reuther, president of the United Automobile Workers, succeeded to Murray's office. George Meany, onetime Plumbers' Union official and later secretary-treasurer of the AFL, succeeded Green. Reuther and Meany immediately initiated action toward achieving a no-raiding pact, which was ratified by the AFL and CIO conventions. In February 1955, Reuther and Meany negotiated an agreement which brought the CIO back into the AFL fold. By the end of 1955, both AFL and CIO conventions had ratified the pact. A new organization—known as the American Federation of Labor and Congress of Industrial Organizations—was born, with George Meany as its head.

The merger overcame two pillars of the AFL foundation which heretofore had been too great a stumbling block—the principle of exclusive jurisdiction and the principle of the autonomous national union.

The doctrine of exclusive jurisdiction provided that each affiliated national union should have a clear and specified job territory and boundary ordinarily defined in terms of work operations, crafts, trades, occupations, or industrial grouping of jobs, and occasionally defined in terms of geography.[17] Under this doctrine, no two unions were supposed to have jurisdiction over the same work operations or area. As a corollary, the AFL, by determining union jurisdictions, also determined the union which the individual employee should join. Of course, since the passage of the National Labor Relations Act (now known as the Taft-Hartley Act) in 1935, workers have designated by election the union that they desire to represent them. Since workers may not follow the dictates of the federation as to union jurisdiction, the principle of exclusive jurisdiction was never fully operative after 1935.

Meany and Reuther did not attempt to merge competing unions when the AFL and CIO merged. Instead, the merger agreement simply provided that jurisdiction actually exercised by each affiliate at the time of merger was to be preserved intact and that established collective bargaining relationships supplanted historical jurisdiction as a basis for unions' territorial or organizing rights. For unorganized groups, or for groups outside of the merged federation, a union was supposed to organize on the basis of its historical jurisdiction, with the federation determining priorities and rights in case of a dispute.

The second significant alteration in the fundamental concept of American unionism as developed originally by the American Federation of Labor has been the modification of the principle of autonomy by the requirement that national unions shall be free of corrupt and totalitarian influences if they are to maintain AFL–CIO affiliation. The AFL-CIO set up codes of ethics and an Ethical Practices Committee, but it could only enforce its codes by expelling an affiliate. This it did, in 1957, with three

---

[17] John T. Dunlop, "Structural Changes in the American Labor Movement and Industrial Relations System," in Industrial Relations Research Association, *Annual Proceedings* (New York, 1956), p. 13.

unions, including the country's largest, the Teamsters. Under James R. Hoffa and later Frank Fitzsimmons, however, the Teamsters declined to purge its ranks of persons of ill repute and proceeded to compete for the right to represent workers in many jurisdictions. The AFL–CIO has not again shown a disposition to expel recalcitrant affiliates.

Other unions which have remained outside of the AFL–CIO fold include the surviving organizations which were expelled from the CIO for Communist domination, and the United Mine Workers, whose membership in the coal mines declined with employment from 500,000 to about 75,000, and the Brotherhood of Locomotive Engineers, which has always remained independent. The other operating railroad "brotherhoods"—the Locomotive Firemen, the Trainmen, and the Switchmen—decimated by declining employment in their industry—merged in 1969 under the name of the United Transportation Union which is affiliated with the AFL–CIO.

Although both Meany and Reuther hoped that membership in the merged Federation would spur unions in overlapping jurisdictions to unite, this happened very slowly until recently. Now it has hastened, largely as a result of basic economic considerations—declining memberships and rising costs of operations—plus the aging of leaders who, with impending retirement, were more favorably disposed to mergers. The already noted railroad unions merger is a case in point, and several others have occurred in that industry. Similarly, the former CIO Packinghouse Workers, substantially weakened as the meat-packing industry shut down its obsolete, large urban facilities, merged with the former AFL Meat Cutters and Butcher Workmen in 1968. In other cases, weaker unions have found a home in strong organizations anxious to expand their jurisdictions. Thus, the United Steelworkers has successively taken over the Mine, Mill and Smelter Workers, the United Stone and Allied Products Workers, District 50, formerly United Mine Workers, and several small independents. Some 80–90 unions had been involved in mergers by mid-1972, leaving competing and overlapping jurisdictions still very prevalent.[18]

Of more significance than the slowness of amalgamation of competing unions in precluding basic labor unity after the AFL–CIO, was the estrangement between George Meany and the late Walter Reuther. Meany continued to hold the reins of power and remained vigorous into his late seventies. As he passed 60, Mr. Reuther saw his opportunity to head the merged federation fading. He campaigned for more involvement in social welfare and civil rights causes, for more opposition to the country's involvement in Viet Nam, and finding little support even

---

[18] For a compilation of mergers between the merger of AFL–CIO in 1955 to mid-1970, see Lucretia M. Dewey, "Union Merger Pace Quickens," *Monthly Labor Review*, Vol. 94 (June 1971), pp. 63–70.

among former CIO affiliates, led the UAW out of the AFL–CIO in 1968.

Obviously hoping to replicate John L. Lewis's success of the 1930s, Reuther joined with the Teamsters, whom he had helped to drum out of the AFL–CIO, to form the Alliance for Labor Action, a rival federation. ALA, however, failed to attract a following despite substantial expenditures both in organizing attempts and for civil rights and welfare purposes. Reuther's death in an airplane accident in 1970 cost ALA its driving force. The General Motors strike later that year drained the UAW treasury. In early 1972, the Teamsters and the UAW dissolved the short-lived Alliance for Labor Action.

TABLE 2–1

Union Membership in the United States Selected Years, 1930–72

		Membership as a Percentage of:			
		Total Labor Force		*Employees in Non-Agricultural Establishments*	
Year	*Union Membership (000s)*	*(000s)*	*%*	*(000s)*	*%*
1930	3,401	50,080	6.8	29,424	11.6
1940	8,717	56,180	15.5	32,376	26.9
1950	14,267	64,749	22.0	45,222	31.5
1953	16,948	67,362	25.2	50,232	33.7
1956	17,490	70,387	24.8	52,408	33.4
1958	17,029	71,284	23.9	51,368	33.2
1960	17,049	73,126	23.3	54,203	31.5
1963	16,586	74,681	22.2	55,515	29.9
1966	17,892	78,893	22.7	63,864	28.0
1968	17,900	79,000	22.6	65,000	27.5
1972	19,400	80,500	20.4	76,475	25.4

Source: U.S. Department of Labor, and authors' estimates.

Although neither the Teamsters nor the Auto Workers returned to the AFL–CIO by mid-1972, both may do so, for their relation with the Federation is no longer marred by personality classes. Nevertheless, both have demonstrated that a large union can exist without difficulty outside the Federation; but the ALA experience causes doubt that an AFL–CIO rival can be successfully created in the foreseeable future.

American Unions Today

Table 2–1 shows the growth of union membership from 1930 to 1972 and the percentage of the labor force unionized. The great periods of growth were during World War I (which gains were substantially lost during the 1920s) and the periods 1935–39 and 1940–44. Union membership rose slowly for the first 12 years after World War II, but these gains did little more than to keep pace with the increase in the labor force. Judging from the fact that the nonunion groups of 1944 were still largely nonunion in 1956, it would appear that union growth in the 1944–56 period stemmed principally from expansion in employment by unionized firms.

Union membership reached a peak of 17.5 million in 1956—one year after the AFL–CIO merger—and then began to decline, not only as a percentage of the labor force but in absolute numbers as well, until 1963. The years between 1956 and 1963 saw the membership roles of former CIO affiliates especially hard hit, as, first, recession unemployment occurred, and then automation and increased productivity permitted increased production without increased employment.

After 1962, union membership again moved upward, passing its former peak in 1966, and surging on to a new high of 19.4 million in 1972. One cause was the sustained prosperity of the 1960s. Industry expanded payrolls in the unionized sector, and union memberships rose accordingly. A second reason for union growth in the 1960s was the tremendous expansion of public employee unions. For example, the American Federation of State, County and Municipal Employees grew from 210,000 members in 1960 to 525,000 10 years later, a gain of 150 percent. Other organizations of government employees made similar gains.

Nevertheless, union growth failed to keep pace with the growth of the labor force. Although unions made some gains in such historic nonunion areas as agriculture, where the United Farm Workers Organizing Committee of Cesar Chavez forced union recognition by product boycotts in urban centers, most traditional nonunion citadels remained unorganized. The southern textile and furniture industries, many service industries, and most salaried employment still remained outside of organized labor's power in 1972. Basic, of course, has been the shift from blue-collar to white-collar groups except in such areas as supermarket clerks, who are the largest group in the Retail Clerks' International Association, and in government employment. As Leonard Woodcock, president of the United Automobile workers has noted:[19]

The groups of workers we traditionally have represented are growing smaller. There has been a union breakthrough among white-collar employees, but mainly in government. As for office workers in the auto industry, managements give them the same raises the union wins for production workers, and frequently add something extra for the office group.

Office workers have told us frankly that they are content to stay out of the union because they don't have to pay dues or go on strike but get the same raises. They admit it's the union that wins them their raises.[19]

---

[19] Quoted in *U.S. News & World Report*, February 21, 1972, p. 23.

Except in periods of great social change like the 1930s, union membership has been closely tied to the business cycle, rising in prosperous times with increased employment and declining as production and employment decrease. The expansion in public employment during the 1960s not only increased expected gains of a prosperous period but also added a group to union rolls who are relatively insulated from cyclical fluctuations. Increased unionization of public employment, and of such semipublic areas as hospitals, universities, and the other nonprofit sectors, adds a new dimension to collective bargaining and public policy which is discussed in Chapter 22.

Meanwhile, unions remain a tremendous and powerful force. Despite the decline in the proportion of the labor force which they represent, they are the dominant influence in wage determination and in determining the rules and regulations under which people work. For the nonunion sector is heavily influenced by union policies and follows closely (or jumps ahead of) that which unions obtain for their members. As AFL–CIO President George Meany has noted:

> We [organized labor] have never had a large proportion of the labor force in this country—nothing like Britain, nothing like the Scandinavian countries, nothing like the Germans. . . .
>
> We've done quite well . . . we've delivered more to the American worker than any labor movement that ever existed. . . .
>
> With all our complaints, we have the highest standard of living in the world.
>
> Why should we worry about organizing groups of people who do not appear to want to be organized? If they prefer to have others speak for them and make the decisions which affect their lives, without effective participation on their part, that is their right.[20]

Concentration of Union Membership

In 1972, the six largest unions had approximately 34% of the total union membership. These unions—the Teamsters, the Automobile Workers, the Steelworkers, the International Brotherhood of Electrical Workers, the Machinists, and the Carpenters—all claimed more than 800,000 members, with the first three claiming more than 1 million each and the Teamsters in excess of 2 million.

Table 2–2 shows that over the years the six largest unions have generally accounted for about one third of the total union membership. Although the makeup of the six largest has changed from time to time, the Carpenters have always been represented in the group, and the Miners were represented until very recently.

The elimination of the United Mine Workers from the Big Six is a direct result of the decline in employment in the coal mining industry.

---

[20] From an interview in *U.S. News & World Report*, February 21, 1972, p. 27.

TABLE 2–2

The Six Largest Unions, 1900–1972

Year	Six Largest Unions (In Order of Membership)	Membership of Six Largest	Total Union Membership	Percentage of Total Union Membership in Six Largest
1900	Miners Carpenters Railroad Trainmen Cigarmakers Locomotive Firemen Locomotive Engineers	335,800	868,500	38.7
1920	Miners Carpenters Machinists Railway Clerks Railroad Trainmen Railway Carmen	1,649,000	5,047,800	32.6
1929	Carpenters Miners Railroad Trainmen Electrical Workers* Clothing Workers Painters	1,028,200	3,442,000	29.8
1953	Automobile Workers Teamsters Steelworkers Machinists Carpenters Miners	5,750,000	16,948,000	34.4
1964	Teamsters Automobile Workers Steelworkers Machinists Electrical Workers* Carpenters	5,850,000	16,800,000	34.2
1972	Teamsters Automobile Workers Steelworkers Electrical Workers* Machinists Carpenters	6,650,000	19,500,000	34.1

° International Brotherhood of Electrical Workers.

Source: Leo Wolman, *Ebb and Flow in Trade Unionism* (New York: National Bureau of Economic Research, 1936), for data for 1900–1929; U.S. Department of Labor, for 1953 and 1964; authors' estimates for 1972. Canadian membership excluded from total membership.

On the other hand, the Brotherhood of Carpenters and Joiners has been able to maintain its place in the Big Six not only because of the postwar boom in building construction and the continued importance of this trade but also because this union has branched out and organized, on an industrial basis, woodworking and furniture plants and lumber workers.

The International Brotherhood of Electrical Workers with a membership of 980,000, and the International Association of Machinists and Aerospace Workers with 900,000 members like the Carpenters, are former craft unions which have branched out and organized factory workers on an industrial basis. For example, the Machinists now include aerospace employees in addition to a great variety of metalworking shops. The Electrical Workers include not only electricians but also employees of all classes in public utilities and electrical and communication products manufacturing. In 1967, it passed the Machinists in membership for the first time in 30 years.

The Automobile Workers and the Steelworkers are the only former CIO unions in the Big Six. Their size is largely the result of the size of the basic industries whose employees they represent, but they have augmented their growth by spreading into related jurisdictions. The automobile union now includes aerospace employees and the bulk of the workers engaged in agricultural implement manufacture. The Steelworkers have enrolled thousands in metal fabricating, metal mining, and chemicals. Much of the recent membership increase recorded by the Steelworkers results from mergers with other unions, notably the Mine, Mill and Smelter Workers, and District 50, formerly United Mine Workers.

The Teamsters is the country's first 2-million-member union. It has not only taken advantage of the great growth in the distribution and service industries within its traditional jurisdiction, but since its expulsion from the AFL–CIO, has organized employees in any industry where it could. Moreover, the Teamsters is not only the largest union but also the most powerful. Not only do trucks carry the bulk of goods in our economy but also usually complete the delivery of items shipped by rail, air, or water. Hence, if trucks stop, little moves. Their strategic position insures the Teamsters' power.

In the 1970s, one union, the American Federation of State, County and Municipal Employees, could easily become one of the six largest unions, if not the largest. During the 1960s, it grew 150 percent. With nearly 6 million noneducational employees projected for state and local government by 1980, membership in AFSCME could then be more than double its current 550,000.

Labor in Politics

Gompers' "voluntaristic" philosophy advocated separation of unions and political parties—but not union aloofness from politics. Thus, under

Gompers' leadership the AFL avoided involvement with any political party but attempted to throw its weight to any candidate with a prolabor record or platform, and against those considered antilabor, regardless of the party to which the candidate belonged.

Although the AFL–CIO today has not altered its official position and maintains ties to many Republicans, it is heavily committed to, and involved in, the Democratic party. With finances and field workers it has provided major support for Democratic candidates, including presidential ones, during the last decade and is now a great power in that party. Moreover, by allying itself with various groups, such as those backing civil rights legislation or old-age benefits, the AFL–CIO has built effective allies which are of immense aid in generating support for candidates and issues.

The AFL–CIO role in politics is likely to increase, not decline. The election reform law of 1972, which purported to limit campaign spending, actually weakened controls on union use of funds for politics. The Taft-Hartley Act restricted the use of union dues in political campaigns, but a clause in the 1972 election law overruled court decisions which allowed criminal prosecution of union officials who made political contributions from union treasuries.[21] Thus unions are freer than at any time since 1947 to spend their members' dues in behalf of political candidates, and as they did in 1972, will continue to do so.

In respect to politics, unions are not different from corporations. Corporation officials utilize primarily economic weapons, both in their dealings with labor and in the other facets of their business relations. Like union officials, corporation officials are conscious of the political world about them and of the desirability of a favorable political climate. Lest it be assumed that labor unions are the only special-interest group active in politics, it is well to remember not only the activities of businessmen but also those of farm organizations, the American Medical Association, and other professional societies, as well as a host of others, all of whom are laboring hard for a favorable political climate in which to carry on their basic economic activities.

Because America remains a land of plenty, replete with opportunity, its labor unions remain conservative. Today, unions are as uninterested in socialization of business as they were in 1900. Likewise, the aims of American unions have not changed over the years. The words of Samuel Gompers could describe the basic aims today as they could 50 years ago—"the best possible conditions obtainable for the workers . . . more —always more."

In refusing to accept the highest standard of living ever achieved by workers anywhere as being beyond improvement, present-day American

---

[21] For the story of how the AFL–CIO managed this coup, see Jerry Landrauer, "How Two Legislators, Unions Work to Undo Fund-Raising Curbs," *Wall Street Journal*, January 18, 1972, p. 1. See also Victor Riesel's syndicated column, *Labor's Political 100 Million?*, mimeo copy, February 11, 1972.

labor is following in the footsteps of its forefathers. America has been built by those who refused to be satisfied with the best that existed, and then did better. This applies to worker, businessman, farmer, and professional man. The worker who wants more wages, the businessman who goes after record profits, the farmer who seeks higher corn prices—all are acting like perfectly normal Americans.

The Young, the Female, and the Black

As union members more and more achieve middle-class status, they run the danger of antagonizing segments of our society who have traditionally been their supporters. The rush of young people into the labor market at a time when most union officials are middle-aged or older has created clashes within the union. One longtime union official noted: "The young worker never experienced the Big Depression. He is well educated and has been taught to be independent. He doesn't feel the work ethic that is so important to his parents."[22] Another union official pointed to another problem: "Often when a man gets hired in a plant that has a union shop [compulsory union membership] . . . his introduction to the union is a deduction of $20 or so union affiliate fee on his paycheck. That's not a good introduction."[23]

In view of the sizable sector of the labor force which is under 25 years, and which is projected in this decade to remain below 25, union leadership, as well as membership, must surely begin to reflect that fact. As we shall note in the following chapter, union leadership, despite recent changes, is relatively static. Youthful restlessness could change that.

Union leadership also gives little recognition to women; yet women now comprise nearly 40 percent of the labor force and a significant but lagging share—20 percent—of union members. In this age of women's liberation and increasing recognition, it can still be reported that no woman heads a national union, very few are union officials of any kind, and none has ever sat on the AFL–CIO Executive Council. Obviously, this can be an increasing problem for American unions.

Although the AFL–CIO and many unions have supported most civil rights legislation, there is much white-black controversy within unions as in society. One reason is that at the local level, unions and union members, and particularly those very visible ones in the building trades, have more often than not opposed practical equal opportunity for blacks. As a result of this, relations between black groups and unions have become very strained in recent years.

The black-union relationship could well become further embittered in future years because of the middle-class outlook of union members, and

[22] Comment of Joseph A. Beirne, president of Communications Workers of America, reported in *U.S. News & World Report*, February 21, 1972, p. 25.

[23] Comment of Leonard Woodcock, president of United Automobile Workers, quoted in *U.S. News & World Report*, February 21, 1972, p. 25.

their lack of sympathy with those at the bottom of the income scale where blacks predominate. The result could seriously weaken unions, despite the existence of the thousands of black union members, because it would mean that a strong voting bloc and pressure group which has generally voted with unions would turn against unions, and support curbs on the union movement.

Within unions, a number of black separatists groups have been formed, but little· success has been achieved by them. Thus, in Detroit UAW locals, blacks who have won local officer positions have espoused working within the UAW rather than radical or separatists aims.[24] In the urban transit industry, strong efforts of the predominantly black work force in major cities to win control of locals has been stymied by union policies that permit pensioners to vote. The latter, being predominantly white, have kept incumbent whites in office despite the social change in working personnel.[25]

Black members of unions are still poorly represented at top union echelons. Slow turnover in union officialdom, and the fact that blacks are a minority of most memberships ensure this situation, but its continuation is certain to be a focal point of dissent and controversy in the labor movement.

The Impact of Controls

Perhaps as significant as the changing character of the work force on the future growth of unionism is the impact of wage and price controls. Will unions be able to "produce" for the membership under wage restraints? Certainly, the experience during World War II and during the Korean War not only left the labor movement's strength intact but may well have expanded it. If unions break through the restraints and obviously contribute to further inflation, what will be the impact? In Europe, there is no evidence that unions have been hurt by such developments.[26]

In a later chapter, we shall explore the socioeconomic problems involved in wage and price restraints. In a real sense, these restraints were instituted in the United States because the wage-setting mechanisms under

---

[24] Herbert R. Northrup, "The Negro in the Automobile Industry," in *Negro Employment in Basic Industry* (Studies of Negro Employment, Vol. I [Philadelphia: Industrial Research Unit, Wharton School of Finance and Commerce, University of Pennsylvania, 1970]), Part II, pp. 99–104.

[25] Philip W. Jeffress, "The Negro in the Urban Transit Industry," in Herbert R. Northrup et al., *Negro Employment in Land and Air Transport*, (Studies of Negro Employment, Vol. V [Philadelphia: Industrial Research Unit, Wharton School of Finance and Commerce, University of Pennsylvania, 1971]), Part IV, pp. 85–90.

[26] On the European experience with controls, see Lloyd Ulman and Robert J. Flanagan, *Wage Restraint: A Study of Incomes Policies in Western Europe* (Berkeley, Calif.: University of California Press, 1971).

collective bargaining had too great an inflationary result. Perhaps the labor movement has achieved such power in the United States that restraints are essential. We shall also explore this question—as well as whether the wage and price controls are satisfactory as restraints—in subsequent chapters.

QUESTIONS FOR DISCUSSION

1. Do you think union growth will be faster or slower in 1975–1980 than it was in 1965–70? Support your answer.
2. Why did not the Alliance for Labor Action survive as a rival of the AFL–CIO?
3. If you were the president of the Brotherhood of Locomotive Engineers, an independent union, would you support affiliation with the AFL–CIO? Why, or why not?
4. Has the Teamsters' Union been damaged by its expulsion from the AFL–CIO? If so, in what manner? If not, why not?

SUGGESTIONS FOR FURTHER READING

BERNSTEIN, IRVING. *The Lean Years. A History of the American Worker, 1920–1933*. Boston: Houghton Mifflin, 1960.

———. *The Turbulent Years. A History of the American Worker, 1933–1940*. Boston: Houghton Mifflin, 1970.

Two well written volumes describing pre-World War II worker problems and unions in a very sympathetic manner.

DEWEY, LUCRETIA M. "Women in Labor Unions," *Monthly Labor Review*, Vol. 44 (February 1971), pp. 42–48.

An analysis of why women lag in membership and position in the labor movement.

GALENSON, WALTER F. *The CIO Challenge to the AFL*. Cambridge, Mass.: Harvard University Press, 1960.

An examination of the effect of the rise of the CIO upon the policies and activities of the AFL.

ROWAN, RICHARD L. (ed.). *Readings in Labor Economics and Labor Relations*, Part II, "Some Aspects of the History of the American Labor Movement," pp. 92–158. Homewood, Ill.: Richard D. Irwin, Inc., 1972.

Various articles by leading authorities on the development, theory, and history of the labor movement.

CASE STUDY READING

Under the guidance of your instructor, read a book or a series of articles about unionism and industrial relations in a particular industry. How does the growth of unionism in the industry you studied compare with the growth of unionism in the country as a whole?

Chapter 3 : UNION STRUCTURE AND GOVERNMENT

The governments of American unions, like those of nations, run the gamut from democracy to dictatorship. The type and structure of a union organization have traditionally depended upon a wide variety of industrial and personal factors, but with the passage of the Labor-Management Reporting and Disclosure Act of 1959 (also known as the Landrum-Griffin Labor Reform Act), federal law became a most important factor shaping union government. Since union government and structure have important repercussions both on union policies and on the economy as a whole, a knowledge of union structure and government is essential background to the economics of labor.

ORGANIZATIONAL STRUCTURE AND ITS DETERMINANTS

Union organization usually commences on either a "craft" or an "industrial" basis, but it soon expands beyond these limitations. Today there are very few craft unions which confine their membership to a particular craft, and very few industrial unions which have not expanded beyond their original industry. Thus, the International Brotherhood of Electrical Workers takes into membership building-trades electricians, railroad shop electricians, shipyard electricians, and electricians wherever else they are employed; but it has also organized all employees of telephone, electrical machinery, and electronic concerns. Likewise, the original jurisdiction of the United Automobile Workers included all employees in and around automobile plants, whether janitor, electrician, tool and die worker, assembly worker, or anything else; now, as the United Automobile, Aerospace and Agricultural Implement Workers, its activities embrace these additional industries also.

Some unions have expanded even further. The Teamsters will accept employees in any occupation or plant. Being outside the AFL–CIO, these unions have no compulsion to respect the jurisdictions of other organizations.

Sometimes, as in the case of the Teamsters, organization structure is determined by leadership power conflicts. More often, technical, market, or government factors are determinative. Early craft unions found that if they did not accept the helpers into their unions, the helpers would take their places in case of strikes. The AFL failed to organize the mass-production industries, partially because it would not accommodate organization structure to organizational needs. The CIO forced the AFL to adopt a more realistic approach.

Technological factors compel changes in union structure. Several craft unions—the Brotherhood of Blacksmiths, Drop Forgers and Helpers, for example—have disappeared from the scene because jurisdiction has been shrunk or obliterated by technical change.

Government policy alters union structure. The National Labor Relations (Taft-Hartley) Act removes some jurisdiction rules from the hands of union leaders and places them in the hands of the workers themselves and the National Labor Relations Board. For example, if a group of textile workers wish to be represented by the Rubber Workers' Union, and if the leaders of that organization are agreeable, they can petition the National Labor Relations Board for an election. The NLRB then decides who is eligible to participate in the election and holds it. If the workers vote for the Rubber Workers' Union, it is that union, which is the legal representative of the workers for collective bargaining, with which the employer must deal, regardless of what union jurisdictional rules provide.

As noted in Chapter 2, the constitution of the AFL–CIO recognized the realities of jurisdictional control under the NLRB by, in effect, giving organized labor's sanction not only to whatever jurisdiction a member union had successfully organized but also to contests among member unions for newly organized groups where two or more unions could demonstrate historical interest. The principle of exclusive jurisdiction as determined by the AFL died, in fact, in 1935 when the Wagner Act became law; the AFL–CIO recognized its burial in the merger agreement 20 years later.

The AFL–CIO constitution did not end either jurisdictional difficulties among unions or jurisdictional conflicts between the rules of the merged federation and the Taft-Hartley Act as interpreted by the National Labor Relations Board. To settle quarrels within the federation itself, a board, headed by an outside impartial umpire, was established as part of the no-raiding agreement which preceded the merger. This board has had considerable success in reducing union raiding and jurisdictional disputes. The NLRB now gives the board an opportunity to settle raiding disputes before it takes action in such a dispute between two or more AFL–CIO affiliates.

The decisions of the National Labor Relations Board affect union structure in other ways. For example, if the NLRB declines a union request to separate skilled from unskilled workers, the petitioning union has the choice of opening its doors to the unskilled as well as the skilled or facing the possibility of losing the right, as a result of the adverse votes of the unskilled, of representing either the skilled or the unskilled. This does not mean that craft unions have to take on an industrial character because of rulings of the National Labor Relations Board. The NLRB, as we shall point out in Chapter 19, has been careful to maintain the rights and jurisdiction of craft unions where that is desired by workers and where the craft is clearly a distinct work group.

In many situations, union jurisdictional lines are not clear. In an industry organized along craft union lines, as is the building industry, technological change and the substitutability of one material for another lead to conflicting jurisdictional claims and to jurisdictional strikes—that is, strikes of one craft against another craft doing the work. On the outcome of such strikes depends which group of workers will do the work and perhaps which union will grow in strength and size. Often in history, conflicts over jurisdiction have led to eventual merger of the contesting organizations.

A dispute over which union will represent workers is different from a jurisdictional dispute, since no matter which union wins out, the same workers will continue to work. In representation matters, the accidents of location often determine the result and therefore the union structure.

If, for example, a metal-fabricating company is located in Detroit, where the United Automobile Workers is strong, it will probably be represented by the UAW; if it were in Pittsburgh, the United Steelworkers would probably win bargaining rights; in Minneapolis, the Machinists, etc. In each case, the friends and relatives of the plant workers are likely to be in the dominant union of the area, and so that union is likely to be chosen by the workers in the metal-fabricating plant to represent them.

DETERMINANTS OF UNION GOVERNMENT

As a union grows and takes into membership workers with different interests, not only its structure but also its government is shaped to meet the needs of the members and to take advantage of the experience which develops. For example, the division of the membership along craft, industry, racial, or geographical lines often results in semiautonomous division within unions and in special provisions for representation for specific groups. Thus, all executive board members in the United Automobile Workers' Union are elected from various geographic areas except two, who are elected "at large" but who, by tacit consent, are a Negro and a Canadian.

Administrative Determinants

Practical administrative problems also determine union regulations. For example, unions discovered at an early date that strike control would have to be centralized to some extent if the unions were to be preserved. This proved necessary to prevent "quick on the trigger" locals from striking on the slightest provocation and thus costing the union and members thousands of dollars for strike benefits, legal and publicity charges, etc. Strike control by national unions takes two forms. In many cases, no strike can be called without approval of the national executive board. In others, any strike which is called without national union approval deprives the strikers of strike benefits or other such national union help.

Effect of Rival Unionism

The development of rival unionism on a mass scale in the 1930s materially affected union government. In many cases, the advent of rival unions forced existing unions to open their doors to members previously barred. For example, some unions which once admitted only skilled workers (Flint Glass Workers and the International Molders and Foundry Workers' Union of North America) admitted unskilled workers in order to prevent their organization by the CIO. A number of other unions, such as the Hotel and Restaurant Workers and the Commercial Telegraphers' Union, removed bars to black workers because of the threat of rival unions. On the other hand, the existence of a union with discriminatory racial policies has often caused rival unions to "soft-pedal" its equalitarian policies in order not to alienate the dominant white membership. The merger of the AFL and the CIO has, of course, reduced the effects of rival unionism on union policy and government.

Imitative Elements

Many union constitutional provisions result merely from the fact that the writers of the constitutions copy similar provisions from the constitutions of older organizations. The constitution of the first permanent union, the Typographical Union, was copied from that of the Right Worthy Grand Lodge of the Independent Order of Odd Fellows, and then it was gradually amended to suit the needs of the union. Likewise, many railroad union constitutions bear a strong resemblance to the constitution of the oldest—the Brotherhood of Locomotive Engineers.

Power Elements

A number of union constitutional provisions can be explained only by the desire to increase the power of given individuals or groups. Thus, James Hoffa was able to have the constitution of the Teamsters substantially rewritten to transfer power from subordinate officials to the union presidency. John L. Lewis had great power given the presidency of the United Mine Workers and reduced the union districts to impotency. Provisions in such union constitutions as the Carpenters' which give a greater vote to craftsmen than to members of industrial locals are aimed at retaining power for the former even though they might not make up a majority of the union's membership.

Effect of Legislation and Court Decisions

Union government, like union structure, is often shaped by laws or the decision of administrative bodies or courts. For example, the adoption of civil rights legislation has forced unions to delete racial bars from their constitutions. Decisions of the National Labor Relations Board, placing certain groups of workers in bargaining units, have compelled unions to alter their admission policies. Likewise, the courts have ruled that union leadership did not have authority under certain union constitutions to take specific acts—for example, to expel a member. In a number of instances the union has thereupon amended its constitution, granting the officers additional authority.

But no act of government has so affected union government as has the Labor-Management Reporting and Disclosure Act of 1959 (Landrum-Griffin). Under this law, members of labor unions are guaranteed basic rights of free speech, free assembly, and access to financial information, and their officers are required to maintain records and to account for union funds. In addition, unions are required to amend their constitutions, if necessary, to conform to this legislation. The law spells out procedures for the election of officers of unions, their terms of office, and frequency of election, and provides rules for the conduct of elections.

THE NATIONAL OR INTERNATIONAL UNION

The "top" organization of American unions is the national or international union. The officers of the national unions are selected either by a convention or by referendum, or by a combination of the two, whereby the convention nominates, with the actual contest being determined by a referendum of the entire membership. Unions are required by the Landrum-Griffin Act to have a national convention at least once every five years. Many do so at shorter intervals.

Although union conventions generally provide for representation of every local, many locals do not send delegates because of the cost. Some internationals have paid the local union convention expenses, but the expense of so doing is usually considered too great. As a result, large segments of the membership can be unrepresented at union conventions.

Because the convention is the supreme governing body of most unions, a fair procedure for electing convention delegates is a requisite of democratic union government. Yet most national union constitutions had very little, if anything, to say about how delegates to conventions were to be selected prior to the passage of the Landrum-Griffin Act, which contains regulations for fair election procedures. Even now, however, top union officials can assure a friendly convention by paying expenses of delegates from locals friendly to them and refusing to pay similar expenses for others—as has allegedly been done in recent United Mine Worker conclaves.

Some conventions are truly deliberative bodies; others are just captive audiences assembled to hear union officers and special guests talk, and to affirm action already decided upon. Even if the convention is truly deliberative with wide participation by the delegates in formulating, discussing, and adopting or rejecting policies and rules, the real work is done in caucus or committee. In some unions, there is an air of the perfunctory at the convention when actually there has been heated debate and wide participation by delegates in caucuses or committees.

To control the convention committees may be to control the convention. A credentials committee will have a powerful voice in determining which of two contesting groups of delegates can be seated with a vote in the convention and who is to be denied access to that vote. The resolutions committee may be able to bottle up some proposals and report out others, thus controlling the priorities and nature of the floor discussion. The appeals committee hears those who have been disciplined by union locals or officers or who otherwise have a grievance against union judicial machinery. Other committees may perform equally strategic functions. Since either the international president or executive board almost always appoints the convention committees, the delegates must overturn the convention machinery to change the convention committees.

If, however, the convention delegates elected their committees after arrival, they would probably have either to accept their officers' recommendations because candidates for committee assignments would not be generally known to the delegates, or, as in one convention of the International Association of Machinists, to spend nearly a week bickering over committee assignments and transact almost no other union business. The IAM abandoned direct delegate election of committees after this experience.

The Referendum

About one fourth of the country's unions elect their officers by direct referendum. The referendum can be a useful tool in promoting union democracy, where the membership has a tradition of participation and a high sense of responsibility, such as in the case of the International Typographical Union, or where procedures for getting nominated and insuring fair and honest elections are carefully adhered to. It is, however, no real substitute for a convention. Union members frequently do not take an interest in referendums, so that the decisions made as a result of them have largely been the decisions of active minorities who took the trouble to vote.

National Union Officers

Most national unions are officered by a president, a secretary-treasurer, and one or more vice presidents. The number of vice presidents will be determined by many factors, for example, whether regional directors bear that title. In addition, most unions have a national executive board which is theoretically the top governing body between conventions. Members of the executive board are often the regional directors or vice presidents.

Although the president, or whoever the chief executive officer of the union may be, is almost always technically subordinate to the executive board, more often than not he is likely to control it. There are, of course, exceptions. In most cases, however, the constitutional power of the union's chief officer is very great; and if he is a forceful personality, he may reduce the executive board to complete subordination, as James R. Hoffa or John L. Lewis did, or simply dominate it, as did Walter Reuther, by stature and force of personality.

Tenure of National Union Officials

The tenure of national union officials has traditionally been long. Indeed, opposition to national union officials in election contests was rare until recently. John L. Lewis was president of the United Mine Workers from 1920 to 1960; William Hutcheson, of the Carpenters from 1915 to 1952 and his son, Maurice, from 1952 to 1972; Daniel Tobin, of the Teamsters from 1907 to 1952; William D. Mahon, of the Amalgamated Association of Street, Electric Railway and Motor Coach Employees of America from 1893 to 1946; and Walter Reuther, of the United Automobile Workers from 1946 till his death in 1970. Most unions have been dominated by one man for many years.

In any election the incumbent has a tremendous advantage. He is already well known to the membership, and his every action is news. The challenger must make himself known outside of his locality and must have an issue which differentiates him from the incumbent. Patronage, the union journal, and other avenues of communication are controlled by the incumbent. In the fairest of elections the challenger faces heavy odds.

In one union, however, contests for the presidency have been the rule rather than the exception. The International Typographical Union stands out for the number and vigor of officer contests. Only three times since 1898 has the ITU presidency been uncontested, and most elections have been determined by narrow margins. Although this is decidedly an exceptional case, there have been an unusually large number of contests for top union offices in recent years.

Does this presage a new infusion of political opposition and democracy within unions? Certainly, provisions of the Landrum-Griffin Act relating to fair elections make opposition to the incumbent less likely to result in economic or physical harm to the challenger and reduce the potential for stealing elections. James B. Carey's henchmen announced in 1964 that he had been reelected president of the International Union of Electrical, Radio and Machine Workers by a margin of 2,193 votes. After court action, and a recount by the U.S. Department of Labor, pursuant to the Landrum-Griffin Act, the Department of Labor announced: "The ballots were miscounted by the [union] Trustees . . . instead of winning the election by 2,193 votes, as reported by the Trustees, Carey lost the election by 23,316 votes. . . ."[1]

One can, however, doubt that the trend toward long tenure of, and little opposition to, union chief executives will be radically altered by the Landrum-Griffin procedures, or by any changes in union institutional mores. For the most part, union incumbents do not depend on stolen elections to keep them in power. Landrum-Griffin Act regulations which provide for honest elections and make provisions for recall and impeachment are not, therefore, likely materially to reduce the length of incumbency of union chiefs. The comparatively large number of union chief executives who were replaced in recent years is the result of several unique combinations of factors. In some situations, clashes within union hierarchies precipitated a change. In others, contests resulted from union expansion, change of labor composition, or simply aging of the bureaucracy. It is likely, however, that the new leadership, once ensconced, will serve many years.

In several unions, nepotism has marked leadership tenure. This is especially true in the building trades unions and in key locals of the Longshoremen. The nepotism and long-term incumbency of top union officials are, of course, not unique in American life. Corporation and university officials frequently are in power for long terms, and there are advantages therefrom. In industrial relations, it may promote stability and understanding between labor and management. A union official who does not fear for reelection may be in a position to act more realistically with management than one who must constantly bear in mind the effect of collective bargaining on his tenure. That experience is a valuable asset, few would deny. Nevertheless, the advantages of active opposition appear to outweigh the disadvantages. New blood means new ideas, new

---

[1] Similarly, in 1972, insurgent Arnold Miller defeated incumbent Tony Boyle in an election run by the Department of Labor after Boyle's "re-election" had been set aside by the courts.

directions, and often, better representation. Union members deserve such effective representation.

Appointive Officials

In addition to elected officials, most national unions have a sizable staff of paid, appointed personnel. They include two groups: the specialists or professionals and the international representatives. The former are the lawyers, economists, statisticians, research and educational directors, etc., whom modern trade-union organizations must employ in order to engage in what has become the highly technical business of running a union and engaging in collective bargaining with management. The latter nearly always come from the ranks of union members.

Professional employees of unions sometimes become key figures in union administration or collective bargaining. Usually, however, the lawyer remains in the background as a chief adviser of top officials. And if these officials fail to secure reelection, their lawyers and other professional advisers are usually swept out of office by the new administration. However important the advice of professionals is to labor leadership, that advice can always be purchased as well from those whose loyalty is above question as from those who served the outgoing administration. With extremely few exceptions, professional personnel have discovered that working for a union permits less deviation from the official administration line than does working for government or business.

International representatives have three main functions: First, they are assigned to organize unorganized shops in the union's jurisdiction; second, they assist local unions in negotiations and collective bargaining; and third, they act as political representatives of those responsible for their appointment. Much has been said and written about "interference" by national union officials who prevented local unions from settling controversies except on terms dictated by the national union. For example, the 1967–68 copper strike, which lasted about eight months, involved basically a demand by national leaders of the Steelworkers that the companies agree to companywide or industrywide bargaining, an issue of much less interest to the local membership.[2]

Frequently, however, the national union is a force for peace. Its officers know the costs of strikes, and its staff builds up prestige by successful, peaceful settlements. Local union officers often are too fearful of the consequences of their actions and too inexperienced. The local officers "get out on a limb" from which they cannot rescue themselves. At this point the international representative can step in and use the prestige of the national union to sell the membership on the need for a reasonable solution.

---

[2] See William N. Chernish, *Coalition Bargaining* (Industrial Research Unit Study No. 45 [Philadelphia: University of Pennsylvania Press, 1967]), chap. 9.

International representatives have little job security, although they may win it for the rank and file through collective bargaining. Theirs is a political appointment (which does not cast aspersions on their abilities), and they must aid the political fortunes of those who appoint them if they are to retain their jobs. The power of patronage in government is always an important weapon in the hands of the incumbent. So also is it in a union. A union official who gave no heed to politics would not last long in office. He must make friends in order to assure his reelection. One of the best ways to do that is to appoint to jobs people who have contributed to his success and who will continue to work for his interest. The international representative is a political appointee and thus the political emissary of the person responsible for his appointment. For, basically,. the union is internally a political organization. It could not be otherwise if it is to be in any way democratic.

Union international representatives, like employees of business, revolt against insecure working conditions. The decline in union membership between 1956 and 1962, the AFL–CIO merger, and resultant layoffs of organizers have led to the formation of unions by union representatives and demands that such bodies as the AFL–CIO, or international unions negotiate with unions of *their* employees. The reaction of labor's top officialdom has been remarkably like that of management 40 years ago—rejecting recognition. The unions of union organizers have repeatedly been forced to go to the National Labor Relations Board to compel unions to recognize unions of their own employees!

INTERMEDIATE UNION GOVERNMENT

To coordinate the activities of local unions, and to act as an intermediary form of government between the local and the national, most unions have established what are termed regional offices, district councils, joint boards, etc. In industrial unions the regional office is the most common. Its jurisdiction varies with the concentration of the industry. For example, the state of Michigan is divided into numerous regions by the United Automobile Workers, and the rest of the country has proportionately many fewer regions because the industry is concentrated in and around Detroit. Similarly, the districts of the United Mine Workers are contiguous with the various coal fields; and those of the United Steelworkers are heavily concentrated in the Pittsburgh–Ohio Valley area.

Building-trades unions, which are organized on a craft basis, frequently have all local unions in an area represented in a coordinating district council. The garment unions call a similar organization a joint board; railroad unions generally coordinate their locals on a single railroad in what they call a system federation.

Whatever the name, the general purpose of these intermediate forms

is the same: coordination of local union activities and joint action of
locals in dealing with management. Generally, the regional office is
headed by an official elected either by the entire union membership or
by the membership of the district or region only. In some unions,
regional chiefs have the title of vice president; in others, such as the
building trades, the head of the district council may be merely the
secretary-treasurer of that council. In any case, the regional office is an
important union position which many local union officials covet.

THE LOCAL UNION

The local union is the part of union structure which the member
contacts directly. The conduct of affairs on the local level is thus frequently the means by which the member judges his union. Like the
government of municipalities, there is much in local union government
which is heartening to those interested in democratic ways and much that
is unsavory; and the latter, as in municipal affairs, is most often attributable to the failure of the citizenry, or members, to concern themselves
with the conduct of their organization. In short, local union government,
like municipal government, too often depends on the character of the
small minority who bear the burden of operating the organization.

Local Jurisdiction and Size

The jurisdiction and size of local unions do not follow a fixed pattern.
Most commonly, the local has jurisdiction over a single plant, and thus
the size of its membership depends upon the size of the plant. One of the
largest locals is No. 600, United Automobile Workers, which has jurisdiction over the 40,000 workers employed in the River Rouge (near
Detroit, Michigan) works of the Ford Motor Company. Other one-plant
locals have only 10 to 100 members.

There are, however, many variations from the one-plant local. Craft
union locals commonly have jurisdiction over an area. Thus, the Bricklayers' Local No. 1 of Louisiana is composed of all union bricklayers in
New Orleans. In larger cities, like New York or Chicago, two or three
such locals may divide the jurisdiction.

Local union membership may also be divided on racial or national
lines. Thus, in many southern cities, building-trades mechanics were
found in separate racial locals prior to the 1964 Civil Rights Act. In New
York, certain locals of the International Ladies' Garment Workers'
Union have been confined to one ethnic group.

Industries in which average plant employment is small are frequently
characterized by multiplant or "amalgamated" locals. Thus, in the Detroit tool and die jobbing shops, which employ an average of less than
25 employees per shop, two United Automobile Workers locals have

jurisdiction—one on the East Side the other on the West Side. In such cases, one shop is considered too small to function as a unit.

Amalgamated locals may also develop for other reasons. A number of unions have amalgamated locals which are quite large, apparently to centralize control. Under the amalgamated system, each plant in the large locals is represented on an executive board. Control of the executive board secures control over all plants. By concentrating all their strength on a few small plants, one faction can win a majority on the amalgamated executive board and hence have complete control over the local.

Local Union Officers

If a local union is small, it usually cannot afford full-time officials. In such cases, its officers work at their jobs but, by agreement with management, take time off for union business. The union compensates them only for actual expenses, which include time off from their jobs at the job rate. In many instances the international union assigns a full-time representative to aid local unions in the conduct of their affairs. The international representative is of special importance where the local cannot afford full-time officers of its own.

The larger local unions usually have one or more full-time officials, who are compensated completely from the local treasury. The top-ranking official may be the president, or the latter may be only a figure-head, with the chief power in the hands of a business agent or manager, or a secretary-treasurer. Custom, accident, and the strength of individuals who have occupied or are occupying these positions are the determining factors.

Only the largest local unions can afford appointed officials to assist elected ones. A few of these do, however, have organizers and other "local representatives" on their payroll. Such appointees help organize new shops, assist in negotiating and administering collective bargaining contracts, and aid the union political fortunes of those elected officials who are responsible for their appointment. They function on a local basis similarly to international representatives on a national basis. Because they are self-sustaining, large locals often operate quite independently of their international union.

Duration of Local Union Office

Most commonly, local officials are elected for a term of one or two years. In contrast to the situation in the national union, the turnover of local officials is high. This is especially true in the smaller locals, where the leaders and the membership are close and challenges to local leadership do not involve expensive campaigning. On the average, it is not likely that the tenure of local office exceeds two or four years. Some of the turnover is accounted for by advancement to higher union positions; some, by the fact that local union officials often accept managerial positions—for example, become foremen; but most of the turnover is accounted for by the desire of the electorate for a change in administration.

Local union officials often have few compensations for their jobs. Their salaries as a rule are not particularly high, and often not very much in excess of what they can earn as workers. There are of course exceptions, with some local officials inordinately overpaid. In the main, however, status is likely to be more important for the full-time official, for full-time union work is more appealing to many than a factory job of equal pay. Against that, however, are the long hours, the necessity to work nights when factory employees are free, and the constant reminder that tenure in office is likely to be short.

The Shop Steward

Besides compensated officials, nearly all local unions have shop stewards or committeemen, who are the union representatives in the plant. They are usually elected by the group they serve. These officials work full time at their jobs; but in addition, they collect dues, handle grievances with management foremen, and generally look after union affairs in the shop. They carry the union's message and represent the union in its daily contacts with members. Their relations with foremen often determine the type of industrial relations which exist in a plant; for whatever may be the union-management relationship at the top level, stewards and foremen are the persons who must carry it out on the shop level where it counts.

Membership Apathy

Despite the evidence that the great majority of local union officials are both undercompensated and honest, a significant number have obviously been neither. Therefore the obligations for fair procedure set forth in the Landrum-Griffin Act specifically apply to local unions as well as to national unions. Local unions must now elect officials by secret ballot at least once every three years. Various guarantees are set forth to insure free elections by secret ballot, reasonable opportunity to nominate candidates, a fair notice of election prior to elections, no discrimination in use of membership lists or campaign literature distribution, and safeguards for a fair count of ballots.

If, however, the Landrum-Griffin Act is to achieve its full effect, the average union member will have to attend union meetings much more consistently than he ever has before. The outlook for such a turnabout in behavior is not promising.

The business of the local is generally conducted at meetings which are either called by local officials or held at stipulated intervals. Unfortunately, these meetings are not, as a rule, either interesting or well attended. The average union member takes his responsibilities as a member lightly. After a hard day's work, he is much more likley to stay home with his family or to engage in recreational pursuits than to attend a union meeting which may be quite unexciting. In short, his attitude toward his union duty is like that of the average citizen toward his responsibilities as a stockholder, organization member, or citizen.

TRUSTEESHIPS

Constitutions of many international unions authorize the international officers to suspend the normal processes of government of local unions and other subordinate bodies, to supervise their internal activity and assume control of their property and funds. These "trusteeships" (or "receiverships" or "supervisorships," as they are sometimes called) are among the most effective devices which responsible international officers have to insure order within their organization. In general, they have been widely used to prevent corruption, mismanagement of union funds, violation of collective bargaining agreements, infiltration of Communists —in short, to preserve the integrity and stability of the organization itself.

In some instances, however, trusteeships have been used as a means of consolidating the power of corrupt union officers, of plundering and dissipating the resources of local unions, and of obstructing the development of free speech, free assembly, and free elections within local unions. The fact that most union constitutions are vague on the explicit terms and powers of trusteeships has permitted and abetted misuse of the trustee function.

The reasons why trusteeships may be initiated are typically vague and indefinite, and provide the international president or executive board more often than not with almost blanket authority to take over a local union or even to subvert the will of the local membership. For example, the constitution of the United Mine Workers provides as follows: "Charters of districts, sub-districts and local unions may be revoked by the international president, who shall have authority to create a provisional government for the subordinate branch whose charter has been revoked." Under this provision, John L. Lewis and his successors instituted trusteeships and maintained them for over 40 years without permitting a resumption of district union governments.

Title III of the Landrum-Griffin Act sets forth detailed regulations for the conduct of trusteeships. Undoubtedly, the existence of this law has curtailed abuses in trusteeship administration by limiting the right of unions to impose trusteeships and by requiring the reporting of facts concerning trusteeships and providing for appeal and possible court reversal of arbitrary actions. Nevertheless, the trusteeships imposed by John L. Lewis in the 1920s were still in effect until 1972. Although the U.S. Department of Labor finally announced in 1964 that it would sue in court to force an end to this undemocratic practice, it was not until mid-1972 that a series of court decisions ordered the trusteeships terminated and elections for officers in the affected districts.

UNION FINANCE

Operating a union in modern American society is an expensive undertaking. Officer and employee salaries, office rent, traveling expenses, postage and other communications costs, publicity, and legal and research activities are some of the daily routine expenses which must be met. In addition, a reserve must be built up; for a long strike, with its increased demands on ordinary services, plus the cost of strike benefits, extra legal and publicity help, etc., can drain the union treasury of several million dollars. As an extreme example the United Automobile Workers and its locals spent $142 million on strike benefits in 1970. This included the disbursements during the General Motors strike of that year. Net worth of the UAW, which stood at close to $100 million a few years before, was down to $5 million at the end of 1970.[3]

Dues and Fees

The funds necessary to operate a union and to service its membership come primarily from the monthly dues paid by the members themselves. In addition, unions derive income from initiation fees and assessments, also paid by members, and from government bonds, property, or other securities in which excess or reserve funds are invested.

In general, the older craft unions have the highest dues and initiation fees. High dues and fees are justified by these unions on the ground that newcomers should compensate the union which has raised wages and standards in the craft, especially since the present high wages permit "Johnny-come-lately" to pay his share so easily. A high initiation fee also serves to discourage applicants and thus give union men a greater part of the available work. The use of the initiation fee as an exclusionist policy is only feasible if entrance to the trade can be controlled by the union. With a few exceptions, only craft unions can exert such control. An industrial union which depends for its bargaining strength on orga-

---

[3] See *Solidarity*, August 1971, for the UAW financial report.

TABLE 3–1

Union Financial Information, Selected Unions, 1970

Union	1970 Membership	Average Monthly Per Capita Dues	Total Receipts	Net Assets
Teamsters......................	1,829,000	$2,840,204	$144,527,184	$86,651,634
Automobile Workers.............	1,486,000	7,493,559	911,966,643	5,139,452
Steelworkers....................	1,200,000	4,516,682	135,963,099	56,577,370
Electrical Workers (IBEW)........	922,000	4,263,348	102,574,768	30,314,750
Machinists......................	865,000	2,569,052	37,345,827	37,210,994
Carpenters......................	820,000	1,990,240	41,810,191	36,034,291
Laborers........................	580,000	642,968	14,229,946	28,149,599
Operating Engineers..............	393,000	590,673	13,086,422	29,027,321
Plumbers........................	312,000	917,397	36,079,955	22,495,175
Electrical Workers (IUE)..........	300,000	909,069	11,548,360	928,890
Railway Clerks..................	275,000	430,500	13,684,676	10,017,410
Rubber Workers.................	216,000	563,356	26,492,665	12,056,977
Oil, Chemical, Atomic............	175,000	585,204	8,568,257	5,137,735
Chemical Workers...............	101,000	328,600	5,223,173	3,462,621
Mine Workers...................	75,000*	305,186	9,694,770	86,319,302
National Maritime Union..........	50,000	333,726	5,889,702	11,029,200
Cement, Lime and Gypsum Workers.....................	36,000	115,494	3,683,330	3,137,345

* Authors' estimates.

Source: U.S. Department of Labor, Bureau of Labor Statistics and Office of Labor-Management and Welfare Pension Reports.

nizing all employees of the industry or firm would defeat its purpose by raising its fees high enough to limit membership.

On the basis of the data filed with the U.S. Department of Labor pursuant to the Landrum-Griffin Act, the authors estimate that national unions had receipts well in excess of $1 billion in 1972. In addition, several billions more are now channeled annually into union-controlled or union-management welfare and pension funds. Table 3–1 summarizes financial information for certain unions, including the six largest, several very wealthy ones, and some whose assets are dwindling as their membership declines—for example, Chemical Workers. It does not, however, include information on union welfare and pension funds, the assets of which in 1968 were estimated at 50 times those of unions,[4] and are probably now substantially greater.

Initiation fees tend to vary from double the monthly dues to much more. Many of the older craft unions charge $100 or more for an entrance fee, usually payable in installments. Where initiation fees of $500 or a $1,000 have been asked, for example, in some of the skilled crafts

[4] By Frank M. Kleiler, former Director, Office of Labor-Management and Welfare Pension Reports, U.S. Department of Labor, *Daily Labor Report*, February 8, 1968.

of the motion-picture industry, such fees are as much bars to admission as they are actual charges.

The extent of union assessments varies considerably. Generally, they occur as a result of an emergency expenditure, for an organizing campaign, or for strike benefits. For example, the United Automobile Workers enacted a $25-per-month assessment in 1971 to help defray expenses related to the strikes, particularly the one involving General Motors Corporation.

The Problem of High Fees

Generally, complaints of high union fees refer to initiation fees rather than to dues. Moreover, as has been pointed out, the basic problem is admission policy and not initiation fees. Any legal attack on what is considered antisocial union fees must be directed to the root of the problem—the extent to which unions should be permitted to exclude persons from employment by excluding them from the union.

There is no one criterion for a "too high" initiation fee. One hundred dollars appears a quite reasonable fee for the Air Line Pilots Association, whose members may earn more than $50,000 per annum; the same fee is outrageous when charged by the Laborers' Union. A fee is large or small relative to the benefits expected, which include primarily prospective earnings.

Most union fees are not excessive by this standard. The main exceptions are found in the building and amusement industry unions. In these industries, union power is great, and union control over jobs extraordinarily complete. Those who are in the unions are thus afforded an unusual opportunity to inflict heavy charges on such applicants as they permit to join.

Section 8(b) of the Taft-Hartley Act makes it an unfair labor practice for a union to charge "excessive or discriminatory" fees. The act further requires the National Labor Relations Board to consider "among other relevant factors, the practices and customs of labor organizations in the particular industry, and the wages currently paid to the employees affected" in determining whether a fee is excessive or discriminatory. The NLRB has had comparatively few complaints under this section and has ordered fees reduced or discontinued in only a few instances.

The Landrum-Griffin Act attacks the problem of union dues and fees from another direction. It prohibits unions from raising dues or initiation fees or from levying assessments, unless a majority of the members of a local union so vote either in a referendum, or by secret ballot at a special meeting for which due notice has been given; or unless a national union votes by referendum or at convention, for which appropriate due notice has been given. Failure to follow these provisions has forced a few unions to rescind dues increases or assessments.

Salaries

Unions are, in general, not distinguished, as high-salaried organizations. The average union staff member receives less than his counterpart in industry, in terms of salary, benefits, and expense allowances. Actually, union officials are paid on the more modest scale which typifies employees of other nonprofit institutions. Of course, the income of the union representative is usually greater, often substantially, than he would earn in his trade. More often, however, the prestige and interest of the office, rather than the money, are the lures which impel a man to seek union office.

As the data in Table 3–2 show, there are, however, a few union officials who receive fairly high salaries and allowances. A salary of from

TABLE 3–2

Union Presidents and Their Salaries, Selected Unions, 1970

Union	1970 Membership	President	Salary	Other Compensation
Teamsters	1,829,000	Frank E. Fitzsimmons	$75,000	$13,309.93
Automobile Workers	1,486,000	Leonard Woodcock	25,071	8,195.00
Steelworkers	1,200,000	I. W. Abel	52,500	15,157.51
Electrical Workers (IBEW)	922,000	Charles H. Pillard	53,444.44	7,437.02
Machinists	865,000	Floyd E. Smith	27,000	7,014.20
Carpenters	820,000	William Sidell	51,600	4,151.39
Laborers	580,000	Peter Fosco	50,000	21,132.00
Operating Engineers	393,000	Hunter P. Wharton	75,000	18,200.00
Plumbers	312,000	Martin J. Ward	47,610	22,585.00
Electrical Workers (IUE)	300,000	Paul Jennings	32,124.88	7,969.35
Railway Clerks	275,000	C. L. Dennis	70,000.08	14,896.57
Rubber Workers	216,000	Peter Bommarito	25,480.76	5,084.72
Oil, Chemical, Atomic	175,000	A. F. Grospiron	24,600	9,181.00
Chemical Workers	101,000	Thomas E. Boyle	26,884.82	2,715.08
Mine Workers	75,000*	W. A. Boyle	50,000	8,098.00
National Maritime Union	50,000	Joseph Curran	97,047.38	1,371.69
Cement, Lime and Gypsum Workers	36,000	Thomas E. Miechur	10,144	807.00

* Authors' estimate; membership not reported to Bureau of Labor Statistics.
    Note: George Meany, president of the AFL–CIO, was voted a salary of $90,000 by the 1971 AFL–CIO convention.
    Source: U.S. Department of Labor, Bureau of Labor Statistics and Office of Labor-Management and Welfare Pension Reports.

$25,000 to $50,000 does not seem large when compared to one varying from $100,000 to $500,000 paid to an industrialist. But unions are, after all, nonprofit organizations whose expenses are paid for by workers' monthly dues; and sometimes, those dues come from workers whose income is very small. Thus, the $50,000 salary of Peter Fosco, long-time president of the Hod Carriers and Building Laborers, is paid for mainly by laborers. And as the number of seamen and railway clerks has declined, the salaries of Joseph Curran, president of the National Maritime Union, and C. L. Dennis, president of the Railway Clerks, have gone up.

The largest unions do not necessarily pay the highest salaries, although the Teamsters is high in both respects. National Maritime Union's 50,000 members paid Joseph Curran $98,419.07 in salaries and expenses, making him the highest paid labor leader in the country, but Peter Bommarito's 216,000 Rubber Workers paid him only $30,565.48. With almost 1.5 million members, the United Automobile Workers paid their president only $33,226; with 25% of the UAW's membership, the Operating Engineers paid $93,200, or almost three times as much, to Hunter Wharton, their president.

We may conclude that union salaries vary with the interest of the chief executives in the subject. Some union officials want more money than others. And because the salaries of the rest of the union bureaucracy depend upon what the top man receives, there is always interest in more money for the top man if he is willing to countenance his subordinates pushing up the scale.

Union Financial Methods

A union with a membership of 100,000 and dues of $10 per month would have a monthly dues income of $1 million and expenditures for numerous items, most of which are purchased in bulk. Obviously it is imperative that unions operate with careful bookkeeping and accounting methods which account for every penny to the membership. Many unions have always done this, but others have not. In addition, local union accounting practice was often inadequate. Careful practices such as were adopted by the Steelworkers, the Ladies' Garment Workers, or the Machinists were not sufficiently common, especially at the local level. The passage of the Landrum-Griffin Act in 1959, and pension and welfare control laws in 1958 and 1962, were designed to safeguard union and welfare funds, now amounting to several billions of dollars.

As a result of these laws, union financial practices have been substantially improved. Although congressional investigators have found that millions of dollars of union and welfare fund assets have been siphoned into the hands of questionable characters,[5] or used, as James R. Hoffa did, for questionable investments in questionable projects run by equally questionable characters,[6] the practice continues, because unless someone complains, the government, under existing law cannot act.[7] Too often employers must share the guilt of dissipating union welfare funds because they have done nothing to stop it after handing over the monies. Both Hoffa and employer representatives on a Teamster welfare fund were convicted of conspiring to misuse such funds.

Union Assets

Based on reports to the U.S. Department of Labor, the authors estimate that international unions had approximately $4 billion in assets in 1972. This does not include the tremendous assets of local or intermediate union bodies; nor does it include the assets of welfare and pension plans, many of which are wholly or partially union controlled, and have assets estimated, as already noted, many times those of unions. Although union assets are enormous, they do not approximate those of major corporations. A few of the major corporations have more assets than all unions combined.

Most union funds are invested in low-return government bonds. Union financial managers want their assets liquid for emergencies, and they want to avoid criticism that could come if they invested in stocks of companies with which they might deal. Attempts to persuade unions to invest in socially desirable projects, such as low-cost housing, or to diversify their investments have largely been unsuccessful.

A conspicuous exception to this rule is the Teamsters, whose funds have been invested in a variety of deals, including real estate, gambling casinos, and hotels. Many of these Teamster deals have shown little return and are the basis for a continuing investigation of relations between Teamster officials and the promoters of these ventures.

In most cases, union wealth is a function of the prosperity of an industry. The brisk demand for automobiles in the 1960s made the UAW the country's wealthiest union until it overspent its assets on building projects and on the General Motors strike. Declining employment so

---

[5] See, for example, "Diversion of Union Welfare-Pension Funds of Allied Trades Council and Teamsters Local 815," in *Hearings before the Permanent Subcommittee on Investigations of the Committee on Government Operations*, (U.S. Senate, 89th Cong., 1st sess., 1965).

[6] Ralph and Estelle James, *Hoffa and the Teamsters. A Study of Union Power* (Princeton, N.J.: D. Van Nostrand & Co., 1965), pp. 213–320.

[7] When a complaint occurs, the courts can act. Thus, the Journeymen Barbers' Union pension fund was put under a court trusteeship after the fund was looted. (*Hood et al.* v. *Journeymen Barbers'* . . . *Union*, U.S. Court of Appeals, 7th Cir. [January 10, 1972].)

reduced the income of several railroad unions in the same period that a wave of union mergers occurred. The assets of the Mine Workers remained high despite a decline in coal miners from 500,000 to 100,000, because royalties for its welfare fund were based on tonnage mined, not number of miners and because the employer and union trustees of the Miners' welfare fund used its assets to further the UMW policy of protecting its investments rather than for its members. Thus, in the period between 1951 and 1969, 14%–44% of the miners' welfare fund monies were left in a noninterest-bearing account in the Washington, D.C., bank controlled by the UMW. Other funds were utilized to purchase public utility stocks in order to force these utilities to buy union-mined coal. A court ruled these acts a breach of trust and a conspiracy, ordered the UMW president to resign as a trustee of the welfare fund, ordered that all relations with the UMW-controlled bank cease, and assessed damages against the trustees of the welfare fund.[8]

ADMISSION POLICIES AND THE RACE ISSUE

The great majority of American unions admit any applicant to membership. "If he is good enough to work in the plant, he is good enough to join the union" sums up the prevailing union practice and attitude.

But unions also tend to accept prevailing practice. The union is the servant of its members, not an innovator. If discrimination exists, it is likely to be satisfactory to white union members. That is why Negro organizations and unions often are at loggerheads. That is why much antagonism exists today between many union and Negro groups.

Although the AFL preached against discrimination in its early period, many of its constituent unions did practice discrimination. Negroes were antagonistic to organized labor in the pre-1932 period because of this fact. But when the CIO was organized, it made a practice of encouraging Negro membership. This, in turn, forced the AFL and its unions to adopt a more tolerant attitude. Unions, and especially the CIO, received heavy Negro support during the next 15 years.

But as black unemployment rose in the late 1950s and the drive of the Negro for more equal status on all fronts continued, the gulf between the aspirations of blacks and unions widened. Racial equality programs ran counter to the vested interests of white union members—and they control most unions. The attempts of blacks to end this discrimination, and the tendency of unions to institutionalize the status quo ran counter to racial harmony.

The reasons for racial discrimination by unions lie in the basic economic and technological conditions of a particular industry. The unions

---

[8] *Blankenship et al.* v. *Boyle et al.*, Civil Action No. 2186–69, U.S. Dis. Ct., D.C., April 28, 1971.

which readily admit all applicants—the United Automobile Workers, the United Steelworkers, the International Ladies' Garment Workers' Union—are organized on an industrial basis, the only type of union structure feasible in a mass-production industry. Such unions derive their bargaining power by admitting all the workers in their industries to membership and by bargaining for them without discrimination. If they excluded any racial or ethnic group, they would weaken their bargaining power. Exclusion would invite the excluded group to join another union and to break strikes. Racial exclusion by unions in mass-production industries is not only impractical, but it endangers the union's very existence.

On the other hand, equal admission practices do not necessarily mean equality of treatment. Union seniority rules often institutionalize existing discrimination in promotion practices, or even add new discriminatory practices. In the steel industry, the United Steelworkers has done little to open up rolling mill jobs, traditionally a white man's preserve, to blacks. Nor did the United Auto Workers, until very recently, substantially aid efforts of blacks to expand their opportunities among the skilled craftsmen of the industry.

There are craft unions that do not discriminate, and industrial unions that do. Many other factors are involved; and in each case, they are mixed in different ways. In the case of the railway unions, for example, much can be explained by their character as fraternal societies. The first two railway unions (the Brotherhood of Locomotive Engineers and the Order of Railway Conductors of America) were fraternal and benevolent societies, and discriminatory rules are traditional in many areas of the fraternal field. As other railway unions came into existence, they copied the bylaws of the older organizations, including the discriminatory rules, as a matter of course, even though they may have become by then more important as bargaining than as fraternal organizations.

Economic factors, however, have been most important in maintaining the discriminatory practices of the railway unions. When employment on the railways declined, the railway unions tried for years to shift to black workers, whom they barred from membership, the burden of unemployment. The Brotherhood of Locomotive Firemen and Enginemen and the Brotherhood of Railroad Trainmen succeeded in getting nearly every railroad in the South either to limit the number of Negroes hired as brakemen and firemen or, more often, to eliminate Negroes from these jobs altogether within a few years. This deprived blacks of jobs which had been open to members of their race since the southern railroads were built.

The AFL–CIO takes a strong position against discrimination in its constitution and in all of its official actions. Nevertheless, it admitted to membership both the Locomotive Firemen and the Railroad Trainmen, after exacting promises that these organizations would delete the offending clauses from the constitutions—which they did, but significantly without altering their practices for many years.

There are many unions which expressly protect the right of workers to join, regardless of race. Such provisions vary from explicit provisions that "no worker otherwise eligible to membership shall be discriminated against or denied membership because of race" (Woodworkers), or that any discrimination because of race will be punishable by a fine of $100 (Bricklayers), to simple provisions that all eligible members, "regardless of race," shall be admitted.

Except in the building trades, racial admission policies are likely to be determined and controlled by the national union. There have been important exceptions. Locals of the United Automobile Workers have discriminated against Negroes, despite contrary national union policies; and locals of the Machinists and Boilermakers have admitted Negroes on an equal basis, in spite of national union discriminatory rules. These local variations have been the exception rather than the rule.

In the building trades, locals have on many occasions discriminated against blacks despite national officer pressure. This industry is still featured by strong local autonomy—and internal racial discrimination. As a result, building-trades local unions have been the targets of numerous civil rights demonstrations and court cases brought by state human relations commissions and by the federal government pursuant to the 1964 Civil Rights Act. Few matters have caused so much bitterness between unions and civil rights groups as the obvious and overt discriminatory practices of some building-trades unions.

Despite the progress in eliminating it, racial discrimination by some unions remains a blot on the labor movement. The fact that the record of the labor movement is about equal to that of most other facets of American life in race relations does not reduce the need to eliminate race discrimination in unions.

CLOSED UNIONS

Sometimes, unions refuse admission to any newcomers or accept only a favored few, for example, relatives of members. Such unions are found almost exclusively among the highly skilled or strategically located groups who alone are in a position to control entrance to the trade. In addition, closed unions may be found in industries where employment is casual or seasonal (maritime, garments). In a case in Philadelphia, one man tried in vain to gain entrance to the motion-picture projectionists' local for about 50 years—an extreme case involving skilled work in a casual trade.[9]

The closed union is usually a local organization. Generally, national

---

[9] *Philadelphia Inquirer*, December 2, 1962, p. 32. Investigation in 1968 indicated that he had never been admitted.

unions are opposed to a policy which limits union membership and may create a sizable group of potential strikebreakers. The local leadership, however, is under pressure to give preference to local members—even at the expense of members from other locals—and closing the union books is one way to achieve this result.

Sometimes, closed unions give limited work permits to nonmembers. This has developed into a racket in many instances, with permit holders charged high fees to work. A number of building-trades union locals have used the permit system to comply with government "goal" or quota requirements on jobs for blacks in federally financed construction. This, of course, serves to avoid admitting the black craftsmen to the union on a permanent basis and thus continues the practice of discrimination in construction in which federal funds are not involved.

The closed union is most common in the building, amusement, and printing trades, the local delivery business, diamond cutting, and mirror manufacturing. In periods of depression, it has extended to the seasonal and casual trades, and even to such industries as mining.

Reasons for Union Exclusionary Policies

The fact that some trade-unions limit their membership should not be regarded as too extraordinary. A great many barriers against economic opportunity are sought by a wide variety of organizational groups —farm, business, and professional as well as labor organizations. Moreover, the policies used by unions to bar admission are like those of other groups. Consider, for example, the historic attempts of the American Medical Association to limit the number of doctors (or to use the AMA's terminology, "prevent overcrowding of the profession"). Constituent groups of the AMA have used licensing laws, race discrimination, discrimination against aliens, denial of licenses to out-of-state doctors, and other equally antisocial means of restricting entry into the medical profession.

Whether a labor organization, a professional society, or a business organization, the reasons for restricting entry are usually the same: work-scarcity consciousness, dictated by fear of unemployment. For example, unions are more likely to close their books in depressions than in prosperity. Also, it is true that race prejudice is only one factor in the discrimination against Negroes. Undoubtedly, a most important reason for such discrimination is the fact that the color line provides a convenient method of limiting the market.

Public policy generally does and should condemn closed unions. Yet the case is often not a clear-cut one. For example, in depressed times, when unemployment among union members in the maritime industry is significant, unions typically "close their books." Because of the hiring hall system, whereby men are employed in rotation for available jobs, the effect of admitting new members would result in a further sharing of unemployment in a particular industry where unemployment among those already attached to the industry is severe and where employment even in ordinary times is casual and intermittent. Nevertheless, if the union books are closed to some, but not to others, on the basis of race, creed, or color, or by some other invidious method, then the action is clearly indefensible—and today also illegal.

JUDICIAL PROCEDURE IN UNIONS

In the conduct of their affairs, unions have found it necessary to establish a list of offenses for which penalties may be assessed against the members. Union constitutions give officers considerable authority to impose a wide variety of sentences upon their own initiative, or after a trial has found the member guilty. Many of the offenses are general in character (action unbecoming a union member is such an offense); others are more specific (strikebreaking, for example).

The penalties vary from a modest reprimand to the serious ones of heavy fines or expulsion from the union, which can mean a virtual blacklist for employment. Union judicial processes are thus a serious matter from the point of view of public policy—namely, to what extent should private governments, such as unions, be permitted to levy fines and to deny persons work?

Anyone familiar with the realities of union organization realizes that unions must have some protection against those who would convert the union into instruments of outside organizations, for example, the Communist party, or those who are agents of the employer, labor spies, or provocateurs. Moreover, if unions were unable to enforce any penalties whatsoever against members, workers who violate collective bargaining agreements could not be disciplined by the union.

On the other hand, the vagueness and general character of offenses found in union constitutions are a grave peril to the civil rights of its members. One of the worst abused is the prohibition against slander. No constitution defines "slander." Yet, it has often been invoked to insulate union officialdom against criticism. The same is true of "creating dissension" or discussing "union business" in public. Such events contributed to the passage of the Landrum-Griffin Act's "bill-of-rights" sections, guaranteeing members' rights to free speech.

Procedure

Charges against a union member are typically filed by another member. Invariably, they must be in writing and be served on the accused. A trial committee is then usually appointed by the local president or elected by the local. The committee hears testimony and renders a decision, which usually is reported to the local membership for action. A guilty verdict often requires more than a majority vote—two thirds or three fourths—usually by secret ballot. Penalties vary from reprimands and light fines ($5) to expulsions and heavy fines ($100–$5,000).

Virtually all unions provide for appeals through the union hierarchy. A frequent course is for appeal to the regional office, thence to the international president and/or executive board, and finally to the international convention.

In addition to this procedure, a number of unions grant their international president specific authority to initiate and/or hear charges against local members or local unions. Other unions permit the president to order a local to try a member and to take action if the local refuses to comply.

Unfortunately, most union constitutions do not provide for a stay of execution of the penalty pending appeal. Thus, even if a member eventually won a case on appeal, he could be denied union membership (and work) in the interim, which could be as long as four years. The ability of unions thus to discipline members has been reduced somewhat by the provisions of the Taft-Hartley Act, which do not interfere with the right of a union to expel a member but prevent that expulsion from causing the member's discharge, except for nonpayment of dues; and by the bill-of-rights sections of the Landrum-Griffin Act, which have provided much more ready access to the courts for redress if a member is wronged. Studies of the impact of these laws in terms of actual redress to the individual indicate, however, that restoration of job rights is often not effectively accomplished; or else that the costs of litigation are too formidable for the individual to undertake.[10] Moreover, U.S. Supreme Court decisions which permit unions to fine members who refuse to restrict production[11] and which permit unions to sue in court to collect fines from employees[12] would appear to have undermined the protections which Congress attempted to legislate.

Analysis of Union Judicial Procedure

Justice requires trial before an impartial jury, a full and fair hearing, and speedy determination of cases, including the appeal. Union judicial procedure has not stood up well under these criteria. There have been

---

[10] See, for example, the articles by Bernard L. Samoff, Regional Director of the NLRB Philadelphia office, "The Impact of Taft-Hartley Job Discrimination Victories," *Industrial Relations*, Vol. 4 (May 1965), pp. 77–94; "Taft-Hartley Job Discrimination Victories," *Labor Law Journal*, Vol. 17 (November 1966), pp. 643–63; and Cyrus F. Smythe, Donald P. Schwab, and Robert Madigan, "Individuals' Procedural Rights in Union Disciplinary Actions," *Labor Law Journal*, Vol. 17 (April 1966), pp. 226–40.

[11] *Russell Scofield et al.* v. *NLRB*, 394 U.S. 423 (1969).

[12] *NLRB* v. *Allis-Chalmers Mfg. Co.*, 388 U.S. 175 (1967). For critical analyses of these decisions, see Jeffrey L. Harrison, "Union Discipline and the Employer-Employee Relationship," *Labor Law Journal*, Vol. 22 (April 1971), pp. 216–21; and note "Fair Representation and Union Discipline," *Yale Law Journal*, Vol. 70 (March 1970), pp. 730–45.

some significant exceptions to this judgment. The International Typographical Union constitution shows great concern for due process and independent judicial determination for those charged with offenses against the union.

The United Automobile Workers goes even further. It has set up a public review board composed of seven well-known citizens who have no other relationship with the union. The review board receives copies of all complaints lodged with the UAW international executive board. If a union member is dissatisfied with the decision of the executive board, he may then appeal to the public review board, which has not hesitated to overturn the executive board on a number of occasions. Moreover, the public review board has authority to act directly on a matter "if it concludes that there is substance to the original complaint and that the action of the International Executive Board does not satisfactorily meet the problem." The Upholsterers' International Union is the only other union with a similar public review system.

As a matter of fact, those who bring charges under union constitutional processes more often than not may control the staffing of the trial committee appeal bodies. Thus, local officers who may bring charges in most unions either are most usually on the trial committee or appoint that body, this being the case in 77 of the 136 unions studied by the Bureau of Labor Statistics. However, 56 of these unions denied a place on the trial committee and appeal body for anyone who was an accuser or defendant. In addition, the defense is often prevented access to information, and witnesses are sometimes intimidated from testifying for the defense, or prompted to testify for the prosecution. The infliction of the penalty prior to the completion of an appeal has also been a severe hardship in many cases. An appeal to a convention which may not meet for five years is often an empty right, especially if the penalty is enforced meanwhile. Moreover, conventions are large legislative bodies, basically unable to give the time and study to appeals from disciplinary actions or other judicial functions. Since convention committees are usually appointed by union officers, such committees usually recommend denial of appeal from rulings made by these same officers.

Traditionally, the courts have regarded unions as private bodies without a vested public interest. Hence they would not intervene on behalf of a worker disciplined by a union unless the worker was denied the forms of a fair trial, i.e., fair according to the union rules, or else fair in general terms if the union rules contravene public law or policy. Moreover, the courts frequently required union members to exhaust internal remedies before accepting a case—which meant appealing first up the union hierarchy to a convention before bringing the case to the courts. Court litigation is, moreover, costly and uncertain in outcome because of the numerous technicalities involved.

Congress, therefore, intervened by passing the Landrum-Griffin Act, which requires guarantees of freedom of speech and assembly, freedom to resort to the courts or administrative agencies without reprisal, and safe-guards against disciplinary action (except for nonpayment of dues) unless served with written charges, given time to prepare a defense, and afforded a fair hearing, regardless of any contrary provision in a union constitution. Moreover, if the union procedure takes longer than four months, the judicial requirement to exhaust internal remedies is waived, so that court appeal is facilitated. Nevertheless, appeals to the courts continue to be costly and lengthy, although an increasing number of union members are using this avenue of redress.

DEMOCRACY AND BUREAUCRACY

Democratic government is frequently confused with "good" or effi-cient government. Some of the best-run unions in the country from the point of view of economic returns to membership, responsibility, financial integrity, etc., cannot be considered democratic. The Amalgamated Clothing Workers and the United Steelworkers are cases in point. On the other hand, the excessive delegation of authority, both executive and legislative, to union officials, who in turn employ a large appointive bureaucracy, is not necessarily a structural defect of large political units. It endangers democratic principles but is not proof of lack of democracy.

Moreover, union constitutions meet fairly well the key structural requirements of democratic government—general suffrage, free election of legislators, and control by the legislators of expenditure of funds and other executive actions. To be sure, the governments of unions frequently vary widely from the constitutional forms; and in actual fact, most unions are operated by political machines, the members of which have a vested interest in perpetuating themselves in office. This is, however, no unique indictment, since virtually all organizations are run by active minorities.

The most valid tests of democracy are found in the extent to which a union—or any other organization—adheres to principles laid down in the Bill of Rights—the first 10 amendments to the Constitution. For example, are union members protected in the rights to free speech, assembly, and press to the extent that they can, without fear of reprisal, criticize their leaders and work openly for the defeat of those leaders? Is there a judicial system within the organization which protects individual members in the exercise of these rights and which effectively insures a fair trial for those accused of crimes against the organization?

On the bases of these standards, Congress, in the light of evidence such as presented in this chapter, found unions so wanting as to require a legislative bill of rights for union members imposed by law.

LABOR RACKETEERING

Deficiencies in trade-union government which have been discussed in this chapter do not necessarily involve "racketeering," as the term is commonly used. What racketeering involves is the conversion of the union to the private benefit of the union official. A union official may engage in all sorts of undemocratic practices and still not convert the union into an instrument utilized primarily for his own benefit. Dave Beck, however, was different. Born in poverty, he worked himself up from laundry driver to the presidency of the country's largest union, the Teamsters. Not satisfied with the power, prestige and affluence of office, he used the union as a vehicle for personal moneymaking, greedily turning almost every opportunity to his profit. Finally, he was forced out by Senate committee revelations and an indictment for income tax evasion, for which he was later convicted.

Not all labor racketeers grow up in the labor movement. Some are full-fledged lawbreakers before they become union functionaries. An example is Johnny (Dio) Dioguardi, alleged Mafia member, who was brought into the Teamsters by Hoffa. Dioguardi created a number of "paper" local unions which sold protection to employers, and which also gave Hoffa the votes to control the New York City District Teamsters' Council.

Causes of Racketeering

Labor racketeering is likely to flourish in those industries in which employment is unstable and strikes are extremely costly. In such instances, notably trucking, the building trades, the longshore, and the amusement industries, the labor force changes so fast that opposition to leadership is difficult. More often than not, there are more men than jobs, so that the power of dispensing jobs is great, and the fear of unemployment inhibits opposition. When opposition within the union arises, a beating or a murder can squelch it. Employers, meanwhile, acquiesce in order to avoid strikes, property damage, or physical beatings.

Racketeering and Public Policy

Racketeering is thus a cancerous growth on the labor movement. It affects only a small portion of unions, but a significant enough group to be of public concern. Moreover, union racketeering is often a part of a larger setup featuring crooked business and political deals.

Obviously, such racketeering is more of a police than a labor relations matter. Too often, local authorities are unable or unwilling to cope with the situation; and sometimes, state officials are in no better position. A bistate authority established by New York and New Jersey is now trying to control crime on the New York City waterfront. Among the laws it must enforce is one barring those recently convicted of felonies from serving as union officials. A similar provision has been incorporated in the Landrum-Griffin Act. It has made it more difficult for racketeers to utilize unions as fronts for rackets but has certainly not ended the problem.

THE GOVERNMENT OF THE AFL–CIO

The government of the American Federation of Labor reflected the deliberate desire on the part of the founders of that organization to lodge the principal power in the hands of the national unions. The AFL constitution gave its president no authority to intervene in the affairs of its constituent unions. Consequently, a mild-mannered leader like William Green took refuge in his lack of authority when pressured to act against an affiliate. Stronger personalities, like AFL founder Samuel Gompers or George Meany, used the prestige of office to assert leadership when an affiliated union misbehaved, without violating the technicality that national unions are autonomous bodies.

Since the CIO was organized by former AFL unions, it is not surprising to find that its constitution was similar to that of the AFL. Thus the CIO constitution gave the president no statutory authority over affiliated unions. Until the death of Philip Murray in November 1952, however, the CIO executives, Murray and John L. Lewis before him, had great influence over affiliated unions. This was true because Lewis and Murray had, each in his own way, strong leadership personalities, and because both were the heads of powerful affiliated unions besides heading the CIO itself: Lewis of the Mine Workers, which he later took out of the CIO which he did so much to found; and Murray of the Steelworkers. It was also true because Lewis and Murray helped to organize many of the unions affiliated with the CIO, and other leaders in the CIO looked up to them and greatly respected their judgment. After Walter Reuther succeeded Murray as CIO president, he had the backing of the auto workers of which he remained president, but much less complete support among other CIO unions. This perhaps contributed to his willingness to merge the CIO with the much larger AFL.

Figure 3–1 describes the formal governmental structure of the AFL–CIO. It is much like that of the AFL (and the CIO, which was modeled on the AFL). The Executive Committee is a new development, which stems partially from the fact that the Executive Council was almost doubled in size after the merger.

The supreme governmental body is the convention, which meets biennially. Between conventions, the federation is ruled by its Executive Council, composed of the heads of 27 union officials who are vice presidents of the federation, plus the AFL–CIO's only two full-time salaried officers, the president and the secretary-treasurer. The Executive Committee, which meets bimonthly, is a committee of six members of the Council, elected by the Council, plus the president and the secretary-treasurer. AFL–CIO vice presidents receive no salaries from the federation.

National union control of the AFL–CIO conventions is insured by the method of representation. Each national union is entitled to send delegates to the convention in accordance with a formula based upon the membership for which monthly per capita tax has been paid to the AFL–CIO.

In contrast, directly affiliated locals—that is, local unions which are affiliated with no national union but are attached directly to the federation —are accorded just one delegate, as are city and state federations and departments.

FIGURE 3–1

Structure of the AFL–CIO

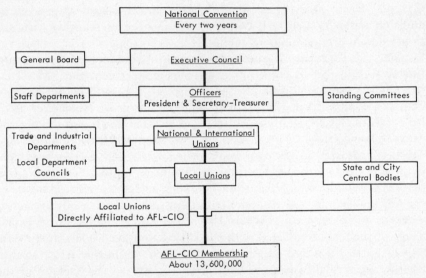

Source: U.S. Department of Labor, Bureau of Labor Statistics.

Most delegates to AFL, CIO, and now AFL–CIO conventions are officials of affiliated unions. The rank and file are more apt to be represented directly at conventions of affiliates. This does not, of course, imply that the AFL–CIO conventions do not represent rank-and-file opinion.

The AFL and CIO organized local unions for direct affiliation only when no affiliated national union had jurisdiction over the persons involved. After the merger, most of these unions were turned over to a national union. City and state councils are coordinating bodies which were chartered by the AFL and the CIO in cities and states for the purpose of giving direction and leadership to affiliated unions and to represent the AFL or CIO point of view before city and state officials. Often the leaders of these central bodies have considerable influence in their areas. They assist unions with bargaining, represent them before public bodies, and generally aid and coordinate their activities. The merger agreement provided the state and city AFL and CIO organizations had until December, 1957, to merge voluntarily. After that, the AFL–CIO was supposed to force merger. By the deadline, less than half had merged. It was 1963 before Meany finally forced some recalcitrant state and local bodies to merge, and as late as 1972, some which did merge either split apart, or former AFL or CIO unions disaffiliated from state or local bodies.

The Industrial Union Department was created to give the CIO unions a coordinating body within the merged federation. Other unions with industrially organized segments have since joined this department, but it remained at first a focal point for the old CIO group, and a platform for Walter P. Reuther, head of the department, to expound his views as he formerly did when president of the CIO, and to coordinate organizing, negotiating, and research efforts. Since the mid-1960s, the Industrial Union Department (IUD) has attempted to coordinate bargaining among unions which deal with the same company or industry. Such "coalition" bargaining tends to transfer the locus of union power from the various local and national unions to the IUD and greatly to enlarge the scope of bargaining, and therefore the impact of strikes. More recently, the IUD has proposed extending coalition bargaining across national boundaries in order to bargain on a coalition basis with multinational corporations. How such arrangements would work out in practice remains to be seen.[13]

The Union Label Trades Department promotes "union-made" goods. The four other departments act as bargaining agents, activity coordinators, and jurisdictional dispute mediators among railroad shopmen (Railway Employees Department), shipyard workers (Metal Trades Department), building tradesmen, and maritime workers. One international union can be a member of several AFL–CIO departments; the International Brotherhood of Electrical Workers, for example, is affiliated with all but the maritime trades group.

The AFL–CIO services its affiliates with a wide variety of functions, coordinating their activities, mediating disputes among unions, supplying news, publicity, economic and legal assistance, and leading and coordinating political activity, including lobbying at all governmental levels. The federation receives its funds from a per capita tax of 4 cents per month which each international union supposedly pays on each of its members. We say "supposedly" because sometimes the larger unions tend to report to the AFL–CIO a membership considerably less than they have in order to keep down their cost of belonging to the federation. As a result, AFL–CIO membership figures which are based upon the per capita taxes received may not be accurate.

The power of the AFL–CIO over its affiliates is greater than that which was held by the old AFL, but it remains limited despite the

---

[13] We shall discuss this issue further in Chapter 4.

vigorous leadership of George Meany, president of the AFL since 1952, and of the combined federation since the merger. Article VIII (7) of the AFL–CIO constitution establishes procedures to implement the doctrine, adopted in the new merger constitution, that affiliated unions shall be free of corrupt influences and totalitarian agencies. The Executive Council is empowered to conduct an investigation, to direct an affiliated union to take action on these matters, and on a two-thirds vote to suspend an affiliate pending action by the convention. This was the procedure followed in the suspension of the Teamsters' Union and other unions which the convention then expelled.

The AFL–CIO, for a short period, regulated the conduct of its affiliates to a degree not even considered by the AFL of William Green's recent, yet bygone, days. The passage of the Landrum-Griffin Act, however, lessened federation interference in the affairs of its affiliates. For with the enactment of legislation, the government took over the policing of union government and finances, and did so after the AFL–CIO expulsion of the Teamsters had demonstrated the basic lack of ability of the AFL–CIO to curb large affiliates which could "go it alone" after expulsion—the federation's most drastic penalty. Evidences of racketeering in such affiliates as the Painters have since elicited no action from the AFL–CIO headquarters.

QUESTIONS FOR DISCUSSION

1. Explain why the tendency toward increasing centralization of unions has occurred.
2. What do you think is the greatest weakness in union government? What remedies would you propose?
3. Why do you think discrimination and racial prejudice exist among unions?
4. Go to a local union meeting. Observe the conduct of affairs. Compare it with the local's constitution, and report to your class who runs the local—and how.

SUGGESTIONS FOR FURTHER READING

Bok, Derek C., and Dunlop, John T. *Labor and the American Community*, pp. 42–206. New York: Simon & Schuster, Inc., 1970.

Chapters dealing with union government, administration, minority rights, and AFL–CIO leadership.

Hutchinson, John. *The Imperfect Union. A History of Corruption in American Trade Unions*. New York: E. P. Dutton & Co., Inc., 1970.

An analysis of the character and extent of union corruption, utilizing especially the McClellan Hearings which led to the passage of the Landrum-Griffin Act.

Northrup, Herbert R. et al. *Negro Employment in Land and Air Transport*. Studies of Negro Employment, Vol. V. Philadelphia: Industrial Research Unit, Wharton School of Finance and Commerce, University of Pennsylvania, 1971.

Studies of the effects of company, government, and union policies upon black employment in four transportation industries.

ROWAN, RICHARD L. (ed.). *Readings in Labor Economics and Labor Relations*, Part III, pp. 159–276. Homewood, Ill.: Richard D. Irwin, Inc., 1972.

A series of significant articles on union structure, government, and administration.

PART III

Collective Bargaining

Chapter

4

ORGANIZING AND

NEGOTIATING

How do workers become organized in a union? What happens when collective bargaining begins? What are the wage and nonwage issues which concern labor and management in the collective bargaining process? What about strikes, "industrywide bargaining," "coalition bargaining," and "labor monopoly"? These vital questions will be the subject of our discussion in this and the following three chapters.

ORGANIZING

The unorganized plant may be called to the union's attention in a variety of ways. Often employees contact the union to interest it in establishing a local union for them. Other times the employers with whom the union deals stress the competition of nonunion firms and give the union representatives names and places as well as facts and figures. And frequently, the union will itself map out a drive to bring the nonunion plants within the fold.

The nature of the organizing campaign will depend upon the skill of the union leadership and its objectives. For a small group, the union drive may consist exclusively of personal contact of workers by the union representative. Organizing campaigns involving large companies include radio and newspaper publicity, leaflet handouts, large public meetings, and other methods of arousing enthusiasm in addition to the essential personal contacts.

As soon as possible, the organizers attempt to establish contact with sympathetic workers in the plant. Such workers act as volunteer organizers within the plant and form the nucleus of the budding union organization. As the union following increases, membership meetings are held, and a program for building a local union is developed.

Today in most industries the large firms have been organized. Increases in membership come only from the laborious task of attempting to unionize relatively small firms. Where large companies still remain unorganized, they are "tough nuts to crack." If they have held out this long against union organization drives, the employees involved are not likely to be interested in unionization. The employees of government, federal, state, and municipal, and of nonprofit institutions, such as hospitals, are now the most inviting organization targets. These groups include large numbers of unorganized employees who have recently demonstrated a strong interest in unionization.

Winning Union Recognition

Whereas once the question of whether employees desire union representation could be determined only by force, the Taft-Hartley Act provides that "representatives . . . selected for the purposes of collective bargaining by the majority of the employees in a unit appropriate for such purposes shall be the exclusive representatives of all the employees in such units for the purposes of collective bargaining. . . ." Congress gave to the National Labor Relations Board the power to conduct elections or otherwise to determine what union, if any, shall represent a given group of workers for collective bargaining. Once a union is certified by the NLRB as the bargaining agent, the Taft-Hartley Act provides that an employer must deal with it.[1]

WHEN THE UNION ENTERS

A union organizing campaign, by its very nature, upsets existing relationships and unbalances emotions within a plant. The job of the union organizer is in many respects that of initiating the transfer of the employee's loyalty from the employer to the union. To accomplish this, he is likely to point up existing or imagined grievances, to promise extraordinary and often unattainable benefits, to appeal to the worker to join with his fellows at the peril of being a social outcast, and to give impetus to the impulse of aggression and hostility which exists dormantly within most individuals.

The purpose of the union, of course, is to win the representation election conducted by the National Labor Relations Board, or otherwise to gain recognition from the employer as the bargaining agent. To accomplish this purpose, the union must sell itself to the workers; and as in political campaigns, almost no holds are barred. Under such circumstances, the employer finds himself under extraordinary temptation to develop a keen emotional animus toward the union and its personnel. Many employers believe that they must keep the record straight for their employees, that they should advise their employees to vote in representation elections so that decisions will not be made by default, and that they should correct grievances which are called to their attention by

---

[1] See Chapter 19.

the union organizing campaign. Employer communication to employees in such situations is becoming more and more common.

Employers who attempt to convince their employees that they are better off without a union may be charged with violating the Taft-Hartley Act by intimidating workers in the free exercise of their rights to choose their bargaining agent. Union organizers, on the other hand, complain that they are often denied equal opportunity and facilities to get their viewpoint across to employees; and when they stage mass rallies or picket at the factory gate so as to influence employees leaving or entering the plant, they may find that the employer has obtained an injunction prohibiting such activity. Some of these problems involved in the exercise of free speech by employers and picketing for organization purposes will be discussed in Chapter 19 in connection with analysis of the Taft-Hartley Act.

Problems of Early Adjustment

When the election is over, and if the union wins bargaining rights, the parties sit down at the conference table to negotiate an agreement which will govern their relationship for the next few years. Then there is a real need for clear heads and mutual understanding, not name calling and emotionally generated heat. But such a change in attitude, although undeniably beneficial to stable labor relations, cannot be achieved overnight. Charges, recriminations, and abusive remarks made in the heat of the preceding battle are not quickly forgotten. The union has the job of making good on as many promises to the employees as it can, and of establishing itself firmly not only with those employees who voted against it but also with those who have been lukewarm. The union representative, therefore, is likely to make extravagant demands and to be unwilling to compromise.

The employer, on the other hand, often retains the view that the employees were better off without the union, and he is disinclined to yield any concessions which would strengthen the union position and thus indicate to employees who were either lukewarm in their adherence to the union or who voted against union representation that there are substantial benefits to be gained through retention of the union as bargaining agent.

As a matter of fact, stable bargaining relations are not likely to be achieved until two developments occur: (1) management accepts the idea that the union is in the plant to stay, and (2) union members and leaders understand that their union is not all-powerful but instead that the basic job of running the business is still largely a management function. Until the new union and management learn to understand their new relationship and achieve a *modus operandi* within this relationship, there is likely to be some strain and strife in union-management dealings.

Management has the opportunity to start bargaining relations off on the right foot by dealing with the union honestly and fairly as a permanent institution and by forgetting any unpleasantness that developed during the organizing campaign. Management can also be helped by employing competent advisers who are experienced negotiators and who understand the significance of the first contract in the long-time union-management relationship. Otherwise management may concede issues that seriously interfere with the profitable operation of the business while fighting the union on other issues which, in the long run, may be less significant. For example, it may be far less costly to grant demands for extra vacation benefits rather than to concede to the union a veto over how many persons are required to man certain machines or whether new and more productive equipment may be introduced, even though a concession on these latter points does not involve any immediate cash outlay.

Union leaders can also ease the tensions by sending in new personnel to conduct negotiation of the contract—persons who cannot be charged with responsibility for any false accusations or violence which may have occurred in the course of organizing the plant—and by having the courage to explain to extremists among its members that some demands are out of the realm of the possible.

Negotiating the Contract

Negotiation of a contract, whether by a new union or an established union, is heavily a matter of effective preparation before negotiations commence but also a contest of wits between the representatives of management and the representatives of the union. In many cases, the general pattern of the contract will have been set before the negotiators even sit down at the conference table. This is true not only of the amount of any wage adjustment sought by the union but also with respect to the general content of the contract. Quite often the union will present the employer with a form of contract used by other organized employers in the same industry or by the same union in another industry. Or it may be that the employer will submit a form of contract which contains various clauses taken from other contracts in the industry or area.

Even if neither party presents a proposed contract, the "big bargains" —like those between the United Automobile Workers and General Motors, the United Steelworkers and United States Steel—or the big bargain in the particular industry or area may well have decided the general tenor of the agreement. But even where the general pattern has been set, the course of bargaining between the employer and union representatives will determine the extent to which the general pattern will be modified to suit the needs and peculiarities of the particular firm involved.

Collective bargaining has been facetiously referred to as "collective arguing." Since both parties sit down together with the intention of bargaining, they may try to conceal the ultimate position they are pre-pared to take and commence bargaining from extreme positions. If the union is prepared to settle for a 25-cent-an-hour increase, it may submit a demand for $1 an hour. Although the union's intention, when it makes such extravagant demands, is usually apparent to a skillful management representative, submission of such demands at the outset of negotiations accomplishes two useful purposes from the point of view of the union. In the first place, there are always certain extreme elements in the union who vociferously urge that large wage adjustments be obtained. The union negotiators must, therefore, present such a demand and retreat from this extreme position only after they appear to have made a last-ditch stand in the face of overwhelming employer opposition. In the second place, human nature is so constituted that management may be readier to settle at a lesser figure, and management representatives will feel that they have done a better job of bargaining, if the union demand starts higher than if it starts lower. The employer cannot, of course, know precisely what the union minimum demand really is. By starting from a high figure, therefore, the union hopes to improve its chances of picking up a few cents an hour which it might not otherwise have obtained had it started at a figure closer to the true minimum.

This method of bargaining is not always either smart or successful. Experienced management negotiators often refuse to make a genuine offer until the union "gets realistic." Often the only result of fantastic union demands is a delay in negotiations or an increase in bad feeling. In a number of strikes in the late 1960s, the union negotiators did not recede from such demands until after a long strike. Apparently these union officials believed that this approach was necessary to convince the rank and file of their militancy.

Collective bargaining frequently looks like a show. Sometimes the purpose of the oratory and gesticulations is to impress the parties on the other side of the table. Sometimes, there may be an actual audience, as is the case when the union business agents bring with them a large negotiat-ing committee representing the membership. Then the business agents are anxious to impress the negotiating committee with their skill as negotia-tors and the fact that the employer is a tough party to deal with. So they play to the galleries. Occasional walkouts by the union or management representatives from the bargaining table have come to be accepted as part of the byplay of collective negotiations.

The union, of course, does not have a monopoly on "acting ability." Employers also have become efficient in the art of predicting dire conse-quences if compelled to grant the union demands. When a representative of an employer association, or an outside consultant or lawyer, handles the company negotiations, he may also engage in theatrics to impress manage-ment personnel on the negotiating committee. Sooner or later, however, both sides get down to business, and usually a contract is hammered out. (See Figure 4–1 for the index of subjects covered in a typical agreement.)

FIGURE 4–1

Index to a Typical Collective Labor Agreement, Showing the Range of Subjects Covered

INDEX

FIGURE 4–1—*Continued*

Dissatisfaction with the "haggling" approach to collective bargaining has induced some employers to come to the bargaining table with a carefully researched and thought-out proposal, offer it to the union, and at the same time announce it publicly to the employees. The bargaining offensive in this instance reverts to the employer, and the bargaining which does occur usually is concerned with possible or minor modifications in the company offer. The effect of this tactic is to force the union to justify to its constituents any attack on the employer's position, for management has communicated its position directly to employees. This approach has been utilized with great success by a few large companies, and is known as "Boulwarism," after L. R. Boulware, a former vice president of General Electirc Company, who publicized it widely.

Satisfying the Constituents

No matter how smart the union may be or how fair the employer (an employer's being fair does not mean inept bargaining on his part), there will always be some employees in the plant who will be dissatisfied with the results. Usually, they are groups to whom the union promised something that was not obtained. They are the union's problem as well as the employer's. Moreover, difficulties in the home may cause some employees to discover "grievances" which are merely figments of their imagination, for their private lives may have upset them emotionally.

These problems require sincere, sympathetic, and honest treatment by both management and union officials. Grievances must be settled, not won. It does no good to prove that a grievance did not really exist. Pent-up grievances, however imaginary, are the sparks that flame into "quickie" strikes. A real attempt must be made to find the sources of the difficulties and to correct them, even if they are totally unrelated to the grievances presented; otherwise, dissatisfaction continues. Even under the best conditions, a new relationship between management and labor may be hindered by an occasional "wildcat" stoppage led by irresponsible elements who cannot be controlled by union officials. As elected officers who desire to retain their positions, union leaders cannot be too tough on contract breakers.

If, however, wildcat strikes or slowdowns continue despite company patience and good faith, it may be because understanding has degenerated into appeasement. Then a firm management hand, discipline of those who violate the contract, and a "no more nonsense" discussion with the union are usually the best methods of ending the trouble.

THE ECONOMIC SETTING OF COLLECTIVE BARGAINING

The labor relations policies of the textile and pulp and paper industries in the South are completely opposite in most instances despite the fact that both are located in the same region and often in the same or neighboring communities. The textile industry fights unionization tooth and nail, whereas the pulp and paper industry has stressed accommodation, peaceful union recognition, and high wages.

The answers to this seeming paradox lie in the different economics of the two industries. The textile industry has a high labor content, with its ability to operate profitably heavily dependent upon the availability of a large supply of semiskilled labor. Unionization presents a threat to the profitable operation of the enterprise and to the ability of the industry to meet foreign competition, with its much lower labor costs.

In contrast, the economics of the pulp and paper industry is featured by huge investments in buildings, equipment, and timber reserves, a relatively low turnover of capital, and a low percentage of labor costs relative to total costs. With fixed costs so high, there is tremendous pressure on the pulp and paper industry to operate its facilities 24 hours per day, seven days per week. To accomplish this with a minimum of interruptions, the industry has extended voluntary recognition to unions and paid high wages. The unions in turn have given the companies a relatively free hand in plant operations and have generally cooperated in peaceful settlements. In addition, the unions have aided in recruiting personnel to the often inaccessible locations where mills must be located.

The nature of collective bargaining is always heavily dependent upon its economic setting. The employment relationship is an economic relationship. The character and extent of competition, the relation of wage costs to total costs, the demand for the product, the capacity of the industry to pass on higher costs to the consumer (that is, the elasticity of demand for the product), and the size of the market all directly affect the nature and results of collective bargaining. Misjudging any of these factors can directly and adversely affect the demand for the product and thus for labor. Hence not only the results of bargaining but also the organization of bargaining arrangements (or lack thereof as in the case of the textile industry) reflect the economics of the industry. Whether, for example, employers bargain for themselves or through an association, as will be discussed in Chapter 7, depends largely upon these economic variables. The ability of a company to set up subsidiary plants where unions are weaker instead of concentrating them in one area where a strike can close down the entire company can depend on the capacity of the company to afford more than one operation and the investment required to make a plant profitable. A company whose plants manufacture unrelated products has much more bargaining power than one with assembly operations and parts plants all of which are interdependent. A company which supplies parts, such as glass or rubber tires, to another industry which, like the automobile industry, cannot operate without these parts, is usually reluctant to take a strike which could shut down its big customer. In such industries wages are usually very high.

Other examples could be given to show the dominance of the economic setting in collective bargaining. Within the economic constraints, other factors are significant. The social setting of collective bargaining illustrates this fact.

THE SOCIAL SETTING OF COLLECTIVE BARGAINING

The attitudes and issues which develop in the process of collective bargaining are profoundly affected by the social environment in which workers and employers live and work. Although collective bargaining technically concerns only the conditions and terms of work in a particular plant or company, the demands made by workers and the reactions of employers to such demands may reflect broad sociological patterns affecting the community, or even the country as a whole. The struggle between management and unions is to some extent a struggle for status—for recognition and respect and security. This contest is not confined to the factory. It can be seen in the attempts of labor and management to gain the favorable attention of public opinion. It is likewise to be seen in attempts of labor and management groups to influence the election of public officials. Union officials who live in a small-town atmosphere of hostility to unions are not likely to sit down with management with anything other than an attitude of suspicion and distrust.

Ethical and cultural patterns in the community leave a characteristic imprint on collective bargaining relations. Steelworkers have frequently been Italian-born or Polish-born; garment workers, Jewish and Italian in background; automobile workers, often Southerners, white and black. These diverse cultural and ethnic backgrounds undoubtedly influence union policies and the course of collective bargaining in particular industries and localities.

Likewise, some of the frictions which develop in a plant may be attributable to deep-rooted tensions in the community growing out of racial conflicts. Antagonism between black workers and white foremen may merely mirror the broader struggle for status of underprivileged black citizens who are discriminated against in the community and of white citizens taught early in life to "keep the Negro in his place."

In 1972, 23 percent of the work force was under 25 years of age. Youths today are quite different from their counterparts of 20 or 30 years ago. They are American born, usually of at least two generations, and better educated than ever before. They have grown up in an era of full employment, rising standards of living, and prosperity. They have seen unions stall great industries and union leaders command the respect of management and public officials. But they are questioning many policies of unions and companies. Excessive stress on pensions and security, for example, seems unnecessary to them in the light of their experiences and value scales. They want high wages and they want them now. When unions have not delivered to their satisfaction, they have not hesitated to reject settlements and to stay on strike. Sometimes, such rejection is more a revolt against union leadership than unhappiness with the proposed agreement. But an active, restive, well-educated, and uninhibited rank and file adds a new dimension to collective bargaining.

As these young people grow older, they will undoubtedly become more hesitant to strike, more stable in their relationships. Nevertheless, they will be affected by their environment, which is different from that of their elders, and this will affect union-management relations. They will, for example, be more used to interracial work forces and less concerned about minority workers in management positions. They will also have different attitudes toward women at work, for already in 1972, females comprised 40 percent of the labor force and by then had accounted for 60 percent of the growth in the labor force during the previous 20 years. As this increased participation of women workers continues, it will place emphasis on such matters as equal pay for equal work regardless of sex, synchronized vacations for husband and wife workers, and maternity leave and part-time work opportunities to allow mothers to work and still care for families.

THE COLLECTIVE AGREEMENT

A collective bargaining agreement today is customarily a lengthy document, often drawn in final form by an attorney, which sets forth the basic rules and standards which will govern the relationship of the employer and employees for the duration of the contract. The contract terms are binding not only on union members but also on all employees, whether members of the union or not, who are included within the bargaining unit. Union contracts customarily include clauses governing wages and hours, vacations, grievance procedure, union security, rights and responsibilities of management and union, promotion, layoff and discharge, and various working conditions peculiar to the plant or industry, as indicated by the table of contents of the contract reproduced in Figure 4–1.

Bargaining during the Life of the Agreement—Grievance Disputes

The typical union-management agreement, contains provisions—grievance machinery—for the settlement of disputes arising out of contract interpretation and application. The grievance machinery usually includes a series of steps, with a higher level of union and management authority participating at each step. To induce settlement without a work stoppage, more and more contracts provide for a terminal step of arbitration, to which are referred disputes that the parties cannot settle in any of the earlier stages. This type of arbitration is found in more than 90% of the contracts negotiated in recent years.

The grievance procedure is in fact more than a process which provides for the peaceful settlement of disputes arising out of contract interpretations. It is also a mechanism through which misunderstandings can be straightened out and problems solved. It permits representatives of management and labor to meet regularly and to obtain greater understanding of each other's problems. Finally, it is a vehicle for continued collective bargaining.

Collective bargaining does not end when the agreement is signed. It simply takes a different form. Union officials are just as alert to the possibility of obtaining additional benefits for their membership after a contract is signed as before. If, for example, the union can induce management to make an exception on vacation policy for one worker, that exception can be made the basis of a demand for liberalization of vacations in the next contract negotiations, either with this company or with other companies with which the union deals. Various groups in the shop may try to gain by direct action or pressure what they failed to achieve in bargaining over the new contract. If a rival for the union leadership can make gains in this manner, he might insure his election to the top union job next time.

Management may also do more than rest upon the contractual status quo. Plant managers and supervisors, anxious to maintain their control and profit positions, sometimes attempt to water down the agreement in practice. The contract is, in a real sense, only a temporary resting place.

In most instances, bargaining during the life of the contract is different from bargaining over a new contract. That is true because the bargaining after the contract has been signed is basically over the interpretation and administration of the agreement, whereas before the agreement is signed, it is the language of the agreement which is in dispute. Thus, some observers liken the negotiation of the agreement to the legislative function of writing laws, and the interpretation and administration bargaining which goes on after the agreement is signed to the judicial function of interpreting laws which the legislature has enacted. Like judges, the parties can substantiallly alter meaning and intent by interpretation.

Nevertheless, the attitudes of unions and managements toward interpretation and toward bargaining over new contracts are in many ways quite different. For example, whereas, as already noted, most agreements provide for the arbitration of grievance disputes—that is, disputes over contract interpretation—only about 2% provide for the arbitration of disputes over new or reopened agreements. In other words, unions and managements are willing to allow a third party to settle a dispute over an interpretation of an agreement when they cannot agree on the interpretation; but when it comes to the actual negotiation of the agreement, they want no outsider to do it for them.

Now, this is sensible, because no one is as qualified to write a contract as the parties who have to live with it. On the other hand, if the company is going to get out production, and if the workers are to receive steady pay, then the parties have to agree on a practical method which insures that production will not be interrupted by disputes over contract interpretation and administration. Then, if either party is too dissatisfied with the results of the decision of the outside arbitrator who interprets the disputed clause in the agreement, that party can attempt to have the contract altered at the next negotiation.

Figure 4–2 shows typical grievance machinery from the time a grievance is raised until it is settled by arbitration. Before an arbitration can occur, the arbitrator, or in some cases, board of arbitrators, must be selected. Some agreements provide either for a permanent arbitrator selected by the parties, or a permanent number of arbitrators who rotate by case. More often the arbitrator is selected for each case, or group of

FIGURE 4–2

General Pattern of Grievance Machinery in Large Plants

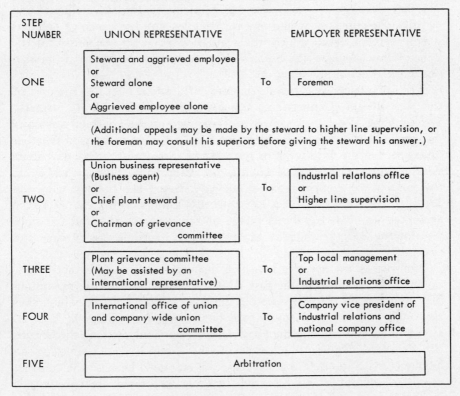

STEP NUMBER	UNION REPRESENTATIVE		EMPLOYER REPRESENTATIVE
ONE	Steward and aggrieved employee or Steward alone or Aggrieved employee alone	To	Foreman
	(Additional appeals may be made by the steward to higher line supervision, or the foreman may consult his superiors before giving the steward his answer.)		
TWO	Union business representative (Business agent) or Chief plant steward or Chairman of grievance committee	To	Industrial relations office or Higher line supervision
THREE	Plant grievance committee (May be assisted by an international representative)	To	Top local management or Industrial relations office
FOUR	International office of union and company wide union committee	To	Company vice president of industrial relations and national company office
FIVE	Arbitration		

cases. Most contracts provide that if the parties cannot agree on a selection, either the Federal Mediation and Conciliation Service, or a private, nonprofit organization, the American Arbitration Association, will be asked to submit a panel from which the arbitrator can be chosen, or even to name the arbitrator.

Typical Grievance Cases

In a certain year, two important holidays—July 4 and May 30 (Memorial Day)—came on Saturdays. What happened if the contract called for provisions for special pay or for leave with pay on these days and Saturday was not a workday? The answer is that it all depends upon what the contract says. For if a dispute over contract interpretation goes to an arbitrator, his job is to decide the dispute in the light of what the contract actually says and means.

This dispute arose at the Hanson & Whitney Company of Connecticut, which deals with the Electrical, Radio and Machine Workers. Here the decision went with the company's contention that it was not obligated to pay for these holidays not worked because the contract stated (1) that the regular workweek was Monday to Friday, inclusive, and (2) that the company would pay for time lost in observance of holidays which were observed during the regular workweek. Obviously, in the light of this language, the union's claim for pay for a Saturday holiday not worked could not stand up.

The same issue arose before the same arbitration board in the case of the New Britain (Connecticut) Gas Company and District 50, formerly United Mine Workers, but here the language of the contract was quite different. This contract provided that holidays were to be paid whether falling within the workweek or not; and furthermore, that holiday hours were to accumulate and be counted in determining hours worked for the purpose of computing overtime pay. Since the holiday came on Saturday after the employees had worked 40 hours during the week, the arbitrator decided that the language of the contract required not only pay for the Saturday holiday but pay at the overtime rate of time and one half.

Seniority is another area in which disputes are frequently hotly contested. This is especially the case when the issue involves the promotion of a junior man over a senior one under a contract clause which says that both seniority and ability will be factors in promotion.[2] For example, in a case involving the Hercules Powder Company and the Chemical Workers' Union, the action of the company in promoting an employee with less than top seniority was sustained because the contract read that seniority would prevail *"only if* factors of ability, aptitude and training are relatively equal." The words "only if" made it clear that seniority was a secondary, not a primary, criterion for promotion. On the other hand, the action of the Southern Bell Telephone Company in promoting a junior employee was overturned by the arbitrator in a dispute with the Communication Workers because the pertinent contract clause read that "seniority shall govern if other necessary qualifications of the individuals are substantially equal"; but the company wrongly interpreted the clause to permit it to promote the best qualified who was not "substantially" superior to the most senior employee in line for promotion.

---

[2] Seniority is discussed in Chapter 6. The terms *senior* and *junior* are used to denote length of service with a company, not age or experience.

Among the most difficult cases are those involving discipline. Often the issues are not sufficiently clear, and the evidence is blurred. For example, an employee may have deserved to be discharged for his conduct; but if the employer does not follow the procedure outlined in the contract, the arbitrator may have to reinstate the employee because contract procedure must be followed if an action is to be sustained in arbitration. In other cases, union officials will carry discharge cases to arbitration because the rank and file demands that officials fight for the membership, right or wrong. Even if the arbitrator sustains the discharges, the union official can take credit for putting up a good fight.

These cases illustrate not only how grievance disputes are settled but also why contract interpretation is so important to both labor and management during the life of the agreement. By settling disputes over interpretation and administration, and by working out disagreements, labor and management use the grievance machinery to turn a dry-reading contract into a way of working together.

Grievances are important to the union leadership in other ways. They afford an opportunity to gain the workers' loyalty and support by effectively arguing workers' causes with management in the many disputes which are processed through the grievance machinery. Furthermore, operation of the grievance machinery provides opportunities for thousands of workers to serve as union stewards and committeemen, and thus to gain familiarity with the process of collective bargaining. Several hundred thousand union members now serve in these minor positions. By participating in the grievance machinery, these men are training themselves for future union leadership and at the same time doing something which raises them above the monotony of tending a machine.

Management's representatives in the shop, the foremen, usually find that dealing with a union makes their job much more difficult. Once the union is in, the foremen's commands are subject to union challenge. But the foreman who learns to deal effectively with the union is training himself for a bigger job—for this foreman has learned to deal with people in a situation where not only command but also leadership achieves results.

Arbitration Loads, Delays, and Problems

In recent years, the arbitration machinery set up by companies and unions has been showing signs of strain. In general this is not true where contracts cover only one plant and one local union. There most disputes continue to be settled by the foreman and the union shop steward, and only a few will go to arbitration. Where multiplant contracts exist, the situation is likely to become more formalized and slower of resolution. Decisions involving one plant affect others, and often local officials, both union and company, are reluctant to settle without checking with their superiors. Frivolous cases often add to the list because local union officials avoid processing them or conceding their lack of merit for fear of alienating constituents.

To attempt to deal with such problems and their increasing grievance load, the United Steelworkers and the major steel concerns, following the recommendation of a joint committee which studied the problem, established an expedited procedure in 1972. It provides for the elimination of some of the grievance steps in cases which by agreement involve "an issue of limited contractual significance and complexity" and for their submission to an arbitrator from a rotating panel of 20 in informal hearings, with no briefs or transcripts. The arbitrator must issue a brief decision within 48 hours after the hearing is completed.[3]

The steel industry experiment to unclog the arbitration system is extremely important. Unsettled issues breed discontent, poor productivity, and strikes. Moreover, arbitration since 1960 has been clothed with great powers, for in three famous cases then, the U.S. Supreme Court ruled that unless a specific exclusion is written into a labor agreement, all issues arising between the parties to a contract were arbitrable.[4] Thus, such matters as plant moves, contracting out, and other facets of managerial decisions about which the union may have failed to gain a voice in the contract negotiations, may still be subject to arbitration. Such matters cannot be decided rationally or fairly a year after the fact.

LONG-TERM CONTRACTS

In 1948, a new bargaining style was established when General Motors Corporation and the United Automobile Workers negotiated a two-year contract, and then followed in 1950 with a five-year agreement. In 1951, 70% of the union contracts examined by the Bureau of Labor Statistics were of one year's duration. Five years later, the Bureau reported that only 35% of the contracts in its file were for a period of one year or less, whereas 65% covered periods of two years or more. By 1964, the Bureau's records indicated that contracts for periods of two years or more were the overwhelming favorite of unions and companies, and this practice continued to 1972. The imposition of wage-price controls in late 1971, and the resultant uncertainty about future wage movements, however, led to a flurry of union demands for one-year agreements.

Nevertheless, the popularity of the longer contracts is likely to en-

---

[3] The authors are indebted to Mr. Ben Fisher, Director, Contract Administration Department, United Steelworkers of America, for materials on the steel procedure. See also *Steel Labor*, February 1972, p. 5.

[4] *United Steelworkers of America* v. *American Manufacturing Co.*, 361 U.S. 564 (1960); *United Steelworkers* v. *Warrior and Gulf Navigation Co.*, 363 U.S. 574 (1960); and *United Steelworkers* v. *Enterprise Wheel and Car Corp.*, 363 U.S. 593 (1960).

dure. Both unions and managements prefer to avoid possible interruptions in their relationships every year. Annual negotiations can cause such regular uncertainties in production schedules and deliveries that profits and jobs are endangered, and this is obviously worth avoiding.

The trend has, however, definitely been away from the "formula bargaining" devised by General Motors and the United Automobile Workers in 1950. This formula provided for quarterly cost-of-living adjustments based upon movements of the consumer price index plus annual wage increases regardless of the movement of prices. Then, as prices rose in the late 1960s, unions again sought and won automatic cost-of-living adjustments as a condition of signing long-term agreements. These had been abandoned in most industries in the late 1950s or early 1960s.

Human Relations Committees

Following the 1959 steel strike, the United Steelwokers and the Kaiser Steel Corporation set up a committee composed of three well-known arbitrators plus representatives of each side to try to work out some of the problems which had led to the strike. Later the larger companies in the basic steel industry and the Steelworkers established a joint Human Relations Committee to meet regularly on joint problems. These committees achieved much publicity and had seemingly good results of disposing of troublesome issues without resort to strike. Most of them have worked quietly on particular problems which required considerable analysis and discussion before a settlement could be reached and which therefore could have caused problems in negotiations if not handled carefully. Others, particularly the Kaiser program, seemed to have been overballyhooed and ended in a strike and mutual dissatisfaction when the initial high payoffs dwindled.

Beginning in the early 1970s, a new union-management emphasis arose—joint committees to improve productivity. Again the steel industry and the United Steelworkers were prominent. Their problem was very real: How to improve productivity so that American steel producers, with their much higher wage costs, could compete with foreign producers and their much lower priced labor? Similarly, locals of the United Rubber Workers in Akron, Ohio, have been working with management to examine their practices and thus stem the flow of work from Akron to newer plants elsewhere. There is little new about such programs of joint labor-management activity. They have been historically established when jobs are at stake. Whether successful in their objectives, their application is likely to be limited because they cannot usually stem the basic economic tides which affect the parties involved.

A collective bargaining system, as the next few chapters will emphasize, grows out of the experience of the parties, which, in turn, is based upon the structure and problems of the industry involved, the general economic situation, the personalities at work, and a host of other things. What is applicable in one place may not be in others. There is no panacea for the solution of problems. They must be met, examined, and handled, and no two groups do that exactly alike.

As to the use of neutrals, as in the Kaiser plan, there can be no doubt that there are situations where an objective study, a different point of view, or a new look can be most helpful and appropriate if a particular problem or problem area is to be handled to successful conclusion. There is, however, no substitute for experience, and no crutch for responsibilty. Management and union officials cannot, in the final analysis, share their responsibility and accountability. If the business is not profitable, it is the management's responsibility; if the union members are dissatisfied with their contract or its administration, they hold the union leadership accountable. Third parties or neutrals may help to bring agreement, but those responsible must achieve the agreement and live with it.

THE SCOPE OF BARGAINING AND
MANAGERIAL PREROGATIVES

Union policy with respect to wages has always been phrased in terms of "more—always more." Management fears that unions intend to apply this same policy to the scope of collective bargaining. Rulings by the courts in expanding the jurisdiction of arbitrators, and of the National Labor Relations Board in requiring bargaining over actions, such as the contracting-out of work, which are initiated on purely economic grounds, have, as will be discussed in subsequent chapters, added to management's fears and sharpened the debate over "management's right to manage" and the unions' right to encroach thereon.

Managerial prerogatives may mean different things to different people. For the most part, however, the term is used by the group in society who may be termed the "professional managerial class." These are the managers of large corporations, as distinguished from the stockholders, who are the owners. These people, who include in their ranks the whole array of business executive and administrators from president down to foreman, are a group set apart from both labor and owners. In a very real sense the conflict over managerial prerogatives and functions is part of the struggle of this group for status and recognition—a struggle which is as important to this group as is the struggle by union leaders for recognition and public respect. Some take the view that the function of the union is primarily one of limiting the power of the managerial class to determine the distribution of the total product of industry and the share of individuals and groups in it.

But the conflict over managerial prerogatives is also a part of the conflict between management's desire and need to innovate and employees' attempts to achieve "security" by institutionalizing the status quo. The history of labor relations is replete with examples of employees, acting through unions, "winning security" by restricting management's freedom to innovate or to change, only to find that their "victory" created a high-cost situation which lost the very jobs they sought to protect. For if innovation and change are blocked in one plant or industry, other companies will innovate and change, with resulting cost differentials and consequent effects on sales, profits, and employment.

Nevertheless, there is no clear pattern of practice from one industry to another as to what is solely a management function. In Chapters 5 and 6, we shall find that unions have been able to influence—or, on occasion, to control—a wide variety of actual managerial problems which relate both to the wage and to the nonwage aspects of collective agreement. Thus, unions assist in advertising and distribution; influence and affect price policies, directly or indirectly; control or limit entrance to the trade; act as employment agencies or otherwise control hiring; affect the rate of technological advancement and, therefore, management organization of the factors of production; and in other ways participate in what management traditionally has considered its proper functions. Obviously, a definition of managerial functions which would have any real meaning would be very difficult.

Actually, collective bargaining affects all phases of business activity. Paradoxically, the companies which recognize this fact are the ones which have been best able to retain "management's freedom to manage." Before making decisions on plant location, contracting-out, work scheduling, or even new-product development and manufacturing, companies such as General Motors or Armstrong Cork, consider the employee relations aspects and work to eliminate complications and problems which might otherwise arise. They thus avoid challenges in sensitive areas and are prepared to meet opposition if it arises, not on an emotional but on a factual basis.

Looking at the problem another way, it is important to recognize that unions are, in a real sense, a management-regulating device. The extent to which this management regulating or restraining becomes participation is sometimes only a matter of degree. This is true despite the fact that most unions disclaim any desire to participate in management as vehemently as management denies the right of labor to participate in management. Yet in the light of the vast participation of unions through collective bargaining machinery in activities which directly or indirectly affect all phases of company management, there is already labor participation in management.

The extent to which labor participation should exist in management decisions, or whether it is socially desirable, remains a matter of debate. Certainly, solution of the problem of the extent of union participation and influence in management is one of the great problems of our time. In fact, the issue of union impingement on managerial prerogatives is merely another aspect of a greater issue—namely, the role of unions in our society. One may therefore agree with the view (often expressed in anger or sorrow by businessmen) that there are in fact no limits to union interests in management. Union penetration of former managerial prerogatives is likely to be greatest in the areas most closely associated with industrial relations. Personnel management is thus today much less a sole management function than is business finance. Since, however, industrial relations affect all aspects of a business, union interest in corporate financial methods should not be surprising. Nor is such interest new. The railroad unions, for example, have criticized the financial methods of the railroads, charging that they carry an oversized bonded indebtedness which tends to siphon off earnings and thus to permit the railroads to plead inability to pay wage increases. Many other examples could be cited involving production, sales, engineering, and other management functions in which unions have taken an effective interest.

But although unions have taken an *interest* in management functions beyond the personal field, that interest has not altered management decisions, at least in the mass-production industries. Thus, the decisive considerations in the automobile or steel industries, both before and after the spread of unionism, have been economic and center in the advantages which accrue to the largest producers by virtue of their ability to spread their costs. The unions have effected changes and altered ways of thinking, but the basic decisions outside of the personnel field are made by management and controlled by the economics of these industries. When management has lost this control, or when the economics of the situation have been disregarded, the inevitable result has been economic loss—sales, profits, and employment have declined, or the companies have gone out of business.

SETTING UNION POLICY FOR COLLECTIVE BARGAINING

Who sets union policy in collective bargaining—and how? There is, of course, wide variation among unions, but several clear trends have developed over the years. One is the shift of control from local unions to national unions. This is in line with the trend toward centralization of national union power, which we noted in Chapter 3.

The Shift to National Control

The trend toward national union control of collective bargaining is not new; it was noticeable at the turn of the century. In recent years, however, it has gained momentum, for several reasons.

In the first place, national unions have been forced to take over authority from locals in order to insure that uniform wage and working conditions and policies pertaining thereto will be followed where the national union believes such uniformity is essential. This is especially important when union members travel, as in the case of musicians, actors, or building workers. Although these unions negotiate on a local basis, their negotiations are often either guided by the national union or controlled by the national union to insure uniformity within limits and to prevent jockeying to secure superior settlements.

Even where the tradition of local control is strong, national unions sometimes regulate the limits of local union bargaining. Local agreements in the Typographical Union must be submitted to national headquarters for approval. The United Automobile Workers has created national departments which do the primary bargaining with such multiplant concerns as General Motors, Ford, and Chrysler.

When collective bargaining goes from the local to the national stage, the power of the local union wanes. Centralization of authority within the United Mine Workers has obviously been furthered by the development of national collective bargaining. On the other hand, regional systems of collective bargaining, such as exist in the parts of the pulp and paper industry, have the effect of creating semiautonomous departments within national unions. Especially if the region is large, it becomes self-sufficient and needs little national assistance in bargaining. Its officers and members are then not likely to submit meekly to close national union supervision. Moreover, even when bargaining is nationwide, purely local conditions are left for local bargaining. The coal miners are a case in point.

Too tight national union control of local bargaining has often brought strong local reactions. Agreements made by national union leaders have on a number of occasions been repudiated by local union members who felt either that their interests were insufficiently considered or that they were not sufficiently consulted beforehand.

Within a single organization, there may be conflict between "high-wage" and "low-wage" locals over the extent of national control. The former, fearful that they will lose business to the latter, are likely to desire strong national control in the interests of uniformity. Because of the marginal character of many employers with whom the low-wage locals deal, they are likely to oppose these policies.

Federation Control

As noted in Chapter 3, certain departments of the AFL–CIO play a role in the collective bargaining process. For many years, the Railway Employees Department has coordinated bargaining for the railroad shop-craft unions; the Building Trades Department and the Metal Trades Department have local or regional affiliates which perform the same task in local or regional bases. By such departmental confederations, craft unions have been able to deal on an industrial basis with employers. But historically, the coordinating department official has had little authority or power except to carry out the desires of the national or local unions.

An attempt at more far-reaching coordination, or coalition, has been undertaken by the Industrial Union Department, which has attempted to bring into one bargaining group industrial and craft unions which deal with one company or one industry. Under this coalition program, the representative of the Industrial Union Department assumes a key role in the bargaining, becomes the key strategist, and often the key spokesman as well. The aim of the program is to bring maximum union pressure on the company and to promote union mergers and amalgamations by demonstrating the effectiveness of coalition efforts.[5] If successful, this program would result in taking the bargaining process and its control one step further from the local union and would, of course, dilute national union control of bargaining as well. The final step now advocated by the Industrial Union Department in dealing with multinational corporations is multinational bargaining—that is bargaining between the corporation and representatives of employee unions from all countries in which the corporation has facilities. Such meetings have already been held between a few companies and unions in a number of European countries and could become more common if political boundaries diminish in significance and corporate expansion continues on a worldwide basis.[6]

The Formulation of Demands

Although negotiations may be controlled to a considerable extent by the national officers, it is typically the local members who formulate demands. Actually, of course, most demands other than those for higher wages or specific working conditions are usually articulated by union officials, or in the case of many unions, developed by the leadership. Sometimes union officials even push demands that are not popular with the rank and file. In times of unemployment, it is not uncommon, for example, for the leadership to be demanding shorter hours and work division while the rank and file that is working want more overtime. In general, however, the leadership must keep its ear to the ground and attempt to articulate what is of interest to the rank and file. Otherwise both the political support of the officials and the opportunities for contract settlement are endangered.

---

[5] For an analysis of this program, see Willian N. Chernish, *Coalition Bargaining* (Industrial Research Unit Study No. 45 [Philadelphia: University of Pennsylvania Press, 1969]).

[6] Based on preliminary information of a study of multinational bargaining under way at the Industrial Research Unit of the Wharton School.

Customarily, demands are formulated at local meetings, in some cases on the basis of leadership proposals, in others after presentation by a special committee, and in still others after direct suggestions from the floor. When more than one local is involved, union rules often call for joint committees of the locals to unify demands. Regional bargaining requires machinery once utilized in the Pacific Coast paper industry, where the locals submit their amendments to a general meeting held just prior to bargaining conferences. Demands of unions engaged in national bargaining are usually formulated at national conventions (miners, steel-workers) or at special national conferences (railway employees).

One of the effects of rank-and-file formulation of demands is likely to be that the demands are excessive, both in number and in amount. Everyone has his favorite recipe. This, in turn, leads on occasion either to disgruntlement with results or to strikes because extraordinary demands either are not met or are insisted upon in the face of employer resistance.

Negotiating Personnel and Its Powers

The negotiating committee in most unions is appointed with an eye to representation of the various groups within the organization. The various crafts, geographical areas, races, or nationalities are likely to be represented on any negotiating committee. It is quite common for union constitutions to require that negotiating committees provide for adequate geographical or trade representation. Craft groups in industrial unions especially insist on representation. Only a few unions, such as the Laborers' Union, grant almost blanket power to union officials to act automatically as the negotiating committee.

In actual practice, negotiations are frequently carried on by a sub-committee of the negotiating committee. This is often a practical necessity, since negotiating committees are frequently too large and negotiations become unwieldy when all members participate. Some union constitutions provide for the election of a subcommittee. Others do so in practice. In still others, the union president becomes the subcommittee, particularly where he has a considerable standing and prestige with both employers and the membership.

The power of negotiating committees or subcommittees varies considerably. At the local level the committee is rarely given full authority to settle without rank-and-file approval of the terms. However, it is quite usual for the rank and file to give a negotiating committee power of settlement after negotiations have proceeded for some time or have reached an impasse where a prompt decision is essential.

In general, it is probable that most local leaders would not want complete power of settlement. The reason is that if they make an agreement without specific rank-and-file approval, they will be held strictly accountable for the results, and the net effect of the accounting may well be defeat for reelection.

On the other hand, most national leaders would prefer the power to settle. They feel that they are capable of securing the best settlement possible, and that the rank and file, which is often without knowldege of the peculiar problems involved in negotiations, will demand more than can possibly be obtained and thus force the union into costly strikes which it has no hope of winning.

The case for granting union officials the power of settlement is formidable. Nevertheless, the requirement that all terms be referred to the rank and file is a power check on union leadership which is probably best retained. Moreover, even in cases where union leadership possesses the right to settle, rank-and-file revolt may effectively curtail that right simply by refusing to work under the new contract. Although rank-and-file rejection of contracts has been alleged to be a serious problem, careful research has demonstrated that it is not pervasive, but that when it occurs, it is the result of a fundamental failure on the part of union officials and managements to communicate properly with the rank and file.[7]

There is a great deal of educational value in worker participation in collective bargaining. With the exception of times when there are political contests within the union, negotiations for new contracts cause the greatest turnout to meetings and the greatest general worker interest. Service on negotiating committees, participation in discussion over terms of settlement, and the interest which these activities arouse build union leadership for the future and assure an element of democracy in unions.

National collective bargaining, however, does not appear to afford the opportunity for full discussion for settlement on the local level unless it is possible to have the contract discussed and voted upon at local meetings all over the country. With hundreds of locals involved, as in the case of the United Steelworkers, this is impractical. Moreover, the referendum is no substitute, since it does not permit argument and discussion, which are the essence of the educational process. A truly representative national bargaining committee with an effective voice in negotiations appears to be the most practical body to approve or reject contracts where national or regional collective bargaining exists. The difficulty of obtaining effective rank-and-file participation in national collective bargaining is one reason why local strikes have become so common in such industries as automobiles after the national bargaining has been concluded. Local issues and local participation require consideration that cannot be given at the national level, and a strike may be the only method of effective participation for the local rank and file.

---

[7] Donald R. Burke and Lester Rubin, "Is Contract Rejection A Major Collective Bargaining Problem?" scheduled for publication in 1973 in *Industrial and Labor Relations Review*. Manuscript in authors' possession.

Under such circumstances, the settlement of the national contract may be only the beginning of labor problems for the company, not the end. Obviously, if through coalition bargaining or multinational bargaining, the scope of bargaining is further expanded, the rank-and-file participation will be even more eroded and the resultant problems will increase.

SETTING MANAGEMENT POLICY FOR COLLECTIVE BARGAINING

"When employees want to deal with management through a union, the most fundamental, question is how far management should be guided by definite policies."[8] The absence of policies means that all decisions are made on a spur-of-the-moment or opportunistic basis. The usual result in such cases is that management sacrifices the long-run needs of the business to maintain its competitive position for assurances of uninterrupted production at the moment. For example, in the 1940s and early 1950s, the Studebaker Corporation of South Bend, Indiana,[9] and the Alexander Smith Carpet Company of Yonkers, New York, were cited as outstanding, liberal companies which handled union relations well. By 1966, both were out of business. Opportunistically attempting to buy good labor relations, these and many other companies allowed their costs to grow until they could not compete. Not only were the stockholders and business managers losers—their employees lost their jobs, and the local unions representing these employees lost their members.

A management guided by well-thought-out policies does not mean a rigid management. New situations and problems constantly arise, and experimentation is necessary. But such experimentation is far different from action by opportunism, or from complete concern with the immediate and disregard of the future. As the authors of an outstanding work noted:

A few firms are in a position to dictate the nature of their relationship with the union; many small firms must take what conditions the union offers and get along as best they can; most firms, however, are more or less an equal match for the union, and the quality of their relationship with the union depends on the skill shown in negotiating and administering the agreement. The

---

[8] Sumner H. Slichter, J. J. Healy, and E. R. Livernash, *The Impact of Collective Bargaining on Management* (Washington, D.C.: Brookings Institution, 1960), p. 10.

[9] When the UAW's Walter P. Reuther in 1945 reported to General Motors' chief negotiator that Studebaker had granted a substantial wage increase, the General Motors spokesman retorted: "I wouldn't want our plants run like Studebaker's are run" (Robert M. MacDonald, *Collective Bargaining in the Automobile Industry* [New Haven: Yale University Press, 1963], pp. 364–65). Professor MacDonald's study, in contrast to earlier, less incisive ones, found Studebaker featured by costly and poorly administered labor practices, brought on chiefly by inept handling of labor relations by top management and by inadequate training of supervision.

best goal for most firms is a stable relationship with the union on terms that permit the firm to be competitive and to adapt itself to changing conditions.[10]

This "stable and competitive" relationship can be achieved only if the top management of a company understands its importance and is willing to invest the time, talent, and funds to obtain this objective. Only top management can make some of the necessary decisions. For example, will the company be willing to take a strike in order to prevent it from being saddled with a work rule which one day might weaken its competitive position? "Unless top management takes a firm position in advance against accepting uneconomic practices, subordinate officials will tolerate them rather than assume the responsibility of failing to meet production standards."[11]

MANAGEMENT ORGANIZATION

To implement its policies, management must set up an organization capable of handling both union relations and other aspects of the personnel function. Because union relations involve a time-consuming process, and a talent not necessarily held by production or sales executives, a special management representative or department is usually assigned to handle personnel. If union relations are conducted on a part-time or off-hand basis, the net effect is likely to be expensive concessions made to the union "so we can get back to our main business of cutting metal or shuffling paper." Small companies which cannot afford full-time personnel departments often hire skilled lawyers or consultants for this purpose.

The companies noted for the most successful administration of their labor relations assign this responsibility to executives of stature and resourcefulness, compensate them and afford them status accordingly (for example, name a vice president to the top personnel post), and see that they are a part of the top councils of the concern. Such persons can recommend policies or changes in policies, argue with other top executives about the merits of various issues, and see that the labor relations point of view is considered in basic production and sales policies. Problems can then be met and handled before controversies arise.

Keeping Line Supervisors Informed

Equally as important as setting policy and putting effective leadership in charge of union and personnel relations is the need for top management to make clear to its subordinate officials, supervisors, and foremen what it expects of them in handling the union relationship. Unless this is done clearly and effectively, policies at the shop level will

---

[10] Slichter, Healy, and Livernash, *Impact of Collective Bargaining*, p. 11.
[11] *Ibid.*

bear little relation to the pronouncements from company headquarters, for the foremen will work to "get along" at whatever cost it requires. Such "getting along" can mean quiet but costly concessions which, in practice, whittle away managerial control of the shop, reduce productivity and efficiency, and injure the competitive position of the company.

The best managed companies, therefore, spend considerable time, effort, and money on foremen selection and training, in an effort to insure effective management, including employee relations management, at the shop level. Foremen are instructed in such companies on techniques of handling people, grievance settlement, and union contract interpretation.

It is most important, also, that top management back up its supervisors and practice what it preaches. If executives of a company advise foremen to take a strong stand against a union demand or action and then yield to the union under the threat of a strike, the word will go through the shop grapevine that management does not mean what it says. The union will take the action to mean that it can induce a change in company policy by a show of force, and foremen will see such executive inconsistency as advice to them to concede readily and quietly to union demands.

The Management Bargaining Committee

From the point of view of the employer, bargaining with the union may be on an individual plant basis or on a companywide basis, or the employer may be one of a number of employers who bargain together in an employers' association. If bargaining is between a local union and a single plant of a large corporation, negotiations may be conducted by the local personnel director and/or the plant manager, subject to instructions from company headquarters. On the other hand, if all of a number of plants of a company are involved, the industrial relations director of the company is likely to conduct negotiations. In regional or industry-wide bargaining, employers are usually represented by committees or officers designated by the employers' association. On all levels of collective bargaining negotiations, employer representatives may include the company attorney or consultant, whose function may be to participate actively in negotiations, to give behind the scenes, or in some cases merely to reduce to contract form the bargain reached by the parties.

As in the case of unions, there is considerable diversity in the amount of authority given the management representatives at the bargaining table. In some cases, they may be able to make final decisions on all aspects of the contract; in other situations, they may be able to agree only to minor changes and concessions, and they must obtain the approval of the president before committing the company to anything substantial. Large outlays, such as those involved in the establishment of a pension system, sometimes require approval of the board of directors as well as of the president.

Within the management organization, some of the same type of pulling and hauling for the power of decision making occurs as goes on within the union. In some cases, the financial officer exercises powerful influence whenever a money matter is involved. In other companies the dominant voice is that of the top production man; in still others the top sales executive exercises the most influence. The extent to which the advice of the chief personnel official is accepted in such situations is a measure of the standing and influence of both himself and his function.

Whenever a company must determine whether to take a strike or to accede to a union demand, a decision must be made on the basis of the current position of the company and the prospects and choices involved. Obviously the final determination in such matters must be made by the top executive of the company. In such instances the current sales and the financial and production situations must be evaluated. The decision cannot be made on the basis of industrial relations alone but must be made on the total needs of the company. A company which can stockpile inventory is obviously in a stronger position to resist union pressure than one which sells a nonstorable service. Automobiles or steel can be warehoused or built ahead; daily newspapers, air transport companies, or restaurants cannot accomplish this. The demand for some products can be postponed; for others it cannot. Management decisions must reflect the realities of the company's industrial situation.

Because a strike involves losses now and concessions *may* be serious in the future from the point of a company's competitive position, there is a great temptation for businessmen to decide questions involving labor relations on a short-run basis. Yet the failure of management to evaluate correctly the long-run implications of costly concessions made to avoid labor strife has been fatal to many companies. Undue concessions made at the point of a strike threat, or actual strike, are too often an invitation to further strife. For by yielding to such coercion, management is in effect telling union officials and members that a strike threat or a strike pays off. If this feeling becomes general, it can easily result in a long, bitter strike at some future date—if not a series of shorter walkouts—but in any case, it can be quite costly to the business.

Moreover, if a company yields to an uneconomic demand, or a series of demands, it may be digging its grave by incurring a cost which does not permit it to compete in the product market. This can mean not only loss of profits but also loss of jobs and hence union members. A short-run decision which ignores long-run considerations can be disastrous to both employer and union.

Of course, not all business decisions, any more than all union decisions, are based upon economic calculation. Instances of businessmen forcing a strike to win leadership over rivals in their own firm are not unknown. Likewise, industrial relations decisions based upon emotions rather than economic facts occur every day in managerial ranks. Businessmen, like union leaders, are people, and anything but infallible.

QUESTIONS FOR DISCUSSION

1. If you were the personnel manager of a plant and a union began an organizing campaign, what actions would you take? If you were a business agent of a union, how would you attempt to recruit workers?
2. Why do you think long-term contracts have become so important? What are the economic implications of this development?
3. What are managerial prerogatives? Is it a good idea to define them by law? If you were a manager, how would you protect your prerogatives?

SUGGESTIONS FOR FURTHER READING

CHERNISH, WILLIAM N.   *Coalition Bargaining.* Industrial Research Unit Study No. 45. Philadelphia: University of Pennsylvania Press, 1969.
   An analysis, with numerous case studies, of the union drive for expanded bargaining units and its implications.

DUNLOP, JOHN T., and CHAMBERLAIN, NEIL W.   *Frontiers of Collective Bargaining.* New York: Harper & Row, 1967.
   Thirteen authors examine a wide variety of labor relations problems and comment on their significance and impact.

SIEGEL, ABRAHAM J. (ed.)   *The Impact of Computers on Collective Bargaining.* Cambridge: The MIT Press, 1969).
   A series of articles estimating how the computer is affecting, and will in the future affect, collective bargaining.

SLICHTER, SUMNER H.; HEALY, J. J.; and LIVERNASH, E. R.   *The Impact of Collective Bargaining on Management,* chaps. i–ii, xxi–xxx. Washington, D.C.: Brookings Institution, 1960.
   These chapters of this outstanding work deal with management issues in collective bargaining, grievance handling and arbitration, and managerial handling of industrial relations.

Chapter 5	THE CONTENT OF COLLECTIVE BARGAINING: WAGES

Collective bargaining is basically a method of determining wages and working conditions for employees. In this chapter, we shall examine the wage content of collective bargaining; in the following chapter the working conditions which form the "industrial jurisprudence" of bargaining will be our subject. Then, in Chapter 7, we shall discuss some key questions resulting from the bargaining process.

WAGE—A COMPLEX TERM

A better insight into the nature of the collective bargaining process is provided by considering just what is encompassed by the term *wage*. There is a natural inclination to use this term as if it were a rather simple component and as if the only variable which had to be determined in setting the wage was its amount. Actually, however, the wage is a highly flexible form of compensation and may vary considerably both as to form and as to content. For example, it may be based on payment by the piece, payment by the hour, or participation in a complex profit-sharing plan. It may or may not include group insurance, pensions, and similar fringe benefits. For example, a labor-management negotiation may result in a 35-cent-per-hour "package," composed of 25 cents in wages, 5 cents in pension improvements, and 3 cents in insurance and miscellaneous benefit improvements, and 2 cents in holiday and vacation allowances.

Only the first item—the change in the wage rate itself—relates directly to what has traditionally been termed *wages*, whereas the other items of the wage package fall in the category of supplementary or fringe benefits. Moreover, to the company wages are a cost whereas to the worker they are income. Those who think in terms of social needs regard wages as a right to income, not payment for work. Demands for guaranteed annual wages reflect the merging together of wages paid by the hour and salaries paid by the week, month, or year, with guaranteed income for present hourly as well as for salaried workers. The importance of wages is further emphasized by the fact that wages and salaries comprise about 65% of national income, a potent factor in national income determination and in the impact on the business cycle and the state of the economy. What some of the major forms of wage payment are, and management and labor attitudes toward them, will be considered in this chapter. As a background, it will be useful first to consider the various types of wage data which are published, so that the reader may be familiar with the content as well as the limitations of such statistics.

ANALYSIS OF WAGE DATA

The union leader, bargaining with an employer, may be primarily interested in setting a high rate for a particular job in the collective bargaining agreement. The employees, on the other hand, may be more interested in their actual take-home pay. And the employer is likely to be concerned with the overall cost of labor, including all fringe benefits paid by him. Because of these varied interests in employee compensation, a number of statistical series are published which analyze wage changes from different points of view. Seven major types of data can be distinguished.

1. *Wage rates* represent the actual price for particular jobs. Because of the great diversity of such rates, not only from industry to industry but also from company to company within the same industry, there are no overall compilations of such rates published regularly by any agency of the government or by private research organizations. However, the Bureau of Labor Statistics of the U.S. Department of Labor publishes studies of wage rates for industries and for occupations in states and metropolitan areas.[1] Such studies report the average rates in plants, often by occupation, occupational groups, and area.

2. *Straight-time average hourly earnings* are the average wages earned, exclusive of overtime pay. They include incentive pay, but generally exclude payment for work on weekends, holidays, and late shifts. The Bureau of Labor Statistics also publishes studies of straight-time earnings for particular jobs in various industries.

3. *Gross hourly earnings* include all wage payments to employees, including overtime, premium pay for holidays and weekend pay, etc., and therefore normally exceed straight-time earnings. Some statistical series report earnings *per hours worked,* and some report earnings *per hours paid for.* If a man is paid for a holiday on which he does not work, should the hours in the holiday be added to hours worked during the rest of the week to obtain the hours figure to divide into total earnings so as to arrive at average hourly earnings? The Bureau of Labor Statistics says yes; the Bureau of the Census says no. As a result, hours of work as used

---

[1] The U.S. Bureau of Labor Statistics studies are reported or summarized in the *Monthly Labor Review,* published by the U.S. Department of Labor, and often issued in more complete form as separate bulletins. The Bureau's other monthly journal, *Employment and Earnings,* contains the tabulated earnings data.

by the Bureau of the Census in its series have averaged about 5% less than hours paid for as reported by the Bureau of Labor Statistics.[2] The most complete gross hourly earnings data are published in the form of a monthly series by the Bureau of Labor Statistics covering 21 broad manufacturing industry groups, about 300 manufacturing industries, and 30 nonmanufacturing industries, including trade, construction, and mining.[3]

4. *Weekly earnings* reflect the average number of hours worked per week in relation to gross earnings per hour. Weekly earnings data are published monthly by the Bureau of Labor Statistics and are also compiled by various state departments of labor, and trade associations.

5. *Weekly take-home pay* refers to the amount left in the weekly pay check after deductions for federal, and in some areas state and/or local income taxes, social security taxes, union dues, health and welfare programs, group insurance, and other benefits. The Bureau of Labor Statistics publishes a monthly calculation of "spendable average weekly earnings," which is defined as gross average weekly earnings less an amount estimated for federal income and social security taxes.[4] By excluding other deductions from paychecks, this average overestimates take-home pay.

6. *Annual earnings* of employees are not published in any regular series. Studies of various industries are made from time to time by the U.S. Bureau of Labor Statistics. In addition, the U.S. Department of Commerce publishes data for 84 industries and industry groups for "full-time equivalent" employees.[5] These are not actual earnings figures but rather computed figures derived by dividing wages and salaries in an industry by the number of full-time workers. For industries having a substantial number of part-time employees, the U.S. Department of Commerce reduces these to an equivalent number of full-time employees.

7. *Fringe benefits* run the whole gamut of pay from "coffee-break time" to employer payments for unemployment insurance. There are no reliable statistical series showing the cost of fringe benefits for industry as a whole, or even for all manufacturing industries. Since 1947, the Chamber of Commerce of the United States has made a biennial sample study of the extent and nature of fringe benefits.

BASIC WAGES

Since many different types of payment are included in labor's total compensation, it is convenient to distinguish two major categories which

---

[2] The significance of this difference in methodology in relation to fringe benefit payments is explored later in this chapter.

[3] These data are found each month in *Employment and Earnings*.

[4] *Ibid.*

[5] Published as a supplement to the U.S. Department of Commerce monthly publication, *Survey of Current Business*.

together make up total compensation: basic wages and supplementary (or fringe) benefits. Basic wages may be defined as the payment for hours actually worked, based on time or output. This includes payment at a higher rate for overtime and premium pay for working night shift, Saturday, or Sunday, and so forth. Supplementary benefits cover all other types of compensation, including vacation pay, Christmas bonuses, pension benefits, dismissal pay, and so on.

Basic Wages: Time Payment

The great majority of American workers are paid by the hour, day, week, or month—i.e., by time. For manual workers, rates are typically set by the hour or the day; for white-collar and supervisory workers in private industry, by the week, half month, or month, or, less frequently, by the year. Management employees are often paid at an annual rate of pay. Workers paid on an hourly or daily basis (as well as those who are on an incentive basis where the incentive is computed on the basis of hourly or daily output) are usually referred to as "wage earners." Workers paid by the week or longer time interval are usually referred to as salaried workers.

Time pay customarily varies to provide extra compensation to employees who have to work at undesirable hours. Nearly all collective bargaining contracts now provide for premium pay at the rate of time and one half for Saturday, or for the sixth day of the week, and double time for Sunday, or the seventh day, and also for extra compensation for evening and night shifts.

Since paying for results is deeply ingrained in managerial philosophy, many employers criticize time payment systems because output and earnings are not directly related. Unions, however, frequently prefer time pay because it compensates workers on a uniform basis and prevents the speedier workers from making it hard for the slower members of the union. Nevertheless, union and managerial attitudes toward the form of wage payment are more the reflection of economic, technological, and historical conditions than of a basic ideological preference for one type of payment rather than another. For example, the United Automobile Workers is widely credited with eliminating incentives in the automobile industry. Yet, incentive plans at Studebaker and Kaiser-Willys were abandoned at managerial insistence after they became unworkably high-cost—a move reluctantly acquiesced to by local unions after much strife.[6]

Payment on the basis of time work prevails in more than 70% of manufacturing industry, and throughout the building and service trades,

---

[6] Robert M. MacDonald, *Collective Bargaining in the Automobile Industry* (New Haven, Conn.: Yale University Press, 1963), pp. 112–31.

public utilities, and transportation, although the last industry also incorporates such factors as mileage and trips in its pay scale. This is the most practicable method of payment for most jobs in the business world.

Basic Wages: Incentive Payment

Piecework and other forms of incentive payment relate compensation and output, so that earnings fluctuate more or less in accordance with actual output, thus providing a direct financial stimulus to workers to increase their efforts and output. About 30% of workers in manufacturing receive their basic wages through some form of incentive payment. Such payment is common in apparel, textiles, footwear, and some of the metalworking industries. There is frequent variation, however, even among companies in the same industry. Bonuses and commissions are also frequently paid in retail and wholesale trade as a stimulus to the efforts of individual salesmen.

In general, incentive systems work out best in industries where labor cost is a large percentage of total cost, where competition is keen, and where the output of the individual worker is easily discernible. Clothing and textiles are good examples of industries which meet these requirements. In general, incentive compensation is not practical where emphasis is on quality rather than quantity, where individual output or performance cannot be measured with precision, and where mechanical contrivances control the speed of employees' work. Automobile assembly, chemical manufacture, and machine tool design are examples of industries in which these conditions apply. Automation and improvement in methods or machine design cause earnings of employees paid on an incentive basis to increase rapidly and get out of line with others in the plant. This is a frequent cause of labor strife. Those receiving the high wages resist change, others resent the out-of-line wages, and management must often take a strike in order to get the incentive rates (and labor costs) back into line. Otherwise a company risks loss of business because of noncompetitive prices resulting from the runaway incentive payments.

Incentive plans vary from simple payment by the piece, or unit of work, to complicated formulas which provide a bonus for production in excess of an established norm. The most common of the latter are standard hour plans. In such a plan, a piecework rate of 20 cents per piece multiplied by a 10-piece-per-hour standard equals $2. Workers would be expected to produce this under normal conditions at a normal workpace. For higher production, a bonus or incentive would be paid. Incentive plans may be figured on the basis of an individual's output, which is most common, but also on the output of a related group, or even on the output of an entire plant. Group incentives are applicable only to closely related operations where individual performances are linked. Plantwide incentives have the advantage of keeping all employees interested in high production, but since it is difficult, if not impossible, to relate the work of many employees, for example, maintenance personnel, to output, it is possible for some employees to loaf and still reap the bonus.

Union Attitudes toward Incentive Wage Methods

Union policy toward incentives has always varied considerably from industry to industry, and is far less important in determining the extent of incentives than are the basic economic and technological forces in the industry; or, as in the case of steel, the historical fact that the industry grew up with this form of payment in contrast, for example, to the aerospace industry, which started and adhered to a time method of payment. There is no evidence that the United Steelworkers has made any attempts to alter the basic method of payment in the steel industry.

Nonunion competition has historically been an important circumstance conducive to union acceptance of incentives. Before men's clothing was so thoroughly organized, the threat of nonunion competition was one of the most important reasons why the union therein not only did not oppose incentives in piecework but actually promoted them. In addition, the Amalgamated Clothing Workers, which has been as favorably disposed toward piecework as any union, has promoted its installation because only through piecework could the workers in the clothing industry increase earnings without increasing labor costs. In general, unions accept the method of payment in an industry. They may favor incentives where manual skill and labor costs are extremely important, where nonunion competition exists, where the unit of production can be defined with precision, where standards of work are fairly stable, and where piecework incentives have worked reasonably satisfactorily over a long period of time. The great majority of unions do not take a strong stand either for or against incentives as such, but instead they attempt to exert influence over how incentives work in practice—which, if successful, can have profound effects on the results of incentives.

Union Control of Incentive Systems

The United Mine Workers requires payment for "dead work" and compensation for other unfavorable conditions; the Textile Workers' Union fights management on the work load or stretch-out issue without opposing incentives per se; and the United Steelworkers is vitally concerned with methods of computing tonnage rates without attacking the basic system itself. A strong union, by placing numerous restrictions on the incentive system, may succeed in "demoralizing" it—creating substantial inequities in earnings and effort; raising substantially average hour yields or bonuses; and effectively divorcing productivity and earnings by instituting various guarantees which insure high "incentive" bonuses, whether or not production quotas are met. Usually, union pressure to accomplish this is accompanied by relaxed managerial control and managerial impatience to "get production out of the door no matter what the costs"—which can be substantial.[7]

A union drive to control an incentive system usually takes a number of years. As a rule, the battle for control is waged on two fronts—through negotiation for changes in the contract and the day-to-day shop operations revolving around rate setting on new jobs and the grievance procedure. By gradually winning guarantees for machine downtime, by negotiating out-of-line rates and then bringing other rates up to those already out of line, by harassing supervision and time-study departments with grievances, and by slowdowns or walkouts at critical delivery periods, the standards can be effectively reduced, and the incentive system can be turned into a featherbedding device for higher pay with less work. Unless management is eternally vigilant, an experience can develop such as that at a ball-bearing plant in Philadelphia where each day the employees stopped work after five or six hours and just loafed because they had made a "day's pay" under the demoralized incentive. Only the purchase of property in Tennessee and plans to relocate there ended this practice—which grew up as a result of union pressure and ineffective managerial response.

Although sound collective bargaining relationships exist in numerous plants where incentive systems are utilized, there is considerable evidence that incentive plans do complicate industrial relations and can contribute to industrial strife. So many factors, frequently intangible and unmeasurable, affect a worker's earnings that unless mutual goodwill exists, continued bickering is often the result. For example, if a machine breaks down or materials stop flowing, should the worker receive base pay or average hourly earnings of a previous period?

Another problem arises from the fact that in the average plant an incentive system can be applied to only a part of the employees; maintenance personnel and employees whose speed of work is entirely machine controlled remain on time work. This creates demands for bonuses or wage increases to nonincentive workers in order to equalize earnings. Managements sometimes further complicate matters by reducing maintenance on the grounds that workers on incentives will "find a way" to produce. Contrary to the belief that incentive pay permits less management, experience demonstrates that installation and effective administration of an incentive system requires increased management ability and frequently substantial additions to management payroll in order to provide the staff people—the accountants, time-study experts, and personnel men—who are needed to make the plan work.

---

[7] Sumner H. Slichter, J. J. Healy, and E. R. Livernash, *The Impact of Collective Bargaining on Management* (Washington, D.C.: Brookings Institution, 1960), pp. 490–529.

Measured Daywork

The realization that incentive systems have disadvantages as well as advantages for management has encouraged the search for a method of wage payment which combines the simplicity of time payment with the control of worker efficiency which is a feature of effective incentive systems. This interest has been furthered by technological advances which reduce worker control over speed or effort. In most plants, however, many employees with remarkably little effort can raise their efficiency considerably. Measured daywork plans offer pay by the hour in association with some type of control of worker efficiency by means of production standards. To make such a system work, management must establish meaningful standards, be able to justify their fairness and objectivity, and adhere to the standards under pressure. If the standards are to be meaningful, they must be met, and those who refuse to meet them must be disciplined. Otherwise, no one will make an effort to meet them. This, in turn, requires managerial objectivity and fairness in setting standards, for if the employees as a whole do not think the standards are fair, then a concerted effort to break them can often succeed.

If, however, management is convinced that the standards are fair, and remains so convinced after carefully evaluating grievances concerning them, it must be willing to back up this opinion. To many companies, this means defending their position before arbitrators. Other companies feel even stronger about the need to maintain control over production standards, which can indeed mean control over productivity and hence profits and competitive position. The General Motors Corporation, for example, regards such control as so significant that it prefers to permit unions to strike over production standards in order to exempt such disputes from arbitration. General Motors management believes that this results in better production standards from the company point of view, not only because it leaves production standard determination in the hands of management but, equally important, because the importance of standards setting is emphasized by this procedure. If the standards are set too loose, the cost and competitive position of the plant or operation are jeopardized; if they are set unfairly, a costly strike can occur. Plant management is thus under exacting pressure to set proper standards at all times.

Production Standards and Effective Employee Relations

Loose work standards and inefficient methods not only contribute to a lack of profitability of the enterprise but also do not usually result in sound employee relations or to the absence of strikes. As the authors of the most authoritative book on collective bargaining's impact on management point out:

Logically it might be expected that a fairly high task level, creating a strong competitive position for a plant, would lead to serious union-management conflict. While the possibility of conflict cannot be ruled out, observation tends ιo support the view, when reasonably qualified, that the reverse is true. It is the demoralized incentive plans and the poor daywork plans that are associated with union-management conflict. Efficient plans tend to have satisfactory to good union-management relations.[8]

The reasons for this apparent paradox became clear, if they are not already, as the reader's study progresses through the many facets of industrial relations and labor economics. Among them are the following:

1. Loose standards, whether incentive or daywork, lead inevitably to high costs and poor competitive position, and result in layoffs and unemployment. The effect is to generate insecurity, poor morale, unrest, and strife.
2. Loose standards usually are preceded by managerial yielding to short strikes, threats of strikes, or slowdowns in order to keep production going. But by yielding to this pressure, management incites more of it. Eventually, the employees go too far, and a long and bitter strike does occur.
3. Loose standards create inequities. People doing similar work are paid different rates or earnings. This creates unhappiness, unrest, and constant demands for changes.
4. Well-run plants, in contrast to poorly run ones, feature uniform treatment of people similarly situated. Threats of force to change what is considered proper are firmly resisted. By experience, employees learn that such action will not yield results; hence, they do not resort to it. Where this is combined with cost-consciousness and sound and humane management, the result is steadier work and well-understood conditions. Feeling secure and knowing where they stand, employees and their union representatives are more likely to work things out with management on a peaceful, logical basis because they have learned that it pays to do it that way.

PROFIT-SHARING PLANS

Incentive systems, whether they be piece-rate or group plans, are generally related to physical production. Profit-sharing plants attempt to go a step further and distribute to workers a share in the profits of the business after all ordinary costs, such as wages, materials, and overhead, have been met. Profits have no necessary or close relation to physical production or employee effort—and this is one of the inherent weaknesses in profit-sharing plans. Employees may exert extra effort, yet profits may decline because competitive conditions compel a reduction in prices; on

---

[8] *Ibid.,* p. 551.

the other hand, physical production may decline, yet profits may rise because the employer has made a favorable purchase of raw materials, or for many other reasons.

Despite the lack of close connection between employee effort and profits, many employers believe that profit sharing is the best means to obtain maximum cooperation between labor and management and to eliminate friction in labor relations. Profit-sharing plans have existed for over 150 years. Today, well over 2 million workers are covered by such plans.[9] By permitting profit-sharing payments to a trust to qualify as employer expenses if not in excess of 15 percent of employee compensation, and by permitting such payments, after remaining in trust for a specified time, to be received as capital gains subject to a 25 percent maximum tax, federal tax law has spurred the growth of such plans.

Profit-sharing plans are most likely to be found where profits are reasonably large and consistent, the labor force stable, and unions not strong. Obviously, if the first two conditions do not prevail, there are few profits to share and few employees to share such profits regularly. However great a plan on paper, it is meaningless if it does not produce results.

Unions have traditionally opposed profit sharing. Such an employee-employer "partnership" makes employees more difficult to unionize.[10] Moreover, profits are affected by managerial actions over which collective bargaining has no effect. Thus one union official commented that under profit sharing, a union either

. . . must demand a voice in areas where it has never demanded a voice before . . . ; or it must be willing to have its return for its employees under that plan regulated unilaterally by company decisions. For example, . . . the company could double the number of foremen . . . raise executive compensation, executive bonuses, stock options. . . . Decisions whether to borrow money, whether to expand . . . on depreciation, tax changes . . . and all affect the results of a profit-sharing plan. Therefore either the union has to have a voice [in these matters] or have to be agreeable to having its compensation set unilaterally. And the Steelworkers Union is not interested in doing either.[11]

Such union opposition to profit sharing is remarkably similar to that expressed by the General Electric Company when it abolished profit sharing for wage earners because

---

[9] Data from U.S. Bureau of Labor Statistics.

[10] See Charles Schotta, Jr., "The Distribution of Profit-Sharing Plans: An Analysis," *Southern Economic Journal*, Vol. 30 (July 1963), pp. 45–49; and Edward R. Czarnecki, "Effect of Profit-Sharing Plans on Union Organizing Efforts," *Personnel Journal*, Vol. 49 (September 1970), pp. 763–73.

[11] Statement of Marvin Miller, then assistant to the president, United Steelworkers of America, before the National Industrial Conference Board meeting of January 16, 1964.

. . . an individual employee seemed to realize that his performance on the job had little or no effect on what he got from the general profit-sharing plan . . . Wage earners do not have direct control over pricing policies, design, manufacturing technology, credit and collections, managerial efficiency and a host of other factors and forces that contribute to profit or loss. So wage earners should not be penalized when a company loses money nor rewarded by a share of the profits when a company makes money.[12]

Employers also oppose profit sharing with unionized employees because they do not desire to bargain over what share of profit will go to employees, which would be required under the Taft-Hartley Act. This is one reason why the late Walter Reuther found General Motors, Ford, and Chrysler uninterested when, departing from typical union policy, he made a contract with American Motors in 1961 providing for sharing profits. That company hoped to exchange profit sharing for union surrender of restrictive practices. The sales and profit declines of the company, plus union unwillingness to make concessions, caused an early demise of the plan.

Gain Sharing, Buy-Out Formulas, and Scanlon Plans

The American Motors profit-sharing plan is similar to other "formulas" which attempt to "buy out" union restrictive practices. Longshoremen on the West Coast gave up numerous featherbedding practices in return for higher wages and employer contributions to funds providing welfare, disability, and retirement benefits. This seemed to have had the desired result, although other problems, notably jurisdictional disputes with the Teamsters' Union and an intraunion power struggle broke the period of labor peace in 1971–72, which the buy-out formula induced more than a decade earlier.

The Kaiser Steel plan, noted in the previous chapter, was originally a combination buy-out formula for restrictive practices, a substitute for a demoralized incentive plan, and a public relations device for the company. Wide publicity was given to its monthly bonus distributions. Like many profit-sharing plans, it disintegrated when sales and profits fell and bonuses declined. A bitter strike occurred in 1972 over its terms.[13] Perhaps this was inevitable because it was based on an impossible premise: that there was to be no relation between company profitability and work bonuses based on "efficiency." Such a premise obviously ignores the reality of what occurs to efficiency when plant utilization declines as a result of lagging sales.

Scanlon plans, developed by the late Joseph Scanlon, onetime Steelworkers' union official, are designed to give employees an incentive to

---

[12] General Electric Company, *Union Relations Bulletin,* January 16, 1958.
[13] *Wall Street Journal,* February 24, 1972, p. 36.

improve production methods and to suggest cost savings. They often are substituted for demoralized incentive plans. A plantwide incentive—or bonus—potential replaces the existing incentive with the aim of producing teamwork efforts to achieve higher efficiency and productivity. "The incentive toward teamwork is provided most commonly by giving the employees a large share (usually three-fourths) of the savings in labor costs. The savings are measured by ascertaining the extent to which the ratio of payroll to sales value of production is reduced below the previous normal ratio."[14]

Scanlon plans require a great deal of mutual trust and cooperation among employees, unions, and management if they are to work. They have been most successful among small firms which have been in trouble competitively, and in which employer-employee relations have been on a high plane of mutual confidence. On the other hand, such plans are not without problems, since bonuses are paid to all, regardless of the contribution of each to the savings. Moreover, under such plans there is a tendency for the parties to become overimpressed with initial successes and to believe that necessary overhead, such as industrial and methods engineers, maintenance outlays, and adequate supervision, can be dispensed with because "the worker knows best how to cut costs." Under such conditions a Scanlon plan can become as demoralized as an incentive plan and can result in the payment of bonuses which would not have been paid if proper consideration had been given to expenses required to maintain future profitability. This seems to have occurred in the case of the widely publicized Scanlon plan at the LaPointe Machine Tool Company, and may well be much more typical of long-run results of such plans than the Scanlon enthusiasts have set forth.[15]

FORMALIZATION OF WAGE STRUCTURE

In most of American industry, wages are tailored to the job rather than to the man. Management could, of course, attempt to pay each worker an amount equal to management's estimate of the worth of the individual, taking into account his age, health, skill, length of service, and

---

[14] Slichter, Healy, and Livernash, *Impact of Collective Bargaining*, p. 865. This explanation is given: "Suppose the normal ratio is found to be 35 per cent, which means that if a plant were selling $1 million of goods a year, payroll would normally be $350,000. If the workers by improving their efficiency were able to produce $1 million of goods for a payroll cost of $310,000, three-fourths of the saving or $30,000 would be paid to them as a bonus."

[15] For an analysis of the LaPointe situation, see Herbert R. Northrup and Harvey A. Young, "The Causes of Industrial Peace—Revisited," *Industrial and Labor Relations Review*, Vol. 22 (October 1968), pp. 31–47. For a further and very careful critique of the Scanlon approach, see R. B. Gray, "The Scanlon Plan—A Case Study," *British Journal of Industrial Relations*, Vol. 9 (November 1971), pp. 291–313. For the favorable side, see F. G. Lesieur (ed.), *The Scanlon Plan* (Cambridge, Mass.: M.I.T. Press, 1958).

similar factors. This practice is followed to some extent with respect to supervisory and executive employees and in the hiring of employees such as musicians and radio performers, whose individual talents vary greatly. In a large industrial establishment, however, such piecemeal establishment of a wage structure would be expensive, time-consuming, and impracticable. As a consequence, most industrial establishments have adopted formalized wage structures.

Formal wage structures are generally of two kinds. A "single-rate establishment" pays the same rate to all experienced workers in a job classification. This means that a lower rate may be set for trainees, but once a man has acquired what is considered the minimum experience necessary to qualify him for the job, he is paid the same rate as all other experienced workers performing the same work, regardless of variation in length of service and other factors. A "rate range establishment," on the other hand, sets up a range of rates for a particular job and provides that specific rates for individual workers within the range are to be determined by merit, and/or length of service.

Job evaluation involves the establishment of a rational internal wage structure. Although such an evaluation may be accomplished in many ways, it usually is done in three steps: Jobs are described in terms of a formula giving due account to skill, responsibility, working conditions, effort, etc.; and finally, jobs are grouped into a hierarchy of grades and wage or salary rates or ranges established for the grades.

Job evaluation developed as a management device aimed at simplifying the wage structure and its administration and preventing "whipsawing" of rates—that is, using one out-of-line job to gain a wage increase and then using that wage increase to press for others. Except in a few industries, such as steel, job evaluation has not enjoyed formal union support. It does, however, usually gain union acceptance. This occurs because whereas the introduction of a job evaluation plan upsets internal wage relationships and thus is often not politically supportable by union leadership, once the plan is introduced, it stresses payment on a job rather than on a personal basis, and hence reduces friction and dissension among union ranks. For employers, job evaluation simplifies wage administration and helps to prevent individual supervisors from letting individual wage rates rise out of line.

Within job evaluation plans, most unions prefer single rates to rate ranges. In the automobile industry, union pressure has virtually eliminated rate ranges.[16] Many employers prefer ranges, with the right to reward merit within the range. Other employers have found that ranges of this type can be maintained only by strict control because otherwise pressure on the foremen to recommend increases within the range soon puts most employees at the top of the range. Some ranges are, in effect, just nominal,

---

[16] MacDonald, *Bargaining in the Automobile Industry*, pp. 83–133.

for the contract may provide that employees receive a wage increase every few months until they reach the top of the grade. The most effective rate range plans place strict limits on the manner and/or number in the grade who can achieve the top rate and permit automatic increases only to the midpoint of the range—if at all. Since the midpoint of the rate range is, theoretically, the same as a single job rate would be, an average of the workers' rates in any grade which exceeds the midpoint means that the plant is paying more for a range rate than it would for a single-rate structure.

SUPPLEMENTARY OR FRINGE BENEFITS

Wage supplements, commonly called fringe benefits, are of two types: those imposed by government, such as Social Security, and those provided by employers, often pursuant to union agreements, as direct benefits for employees. Government benefits are discussed in Chapter 17. Here we are primarily concerned with fringe benefits as wage supplements. Employers have granted to their employees, health and accident insurance, life insurance, holidays and vacations with pay, pensions, paid sick leave, annual wage guarantees, and many other fringe benefits. Among the newest fringes are prepaid dental and psychiatric care, group automobile insurance, and prepaid legal services. Supplemental compensation is now a significant portion of total labor cost, and therefore an important factor in labor negotiations. It is also a source of public concern both because of the billions of dollars involved and of the impact of costs and benefits on the level of employment and income in the economy.

Nature and Extent of Supplementary Benefits

There is no reliable statistical series published showing the cost of all supplementary benefits for industry as a whole, or even for manufacturing industries. This is understandable when we consider that supplementary benefits include such things as pay for "coffee-break" time, suggestion awards, free meals, and a whole gamut of similar benefits. Few employers have the time to calculate the cost of all these miscellaneous benefits. Despite the increasing emphasis placed upon fringe benefits in union negotiations, many employers do not know precisely their fringe costs.

If we include in supplementary benefits only employer contributions legally required for various types of social insurance, such as old-age and surivors insurance, unemployment insurance, railroad retirement insurance, and in addition, employer contributions to private pension and welfare funds, then Figure 5–1, which is based on U.S. Department of Commerce statistics, indicates that in 1970, employers had spent in the neighborhood of $50 billion on such payments per annum.

FIGURE 5–1

Employee Benefits in Private Industry

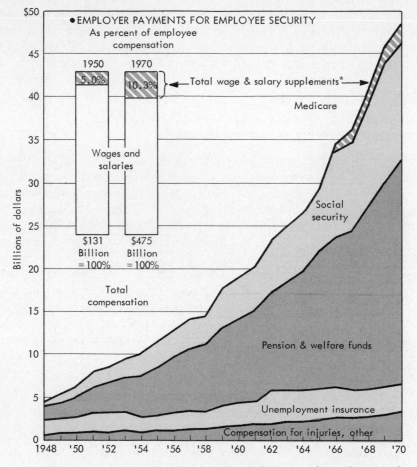

° Includes some minor items, less than 1% of total, that are not for employee security.
Source: Data, U.S. Department of Commerce; chart, The Conference Board. Reproduced by permission.

The data in Figure 5–1 reveal a big jump in fringe benefit costs since the 1940s, when private pension, insurance, and welfare plans became increasingly important. The trend since then has continued almost steadily upward, and promises to do so as long as union negotiators stress "security" in their bargaining. In connection with the chart, The Conference Board points out:

Supplements to wages and salaries continue to rise sharply and to increase as a proportion of total employee compensation in private industry. All of the relative gain is being accounted for by payments for the security of employees in their retirement years. Total wage and salary supplements came to 10.3% of total employee compensation in 1970, compared with 5.0% in 1950, according to the U.S. Department of Commerce.

Since 1960, annual employer contributions for Social Security (excluding medicare) and into private pension and welfare funds have soared 181% and 167%, respectively, compared with a 92% increase in aggregate wages and salaries; private employers are currently paying about $2 billion a year for medicare, which became effective in 1966. On the other hand, contributions for the security of employees during their working years—unemployment insurance and workmen's compensation—have increased only 50% since 1960.

In addition to wage and salary supplements, employers provide many built-in benefits, such as paid vacations, holidays, and sick leave, which are part of basic wages and salaries. When both types of employee benefits are counted—as is done by the U.S. Chamber of Commerce—the ratio to wages and salaries is, of course, greater than for supplements alone. Because of this basic difference, the data in Table 5–1 are not comparable to those in Figure 5–1.

Hence the data in Figure 5–1 tell only part of the story. Biennial studies by the Chamber of Commerce of the United States indicate that payments for vacations, holidays, rest periods, and other time not worked constitute almost one half of total fringe benefit costs.

The growth of fringe benefit costs is also shown in Table 5–1, which is based upon data supplied by 137 identical companies in each of the Chamber of Commerce's biennial surveys since 1951. Fringe payments in this calculation rose from 20.2% of payroll in 1951 to 34.3% in 1971, an increase of 69.8%. Because wage rates were also rising during this same period, fringe benefits calculated on a cents-per-hour basis and on an annual-dollars-per-employee basis increased more rapidly than on a per-cent-of-payroll basis. Fringe benefits for these companies increased from 34.5 cents per payroll hour in 1951 to 143.5 cents in 1971, an increase of 359%! On a dollars-per-year-per-employee basis, such benefits rose from $708 in 1961 to $2,970 in 1971—an increase of 319.5%.

As can be seen from Table 5–1, the two major classes of fringe benefits are "pension and other agreed-upon payments" and "payments for time not worked." The former rose from 6.5% of payroll in 1951 to 12.6% in 1971; the latter rose from 7.2% to 11% during the same period.

Payments for pensions and other agreed-upon payments, as used in the Chamber of Commerce survey, include pension plans; life insurance; sickness, accident, surgical, medical care, or hospitalization plans; contributions to supplementary unemployment benefit plans; and dismissal or termination pay allowances. All of these have been very much in the forefront of union demands during this entire period. The phenomenal growth of such benefits during these years was due to a number of factors—the freezing of wages during World War II, NLRB decisions holding that such benefits were subject to collective bargaining, and favorable tax treatment under federal income tax legislation accorded to employer-

Table 5-1

Comparison of 1951–71 Employee Benefits for 137 Companies

Item	1951	1953	1955	1957	1959	1961	1963	1965	1967	1969	1971
All industries (137 companies)											
1. As percent of payroll, total	20.2	21.6	23.2	24.6	25.8	27.1	27.9	27.8	29.9	31.6	34.3
a) Legally required payments (employer's share only)	2.9	2.8	3.0	3.1	3.6	4.1	4.6	4.2	5.0	5.3	5.6
b) Pension and other agreed-upon payments (employer's share only)	6.5	7.3	8.1	8.4	9.2	9.3	9.5	9.8	10.3	10.8	12.6
c) Paid rest periods, lunch periods, etc.	1.6	1.9	2.1	2.2	2.1	2.4	2.4	2.5	2.9	3.1	3.2
d) Payments for time not worked	7.2	7.4	7.7	8.6	8.8	9.2	9.4	9.4	9.8	10.4	11.0
e) Profit-sharing payments, bonuses, etc.	2.0	2.2	2.3	2.3	2.1	2.1	2.0	1.9	1.9	2.0	1.9
2. As cents per payroll hour	34.5	40.8	47.9	55.4	63.3	71.6	79.8	85.3	100.7	118.0	143.5
3. As dollars per year per employee	708	844	997	1147	1308	1486	1666	1790	2095	2460	2970
All manufacturing (56 companies)											
1. As percent of payroll, total	18.0	19.7	21.7	23.7	24.7	26.1	26.8	27.0	29.6	31.5	34.9
a) Legally required payments (employer's share only)	3.2	3.0	3.4	3.5	4.1	4.7	5.2	4.8	5.6	5.9	6.4
b) Pension and other agreed-upon payments (employer's share only)	4.8	5.7	6.5	7.2	7.8	7.9	8.2	8.7	9.5	10.2	12.4
c) Paid rest periods, lunch periods, etc.	1.8	2.3	2.7	2.7	2.6	2.9	3.0	3.0	3.4	3.5	3.6
d) Payments for time not worked	5.7	6.1	6.4	7.5	7.7	8.2	8.3	8.7	9.2	9.8	10.7
e) Profit-sharing payments, bonuses, etc.	2.5	2.6	2.7	2.8	2.5	2.4	2.1	1.8	1.9	2.1	1.8
2. As cents per payroll hour	31.0	37.4	44.7	52.9	61.5	69.1	75.6	82.2	97.1	114.8	143.2
3. As dollars per year per employee	657	798	946	1111	1259	1443	1598	1760	2057	2453	3014

All nonmanufacturing (81 companies)

1. As percent of payroll, total..........	21.7	22.9	24.2	25.3	26.5	27.7	28.7	28.4	30.1	31.7	33.8
a) Legally required payments (employer's share only).................	2.7	2.6	2.7	2.9	3.2	3.6	4.2	3.9	4.6	4.9	5.0
b) Pension and other agreed-upon payments (employer's share only)...........	7.7	8.4	9.1	9.3	10.1	10.3	10.5	10.5	10.8	11.3	12.7
c) Paid rest periods, lunch periods, etc......	1.4	1.7	1.7	1.9	1.7	2.1	2.0	2.1	2.6	2.8	2.8
d) Payments for time not worked..........	8.2	8.3	8.6	9.3	9.6	9.8	10.1	9.9	10.2	10.8	11.3
e) Profit-sharing payments, bonuses, etc....	1.7	1.9	2.1	1.9	1.9	1.9	1.9	2.0	1.9	1.9	2.0
2. As cents per payroll hour..............	36.9	43.0	50.1	57.1	64.6	73.4	82.7	87.4	103.1	120.1	143.7
3. As dollars per year per employee........	742	875	103	1172	1341	1515	1711	1809	2119	2465	2941

Source: Chamber of Commerce of the United States.

sponsored programs. These factors, together with a growing acceptance
by employers of responsibility for worker security, accounted for the
tremendous growth of these plans during this period.

Today fringe benefits are so pervasive in American industry that paid
holidays and vacation are almost universally provided, and over 90% of
employers make payments for welfare programs of various kinds. Moreover, each year the liberality of these programs increases. Whereas health
plans once covered only basic hospital care, now some include dental and
psychiatric care and free eyeglasses; 6 holidays with pay have advanced to
10 and 12 and one week's vacation to four with even a three months
sabbatical at intervals; time off with pay and benefits seem not only to
expand but find new ways of expression.

KEY FRINGE ISSUES

In terms of costs, problems and pervasiveness, two fringe benefit items,
pensions and insurance against illness, are surely the most significant. A
third, supplemental unemployment benefits (SUB), deserves special mention also, because it has moved key groups of employees toward
guaranteed income, although SUB coverage is much more limited than
guaranteed income. Pensions and SUB are both designed to provide additional security to those already receiving benefits from governmental
"social security" programs, which are discussed in Chapter 17. To some
extent this is true about illness protection, or health insurance, as it is
commonly termed. The direct costs of these fringe benefits, and their
significance in the total employee compensation picture, all require that
they be discussed as "wages."

Pensions

The great growth of pensions has come in recent years as a result of
collective bargaining pressures and the tax code which provides that
employer contributions to a pension plan are tax-deductible business
expenses. Since 1940, retirement benefits have grown much faster than
wages. About one half of the labor force, 41 million persons, are now
covered by private pensions, including those negotiated in collective
bargaining; approximately 16 million retired persons now draw benefits
estimated at $15 billion from funds with assets estimated at $220 billion.[17]

Figure 5–2 sets forth the details of pension fund growth and financing
since 1950. In introducing this "Road Map of Industry," The Conference
Board says:

---

[17] Gilbert Burck, "That Ever Expanding Pension Balloon," *Fortune*, Vol. 84
(October 1971), p. 101. Burck's data include state and municipal government pensions and thus his figures differ with those of The Conference Board.

Private pensions, whether measured by fund assets, coverage, benefits paid, or number of beneficiaries, have been growing faster than government pensions. Assets of all private pension funds (insured and noninsured) reached $136.3 billion (book value) at the end of 1970, according to estimates by the Securities & Exchange Commission. This represents a growth in total assets of $7.8 billion for the year, or 5.7%, compared with $10.5 billion, or 8.9%, in 1969. While growth in assets of private funds was still substantial, the rate of increase in both 1969 and 1970 was below that of the Fifties and most of the Sixties.

The Board further notes:

Assets of private pension funds have grown faster than either public or government funds. ("Public" refers to civil service and state and local retirement funds; "government" refers to the Railroad Retirement, Federal Old Age and Survivors Insurance, and Federal Disability Insurance funds.) Since 1950, assets of private funds have grown an average of 12.8% a year, while public and government funds increased their assets at 8.0% and 2.7% rates, respectively. Extraordinary expansion of noninsured fund assets has been directly responsible for the rise in private pension plan assets. (Noninsured funds are those financed through, and administered by, trustees—usually banks; insured funds are those operated by insurance companies.) In the last 20 years, assets of noninsured funds have grown from slightly over half of total private fund assets to more than two thirds of the total. The increase in the share of the noninsured funds probably is primarily attributable to the realization of capital gains from the sale of corporate stocks. Corporate stocks have grown from 17% of the noninsured funds investment portfolio in 1950 to 55% at the end of 1970. Largely as a result of a widespread decline in stock prices, however, the 1970 increase in stockholdings was less than in previous years.

A note by Karen Kelly appearing on this section of Road Map No. 1679 states:

Private pension fund assets constitute the nation's largest and fastest growing pool of private capital. But benefit expectations and demands of prospective pension recipients may well be growing faster than the funds that will be available to meet them. Pension costs will be boosted in coming years as wage levels rise and demands for benefits more in line with pay strengthen. A likely continuation of the trend toward earlier retirement will further increase pension costs. Already, some strong unions are pressing for earlier retirement at full pay.

Growth in demand for less rigid "vesting" provisions, however, is the most important factor causing worry about escalation of future pension costs. Vesting provisions establish an employee's right to collect a deferred pension if he leaves his job before he is eligible for retirement. Most plans have some vesting provisions, but with such stiff age and length of service requirements that employee turnover would likely wipe out pension credits before they become obligations. Many changes in private pensions are now being proposed and considered, including, for example, requirements that benefits be fully vested after 10 years of service, or partially vested after a combination of age and years of service. In the past, vesting legislation has been fought by many employers; should such legislation become law, pension costs would soar. Higher costs, of course, will require greater company contributions or better investment performance than in the past, or both.

The retirement benefits provided by private pension plans vary a great deal from employer to employer. The amount and type of pension benefit provided in collectively bargained plans is usually a fixed dollar amount, regardless of the employee's earnings. A formula frequently used to determine the employee's benefit is one which provides a dollar amount (such as $5 to $10) of monthly pension for each year of service the employee has completed at retirement. In plans covering salaried and nonunion personnel, the benefit formula usually is related to the employee's earnings and length of service. Many pension plans also make provision for death, termination of employment, or total disability.

Pension plans frequently require a minimum number of years of service and achievement of age 65 to be eligible for retirement. Most plans in the past have provided for retirement at an earlier age but at greatly reduced pensions. If the employee is disabled, the reduction is waived. In recent years, there has been great stress on early retirement at

FIGURE 5–2

Private Pension Funds

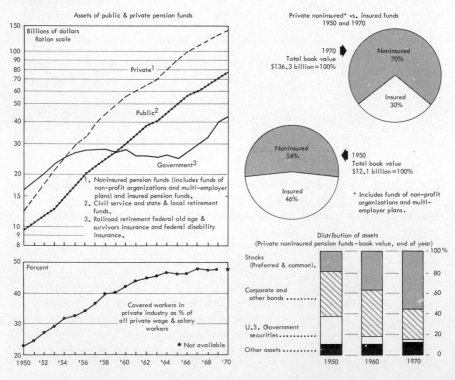

FIGURE 5–2 (Continued)

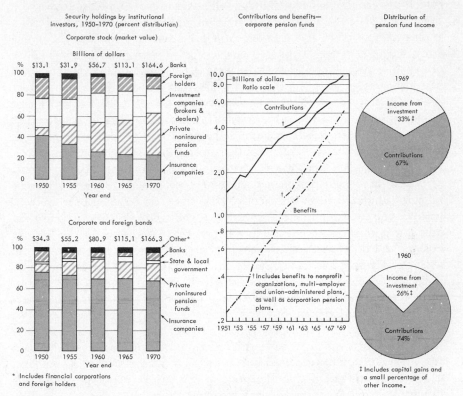

Security holdings by institutional investors, 1950–1970 (percent distribution)

Corporate stock (market value)

Corporate and foreign bonds

Contributions and benefits—corporate pension funds

Distribution of pension fund income

1969
Income from investment 33%‡
Contributions 67%

1960
Income from investment 26%‡
Contributions 74%

† Includes benefits to nonprofit organizations, multi-employer and union-administered plans, as well as corporation pension plans.

* Includes financial corporations and foreign holders

‡ Includes capital gains and a small percentage of other income.

Source: Road Maps of Industry, No. 1679, The Conference Board. Sources of data: Securities & Exchange Commission; Social Security Administration, The Conference Board.

full pension for those who complete 25 or 30 years service. This has been carried to extreme measures in some cities, which now provide for retirement at half the last year's salary for those age 50 who have completed 25 years service. In New York City, this swamped the pension fund, as employees "rushed to the exits" in order to collect a pension and then obtain employment elsewhere. Such early retirement features raise a grave question whether obligations can be met. In New York City, for example, the annual pension costs for 1975 have been estimated at $750 million.[18]

The increasing dependence of employees on private pensions has spurred demands for government controls. Most persons who depend

---

[18] E. S. Willis, "Pension Opportunities and Problems: Issues in Collective Bargaining and Government Regulation," in Richard L. Rowan (ed.), *Collective Bargaining: Survival in the 70's* (Labor Relations and Public Policy Series, Report No. 5. [Philadelphia: Industrial Research Unit, Wharton School of Finance and Commerce, University of Pennsylvania, 1972]), p. 363.

on pensions eventually receive them, but there are many instances in which the promise is never fulfilled. One reason is that an employee may not have worked at a company long enough to "vest," that is establish a right to a pension at age 65, even though he does not work at that company when he reaches the retirement age. Vesting has become more common, especially for those with long service who are over age 50. A reasonable proposal put forward by a noted pension authority would require vesting for all those who achieve "the rule 50"—that is, when any combination of age and service equals 50.[19] Since the costs of pensions are a function of turnover of covered employees, among other factors, this would increase the costs of plans that do not provide such vesting.

A more fundamental reason why employees sometimes do not receive promised pensions is that inadequate provision is made for their payment by not "funding" them sufficiently. If insufficient funds are set aside to pay pensions and the money is not there, the employee can depend then only on company solvency when he retires. Companies do go out of business without meeting these obligations. Studebaker was a classic example. There is now considerable interest in providing legislation which will require minimum funding standards that require pension obligations to be set aside in trust funds, or through insurance companies, in a prescribed manner. Even so, however, if the company fails this would not suffice to insure more than a partial pension for many, because those thrown out of work may have only part of their promised pension paid for when the company ceased operations. To overcome this eventuality, it has been advocated that the government insure pensions by an additional charge on all companies providing them.

The steady increase in pension costs as a result of early retirement options which increase those costs rapidly (by requiring that the pension be paid longer to an employee who has earned it over a shorter period) and union pressure which has steadily upped pension benefits, raise the very serious question of how much pension the economy desires at what costs. One estimate is that if retirement for everyone is lowered to 60 from 65, the effect in hours worked would be the same as if the workweek were lowered to 31.5 hours, and retirement at 55, as if lowered to 27 hours.[20] Such a loss of manpower would be highly inflationary, for it could not possibly be offset by productivity increases. If benefits, particularly pensions, keep increasing rapidly, the schism between younger workers, who usually want wages now, and older ones more interested in benefits, could cause grave problems for unions and managements. What needs often to be determined is which is desired more; the time when both could be increased rapidly may well be drawing to a close.

In this regard, two contrary trends may be at work. On the one hand,

---

[19] Dan M. McGill, "Private Pensions and Public Policy," *ibid.*, p. 385.
[20] Burck, "Ever-Expanding Pension Balloon," p. 102.

the labor force is younger, on average, than ever before, and as noted in Chapter 1, will continue to be predominantly young for many years. This would seem to presage a greater interest in wages rather than pensions. On the other hand, the stabilization program of the Nixon administration, like those during World War II and the Korean War, restricts wage increases but gives a relatively free rein to pensions and other fringes. The result could be an abnormally large increase in pensions at a time when they would be expected to grow more slowly.

HEALTH AND WELFARE PLANS

Privately organized protection against the cost of sickness has grown at a tremendous rate in recent years. Hospitalization insurance has become so popular that by 1971, 181.5 million people, nearly 90% of the civilian resident population, had such protection. Other types of medical care insurance have also become increasingly important, though not so prevalent as hospitalization benefits. In 1970, surgical expense insurance covered 93% of those having hospitalization insurance and 80% of those with hospital insurance also had regular medical expense protection. Insurance companies provide about two thirds of this protection, Blue Cross–Blue Shield, the bulk of the rest, with independent plans covering the balance of about 5%.[21]

Health insurance coverage grew very rapidly during the 1960s, increasing those covered by nearly 40%. Major medical expense also grew rapidly, as Figure 5–3 shows, for both primary breadwinners and their dependents. This form of coverage is designed to help absorb the cost of serious or catastrophic illness or accidents. Usually major medical plans provide for a deductible amount, which is equivalent to the benefits paid under a basic plan covering ordinary hospitalization, surgical, and medical costs. When the primary coverage has been used up, and perhaps after a "corridor deductible" of $50–$200, the major medical plan takes over and pays 80% of all the illness expenses up to $25,000 or even more. Such coverage is extremely important when a severe accident occurs or a chronic illness lingers.

Unions have pushed hard for health insurance coverage under collective bargaining since World War II, and today few contracts exclude such coverage, which tends to be ever more elaborate. New features include psychiatric care, prepaid eye treatment and glasses, prepaid dental care, and annual physical examinations. As in the case of pensions, the costs of such programs have grown enormously, and under union pressure, the bulk of the plans call for the employer to bear all costs for employees and their dependents, whereas once the cost of the latter's coverage, especially, was deducted from the workers' paychecks.

---

[21] Data from the Health Insurance Institute.

In 1970, the American public spent $46 billion on health care, 148% more than in 1960.[22] With the costs of health care rising faster than almost anything else, it is not surprising that both unions and management are interested in controlling the cost of providing health insurance. The union position seems to be to transfer the costs to the general taxpayer through a form of government health insurance. Presumably in that case welfare plans would be either incorporated into the national system, or, like union-bargained pensions, supply additional benefits on top of the

FIGURE 5–3

Number of Primary Insureds and Dependents Protected by Major Medical Expense Insurance (issued by insurance companies, in the United States)

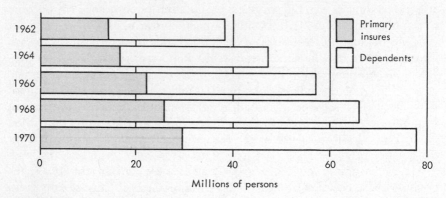

Source: *Source Book of Health Insurance Data, 1971–72* (New York: Health Insurance Institute, 1972), p. 28.

tax-supported programs. Since the history of all prepaid health care demonstrates that its availability will greatly increase its usage, one could expect costs to rise under a national program, but they would fall on a different group. Unions also see an additional benefit in national health insurance during strikes, for presumably coverage would not then be interrupted. Now employers can refuse to continue coverage after a strike lasts 30 days because their contractual obligations to do so ceases. Usually in such instances the union pays the costs until the strike is settled. Apparently the desire to avoid the enormous costs of another month's premium put much pressure on officials of the United Automobile Workers to end the General Motors strike of 1970 when they did.

For employers, a basic problem of health insurance is that they do not control the costs. They bargain generally to provide certain benefits, and then are faced with spiraling hospital and other costs which they must pay. This has greatly increased interest in prepaid group care, where there is provided stipulated services by a group of doctors, facilities, and

[22] *Ibid.*

medical care specialists at agreed-upon costs. Here the payers of the service have a greater voice in costs than where they merely agree to pay for benefits. The best known of these plans is the one begun on the West Coast by the late industrialist, Henry Kaiser.

Despite their high and rising costs, health insurance programs are not designed to cover accidents or illness occurring, or resulting, directly from employment. This is the function of workmen's compensation, the oldest form of social insurance, which is discussed in Chapter 17. In addition, temporary and permanent disabilities are also dealt with under state and federal legislation, and as noted, are also provided for in many pension plans.

As noted in Chapter 3, a continuing social failure has been the inadequate regulation of fiduciary responsibility for trustees of welfare and pension plans. It is likely that this will shortly be changed, for there is much pressure for congressional action. Huge amounts of money thus held have been squandered, improvidently invested, or otherwise used for purposes for which the monies were not intended. Most, indeed the great majority, of funds are prudently held and invested and serve their stated purposes. Unfortunately, some are not, and so federal regulation is required to insure their integrity.

Supplemental Unemployment Benefits

SUB plans are by no means as pervasive as are pension and health insurance programs, being largely confined to industries which deal with the automobile, rubber, and steelworker unions, plus a few others. Essentially, most of these plans provide for the establishment of funds which pay out benefits to those laid off over and above what state unemployment compensation programs provide. Additional benefits are provided for "short weeks" so that the employer can divide up work by closing down, as in the automobile industry, an assembly line for two days per week and workers receive compensation which about guarantees five days pay for three worked. This, of course, moves employees closer to the much sought after annual wage.

One reason why SUB plans have not achieved greater popularity is that they are significant only to those more recently employed. The senior men are usually fairly secure and do not want monies bargained to go to funds from which they stand to reap little benefit. To accommodate these feelings, some contracts permit senior men to take layoffs instead of working, as will be noted in the following chapter. Even here, however, SUB funds do not provide real protection in very heavy layoffs but are of greater help in seasonal swings such as occur in automobiles. In aerospace, for example, where the end of a contract can mean mass layoffs, SUB plans have run out of funds before layoffs hit senior men. Thus, in an eastern helicopter plant, where employment declined from a peak of 13,000 to 4,000 after the pullout from Viet Nam began, the SUB fund was exhausted by the time that the labor force was reduced to 8,000. The next 4,000 laid off received no SUB benefits, although most had more seniority than those laid off previously. In such circumstances, SUB seems neither fair nor appropriate. In its place several aerospace companies provide for a lump-sum dismissal payment, based upon seniority, or a similar mechanism which recognizes, rather than discriminates against, length of service.

WAGE COSTS, FRINGE BENEFITS, AND TAKE-HOME PAY

It is apparent that, bit by bit, American industry is obligating itself to underwrite the economic needs and the economic risks of the worker. Industry today provides a cradle-to-grave security program for employees similar to government programs in England and other countries.

TABLE 5–2

Item	Weekly Cost to Employer
Federal Old-Age, Survivors, and Disability Insurance tax	$ 8.00
Unemployment insurance taxes	3.25
Workmen's compensation premium	2.00
Private pension contribution	9.00
Group insurance contribution	4.00
Supplemental unemployment benefit plan contribution	3.00
Pay for holidays, vacations, rest periods, and other time not worked	22.00
Employee facilities, services, and other miscellaneous benefits	3.75
Total	$55.00

As more and more costs go into fringe benefits, payment by the hour for time actually worked will become less important. Does this mean that our traditional modes of payment will eventually be outdated? Many questions which cannot be answered today are a matter of concern to business and labor leaders alike.

At the same time as the employer's cost of employing a worker has been increasing because of fringe benefits, employee take-home pay has been subjected to major deductions in the form of withholding for federal income taxes, state income taxes, union dues, charitable contributions, etc. The result has been a growing gap between spendable earnings and labor costs. For example, assume that a company employs a worker at $200 weekly pay. The company could have, in addition to this direct wage cost, indirect costs associated with the employment of this worker as shown in Table 5–2. On the other side of the coin, the employee's paycheck might well reflect deductions such as those in Table 5–3.

In this company, therefore, the employer looks upon his labor costs as $255 per week for this particular employee, while the employee only receives $154.50 in his pay envelope. The employee is, of course, aware of these various indirect benefits and of the manner in which his pay has been diverted. The problem facing industry, however, arises from the fact that to a considerable extent, these amounts are likely to be discounted in the employee's thinking. Although "package" settlements, which provide that much of a bargain wage adjustment shall be taken in the form of fringes, are especially popular with employees who are security-conscious, even such employees also tend to think in terms of "take-home" pay—that is, the amount actually received in the pay envelope. Continued emphasis on fringes, therefore, can tend to increase

TABLE 5–3

Item	Weekly Cost to Employee
Statutory deductions (federal and state income tax withheld; withholding for federal Old-Age, Survivors, and Disability Insurance)	$38.00
Union dues	1.50
Group insurance premiums for dependents' coverage and contributions to company thrift plan and charitable drives	6.00
Total	$45.50

the cost to the employer without increasing the immediate satisfaction of the employee.

Fringe Benefits and Employment

A characteristic of many fringe benefits is that they are attached to the individual employee rather than to the overall wage bill of the employer. Thus, the worker receives vacations, holidays, pensions, group insurance, etc., whether he works 35 hours, 40 hours, or 50 hours per week. Of course, his earnings may change the amount he receives as benefits; but within broad limits, such fringes are often like the government social security program (old age): After a basic amount of payroll cost, there is no additional charge.

This means that fringe benefits can make it cheaper to work employees overtime than to hire new employees. For example, assume that fringe benefits cost an employer 75 cents per hour and government-imposed benefit programs (social security, and unemployment and workmen's compensation) add another 25 cents. Add to these the costs of recruiting, indoctrinating, and employing new personnel, which can be substantial, and frequently employers find that it is cheaper to employ existing employees at overtime rates (time and one-half basic rates) than it would be to hire new employees. This fact accounts for proposals to increase the overtime rate to double time as a means of discouraging overtime.

Fringe benefits, by adding to the employers' marginal costs, may adversely affect both the amount of employment and its character—that is, whether existing employees are worked more hours or new employees are added to the payroll. The cost of security for some may be less employment—and less security—for others. Whether, however, adding to the cost of overtime, and hence to the employers' overall cost, would lessen or increase the propensity to employ is, of course, very doubtful. We shall return to this issue in our discussion of the hours of work question in Chapter 16.

SUMMARY

We have seen that the wage issue is not a simple question of how many cents per hour a worker should be paid. Wages—in the sense used in this text—can encompass a wide range of benefits, from maternity care for a worker's wife to extra pay for working after 6 P.M. Wages are naturally important to a worker because they mean purchasing power for him and his family. But wages also have another dimension in our society which should not be overlooked. The worker, in common with other members of the community, views his wage as a symbol of his standing in the community. It is an aspect of his status in our economic society. That is why benefits such as a third week of paid vacation, for example, are so important. If John Jones is at home cutting the lawn while Bill Smith is working at the plant because his company did not give the third week of vacation, you can bet that Mrs. Jones and Mrs. Smith are discussing the injustice of it all and that Bill Smith—and eventually his employer—will hear about it!

In the next chapter, we shall consider other problems arising out of the employer-employee relationship which do not directly involve wages but are important issues in the collective bargaining process.

QUESTIONS FOR DISCUSSION

1. Discuss the various forms of incentive payment. Is it true that unions oppose piecework and favor time payment? Support your answer.
2. Discuss the pros and cons of profit sharing versus gain sharing.
3. Discuss the relationship of fringe benefits as a cost to the employer and a return to the employee. Do you think the trend of fringe benefit costs will continue to rise; and if so, what are some of the implications of this trend?
4. To what extent if any do you think that the federal government should regulate pensions? What issues might be the most important to regulate?

SUGGESTIONS FOR FURTHER READING

Levinson, Harold M. *Determining Forces in Collective Wage Bargaining.* New York: John Wiley & Sons, Inc., 1966.

A scholarly analytical study of wage changes in four industries, emphasizing the power factors in collective bargaining which have contributed to the wage trends.

McCONNELL, CAMPBELL R. (ed.). *Perspectives on Wage Determination: A Book of Readings.* New York: McGraw-Hill Book Co., 1970.

A excellent collection of articles on many facets of wage determination.

MUNTS, RAYMOND. *Bargaining for Health. Labor Unions, Health Insurance, and Medical Care.* Madison, Wis.: University of Wisconsin Press, 1967.

An excellent history and analysis of union policies in the health insurance area.

ROWAN, RICHARD L. (ed.). *Collective Bargaining: Survival in the 70's?* pp. 359–92. Labor Relations and Public Policy Series, Report No. 5. Philadelphia: Industrial Research Unit, Wharton School of Finance and Commerce, University of Pennsylvania, 1972.

Pension issues now before the country are summarized and commented upon from different points of view by Professor Dan M. McGill and Mr. E. S. Willis.

SLICHTER, SUMNER H.; HEALY, J. J.; and LIVERNASH, E. R. *The Impact of Collective Bargaining on Management,* chaps. xvii–xx. Washington, D.C.: Brookings Institution, 1960.

These chapters of this outstanding work contain comprehensive and realistic analyses of wage incentives, measured daywork, evaluated wage structures, and other wage structure considerations based upon extensive field work and careful evaluations of the problems encountered. The discussions are still current although written more than a decade ago.

| Chapter 6 | # THE CONTENT OF COLLECTIVE BARGAINING: INDUSTRIAL JURISPRUDENCE |

The process of collective bargaining, as we have seen from the previous chapter, is a method of determining the price of labor, that is, of fixing wages. An additional important function of collective bargaining is to formulate the rules and regulations governing the employment relationship.

Where there is no union, management's labor policies may be liberal or restrictive; but in either case, they are *management's* policies. Management is free to discharge, to promote, to hire, or to lay off in any legal manner in which it desires. But when a union represents the employees, these functions and many others which were once the prerogative of management become subject to a variety of rules. Some of the rules are written into an agreement between union and management; others are simply accepted by both parties and remain unwritten; and still others are embodied in federal, state, or municipal laws, often as a result of pressure by unions or employers. These rules embody the system of "industrial jurisprudence" by which the relation of union and management is regulated.[1]

No Uniformity of Rules

A system of industrial jurisprudence is basically the result of American workers' demands that industrial relations be conducted according to rules which they have a voice in formulating. Only if such rules are in effect do unions and employees feel that persons equally situated will be guaranteed equal treatment in promotions, layoffs, discipline actions, and in meeting technological change; and only if such rules exist can the union in most situations influence substantially the handling of people and main-

---

[1] As the term was used by the late Professor Sumner H. Slichter in his path-breaking book, *Union Policies and Industrial Management* (Washington, D.C.: Brookings Institution, 1941), p. 1. A second edition, completed by Professor Slichter just prior to his death in 1959 and coauthored by Professors J. J. Healy and E. R. Livernash, was published in 1960 under the title, *The Impact of Collective Bargaining on Management* (Washington, D.C.: Brookings Institution).

tain its own status as a significant organization capable of exerting effective pressure on managerial decision making.

The type of rules developed in a particular industry or shop reflects the problems encountered there. The industrial pattern—including the extent of product competition, the character of the labor market, the degree of union and nonunion competition, the rate of technological change, and a host of other socioeconomic factors—determines particular union policies. What one union finds suitable in a particular situation, another in a different locale will reject as unworkable. Union policies are a function of their environment. Hence we find a wide variety of policies pursued by various unions.

Union Security[2]

A primary aim of most unions is "union security," and this usually involves some form of compulsory union membership and automatic dues checkoff. Whether a union will demand a "closed shop" (under which employees must join the union as a prerequisite to employment) or a "union shop" (under which the employer may hire anyone he chooses, but after a probationary period of 30–90 days all employees must join the union as a condition of employment) will vary with the type of employment and labor market. In general, the closed shop is found among skilled and strategically located trades and in industries in which employment is casual and intermittent. The closed shop differs from the union shop primarily in that it is not only a means of "union security" but also a method of controlling entrance to the job or trade. Other forms of union security, including methods of "checking off" dues and thus assuring unions of a flow of funds, are described in Table 6–1. Approximately 80% of the nearly 18 million persons covered by collective bargaining agreements in private industry work under some form of union security provisions.

Except in underdeveloped countries, union security provisions are not common outside of the United States and Canada.[3] In America, the closed or union shop became a necessary weapon for union survival. Only with such protection could the union count on effective protection from employer discrimination against union members. In many cases the closed- and union-shop provisions were necessary to induce workers to join the

---

[2] For a more complete analysis of this subject, with emphasis on the legal and public policy aspects, see Herbert R. Northrup and Gordon F. Bloom, *Government and Labor* (Homewood, Ill.: Richard D. Irwin, Inc., 1963), chap. viii.

[3] In many underdeveloped countries, unions have found that it is impossible to collect dues and to maintain an organization without at least a checkoff. In New Zealand and in some of the Australian provinces, workers are required by law to maintain membership and to pay dues to the union which represents them before state arbitration courts. The British industrial relations law which became effective in 1972 has similar features but also restricts compulsory unionism.

TABLE 6–1

Types of Union Security and Checkoff

Union Security Terms	Checkoff Terms

Closed Shop—Employer agrees that all workers must belong to the union to keep their jobs. He further agrees that when hiring new workers he will hire only members of the union.

Union Shop—Employer agrees that all workers must belong to the union to keep their jobs. He can hire whom he wants; but the workers he hires must join the union within a specified time (usually 30 days) or lose their jobs.

Modified Union Shop—Employer agrees that all present and future members of the union must remain in the union for the duration of the contract in order to keep their jobs. (Present workers who are not in the union and who do not join the union in the future can keep their jobs without union membership.) The employer further agrees that all new employees must join the union within a specified time (usually 30 days) or lose their jobs.

Agency Shop—The employer and the union agree that a worker shall not be forced to join or stay in the union to keep his job. The worker has the choice of joining or not joining. But if he elects not to join he must pay to the union a sum equal to union dues. This sum represents a fee charged him by the union for acting as his agent in collective bargaining and in policing the union contract.

Maintenance of Membership—Employer agrees that all present and future members of the union must remain in the union for the duration of the contract in order to keep their jobs. (Workers who are not in the union and who do not join the union in the future can keep their jobs without union membership.)

Revocable Maintenance of Membership—Employer agrees that all present and future members of the union must remain in the union to keep their jobs. But he specifies that workers can leave the union during specified periods (usually 10 days at the end of each year) without losing their jobs.

Preferential Hiring—Employer agrees that in hiring new workers he shall give preference to union members.

Voluntary Irrevocable—Employer agrees to deduct union dues and other monies from the worker's wages only if the worker signs a form authorizing him to do so. This generally requires that the worker's authorization shall not be irrevocable for more than 1 year or beyond the termination date of the contract, whichever is sooner.

Year-to-Year Renewal—Employer agrees to deduct dues and other monies from the worker's wages if the worker signs a checkoff authorization. If the worker does not revoke his authorization at the end of a year or at the contract termination date, it goes into effect for another year.

Voluntary Revocable—Employer agrees to deduct union dues and other monies from the worker's wages if the worker signs a form authorizing him to do so. The worker can revoke this authorization any time he sees fit.

Automatic—Employer agrees automatically to deduct dues and other monies from the worker's wages and turn the money over to the union.

Involuntary Irrevocable—Employer agrees that to secure and keep his job a worker must sign a form authorizing the employer to deduct union dues and other monies from his wages.

Source: J. J. Bambrick, *Union Security and Checkoff Provisions* (Studies in Personnel Policy, No. 127 [New York: National Industrial Conference Board, 1952]). Mr. Bambrick's definitions have stood the test of time and remain current.

union, not so much because of their reluctance to join but because of their fear of consequences in the form of employer retaliation if they joined voluntarily.

In other democratic countries, unions found less need of union security, for they often grew at a more rapid rate than those in the United States and encountered much less employer opposition. Complete union membership was achieved not by union security provisions in contracts but by direct action among employees. Men unwilling to join unions in European democracies are usually compelled to do so either because union men will not work with them or because they find that failure to join unions means social ostracism or other types of effective pressure. Such methods proved ineffective in America because of employer opposition to unions and the lack of class-consciousness on the part of employees.

Theoretically, the passage of the National Labor Relations (Wagner) Act in 1935 eliminated much of the need for union security by outlawing employer discrimination against workers because of union membership and by requiring employers to bargain with duly certified unions. Nevertheless, union security demands lost none of their intensity. This was true partly because union leaders and members believed, often with considerable justification, that employers were opposed to unions and could circumvent the law; partly because, emotionally, they could not imagine successful unionism without the closed or union shop; and partly because of the rise of rival unionism on a scale theretofore unknown. The existence of a union security provision deters raiding by rival unions and thus gives unions "security" from another angle. The merger of the AFL and the CIO in 1955 further outmoded this union argument in favor of security needs.

Like union arguments in favor of union security, which attempt to couch the issue in terms of the survival of collective bargaining, employer arguments against compulsory unionism are usually set forth in highly emotional language—that is, in terms of individual liberty, "right to work," or "freedom from domination by union bosses." In actual fact, there are very real power issues involved: power of a union in relation to its members and power of a union in bargaining with management. These are vital concerns of both labor and management.

Power over Members

That the union security issue is concerned with union coercive power over its members seems undeniable. Power over the membership involves, of course, the right of a union to fine, to discipline, or to effectuate the discharge of a member for violation of union rules or conduct, or for the completely indefensible reasons of opposing, antagonizing, or otherwise offending union leadership. Students of labor relations have always recognized that a union must have some authority over its members, particularly when a majority has taken a legitimate position in favor of a legitimate objective. Otherwise, anarchy in industrial relations could result. For example, few disagree with the right of a majority to accept a settlement offered by an employer, or to reject the settlement and to choose a strike. But should a union have the power to fine or to discipline a member who crosses a picket line and returns to work during a strike, and thus makes the achievement of the strike goal more difficult for the majority? Questions like this involve complex moral and economic issues which each citizen may answer differently and which the legislatures and the courts likewise find difficult to determine. The U.S. Supreme Court, by the narrow margin of five justices to four, ruled that a union could fine members for refusing to stay on strike and that unions could sue in the courts to collect the fines.[4] The complexities of such questions and their difficulty of resolution have induced the Congress and state legislatures to move into this field of regulation—either by a "bill-of-rights" guarantee, such as is contained in the Landrum-Griffin Act, or by limiting or controlling union security provisions.

The Taft-Hartley Act of 1947 outlawed the closed shop, placed restrictions on other forms of union security, and expressly permitted the states to legislate in this field, regardless of federal law. Once a union security provision was legally negotiated, the union was not restricted in its admission or disciplinary actions, but it could require the discharge of an employee pursuant to a legal union security provision only on the ground that the employee had failed to tender the regularly required initiation fee or dues.

Discharges and Checkoff

Expelling a man from a union for nonfiscal reasons, or for declining to pay a special fine or assessment, cannot thus expel him from his job unless an employer conspires with a union to violate the Taft-Hartley Act. Undoubtedly, this happens when the parties mutually agree to rid themselves of a "troublemaker" to both. Nevertheless, the existence of this provision has restrained arbitrary union discipline of members, and especially arbitrary union-inspired discharge of members.[5]

The Taft-Hartley Act in this respect did not attempt to protect a person's right to belong to a union. It protected the person's right to remain on the job under a union-shop provision as long as he tendered his regular union dues. The sections of the Landrum-Griffin Act dealing with

---

[4] *National Labor Relations Board* v. *Allis-Chalmers Mfg. Co.*, 388 U.S. 175 (1967).

[5] There is still considerable use of union security provision to deny job opportunities, but much less than before Taft-Hartley became law. See Mack A. Moore, "The Conflict between Union Discipline and Union Security," *Labor Law Journal*, Vol. 18 (February 1967), pp. 116–23.

individual union rights, which are discussed in Chapter 20 added protection to the individual against arbitrary expulsion from the union.

Closely allied to this union security restriction in the Taft-Hartley Act was the act's ban on the compulsory checkoff. The checkoff of membership dues was made lawful only where individual employees execute a written assignment of wages for not longer than one year, or for the duration of the applicable union contract, whichever is shorter. In general practice, such assignments are in effect until revoked. But it is now unlawful for an employer and union to agree to turn over a portion of an employee's wages to a union without that employee's express written permission—certainly a highly defensible public policy.

Ban on Closed Shop

The Taft-Hartley Act outlawed the closed shop (see Table 6–1, for definitions) and other forms of preemployment preferential treatment of union members. The writers of the act were impressed with the fact that unreasonable denial of work had occurred as a result of union control of hiring, and this they were determined to eliminate.

There is general agreement, however, that this provision tended largely to drive the closed shop underground instead of out of existence. We shall examine in following sections of this chapter why control of hiring through the closed shop is so vital to unions in the building, maritime, and other trades where employment is intermittent. In Chapter 3, we also noted how the closed shop is used to bar persons deemed unacceptable to the members—for example, to discriminate against minorities. There is no question that unions in the building trades, for example, have used the power inherent in closed-shop arrangements to deny blacks job opportunities.

Despite the obviously discriminatory activities of the building trades unions, Congress in 1959, while enacting the Landrum-Griffin Act to promote union democracy, actually loosened Taft-Hartley restrictions applying to the construction industry. It legalized "prehire" aggreements (that is, arrangements to employ union personnel before a job starts). Such agreements may now make union membership compulsory 7 days after employment (rather than 30 days, as is the Taft-Hartley requirement in other industries), provided that the state law permits union security provisions. Construction union contracts also can require an employer to notify the union of job opportunities and to give the union an opportunity to refer qualified applicants for employment, and can specify minimum training or experience qualifications for employment. The net effect of these provisions was to restore a considerable amount of legality to the actual practice in the construction industry. Then, five years later in 1964, Congress enacted the Civil Rights Act, Title VII of which forbids discrimination by unions or employers on grounds of race, color, creed, or sex. The net effect has been a flood of street demonstrations and of lawsuits aimed at unions and contractors in the building industry, and massive federal programs aimed at forcing unions and companies in this industry to open up jobs for blacks and to cease using the closed shop as a device for racial discrimination.

The Taft-Hartley Act also provided that a union could negotiate legal forms of union security only after a special vote of the membership. This was based on a belief that employees would reject compulsory unionism. The opposite proved to be the case. Between 1947 and 1951, when these elections were conducted, over 75% of the 6,545,001 eligible employees voted for the union shop and authorized negotiations for it in 97% of the cases.[6] The net effect was twofold—a bipartisan movement to repeal this voting requirement, which was accomplished by the Taft-Humphrey amendments of 1951; and a general spread of union-shop agreements throughout industry. Companies such as General Motors and United States Steel, which had accepted maintenance-of-membership provisions only under National War Labor Board compulsion, now agreed to the union shop after their employees had voted in favor of it.

"Right-to-Work" Laws and the Union-Management Power Relationship

In the long run, the most significant provision of Taft-Hartley relating to union security is probably Section 14(*b*), which provides that "Nothing in this Act shall be construed as authorizing the execution or application of agreements requiring membership in a labor organization as a condition of employment in any State or Territory in which such execution or application is prohibited by State or Territorial Law." This provision ran counter to the usual principle that state laws are superseded by federal legislation on the same subject matter.

Thus, the clear purpose of Section 14(*b*) was to give states the right to legislate in this field; and 19 did, outlawing union security provisions altogether.[7] The issue of whether a state should outlaw union security provisions remains very much alive in several states.

Because of the emotional content of the arguments pro and con on the union security issue, and hence right-to-work laws, some observers have expressed the belief that the issue itself is largely symbolic and political rather than economic and significant in the union-management relation-

---

[6] Data from *Monthly Labor Review, August* 1953, p. 837. An analysis of these votes is presented in Northrup and Bloom, *Government and Labor*, pp. 236-41.

[7] Alabama, Arizona, Arkansas, Florida, Georgia, Iowa, Kansas, Mississippi, Nebraska, Nevada, North Carolina, North Dakota, South Carolina, South Dakota, Tennessee, Texas, Utah, Virginia, and Wyoming. Indiana which had such a law, repealed it; Louisiana has such a law applying only to agricultural employment.

ship.[8] Yet, even the Taft-Hartley union-shop polls found a significant minority of workers who declined to support the union shop. This minority—about 23%—is a substantial number of members (and dues)— enough to affect a power balance, to pay considerable strike benefits, or to employ a squad of union organizers.[9]

Other investigations support the view that in the absence of compulsory union provisions, a significant minority of employees in bargaining unions remain nonunion.[10] By restricting union income, state right-to-work laws most certainly affect the union-management relationship more basically than in a symbolic manner.

CONTROL OF ENTRANCE TO THE TRADE

Attempts to control entrance to the trade are limited largely to craft unions. Except for a few, such as the United Mine Workers, who have been able to utilize license laws in a few areas, industrial unions do not find it feasible to control entrance. Their members learn their tasks by experience. They permit the employer to recruit the work force and exert their control in other ways.

Craft unions, however, have found that control of entrance is an effective method of increasing their bargaining power. Their efforts take two principal forms: regulation of apprenticeship and support of licensing legislation.

Regulation of Apprenticeship

Apprenticeship is a way by which young men who meet certain standards of age, education, and aptitude can learn a trade by working at it under close supervision and usually combine such practical learning with appropriately related part-time schooling. Nearly all unions whose membership includes journeymen, for which apprenticeship is customary, attempt to regulate the terms and conditions under which apprentices are employed. From a pre–World War II figure of 17,300, the number of apprentices grew to a high of 230,283 in 1950, then declined steadily to 158,616 in the mid 1960s. The trend turned upward again so that by 1971, approximately 280,000 apprentices were reported.[11] About 65% of all

---

[8] This seems to be the conclusion of Professor Frederic Meyers, *"Right to Work" in Practice* (New York: Fund for the Republic, Inc., 1959). For a critique of Meyers' conclusions, see John M. Glasgow, "The Right-to-Work Law Controversy Again," *Labor Law Journal*, Vol. 18 (February 1967), pp. 112–15.

[9] See Northrup and Bloom, *Government and Labor*, pp. 235–38; and Glasgow, "Right-to-Work Law Controversy," pp. 112–15.

[10] Glasgow, "Right-to-Work Law," pp. 112–15.

[11] Phyllis Groom, "Statistics on Apprenticeship and Their Limitations," *Monthly Labor Review*, Vol. 87 (April 1964), pp. 392–93. Recent data courtesy Bureau of Apprentice Training, U.S. Department of Labor.

registered apprentices are in building construction, 15% in metal trades, 8% in printing trades, and the balance widely dispersed throughout industry.

Apprenticeship is only one of the many ways in which a vocational aptitude may be gained. In most occupations, training is learned on the job, in trade or vocational schools, in the Armed Forces, or in federal or state training courses, or probably principally, by "picking up the trade" —that is, working with journeymen on a variety of jobs until proficiency is obtained. Only about one fourth of all unions actually participate in apprenticeship regulation. Moreover, most employees who do work in apprenticeable trades have learned their trade without having served an apprenticeship. Thus, studies have estimated that as many as 80% of all carpenters and 30% of the electricians became journeymen without serving apprenticeships.[12] These studies also show that it is more difficult to become a journeyman in the electrical, mechanical, and plumbing trades without formal training than in the carpentry, painting, or trowel trades (bricklaying, cement finishing, etc.).

Unions control apprenticeship by a variety of regulatory devices. One is to establish qualifications which are both artificially high or subjective. Requirements that applicants be high school graduates, aged 17–25, be proficient in mathematics and pass exacting tests, have a basis for the advanced mechanical trades but not for the less exacting ones. Indeed, those who can qualify under such rules usually prefer a college education instead of apprentice training. Even if a prospective candidate passes these tests, he may be subject to interviews which rate him on purely subjective grounds. Opportunities for racial discrimination or for exclusion merely to maintain union craft monopolies are thus readily available. In 1972, for example, after consistent government prodding, only 6% of all apprentices were black, a substantial increase in five years, but still substantially below a reasonable or fair share. Moreover, in the electrical, plumbing, and mechanical trades, the proportion was far less—2%–3%.[13]

Another common method of regulating apprenticeship is to control the proportion of apprentices to journeymen. This protects journeymen against any tendency on the part of employers to displace journeymen with apprentices. Agreements in the building or printing trades normally contain provisions for the employment of one apprentice to every four to eight journeymen. In addition, many unions negotiate agreements which place an absolute limit on the number of apprentices who can be hired.

---

[12] See, for example, Howard G. Foster, "Nonapprentice Sources of Training in Construction," *Monthly Labor Review*, Vol. 43 (February 1970), pp. 21–26.

[13] See U.S. Department of Labor, Labor-Management Services Administration, *Admission and Apprenticeship in the Building Trades* (Washington, D.C.: U.S. Government Printing Office, 1971). Data on race from Bureau of Apprentice Training, U.S. Department of Labor.

In addition to controlling the number of apprentices by a direct limitation, unions can also control apprentice training by controlling the wages of apprentices. The higher the wages of apprentices are set, the more costly it is for the employer to use apprentices. Thus, a liberal ratio of apprentices to journeymen may be nullified by an unreasonable rate for the use of apprentices.

Few unions require the serving of an apprenticeship as a condition of membership. Perhaps more would do so if they completely controlled entrance to their trade. The fact of the matter is, however, that so many Americans either pick up a trade without formal training or have secured their training by other means that unions could not sustain a requirement that apprentice training be an absolute prerequisite to membership.

The reasonableness of union apprentice regulation varies from industry to industry. There has been considerable evidence in certain trades, including building and printing, that union apprentice regulations have been utilized to prevent newcomers from winning a place in the industry; and in other cases, such limitations have actually created artificial shortages of labor. Moreover, in many of these trades, apprentice regulations have been utilized to confine apprentice training to friends or relatives of journeymen and to exclude Negroes and other minority groups from participation.

Discrimination against blacks in apprenticeship participation has been a serious matter because there are few other ways in which they can learn these trades. Not having friends and relatives in jobs, except in the southern trowel trades (bricklaying, plastering, and cement finishing) where there has been a tradition of Negro craftsmen since slavery days, blacks have been compelled to depend upon formal training if they desired such skilled work. Informal training based on working with family or friends, or otherwise picking up the trade, a common method of instruction, depends on contacts largely unavailable to blacks. Yet the formal plans in such fields as building construction have been in practice reserved for whites only, with very few exceptions until recently.

Because of this exclusion, combined with a shortage of craftsmen in many cities, the U.S. Department of Labor has instituted plans (termed "Philadelphia Plans" because the first one was instituted there) in key cities throughout the country which require that certain percentages of work in key crafts be performed by black craftsmen. In addition, where government funds are involved, these plans provide for "learner" and "advanced learner" categories so that journeymen proficiency can be acquired by means other than apprenticeship. These plans have resulted in substantial increases in many cities in black craft worker utilization. Often, however, the goals of the plans are not achieved because local unions have frustrated their intent, particularly by permitting blacks to work under permits instead of admitting them to membership, thus setting the stage for eliminating the minority workers if the government reduces its pressure for equality. Moreover, such local union tactics are designed to exclude blacks from nongovernment work.[14] Another problem is that qualified black applicants are often scarce. Those with the requisite backgrounds, particularly in high school mathematics, are as their white counterparts, more likely to be interested in a college education than in apprenticeship training. Many blacks whose schools are either in the city slums or in largely segregated southern areas, find that their training has been inferior. Special training and assistance is now recognized as required if blacks are to gain a fair share of skilled craft work.

Unions perform some definite services in regard to apprentice training. The existence of a strong union prevents an employer from keeping an apprentice on a particular task he has mastered instead of giving him a well-rounded mechanical education. The temptation for employers to confine apprentices to a small section of the mechanic's job is very great, for in such cases they are receiving work of mechanic's quality for apprenticeship wages.

On the other hand, union apprenticeship terms are often obsolete. It is highly doubtful whether today three to five years is a necessary term for learning many of the building crafts which require apprenticeships of that duration. These terms could be shortened, but unions fear to do this because their rules and restrictions are based on the number who can be expected to become journeymen after long apprenticeships. Any reduction in the terms would probably be accompanied by a reduction in the percentage of apprentices permitted in union agreements.

Apprentice training as a whole is not likely to be a very efficient method of providing qualified labor when it is needed. Typically, during periods of depression, no apprentices are trained, so that in following periods of prosperity, there is a great shortage of skilled labor. Then in the prosperity period the number of apprentices being trained increases tremendously. By the time some of these apprentices become qualified journeymen, business conditions and their opportunities for employment have worsened.

Licensing Legislation

The great interest of recent years in breaking down barriers to the employment of the disadvantaged and to integrate blacks into all segments of the labor force and society has focused interest on the manpower implication of licensing legislation. Such legislation by states or municipalities has been utilized by many groups in society to limit en-

---

[14] For a study of "Philadelphia-like" plans in two cities, see Richard L. Rowan and Lester Rubin, *Opening Up the Skilled Construction Trades to Blacks: A Study of the Washington and Indianapolis Plans for Minority Employment* (Philadelphia: Industrial Research Unit, Wharton School of Finance and Commerce, University of Pennsylvania, 1972).

trance to occupations, professions, and even trades. Union groups which sponsor such laws include plumbers, electricians, barbers, taxi drivers, and many others. Generally, they work closely with employer counterparts, and the laws give unions and employer associations prominent places in their administration. Ostensibly, they are enacted in the interest of the safety of the consumer. Actually, their real purpose from a union point of view is to limit entrance into the trade and to increase union bargaining power by making it more difficult for employers to employ strikebreakers.

Several careful studies of licensing legislation have recently been made.[15] They indicate that licensing laws are frequently abused and that their value to the consumer varies considerably. For example, such laws may be used as a vehicle for race discrimination, or to restrict artificially the number of qualified mechanics.

The problem of licensing legislation extends beyond unions. The medical, legal, dental, and the other professions which advocate licensing legislation have encountered the same problems. Studies of the practices of physicians and pharmacists indicate that there is considerable use of licensing laws to limit competition and to monopolize services and markets. Licensing laws which are sold to the public as a means of protecting the consumer are easily perverted into tools for enhancing restrictive practices or furthering monopoly control.

CONTROL OF HIRING

In an unorganized labor market the employer controls both hiring and layoffs. When a union enters the picture, it must secure some voice in at least one of these vital matters. Otherwise, the union can be of little service to members who fear discrimination because of union membership or who want hirings and/or layoffs conducted by rules rather than by employer fiat.

Methods of Controlling Hiring

The most common method of controlling hiring is by means of the closed shop, requiring employers to hire only members of the union or, if

---

[15] Among the studies are, Elton Rayack, *Professional Power and American Medicine: The Economics of the American Medical Association* (Cleveland, Ohio: World Publishing Co., 1967); F. Marion Fletcher, *Market Restraints in the Retail Drug Industry*, (Industrial Research Unit Study No. 43 [Philadelphia: University of Pennsylvania Press, 1967]); *State Licensing of Health Occupations* (U.S. Department of Health, Education, and Welfare, Public Health Service Publication No. 1758 [Washington D.C.: Government Printing Office, 1967]); *Occupational Licensing and the Supply of Nonprofessional Manpower* (U.S. Department of Labor, Manpower Administration, Monograph No. 11 [Washington U.S. Government Printing Office, 1969]); and Edmund W. Kitch et al., "The Regulation of Taxicabs in Chicago," *Journal of Law and Economics,* Vol. 14 (October 1971), pp. 285–350.

no union members are available, persons willing to join the union. Some agreements go further by requiring the employer to hire only through the union office or through a hiring hall which may be controlled by the union, by the union and the employer in cooperation, or by a third body, for example, a government bureau.

Control over layoffs often involves indirect control over hiring, especially if, as on the railroads, employment is declining on a secular basis. In the railroad industry the seniority agreements provide for preference for furloughed men in rehiring in the order of the furloughed men's seniority, i.e., length of service with the company. If there is a large pool of furloughed men, the employer's freedom to hire is restricted almost as severely under this type of seniority agreement as under the closed shop.

As in the case of control over entrance to the trade, control over hiring is practiced mainly by the craft unions. The main exceptions involve, first, such control over hiring as result from control over layoffs (for example, seniority provisions); and, second, control over hiring by industrial unions in industries where employment is casual and intermittent or seasonal, as in the maritime or needle trades. Most other unions do not operate in labor markets which permit them to exert control over hiring. Hence, except indirectly through seniority provisions, most industrial unions concentrate on control of layoffs and do not attempt to restrict employer control of hiring.

Hiring Halls

It is quite common in many industries where the average employer is small and the unions are organized on a craft basis for the employer to hire through the union office. Sometimes, this custom arose more as a convenience to employers who wanted a central hiring office than as a means of union control. Generally, however, it is a result of union demands, provoked by special market conditions. In trades or industries where employment is intermittent or casual—for example, building or maritime—hiring through the union is the only method by which the union can secure equal division of work for its membership and end systems whereby a small portion of the membership secures the bulk of the available work.

Although unions may demand that employers hire through them in order to avoid abuses, the net effect may be the substitution of new abuses for old. For example, in the building trades the business agent has frequently substituted his favoritism for that of the contracting foreman. The opportunities to use job dispensations as a means of building up one's personal political machine within the union are immense, and the temptation is frequently succumbed to. In order to protect themselves against such methods, the rank and file of many unions may require officials to rotate jobs on a first-come, first-served basis. This, however, can place a heavy burden both on employers and on the most efficient men. It severely restricts the right of employers to choose men whom they deem competent. And since, especially in the building trades, where the unions do not control layoffs, the least efficient are the first fired and thus the first in line for new jobs, the efficient men are at a disadvantage once they are laid off.

In the garment trades, where employment is highly seasonal, unions control hiring but permit employers latitude in rejecting employees. Thus, a typical agreement provides that employees of a given craft may be sent in rotation, but the employer has the right to discharge without union complaint during a two-week probationary period. Contracts in other industries vary, some giving the employer the right to reject at least two persons sent by the union office for a job; but upon rejection of a third, the union may challenge the employer to prove incompetency through the grievance machinery.

Formal hiring halls are most common in the maritime industry. Because employment in this industry is casual, there is usually a larger labor force attached to it then there are jobs at a given time. This has encouraged a host of antisocial hiring practices and racketeering at the expense of the workers, such as selling jobs, forcing employees to borrow money at exorbitant rates, or to patronize retail establishments in which employers have an interest, etc. Repeated exposures of these practices led the states of New York and New Jersey, in 1953, to establish a bistate waterfront commission to run hiring halls in the port of New York. On the West Coast, such halls were established in 1934. They are formally under joint union-management control, but since the dispatcher is a union man, the union is the dominant factor in their control. Most seamen's unions also operate hiring halls.

Closed Unions and Hiring Halls

The union which is "closed"—that is, which will not admit new applicants to membership—is generally painted as antisocial. Like all generalizations in labor relations, this is not always so. In the maritime industry, some restriction of entry is actually desirable. One of the causes of favoritism and racketeering in hiring on the waterfront is the fact that, especially in depressed times, unemployed workers drift there, often attracted by the high hourly rates. If the "drifters" are granted free entry into the organization, the hiring hall becomes a vehicle for sharing poverty rather than sharing work. The unions must therefore either refuse admission to newcomers or enforce some sort of seniority regulations which modify rotation schemes and give preference to the workers who have been longest attached to the industry. The former policy is more often pursued because the admission to membership of workers for whom there are no jobs provides a hard core of opposition to incumbent union officers. Moreover, the "unemployed brothers" are likely to congregate in the union hall and to be able to attend all meetings. They thus are in an excellent position to control union policy out of proportion to their numbers.

CONTROL OF LAYOFFS

The interest of a union in layoff policy stems from two sources: the worker's desire to know where he stands—to know what chancee he has of retaining his job in case of a reduction in the labor force—and the union's desire to maintain some control in the employment process, which it can do only by a voice either in hiring or layoffs. Since, for reasons already noted, few unions can control hiring, most attempt to have a strong voice in the procedure which governs layoffs. The most common method of handling layoffs is by seniority.

Seniority

Seniority agreements generally provide that employees in a plant or subdivision thereof shall receive preference in layoffs and rehiring in the order in which they were hired. In some cases, as on the railroads, seniority agreements are quite rigid, the only requirement being ability to perform the job. In other cases, seniority provisions are much weaker, giving the employer the opportunity to select a more competent person over one with greater seniority. A few agreements provide for retention by the employer of a small percentage of personnel in slack times, regardless of seniority, so that the plant will be manned by a key basic work force. Many agreements place the union shop steward or committeeman at the head of the seniority roster.

Seniority is most common in the railroad, automobile, iron, steel, rubber, electrical products, and other mass-production industries. In the mass-production industries the extent of the seniority district or unit varies considerably. Sometimes the seniority district is the plant, sometimes a plant division, or a department, or an occupation, or some combination thereof. In general, management prefers the smallest possible seniority districts, with no provisions for workers to hold seniority in more than one district. Under such regulations, layoffs and rehiring do not involve much dislocation in the plant and hence do not interfere materially with the efficient organization of personnel.

Union and employee preference as to the size of seniority districts varies considerably. In general, in times of unemployment, skilled workers prefer wide seniority districts and unskilled workers narrow ones. This is because skilled workers can replace unskilled ones but not vice versa. Hence the wider the seniority district in times of layoffs, the greater the chance for the skilled worker to find a spot by exercising his seniority, and the greater the chance that the unskilled worker will be pushed out of a job. In times of prosperity the opposite is likely to be true because expanding employment gives unskilled workers the opportunity to advance in the occupational hierarchy, and this they like to do without sacrificing their seniority in their former jobs. On the other hand, skilled workers see in expanding employment more competition for jobs when times become depressed. Hence they favor narrow seniority districts during prosperous periods.

Seniority and Race

A combination of narrow seniority districts and discriminatory employment practices has been used for many years in the southern pulp and paper and tobacco industries, as well as in iron and steel plants in many parts of the country, to confine blacks to less desirable jobs in these industries. The seniority practices in these industries were not discriminatory per se. Rather they were developed out of the needs of the industry. For example, in pulp and paper, a person worked his way up the paper machine hierarchy of jobs to the top job of machine tender. No one else in the plant could bid on any paper machine jobs except the lowest one, no matter how much plantwide seniority he had, unless he was in the paper machine line of progression. The nature of the job requires long service on the machine to be able to hold the top job. Blacks, however, were employed only for certain jobs, and seniority lines were perverted to deny them the right to bid on even bottom jobs in seniority lines. This led to the development of the "rightful place" doctrine under which the "affected class"—that is, blacks employed before hiring was nondiscriminatory—were permitted to advance on the basis of plantwide seniority, instead of occupational seniority, after they were placed in a progression line.[16] The result has been a rapid upgrading of some blacks in a number of southern industries. Unfortunately, many blacks employed for laboring jobs in the period prior to the 1964 Civil Rights Act lack the educational qualifications to handle the more complicated mechanical and machine-tending positions. Those employed since job discrimination was outlawed do, however, have the necessary qualifications.

In the automobile industry, seniority districts are very broad, since more than half of the jobs are semiskilled. It is easy for persons to move

[16] The key court cases setting forth this principle are *Quarles v. Philip Morris, Inc.*, 279 F. Supp. 505 (E.D.Va. 1968); and *U.S. v. Local 189, United Papermakers, et al.*, 282 F. Supp 39 (E.D.La., 1968); affirmed 416 F.2d 980 (5th Cir., 1969); cert. denied 397 U.S. 919 (1970). The impact of these cases is discussed in Herbert R. Northrup and Richard L. Rowan, *Negro Employment in Southern Industry* (Studies of Negro Employment [Philadelphia: Industrial Research Unit, Wharton School of Finance and Commerce, University of Pennsylvania, 1970]), Vol. IV, Parts I and III.

from job to job and for relatively unskilled personnel to master many of the operations. This is a significant reason why the automobile industry is one of the largest, if not the largest, employer of blacks, who, as we have noted, are relatively less educated and less well represented in jobs requiring a high skill.

Other Effects of Seniority

The widespread use of seniority provisions in industrial relations has other salutary and unfortunate effects. The most important argument in favor of seniority is that it affords the worker knowledge of his position vis-à-vis his fellow workers. Although seniority is frequently confused with security, it should not be, since, if the plant in which the worker holds seniority ceases to operate, seniority is of little value. Moreover, for every worker whom seniority retains on the payroll, another must be discharged. Seniority, however, is an impersonal criterion and rules out the personal favoritism workers fear so much. And it does have a sort of rough justice, since it gives preference to those who have worked the longest and who presumably have the greatest equity in their jobs.

On the other hand, seniority can put a premium on mediocrity. The person who is least willing and able to take advantage of opportunities in other plants, or who has least ability and therefore does not receive such opportunities, is the one who stands the greatest chance of reaching the top of a seniority roster. For those who like to get ahead by standing still, seniority is a godsend. For those who yearn for the opportunity to advance quickly on merit, seniority is a bane.

In some instances, seniority may improve managerial efficiency. The fact the employers can no longer discharge workers at will forces them to improve selection and training facilities. Moreover, union controls prevent the degrading practice of buying favors from foremen and other such favoritism on the job. From the community point of view, seniority gives the not-quite-so-efficient worker an opportunity to improve instead of being cast out or passed over in promotions. It also protects the older worker from being laid off in times of slack employment.

Seniority causes many internal union problems. For example, there is frequently dispute over what constitutes length of service. Occasionally, service is interrupted for one reason or another, and a wide divergence of opinion is likely to arise both between employer and union and among employees as to whether breaks in seniority for one or another reason should be overlooked. Internal union disputes over seniority provisions and their interpretation have resulted in lengthy and costly litigation.

Seniority provisions have an effect on strikes. Generally, senior men are less willing to strike because they have more to lose. Once on strike, senior men are likely to be apprehensive at the slightest hint that their jobs are being filled. Junior men are usually more willing to strike but may be tempted to return to work in order to leap from the bottom to the top of the seniority roster. Once men return to work, strikes may drag on over the issue of whether the strikebreakers can maintain their place on the seniority roster.

Juniority

Pay to employees who are not working has now reached a stage in some industries where it literally almost pays not to work. In the rubber tire, farm equipment, and automobile industries, for example, the differential which a worker receives for working (that is, wages less paycheck deductions as compared with what a laid-off employee gets from state unemployment compensation plus supplemental unemployment pay) can amount to as little as $10 to $25 per week. In view of this fact, some agreements in these industries permit a senior employee to take layoff instead of working where the layoff is involuntary and the senior man's job is directly affected. Thus, the junior man stays on the job, the senior man takes leisure with pay. This is the first recognition in union contracts that layoffs may be preferable to working and that the penalty for juniority may be a requirement to stay on the job. At one rubber company, nearly every senior man involved has taken the layoff instead of accepting a lower rated job. They can accumulate seniority for two years on layoff, which permits some to reach retirement age. Management considers such juniority an advantage because it eliminates multiple bumping and the high costs of retraining and lost production associated with wide shifts in personnel throughout the plant.

Division of Work

Division of work was once much more widely utilized as a layoff control than it is today. The reason is the combination effect of higher layoff benefits and higher paycheck withholding. Division of work can reduce take-home pay very close to the level of benefits paid under state unemployment compensation systems. When supplemental unemployment benefits are added to state benefits, as in the automobile and steel industries, take-home pay under a division-of-work system can even be less than benefits for not working. Since division of work is also usually less efficient than laying off unnecessary men, it now has little popularity except in special situations, such as in the seasonal garment industry.

There is, however, one situation in the automobile industry where a form of division of work is used and combined with a special form of unemployment pay. Instead of laying off assembly-line workers, companies now often put their labor force on two- or three-day weeks. Employees then receive "short-week pay" to make up some of the lost pay. Manufacturers prefer this because they do not have to slow up the line and reassign each and every job that is left. If, however, business does not improve in time, then layoffs are made and jobs restructured accordingly.

Dismissal Wages

Dismissal compensation is fundamentally a device to mitigate losses resulting from permanent dismissal rather than temporary layoffs. It is utilized in instances in which employees are severed from the payroll as a result of plant abandonment or movement to another area, or as a result of a permanent decrease in the working force. In cases of permanent severance of employees who are near, but have not achieved, the retirement age, a dismissal wage may be used to make up earnings until the employee reaches the age when he is eligible for a pension. Dismissal pay usually provides a schedule of payments based upon length of service. It is very common in the newspaper industry, which has seen many concerns go out of business in recent years. It is also widely used in defense-oriented industries where heavy layoffs resulting from changes in governmental procurement policies are common. In many other industries, companies and unions have negotiated a dismissal pay schedule after the decision has been made to go out of business or to close a plant.

PROTECTING AGAINST LAYOFFS

Seniority, division of work, and dismissal wages are all means to *mitigate* the effects of layoffs. But unions also strive to protect their members against layoffs. Among the methods utilized to do this are provisions for retraining, limiting of contracting-out, and "make-work" or "featherbedding" restrictions.

Retraining

Widespread displacement of blue-collar employees in the mass-production industries during the late 1950s generated considerable interest in retraining by industry, unions, and government. The federal government began a program in 1961. Vocational education by government is not new, but the Manpower Development and Training Act of 1962 marked a broader entry into the training and retraining field which was especially aimed at the unemployed and which more recently has been designed to help "disadvantaged" persons, particularly Negroes and members of other minority groups, obtain jobs in industry. Other programs have been designed to assist those already employed to qualify, through basic education and/or training, for upgrading. Although many of these training programs may have opened up new opportunities for the disadvantaged, their success has often been found to be somewhat limited.[17] To attempt to open up more skilled construction jobs for blacks, the Nixon administration has sponsored numerous training programs in that industry, some under union sponsorship, others as part of the "Philadelphia-like" plans designed to qualify minorities for skilled work. The success of these programs has varied considerably from city to city.

From the union point of view, interest in training already displaced workers or those never employed is secondary to attempting to gain retraining for those still on the job but threatened by displacement. In the last decade, the authors have observed an increasing union interest in provisions designed to give training (often at employer expense) to employees to qualify them for new opportunities. In addition, many of the larger companies make available opportunities for employees to take appropriate training on their own time and at their own expense. If the pace of technological change continues, one may expect a rising interest in such retraining, and perhaps it may become a major focus of union demands in some industries.

Another union proposal—the training of blue-collar personnel for white-collar jobs—is likely to meet with more employer resistance. Many blue-collar workers do advance to white-collar jobs. But industry is likely to go slowly to advance union-oriented factory workers to its as yet largely unorganized office work force.

Contracting-Out and Part-Time Work

Few issues in recent years have generated more heat both between companies and unions, and among unions themselves, than has the contracting-out of work. Most manufacturing enterprises do not make everything they assemble. They "contract out" or buy parts from various suppliers. In turn, such companies may make parts for other companies if they have capacity in some departments. The reasons for this are manifold but basically fall into two categories: (1) The ability to make parts or items better and cheaper varies among companies; therefore, it is often not good business for a concern to make all of its parts. (2) Some parts or components are not required in sufficient volume to make it profitable for a company to tool up, purchase equipment, or employ or train labor in order to make them itself. And of course, much contracting-out takes

---

[17] For a study of a broad retraining and resettlement program in the meat-packing industry in which there has been considerable technological displacement and plant closings, see George P. Shultz and Arnold R. Weber, *Strategies for the Displaced Worker* (New York: Harper & Row, Publishers, 1966). For an analysis of less successful training, see Richard L. Rowan and Herbert R. Northrup, *Educating the Employed Disadvantaged for Upgrading. A Report on Remedial Education Programs in the Paper Industry* (Philadelphia: Industrial Research Unit, Wharton School of Finance and Commerce, University of Pennsylvania, 1972).

place because firms often find parts companies that have lower labor costs and can do the job for less.

From time to time, also, the ability to make parts varies. Capacity might be reached so as to force a company to contract out work in order to meet delivery dates. When orders decline, work previously contracted out may be done within the company. Loading and manning factors also may force contracting-out. For example, one department may be overloaded while another is short of work. Yet the short-of-work department may not have the skills or equipment to aid the overloaded one.

In recent years, there has been an increase in another type of contracting-out—that of such services as typing and secretarial work, janitorial service, plant guarding, even engineering work, and in some chemical and petroleum concerns, all maintenance work. Companies have found that it is cheaper to pay an agency to supply temporary office help in order to meet peak loads than it is to have employees on the payroll who cannot be kept busy. High wages and fringe benefits have raised the costs of employing guards and janitors to a point where it is economic to contract out such work.

Companies supplying contract labor have had no difficulty in finding workers who desire this type of employment. Temporary employees are the fastest growing segment of the labor force, with almost 10 million persons so occupied. The married woman who wants to work only a few days per week, or a few hours each day while her children are in school, the teacher or fireman who "moonlights" during off hours for more income, the student putting himself through college, all swell the part-time labor force. Unions in industrial plants are opposed both to contracting-out and to using part-time labor. Being responsive to fears of the people in the plant that contracting-out costs them jobs, and finding that part-timers have little interest in becoming union members or dues payers, unions have naturally put pressure on management to restrict such practices. Some of these restrictions are very tight and deny essential managerial flexibility required to maintain delivery schedules or profitable operations. Other clauses simply require management to notify unions why contracting-out is necessary. Many managements do this anyway, in order to allay fears and otherwise avoid controversy or support for restrictive union demands. The National Labor Relations Board now requires that management bargain at least on the impact of such contracting-out on employees; such decisions can also be subject to arbitration under the contract unless the agreement contains a specific disclaimer to the contrary.

The building-trades unions, in contrast to those in industrial plants, not only are unopposed to contracting-out or to the use of temporary help, but enthusiastically support such measures as a means of furthering the employment of their members. The building-trades unions have worked with a number of contractors to promote the idea of having all maintenance work done by contract labor, and this policy has been adopted by a large number of petroleum and chemical firms. The companies using contract maintenance have been well satisfied with it and believe that it provides a sound solution to their needs for a varying number of maintenance employees at different times.[18] The industrial unions, of course, regard contract maintenance as an invasion of their jurisdiction and a method of denying work to their members. Because of such opposition, contract maintenance is most·likely to be found in new or unorganized plants in the future.

"MAKE WORK" OR "FEATHERBEDDING"

Insecurity of the worker in modern industry has led employees to "make work" by adopting a variety of policies. These make-work or "featherbedding" arrangements often exist among unorganized as well as organized employees, but the entrance of a union can have the effect of formalizing and strengthening them.

Restrictions on Output

Restrictions on output, direct or indirect, are the most common make-work practice. Formal restrictions are not very common in industry, although reference to them sometimes occurs in union literature or even in collective bargaining contracts. Usually, however, the restrictions are disguised as health protective devices or, more likely, simply based on tacit understanding among employees. Restrictions, both formal and informal, are more often found under incentive than daywork systems because workers often fear that a "world beater" among them will earn so much that he will force the more average employees either to quit or to work at an exhausing pace.

Restrictions on output and other forms of make-work policies are also the result of fear on the part of employees that they will work themselves out of a job. Most employees believe that there is a given amount of work and that by stretching it out, each employee will receive more. This notion is, of course, fallacious. If employees restrict production, the result is higher costs and higher prices; consumers buy less of the product; and in the end, employment opportunities are diminished. In industries such as building construction, however, the individual worker may stretch out his immediate employment by slowing up on the job, even though the long-run effect of the slowdown may well be less work because of resultant high costs.

Limits set on output are usually enforced by social pressure rather

---

[18] See James H. Jordan, "How to Evaluate the Advantages of Contract Maintenance," *Chemical Engineering*, Vol. 75 (March 25, 1968), pp. 124–30.

than by union rule. True, sometimes men have been fined for getting out too much work. More often, whether the plant is unionized or not, the speed of work deemed appropriate by the majority is enforced by their refusing to engage in social relationships with other workers who "speed up." The latter, finding themselves outcasts from the groups to which they belong, are likely to conform to the "social output" very quickly.

Limits on output frequently become more obsolete as machinery improves and worker efficiency rises. As time passes, such restrictions are often self-defeating. The result may be either loss of membership in the union or inability to organize nonunion shops because the lack of restrictions in the latter establishments can permit nonunion employee earnings to rise above union earnings. Since the national union leadership is likely to be more interested in organizing nonunion shops than is local union leadership, severe restrictions on output favored by locals are often vigorously opposed by national unions.

Restrictions on output may be effected by indirect methods. Thus, instead of setting a quota, the same results may be achieved by retarding speed of performance—for example, by limiting the number of machines a man may tend or, as in the case of the Painters' Union, limiting the width of the brush or size of the roller.

Restrictions on output may also be achieved by excessive safety or quality controls. When the New York bus drivers want to slow down, they observe all safety regulations. The result is to put buses an average of 30 minutes behind schedule on moderately long runs.

The 1971 federal Occupational Safety and Health Act provides numerous opportunities for utilizing safety as a means of restricting output or pressuring management. Complaints can be made to the U.S. Department of Labor, and whether they are real or contrived, the complaints must be investigated and sometimes production may be slowed or halted —as will be discussed in Chapter 17. The construction unions have adopted numerous rules in the name of safety which are in fact featherbedding devices. Instances exist in which an operating engineer is paid $300–$400 per week for starting and stopping two or three gasoline engines smaller than those on most home lawn mowers; or in which union electricians must be on hand where temporary lights are used. They are paid $7 to $10 an hour, around the clock, to watch the lights burn.[19]

Unnecessary Work and Unnecessary Men

Some of the most obvious featherbedding results from union requirements that unnecessary work be done, that work be done by time-consuming methods, or that unnecessary men be hired. The building,

---

[19] For numerous other examples, see "Low Productivity: The Real Sin of High Wages," *Engineering News-Record*, February 24, 1972, pp. 20–23.

amusement, and railroad industries are characterized by a good deal of such union policies. For example, it is standard practice for the Plumbers' Union to require that pipes be threaded on the job, even though it is far more economical to do the threading in the shop. The International Typographical Union requires that when plates or papier-mâché matrices are exchanged, as they frequently are, the matter be reset, read, and corrected within a stipulated period, and that proof be submitted to the union chairman in the office. The Meat Cutters often require that pre-wrapped meat be rewrapped on the job. In 1968, the Brotherhood of Railroad Trainmen demanded that railroads eliminate the use of radio telephones by crewmen and go back to the hand signals and lanterns of the age of the coal-burning locomotives. According to the union, this would mean more jobs and would increase safety!

The employment of unnecessary men is typified by the manner in which the Brotherhood of Locomotive Firemen and Enginemen was able for years to maintain a "fireman" on diesel engines, even though his firing function did not exist; or by the excessive complements carried by American ships—about one third more than by foreign ships. By refusing to permit workers to do jobs outside of their narrowly defined craft jurisdictions, unions in the building, amusement, and railway industries likewise prevent the most effective utilization of manpower and thus require the employment of unnecessary men.

Seniority, Job Ownership, and Featherbedding

Featherbedding was once considered primarily a problem involving craft unions and craft-organized industries. But it appears also in manufacturing enterprises organized by industrial unions. The avenue by which featherbedding most often enters such an industrial situation is through an expansion of the concept of seniority.

The argument goes like this: If a man has seniority in a particular occupation, then he alone can perform the work, even though other persons are qualified to do it. By seniority, he acquires exclusive ownership in his job. Then only a person in that craft can be assigned to the job if the person who "owns" the job is not available.

Similarly, according to this reasoning, if an employee "owns" a job, the employer is no longer permitted to contract it out; and if, in the exercise of what he thinks is his management function, he does so, the employee is entitled to be paid for not working. In a similar view, the National Labor Relations Board has ruled that no contracting-out can be undertaken without consultation with the union—presumably to protect the employees' rights to their seniority.

Few managements could have believed that signing a seniority agreement would mean turning over job ownership as well. Although in the past, industrial unions generally have not sought such an interpretation of seniority, they are increasingly doing so. The pressure is strongest in times of layoffs, when the principle of job ownership can save a man's job. Of course, the added cost involved may eventually result in additional unemployment, including the worker whose job was supposedly saved. But this possibility usually does not seem imminent to those advocating restrictions.

A related idea is that of job confinement—if a job is owned by a particular craft, its limits must be confined or circumscribed. Recently, a strike over this issue occurred at a large machine shop, when some small groups of chippers and flame gaugers were instructed to squirt oil on castings so they could see where they were working. Through their local unions the groups charged that squirting oil from a can was outside the jurisdiction of their jobs, and demanded that somebody else do the work.

In no industry are job ownership and make-work practices more prevalent than in newspaper publishing. Yet such practices have certainly not brought with them worker security. Rather, by adding to costs and by decreasing productivity, they contributed to the demise within three years of four newspapers in New York City and many elsewhere.

Make-Work Legislation

A number of laws have been passed at the prodding of special-interest groups which are ostensibly in the interest of the consumer but actually go considerably beyond that. In this category are laws which require a "full" railroad crew and which often result in the employment of unneeded personnel. Licensing laws frequently require a skilled man to do an unskilled job, such as an electrician to replace a light bulb. Unions build on such laws by having skilled craftsmen unload materials, lay pipe, build forms, or break through walls—all jobs that laborers could well perform. In addition, building codes often discriminate against prefabricated materials which are adequate, or even superior, but which can be produced cheaper in factories than work can be done on the job.

Comments on "Make Work"

Make-work rules are a wasteful method of dealing with the problems of unemployment and insecurity, since they add to the cost of production and, as a result, curtail total employment. In many cases, make-work provisions so raise costs that wages are lower than they might otherwise be. An excessive use of make-work rules may seriously limit a union's effectiveness, for it may cause internal dissension between those favoring limits and those favoring higher earnings. Also, as already noted, limits on work may permit nonunion earnings to exceed union ones and thus prevent a union from organizing nonunion workers who are not interested in decreased earnings.

Make-work rules do not eliminate the intermittent employment which is found in the building and amusement industries, where their use is common; nor have make-work rules halted the secular decline in railway employment. Actually, by attracting more labor to an industry than is needed, make-work rules aggravate these evils.

Make-work policies present a difficult problem in terms of public policy. One method of attempted regulation is illustrated by the Taft-Hartley Act and a few similar state laws. Section $8(b)$ (6) of the Taft-Hartley Act makes it an unfair labor practice for a union "to cause or attempt to cause an employer to pay or deliver or agree to pay or deliver any money or other thing of value in the nature of an exaction, for services which are not performed or not to be performed." This clause was sometimes referred to as the "antifeatherbedding" provision; but actually, its scope has been construed by the courts and the National Labor Relations Board to be much more limited than the practice of make-work rules which is ordinarily encompassed within the term "featherbedding." Although make-work rules are wasteful and costly to the public, it is doubtful whether they can be dealt with effectively by legislation. What agency, for example, is to pass judgment on how fast a man should work, or how many men should be required to operate a given machine, or at exactly what point a job requires a skilled craftsman and at what point little skill is necessary?

To be sure, extreme cases are easy to detect. Legislation, however, would have to leave extraordinary discretion to a government bureau. To do its job, that bureau would be compelled to pass judgment on a variety of labor relations matters and would thus end up regulating industrial relations to a degree which neither labor, business, nor the public would find desirable.

There is another aspect to make-work rules and public policy which cannot be ignored. Restriction of output on the part of labor organizations is only one type of such restriction in the economy. Many businessmen restrict output in order to keep prices high. Numerous professional societies have urged enactment of legislation which would permit only licensed personnel to pursue a profession, but the definition of the profession often goes beyond the need for professional competence. In New Jersey the State Bar Association attempted unsuccessfully to have the negotiation of labor-management contracts declared the practice of law. If the attempt had succeeded, nonmembers of the state bar would have been unable to compete with lawyers for the right to aid labor and management unless no compensation was accepted. Farmers continually restrict production, plow under crops, and let fruit rot on the trees in order to bolster prices. Indeed, farmers are often encouraged to do this by law! Should only labor restrictions be regulated? Equality of treatment under the law would seem to require that all groups be equally affected or unaffected by legislation.

Before advocating legislation, it is well to realize that many featherbedding practices are the result of managerial mistakes or inadequacies. For example, the fireman issue on the diesel engine arose because railway management believed in 1936 that diesels were only a special-purpose engine that would never replace steam. "Bogus" work in printing derived from managerial desire to charge advertisers a full rate and was once actually encouraged by newspaper publishers. Wasteful ship crew and longshore complements grew out of cost-plus practices during World War II and employer profits on such overmanning. Numerous other featherbedding rules have resulted from managerial failure to make decisions on a long-run instead of an immediate-profit basis.

TECHNOLOGICAL CHANGE AND AUTOMATION

The introduction of new machinery or methods may be beneficial to union members by easing the physical strains or improving the safety of the job, or by bringing in more work and hence increasing employment. In some cases, unions have agitated for technological improvements. Lighter, faster trucks have created more jobs for truck drivers; and larger, faster airplanes have made more jobs for pilots. There are many other such examples.

On the other hand, many technological developments affect workers adversely, at least immediately. They make the job more hazardous or more difficult, or they may reduce employment in particular plants. For example, paint spraying can cause lead poisoning; the substitution of the one-man streetcar for two-man operation certainly makes the job of the operator more difficult; the introduction of the continuous strip mill resulted in the abandonment of many hand-rolled steel mills; and the diesel engine eliminated the need for firemen.

Obstruction

The adverse effects of technological change have led a number of unions at various times actively to oppose shifts in methods of production. Opposition to technological change may take several forms. The most common is refusal to work with new machines. Workers can also reduce output, demand prohibitive pay, or even ask for legislation in their fight against change.

Few industrial unions adopt obstruction policies, although occasionally some of their locals may do so. The reason is that the average technological development does not affect all members of an industrial union; and therefore, it cannot go "all out" for the interests of a minority of its members. On the other hand, all members of a craft union are likely to be directly affected by an alteration in the methods of production.

In some cases, obstruction has been successful. Thus, plumbers have prevented the use of pipe-threading machines, and the bricklayers of automatic bricklaying equipment. But this "success" has been limited in the case of the plumbers by the use of tubing instead of piping, and connections by soldering and other means which avoid threading; and in the case of bricklaying by other means of facing, such as glass, poured concrete, or aluminum.

Opposition to technological change can rarely be successful for long, for if the new methods are superior, some enterprising manager will find a way to use the new technique or to surmount the old one by a substitute process or technology. Then the union will have to decide whether to give up its opposition or to see its members unemployed. At this point, national union leaders, anxious to preserve the union, may find themselves at odds with members or local leaders whose prime objective is to work out their lives—or as long as possible—on the old techniques and methods which they know.

Worker opposition to technological change dates back at least to the Industrial Revolution, when the textile workers of Lancashire smashed newly installed machines.

The appearance of something new, whether in the form of a new labor-saving device, a new incentive system, a new kind of supervision, or a new process, seems to sound an alert among men at work; they mount guard, as it were, suspicious in advance that the change bodes them no good. The problem that emerges becomes particularly baffling when time and time again it appears immaterial whether an innovation affects the workers adversely or not. Indeed, even when it promises them substantial benefit, they still may pull and haul and balk.[20]

Union policies of obstruction are basically reflections of workers' fears that changes will affect them adversely. The union acts to solidify the obstruction or to fight it, but not to create it. Moreover, in many instances, union obstruction has served a good purpose. Opposition of the streetcar motormen to the one-man car led to the invention of the safety-door brake; the fight against the paint spray has helped to develop effective "waterfall" and blower systems to control fumes; and numerous other examples exist of safety measures taken to offset union claims of "health hazards" which, in fact, stem largely from rank-and-file opposition to change.

Perhaps even more important than forcing improvements in machines, union obstruction policies have compelled industry to consider

---

[20] B. M. Selekman, *Labor Relations and Human Relations* (New York: McGraw-Hill Book Co., 1947), p. 111.

human costs in introducing new methods. Abandoning a plant or eliminating a skill causes tremendous hardship to those affected. By slowing the process or forcing management to make concessions, union obstruction to technological change has reduced the number of employees rendered temporarily useless by progress. On the other hand, there are many cases, particularly in the building, printing, and other trades, where union obstruction policies have increased consumer costs without apparent benefit to the community.

Competition

If a union finds that a policy of obstruction is failing (usually because nonunion shops are utilizing the new technique and causing unemployment in the union shops), it may attempt to compete with the new method. This takes the form of wage or working rule concessions to employers who retain the old techniques or, in rare instances, of the formation of cooperatives by displaced employees who seek to maintain old methods of operation.

Essentially, the policy of competition is a short-run device adopted for the purpose of slowing the advancement of new techniques and preserving the working lives of employees who would otherwise be displaced. If the new technique is sufficiently superior, wage and working rule concessions are not likely to halt its introduction. Nor can cooperative plants producing by less efficient methods hope to compete permanently with more modern plants.

A policy of competition, nevertheless, is not without social benefit. By providing temporary employment for workers who might otherwise be unemployed, it mitigates the hardships of change. Moreover, as in the case of obstruction policies, competition forces improvement in new machines, which are often crude when first introduced, and therefore a policy of competition can result in the reduction of costs and of prices.

Control

In most cases, opposition to technological advancement and union attempts to compete with new techniques are temporary measures. Sooner or later, the union members must decide whether they want the union to survive. If they do, they must work out an agreement with management which permits use of the new invention. In short, the union must adopt a policy which gives it some control over the working conditions which develop under the new technique.

The policy of control may take many forms. In the supermarket industry, for example, the Amalgamated Meat Cutters and Butcher Workmen has generally obstructed the concept of central meat cutting instead of having butchers in each store. Some locals, however, have provided in their contracts that if central meat cutting is introduced, butchers in the stores will receive first opportunity for the jobs and their union will be recognized as bargaining agent in the central plants.[21] In the steel industry, the United Steelworkers has insisted that some of the benefits of machinery go directly to the workers. This has been used as a talking point in wage negotiations and also to implement union arguments that men laid off as a result of new techniques should be given the first opportunity for new job openings. In other cases, unions have negotiated dismissal compensation for men laid off. This tends to lessen rank-and-file opposition to a policy of control. A final method of control is for the union to negotiate high wage rates for work on new machines, which slow down the introduction of the new technique by making it relatively more expensive. As a result, the effect on the working force may be temporarily lessened—unless the net effect is to make the whole operation so high cost that everyone concerned loses his job.

The willingness of a union to adopt a policy of control depends on a variety of factors. Industrial unions are more likely to favor control policies than are craft unions because a new technique often helps one part of the industrial union membership even though it hurts another part. Moreover, craft unions may be unwilling or unable to organize employees operating the new machines, or their members may be unwilling or unable to learn new techniques or to work on new machines. Even if workers are willing and able to be retrained, the new technique may be started in a new plant or industry, and the opportunity to work the new technique may simply be unavailable to those utilizing the old methods or equipment.

Unions are much more willing to accept new techniques and methods if jobs are visibly at stake. Competition of nonunion or foreign plants, or of substitute methods or products, and consequent loss of sales and jobs, make clear to employees that costs must be lowered if jobs are to be saved. As such competition strikes closer to home, opposition to technological change tends to decline.

The vast number of technological improvements which have been introduced and their initial ill effect on workers raise the question of why more unions have not adopted policies of obstruction rather than control. The main reason appears to be that most inventions are introduced in times of prosperity and full employment, and indeed contribute to the prosperity. In such times, reemployment of displaced men is more easily effected, and opposition to new techniques is consequently lessened.

---

[21] Herbert R. Northrup and Gordon R. Storholm, *Restrictive Labor Practices in the Supermarket Industry* (Industrial Research Unit Study No. 44, Philadelphia: University of Pennsylvania Press, 1967).

AUTOMATION FUNDS AND DISPLACEMENT

Automation

Technological developments since World War II have moved along three basic lines. These developments, termed "automation," can be divided into three fundamental groups.[22]

1. The integration by means of mechanical engineering techniques of conventionally separate manufacturing operations into lines of continuous production untouched by human hands.
2. The use of "feedback" control devices or servomechanisms which permit individual operations to be performed, tested, and/or inspected, and controlled without human control by means of electrical engineering or electronic techniques.
3. The development of computing machines which can record and store information and perform complex mathematical operations on such information largely by means of electrical engineering developments.

The effect of automation on labor utilization has been and is potentially spectacular. Labor displacement in some industries has been severe and in other industries promises to have effects that are even more drastic. In the longshore industry, for example, where ships have been loaded and unloaded by substantially the same methods for many years, an innovation known as "containerization" has been developed. This is the principle whereby products to be transported in ships are loaded in large, fully enclosed containers at the factory or warehouse and the containers are moved directly by cranes from the dock into the vessel (and unloaded by the same method), thus eliminating all manual loading and unloading of ships at the dockside. Adoption of this method affords major reductions in costs and improvement in efficiency of stevedoring operations.

Meat-packing is another industry in which automation has already had profound effects on employment. Manual handling of carcasses has been replaced by conveyors; dressing knives are driven by electric motors; hand curing of bacon and ham has given way to "pickling" by needle injections; automatic machines slice, weigh, and package bacon, and stuff and pack sausage. As a result, employment in the meat-packing industry has declined by about 50,000 in an era in which the consumption of meat has steadily risen.

Such problems have led to special collective bargaining action. The West Coast longshore agreement in effect provided that the employers "buy out" the restrictive practices and opposition to technological

---

[22] These definitions were first set forth by G. B. Baldwin and G. P. Shultz in "Automation: A New Dimension to Old Problems," in Industrial Relations Research Association, *Annual Proceedings* (Detroit, 1954), pp. 114–28.

change by establishing a fund for improved pension and welfare benefits, provisions for early retirement, and other additions to the welfare package of the longshoremen. Since this contract was first negotiated in the early 1950s, employment on West Coast docks has actually risen because of general prosperity and its impact on shipping, and because of the requirements of the Vietnam war. A strike in 1971–72 involved other issues and did not end the new rules. It did, however, reveal some fear of declining work incident to the withdrawal from Vietnam. Whether productivity will remain high if slack work occurs remains to be seen.

Armour and Company and the union of meat-packing employees also set up a fund. Its purpose was to study the effects of automation and to attempt to transfer and to retrain employees, or to otherwise improve the opportunities of the displaced. As a result of such efforts, some success occurred in retraining and relocation of displaced packing-house employees.[23]

Automation funds of lesser magnitude, or arrangements of a similar nature, have been developed by the American Federation of Musicians, the International Ladies' Garment Workers' Union, and the East Coast longshoremen's union.[24] In addition, the Kaiser and Scanlon plans, discussed in the preceding chapter, have similar aspects insofar as they are attempts to deal logically and consistently with the problem of technological displacement. Likewise, the efforts of unions in the steel and brewing industries to negotiate long vacations or "sabbaticals" are motivated principally by the desire to mitigate the impact of technology on employment by sharing the work.

But basically, neither automation funds nor the other arrangements discussed emphasize benefits for displaced workers. Rather, the benefits are designed either entirely or primarily for the purpose of sharing the savings of automation with those employees who are retained on the payroll. Thus, such funds are like an extension of the basic policies of unions which concentrate on high wages for those left on the payroll. Since both managements and unions are interested in present and future employees, not former ones, this should not be surprising—but it should also emphasize that automation funds are designed primarily for those who remain to share in the fruits of technology, and not to care for the displaced. In effect, automation funds are a method of union control of technological change; contributions to the fund add to industry's costs of innovating and can therefore slow it down without completely obstructing the innovation.

---

[23] See Shultz and Weber, *Strategies for the Displaced Worker*, for a discussion of the Armour program.

[24] A discussion of the various automation funds is found in Thomas Kennedy, *Automation Funds and Displaced Workers* (Boston: Graduate School of Business Administration, Harvard University, 1962).

EFFECT OF UNION ORGANIZATION ON EFFICIENCY

In many firms, prior to the advent of union organization, management depended upon payment of low wages to keep costs down to a competitive level. Union organization, by removing wage rates from the competitive sphere, can produce a desirable change in emphasis from wage levels to production costs and thereby diminish the divergence in technical standards between the least efficient and most efficient firms in the industry. If the effect of union wage pressure is to make inefficient managers better innovators, the general level of efficiency in industry will benefit. And of course, to the extent that the least efficient firms are eliminated, an automatic increase occurs in the statistical average efficiency of firms left in industry.

Union organization may increase "social efficiency" by slowing down managerial action designed to displace persons or by forcing managers to consider such things as retraining existing employees instead of replacing them. The net effect can be to prolong the working life of people and thus to add to the overall ability of the population to support itself.

Union organization, by raising wages in union plants, increases the cost advantage of nonunion competitors and compels union firms to increase efficiency in order to remain in competition. Moreover, the presence of a strong union with alert shop stewards compels management to justify many production methods and rates, and therefore encourages a more careful examination of costs and production policy. Although union wage pressure probably produces a small net gain in labor efficiency, the difficulties encountered by union plants in holding their markets indicate that the gain is insufficient to offset the increased price of labor.

Union influence upon technical efficiency has a time dimension. Probably the greatest increase in efficiency is forthcoming when an industry is newly organized. Then the wastes may be more obvious and abundant; but after a while, when the backlog of waste is largely exhausted, a point of diminishing returns must be reached. Furthermore, as unionism itself matures and its power in industry grows, it is more likely to bring its own wastes to industry. As a general rule, the more strongly entrenched the position of a union in an industry, the less it is concerned with the efficiency of the individual firms under its jurisdiction. Consequently, even though the possibilities of raising the level of industrial efficiency are considerable, there is room for skepticism regarding the contribution which unionism will make in this respect in the future. Managements in the railroad, printing, apparel, and construction industries have been subjected to union wage pressure over a long period, but it is certain that they are not conspicuously more able, thorough, and alert to technological developments than managements in other industries.

UNFAVORABLE EFFECT OF UNION RULES

On the whole, union organization probably tends to diminish industrial efficiency rather than to improve it. The rise of unionism has led to a multiplication of union rules and restrictions which limit the freedom of the employer to revise costly operations and to introduce improved techniques of production. There is no immediate prospect of eliminating the many needless make-work rules which are found at present in organized plants in various industries. Although union wage pressure affords some simulus to invention and technological progress, it is doubtful whether general union wage adjustments occurring more or less simultaneously over a broad area of industry provide much stimulus to the rate of mechanization. Moreover, whatever stimulus is forthcoming from this source tends to be offset by the restrictive influence of union policies which retard the rate of introduction of labor saving methods and machinery.

Despite the fact that the leaders of organized labor condemn opposition to laborsaving machinery, the policy still is practiced by individual unions. It is easy for leaders to generalize in sweeping terms about the futility of attempting to stem the advance of progress; but if the individual worker see in his union a possible barrier to introduction of a new improvement which threatens his job, he is likely to use it. Union organization has not altered the feelings or attitudes of the average worker toward laborsaving machinery, but it has given him the strength to resist or retard technological change, whereas previously he could only voice weak protest.

Management, by and large, is compelled by the profit motive to be interested in reducing costs and improving the quality of the product. These twin objectives of employers ordinarily place management on the side of efficiency in the collective bargaining process. Unions—at least where nonunion competition is not a major problem—are interested primarily in improving earnings and working conditions, and in introducing order, tenure, and stability into the employment relationship. These objectives have important value from the point of view of the community and society; but we should recognize that in many cases, they will conflict with productive efficiency.

QUESTIONS FOR DISCUSSION

1. Do you feel that a union is ever justified in opposing technological change? Can you support your answer from experience?
2. Why is contracting-out so emotional an issue? How is it concerned with union policy and management rights? Why is it so much more in controversy today than formerly?
3. Why is apprenticeship so important to Negroes? What would you do to attempt to increase the number and proportion of black craftsmen?

4. Seniority has many ramifications. Discuss its relation to job security and union security, and how it can affect these two objectives of most unions. Discuss also the impact of seniority on blacks.

SUGGESTIONS FOR FURTHER READING

LEVINSON, HAROLD M. et al. *Collective Bargaining and Technological Change in American Transportation.* Evanston, Ill.: Transportation Center at Northwestern University, 1971.

A detailed study of the interaction of collective bargaining and technology in the trucking, railroad, maritime, and air transport industries.

"Low Productivity: The Real Sin of High Wages," *Engineering News-Record,* February 24, 1972, pp. 18–23.

A popular account, replete with examples of the malaise of featherbedding now extant in construction.

MARSHALL, F. RAY, and BRIGGS, VERNON M., JR. *The Negro and Apprenticeship.* Baltimore, Md.: Johns Hopkins Press, 1967.

A study of the problems involved in the attempts to open up apprenticeship to blacks.

Occupational Licensing and the Supply of Nonprofessional Manpower. U.S. Department of Labor, Manpower Administration, Monograph No. 11. Washington, D.C.: U.S. Government Printing Office, 1969.

A survey of the numerous licensing restrictions on job entry.

ROWAN, RICHARD L. (ed.). *Readings in Labor Economics and Labor Relations,* Part IV (c), "Issues in Jurisprudence," pp. 343–62. Homewood, Ill.: Richard D. Irwin, Inc., 1972.

Three articles on the union shop, featherbedding, and property in work.

SLICHTER, SUMNER H.; HEALY, J. J.; and LIVERNASH, E. R. *The Impact of Collective Bargaining on Management,* chaps. ii–xii. Washington, D.C.: Brookings Institution, 1960.

The basic work on industrial jurisprudence.

Chapter 7

MULTIUNIT BARGAINING, STRIKES, AND THE LABOR MONOPOLY ISSUE

In this chapter, we continue our discussion of collective bargaining practices, taking up three of the most controversial issues—multiunit bargaining (often called industrywide bargaining), strikes, and the question of whether unions are monopolies.

MULTIUNIT BARGAINING

Multiunit bargaining is simply a term used to denote a collective bargaining arrangement which covers more than one plant. Multiunit bargaining takes many forms. One such form occurs when a single management controls two or more plants which are organized by a single national union. Negotiations between the United Automobile Workers and the General Motors Corporation or between the United Steelworkers and the United States Steel Corporation are two of the best-known examples of this type of bargaining. Both negotiations are between one management and one union, but they each establish basic wages and employment conditions for many separate plants throughout the country. Moreover, the settlements reached in these bargaining conferences provide the key wage bargains for much of the economy.

A second type of multiunit collective bargaining involves bargaining between one or more national unions and a representative of two or more managements in a single industry. For discussion purposes, such bargaining is usually subdivided on a geographical basis into local, regional, and national types. Local multiunit bargaining is by far the most common. It occurs in service industries of many kinds, building construction, amusements, retail stores, clothing, and many other industries in which the competitive market is predominately local. Frequently, it is difficult to distinguish the practical difference between the second type of bargaining on a national basis where the employers are represented by an association or other bargaining representative and the situation where a national union bargains at one and the same time with a number of multiunit employers. This is the situation in the steel industry. Each of the steel companies theoretically bargains independently with the United Steelworkers; but as a practical matter, they all look to the United States Steel Corporation to set the pattern.

Among the industries in which regional multiunit bargaining is common are pulp and paper, lumber, nonferrous metal mining, and maritime and longshore work.

National multicompany bargaining is frequently termed "industry-wide" bargaining, but the latter term is inaccurate in most cases. Even the widely known bargaining in the railroad industry, which is national in scope and very inclusive, is not actually completely industrywide.

National collective bargaining is itself divisible into two groups. In the first type a sizeable segment of an industry throughout the country bargains with a national union or unions. The gradual extension prior to World War I of bituminous coal bargaining from local areas to districts and hence regionwide agreements, climaxed by the "central competitive field" agreements covering mainly Pennsylvania, Ohio, Indiana, and Illinois; the disintegration of this system in the 1920s because the unionized mines could not compete with the nonunion southern mines; and finally, the rise of national bargaining after 1934, afford the most vivid and well-known example of this development. Then, in the late 1940s, this bargaining split into northern and southern groups.

Railroad history provides another example. Single railway system bargaining developed, under the impetus of union "concerted movements," into regional conferences; then, during World War I, when the federal government took over the railroads, national bargaining was adopted. It relapsed into regional bargaining in the early 1920s, but national bargaining was again revived by the railroads in 1931 for the purpose of securing nationwide decreases. Since then, national bargaining has continued.

The railroad and bituminous coal situations have one significant difference which derives from the structure of their respective unions. Bituminous coal deals with one industrial union. Its negotiations settle matters for all employees at one time. Railroads deal with 20-odd craft unions. On most occasions the railroad unions have split into two, three, or four groups. National conferences are held with each group by the carriers. A settlement with one group must be made with the demands of the others in mind, thus greatly complicating bargaining.

Quite different either from the bituminous coal or the railroad situations, where most workers in an industry are involved in the national bargaining, is the second type of industrywide bargaining. This is the situation where only one craft of workers bargains, as in wire weaving, tile laying, sprinkler installation, elevator installation and repair, and wall-paper crafts. Despite the fact that only a small segment of a particular employer's work force is involved, the bargaining is national in scope. A small, well-organized craft, desirous of maintaining its standards throughout the country, and an important industry segment providing nationally used products and/or services, participate in these multiunit bargaining arrangements.

Still another type of multiunit collective bargaining cuts across industry lines. In such cases, bargaining occurs between an employer association, or division thereof, representing numerous industries and the union or unions holding bargaining rights for the workers in these industries. Bargaining of this type has developed most fully in the San Francisco metropolitan area and has spread to several other western cities and to Hawaii. In San Francisco the aggressiveness and scarcity of labor led employers to organize and bargain on an areawide basis as early as the "Gold Rush" days, but modern master agreements date from the union drives of 1934. Then the use of "whipsaw" tactics by unions—striking employers one at a time in order to raise wages—led to the formation of the San Francisco Employers Council in 1938. Today the Council coordinates all negotiations for its members.

Coordinated, or coalition, bargaining, as noted in previous chapters, has been developed by the AFL–CIO Industrial Union Department as a means of increasing union leverage on companies which deal with a number of unions at various plants throughout the United States and Canada. The IUD has attempted to coordinate efforts of unions to obtain common termination dates of contracts with a particular company, or with several companies in an industry, and then threaten to shut down all the plants if the managements refused to deal on a coalition basis. The IUD drive has been resisted for the most part by industry, but has achieved some success in electrical manufacturing.[1] More recently the IUD has joined with other unions, foreign and domestic, in an attempt to bargain on a multinational basis. Serious attempts on this front are likely to occur in the 1970s.

The Extent of Multiunit Collective Bargaining

Table 7–1 summarizes the findings of a survey as to the extent of multiunit collective bargaining. Because of the variations within industries, it has been necessary to include some industries under more than one heading.

In the left-hand column, titled "Single Company," are listed industries in which exist significant numbers of companies having several plants which deal on a companywide basis with unions. These industries are mostly the so-called "heavy" or "basic" industries, characterized by large investments, mass production, and a small number of large multiplant companies.

The three center columns are devoted to multicompany, multiunit

[1] See William N. Chernish, *Coalition Bargaining* (Industrial Research Unit Study No. 45 [Philadelphia: University of Pennsylvania Press, 1969]).

TABLE 7–1

Extent of Multiunit Collective Bargaining*

| Single Company | Multicompany | | | Multi-industry |
	National	Regional	Local Area	
Automobile	Anthracite	Fishing	Building construc-	San Francisco
Electrical supplies	coal	Canning and	tion	Tacoma
and equip-	Bituminous	preserving	Building materials	Reno
ment	coal	foods	Longshoremen	Sacramento
Farm equipment	Iron and steel	Lumber	Trucking (local de-	Los Angeles
Flat glass	(basic)	Pulp and paper	livery)	Phoenix
Office equipment	Railroads	Agricultural	Warehousing	Denver
Rubber	Pottery	growing	Amusements and	Hawaii
Meat packing	Pressed and	and har-	theaters	Albuquerque
Rayon textiles	blown	vesting	Hotels and restau-	
Shipbuilding	glass	Clay sewer pipe	rants	
Woolen textiles	Glass con-	Cement	Laundries	
Nonferrous metal	tainers	Maritime (all	Cleaning and dyeing	
manufactur-	Trucking	classes)	service	
ing	(over the	Seamen	Building service	
Nonferrous metal	road)	Longshore-	Retail stores	
mining	Wire weaving	men	Department stores	
Pulp and paper	Wallpaper	Furniture	Charitable organ-	
Tobacco	Tile laying	Motion-picture	izations	
(cigarettes)	Sprinkler fitter	production	Metal job shops	
	installa-	Hosiery	Machine	
	tion	Cotton textiles	Tool and die	
	Elevator in-	Woolen textiles	Pattern	
	stallation	Dyeing and	Foundry	
	and repair	finishing	Steel products	
	Men's and	textiles	(nonbasic)	
	boy's	Cotton gar-	Jewelry and	
	clothes	ments	silverware	
	Work clothes	Leather	Newspaper printing	
	Stoves	(tanned,	Book and job print-	
		curried,	ing	
		and fin-	Women's clothes	
		ished)	Millinery	
		Shoes	Fur	
		Trucking	Leather products	
			and gloves	
			Shoes	
			Confectionery	
			products	
			Meat packing	
			Dairy products	
			Baked goods	
			Malt liquors	
			Beverages	
			(nonalcoholic)	
			Tobacco (cigars)	
			Furniture	
			Knit goods	
			Silk and rayon	
			textiles	
			Paper products	
			(boxes, etc.)	
			Garage main-	
			tenance men	

* Coordinated or coalition bargaining has been attempted in many industries, notably electrical manufacturing, nonferrous mining and manufacturing, chemicals, and drugs.

bargaining. It will be noted that in only a few industries does national collective bargaining exist.

Local multiunit bargaining embraces by far the most industries involved. Multi-industry bargaining, as in San Francisco, is confined to western areas and Hawaii.

From this table, it is clear that multiunit bargaining in the United States embraces an enormous portion of American industry. Multiunit bargaining also varies according to issues. Pensions, for example, are bargained nationally in electrical construction, but most other issues are bargained locally. A wide range of such varied practices exists in industry.

Reasons for Development of Multiunit Collective Bargaining

The reasons for the development of the various types of multiunit collective bargaining vary from industry to industry. Sometimes the union is responsible for initiating such bargaining. In other cases the employers take the initiative.

Equalizing wage costs has been an important reason why unions have supported multiunit collective bargaining. In the railroads, for example, the brotherhoods found that the individual railroads were using the competition of other lines as a reason for objecting to wage increases. This led the brotherhoods to support first regional and then national bargaining. In the needle trades, wages are the most important cost factor. Both the unions and the employers discovered at an early time that unionism could not exist unless it equalized wage costs. This resulted in marketwide bargaining in the various branches of the industry; since most markets are local in scope, bargaining is local in scope. The exceptions are the men's clothing industry, which has expanded into a national bargaining situation, and the work clothes industries, where the union label has induced various manufacturers throughout the country to enter negotiations with the United Garment Workers.

The equalization of competition has played an important role in the development of multiunit collective bargaining in lumber, pulp and paper, pottery, and the various branches of the glass industry. In some of these industries, initiation came from the employers' side. In such industries as electronic manufacturing, the metal-jobbing shops of various types, and book and job printing, as well as others, the pattern is similar to that in the garment trades. Wages are a significant, if not the most significant, cost item, the plant labor force is small, and the degree of competition high. All these factors tend toward the development of multiunit collective bargaining once the workers become unionized.

In industries in which an employee typically works for more than one employer, multiunit collective bargaining is virtually essential for both employer and union. These industries include the maritime trades, the building trades, and the needle trades. In such industries, failure to equalize wages and working conditions would have the effect of permitting some employers to pay less wages to workers who also work for other employers paying higher wages. From the union point of view, this is an intolerable situation, and it is equally so from the employer's viewpoint. For example, in the building industry the low-wage employer would be able to outbid high-wage competitors—and solely because the union allowed him a favorable rate. This would injure the union's relations with other employers. Hence the only solution from the point of view of both employer and union is multiunit bargaining over the extent of the market.

Another reason why both unions and employers prefer multiunit bargaining is that it eases contract enforcement. From the union point of view, this is very important in such industries as building or trucking, or in any others where the size of the firm is small and the employees bear a very close personal relation to their employers. There is a tendency in such industries, particularly when work is slack, for the employer to ask, and often to receive, wage concessions from his workers and to keep the concessions secret from the union. This enables the employer to get more work at the expense of his competitors. It also, however, takes business from the more contract-conscious competitors and threatens the entire union wage structure. Under a multiunit arrangement, such local deals are more difficult, especially since most arrangements contain explicit provisions enumerating severe penalties for any deals or kickbacks.

Multiunit bargaining simplifies negotiations in industries where there are scores of small employers. It also enables small companies represented by an association to employ skilled attorneys and industrial relations specialists whom they could not afford on an individual plant bargaining basis.

Unions like multiunit bargaining because it makes it more difficult for a rival union to gain a foothold in the industry. A history of bargaining with an employers' association will tend to induce the National Labor Relations Board to designate the multiplant group as the appropriate unit for bargaining purposes and thus block the efforts of a rival union to pick off individual plants. Employers also favorably regard the protection against rival unions afforded by multiunit bargaining, since the resultant stability of labor relations in the industry may produce moderation on the part of union leaders who feel sufficiently secure against rivals to display economic statesmanship. Of course, if a rival union can win a majority of votes for the entire multiplant unit, it can take over bargaining rights for all of the plants even though it might lack a majority in some of them. This is what a newly formed union, the Association of Western Pulp and Paper Workers, was able to accomplish in the western pulp and paper industry in 1964 after these employees had been represented by AFL–CIO unions for 30 years.

Multiunit bargaining alters the power structure within a union. Thus, James R. Hoffa pushed for national bargaining in the over-the-road trucking industry as a means of cementing his power in the union. By concentrating power for negotiations at the national level, the national leaders reduce the importance—and the independence—of the local and regional leadership. National and regional negotiations greatly enhanced centralization of authority in the United Mine Workers. It could have been expected to encourage a similar trend in the Teamsters' Union, which is one reason, after Hoffa was jailed, that the union vice presidents encouraged a return to regional bargaining.

One of the most important reasons why employers have initiated or defended multiunit bargaining is the protection it gives them against loss from strikes. In industries such as transportation, building construction, amusements, services, or retail trade, a strike can result in a loss of business which is never regained because the company deals in a perishable good or service. If the union can pick off employers of such industries one at a time, employers are, more often than not, helpless to prevent the union from achieving even the most outrageous demands. But when employers form a common front, the union power is blunted because a strike means a strike of the entire industry. This, in turn, results in a serious loss of employment to all union members; and, perhaps even more important, no employer benefits from the loss of business of an employer who is struck. The logical development of such a situation has occurred in the West Coast maritime industry, where strikes have been answered either by industrywide lockouts or by the payment of benefits to struck concerns.

On the other hand, many employers who have their employee relations well controlled oppose multiunit bargaining because it might permit the union to spread throughout the industry gains won from weaker bargaining companies. The automobile companies oppose joint bargaining because the larger the group involved, the greater the propensity for government intervention, which often takes the form of pressure on the companies to give more to avoid a work stoppage.

The accident of location is also important. Multiunit bargaining is more common on the Pacific Coast than in any other area in the United States. The importance of the maritime and lumber industries and the historical shortage of labor in that area have probably been important factors. But the development of a citywide multiunit system in San Francisco has encouraged a similar development in other western cities and in Hawaii.

Multiunit Bargaining as a Problem

The basic public interest in multiunit bargaining arises out of the effects of work stoppages and of wage increases. A strike which shuts down either a whole industry or a major portion thereof causes serious public inconvenience. A wage increase which is achieved by a large number of workers under conditions which insure widespread publicity, such as when the Steelworkers' Union bargains with United States Steel, can result in public dissatisfaction with the large multiunit strike and with the wage bargain. Such settlements, particularly when effectuated by use of the strike weapon on a large scale, may be highly inflationary, give rise to charges of union monopoly, as discussed later in this chapter, and encourage government intervention in negotiations and strikes. Although government intervention is designed to protect the public interest, it has, in fact, often encouraged higher and more inflationary wage settlements because government officials are usually interested primarily in avoiding strikes and pressure employers to offer additional benefits in order to keep the peace.

Multiunit bargaining, by its very nature, tends to remove the bargaining from local pressures. Although this may have some advantages in creating an atmosphere conducive to reasonable settlement, it also frequently results in ignoring key local issues, or in referring them back to the plant level for further negotiations. As a result, there has grown up in such industries as automobiles and rubber products a situation which poses a double threat to industrial peace. Negotiations are held on the national level at which basic economic issues (wages, holidays, vacations, and benefits) are settled, together with other items of national significance. Other issues are handled locally after national negotiations. Management is then faced with bargaining over a host of problems, such as work standards, seniority, and other work rules, which the literature of collective bargaining calls "noneconomic," but which may be very costly indeed. Such items have a direct effect on productivity, number of labor hours needed, and equipment utilization, all of which help to determine the profitability of the enterprise. Yet, because wages and benefits have already been determined, local managers often have no funds for counter offers, nor can they do much but oppose further increases in costs. Long local strikes, disgruntled local employees, and a high turnover of local union officials who cannot "produce" for the rank and file are frequent results of multiplant bargaining even though agreement at the national level may have been achieved.

Multiunit bargaining can also involve the entire bargaining group in disputes which are of interest to only one small part. For example, an issue over discipline in one factory in 1965 almost shut down most of the industry because local union officials in that plant had extracted a promise of action there from national leaders as a condition of settlement. Frequently in such national negotiations, days will be spent discussing such an issue, and then it will be referred back for local determination anyway. If issues of this sort get out of hand, or if either party is spoiling for a fight, the entire multiunit bargaining group can have a strike. The stakes are higher and the damage greater in multiunit bargaining when labor peace fails.

STRIKES

To many Americans, the strike epitomizes the union. Headlines are made in industrial disputes. They are the sensational aspects of union policies and managerial counterpolicies. Yet, strikes are surprisingly few in comparison to either man-days worked or the number of collective agreements negotiated. (See Table 7–2.) For example, the average annual number of man-days lost in the United States because of strikes during

TABLE 7–2

Strikes and Lockouts in the United States, Selected Years, 1917–67 (private, nonfarm only)

Year	Number of Stoppages	Number of Workers Involved (Thousands)	Man-Days Idle (Million Days)	Percentage of Working Time Lost
1917	4,450	1,227	n.a.	n.a.
1919	3,630	4,160	n.a.	n.a.
1921	2,385	1,099	n.a.	n.a.
1925	1,301	428	n.a.	n.a.
1929	921	289	5.4	0.07
1933	1,695	1,168	16.9	0.36
1937	4,740	1,860	28.4	0.43
1941	4,288	2,363	23.0	0.32
1944	4,956	2,116	8.7	0.09
1946	4,985	4,600	116.0	1.43
1947	3,693	2,170	34.6	0.41
1950	4,843	2,410	38.8	0.40
1952	5,117	3,540	59.1	0.57
1956	3,825	1,900	33.1	0.29
1959	3,900	1,850	68.0	0.61
1961	3,367	1,450	16.3	0.12
1963	3,614	941	16.1	0.13
1965	4,405	1,960	25.4	0.19
1967	4,595	2,870	42.1	0.30
1969	5,700	2,480	42.9	0.24
1971	4,900	3,200	45.0	0.25

Source: U.S. Department of Labor, Bureau of Labor Statistics.

1935–36—a period of great labor unrest—was 16.9 million, or 0.27% of the total annual estimated working time. In 1946, the worst strike year in our history, total man-days lost were 116 million, or 1.43% of the annual estimated working time. In 1959, despite the impact of a steel strike that shut down that industry for several months, total man-days lost were 68 million, or only 0.61% of the annual estimated working time. Almost every hour while strikes occur, a collective bargaining agreement is being peacefully negotiated by a union and a company.

During the latter part of the 1960s, strike incidence began to increase, as unions, strengthened by a tight labor market and pressured by inflation, increased their militancy and sought larger increases which, of course, exacerbated the inflation and helped lead toward the wage-price freeze of August 15, 1971. With the uncertainties of a stabilization period, came a sharp decline in strikes. Experience after World War II, and in Europe, indicates that an end of stabilization may be featured by a rash of strikes. This could, of course, occur here, but may not, since unions demands although curtailed by the wage-price stabilization program, have not been so frozen as to preclude all wage movement.

Although the strike data in Table 7–2 show minute strike losses, they do not tell the whole story. Those laid off because of strikes, for example, are not included. Thus, a strike of 10,000 signalmen in 1971 shut down the nation's railroads. If this strike had been permitted to continue (Congress enacted a special law ending it), it would have shut down numerous plants dependent on railroads for the movement of goods. Employees laid off from these plants would not have been counted as "workers involved" in a strike—yet they surely were.

The data in Table 7–2 are deficient in another way. They exclude the volatile public sector, where strikes are illegal, but occur with increasing frequency. Between 1960 and 1970, the number of work stoppages by government employees increased from 36 to 412, the total workers involved from 28,600 to 335,500, and the man-days idle from 58,401 to 2,023,000.[2] The issues, policies, and concepts involved are sufficiently unique that we shall discuss them separately in Chapter 22. It is important here to note, however, that such stoppages not only add to strike idleness but raise serious questions after the appropriateness of strikes.

Strikes have significance far beyond the number of man-days lost because they impact throughout the economy and disadvantage both government and the public. The very right of unions and companies to disrupt the economy is now under serious question. We shall return to this question in Chapters 21 and 22, where these public policy matters are concerned. Here we consider why strikes rise out of labor-management disputes.

Classification of Work Stoppages

Strikes may be classified in three general categories: (1) economic strikes, concerning wages, hours, and working conditions; (2) strikes to achieve recognition or to eliminate unfair labor practices by employers; and (3) strikes involving conflicts between unions.

The first category—the "bread-and-butter" type of strike—has consistently been the major type of strike in this country, except during the period from 1934 to 1941, when the great upsurge of union organizing

---

[2] U.S. Department of Labor, Bureau of Labor Statistics, *Government Work Stoppages, 1960, 1968, and 1970* (Summary Report, November 1971).

effort pushed to the forefront the second category of strikes. Wages are the most usual but by no means the only reason for economic strikes. For example, the longest major strike in the last several years—that affecting the nonferrous metal industry—was, as already noted, over an unsuccessful demand of the unions for industrywide and companywide bargaining.

Strikes of the second category are intended to eliminate an unfair labor practice by an employer, such as refusal to bargain or discrimination against union activity. Organization strikes, which also fall in this category, have become relatively unimportant in recent years as a result of the high percentage of organization already achieved in industry, the consequent retardation in the rate of growth of unions, and the existence of peaceful methods of determination of a collective bargaining representative under state and federal law. An exception is in the area of public employment, where an increasing number of strikes have occurred over the recognition issue in states which provide no machinery for this purpose.

The third class of strikes is a result of union rivalries over jobs and membership. It includes the jurisdictional strike, which involves a contest between unions as to which group of workers will perform a specified piece of work. It also includes the rival union organization strike, in which rival unions seek to compel the employer to recognize the one rather than the other as the exclusive bargaining agent for certain or all of his employees. Despite the fact that both voluntary machinery through the AFL–CIO and public methods provided by the National Labor Relations Board and state agencies are available to settle such disputes, they continue to exist. Disputes over construction and maintenance work in industrial plants between industrial and building-trades unions, involving the already discussed contracting-out issue, show no signs of abating.

The Taft-Hartley law makes it an unfair labor practice for a union to engage in a strike or refuse to work on goods or perform services where an object is "forcing or requiring any employer to assign particular work to employees in a particular labor organization or in a particular trade, craft, or class rather than to employees in another labor organization or in another trade, craft, or class, unless such employer is failing to conform to an order or certification of the Board determining the bargaining representative for employees performing such work." The same law also forbids strikes aimed at compelling an employer to bargain with one union where another union has been certified by the National Labor Relations Board as the proper representative of the employees. Despite these provisions in the law and the efforts of the AFL–CIO, jurisdictional and rival-union strikes will undoubtedly continue to inconvenience the public from time to time. The question of whether the Carpenters or the Metal Workers should install metal frame windows may seem to be a small reason to tie up millions of dollars of building construction; yet, to the workers involved, it is an emotionally charged issue upon which their very daily bread may depend in years to come. However, strikes over such issues are relatively unimportant in the over-all strike picture. Since 1942, jurisdictional and rival-union strikes have aggregated less than 6% of all strikes from labor-management disputes each year.[3]

Strikes are usually classed in terms of union demands or objectives, but this does not mean that all strikes are the "fault" of the unions. Some strikes probably can be more properly classed as management lockouts. Suppose, for example, that the steelworkers, through negotiations with the steel companies, have won agreements for wage increases of 10 cents an hour; then suppose that one of the companies refuses to go along with the arrangement. Even if this employer has good reason to balk, he knows that the union cannot agree to give his company such a special deal. He would, in effect, be inviting the union to strike, for it could probably do nothing else and still retain the loyalty of its members. Yet the actual decision to strike would be made by the union. Consequently, the strike would be classed as an economic walkout, even though it might be a truer description of the facts to call it a management lockout.

Noneconomic Factors in Strikes

There have been a number of attempts to state a theory of industrial disputes in terms of purely economic calculation. The assumption is that such calculation is utilized by the parties to determine whether a strike would be advisable. If the parties correctly determine each other's propensity to resist and to concede at given wage rates and strike-length periods, then, according to such analyses, they will come to an agreement without a strike at the precise point beyond which neither would concede further without a strike.[4]

The main fault with this analysis is that it does not go far enough. The decision whether to strike for higher wages or to accept a peaceful

---

[3] Data from monthly reports of the U.S. Department of Labor, Bureau of Labor Statistics.

[4] Dr. Allan M. Cartter's book, *Theory of Wages and Employment* (Homewood, Ill.: Richard D. Irwin, Inc., 1959), is a good example. He defines each party's bargaining attitude as follows:

$$\text{"X's bargaining attitude} = \frac{\text{Cost of disagreeing with Y}}{\text{Cost of agreeing on Y's terms}}.$$

. . . When one's bargaining attitude is equal to unity it is just as costly to disagree as to agree on the other's terms, and we can anticipate that when either party finds itself in this position the bargain may be completed on the other bargainer's offered terms." (Page 117.)

In fact, even if we ignore noneconomic factors, experienced negotiators will come to an agreement when the cost of agreement somewhat exceeds the cost of disagreement. The cost of agreement is a known factor. The cost of disagreement is relatively unknown because no one can determine the length of a prospective strike.

settlement at a lower rate does, in fact, depend to a considerable extent on the parties' estimates of the relative resistance or concessions which they can expect of the other. But in addition, such a decision is also influenced by many noneconomic considerations which in some circumstances may make a strike for an additional cent an hour necessary, even though it is unsound on a purely economic basis.

The union is not a purely economic unit; it is a body politic. Its first consideration is ever the strength of the organization and/or its leadership. The General Motors strike of 1970 was designed to win a large wage increase for the membership and renown for the United Automobile Workers' new president. The nonferrous metal strike of 1967–68 had as its main objective the strengthening of the bargaining position and .reputation of the Steelworkers, which had recently merged the Mine, Mill and Smelter Workers into its ranks. In each case, it will take the members many months, even years, to recover their economic losses from such strikes. Yet union leaders talk about "gains" resulting from such strikes—gains which are only such if the union or its leaders are considered separately from the rank and file.

Even where a dispute revolves solely around the size of the wage increase, unions will frequently go out on strike for a few cents more per hour, despite the fact that it is apparent that the wage loss incurred during the strike will far exceed the benefit which may be won in the final settlement. The union—particularly one in the formative stage—may derive more benefit from a wage increase of $1 a day after a strike than it would from a wage increase of $5 without a strike. The union leaders may need the rallying power of a strike to solidify the sentiment of the membership and to consolidate their own control.

Work stoppages may also result from noneconomic preferences of employers. The willingness of employers to take a strike over a principle cannot be measured on an economic calculation chart. What, for example, is it worth to a company to refuse to grant the union shop even if that involves a strike?

Whatever the cause of strikes, the computation of their costs in terms of lost wages or production is not simple. In some industries which produce a perishable or nonreproducible product or service—such as the amusement trades, passenger transportation, and newspaper publishing—business lost can rarely be regained, and therefore the cost of the strike will bear a close relationship to the revenues and wages lost during the walkout. On the other hand, in other industries, time lost by strikes may be made up during the year. Most coal strikes, for example, have not caused miners to lose more working time during an average year than they would otherwise lose from overcapacity in the industry. The average number of days worked per miner per year remains approximately the same in heavy strike years as in years of labor peace. Although this is an extreme case, the situation is somewhat comparable in all industries which produce a storable or postponable product, i.e., a product which, if not produced and sold today, can nonetheless be produced and sold tomorrow. This illustrates the point that the "real" cost of strikes is higher in times of full employment than in periods of less than full employment. For in the latter periods a strike may only determine when idleness, which would occur anyway, will take place.

Strike Tactics

Unions attempt to time a strike so that it will put the greatest pressure on the employer to settle. For this reason, union negotiators attempt to have the term of a collective bargaining agreement end in the employer's busiest season. Employers, of course, prefer to have contract negotiations and any strike action fall in their slack season.

Generally, a strike is preceded by a formal strike vote adopted by the union membership at a meeting at which the last offer of the employer is presented. Occasionally, the membership does not go along with the union leadership and votes to return to work; but usually, most union members support their leadership on a strike vote because they view the vote as a tactical move which psychologically strengthens the hand of their representatives in dealing with the employer.

Strikes sometimes develop without any preliminary formal action. Such unpremeditated walkouts, usually called "wildcat" or "quickie" strikes, are generally of short duration and are a way in which workers let off steam as a result of tensions and grievances which build up in modern industry. In some situations, however, frequent "spontaneous" walkouts of a few hours' duration may be part of a plan by the union leadership to gain concessions from management during the term of the contract without technically violating a no-strike pledge contained in the contract. Although picket lines are informational in theory, they also carry with them a threat of force. In most strikes, workers tend to support the walkout and do not attempt to work. Moreover, employers often do not attempt to operate during a strike unless they do so with salaried employees and supervisors. Where workers attempt to work, however, they are often met with force or threats for which police protection is more likely to be inadequate than protective.[5] The U.S. Supreme Court has strengthened the hands of unions in dealing with members who oppose strikes by ruling that a union could fine employees who crossed picket lines and then institute legal proceedings to collect those fines.[6]

---

[5] On this point see Frank H. Stewart and Robert J. Townsend, "Strike Violence: the Need for Injunctions," *University of Pennsylvania Law Review*, Vol. 114 (February 1966), pp. 459–86.

[6] *National Labor Relations Board* v. *Allis-Chalmers Manufacturing Co.*, 388 U.S. Supreme Court, 175 (1967).

Automation and Strikes

Automation has had a profound effect on union strike tactics in several industries. Several strikes in oils and chemicals have resulted in severe union defeats, since supervisory employees can keep the plant running at near capacity because of the ease of operating automatic equipment. Long-distance dialing has made telephone strikes ineffective for the same reason. Electric light and power strikes now occur with no interruption of service. To the extent that automation operates equipment with minimum manual requirements, unions are finding that the strike is becoming an outmoded weapon.

Strike Benefits and Strike Subsidies

Union leaders recognize that the ability of a union to withstand a long strike depends in major part on its members' economic staying power. Since the average union member's savings are quickly exhausted by a strike, most unions pay strike benefits. Some, like the United Automobile Workers, pay benefits to all workers on a strike authorized by the international union executive board. Other unions, such as the United Steelworkers, pay benefits only to those in need. Strike benefits rarely exceed $40 per week and are often less, but even so, quickly use up large strike funds.

During a strike, unions frequently receive gifts or borrow from other unions to help to defray the costs of strike benefits, publicity, legal fees, and other expenses which accompany a strike. In large strikes, such fund raising is sometimes coordinated by the AFL–CIO, whose direct resources to assist striking unionists are meager.

The meager amount of most strike benefits once required that the average unionist depend heavily on his own resources. This has changed since striking workers now have access to food stamps, welfare of various kinds, and on the railroads, in New York and in Rhode Island, to unemployment compensation as well. It is estimated that $25 million in tax-supported funds was paid to General Electric strikers in 1969–70, and about $30 million to General Motors strikers later in 1970. In New York in 1971–72, striking telephone workers received $75 per week in unemployment compensation for five months after rejecting a contract that was accepted by sister local unions in every other state. Such subsidization of strikes has become increasingly common and promises to have an increasingly unfortunate impact on collective bargaining in which the strike plays a key role.[7]

---

[7] See Armand J. Thieblot, Jr., and Ronald M. Cowin, *Welfare and Strikes: The Use of Public Funds to Support Strikers* (Labor Relations and Public Policy Series, Report No. 6 [Philadelphia: Industrial Research Unit, Wharton School of Finance and Commerce, University of Pennsylvania, 1972]).

In a famous article which drew upon his experience as chairman of the World War II National War Labor Board, Professor George W. Taylor described the function of the strike in the collective bargaining system "as the motive power which induces a modification of extreme positions and then a meeting of minds. The acceptability of certain terms of employment is determined in relation to the losses of a work stoppage that can be avoided by agreement. In collective bargaining, economic power provides the final arbitrament."[8]

If, however, one party—labor—to the collective bargaining arrangement is subsidized with public monies then the strike cannot fully perform its function of inducing agreement because it hurts only one party but not the subsidized one. A careful empirical study of how welfare and other tax-supported benefits paid to strikers affect the results concluded that they greatly reduced the workers' pressure for settlement and thus tended to make strikes last longer and result in higher bargains.[9]

Employer Strike Funds

Employers, too, have been searching for and finding ways to strengthen each other in a common stand against strong unions. One technique is through mutual assistance pacts such as exists among major airlines. Under the terms of this pact, airlines which have been shut down by a strike route prospective passengers to other lines. Participating companies pay over to the struck lines their increased receipts less expenses. Members of the Hawaiian Sugar Planters Association, who bargain on an industrywide basis, also have a mutual support program intended to distribute long-term strike losses evenly among the 26 island plantations. Other groups that have developed strike insurance plans include the railroads and the five largest manufacturers of rubber tires.[10] There also appears to be increased interest by employers in industrywide bargaining and bargaining through employer associations. Courts have sanctioned the right of all employers in a joint bargaining group to shut down when the union strikes one of the group in an attempt to divide and conquer.

The right of labor to strike and the right of management to resist such strikes by lockout and other measures are rights which are entitled to protection so long as they do not create a war of attrition inimical to the public interest. The continued existence of the right to strike as we know it may well depend upon the moderation with which this weapon is used in the next few years. Unfortunately, the decision to strike and

---

[8] George W. Taylor, "Is Compulsory Arbitration Inevitable?" *Proceedings of the First Annual Meeting* (Industrial Relations Research Association, 1948), p. 64.

[9] Thieblot and Cowin, *Welfare and Strikes.*

[10] See John S. Hirsch, "Strike Insurance and Collective Bargaining," *Industrial and Labor Relations Review*, Vol. 22 (April 1969), pp. 399–415.

to tie up an entire industry now frequently devolves upon one or two men, because of the growing scope of industrywide bargaining. The pressures on such leaders of management and labor are often such that considerations other than the general public interest are dominant. This brings us to the important question of whether unions are monopolies. Later we shall again question whether strikes can be tolerated in our economy (see Chapter 21).

UNIONS AND MONOPOLY POWER

The growing strength of organized labor and the power of unions to shut down large segments of our economy through strikes have led many writers and statesmen to ponder whether restrictive measures are not necessary in order to prevent unions from destroying or seriously impairing the free enterprise system in this country. Persons dealing with this problem frequently justify their recommendation for action by labeling unions as monopolies. In some cases, their concern is with the supposed harmful *results* of union bargaining power; in other cases, with the *power* of unions, whether or not in fact exercised, to harm the general public. Some critics of unions assail the strike as the aspect of unionism most inimical to the public welfare; others attack industrywide bargaining or the power of exclusive representation granted unions which are certified as bargaining agents under the National Labor Relations Act. One thing emerges clearly from the epithet hurling and name calling— there is a need for a reexamination of the whole question of whether or not unions are monopolies and, if so, whether or not unions wield monopoly power which is detrimental to the public welfare.

Aspects of Union Monopoly Power

There are certain ways in which it might be said that unions act like a monopoly:

1. In economic theory, one test of a monopolist, as contrasted with a pure competitor, is the ability to fix prices. Unions and monopolists are alike, since they both fix prices and both hope to sell as much of their respective "product" at the fixed price as they can. It is true that the union does not attempt to fix the price of labor with the same objectives in mind as those which motivate a monopolist in setting the price of his product. Presumably, a monopolist fixes a price which will maximize his profit, and in determining this price, he takes account of the fact that the quantity of his product demanded will be less at a high price than at a lower price. Unions, however, are not profit-making organizations. They are not motivated in all cases by purely economic objectives. Unions do not consistently seek to obtain the highest wage possible or the highest maximum income for their membership or the wage consistent with the largest number of jobs for the membership.

Often, unions will strike for another cent or two above what employers have been willing to concede, even though it is apparent that the strike is bound to cost the membership money when the gains achieved are balanced by the losses sustained during the strike. Moreover, recent studies suggest that in fixing wage rates, except in situations of sharp nonunion competition, unions do not take account of the fact that the higher the wage rate, the smaller may be the employment of union members. In other words, unions do not behave like the calculating monopolist of economic theory.

However, strong unions do, within limits, have the power to fix the price of labor. It is in this "monopoly power" that some writers find the great threat to the continuance of the free enterprise system. Charles E. Lindblom, for example, in his book entitled *Unions and Capitalism*, wrote: "The union is a monopoly because it can and does raise the price of labor to levels which will in a competitive price system inevitably cause waste, unemployment, inflation, or all combined."[11] Lindblom stated that the foundation of union monopoly power is the strike. He found that unions were able to maintain a monopoly price for union labor, even though there was competing labor available at a lower price, by coercing the employer into submitting to the union. "Union monopoly regulates the wage rate therefore not by sustained control of supply but by control of the buyer who is the employer. The technique is the strike."[12]

Lindblom viewed the strike not as a refusal to work but as a punitive measure designed to force the employer to submit to the union. To him, the strike with its concomitant picket line was a means of shutting out the competition of union workers. Lindblom's conclusion was, that by use of the strike weapon, unions can force up the price of labor so high as seriously to misallocate resources, restrict output in expanding industries, and threaten the economy with continuing inflation and unemployment.[13]

2. A union is like a monopoly because, once certified by the National Labor Relations Board (and unless decertified), a union has, by law, an area of operation in representing workers in the bargaining unit in which competition from other unions is prohibited. Under the Taft-Hartley Act, employees bargain through unions of their own choosing which the employer must recognize as the exclusive bargaining agent. A majority of persons voting in the election determine the bargaining agent for all of the workers in the bargaining unit. As long as a union remains the certified bargaining agent, it has the exclusive right to represent workers in

---

[11] Charles E. Lindblom, *Unions and Capitalism* (New Haven, Conn.: Yale University Press, 1949), p. 22.

[12] *Ibid.*, p. 58.

[13] Whether union wage policies cause inflation will be discussed in Chapter 13.

their relations with the employer. When this power is combined with a union shop, which requires new workers to join the union as a prerequisite to holding their jobs, the union has, in effect, obtained a monopoly over job opportunities with the particular employer. Nonunion workers or members of other unions cannot work for the employer. We noted in Chapter 6 how compulsory unionism increased the power of union leadership both over the rank and file and in its relations to the employer.

3. A monopoly which controls the source of supply of a product essential to the public can cause the public serious inconvenience and harm by shutting off the supply of that product. Unions frequently are accused of exercising this type of monopoly power, particularly when a strike shuts down an entire industry. In recent years, there seems to have been a growing feeling in some circles that the basis for this type of union power lies in the practice of multiunit collective bargaining. To many people, major strikes involving multiunit arrangements in steel, automobiles, and other industries seem like a battle between Goliaths from which the public is certain to emerge as the major loser.[14]

4. Monopoly in the public mind is frequently associated with great aggrandizement of financial and economic power. The power of large unions to affect economic activity through the use of strikes is well known. Unions have also become great financial institutions. National union assets, including those under their control in welfare funds, now exceed several billion dollars, as we noted in Chapter 3. When unions with such assets as the Teamsters or the United Steelworkers bargain with the individual employer who is not one of the major corporations, the scales may be so tipped in favor of the union that the individual employer can do little else but acquiesce to any demands made by the union, however illogical or uneconomic.

5. Under the antitrust laws of the United States, the test of monopoly is the power to restrain interstate commerce. The actions of unions frequently have this effect. As a matter of fact, any large-scale strike is likely to halt the free flow of products in interstate commerce. Furthermore, unions have frequently taken action deliberately aimed at restricting the flow of goods in interstate commerce. Thus, for example, the U.S. Supreme Court ruled that it was unlawful for Local No. 3 of the International Brotherhood of Electrical Workers to agree with New York City electrical contractors to purchase equipment only from local manufacturers with whom it had closed-shop agreements and to agree with such manufacturers to sell only to contractors who dealt with Local No. 3. *But the Court, in effect, held that if Local No. 3 accomplished this without conspiring with employers, then it was permissible!*[15]

---

[14] We shall return to this subject in Chapter 21.

[15] *Allen-Bradley Co.* v *Local 3, International Brotherhood of Electrical Workers*, 325 U.S. 797 (1945).

The extended immunity granted to labor from the antitrust laws was carried to its logical conclusion in other decisions. The American Federation of Musicians was permitted to maintain a nationwide boycott of recordings by refusing to have its members make such recordings;[16] a hod carriers' union was permitted to prevent usage within its jurisdiction of a low-cost cement-mixing machine except under conditions which made the use of such machines financially impossible;[17] building-trades unions were permitted to boycott materials because they were produced by companies where rival unions were bargaining agents or because they were prefabricated instead of being put together on the job;[18] and unions were allowed to picket or boycott a company solely on the ground that it dealt with a rival union and despite the fact that if the employer recognized the picketing or boycotting union, he would violate the National Labor Relations (Wagner) Act.[19]

6. Unions have been able to destroy individual businesses and deprive persons of their livelihood with immunity. In the famous case of *Hunt* v. *Crumbach*,[20] a union refused to permit members to work for one particular employer and refused to permit his employees to join the union. As a result, they completely destroyed his business in revenge for his previous hostility. The majority of the U.S. Supreme Court held that this was a legitimate exercise of the unrestricted right of concerted action with which labor organizations have been endowed by federal law. In a vigorous dissent, the late Justice Jackson pointed out that with this decision "the labor movement has come full circle. . . . This Court now sustains the claim of a union to the right to deny participation in the economic world to an employer simply because the union dislikes him. This Court permits to employees the same arbitrary dominance over the economic sphere which they control that labor so long, so bitterly, and so rightly asserted should belong to no man."

Both the Taft-Hartley and the Landrum-Griffin Acts restricted aspects of untrammeled union monopoly power.[21] Recent lawsuits undertaken pursuant to these laws against such unions as the Teamsters and the Mine Workers for breach of contract, closing down nonunion operations by force, or other now illegal acts have cost union treasuries hundreds of thousands of dollars. In addition, the U.S. Supreme Court has ruled in a case involving the United Mine Workers that a union forfeits its exemption from the antitrust laws when it is clearly shown that the union has agreed with one set of employers to impose a wage scale on other bargaining units. One group of employers may not conspire to eliminate

---

[16] *United States* v. *American Federation of Musicians*, 318 U.S. 741 (1943).

[17] *United States* v. *International Hod Carriers' Union*, 313 U.S. 539 (1941).

[18] *United States* v. *Building & Construction Trades Council*, 313 U.S. 539 (1941).

[19] *National Labor Relations Board* v. *Star Publishing Co.*, 97 F. (2d) 465 (1938).

[20] 325 U.S. 821 (1945).

[21] See Chapters 19 and 20 for a discussion of these laws.

competitors from an industry, and the union is liable, along with the employers, if it becomes a party to the conspiracy.[22] On the other hand, the same Court ruled that there was nothing illegal in a union forcing all stores to refrain from selling meat after 6 P.M. even though the stores remained open.[23] Litigation in this area continues to fix the boundaries of legality for union conduct, but in view of some of the excesses of union power illustrated by these cases, it would not be surprising if Congress further limited union power.

In summary, then, the charges against unions are that they fix the price of labor through the use of coercion and force, that they have a monopoly of job opportunities, that they can shut down whole industries, that they have become financial giants by reason of their tax-exempt status and the use of the checkoff of dues, and that they hold the power of life or death over thousands of individual businesses. Labor's answer is that despite the alleged power of unions, the average worker with a family still does not have sufficient take-home pay to maintain an adequate standard of living, that the union shop is simply another application of the democratic principle of majority rule, that industrywide bargaining is necessary to stabilize wage rates between competing employers, that the assets of unions are minute compared to the assets of the giant corporations with which they must bargain, and that while some employers may get hurt by union actions, unions use their power to serve millions of workers not a privileged few.[24]

Unions, however, can hardly expect that their monopoly power can continue to be exercised without restriction in an economy which is generally committed to the principle of fostering competition. Certainly, it is realistic to assume that new regulations of trade-unions will come. The direction which such regulation should take, however, is a subject on which there is little unanimity among labor critics. The great danger is that general legislation will be passed which will cause great harm rather than improvement.

For example, some want a blanket application of the antitrust laws to labor. Yet, these laws are most complex. Tomes have been written as to their application to business, but their meaning in specific cases is often not clear. Meanwhile, proponents of laissez-faire complain that the antitrust laws have not ended business combinations.

We noted in Chapter 6 that attempts to legislate against make-work practices are likely to be both ineffective and dangerous to the free enterprise system because of difficulties of distinguishing featherbedding from legitimate practice. Likewise, blanket condemnation of multiunit bargaining—also a favorite of those desiring remedial legislation—could

---

[22] *United Mine Workers* v. *Pennington*, 381 U.S. 657 (1965).

[23] *Local 189, Meat Cutters* v. *Jewel Tea Co.*, 381 U.S. 657 (1969).

[24] "The Labor Monopoly Myth," *Labor's Economic Review* (AFL–CIO publication), February 1956.

well put small businesses at the mercy of unionism, instead of having the opposite effect. For if small business cannot present a united front against union demands, it often cannot obtain an equitable bargain.

Breaking up unions into local bodies is also a much talked-about remedy. This is a variation of the prohibition of multiunit bargaining which ties up entire industries and has led to proposals that industrywide bargaining be banned. Labor contracts would be required by law to be negotiated only between individual employers and local unions. Obviously, this proposal, if adopted, would disrupt long-standing relationships in many industries and would also prohibit bargaining through employer associations, which many management spokesmen feel has done much to stabilize labor-management relations. It can be argued that thus breaking up unions might actually cause them to be even more monopolistic in determining the selling price of labor. For example, if there were four or five separate unions in the automobile industry, each dealing with a separate employer, each company would still find that it was dealing with a monopoly which could cut off its labor supply. On the other hand, the individual unions would vie with one another to get the highest wage possible from their particular employer. The union in General Motors would be able to push its demands without regard to the ability of Ford, Chrysler, or American Motors to meet those demands. While industrywide strikes might be lessened, the restraint now present in union negotiations, which leads to more or less uniform settlements with the most prosperous as well as the least prosperous companies in the industry, would be removed. The result would probably be a strengthening of the tendency of unions to raise wages and to generate increases in money incomes.

Outlawing compulsory unionism is another proposed solution to union monopoly power. This would probably weaken unions because of its effect on union income, but it would not remove union power over product markets, necessarily reduce the potential for industrywide strikes, or otherwise solve many of the abuses discussed in this chapter.

The problem of union monopoly power thus has many complicated facets. It requires most careful analysis, as well as a general review of existing labor relations law, rather than wholesale attack by oversimplified remedies. In Part VI of this book, we shall discuss our basic labor laws and how they have evolved. The approach of utilizing specific laws, or sections thereof, to attack specific abuses will be seen to be more satisfactory than would a generalized approach through the antitrust laws.

QUESTIONS FOR DISCUSSION

1. If Congress outlawed multiunit bargaining, what would be the effects on industries which now bargain on such a basis?

2. Are unions monopolies? Explain your answer, and compare unions with such aggregations of capital as American Telephone and Telegraph, United States Steel, and General Motors.

3. Do you feel that the future will see more and greater strikes, or fewer? Why? Would you expect such strikes, however many or few, to be accompanied by more or less violence than in the past?

SUGGESTIONS FOR FURTHER READING

DEMENIL, GEORGE. *Bargaining: Monopoly Power versus Union Power.* Cambridge, Mass.: MIT Press, 1971.

A mathematical representation of bargaining where firm monopoly power in the labor market is met by union monopoly power over labor supply.

ROWAN, RICHARD L. (ed). *Collective Bargaining: Survival in the 70's?* pp. 77–105. Labor Relations and Public Policy Series, Report No. 5. Philadelphia: Industrial Research Unit, Wharton School of Finance and Commerce, University of Pennsylvania, 1972.

Includes articles endorsing the application of antitrust laws to unions and the pros and cons of permitting strikers to receive welfare payments.

WEBER, ARNOLD (ed.). *The Structure of Collective Bargaining.* New York: Free Press, 1961.

An analysis by several scholars and practitioners of the varying bargaining structures in key industries, and the public policy implications thereof.

PART IV
Economics of the Labor Market

Chapter 8

THE LABOR MARKET

In the market for labor, as in the market for wheat, buyers and sellers meet and bargain over the price at which a sale is to be made. In the wheat market, one price is ultimately arrived at, determined by supply and demand, which "clears the market." Sellers who want a higher price must accept the market price or they cannot sell their product; buyers who want to pay less than the market price cannot find sellers. Does the market for labor function like the market for wheat? If not, why not? What is the explanation for the great diversity which exists in rates of wages and salaries? These are the questions which we shall seek to answer in the following discussion.

DEFINITION OF LABOR MARKET

The concept of a "labor market" has been given many definitions by various writers, depending upon their points of view and the problems with which they were attempting to deal. On the one hand, the labor market can be viewed as a process by which supplies of a particular type of labor and demands for that type of labor are balanced or seek to obtain a balance. On the other hand, the labor market can be considered in the sense of a manufacturing or trading center, or some other geographical area. During World War II, the War Labor Board defined a labor market area as one in which the wage structure and levels in an industry were fairly uniform. The War Manpower Commission defined a labor market as the widest area in which employees with fixed addresses would accept employment. Somewhat similar is the U.S. Department of Labor Manpower Administration's definition of a "labor area" as an "economically integrated geographical unit within which workers may readily change jobs without changing their place of residence."[1]

The foregoing definitions have the common characteristic of view-

---

[1] U.S. Department of Labor Manpower Administration, *Area Trends in Employment and Unemployment* (January 1972), p. 6.

ing a labor market as a definite geographic area. Some economists, however, feel that the element of locality as a characteristic of the labor market is of limited significance insofar as the determination of wages is concerned. It is argued that unions often make wage decisions without reference to supply and demand influences in a particular geographic area. Thus, the wage demands of the Rubber Workers' Union in a small town in the Midwest will not be determined by supply and demand factors within the local area or even in the same industry but may be related to a pattern of wage increases granted by the steel and automobile industries in other parts of the country.

Even though it may be necessary to go beyond a particular geographic area to find the forces or criteria which determine wage levels within that area, the concept of the labor market as a geographic area is still a useful one. In this discussion, the term *labor market* will be used in the sense of the geographic area within which a particular group of employers and wage earners buy and sell services. For some forms of labor, the geographic area may be a town, whereas for other forms of labor, such as a talented violinist, the geographic limits of the labor market may be the entire Western world.

DIFFERENCES BETWEEN LABOR MARKETS AND COMMODITY MARKETS

Labor markets differ from commodity markets. Each buyer is distinguished from every other buyer. Even if the United States Steel Corporation and the John Brown Tool Company were to offer the same basic rate to machinists, the offers would differ in attractiveness to different workers. Some men like to work for a large company; some like to work for a small company. There are literally hundreds of other respects in which different employers may be distinguished in an employee's mind. Because the sale of labor involves a continuing, and not merely a temporary, relationship with the "buyer," these intangibles are frequently more important in the employee's mind than the employer's offering price.

Diversity of Rates

Diversity of rates for the same type of labor is the norm, not the exception, in the labor market. As we shall see, differences may exist between firms, between industries, and between localities. The continued existence of such differentials is attributable in part to imperfections in the flow of information and in part to the variety of influences deriving from both the product market and the labor market which ultimately determine wage levels. Furthermore, because of differences in the race, sex, or length of service of employees performing the same job, diversity in wage rates for the same job may exist even within a single plant.

Wage Fixing in the Labor Market

Wage fixing, analogous to a quoted price in the product market, is characteristic of the labor market. Whereas, in the commodity market, it is normally the seller who sets the asking price, in the labor market (in the absence of unions) the buyer of labor normally sets the price. The price that is set tends to be "fixed" for some length of time. Employers do not want wage rates to fluctuate with every change in supply and demand conditions. Stability in wage rates is essential for satisfactory business operations. Constant change in the wage schedule of the average company would cost more than it is worth. Moreover, stability is also desirable from the point of view of employees. Frequent changes in wage rates would cause friction and suspicion and would make employees feel insecure. Therefore, in changing wage rates, employers customarily grant general wage adjustments to all employees instead of adjusting rates to individual demand and supply conditions, or at least grant individual wage increases according to some plan or custom.

The majority of multiplant companies do relate their wage scales either to those paid by other firms in the area or to rates for the same industry in the area; some, however, pay the same wage scales regardless of the size of the city or the region of the country in which their plants are located, and others have uniform scales for each region or zone. Still others pay community wage rates, but grant the same adjustments, regardless of area. Some companies raise wages with increases in the cost of living and increases in length of service, while other companies do not. Such differences in company wage policies, in employer evaluation of particular jobs, and in stress on various wage factors all contribute to the existence of a diversity of wage rates rather than a single rate for any grade of labor in a particular locality.

The labor market, therefore, is not characterized by a norm of pure competition. There is no wage which will clear the market, toward which a labor market under actual conditions, even in the absence of collective bargaining, is tending. The labor market is characterized by stability and lack of fluidity and a diversity of rates for similar jobs. A rise in the price of labor offered by a particular employer does not cause employees in other firms who are receiving less than that amount to leave their jobs and flock to the high-wage employer. Sufficiently large differentials will, of course, induce a movement of labor; but within a substantial range, changes in rates by a particular employer may have little effect in causing workers to leave other firms to seek work in the high-wage firm. In order to understand why this is so and why diverse wage rates for the same jobs can continue to coexist in the same area, some understanding of labor mobility is required.

THE NATURE OF LABOR MOBILITY

Labor is not a fluid factor of production. It does not flow readily in response to small changes in its remuneration. One reason is that work—having and keeping a job—is a central status symbol in our profit-oriented society and changing jobs involves a risk of having no work at all. A second reason is that generally the employee must transport himself to the place of work, and this may require an expenditure of time and money. The inadequate state of our public transportation systems in many of our large cities undoubtedly inhibits the mobility of many low-income job seekers.[2]

Problems of the Job Search

How do job seekers obtain information about potential job openings? Information sources can be divided into two types of networks: informal and formal. Informal networks include referrals from employees, friends, relatives, and other casual sources, and walk-ins or hiring at the gate. Formal networks include state employment agencies, private fee-charging agencies, union hiring halls, newspaper advertisements, and school or college placement bureaus.[3] Most studies have found that employees rely most upon informal networks. For example, in a study of the Chicago labor market it was found that in four white-collar occupations, informal sources accounted for about half of all hires, while in eight blue-collar occupations, informal networks accounted for more than four fifths of all hires.[4]

In a perfect labor market, job opportunities would be generally known and available workers would gravitate toward the better paying jobs for which their skills qualified them. In the actual labor market, this process is only dimly visible because information about the various job vacancies and the merits and disadvantages of particular jobs are not generally known. To a large extent, job attachments result from chance, rather than careful economic appraisal. It must be recognized that collating information about potential job opportunities involves incurring costs.

---

[2] See U.S. Department of Labor, *Manpower Report of the President, 1971* (Washington, D.C.: U.S. Government Printing Office, 1971), p. 96.

[3] Albert Rees, "Information Networks in Labor Markets," in John F. Burton, Jr., et al. (eds.), *Readings in Labor Market Analysis* (New York: Holt Rinehart & Winston, Inc. 1971), p. 245.

[4] *Ibid.*

Various job seekers will make different trade-offs between the adequacy of information obtained and the cost of obtaining it.[5]

Although some labor market analysts have assumed that the high rate of unemployment among urban poverty area residents is attributable in part to their lack of knowledge of available job opportunities and their inefficient methods of looking for a job, a recent study of job-seeking techniques conducted by the U.S. Department of Labor found little difference between the methods used by poverty area residents and job seekers in the balance of the population of the cities studied.[6] Direct contact with employers was the method used most frequently regardless of the personal characteristics or labor force status of the job seeker. Other methods, in order of their importance, were checking with relatives, newspapers, and the employment service.[7] White-collar workers were found more likely than blue-collar or service workers to use newspapers, private agencies, and community organizations in looking for work and much less likely to use public employment services.[8] The federal government is now actively seeking through a number of programs to help workers in slum areas get more accurate information about job opportunities.

Changing Jobs

Even after a worker has found a job, his new status as an employee does not broaden his horizon of knowledge about other job opportunities markedly. Generally, wages, hours, and working conditions in other plants are either vague or unknown to him. The lack of knowledge on the part of employees attaches them more firmly to their present jobs. They do not think in terms of changing jobs because they do not know what the alternatives are. They know the conditions under which they work, and they fear to take a chance on the basis of their inadequate knowledge of conditions elsewhere.

Most workers are reluctant to change jobs even if they know that a higher wage can be obtained at a different plant or in a different occupation. One reason is that there is a transfer cost in making such a change. There may be a period of layoff between jobs, or additional training may be required, or perhaps the worker will have to physically move himself and his family to a new city or to a new residence in a different

---

[5] See, for an elaboration of this theory, Armen A. Alchian, "Information Costs, Pricing, and Resource Unemployment," in Edmund S. Phelps et al., *Microeconomic Foundations of Employment and Inflation Theory* (New York: W.W. Norton & Company, Inc. 1970), pp. 27–52).

[6] Harvey J. Hilaski, "How Poverty Area Residents Look For Work," *Monthly Labor Review*, Vol. 94 (March 1971), p. 41.

[7] *Ibid.*, p. 42.

[8] *Ibid.*, p. 43.

part of a city. All of these costs impose barriers to movement. Since a job change may mean loss of seniority and accrued rights under pension plans, employees are generally reluctant to leave a job as long as they regard their conditions of employment generally "fair," even though they may not be the best.

Determinants of Occupational Mobility

Why do workers change jobs? The motivation of occupational mobility is not clearly understood, and much field research is required on this subject if we are to have a satisfactory understanding of movements in the labor market. However, we do have available considerable statistical data suggesting definite interrelationships between worker mobility (both voluntary and involuntary) and age, sex, color, education, type of job, and character of employment. Occupational mobility declines as the age of the worker increases. Much of the occupational change among younger workers is probably voluntary and associated with "shopping around" for jobs, casual occupational attachment while in school, and tenuous home town ties. One recent study found that among young men aged 14 to 24, 55% of the whites and 68% of the blacks made at least one job shift within a two-year period. Three or more job shifts during this period were made by as many as 15% of the whites and 22% of the blacks.[9]

As workers grow older, mobility is impaired by stronger occupational ties, job seniority rights, age discrimination in hiring, higher incomes that reduce incentives to move, and the fear of change itself. Among the older worker group, job shifts are more likely to be involuntary than voluntary.[10]

Statistics suggest that men, both white and nonwhite, are more apt to change occupations than women. This is true with respect to full-time and part-time employment. Part-time workers are more mobile occupationally than full-time workers. This is to be expected since the part-time group includes a large percentage of younger workers, blacks, and the less skilled. Surprisingly, however, the data indicate that women have about the same occupational mobility whether on part-time or full-time jobs.[11] Negro men show a higher mobility rate than white men. The difference in rate between black women and white women is inconclusive.[12]

Job changes occur most frequently in occupations requiring little or

---

[9] Herbert S. Parnes et al, *Career Thresholds, A Longitudinal Study of the Educational and Labor Market Experience of Male Youth* (Washington, D.C.: U.S. Department of Labor, Manpower Administration, 1971), Vol. III, pp. 77–79.

[10] Samuel Saben, "Occupational Mobility of Employed Workers" (Special Labor Force Report No. 84 [Washington, D.C.: U.S. Department of Labor, 1967]), p. 32.

[11] *Ibid.*, pp. 36–37.

[12] *Ibid.*

FIGURE 8–1

Geographic Mobility of the Population, March 1969 to March 1970

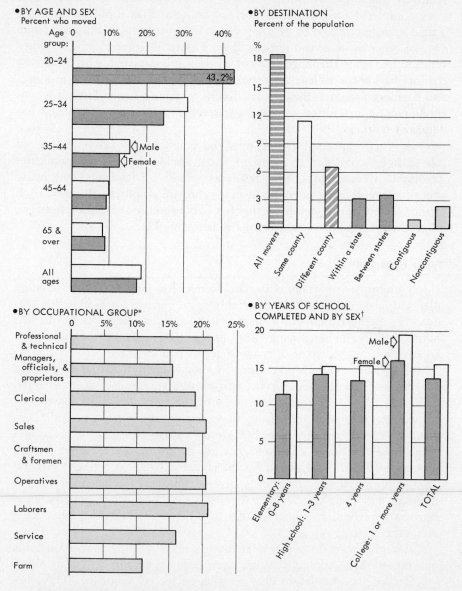

° Employed persons 14 years of age and over.
† Persons 25 years of age and over.
Source: *Geographic Mobility in the Sixties* (Road Maps of Industry, No. 1666 [New York: The Conference Board, May 15, 1971]).

no skill, such as operatives, service workers, and farm and nonfarm laborers. These are also occupations in which unemployement rates are relatively high. Occupational change occurs least among persons who have completed four years or more of college. This simply means that a man who has trained to be a lawyer is likely to stay in the profession. On the other hand, as can be seen from Figure 8–1, geographic mobility tends to be higher the more years of education completed. This is because the job market for college-educated persons tends to be national in scope, and furthermore such persons are likely to have greater knowledge of economic opportunities in other geographic areas than is true of less educated workers.

One other important factor must be considered in any analysis of job changes—that is, that many of them are not wholly economically motivated. Reasons of health, residence, family, friendship, and many other factors all can contribute in motivating an employee to make a job change. These noneconomic factors further lessen the correlation between wage changes and employment in the labor market.

Types of Mobility

Job mobility may take different forms. An employee may change jobs within a particular company. He may change his occupation, his industry, and his employer, or there may be various combinations of these factors. Finally, he may or may not change the geographic location of his employment to the extent of moving across county lines.

Studies by the U.S. Department of Labor indicate that four out of five workers who change occupations also change employers.[13] Furthermore, the same study found that 7 out of 10 of the men and three quarters of the women who changed occupations during the survey period[14] also changed the industry in which they were working. Although job changes which involve change of employers are probably more common than those that do not, as suggested by the above statistics, it is likely that job changes within the confines of a given employer are less likely to be reported, and therefore Department of Labor and other governmental statistics may tend to underestimate the actual mobility which occurs within the firm.

Although we are known as a "nation on wheels," most moves are made over rather short distances. With very little variation each year, about one fifth of the population changes their place of residence. Thus, between March 1969 and March 1970, 18.4% of the population, or 36.5 millions people, changed residences.[15] However, as can be seen from

---

[13] *Ibid.*

[14] *Ibid.*

[15] *Geographic Mobility in the Sixties* (Road Maps of Industry, No. 1666 [New York: The Conference Board, May 15, 1971]).

Figure 8–1, only a small percentage of the persons involved in shift of residences moved over state lines. As has been mentioned, professional and technical personnel stand high in geographical mobility. However, operatives and laborers, who show high occupational mobility, also score high in geographic mobility as well. As might be expected, geographic mobility rates are higher for the unemployed than for the employed.[16]

The Trend in Quit Rates

We have seen that in the labor market both employer and employee are frequently more interested in job stability than mobility. The employee prefers stability in job tenure so that he is not exposed to income loss while changing jobs and can build up rights in valuable job fringes based upon seniority. The employer prefers stability because it means that costs of hiring and training new employees are minimized and he can plan production and operation schedules with the knowledge that adequate personnel are available. Yet, from the point of view of the needs of a dynamic economy with a constantly changing mix of job opportunities, a higher rate of mobility may be required in order to achieve a better utilization of the labor force and to minimize shortages of labor and bottlenecks in production as the economy achieves high employment levels.

Is labor mobility increasing or decreasing in our economy? One way of measuring this trend is to examine so-called "quit rates." Voluntary quits are defined as persons who leave the employ of a company upon their own volition for any reason except to retire, enter military service, or to transfer to another establishment of the same company. Series of such data per 100 employees are available for manufacturing industries over a long period of years. Unfortunately, they are collected only for manufacturing industries, although labor turnover is undoubtedly higher in some nonmanufacturing industries. As the figures in Table 8–1 reveal, quits are relatively small and tend to vary inversely with layoffs and the rate of unemployment.

There has been considerable controversy in the economic literature as to whether or not there has been a long-run tendency for the quit rate in manufacturing to decline. Some writers have raised the question as to whether seniority rights, pensions, and other benefits of job retention had in effect created a "new industrial feudalism" because men could no longer afford to quit their jobs.[17] At least two writers have set forth the

---

[16] U.S. Department of Commerce, Bureau of the Census, *Mobility of the Population of the United States, March 1969 to March 1970* (Current Population Reports, Series P–20, No. 210 [Washington, D.C.: U.S. Government Printing Office, 1971]), p. 1.

[17] The validity of this proposition is explored in Arthur M. Ross, "Do We Have a New Industrial Feudalism?" *American Economic Review*, Vol. 48 (December 1958), pp. 903–20.

thesis that the quit rate in the 1950s had declined from its earlier levels and attributed this decline to such factors as the growth of unionism and the spread of pension plans.[18] On the other hand, other writers examining the postwar period, when maturing unionism and augmented pension plans might have been thought to have retarded mobility, find no evidence of declining voluntary mobility.[19]

TABLE 8–1

Quit Rates and Layoff Rates in Manufacturing, and Unemployment as Percent of Labor Force: Annual Averages, Selected Years, 1947–71

Year	Per 100 Employees		Unemploy-ment Percent
	Quit Rate	Layoff Rate	
1947	4.1	1.1	3.9%
1949	1.9	2.9	5.9
1950	2.3	1.3	5.3
1951	2.9	1.4	3.3
1954	1.4	2.3	5.5
1955	1.9	1.5	4.4
1958	1.1	2.6	6.8
1960	1.3	2.4	5.5
1965	1.9	1.4	4.5
1966	2.6	1.2	3.8
1967	2.3	1.4	3.8
1968	2.5	1.2	3.6
1969	2.7	1.2	3.5
1970	2.1	1.8	4.9
1971	1.8	1.6	5.9

Source: Unemployment rates from *Employment and Earnings* Vol. 18 (March 1972), p. 21; quit and layoff rates from *Handbook of Labor Statistics, 1971* (U.S. Department of Labor Bulletin No. 1705 [Washington, D.C.: U.S. Government Printing Office, 1971), p. 109 and *Employment and Earnings* (March 1972), p. 107.

The trend if any in voluntary mobility cannot be determined merely from a visual examination of the quit rates listed in Table 8–1. What is really relevant is the amount of movement as measured by quit rates in relationship to the opportunity or incentives for movement as measured by the unemployment rate, the extent of interindustry wage differentials, and similar factors. Burton and Parker conclude, after adjusting for in-

[18] E. Clague, "Long-Term Trends in Quit Rates," *Employment and Earnings*, Vol. 3 (December 1956), pp. iii–ix, and J. Shister, "Labor Mobility: Some Institutional Aspects," in Milton Derber (ed.), *Proceedings of the Third Annual Meeting of the Industrial Relations Research Association* (December 28–29, 1950), pp. 42–59.

[19] John F. Burton, Jr., and John E. Parker, *The New Industrial Feudalism: Secular Trends in Voluntary Labor Mobility"* (Occasional Papers No. 33 [A. G. Bush Library of Management, Organization, and Industrial Relations, University of Chicago, 1971]).

centives and opportunities for voluntary mobility, that there is no trend towards declining voluntary mobility in manufacturing industries in the postwar era.[20]

It should be reiterated that the foregoing discussion applies only to manufacturing. Data are not available for other sectors of the economy, and it is quite possible that a different trend may exist there. In any case the great influx of young workers under 25 who are now appearing on the labor market may alter this trend of quit rates, although the anticipated stability of employment in manufacturing may hold quit rates in this sector of the economy down, while those in the service industries, which are expanding, may rise.

LABOR MARKET STRUCTURE

In analyzing various labor markets in this country, we may distinguish them by their geographic location—for example, the West Coast labor market differs materially from that in other parts of the country—or we may distinguish labor markets according to their "structure." A labor market structure has been defined as

a set of "established practices" which are applied consistently in carrying out the various employment functions of recruitment, selection, assignment to jobs, wage payment, transfer, separation, and the like. Established practices are created by law, contract, custom, and managerial policy. Their function is to establish the rights and privileges of employees and to introduce certainty and regularity into the handling of personnel—in short, to create a "rule of law" in employment matters. Their main effect is to limit managerial discretion.[21]

In terms of the foregoing definition, labor markets range all the way from the highly structured to the unstructured, depending upon the presence or absence of rules or practices governing the employment relationship. Thus, public employment characterized by detailed civil service regulations would be an example of a highly structured labor market where managerial prerogatives have been severely restricted. By contrast, the market for domestic servants would be unstructured to a high degree, with great flexibility in the type of relationship which can be worked out between employer and employee.

Structured Labor Markets

Structured labor markets fall into three general categories: (1) the market for public employees, which is structured from entry to exit by

---

[20] *Ibid.*, p. 21.

[21] Orme W. Phelps, "A Structural Model of the U.S. Labor Market," *Industrial and Labor Relations Review*, Vol. 10 (April 1957), p. 403. The writers have drawn heavily on this excellent article for the analysis contained in this section.

legislation and administrative rules; (2) the nonunion labor market in the large firm, in which the structuring aspect emanates from the employer's personnel policies, formulated and administered by a personnel department; (3) the labor market, in which "established practices" derive from collective bargaining agreements and union work rules.

The market for public employees is impersonal, technical, and highly classified. Emphasis is on security of tenure rather than on pay. Entrance requirements are frequently based upon competitive examination. A high proportion of regular, permanent public employees are eligible for civil service status, which carries with it advantages of tenure and opportunities for promotion. However, despite the fact that government, in theory, has unrestricted authority to vary the terms and conditions of employment, as a practical matter the hands of the government administrator in charge of a particular agency are securely tied with the red tape of governmental regulation, so that the public labor market has many of the characteristics of a highly unionized labor market in the private business sector of the economy. The increasing importance of collective bargaining among public employees may further accentuate the formalized structuring of wage and employment practices in this field.[22]

The nonunion structured labor market dominated by employer personnel policies is to be found in three major areas: the large unorganized industrial firm, which, although somewhat exceptional, still exists; the large unorganized firm in the white-collar industries—banks, department stores, insurance companies, etc.; and nonunion employees outside the bargaining unit in large companies which are organized. Large industrial firms which are unorganized retain unilateral control over employment policies but, in practice, are likely to follow rates and policies of their organized competitors so as not to make themselves a target for union organization. In addition, restraints on wages and conditions are imposed by state and federal laws. Large white-collar companies are still the stronghold for structured employment policies dictated by management. This group has become more important in the present decade in terms of share of the total labor market because of the shift of employment toward trade, finance, and related fields, in which this type of structure predominates. White-collar workers in organized companies who are outside the bargaining unit do not have the full protection of the union, but nevertheless benefit in many ways from gains secured by the union for organized employees. Obviously, management cannot afford to have major inequities develop between the two groups of employees, which would either have a bad effect on morale or constitute an invitation to union organization.

Most unionized employment is manual, hourly rated, blue-collar work.

---

[22] See Chapter 22 for a discussion of collective bargaining by government employees.

The employee either may work on a permanent basis for a large industrial concern or may be employed in one of the casual trades, such as construction, where his association with any one employer may be brief. The structure of such a labor market is, in theory, bilateral, resulting from the bargain made by the employer and the union. Where the employer is small and the union strong, as in the building-trades or trucking industry, the union may often dictate the rates of pay, the hours of work, job assignments, promotions, and other aspects of the employment relationship. In larger firms the personnel department may still make policy decisions, but these are generally subject to review and consultation with the union through collective bargaining.

Unstructured Labor Markets

The unstructured labor market is, in general, the market of individual bargains, in which there are few if any rules or regulations affecting employment practices, except governmental enactments setting minimum wages, prohibiting discrimination, etc. This market includes farm labor, domestic help, professional office employees, and employees of small business firms. It has been estimated that this market covers about one third of the civilian employed labor force (excluding proprietors, self-employed, and unpaid family labor). Employment in these markets is apt to be on a personal basis, with little emphasis on formal policies and procedures. Union organization is largely absent, fringe benefits are few, and in many cases the employer is not even subject to the minimal structuring provided by various federal statutes, since most such statutes—the Taft-Hartley Act, the Fair Labor Standards Act, and similar laws—provide exemptions for small local businesses.

Primary and Secondary Labor Markets

In recent years, increasing concern with respect to the high unemployment and low earnings of disadvantaged groups in our urban centers has given rise to a theory of dual labor markets. Under this theory, the urban labor market is divided into two separate sectors: a "primary" market and a "secondary" market, which operate side by side. There is, of course, some movement of workers between the two, but for the most part disadvantaged workers are denied the opportunity of moving from the secondary to the primary market.

The primary labor market is characterized by jobs which offer good pay, good working conditions, and steady employment. The secondary market is characterized by jobs which offer irregular employment, low wages, poor working conditions, and low status. Typical are jobs in restaurants, car wash, day labor in construction, private household work, etc. To some extent, the instability of secondary jobs is matched by the instability of the work force. Since the rewards of secondary employment are low, the penalty for quitting or otherwise losing one's job is also low. Therefore, the secondary market is characterized by frequent job changes and high rates of absenteeism and tardiness.[23]

The operation of urban labor markets has sometimes been described in terms of a so-called "queue theory." Under this theory, workers are ranked by employers in accordance with their perceptions of the workers' productivity and desirability in relationship to the wages they demand. The most preferred, most productive workers are hired first; then, as the labor market tightens, employers are thought to reduce their hiring standards and recruit from the less advantaged.[24] However, there is abundant evidence from recent history that this process does not in fact happen. There can be shortages in the primary job market and continuing irregularity of employment and low earnings in the secondary labor market. Poverty, discrimination, lack of skills—all erect a barrier between the two markets. Recognition of such a barrier implies that reliance cannot be placed simply upon a revival of general business to reduce unemployment among the disadvantaged. Special remedies will be required to deal effectively with this complex problem.[25]

DIVERSITY IN WAGE RATES

We have already observed that even in a local labor market, divergent wage rates may prevail for similar jobs. It is not surprising, then, that diversity is also found when cities are compared with towns or the South with the North, or one industry with another industry. Indeed, diversity of rates is characteristic of the labor market however that term is defined. In the following discussion we shall consider such diversity from four principal points of view: geographical, interindustry, interfirm, and personal.

Geographical Diversity: The North–South Differential

Regional location is an important factor in determining pay levels. It is frequently stated that "wages are lower in the South." This statement is open to several interpretations. The North–South differential may mean that wages in particular industries are lower in the South than in other parts of the country. This is true in some industries, but not in others. Among 26 manufacturing industries studied by the U.S. Bureau of Labor

[23] *Manpower Report, 1971*, pp. 96–98.

[24] See Peter B. Doeringer and Michael J. Piore, *Internal Labor Markets and Manpower Analysis* (Lexington, Mass.: D.C. Heath & Co, 1971), pp. 165–66.

[25] Manpower policies to deal with the problems of the disadvantaged are considered in Chapter 15.

Statistics, the southern wage level ranged from 38.6% below the rest of the country in meat-packing to more than 9% above in synthetic fibers.[26] Likewise, in nonmanufacturing industries the differential ranged from about 30% below in service industries, such as laundries, restaurants and hotels, to only 5% below in bituminous coal. In the basic steel and automobile assembly industries, regional rate differentials have been largely eliminated by collective bargaining agreements.[27]

The North–South wage differential may suggest that in given occupations, earnings are lower in the South than in the North. Although this is true as a general statement, the extent of the differential varies markedly depending upon the occupation. As can be seen from Table 8–2, regional differentials are most pronounced for unskilled plant workers, while differences in the professional and administrative category are insignif-

TABLE 8–2

Pay Levels for Occupational Groups in Four Regions, as Percentage of National Average

Occupations	*U.S.*	*Northeast*	*South*	*North Central*	*West*
Unskilled plant............	100	102	80	109	109
Clerical..................	100	101	96	100	105
Skilled maintenance........	100	95	94	105	106
Technical support.........	100	101	97	101	101
Professional and administrative...........	100	101	99	99	102

Source: Harry F. Zeman, "Regional Pay Differentials in White-Collar Occupations," *Monthly Labor Review*, Vol. 94 (January 1971), p. 53.

icant. The high geographic mobility of persons in the latter category, as already mentioned, means that such employees function in a labor market which is national in scope, and therefore their rates are less subject to regional and local influences.

The North–South differential could also be taken to mean that earnings in certain southern states are much lower than in northern states. This variation is very apparent. In December 1971, gross weekly earnings of production workers in manufacturing averaged about $150 for the nation as a whole. The four states with the lowest weekly earnings were all in the South and Southwest: New Mexico, $109.33; Arkansas, $109.34; North Carolina, $110.15; Mississippi, $110.81; and South Carolina, $113.55.

---

[26] H. M. Douty, "Wage Differentials: Forces and Counterforces," *Monthly Labor Review*, Vol. 91 (March 1968), p. 74.

[27] *Ibid.*, p. 75.

Contrary to what might be expected, however, earnings in Alabama exceeded those in Maine, New Hampshire, and Rhode Island.[28] It is apparent that it is not so much the geographical location as the nature of industry that accounts for much of this variation. Furthermore, even within particular states there can be tremendous variation in compensation. For example, in December 1971, the city with the lowest weekly earnings in the Bureau of Labor Statistics survey was El Paso, Texas, with weekly earnings of only $91.58. Yet the state of Texas as a whole had earnings of $140.49.[29]

The North–South differential may mean that the average wage of all workers in the one region is lower than the average wage of all workers in the other. This is obviously a crude measurement because it compares wages regardless of intraregional industrial mix and variations in skills, city size, and so forth which can affect wage levels. One study concluded that average hourly earnings in the non-South are about 25% higher than in the South. About one third of this differential is attributable to regional differences in the labor force as measured by color, age, sex, and education; about one third is related to regional differences in city size; and about one third of the differential remains, after adjusting for labor force composition and city size.[30]

Many explanations have been advanced as to why this residual differential exists. Some claim that southern labor is less efficient, but after adjusting for educational differences, there is little evidence to support this claim. Union leaders argue that the weakness of union organization in the South accounts for the differential, but North–South wage differentials are much too complex and diverse for such a simple explanation. Differentials vary widely in amounts from industry to industry, whether the industries are unionized or not.

Actually, the most logical explanation of the southern wage differential is the fact that there is an oversupply of labor relative to capital in the South—or to put the matter another way, a relative shortage of capital. The oversupply of labor seems to be particularly acute with respect to unskilled labor. A relative shortage of capital exists in the South even today. While, over the past few decades, there has been a net migration of labor out of the South and a net capital flow in, the southern labor force has been growing at a more rapid rate than that of the rest of the country. Furthermore, Bureau of Labor Statistics projections to 1980 indicate that the southern labor force will continue to grow at a faster rate than will be true for the labor force in the rest of the country.[31] As

---

[28] *Employment and Earnings*, March 1972, pp. 104–106.

[29] *Ibid.*, p. 105.

[30] Victor R. Fuchs, "Hourly Earnings Differentials by Region and Size of City," *Monthly Labor Review*, Vol. 90 (January 1967), p. 25.

[31] Douty, "Wage Differentials," p. 80.

a consequence, the relative surplus of labor is likely to persist and the southern wage differential will decline very slowly.[32]

Union Policy and Regional Differentials

In general, union policy has opposed regional wage differentials. The United Mine Workers, for example, has succeeded in equalizing basic wage rates between the northern and southern Appalachian coal regions; the Steelworkers, with the cooperation of United States Steel and Republic Steel, began to eliminate area differentials in the late 1940s, and the job was pretty much completed in the 1950s. The UAW has ended all area differentials at Chrysler and Ford and has fought to eliminate them at General Motors. The Rubber Workers have been unsuccessful in their attempts to eliminate the regional wage spread. In the early 1960s, however, James R. Hoffa was successful in achieving a uniform national rate for over-the-road truck drivers, eliminating thereby several differentials, including one in the South.

On the other hand, many unions have not opposed southern wage differentials where they regard them as justified by certain circumstances. Because of a poor grade of coal and higher transportation costs, the United Mine Workers continues to sanction wage differentials between the Alabama and the Appalachian bituminous areas. The Textile Workers' Union of America has sanctioned differentials between Virginia and the New York metropolitan area. Very often, local unions in a strategic bargaining situation have been called upon by the national union to forego the maximum wage increase which they might have been able to obtain from local employers simply because the national policy was to establish uniform rates which would be borne by employers generally over a wider geographic area. Uniform wages, these unions feel, increase union solidarity and lessen cleavages within the union ranks.

The difficulty of organizing workers in the South, combined with the low wages of this area, has served as a brake on North–South wage differentials in certain industries. Unable to organize the South, the hosiery and textile workers have seen lower southern rates keep down their wage gains in the North; other unionized mills in the North have either migrated South, where they operate nonunion, or gone out of business. The failure of the United Mine Workers to organize southern coal mines in the 1920s almost destroyed the union. The northern mines were forced to break with the United Mine Workers in order to compete with the low-wage South. The rising number of southern Appalachian mines which

---

[32] *Ibid.*, p. 78, finds that "over the past 60 years there has been little change in the general differential in wages between the South and the remainder of the country." Other investigators, however, have found some evidence that the differential is narrowing. See *Monthly Labor Review*, Vol. 91 (April 1968), p. 44.

now operate nonunion at lower wage and fringe benefit rates is again a severe problem for the UMW.

In these cases, the problem of the regional differential to the union is the problem of union and nonunion competition. The problem of the North–South differential is less acute when the unionized high-wage employers are located in and sell to a market such as the Far West, which, because of distance and geographic factors, is primarily local and is not sensitive to southern competition.

Geographical Diversity: City Size

While average hourly earnings are generally highest in the West and lowest in the South, within each region of this country it has been found that city size has a major impact upon wages no matter what kind of labor is being hired: men or women, white or nonwhite, skilled or unskilled, well schooled or uneducated.

Generally, the bigger the city, the higher the wage. The city-size wage differential is largest in the South and among blacks and workers with limited education. A man in the South, regardless of race, living in or near a city with a population of more than a million, makes 35% more than the average wage earner outside metropolitan areas. A big-city Negro in the South will make 37% more, and a person with fewer than four years of schooling, 63% more.[33]

The reasons for differentials of this magnitude are not fully understood. While differences in cost of living have some relevance to this problem, statistical studies show that intercity differences in cost of living are relatively small compared to differentials in hourly earnings.

Whatever the explanation, the fact remains that these differentials do exist and attest to a lack of fluidity of labor and capital between geographical areas, which is somewhat surprising in our dynamic economy. In recent years, there has been some tendency for industry to move out of the central cities, motivated by the desire to avoid the traffic congestion and high tax rates of those areas as much as anything. This move, if it continues, coupled with the tendency of labor to move to the big cities, could in time narrow the differentials which now exist.

Interindustry Differentials

Marked differences in rates and earnings prevail among various industries for similar jobs, even in the same geographical area. The existence of industrial differentials does not necessarily mean that workers performing comparable jobs are paid at different rates in different industries, though this is sometimes the case. One industry may pay lower

---

[33] *Business Week*, March 11, 1967, p. 175.

rates on the average than another because less skill is required in the industry; because of the larger percentage of women, blacks, or part-time workers employed; because of the location of plants in small towns or rural areas rather than in metropolitan areas; or because of the lack of union organization.

There appears to have been no significant trend toward the broadening or narrowing of industrial differentials in hourly earnings since 1947. The data in Table 8–3 support the thesis of the persistence of inter-industry wage differentials, especially insofar as hourly rates are concerned. There are, of course, changes as some industries decline in employment or profitability and others advance, or new ones arise. But the overall picture seems to be one of maintenance of differentials.

TABLE 8–3

Average Hourly Earnings of Production or Nonsupervisory Workers in Private Payrolls by Industry Division, Selected Years, 1947–71 (in dollars)

	1947	1951	1961	1971
Contract construction	1.54	2.02	3.20	5.70
Mining	1.47	1.93	2.64	4.04
Durable goods manufacturing	1.28	1.65	2.49	3.80
Wholesale trade	1.22	1.52	2.31	3.67
Nondurable goods manufacturing	1.15	1.44	2.11	3.26
Finance, insurance, real estate	1.14	1.45	2.09	3.28
Retail trade	0.84	1.06	1.56	2.57

Source: U.S. Department of Labor, *Manpower Report of the President, 1972* (Washington, D.C.: U.S. Government Printing Office, 1972), Table C–3, p. 217.

Differences among industries in earnings can be attributable to such factors as unionization, region, productivity, degree of concentration within an industry, capitalization relative to labor inputs, and average establishment size. Determination of the degree of influence exerted by each of these factors in isolation is rendered difficult because one or more of these factors is usually interrelated. Thus, for example, it has generally been found that concentrated industries in which a large part of total industry volume is produced by a few firms generally pay higher wages than less concentrated industries. The theoretical explanation of this circumstance would be that such concentrated industries would enjoy higher profits because of the exercise of a degree of monopoly power in the marketplace and therefore could be expected to pay higher wages. However, it has also been found that concentrated industries are also characterized by strong unions, large establishments, and high capital input ratios. Each of these conditions might also be expected to be associated with higher than average wage levels. One study compared the earnings of workers in concentrated industries with workers in non-concentrated industries who exhibited similar personal characteristics, such as age, sex, and educational attainment. Although earnings of workers in concentrated industries were indeed relatively high, it was found that their earnings were no higher than the earnings received by workers with similar characteristics in other industries.[34]

The interindustry wage differential does not seem to have been narrowed substantially by unionism. Yet pattern bargaining, followed by major unions and major industries, may tend to equalize wage adjustments among major industries. This is not contradictory—first, because the adjustments made in bargains tend to be equal but not to equalize the wage structures upon which they were added; and second, because the persistently low-paying industries are often not pattern bargainers even if unionized, which they frequently are not. Thus, the lower wage structure of the latter group of industries tends to be maintained by the interrelated economic and power structure upon which it rests.

Interfirm Differentials

Even within the same industry and geographic locality, different firms will pay different rates for similar jobs. The reason is that an employer offers more than a wage to compensate his employees. There may be more "prestige" in working for one employer than another. Or the plant may be newer, or more accessible. Management representatives, such as foremen, may be more skilled in dealing with employees. It takes a mixture of many qualities to build up the reputation of a company as a good place to work. The wage, therefore, is only one part of the total package of benefits which the employer holds out to his employees.

Some companies have a deliberate policy of paying more than the market, or more than their competitors, for labor, believing that in the long run this will bring them a better type of worker and greater productivity. One investigation based upon a study of metalworking and soft-goods industries found that despite some industry variation, wage differentials based on size of establishment in the order of 20%–25% on a national basis were fairly typical for most of these industries, except textiles and clothing. In large establishments, compensation in the form of fringe benefits averaged about double in cents per hour what was paid by small establishments.[35] However, it is difficult to isolate the effect of size alone on wage rates and earnings. As one book has pointed out, the real

---

[34] Leonard Weiss, "Concentration and Labor Earnings," *American Economic Review*, Vol. 56 (March 1966), p. 115.

[35] Richard Lester, "Pay Differentials by Size of Establishment," *Industrial Relations*, Vol. 7 (October 1967), p. 66.

relation may be with rate of profit, union power, or occupational skill mix, all of which may vary substantially between large and small firms.[36]

Personal Differentials: Sex

While jobs may be alike, no two workers are the same. They bring to their respective jobs different skills, education, motivation, physical strength, and other attributes. We can understand why two workers with different educational backgrounds will be compensated at different rates. We may sympathize with the less educated worker and attempt to provide additional training for him, but there is no national policy which frowns on wage differentials based upon such factors. However, as a matter of national policy we do not approve of wage differentials based solely upon sex or race. Nevertheless, such differentials continue to persist in the labor market.

In 1959, hourly earnings data indicate that women on the average earned only 60% as much as the average male worker.[37] Recent figures on median weekly earnings of workers in spring 1971 show little change in this differential,[38] despite enactment of antidiscrimination laws during the interim and despite the fact that women have moved into higher paid and more responsible positions in industry (see Table 8–4). Of course, such gross data tell us nothing about conditions of remuneration for the same job in the same plant under identical working conditions. A major source of the difference in the median for weekly earnings is that women tend to work fewer hours per week and also have a greater concentration in clerical, sales, and service industries where wages are characteristically low.

The male-female differential can be explained—but it is troublesome nonetheless. For equal years of schooling, the differential between male and female workers in hourly earnings has been much larger than the differential between whites and blacks.[39] The differential varies considerably from one industry or occupation to another. It is least in government employment and largest in service industries such as retail trade where large numbers of women are customarily employed. It is a significant fact that most men work in occupations that employ very few women, and a significant fraction of women work in occupations that employ very few men.[40] One recent study concludes that the differential

---

[36] Albert Rees and George P. Shultz, *Workers and Wages in an Urban Labor Market* (Chicago, Ill.: University of Chicago Press, 1970), p. 7.

[37] Victor Fuchs, "Differences in Hourly Earnings between Men and Women, *Monthly Labor Review*, Vol. 94 (May 1971), pp. 9–15.

[38] Paul O. Flaim and Nicholas Peters, "Usual Weekly Earnings of American Workers," *Monthly Labor Review*, Vol. 95 (March 1972), p. 30.

[39] Fuchs, "Differences in Hourly Earnings," p. 9.

[40] *Ibid.*, p. 14.

TABLE 8–4

Medians of Usual Weekly Earnings of Full-Time[1] Wage and Salary Workers, by Color, Sex, and Industry, May 1971

Industry	All persons	Medians of usual weekly earnings [2]			
		White		Negro	
		Male	Female	Male	Female
Total	$139	$168	$103	$123	$88
Agriculture	80	89	......	63	......
Mining	168	173	......	......	......
Construction	171	181	119	120	......
Manufacturing	141	165	99	125	86
Durable goods	149	167	108	132	95
Nondurable goods	127	160	91	113	81
Transportation and public utilities	161	178	114	131	108
Wholesale and retail trade	119	150	83	110	79
Wholesale trade	153	174	107	116	......
Retail trade	110	141	80	109	77
Private household work	40	......	35	......	44
Finance, insurance, and real estate	131	193	103	118	100
Miscellaneous services [3]	132	173	116	123	92
Business and repair	139	163	110	123	......
Personal services	85	123	71	92	76
Entertainment, recreation	128	169	89	......	......
Professional services	137	182	122	132	99
Medical, except hospitals	104	169	101	......	79
Hospitals	114	145	110	127	92
Welfare, religon	120	141	108	......	......
Educational services	156	189	141	132	120
Other professional services	170	[4] +200	117	......	......
Public administration	165	183	127	156	131
Postal	161	165	......	156	......
Other federal	182	[4] +200	140	149	122
State	148	172	122	......	......
Local	156	174	114	165	124

[1] The full-time worker definition shown in this table, differs slightly from the definition used in other tables. It does not cover persons working less than 35 hours a week because of economic reasons. However, since the number of such persons is very small relative to the total for full-time workers (1 million out of 58 million), their exclusion has only a minimal effect on the medians for the various groups.

[2] Medians not shown where number of workers is less than 75,000.

[3] Includes forestries and fisheries, not shown separately.

[4] Exact median not computed where it fell above $200.

Source: Paul O. Flaim and Nicholas Peters, "Usual Weekly Earnings of American Workers," *Monthly Labor Review,* Vol. 95 (March 1972), p. 35.

in hourly earnings between men and women does not reflect employment discrimination on the part of employers, but rather the effect of the different roles assigned by our society to men and women. Such role differentiation affects the choice of occupation, labor force attachment, location of work, postschool investment, hours of work, and other variables that affect earnings.[41]

Differentials in earnings related to sex result not so much from payment of different rates for the same job as from the restriction of job opportunities. Since many women work only part-time or prior to marriage, they do not gain seniority, acquire skills, or obtain promotion to higher

---

[41] *Ibid.*

paying jobs. Moreover, as a matter of custom, women have generally been afforded employment in jobs which pay less than jobs available to men. When comparisons are made of rates for men and women in the same job in the same establishment, it is found that sex-wage differentials narrow substantially and in some instances disappear.[42]

Nevertheless, discrimination against female workers does exist in the American economy, in violation of federal law. The Equal Pay Act requires employers to pay both sexes equal compensation for work demanding equal skill, effort, and responsibility; but it allows for wage differentials based upon seniority, merit, quality and quantity of work performed, and other factors unrelated to sex. As of June 1971, over $33.5 million had been found owing to nearly 84,000 employees, almost all of them women, as a result of discrimination in violation of the terms of the Equal Pay Act.[43]

Personal Differentials: Race

The earnings of black workers are substantially less than those of their white counterparts. Here, too, there is considerable variation among industries and occupations. Generally, where blacks and whites do the same work in the same plant, the racial differential, once prevalent, has been eliminated. But, as was indicated in Chapter I, blacks are concentrated in the lower paying jobs and in the lower paying industries, have a higher unemployment rate, and receive less pay for the same education. The discrimination suffered by the Negro in the American economy is graphically illustrated by the fact that the average income of black college graduates is about the same as that of white high school graduates in both central cities and suburbs.[44]

During the 1950s, there was no narrowing of the gap in median family incomes between Negroes and other races on the one hand and whites on the other. However, since 1960, the ratio of median family income received by Negroes and other races as a percentage of white median family income has risen from 55% to 64% in 1970.[45] Table 8–5 indicates that the extent of the differential in median income of husbands in skilled and semiskilled occupations varies considerably by region, but the gap has narrowed since 1960 in all areas.

---

[42] John E. Buckley, "Pay Differences between Men and Women in the Same Job," *Monthly Labor Review,* Vol. 94 (November 1971), p. 39.

[43] *Ibid.*

[44] *Manpower Report, 1971,* p. 93.

[45] U.S. Department of Commerce, Bureau of Census, *The Social and Economic Status of Negroes in the United States, 1970* (BLS Report No. 394 [Washington, D.C.: U.S. Government Printing Office, July 1971]), p. 25.

TABLE 8-5

Median Income of Husbands in Skilled and Semiskilled Occupations, 1960–70

	1960			1966			1970		
Area	*White*	*Non-White*	*% of White*	*White*	*Non-White*	*% of White*	*White*	*Non-White*	*% of White*
Total U.S.........	$6,408	$4,213	66	$6,998	$5,032	72	$8,025	$5,979	75
Total South.......	5,546	3,054	55	6,114	3,842	63	7,070	4,758	67
Metropolitan....	6,266	3,551	57	6,752	4,275	63	7,830	5,525	71
Outside metro-									
politan........	4,730	2,394	51	5,464	3,089	57	6,411	4,012	63
Total Non-South...	6,616	5,565	84	7,468	6,094	82	8,402	7,242	86
Metropolitan....	6,838	5,546	81	7,874	6,056	77	8,806	7,286	83
Outside metro-									
politan........	6,068	(X)	(X)	6,711	(X)	(X)	7,616	(X)	(X)

(X)—Less than 75,000 in category.
Source: Ray Marshall, "Trends in Black Income and Employment," *AFL–CIO American Federationist,* Vol 77 (July 1971), pp. 6–7.

DIFFERENCES IN OCCUPATIONAL REMUNERATION

In 1971, the president of International Telephone & Telegraph Corporation received a salary and bonus of $812,494, the highest of any American chief executive.[46] In the same year, the average Class I draftsman earned $6,805.[47] What is the reason for this great disparity of earnings? Does the variation in earnings in a capitalistic society reflect differences in ability, or are other factors responsible?

In the same year, median weekly earnings of white-collar workers were $153, while median weekly earnings for blue-collar workers were $136. Median weekly earnings for private household workers were only $38 (see Table 8–6). How can these differentials continue to maintain themselves in the marketplace? Why is there not continual movement from low-paying to high-paying jobs, so that such differentials would be erased over time? The answers to these questions are complex. Economic theorists attempt to explain the differentials which exist in the marketplace in terms of equalizing differences, nonequalizing differences, and by elaborating a theory of noncompeting groups in the labor market.

Equalizing Differences

Not all occupations are equally attractive to workers. Therefore, even if every worker had freedom of choice as to the type of work he would perform, we would expect that certain jobs which were less attractive would have to offer higher pay in order to attract workers,

[46] *Time,* May 1, 1972, p. 74.
[47] U.S. Department of Labor, *Handbook of Labor Statistics, 1971,* p. 212.

TABLE 8–6

Usual Weekly Earnings of Full-Time Wage and Salary Workers, by Occupation, May 1971

Occupation	Number of workers (in thousands)	Percent distribution by earnings						Median earnings
		Total	Under $60	$60–99	$100–149	$150–199	$200 or more	
All occupations	57,642	100.0	6.3	20.4	30.0	21.0	22.3	$138
White-collar workers	28,284	100.0	4.6	16.1	28.0	20.7	30.7	153
Professional and technical workers	8,849	100.0	3.4	5.2	20.5	26.4	44.5	189
Engineers	1,093	100.0	.1	.5	5.7	15.3	78.3	+200 [1]
Medical personnel	1,065	100.0	3.5	9.3	29.6	29.5	28.2	162
Teachers (except college)	2,415	100.0	4.5	5.6	26.2	32.2	31.5	171
Other professionals	4,276	100.0	3.6	5.1	18.7	25.2	47.4	194
Managers, officials, and proprietors	6,005	100.0	2.7	5.8	17.1	20.5	53.9	+200 [1]
Clerical workers	10,320	100.0	5.2	29.8	42.2	16.4	6.3	115
Steno, typists, and secretaries	2,975	100.0	5.3	28.9	49.1	13.8	2.8	113
Other clerical workers	7,344	100.0	5.2	30.2	39.4	17.5	7.7	116
Salesworkers	3,109	100.0	9.5	21.2	22.9	19.0	27.4	141
Retail sales	1,531	100.0	16.6	36.5	25.7	10.8	10.3	95
Other sales	1,579	100.0	2.8	6.3	20.2	26.8	44.0	188
Blue-collar workers	22,368	100.0	3.5	21.2	34.0	24.6	16.8	136
Craftsmen and foremen	8,565	100.0	1.3	8.6	29.3	31.6	29.2	167
Carpenters	638	100.0	3.0	11.1	28.6	26.1	31.2	164
Other construction craftsmen	1,660	100.0	1.2	9.8	23.7	28.2	37.1	177
Foremen	1,349	100.0	.4	5.3	22.5	27.3	44.6	190
Machinists	523	100.0	.6	4.6	35.4	39.3	20.1	161
Mechanics, automobile	685	100.0	2.3	15.1	36.8	30.8	14.9	144
Mechanics, other	1,322	100.0	.6	7.9	34.7	34.3	22.4	159
Metal craftsmen	545	100.0	1.1	2.9	29.2	37.9	28.9	172
Other craftsmen	1,842	100.0	1.7	9.9	31.5	33.8	23.0	160
Operatives	10,927	100.0	4.2	29.0	36.5	20.8	9.4	120
Drivers and deliverymen	2,121	100.0	2.6	16.6	35.7	26.1	19.0	143
Motor vehicles and equipment	434	100.0	---	6.7	32.3	48.4	12.7	161
Other durable goods industries	3,714	100.0	2.5	24.7	42.3	22.2	8.3	124
Nondurable goods industries	3,074	100.0	4.9	46.2	33.4	11.4	4.1	98
Nonmanufacturing industries	1,584	100.0	10.4	28.6	31.4	21.0	8.8	115
Nonfarm laborers	2,877	100.0	6.9	28.6	38.3	18.6	7.6	117
Construction	674	100.0	4.4	27.4	31.7	21.3	15.1	123
Manufacturing	924	100.0	3.8	27.5	46.5	16.3	5.9	119
All other industries	1,279	100.0	10.3	29.9	35.8	18.9	5.0	113
Service workers	6,283	100.0	21.4	34.6	26.0	11.4	6.6	91
Private household workers	544	100.0	73.9	21.1	3.3	1.1	.6	38
Other service workers	5,739	100.0	16.4	35.9	28.2	12.4	7.2	96
Protective services	952	100.0	1.5	9.3	30.7	32.9	25.7	163
Waiters, cooks, and kindred	1,228	100.0	31.0	39.9	18.4	7.3	3.5	75
Other services	3,558	100.0	15.3	41.6	30.8	8.6	3.5	91
Farmworkers [2]	706	100.0	31.7	39.5	19.6	5.7	3.4	74
Farm laborers	669	100.0	32.8	40.5	19.3	4.9	2.2	72

[1] Exact median could not be computed where it fell above $200.
[2] Includes farm managers, not shown separately.
Source: Paul O. Flaim and Nicholas Peters, "Usual Weekly Earnings of American Workers," *Monthly Labor Review*, Vol. 95 (March 1972), p. 35.

while positions in which working conditions were particularly satisfactory would be able to obtain workers at lower wages. In other words, a part of the differences in wage rates which we observe in the labor market represents a factor which equalizes the attractiveness of various occupations. For example, the low salaries of college professors are partially offset by the short hours of work, the long vacations, and the opportunity for research and study. Women who work as domestics in homes frequently receive more than women who perform clerical tasks in business because, according to our social mores, working as a servant is looked upon as somewhat degrading, and therefore additional compensation must be offered in these jobs to equalize their attractiveness with other positions these women might obtain.

There are many other equalizing factors which balance differences in wages. For example, the clerk in the head office of a large company will be willing to start at a lower wage than a day laborer in the same plant because the opportunities for advancement open to the clerk make up for the deficiency in his entrance salary. Similarly, an occupation in which there is a chance, however small, of making very great earnings—as in the practice of law—is able to attract applicants who are willing to start as clerks at little or no wage. Hazard to life is another factor producing wage differences—the pilot who tests new planes for an aircraft company receives a very high wage in order to compensate him for the risk to life involved in his work.

Another important equalizing difference is the expense of training. The doctor expects a higher remuneration for his work than a carpenter because the expense of his training is so much greater. In 1969, median annual earnings of heads of families employed in white-collar jobs was over $2,000 in excess of the earnings for blue-collar workers.[48] A substantial part of this differential is accounted for by differences in education. White-collar workers are considerably better educated as a group than blue-collar workers. The proportions of each group completing 13–15 years of education are about one fifth for professional, managerial, and clerical and about one fourth for sales workers, compared to only 7% for the blue-collar group.[49] Thus, a part of the higher remuneration of the professional class generally is reimbursement for long years of study. However, as we shall see, differences in remuneration may exist which are not merely equalizing but are out of proportion to the expenses of education and training.

In actuality, most differences in wages in the labor market do not seem to be of an equalizing character. Indeed, they are more often the reverse. Instead of the most unattractive work being the best remunerated, it is usually the poorest paid. It is the ditchdigger and the garbage collector—not the movie actor—who receive the least remuneration for their labor.

Nonequalizing Differences

Broad differences in wages prevail which bear no relation to the relative attractiveness of the work involved. The first great source of such differences is the lack of uniformity in physical and mental capabilities among the working population. Even if every worker had freedom of choice to enter any occupation, it is obvious that few would have the talents—physical or mental—to be great scientists, writers, or boxers. The extent to which such abilities are a result of training and environmental factors is still a subject of debate among psychologists, but it is evident that all workers are not equally gifted by inheritance. Those talents which are prized most highly by the community and which are least common among workers tend to be remunerated with the highest earnings.

---

[48] Robert L. Stein and J. N. Hedges, "Blue-Collar/White-Collar Pay Trends, Earnings and Family Income," *Monthly Labor Review*, Vol. 94 (June 1971), p. 13.
[49] *Ibid.*, p. 20.

Even in more humdrum occupations, such as machine operation or assembly production, differences in ability and dexterity among workers will be reflected in large variations in earnings if the workers are paid by the piece or on an incentive basis. Industrial psychologists have found that individual differences in dexterity, for example, are very great. It is not at all uncommon for some pieceworkers on a job to earn twice that of others doing the same work.

Another important cause of differences is the fact that all occupations are not equally easy to enter. Even in our free enterprise society, in which class lines are not firmly drawn, social strata emerge which render it difficult for the poor son of a laborer to rise to be the head of a great corporation. Examples of such spectacular successes are often cited, but they represent the exception, not the norm.

Differences in ability and in training account for only a part of the wide variations which exist in compensation of members of the labor force. Sometimes the amount of money a person receives for his work will depend more on who his father is or what business his relatives control than upon his own ability or training. Nepotism—favoritism shown to relatives in employment—is a factor not only in politics but also in the labor market.

Noncompeting Groups

The labor market is characterized by a vast number of noncompeting groups, as will be more fully explained at a later point in this discussion. However, in terms of occupational differentiation, five broad strata can be distinguished in the ranks of employees. At the lowest level, in terms of pay and social position, is the common laborer, working either on the farm or in industry and performing work which requires a minimum of skill and a maximum of brawn. His wages are low because there are very many persons in the labor market who can do such simple work and can do no other. Many workers find an entry into such occupations who would be excluded from other types of positions. Thus, the Negro, the immigrant, and various other minority or foreign-born groups make up a large proportion of this lower stratum.

At a somewhat higher wage come the semiskilled. These are workers who have ordinarily had some education and have acquired some knowledge of a technical art but who, for one reason or another, have not served the necessary years of apprenticeship to become skilled artisans.

Above them come the skilled workers—carpenters, boilermakers, bakers, and so on. Most of these men have union cards and the benefit of a considerable period of apprenticeship behind them. That they consider themselves in some respects superior to less skilled fellow workers is demonstrated by the clannishness of the skilled craftsmen in the American Federation of Labor, which, for many years, refused to accept unskilled workmen into membership.

The next group on the ladder of social status—the clerical workers—
are frequently below the skilled and sometimes below the semiskilled in
terms of remuneration. For example, in 1971, craftsmen, the highest paid
classification within the blue-collar group, earned more than the median
for clerical and sales personnel, who are the lowest paid of the white-
collar group (see Table 8–6). Nevertheless, in outlook and social allegiance, clerical workers tend to be allied with the professional and capitalist class. This is a major reason why union organization has made only
slight inroads in this group.

The top group in the labor market, in terms of pay and social prestige,
are the professional workers—the doctors, dentists, lawyers, architects,
engineers, professors, and others who have generally trained for their
occupations in college and through advanced study—and the managerial
groups and self-employed businessmen.

Although there is considerable movement between these groups,
nevertheless, to some extent the strata become self-perpetuating. In other
words, the son of a doctor is likely to become a member of a profession,
while the son of a common laborer is more likely to be a laborer or, at
best, a skilled worker. A study by the Bureau of Labor Statistics of
mobility in the labor market found that there was comparatively little
shifting from blue-collar (craftsmen, operatives, and nonfarm laborers) to
white-collar (professional, managerial, clerical, and sales) occupations.
Only about 12% of the men who changed occupations and held white-
collar jobs in 1966 had been blue-collar workers a year earlier; for women
the comparable proportion was only 5%.[50]

The greatest barrier to movement up the social ladder is the cost and
time required for education and training. The poor laborer would like his
son to go to college, and it may be that the son is bright enough to win a
scholarship. But all too frequently, a career is blighted because the son
must leave school in order to go to work and earn money toward the
support of the family. Family income is related to occupational status. It is
obvious that the farm operator, unskilled worker, or service worker will
have great difficulty in sending a child to college. The GI Bill of Rights
had a major effect on the degree of mobility between these various
groups. It afforded higher education to thousands of men who would
otherwise have been denied the opportunity because of lack of funds.
These men will want their children to have the same opportunity, and
they will be better able to give them this opportunity because they
themselves have left schools and colleges equipped for higher paying jobs
in industry.

If we define as "the skill differential" the percentage difference between the hourly earnings of workers designated as skilled and those
designated as unskilled, then most writers would agree that there has been

---

[50] Saben, "Mobility of Employed Workers," pp. 34–35.

a secular tendency for the skill differential to diminish.[51] Thus, for example, the skill differential was cut by nearly one half during the first 50 years of the 20th century.[52] Although the emphasis of industrial unions, such as the United Automobile Workers, on cents-per-hour increases, which raise rates of lower paid workers relative to higher paid workers, undoubtedly contributed to the narrowing of the differential between skilled and unskilled, other more basic forces were also at work to bring about this change. Even in the building trades, which are organized and bargain on a craft basis, there was a marked narrowing of differentials between skilled and unskilled workers.

One basic reason for the relative improvement in wages of unskilled workers has been the metamorphosis in the type of work performed by "unskilled" workers. The ditchdigger now uses a machine; unskilled labor is now being combined with more capital than in the past, with the result that its productivity and wages have been substantially increased. In this connection, it is perhaps significant that after World War II, the U.S. Bureau of Labor Statistics discontinued its annual survey of the entrance rates of male common labor because of the increasing difficulty of obtaining reasonably comparable reporting among firms and industries for a "common labor" classification of workers.

Another reason for the relative rise in wages of lower paid workers may be the changing conditions of supply for the two groups in the labor market. On the one hand, there has been a substantial reduction in immigration in the past few decades. In earlier years, when large numbers of immigrants were coming into this country, many of the foreign born could be attracted at low rates to jobs involving manual unskilled work. There is also the possibility that with a rising educational attainment of the labor force, there has been a secular increase in the relative supply of skilled workers or of people who would be inclined to gravitate to such jobs rather than to the unskilled level.

At the same time as the gap between unskilled and skilled workers has been narrowed, the differential between unskilled and white-collar workers has also been reduced and in some cases eliminated. Some professional groups now find their average hourly earnings below those of skilled workers, or even below those of essentially unskilled groups such as over-the-road truck drivers. On the other hand, industrial unions, which once concentrated on raising the rates of the unskilled, are now emphasizing percentage wage adjustments to increase the skill differentials as a result of pressure from the craftsmen within their ranks. In some recent settlements, this pressure has resulted in separate and larger adjust-

---

[51] See Melvin W. Reder, "The Occupational Wage Structure," in Campbell R. McConnell (ed.), *Perspectives on Wage Determination* (New York: McGraw-Hill Book Co., 1970). p. 200.

[52] W. S. Woytinsky and Associates, *Employment and Wages in the United States* (New York: Twentieth Century Fund, 1953), p. 342.

ments for skilled workers who otherwise threatened not to abide by the union agreement.

Although various studies document the fact that occupational wage differentials have narrowed when measured in terms of hourly or weekly earnings, over the past 30 years such differentials measured in terms of annual earnings have changed very little.[53] However, studies by the Bureau of Census and the Bureau of Labor Statistics indicate that during the 1960s there was a slightly faster rise in pay for white-collar jobs requiring extended educational preparation than in wages of blue-collar and white-collar jobs requiring little or no training. One exception to this trend must be noted: the earnings of laborers rose relative to those of other groups, probably due to the fact that compensation of persons at this low level in the pay scale received more impetus from increases in coverage and level of the minimum wage provided under federal law.[54]

Unions and Wage Differentials

Traditionally, it was thought that the competitive norm in the labor market was uniformity of rates for comparable jobs and that only imperfections in the market permitted differentials to persist. Based on this premise, it would seem to follow that the introduction of a union into a labor market—since it represents a departure from free competition in the market—would produce even greater variation in wage rates for similar jobs. What has been the effect of unions in practice?

In the first place, in the individual firm the advent of the union compels the employer to reexamine and justify his internal wage structure. As a result, management in organized plants has been compelled to set up job evaluation plans and in general to eliminate unjustified differentials between similar jobs. "Personal differentials have largely been eliminated or brought under formal control in unionized sectors."[55]

In the second place, when unions bargain with a number of companies in an industry, they have—as we have already observed earlier in this discussion—exerted strong pressure to achieve uniformity in rates for similar jobs in the various companies with which they bargain. This has affected area differentials as well as differentials within the same labor market and has tended to eliminate or to reduce both.

Occupational differentials have also tended to diminish over time. Here, the effect of union policies is probably a factor, but other forces in the labor market are likely to have had the most substantial effect.

[53] Arthur Sackley and Thomas W. Gavett, "Blue-Collar/White-Collar Pay Trends: Analysis of Occupational Wage Differences," *Monthly Labor Review* Vol. 94 (June 1971), p. 10.

[54] *Ibid.*

[55] Clark Kerr, "Wage Relationships—The Comparative Impact of Market and Power Forces," in J. T. Dunlop (ed.), *The Theory of Wage Determination* (London: Macmillan & Co., Ltd., 1957), p. 181.

Interindustry differentials have continued to persist over long periods of time. They do not seem to be substantially narrowed by unionism. Likewise, differentials on the basis of race or sex continue to endure.

The interesting question that remains is: Have unions tended to introduce a new type of differential in the labor market—a differential between union and nonunion companies? Published data generally indicate that wages are higher in union than in nonunion plants within the

TABLE 8–7

Average Straight-Time Hourly Earnings[1] of Men in Selected Occupations in Union Establishments as a Percent of the Average for Corresponding Occupations in Nonunion Plants, Selected Manufacturing Industries (average hourly earnings in nonunion plants = 100)

Industry and pay periods	Skilled occupations[2]	Unskilled occupations[2]
Textile mill products:		
Textile dyeing and finishing—Winter 1965–66	103	116
Apparel and other textile products:		
Men's and boys' shirts, except work, and nightwear—		
October 1968	109	104
Work clothing—February 1968	98	100
Furniture and fixtures:		
Wood household furniture, except upholstered—		
October 1968	105	105
Chemicals and allied products:		
Industrial chemicals—November 1965	100	115
Paints and varnishes—November 1965	100	116
Rubber and plastics products:		
Miscellaneous plastics products—August 1969	96	104
Primary metals industries:		
Gray iron foundries, except pipe and fittings—		
November 1967	106	117
Steel foundries—November 1967	104	115
Nonferrous foundries—June–July 1965	108	118
Machinery, except electrical:		
Construction and related machinery—mid-1966	112	117
General industry machinery—mid-1966	99	101
Metalworking machinery—mid-1966	103	111
Office and computing machine—mid-1966	100	103
Special industry machines—mid-1966	105	118

[1] Excludes premium pay for overtime and for work on weekends, holidays, and late shifts.

[2] Pay relatives for skilled and unskilled occupations shown above are averages of regional pay relatives where at least 3 regions were involved. Regions were held constant within industries in computing relatives for skilled and unskilled jobs.

Source: Sandra L. Mason, "Comparing Union and Nonunion Wages in Manufacturing," *Monthly Labor Review*, Vol. 94 (May 1971), p. 22.

same industry.[56] This does not imply that the presence of unions is causally related to the higher level of wages. Unions are more likely to be found in larger plants (in terms of number of employees) and are likely to be more concentrated in metropolitan areas than nonunion plants. With few exceptions studies have indicated that average earnings are higher in large than in small establishments and higher in metropolitan areas than in smaller communities.

As can be seen from Table 8–7, the size of the wage differential varies

---

[56] See, for example, Sandra L. Mason, "Comparing Union and Nonunion Wages in Manufacturing," *Monthly Labor Review*, Vol. 94 (May 1971). pp. 20–26.

considerably by industry, and in a few industries is actually negative. It is also worth noting that in this particular compilation union-nonunion wage differentials were higher for unskilled than for skilled occupations. These findings appear to support the contention that unions have a greater effect on the wages of the unskilled than upon compensation of the skilled. However, care must be exercised in imputing causal relationships to the correlation.

Comparison of data obtained from various studies conducted by the Bureau of Labor Statistics during the past decade suggest that the union-nonunion wage differential is narrowing.[57] However, the data refer only to average straight-time earnings and do not reflect changes in fringe benefits. It is well established that the proportion of total employee compensation directed to payments for nonwage benefits is higher in union than in nonunion plants, and this emphasis upon fringe benefits may have been further accentuated during recent years.

It should be apparent from this brief discussion that it is difficult to isolate the precise effect which unionism has on wage differentials because of the concurring influence of factors such as size of firm and concentration of the industry. Another factor which enters into differentials is the personal element—do the unionized firms attract more productive people? One study found that employees in concentrated industries and in unionized industries had relatively high earnings, but when allowance was made for the personal qualities which might relate to productivity, the concentration effect virtually disappeared and the union effect was reduced to perhaps 6% to 8% and was barely significant statistically.[58]

We shall consider the problem of the effect of union organization upon wage rates in more detail in Chapter 13. At this point, however, it can be stated that even those economists who do not believe that unions can alter basic wage relationships so as to be a source of comparative advantage to their members will concede that unions can alter wage relationships to the benefit of their members in three special circumstances: (1) where unions are new and aggressive and may be offsetting prior monopsony power of employers; (2) where there have been periods of substantial unemployment and in the absence of union contractual arrangements wage rates would tend to fall; and (3) where craft unions control the supply of labor and thereby push up the wage.

Supply and Demand in the Labor Market

We have seen that the labor market differs materially from the market for wheat, which we considered at the beginning of this chapter.

---

[57] *Ibid.*, p. 22.

[58] L. W. Weiss, "Concentration and Labor Earnings," *American Economic Review*, Vol. 56 (March 1966), pp. 96–117.

Diverse rates, rather than a single rate, typically prevail for a given type of labor in the labor market. There is no one market price—even for a particular grade of labor. Buyers and sellers are able to make bargains at a variety of rates.

How, then, do supply and demand fit into this picture? It will be recalled that we have defined the labor market in terms of a geographical area. Because labor is highly immobile, unemployed workers in a labor market tend to remain in the area rather than to seek jobs in a different market. The existence of this excess labor supply has a downward effect on wages—felt more strongly by nonunion than by union workers, but by both nonetheless.

Despite the existence of noncompeting groups, therefore, if there is a decline in business, and therefore in demand for labor in a particular area, which produces some unemployment, this change in demand will ultimately make its influence felt on the whole structure of wage rates in the community. Likewise, if the supply of labor in a local market is reduced, say, by drafting men for the army who would otherwise become additions to the labor force, this influence, too, will have its ultimate effect on wage levels.

Supply and demand—two traditional conceptual tools of economists —have not, therefore, been rendered useless by our changed conception of the labor market. Supply and demand do not interact to produce a single rate in the market, but they do influence the level of the whole structure of diverse rates that characterizes the actual labor market. In the next two chapters, we shall consider in detail what demand and supply mean in terms of labor and the labor market.

QUESTIONS FOR DISCUSSION

1. What factors are responsible for the existence of diverse rates for similar jobs in the same labor market? What effect would you expect union organization to have upon such diversity of rates? Why?
2. Discuss the theory of noncompeting groups. Of what value is this theory in explaining actual differences in remuneration in the labor market?
3. If you were an employer, would you pay national rates or community rates if you had plants in both North and South?

SUGGESTIONS FOR FURTHER READING

BLAU, PETER M., and DUNCAN, OTIS D. *The American Occupational Structure.* New York: John Wiley & Sons, Inc. 1967.

An empirical analysis of the determinants of occupational position and mobility of American workers, with special attention given to the effects of race, religion, migration, and farm background on occupational status.

FLAIM, PAUL O., and PETERS, NICHOLAS I. "Usual Weekly Earnings of American Workers," *Monthly Labor Review,* Vol. 95 (March 1972), pp. 28–38.

An up-to-date article which analyzes data on weekly earnings by race, sex, industry, occupation, and other relevant characteristics.

GALLAWAY, LOWELL E. "The Significance of the Labor Market," in ROWAN, RICHARD L. (ed.), *Readings in Labor Economics and Labor Relations*, pp. 418–27. Homewood, Ill.: Richard D. Irwin, Inc., 1972.

A discussion of the relationship of the labor market, unemployment, and economic growth.

MAHER, JOHN E. "Unions and Wage Differentials," in McCONNELL, CAMPBELL R. (ed.), *Perspectives on Wage Determination*, pp. 218–25. New York: McGraw-Hill Book Co., 1970.

A concise review of empirical studies attempting to measure the effect of unions on wage differentials.

MASTERS, STANLEY H. "An Interindustry Analysis of Wages and Plant Size," *Review of Economics and Statistics*, Vol. 51 (August 1969), pp. 341–45.

Statistical testing and analysis of the relationship between wage levels and plant size.

REDER, MELVIN W. "Wage Differentials: Theory and Measurement," in BURTON, JOHN F. JR., et al. (eds.), *Readings in Labor Market Analysis*, pp. 281–309. New York: Holt Rinehart & Winston, Inc. 1971.

A discussion of the causation and measurement of occupational and interindustry wage differentials in the short and long run.

SAWHNEY, PAWAN K., and HERRNSTADT, IRWIN L., "Interindustry Wage Structure Variation in Manufacturing," *Industrial and Labor Relations Review*, Vol. 24 (April 1971), pp. 407–19.

A mathematical explanation of variations in the interindustry wage structure in manufacturing.

U.S. GOVERNMENT, EQUAL EMPLOYMENT OPPORTUNITY COMMISSION. *Job Patterns for Minorities and Women in Private Industry*, Washington, D.C.: U.S. Government Printing Office, annually since 1966.

These yearly reports show the number and proportions of minorities and women by industry and location for companies employing 100 or more workers.

Chapter 9

THE SUPPLY OF LABOR

We have seen that the labor market is the area in which the supply and demand for particular types of labor seek to obtain a balance. But what do we mean by the phrase "supply of labor"? What are the factors which are responsible for change in supply? Over what time period and from what perspective should variations in supply be considered?

Definition of Supply of Labor

For conceptual purposes—as, for example, in drawing the diagram in Figure 9–1 below showing the relationship between the "supply of labor" and wages—it is sometimes convenient to think of labor as being composed of homogeneous units. We might, for example, assume that the difference in wage rates paid for hours of labor offered by different individuals in the labor market was a rough measure of the value of the labor supplied. We could then convert such actual hours into "equivalent hours" by reducing higher paid hours to the equivalent of the lowest paid hour of work offered in the marketplace.[1]

Obviously such an assumption of homogeneity must be used with care; for it is clear that in actuality heterogeneity of labor is the dominating characteristic of the labor market. Not only is there a multitude of types of labor, running the gamut of skills, professions, and trades, but also no two workers are precisely alike, even though they may both work in the same trade side by side at similar machines in the same plant. Yet despite such heterogeneity there is a degree of substitutability of one kind of labor for another, particularly when training, education and experience can be utilized over time.

It is the heterogeneity of labor, moreover, which produces many of the problems of labor supply which are matters of national concern today. For example, if all labor were homogeneous, there could not be a shortage

---

[1]Milton Friedman, *Price Theory: A Provisional Text* (Chicago: Aldine Publishing Co., 1966), p. 202.

of labor (except due to lack of mobility) as long as one man remained unemployed. Yet in the actual labor market we observe continuing unemployment of large numbers of workers, both with specialized skills and with no skills at all, while at the same time shortages exist for skilled workers in many occupations.

Labor supply can be considered from the short-run as well as from the long-run point of view. The short run can be thought of as a period of time in which decisions are made about whether to sell labor services, at what price, and in what amount, such period being shorter than the time dimension in which decisions are made with respect to education, occupational choice, migration, and family size.[2] The important variables within labor supply in the short run, therefore, become: (1) labor effort, which may be of significance in piece-rate industries; (2) hours of work offered per day, per week, and per year; and (3) number of persons in the labor force, which depends upon labor participation rates and the age structure of the population at a given moment of time.

CLASSIFICATIONS OF LABOR SUPPLY

The supply of labor can be considered from four points of view:

The Supply of Labor Available to an Individual Firm.   This may be large or small, complex or relatively homogeneous, depending upon the size of firm, the ramifications of its operations, and the diversity of its products and plant locations. The labor supply of the United States Steel Corporation, for example, would represent a cross section of the working population. By contrast, the supply of labor to the corner drugstore would probably include only a pharmacist and some clerks.

The Supply of Labor Available to an Industry.   An industry may be defined, for our purposes, as a group of firms producing approximately the same product. The supply of labor to an industry will ordinarily represent a broader class of skills than the supply of labor to an individual firm because of the variation in methods of production used by firms making the same product in different parts of the country. The supply of labor to an industry may, however, be quite limited if the industry draws upon a relatively scarce type of skilled labor. For example, there are comparatively few qualified violin makers in this country. Consequently, the supply of labor available to this *entire industry* in the United States is less than the supply of labor available to an individual firm in other industries (such as, for example, the United States Steel Corporation).

The Supply of Labor Available to a Particular Locality.   This will represent workers of all types employed in a variety of industries within the particular locality. Unless employment in the locality is highly specialized, the supply of labor will normally include a greater variety of

---

[2] Belton M. Fleisher, *Labor Economics: Theory and Evidence* (Englewood Cliffs, N.J.: Prentice-Hall, Inc. 1970), p. 37.

skills and classes of workers than either the supply of labor to an industry or the supply to the average firm. Availability of new workers will depend upon the mobility of workers from other areas and upon the extent to which persons in the area, not normally members of the labor force, can be induced to enter employment.

The Supply of Labor Available in the Economy as a Whole. This is *the* labor force, including workers of all types in all industries in all sections of the country. Since immigration is relatively unimportant, the availability of additional workers in the short run will depend upon the extent to which persons not ordinarily part of the labor force can be attracted into employment.

VARIATIONS IN LABOR SUPPLY

Labor supply is subject to a diversity of influences. Moreover, some influences will affect one element in labor supply (such as hours of work) without affecting another element (such as number of workers available). It is therefore useful to distinguish, on the one hand, the various *causes* of variations in labor supply and, on the other hand, the *components* of labor supply which are subject to variation. We may then select the particular relation between cause of variation and components of labor supply which we wish to study.

The components of labor supply are number of workers, hours of work (i.e., length of workday and workweek), and efficiency. Causes of variation in labor supply include variations in the wage rate, family income, willingness to work, physical strength of the worker, conditions of work, and similar factors. A rise in family income, for example, may influence all three components of labor supply. A rise in family income may make it possible for Johnny to go to college, thus reducing the number of men available for work; it may enable the family breadwinner to buy a cottage at the beach and therefore interest him in securing a reduction in the workweek so that he can spend his weekends at the beach; and it may enable him to eat better, and to see the doctor and dentist more regularly, so that his physical efficiency will be improved.

In the following discussion, we shall be primarily concerned with all three components of labor supply but with only one of the causes of variation: the wage rate. Holding the other causes constant (with the exception of family income), and changing only the wage rate, we shall attempt to ascertain how the amount of labor supplied will vary. This is the conventional way of studying changes in labor supply in the labor market.

Role of Nonwage Factors

It seems probable that the most important single cause of *variation* in the short-run supply of labor is change in the rate of compensation for jobs. The level of wages is, of course, not the only factor employees consider in seeking employment. We know that proximity of the place of employment, congenial atmosphere, employment with friends or relatives, regularity of work, security, and prospect of advancement are all important elements affecting the attractiveness of a job to the individual worker. However, it is the level of wages which normally fluctuates frequently, and it is therefore easier to correlate changes in labor supply with this cause of variation than with others. Any relationship, of course, is going to be rough and approximate; for as we have seen in Chapter 8 in our discussion of the labor market, employees do not normally have accurate information either about existing wage levels in various firms or of changes in such rate levels. Nevertheless, over a period of time, higher wage rates will attract more employees.

Short-Run Supply of Labor

Variations in labor supply may be considered from either the short-run or the long-run point of view. The short-run supply of labor may be defined as the schedule of the varying amounts of labor that would be supplied at varying wage rates. Geometrically represented, the schedule is a curve on a diagram on which the wage rate is measured along the ordinate (Y axis), and the number of workers, or units of labor, is measured along the abscissa (X axis).

As has already been mentioned, the supply curve may be drawn from the point of view of an individual firm, an industry, a locality, or the economy as a whole. For the purpose of explaining geometric representation of supply conditions, we may assume that Figure 9–1 represents supply curves of labor to a firm. The same type of representation, however, can be used to show supply conditions from the point of view of an industry, a locality, or the economy. Figure 9–1 shows two hypothetical supply curves of labor. The line SS' has been drawn parallel to the X axis and intersects the Y axis at a wage of $100 per week. Since SS' is parallel to OX, it indicates that at a wage of $100 per week the employer anticipates that he can get 20 workers or 40 workers or 70 workers. In other words, as much labor as the employer requires can, within limits, be obtained at the same wage rate. Economists describe this situation by saying that the supply curve of labor is perfectly "elastic." Increasing amounts of labor can be obtained without raising wage rates. As we shall see in the following discussion, this is frequently the case when unemployment exists in the labor market.

Suppose, now, that a war crisis arises suddenly and large numbers of workers are drafted into the army. Our employer's supply curve for labor may now be changed abruptly to one which looks like the line ST in Figure 9–1. Because of the shortage of labor in the market, the employer now finds that to get more labor, he must offer a progressively higher wage rate to attract workers away from other firms and to draw persons out of retirement into his factory. Thus, while 20 workers (*OQ*) can be hired for a wage of about $120 per week, if the employer wants to double his labor force to 40 workers, he may find that he will have to raise wages to $140 per week (*RP*). Such a supply curve, which correlates higher wage rates with increased labor supply, is known as a supply curve of less than perfect elasticity.[3] This usually means that the supply of labor is limited relative to buyers' demands and that additional workers or

FIGURE 9–1

Short-Run Supply Curve of Labor to a Firm

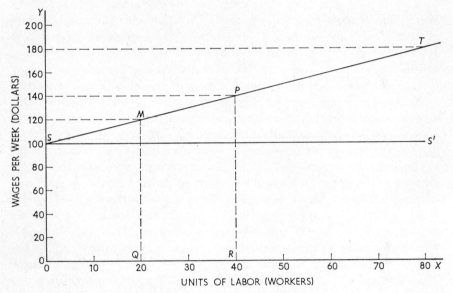

additional hours or units of labor can only be obtained by raising rates of pay.

The more "elastic" a supply curve is, the greater will be the increase in labor associated with a given increase in wage rates. Looked at another way, the steeper the slope of the supply curve, the less elastic it will be. In Figure 9–1, curve *SS'* is more elastic than curve *ST*, and curve *ST* has a steeper slope than curve *SS'*. If the supply curve is vertical, meaning that no matter how wage rates rise or fall, there will be no change in the amount of labor available, the supply curve is said to be "perfectly

---

[3] The concept of elasticity will be utilized from time to time in the following chapters in connection with both supply curves and demand curves. The elasticity coefficient is equal to the percentage change in quantity divided by the percentage change in price (or wage). Algebraically, this relation can be expressed as $(\triangle Y / \triangle X)$ X/Y, where Y equals quantity and X equals price.

inelastic" or of "zero elasticity." On the other hand, if the supply curve is horizontal, as in the case of curve *SS'* in Figure 9–1, any amount of labor (within limits) can be obtained at a constant wage rate. Such a curve is called "perfectly elastic."

Classification of Variations

Much confusion arises in discussions of labor supply because of a failure to distinguish properly between a shift in the entire supply curve and a movement along the curve. The former should be referred to as a "change in labor supply," since "supply" means the whole schedule. The latter should be designated as a "change in the amount of labor supplied," that is, a movement from one *point* on the supply curve to another. This distinction will be clarified if variations in the availability of workers, labor time, and labor efficiency are considered from the viewpoint of whether they do or do not involve an actual shift in the supply curve:

1. A change occurs in the number of workers available in the market.

a) Such a change may be attributable to factors other than a variation in wage rates. For example, the large withdrawals of troops from Vietnam added thousands of GI's to the ranks of the civilian labor force. Where the change in numbers of workers is attributable to nonwage causes, the whole supply schedule of labor shifts its position, either to the right or to the left, depending on whether there has been an increase or a decrease in the number of workers available at given rates.

b) Additional workers may be induced to enter the labor market by the attraction of high wages. To the extent that this is true, there has been a movement along a given supply curve.

2. A change occurs in hours of work.

a) During World War II, hours of work of nonagricultural employees increased from 41 hours in 1940 to a peak of more than 46 hours per week in 1943. In part, the willingness to work these longer hours was motivated by a desire to bring the war to a speedy and successful conclusion. That is, the motive of patriotism would have actuated workers to accept some lengthening of the workweek with no increase in hourly wage rates. To the extent that this was true, there was a shift to the right in the labor supply curve.

b) Workers increase hours of work because of availability of work beyond 40 hours at a premium rate of time and a half. This represents a movement along a given supply curve.

3. A change occurs in efficiency.

a) Music is played in a factory during working hours; and as a result, output increases. There has been a movement of the entire supply curve.

b) On the other hand, if additional efficiency is forthcoming simply as a result of a piece-rate system which rewards additional effort with additional compensation, there has merely been a movement along a given supply curve.

The same distinction in terminology, of course, applies to shifts of the demand curve for labor and to movements along that curve.

THE SUPPLY CURVE OF LABOR TO THE FIRM

As has been mentioned, the supply of labor may be considered in relation to a particular firm, an industry, a locality, or the economy as a whole. The last three types of supply curves are "objective." That is, they represent the "actual" changes in supply of labor which would accompany given changes in the rate of wages, if such variations in supply could be isolated from the general flux in the labor market and measured. The supply curve of labor to the individual firm, however, is of quite different nature. The supply curve of labor to the individual firm, as this concept is normally used by labor economists, is a subjective concept, not an objective fact. It represents the *expectation* of the individual employer as to what the relationship of wage rates and labor supply *will be*.

Of course, we could draw up an objective supply curve of labor for the individual firm. The slope of such a curve would reflect, among other things, differences in worker preference for specified combinations of money income and working conditions, attachment of workers to a familiar workplace or residence, and the size of the firm in question. It is more useful, however, for most economic problems to draw up a hypothetical curve analogous to the demand curves which represent employer expectations. These expectations will be derived in part from past experience; and therefore, many of the elements which would determine the shape of the objective supply curve will enter into the employer's estimation of the shape of the supply curve of labor as he imagines it to be.

Labor Supply to a Large Firm

Because the supply curve of labor to the individual firm reflects the estimates of the individual employer, its slope will depend upon the size of the particular firm involved. A very large firm may have to recognize that any attempt by it to obtain more labor is likely to affect the prevailing wage rate in the locality. In order to obtain 1,000 more workers in a local labor market where there may be only 10,000 qualified workers available in all, a large firm will have to raise wage rates sufficiently to induce workers to leave other jobs. Workers will be reluctant to leave jobs in other firms without such an inducement, since by leaving their current employment, they are likely to lose seniority rights and preferential status with regard to future promotion, health benefits, pensions, and so forth. But when the large firm offers higher wages to attract additional workers, this is likely to produce an increase in wage rates in the community generally, since other employers will also find it necessary to raise wages in order to induce employees to remain. The large firm is thus placed in such a position that any increase in rates it may offer to attract additional workers will likewise have to be offered to all employees already on its own payroll; for if other employers raise rates in retaliation, the large firm would not be able to hold its own employees at lower rates. Moreover, if the workers in the large firms are organized, the union will undoubtedly require uniformity of pay among employees of the same skill. Even if the plant were unorganized, management would probably consider it impracticable from the point of view of employee morale to raise rates for new employees without making a corresponding adjustment in the rates of old employees.

The result in such circumstances is that the addition to the total labor cost of the firm incidental to the employment of an additional worker will exceed the direct labor cost or wage paid to that man. In technical language, this means that the marginal cost of labor (i.e., the addition to the total cost of labor attributable to the addition of one more unit of labor) will exceed the supply price of labor (i.e., the wage offered to the additional worker). Assume that the going rate for labor in the firm is $3 an hour and that 100 men are employed at that wage. In order to attract additional workers, the wage paid to new workers has to be raised to $3.20. The supply price of additional labor, as indicated by the labor supply curve, therefore will be $3.20. But if, as a result of this rise in the wage, all workers already on the payroll have to be given an increase from $3 to $3.20 an hour, the additional cost of $23.20 ($0.20 × 100 + $3.20) attributable to hiring an additional worker will be substantially in excess of his wage ($3.20).

Labor Supply to a Small Firm

The small firm will tend to view its supply curve of labor as being perfectly "elastic" over the relevant range—that is, the employer considers that he can obtain all the additional workers he may need without raising wages. His demand is so small relative to the total supply of workers available that his need for additional workers will not affect wage rates generally. This condition of perfect elasticity may also typify the supply curve for labor in a large firm in times of substantial unemployment. However, the supply curve of the small firm is likely to be perfectly elastic even if there is full employment. For even under condition of full employment, there are some workers leaving other employment for one reason or another, and the small firm may figure it can satisfy its needs from this pool of workers without the necessity of paying higher wages to draw men away from other firms. Consequently, if the small firm has been paying $3 an hour to its employees, it estimates that it can get additional workers for $3, and therefore the marginal cost of the additional labor and its supply price or wage will be the same. The fact that the supply curve for labor to the small firm will tend to be perfectly elastic, while the supply curve to the large firm is more likely to be less than perfectly elastic, influences their respective employment policies. This problem will receive attention in Chapter 10, dealing with the demand for labor.

Why the Labor Supply Curve Slopes Upward

Perhaps the most common cause of an upward slope for the labor supply curve is the need for paying higher wages in order to attract workers away from other firms. As we have seen, insofar as this is the reason for the lack of perfect elasticity in the supply curve, it is more likely to be characteristic of a large than a small firm. But there are other conditions which can produce an upward slope in the labor supply curve, and these are to be found in large and small firms alike. For example, an employer may have to pay penalty rates for overtime if he wishes to get more hours out of his existing labor force. Additional units of labor time have to be remunerated at a higher price, which means that the supply curve for labor to the firm is rising. Another condition which will produce an upward sloping labor supply curve is a scarcity of qualified workers. If additional workers can be obtained at the prevailing wage, but these workers are less efficient, the firm is, in effect, paying an increased price per "efficiency unit." A further possible reason for an upward sloping labor supply curve is increasing "fringe" expenses made necessary by the employment of additional workers. For example, if the only additional workers available are women, the employer may be compelled to expend funds upon separate lavatory facilities, rest rooms, and so forth. The result will be that the marginal cost of employing these additional workers will exceed the wage paid to them.

Effect of Union Organization on Supply Curve

Union contracts customarily fix the wage rates for particular types of labor for a given period of time, usually a year. Once the rate is fixed in the contract, the employer is obligated to pay it, regardless of the amount of labor he employs. Thus, theoretically, a union contract creates a perfectly elastic supply curve for labor.

In practice, however, the results are sometimes different. In a tight labor market the employer may find that even with a union contract, the only way to get more labor is to hire substandard workers and pay them the union rate or to work more overtime. In both cases, his supply curve of labor would be upward sloping: in the former case, because he has to pay more for less efficient labor; in the latter case, because the additional hours worked would have to be compensated at premium rates.

THE SUPPLY CURVE OF LABOR TO AN INDUSTRY

The elasticity of supply of labor to an industry will depend primarily upon the mobility of workers who can be drawn into this industry from other industries. Because most skills in modern industry can be fairly quickly acquired, an industry can ordinarily draw workers away from other industries if it offers sufficient inducement in the form of higher wages. The supply curve of labor for an industry will ordinarily be more elastic than the supply curve for labor in a given locality, because there will be less resistance to the movement of workers away from industry to industry within a given locality than there will be to movement away from or into the locality. The supply curve of labor for an industry will ordinarily be more elastic than the supply curve of labor for the whole economy, because it will be easier to induce employees to leave other industries to work in this particular industry than it will be to induce additional men, women, and children who are not normally members of the labor force to enter the labor market.

The supply curve of labor for an industry will be of zero elasticity —i.e., more workers would not be attracted to the industry no matter how high a wage was offered—only in the rare case when the industry uses a type of highly skilled labor which is not employed by other industries and when the skill is not one which can be easily acquired in a short period. It should be observed that even if the elasticity of labor supply to a particular industry was zero, an individual employer in such an industry might still imagine that the supply curve of labor to his firm was perfectly elastic. He might calculate that even though the industry as a whole could not obtain more workers, his own needs were so small relative to the amount of labor available to the industry that he would be able to attract a few additional workers without being compelled to offer a higher wage.

THE SUPPLY CURVE OF LABOR TO A LOCALITY

The slope of the supply curve of labor to a locality will depend in large measure upon the nature and location of the locality in question. If a shortage of labor were to develop in New York City, additional workers would be attracted from all over the country because of the advantages (other than the job opportunity) which New York has to offer. On the other hand, if a labor shortage were to develop in a little mill town in a backwoods region, even a very high wage rate would not induce many workers to migrate there, leaving their present homes and occupations.

Although many workers, particularly older ones, are reluctant to sever local ties, nevertheless there is a considerable amount of geographical mobility in this country. On the average, during each year over 6% of the civilian population moves its residence across county lines and 3% across state lines.[4] During prosperous periods, the rate of mobility out of labor-surplus areas is higher than in periods of depression. But it is also true from our observation, that lower income groups are often the least willing to relocate.

Many of the characteristics of the supply curve of labor to a locality are also true of the supply curve to the economy as a whole; therefore, these aspects can be conveniently considered together in the discussion below.

THE SUPPLY CURVE OF LABOR FOR THE ECONOMY

Discussions of the supply curve of labor for the economy as a whole are generally phrased in terms of reactions to changes in real wage rates. The assumption is made that the flow in and out of the labor force as well as the change in hours and effort forthcoming from individual workers is made in relation to changes in real wages,[5] rather than in monetary terms. However, there is considerable argument on this point, and some economists speak of a "money illusion" and maintain that workers do in practice react to changes in money rates. In the following discussion, we shall assume that the rise in money rates represents a rise in real wages as well.

For many years, labor economists generally held the view that, except during periods of substantial unemployment, the short-run supply of labor for the economy as a whole was likely to be somewhat inelastic above the prevailing wage. It was assumed that a rise in the rate of wage offered would not substantially increase the number of workers available. As soon as all average workmen were employed, the amount of labor supplied could be increased only by bringing in submarginal workers or people who were not ordinarily part of the labor force—such as women, youths, and older men. The additions which could be expected from these sources in peacetime, within normal wage ranges, were thought to be relatively small. During World War II, patriotism and the lure of very high wage levels did attract many of these groups into the labor market, but this experience was viewed as an exceptional circumstance.

[4] U.S. Department of Commerce, Bureau of Census, *Pocket Data Book USA, 1971* (Washington, D.C.: U.S. Government Printing Office. 1971), p. 51.

[5] Some economists, such as John M. Keynes, argue that workers, individually and in groups, are more concerned with *relative* than *absolute* real wages. Thus, they may withdraw their labor if their wages fall relative to wages elsewhere, even though they would not withdraw if real wages fell uniformly elsewhere. For a discussion of this point, see James Tobin, "Inflation and Unemployment," *American Economic Review*, Vol. 62 (March 1972), p. 3.

In recent years, however, studies of labor market performance has suggested that there is a trend toward growing responsiveness on the part of labor supply. A prime source for the greater degree of elasticity which seems to have evidenced itself in recent years is the growing size and importance of a discretionary labor force. The increased number of part-time workers, the greater participation of women in the labor force, and the growing tendency of older workers to combine early retirement with some reduced rate of participation in the labor force have created a large body of intermittent or multiple-job holders who flow in and out of the labor force with considerably more rapidity than members of the primary labor force.[6]

FIGURE 9–2

Short-Run Supply Curve of Labor for the Economy

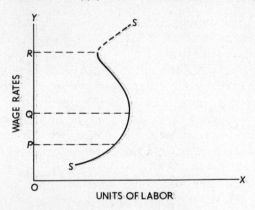

Thus, for example, in 1969 only about 7 out of 10 of the 92.5 million men and women who worked at some time during that year were in the labor force all year.[7] This group, which might be called the "primary labor force" included 59 million men and women who worked all year, 50 weeks or more, primarily at full-time jobs, and another 5 million persons who were in the labor force for periods of less than a full year.[8]

In Figure 9–2, the prevailing wage rate is indicated along the Y axis, while units of labor supplied are measured along the X axis. The curve lettered SS' represents an approximation to the short-run supply curve of labor for the economy in normal times. If we assume that wage rate OP is a bare subsistence wage, then below that rate, workers will not be

[6] Jacob Mincer, "Labor-Force Participation and Unemployment: A Review of Recent Evidence," in J. F. Burton, Jr., et al., *Readings in Labor Market Analysis* (New York: Holt, Rinehart & Winston, Inc., 1971, pp. 79–105).

[7] Howard V. Hayghe, "Work Experience of the Population in 1969," *Monthly Labor Review*, Vol. 94 (January 1971), p. 45.

[8] *Ibid.*

strong enough to work as many hours or in as great a number as at wage *OP*, and the supply curve will therefore reflect this diminution in the number of units of labor supplied by sloping sharply to the left. At and slightly above wage *OP*, we may assume that earnings are very low relative to the standard of living; and as a consequence, workers with families will be compelled to send their children to work at an early age. Also, many women will have to work at this low wage in order to help their husbands support their families. As the wage rate is raised to a more satisfactory level, men are better able to maintain their families on their own wages. Thus, at a wage of *OQ*, earnings of the family breadwinner will be sufficient so that children can remain in school for more extended education and women can remain in the home. Likewise, individual workers will opt for shorter hours and longer vacations so that they can use the higher income for more leisure activities. Consequently, the amount of labor offered on the market will tend to diminish, and the supply curve will slope to the left. As indicated by the discontinuous part of the curve above wage *OR*, it is possible that at very high wages—as was the case during the war years—women and youths will again be induced to enter the labor market. Likewise, older men who were ready for retirement may postpone the event, and even men over 65 may enter the labor market. Therefore, it is possible that at such high rates the supply curve may again slope to the right.

Economists seek to explain the reactions of labor supply to changes in real wage rates by assuming that at various wage rates a balance is reached between the desire for leisure and the desire for income on the part of individual workers and family units. If wage rates rise, two offsetting influences come into play. On the one hand, the so-called "substitution effect" will tend to induce workers to substitute work for leisure, since higher wages now make work more attractive. On the other hand, the so-called "income effect" may induce a worker to reduce his hours of work because with higher income he now can afford to buy a boat, have a summer cottage, and so on, and he therefore needs additional time to enjoy these acquisitions.[9] The "backward sloping" portion of the supply curve is explained by the assumption that as real wage rates rise, for numbers of workers the income effect dominates the substitution effect and results both in fewer hours of work being offered and in the withdrawal from the market of other family members.

Statistical Investigations into the Supply Curve for Labor

Various attempts have been made to determine what would happen to labor supply if earnings were lower or higher than the prevailing rate. These studies have generally been based on one of two approaches: Labor

---

[9] The interrelationships between income and leisure are explored in the mathematical appendix at the end of this chapter. See also Chapter 16.

force size is measured at different moments of time as earnings vary, or simultaneous measurement is made of labor force and earnings in different labor markets to determine what, if any, is the normal interrelationship. One of the earliest investigations in this field was made by Paul H. Douglas, who used the latter approach and, after examining earnings and labor force size in 38 large cities, found evidence of an inverse relationship.[10] Clarence D. Long, who published a comprehensive study of this problem, confirms that variations in the proportion of a city's population in the labor force, i.e., its participation rate, appear to be inversely associated with variations in its average income per equivalent adult male worker.[11]

A somewhat allied question is the problem of what happens to the labor force in times of depression. If there is an inverse relationship between earnings and labor supply, then, as earnings diminish in times of depression, additional workers should be expected to enter the labor force in an attempt to supplement family income. This "additional workers" theory, as it is called, is held by many economists, but it has been rejected by others. Recent empirical research suggests that labor supply is inversely related to the level of unemployment. This implies that as wages drop and unemployment rises, although some secondary workers enter the labor market in order to supplement family income, more depart or delay their entrance until a more favorable labor market situation develops.[12] Thus, the converse of the "additional workers" theory is the "discouraged workers" theory, which in effect postulates that labor force participation will fall as unemployment rises because lack of jobs in the labor market will cause persons to delay entry into, or to withdraw from, the labor force.

The reactions of various groups within the labor force to changes in wage levels at a moment of time are not necessarily the same as over a longer period of years. Data indicate that among families at a given moment of time, the labor force participation rate of married women living with their husbands is lower the higher the income received by husbands. For example, in 1970 the participation rate of wives of blue collar workers whose husband's income was between $4,000 and $7,000 was 48%, while the rate for wives whose husbands earned between

[10] Paul H. Douglas, *The Theory of Wages* (New York: Macmillan Co., 1934), chap. xi. See also Paul H. Douglas and Erika Schoenberg, "Studies in the Supply Curve of Labor," *Journal of Political Economy*, Vol. 45 (February 1937). pp. 45–79.

[11] Clarence D. Long, *The Labor Force under Changing Income and Employment* (National Bureau of Economic Research, General Series No. 65 [Princeton, N.J.: Princeton University Press, 1958]), p. 5. For a current survey and discussion of earlier studies, see Fleisher, *Labor Economics*, chap. iii, "Evidence Bearing on the Theory of Labor Supply," pp. 56–91.

[12] See U.S. Department of Labor, *The U.S. Labor Force: Projections to 1985* (Special Labor Force Report No. 119 [Washington, D.C.: U.S. Government Printing Office, 1970]), p. 10.

$15,000 and $20,000 was 34%.[13] This would seem to support the theory of the backward sloping supply curve. However, over a period of years there has been a marked rise in the labor force participation rate of married women in the presence of rising incomes and higher wage levels of their husbands. This trend represents the combined influence of a host of social and economic factors which are reshaping the role of women in our society.

Hours of Work

The slope of the short-run labor supply curve will depend in part upon the relationship between the rate of wages and the number of hours employees are willing to work. Here again we are faced with the conflicting influences of the substitution effect and the income effect. A longer workday or longer workweek not only spells greater fatigue for the worker but also means that he will have less time to devote to his family, recreation, education, and other pursuits. It is understandable, therefore, why premium pay is offered for longer hours of work. On the other hand, we also know that as take-home pay rises, some workers become more interested in a reduction of hours worked so they can have more time for leisure. It is apparent that this is an era of complex motivation. The subject of hours of work will be discussed in greater detail in Chapter 16.

CHANGE IN EFFICIENCY

The supply of labor can also be varied by a change in efficiency of workers. Just as an increase in wage rates may increase the amount of labor supplied by inducing additional workers to enter the market, so an increase in wage rates may increase the efficiency of a given work force. When wages are at a very low level, an increase in wages will tend to improve efficiency by contributing to the physical well-being of the workers. Workers who are well fed and afforded proper housing facilities are capable of putting forth more effort than employees whose incomes are so low that they cannot properly provide for these basic needs. But once wage rates reach a level at which the worker can maintain a satisfactory standard of living, it is doubtful whether further wage increases have much effect on efficiency solely by reason of their reaction on physical well-being.

However, without regard to possible improvement in physical condition, a rise in wages may induce employees to work harder. A positive relation between wage increases and increased effort is more likely to be found in piece-rate industries than in industries where payment is by the

---

[13] R. L. Stein and J. N. Hedges, "Blue-Collar/White-Collar Pay Trends: Earnings and Family Income," *Monthly Labor Review*, Vol. 94 (June 1971) p. 22.

hour. If the piece rate is raised, the worker can directly increase his take-home pay by producing more units of product, whereas in an industry where payment is by the hour, the worker is likely to feel that his increased effort would simply increase the employer's profit without any direct, immediate benefit to himself. Thus, it is principally in industries using incentive pay plans that variations in efficiency are likely to have any close relationship to changes in wage rates. Approximately 30% of the plant workers in manufacturing industries are paid on an incentive basis.

On the whole, under modern industrial conditions in a high-wage economy, wage changes probably have comparatively little effect upon worker efficiency. Because of the high degree of mechanization in American industry, the speed of the production line rather than individual worker effort is the controlling determinant of labor efficiency.

LONG-RUN SUPPLY OF LABOR

Classical economists viewed the long-run supply of labor as highly flexible. They believed that labor supply adjusted itself to "the natural price of labor"—i.e., the level of real wages which was necessary "to enable laborers one with another to subsist and to perpetuate their race without increase or diminution."[14] This wage was conceived of as an equilibrium rate. If real wages rose above this subsistence level, births would increase, deaths would decrease, population would consequently expand, and, with an unchanged demand for labor, wage rates would necessarily fall. On the other hand, a fall in wage rates below the subsistence level would produce an increase in deaths and a decrease in births. Marriages would be postponed, and married persons would delay having children. Consequently, the supply of labor would decline below the equilibrium level, with the result that wage rates would be bid up to the "natural" wage.

The theory was phrased in terms of a subsistence wage because of the belief, then current, that population tended to increase faster than the means of subsistence. Population was thought to double itself every 25 years—thus increasing at a geometrical rate—while food production increased only in an arithmetical ratio. However, population was prevented from getting too far out of line with subsistence by certain "positive checks," such as vice, pestilence, war, and famine, and "preventive checks," such as postponement of marriage.

Although geometrical increase in population growth and subsistence wages have characterized the history of many underdeveloped countries, particularly in Asia and Central America, the experience of the older

---

[14] David Ricardo, *Principles of Political Economy and Taxation* (Gonner, ed.; London: George Bell & Sons, 1913), p. 70.

countries in Europe and more recently of the United States suggests that the highly industrialized Western nations are entering an era of much slower population growth as a result of changes which have occurred in the science of contraception, attitudes toward size of family and abortion, and the costs of education and other incidents of child-rearing.

Population Projections for the United States

In 1971, the birthrate in the United States dropped to the lowest level in all of American history—to a level even below that experienced in the Great Depression.[15] From a high of 4.3 million births in 1957, the number of births per year dropped to 3.7 million in 1970.[16] That this trend has developed in recent years is all the more remarkable because the number of women of childbearing age in the population has been steadily increasing. It is apparent that fundamental changes in attitudes toward size of family and childbearing are now making their impact felt upon the population statistics.

Because of difficulties in estimating the future behavior of fertility rates, the U.S. Bureau of Census customarily issues a number of projections of population growth based upon different assumptions as to fertility. These long-range population estimates are projections, not forecasts. That is, they do not purport to incorporate an opinion as to what will happen, but simply indicate what can happen if certain assumptions hold true. Based upon new projections issued in 1970, the population increase between 1970 and 1980 could vary from a low of 20.4 million to a high of 31.3 million.[17] If the low figure proves to be more accurate, then the trend which developed in the past decade will continue. From 1950 to 1960, population increased by 28.3 million; from 1960 to 1970, it increased by only 24.3 million.[18]

Although the projected increases in population are still substantial, the possibility of Zero Population Growth (ZPG) by the end of the century is now a distinct possibility. The birthrate in 1971 was running at the rate of about 17.2 per 1,000. The death rate was 9.6 per 1,000. Aside from immigration, this produces an additional 7 people for every 1,000 or 0.8% annually.[19] But the death rate is rising as the population grows older. Moreover, strong pressures are developing to reduce immigration. If the birthrate should continue to fall, the rate of population growth may

---

[15] Ben J. Wattenberg, *The Demography of the 1970's: The Birth Dearth and What It Means* (New York: Family Circle Inc. 1971), p. 2.

[16] *The 1972 World Almanac* (New York: Newspaper Enterprise Association, Inc., 1971), p. 78.

[17] U.S. Bureau of Census sources, cited in National City Bank, *Monthly Economic Letter*, December 1970, p. 7.

[18] *Ibid.*

[19] *1972 World Almanac*, p. 86.

FIGURE 9–3

We May Be On The Way to ZPG

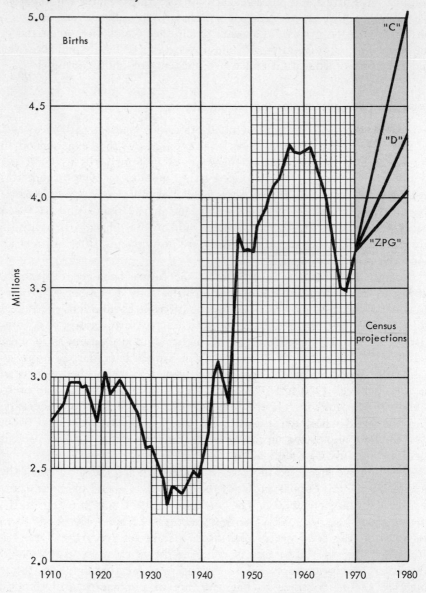

Note: Total births are well below the levels of a decade ago, but they started to increase in 1969 and seem bound to continue to do so until at least 1980, if only because so many young women will be arriving at the main ages of childbearing. All three of the Census Bureau projections charted here seem within reach; a fourth, which assumed that women on the average would have 3.1 children each in the 1970s, already seem beyond reach.

The "C" projection assumes that they will try for 2.8 children each. The "D" projection assumes an average of nearly 2.5, which is actually about the current pace of childbearing. The projection labeled "ZPG" refers to an average of 2.1 children, a rate at which population growth would eventually slow down to zero. Some demographers think we are already approaching that rate.

Source: Lawrence A. Mayer, "New Questions about the U.S. Population," *Fortune,* Vol. 83 (February 1971), p. 82. Reproduced by permission.

closely approximate ZPG by the end of the century. Figure 9–3 illustrates the dramatic decline which occurred in the number of births from their peak in 1957. The ZPG curve in births would require that women on the average limit themselves to 2.1 children each.[20]

Population Growth and the Labor Force

The growth of the labor force—and therefore of labor supply—reflects the influence of two factors—the changing number of persons in the population of working age and the labor participation rate. With respect to the former, the retardation in the rate of growth of population will have a marked effect upon labor force growth and composition. At an annual growth rate of 1.7%, the total labor force is expected to exceed 100 million by 1980. After that, it is anticipated that the rate of growth will slow somewhat, to 1.2%. At this decelerated rate, the labor force will reach an overall total of 107 million by 1985.[21]

As was observed in Chapter 1, the changing age composition of the population will have a significant effect upon the importance of various age groups in the labor force. The teen-age labor force with all its special problems will grow much more slowly, while the largest increases will come in the age group of early career workers, age 25 to 34 years. Women will continue to increase their proportion in the total work force.

By and large the basic participation rates of the past decade are expected to continue during the seventies. Labor participation rates for students are likely to show some increase as students seek part-time employment to assist parents in meeting the mounting costs of higher education. Women will continue to increase their proportion of the labor force: U.S. Department of Labor projections indicate that women will contribute 43% of the net labor force increase between 1968 and 1980, thereby expanding their proportion in the total labor force to almost 37%.[22]

Immigration

In considering the various factors which enter into the long-run supply of labor, mention must be made of net immigration. Because of our restrictive immigration policy, the effect of immigration upon the

---

[20] Lawrence A. Mayer, "New Questions About the U.S. Population," *Fortune* Vol. 83 (February 1971), p. 82. National birth statistics for the first quarter of 1972 indicated that the total fertility rate had dropped sharply, even below the declining 1971 rate, and that births were—at least temporarily—virtually at the replacement rate. See *New York Times*, June 4, 1972, p. 4E.

[21] S. C. Travis, "The U.S. Labor Force: Projections to 1985," *Monthly Labor Review*, Vol. 93 (May 1970), p. 3.

[22] U.S. Department of Labor, *U.S. Labor Force: Projections to 1985*, p. 5.

labor supply has been minimal and this is likely to be the case during the 1970s. It is estimated that during the decade of the seventies the labor force will be augmented by about 1 million immigrants.[23] This number represents less than 3% of the increase anticipated in the labor force during the decade.

SUMMARY

We have seen how supply is related to wage rates and have considered the meaning and content of labor supply from the point of view of the firm, the industry, and the economy. In the next chapter, we shall consider the other side of the picture—the demand for labor. After we have explored thoroughly both the demand and the supply for labor and their relationship to wage levels and employment, we shall be prepared in Chapter 11 to tackle the problem of wage determination as it occurs in the labor market.

APPENDIX: THE SUPPLY CURVE OF LABOR

The supply curve can be derived from a consideration of the individual's work-leisure decision. For purposes of this analysis, we assume that an individual's satisfaction depends on both income derived from working as well as leisure. His utility function is

$$U = f(y, \Lambda) \tag{1}$$

where y and Λ denote income and leisure respectively. The decision facing the individual is to allocate hours to work, thus earning income y or to leisure Λ, the constraints on his ability to maximize satisfaction being the wage rate w and the total number of hours in the day, T. In (1), it is assumed that the individual buys the various commodities in fixed proportions at constant prices, and income is therefore treated as generalized purchasing power.

The rate of substitution of income for leisure is given by

$$-\frac{dy}{d\Lambda} = \frac{\delta f / \delta \Lambda}{\delta f / \delta y} \tag{2}$$

By definition,

$$\Lambda + H = T \tag{3}$$

---

[23] "The U.S. Economy in 1980: A Preview of BLS Projections," *Monthly Labor Review*, Vol. 93 (April 1970), p. 27.

where H is the number of hours of work performed. The budget constraint is

$$y = wH \tag{4}$$

Substituting (3) and (4) into (1), we have

$$U = f(wH, T - H) \tag{5}$$

The first order condition for maximization of utility is

$$\frac{dU}{dH} = -\frac{\delta f}{\delta \Lambda} + \frac{\delta f}{\delta y} \cdot w = 0 \tag{6}$$

which yields on substitution into (2)

$$-\frac{dy}{d\Lambda} = \frac{\delta f/\delta \Lambda}{\delta f/\delta y} = w \tag{7}$$

This states that the rate of substitution of income for leisure equals the wage rate. The second order condition states that

$$\frac{d^2U}{dH^2} = \frac{\delta^2 f}{\delta \Lambda^2} - 2\frac{\delta^2 f}{\delta \Lambda \delta y} + \frac{\delta^2 f}{\delta y^2}w^2 < 0 . \tag{8}$$

Equation (7) is a relation based on T and w and is the individual's offer curve for work and states how much he will work at various wage rates.

The same analysis can be presented diagramatically in terms of indifference curves as in Figure 9–4. Each curve indicates all combinations of income y and leisure Λ yielding the same satisfaction or utility. Points northeast of any point represent higher levels of utility and no two curves cross each other. The objective of the consumer is to reach the highest indifference curve possible. The constraint on this is the straight line determined by the wage rate and the number of hours available, T. With a wage rate w_1, the individual can choose between having all T hours of leisure (Point A) and earning income equal to w_1T by working all T hours (Point B). Also, he can trade income for leisure by moving along the line joining the two points A and B. Points on or below the budget line are feasible. The slope of the line is derived by substituting (3) into (4) and differentiating with respect to Λ to obtain $dy/d\Lambda = -w$.

In order to maximize utility, the individual tries to reach the point at which the straight line is just tangential to an indifference curve as in Point C which is identical to condition (7). If the wage rate increases to w_2, the budget line changes to AD while the optimum point becomes E. By thus increasing the slope of the budget line, the amount of leisure consumed is changed. The locus of all the points of tangency yields the labor supply curve AA.

The relationship between the rate and the amount of work offered by the individual is given in Figure 9–5, and is usually backward bending. This is based on the hypothesis that as wage rates increase beyond a point, an increase in wage income induces the individual to increase leisure

Figure 9–4

The Work-Leisure Decision

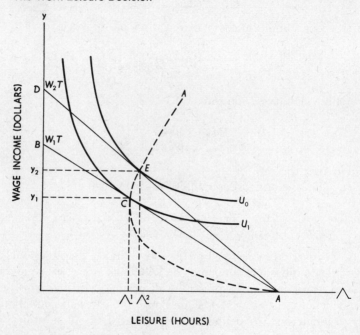

Figure 9–5

Individual Supply Curve of Labor

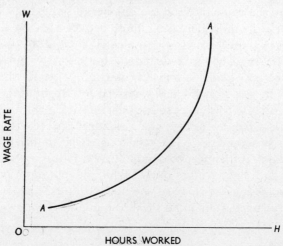

rather than working hours, as the income effect overcomes the substitution effect.* If a homogeneous labor force exists with a single wage rate, the individual labor supply curves can be aggregated to obtain the labor supply curve for the entire economy.

QUESTIONS FOR DISCUSSION

1. Discuss how recent changes in population growth will affect labor supply in years to come.
2. Under what circumstances will the supply curve of labor to a firm be elastic? Inelastic? Draw a supply curve which is perfectly elastic. Draw a supply curve which is less than perfectly elastic.
3. Discuss the difference between a change in the supply of labor and a change in the amount of labor supplied. What circumstances are likely to cause a change of the former type? Of the latter?

SUGGESTIONS FOR FURTHER READING

Bowen, William G., and Finegan, T. Aldrich. *The Economics of Labor Force Participation.* Princeton, N.J.: Princeton University Press, 1969.
   A comprehensive study of participation rates and trends of various groups in the labor force based on data for census years 1940, 1950, and 1960.

Fair, Ray C. "Labor Force Participation, Wage Rates and Money Illusion," *Review of Economics and Statistics,* Vol. 53 (May 1971), pp. 164–68.
   An attempt to determine through statistical analysis the degree of money illusion on the part of labor force participants.

Hicks, J. R. *The Theory of Wages,* chap. v, pp. 89–111. 2d ed. London: Macmillan & Co., Ltd. 1963.
   An analysis of factors governing the individual supply of labor expounded from the classical point of view.

Mayer, Lawrence A. "New Questions About the U.S. Population," *Fortune,* Vol. 83 (February 1971), pp. 80–85, 121–24.
   A provocative article on changing patterns of population growth, their causes, the likelihood of ZPG, and consequences for the United States.

Mincer, Jacob. "Labor-Force Participation and Unemployment: A Review

---

* The relationship between the total effect of a wage change on the number of hours worked is given by the Slutsky equation

$$\frac{\delta H}{\delta w} = \left(\frac{\delta H}{\delta w}\right)_{U = \text{const.}} - H\left(\frac{\delta H}{\delta y}\right)_{w = \text{const.}}$$

The first term on the right-hand side is the substitution effect, or the rate at which the individual substitutes work for leisure when the wage rate changes and he moves along the *same* indifference curve. The second term is the income effect, the change in number of hours worked relative to changes in income with the wage rate held constant. The sum of the two is the total effect on number of hours worked for a given change in the wage rate.

of Recent Evidence," in BURTON, J. F. JR., et al., *Readings in Labor Market Analysis*, pp. 79–105. New York: Holt Rinehart & Winston. Inc., 1971.

A discussion of the responsiveness of the labor force to economic factors in the labor market.

Population Estimates.   Current Population Reports, Series P–25. Washington, D.C.: U.S. Department of Commerce, Bureau of the Census.

These reports issued on a continuing basis are a basic source for data on population growth with detailed breakdown with respect to age, sex, color, and so on.

ROSEN, SHIRLEY, and WELCH, FINIS.   "Labor Supply and Income Redistribution," *Review of Economics and Statistics*, Vol. 53 (August 1971), pp. 278–82.

Estimates of labor supply functions bearing on the question of whether or not provision of unemployment compensation, public assistance grants, and other income supplements create a withdrawal of recipients from the labor force.

SAWERS, LARRY,   "Urban Poverty and Labor Force Participation: Note," *American Economic Review*, Vol. 62 (June 1972), pp. 414–21.

A statistical analysis of labor force participation response on the part of black women and white women in poor and nonpoor areas.

Chapter 10

THE DEMAND FOR LABOR

During the course of a year, at least 6 million enterprises —3 million farms and as many nonagricultural establishments—use some hired labor. How do these employers decide how much labor to employ and what price to pay for it? What determines whether the employer will hire more men or use machines to perform a particular job? These are problems relating to the demand for labor which we shall consider in the following discussion.

In examining the demand for labor, we shall consider in some detail a theory known as the marginal productivity theory, which attempts to explain the determination of the demand for labor. This theory is widely held by economic theoreticians; but in recent years, it has been attacked as unrealistic by a number of labor economists. Despite such criticism, the marginal productivity theory is still a doctrine to be reckoned with in any study of the functioning of the labor market. It has demonstrated remarkable flexibility, and as will be pointed out in the following discussion, its advocates claim that it is quite compatible with some of the newer theories of wage determination which emphasize the bargaining aspect in wage-employment relationships. In this chapter, we shall consider some of the merits and shortcomings of this theory and compare it with other theories which seek to explain the demand for labor.

THE WAGES FUND THEORY

One of the earliest theories which sought to explain the demand for labor was the so-called "wages fund" theory, which became popular in the latter part of the 18th century and the first part of the 19th century in England and France. Economists sought to explain the determination of the aggregate amount of funds which employers were prepared to expend in hiring labor. The amount of such funds available for paying wages and salaries was conceived of as substantially fixed at any given period of time. In some discussions, this fund was referred to as "capital."

The wages fund theory declared that the rate of wages is determined by the ratio between this "capital" and the working population.[1] The theory was never clearly formulated, and there was much confusion as to the precise meaning of its terminology. Some formulations of the theory amounted to no more than a truism. To explain the rate of wages by saying that it is a result of the proportion between the number of employees and the amount expended upon their wages by employers is simply to state an arithmetical proposition, not an economic theory. On the other hand, to maintain that there is a definite and fixed fund which is available for payment of wages is clearly erroneous. Wages fund theorists believed that the fund could not be expanded at the expense of profits—that diminution in profits would also reduce the wages fund. But this conclusion rested on the implicit assumption that employers earned only "normal profits," that is, profits at the minimum level necessary to induce an employer to stay in business. As long as there are surplus profits, so that a reduction in profit will not force employers out of business, the wages fund can be expanded by diverting profits to wage and salary payments.

But there is a sense in which the wages fund theory has some validity. In our modern economy, most products are produced by "roundabout" methods of production. That is, the various commodities which constitute the real wage of labor represent the result of a long "period of production." At any given moment, only a certain amount of finished products are emerging from the long production line represented by our entire productive process, just as on the production line at River Rouge, most of the cars are in an incomplete stage, with only a few ready to be driven off and purchased by consumers.

If the flow of finished products cannot be substantially increased in the short run, an increase in money wages paid to employees may simply produce a rise in prices without augmenting workers' real wages. Thus, in the short run the rate of *real* wages is, to some extent, limited by the size of the "subsistence fund" representing the efforts of past labor which must support current labor until new products emerge from the productive process. However, such a wages fund is flexible over time. Contrary to the view of the proponents of the old wages fund doctrine, an increase in the working population need not reduce the wage rate. On the contrary, when time has permitted the larger number of workers to be better organized so as to achieve a more efficient division of labor, there may be an increase in current output of finished goods which will raise the level of real wages.

The wages fund theory was originally propounded as a means of explaining the determination of the level of real wages. In time, however, it was converted into a doctrine which could be used to prove that

---

[1] J. S. Mill, *Principles of Political Economy* (Ashley, ed.; London: Longmans, Green & Co., Ltd., 1909), pp. 343–44

attempts by workers to raise their real wages were futile. This perversion of the doctrine ultimately led to its recantation by one of its famous proponents. He conceded that the wages fund was not fixed, that the whole of the capitalists' means was potentially capital (in the sense of advances to labor), and that the amount which actually became capital depended on capitalists' personal expenditures.[2]

THE MARGINAL PRODUCTIVITY THEORY

Following the demise of the wages fund doctrine, the marginal productivity theory became the theory generally applied by economists to explain the functioning of the market for labor. At first, marginal productivity attempted to encompass a theory of wages—that is, it sought to explain the determination of wage levels. This stage of the doctrine is closely associated with the work of John Bates Clark, who, in his influential treatise entitled *Distribution of Wealth*,[3] enunciated a theory which rested on three basic assumptions:

1. Rational employers, in an attempt to maximize profits, will be guided by the marginal productivity of a factor in determining the relationship between a factor's return and its utilization. This premise might be called the "marginal productivity principle" and explains employer demand for the factors of production.
2. Perfect competition exists, so that market forces tend to equalize rates of return for all factors over time.
3. Long-run general equilibrium exists in all markets—which implies a stationary state in which technological progress and changes in demand and supply are absent.[4]

Under the above-stated restrictive conditions, the aggregate labor supply is fixed; and assuming a homogeneous class of labor, it is true that the general level of wages for such labor will be determined by its marginal product.

However, in subsequent writings, other economists attacked the assumptions numbered 2 and 3 above as artificial and remote from the labor market of reality. In the writings of Alfred Marshall[5] and others, wage determination was explained by the interaction of supply and demand in the marketplace, with marginal productivity being used as a tool

---

[2] The recantation was made by John Stuart Mill. See Erich Roll, *A History of Economic Thought* (rev. ed.; New York: Prentice-Hall, Inc., 1942), p. 402.

[3] John Bates Clark, *Distribution of Wealth* (London: Macmillan & Co., Ltd., 1899).

[4] See Allan M. Cartter, *Theory of Wages and Employment* (Homewood, Ill.: Richard D. Irwin, Inc., 1959), chaps. i–iii, and especially pp. 18–19.

[5] Alfred Marshall, *Principles of Economics* (8th ed.; London: Macmillan & Co., Ltd., 1920).

to explain the demand for labor. This is the sense in which we shall use the term *marginal productivity* theory in this text. It is *not* a theory of wages; it *is* a theory of demand for factors of production.

According to this theory, employers have a "demand for labor" just as they have a demand for coal, or electricity, or raw materials, or any other of the "means of production" which are required to manufacture a finished product. In considering labor as a means of production, these economists do not, of course, overlook the fact that labor is highly personalized and, therefore, for many problems in the field of labor economics, cannot be treated as the equivalent of so many hours of "energy" on the same level as a lifeless thing like a machine. However, they contend that from the point of view of an employer seeking to operate his plant in the most efficient manner possible, the outlay for labor is a cost of production in the same sense as the outlay for electricity or raw materials. In the employer's calculations, labor becomes merely one of the many factors which can be combined in various proportions to yield varying amounts of physical output.

What determines an employer's demand for labor, according to this theory? Marginal productivity theorists point out that an employer's demand for labor is obviously not determined simply by the physical requirements for production in a given plant. Most plants in our country could physically turn out a larger quantity of goods than they do and could physically utilize larger work forces. The reason they do not do so must be because at some point it becomes unprofitable to produce a larger amount—either because costs rise or prices fall, or both. Therefore an employer's determination as to actual output must be made with an eye on revenue and costs. Likewise, an employer's utilization of labor must be determined by weighing the cost of employing additional labor against the contribution the added labor is expected to make to the revenue of the firm.

Of course, any such determination made by employers must of necessity be very rough and approximate. The average employer cannot estimate accurately the marginal contribution to revenue which will be made by employment of additional labor. Revenues depend not only upon output but also upon prices; and prices are, of course, subject to constant change and fluctuations in our economy. Nevertheless, these economists argue, as a general rule of economic conduct, it would seem logical to assume that if employers wish to maximize their profits, they will hire additional labor only if its cost is less than the anticipated marginal contribution of the labor to the revenue of the firm.

This principle of weighing marginal revenue contributed by a factor against the added cost incurred through its use is the heart of marginal productivity theory. The marginal productivity theory is generally stated in the form of two propositions: (1) Employers will not ordinarily pay labor (or any other factor of production) more than that factor adds to the revenue of the firm; and (2) the forces of competition tend to make employers pay labor (or any other factor) a wage (or price) approximately equal to the full value of its marginal contribution to the revenue of the firm, except in certain special circumstances which we shall consider later in this discussion.

It is important to note that the theory states only a tendency. In a dynamic society such as ours, where prices are always changing, the contribution which employment of additional quantities of labor will make to the revenue of a firm is also subject to continual change. Employers, however, do not change wages or hire or fire workers every time they make a price change. Consequently, the most that can be expected is that whenever employers make adjustments in output, size of the plant, labor force, and capital equipment, they will do so with the objective in mind of attempting to secure as close an equivalence as possible between the "marginal cost" of a factor of production—that is, the additional cost incurred by employing an additional unit of a factor of production—and the marginal revenue product of the factor—that is, the addition to revenue of the firm attributable to employment of the additional unit of the factor.

The Role of Profit Maximization

The two propositions of the marginal productivity theory stated above are simply logical deductions from a premise basic to the theory, namely, that businessmen normally seek to maximize profits. As we shall see later in this chapter, a businessman who finds that with a given amount of labor, he is obtaining a marginal revenue product in excess of the marginal cost of labor, can actually increase his profit by employing more labor until the marginal cost and marginal revenue product of labor are equated. Therefore, if businessmen are interested in maximizing profits, and if they attempt to make estimates of cost and revenue of the marginal type we have considered, there would be some tendency for the wage of labor to approximate the marginal revenue product of labor in the particular firms in which it is employed.

Not all businessmen, however, are motivated by the desire to maximize profits. Recent studies have indicated that the desire for prestige, for power, and for security may be dominant motives in the minds of many employers. Such motives may frequently dictate a policy which is inconsistent with maximizing profit. Some employers may be interested only in "satisficing" profits, rather than in maximizing them. This means that they set a target level of profits based upon a "fair return on investment," which may be less than the maximum profit that can be earned.[6]

---

[6] See Philip Kotler, *Marketing Management* (Englewood Cliffs, N.J.: Prentice-Hall, Inc., 1967), p. 131.

Employer motivation is complex. Marginal productivity theorists concede that motives and objectives other than profit maximization influence employer behavior, but they contend nevertheless that the behavior of most employers can best be explained in terms of long-run profit maximization. Critics of the theory, however, take issue with this assumption and argue that noneconomic motivation is so common that a realistic theory cannot be based on profit maximization. Here is the first of the major cleavages between this theory and other theories of labor demand.

Long-Run Adjustments

The marginal productivity theory is a theory of long-run tendencies. Employer behavior which appears uneconomic from the short-run point of view may actually be designed to maximize profits in the long run. Moreover, in the short run, employers cannot freely change the combination of the factors of production. Suppose an employer has been producing a product using 10 men and a machine. If the price of labor doubles, he may find that he would be better off using half as much labor and a larger, more complicated machine. But it may be impracticable for him to junk his existing machine immediately, or possibly the larger machine cannot be accommodated in his existing plant. Consequently, several years may elapse before he is able to make the adjustment which the marginal productivity theory states he should make if he wishes to maximize profit.

DEMAND FOR LABOR IN THE INDIVIDUAL FIRM

The marginal productivity theory may be considered from the point of view of the individual firm or of the economy as a whole; or stated another way, marginal productivity principles determine the nature of the demand curve for labor, and the demand curve for labor may be examined from the point of view of the individual employer or of the economy as a whole. In the following discussion, we shall be concerned only with the application of marginal productivity principles by the individual employer. Later in this chapter, we shall consider the problem of applying marginal productivity principles to the economy as a whole.

In the context of individual firm analysis, the marginal contribution of a factor is determined by its effect on the *revenue* of the particular firm. If we say, as a paraphrase of the theory, that employers try to pay labor what it is worth, the term "worth" must be understood in a strictly economic sense, without any moral or social connotations. The advertising executive who thinks up new slogans for dog food has a high worth to his agency because his efforts add a lot to the revenue of the firm. The value of his "product" from the social point of view may be nil. The marginal productivity theory was originally enunciated in terms of a theoretical economy in which perfect competition prevailed. In such a system, factors of production would tend to be allocated in a manner such that the optimum aggregate national product would be obtained, and the value of the marginal product of particular employees would be some index of its social worth. This theoretical problem need not concern us, however, at this point. We know that our economy is not perfectly competitive, nor is there such a tendency in that direction to warrant using perfect competition as a norm in our discussion.

Significance of Monopolistic Competition

In the following analysis, we shall assume—what is a fact—that we have an economy characterized by "monopolistic competition." In such an economy, there is in each industry a number of firms, each selling a product which is slightly differentiated from the other. Each producer is in competition with other producers; but to some extent, he is a monopolist in his own little market. Hence the term "monopolistic competition." If the individual producer raises his price, he does not lose all his customers because some customers still prefer his product and will pay the higher price. In other words, while there are competitive products, they are not perfect substitutes in the minds of consumers; and to the extent that such substitution is imperfect, the individual producer is somewhat in the position of a monopolist who can raise his price without losing customers because he has a monopoly of the product. Similarly, when the individual producer lowers his price, he increases his business but does not take away all his competitors' business because some of their customers will remain loyal and buy their products despite this producer's price reduction.

We may assume, therefore, that the average employer with whom we shall be concerned will, in estimating his labor requirements, have in mind the fact that additional units of his product can be sold only at a lower price, which is required in order to take away some of the business from his monopolistic competitors and make it possible to market the larger volume. If additional output can be sold at a lower price, this will also mean that the marginal contribution to revenue made by additional employees will tend to decline. Therefore, the more workers the employer hires, the less he can afford to pay to each additional worker. In geometric terms, this means that the employer will have a downward sloping demand curve for labor.

Geometry versus Reality

Of course, employers do not normally think in terms of geometrical curves. As a matter of fact, they usually would not even have sufficient data to plot a demand curve for labor if they wanted to! The concept of a demand curve for labor is simply an aid which helps economists to understand how employers make decisions involving the employment of labor. The employer must have some rough idea of the various wages he would be willing to pay for varying amounts of labor, based upon his estimates of the additional revenue which such labor could produce for him. The demand curve for labor is simply a geometric representation of this idea.

FIGURE 10–1

Demand Curve for Labor

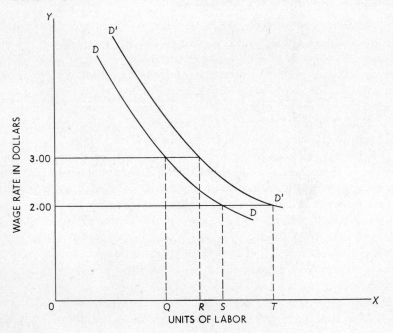

The demand curve for labor of a hypothetical employer is shown by line *DD* in Figure 10–1. The demand curve for labor shows the various amounts of labor the employer would be willing to employ at various wage levels. As in the preceding chapter, we shall assume, for illustrative purposes, that labor is homogeneous so that we can talk about "units of labor" or "additional labor" without need for concern about personal differences. The lower the wage level, the more labor the individual employer feels he can profitably employ. Thus, at the wage of $3, this employer estimates he could employ only *OQ* units of labor, whereas if the wage rate falls to $2, he would employ *OS* units of labor. Such increases are referred to as changes in the quantity of labor demanded because they involve changes along a given demand curve. Sometimes, however, the entire demand curve for labor will shift. This may happen, for example, when there is an upturn in business, such as occurs during the business cycle. A shift in the demand curve for labor means that at every wage rate the employer is now willing to hire more labor than he was previously. For example, in Figure 10–1, if the demand curve shifts to position *D'D'*, then at the wage of $3 the employer will demand *OR* units of labor instead of the smaller amount *OQ* indicated by the previous position of the demand curve. This situation involves an *increase in the demand for labor*, whereas increased employment due to a reduction in wage rates is distinguished by economists as an *increase in the quantity of labor demanded*. A similar distinction in terminology was met in the last chapter in connection with changes in supply.

THE LAWS OF PRODUCTION

We have seen that in monopolistic competition the demand curve for labor is downward sloping because of conditions in the market for the employer's product. There is also another and more fundamental reason why the demand curve for labor has this shape. This is found in the so-called "laws of production"—the law of diminishing returns and the law of scale. These two laws would have the effect of producing a downward sloping demand curve for labor *even if the employer estimated that he could sell additional units* of his product with no reduction in price. These laws affect the amount of additional *physical* product which can be produced by adding additional amounts of one factor of production to other factors. They are laws of physical, not monetary returns.

The Law of Diminishing Returns

The law of diminishing returns is concerned with the effect on total output of adding successive amounts of one factor of production to another factor or group of factors which is held constant in amount. Thus, we may wish to know the effect on total product of adding additional workers to assist in the cultivation of one acre of corn. Or we may wish to know the behavior of total output of shoes as the amount of capital per worker is increased. The universal rule in such cases is that, with a given state of technology, the application of successive units of *any* variable factor to another fixed factor will, after a certain point is reached, yield diminishing returns. Or to put the proposition a little differently, additional units of labor added to another factor—say, capital —will, beyond a certain point (i.e., the point of diminishing returns), produce diminishing marginal increments in total physical product.

Significance for Marginal Productivity Theory. This law of diminishing returns is of fundamental importance to marginal productivity determination. Its relation to marginal productivity theory can best be illustrated if, for the moment, we direct our attention exclusively to physical product. Suppose that additional units of product can be sold at the same price, so that the employer is concerned primarily with the changes in total physical product attributable to employment of additional labor. Suppose, further, that labor itself is paid in physical product rather than in money. Under these conditions the marginal productivity theory would say that there is a tendency for the wage of labor to equal the marginal physical product it produces.

There could be no such tendency, however, if industry operated in a range of increasing rather than diminishing physical returns. This can be seen from the following example, which illustrates production under increasing returns. If increasing returns prevail, the addition of more labor to a fixed amount of another factor will produce more than proportionate increases in total product, with the result that the marginal physical product of labor will continually rise. The marginal physical product of labor is the increase in total product attributable to the addition of a unit of labor. Suppose that all workers are of equal ability (so that they have to be paid the same wage) and that employment of additional labor increases total product as follows:

Men	Total Product	Marginal Product
1	4	..
2	10	6
3	17	7
4	25	8

The addition of a fourth worker increases output by eight units. But the employer could not afford to pay a wage rate equivalent to 8 units of product, since all workers have to be paid the same wage, and payment of an hourly wage of 8 units of output would involve a wage bill of 32 units, which is in excess of total product.

In practice, employers operate within the range of diminishing returns. Therefore the marginal product of labor will be decreasing, not increasing, as in the above hypothetical example. In the following illustration, the addition of the fourth man increases total product from 14 to 17 units:

Men	Total Product	Marginal Product
1	4	..
2	10	6
3	14	4
4	17	3

The marginal physical product (i.e., the increase in total product attributable to the addition of the last unit of the variable factor) of the fourth man is three units, and the employer therefore can profitably pay up to three units as his wage. Because of diminishing returns, the wage bill will not exhaust total product—the wage bill would be only 12, while the total product would be 17. Moreover, there would be a limit to the output of the firm—there would be no incentive to expand output beyond the point at which the marginal product of labor equaled its wage. The demand curve for labor under these circumstances would be downward sloping—even though prices were not affected by increasing output—simply because the marginal contribution to total physical product made by additional workers was declining, and therefore the wage which the employer could afford to pay for such additional labor would also decrease as employment rose.

The Law of Scale

The law of diminishing returns, as we have seen, is concerned with the effect upon total physical output of adding increasing amounts of variable factors to an unchanging amount of a fixed factor. The law of scale, on the other hand, concerns the effect upon total product of increasing *all* factors together. For example, if we double the amount of capital and the quantity of labor and the amount of land, will output likewise double? Will the increase in total product be greater or less than in proportion to the increase in the quantity of factors?

Significance for Marginal Productivity Theory. Why is this problem relevant to marginal productivity determination? The size of the marginal physical product contributed by a particular worker will depend upon the size of the establishment in which he is employed. Take the example of Jones the shoemaker. If Jones is employed in an establishment having only 10 employees, chances are that most of his work will be done by hand. Moreover, he will probably have to make the entire shoe himself, since the number of employees will be too small to permit efficient division of labor. However, as the size of the establishment grows, there will come a point—say, when 100 men are employed—at which it will pay the employer to utilize expensive machinery designed to perform individual operations such as lasting, cutting, and so on. Moreover, the workers can be arranged in a production line, each worker performing only a specialized operation at which he soon becomes highly proficient.

As a result of the introduction of machinery and division of labor, efficiency of operation will increase. Consequently, the physical productivity of a worker in the large factory will be greater than the physical productivity of a worker in the small plant. Here, we have a situation in which an increase in the amount of labor and capital produces a more than proportionate increase in total output. This consequence is fundamentally attributable to the fact that machinery can only be introduced in "chunks." A conveyor belt and production line cannot be advantageously used with only 10 employees, and the small firm cannot use half a machine. As the size of a firm grows, various "indivisible" chunks of other factors become profitable to use; and such utilization, impracticable in a smaller plant, may produce a substantial improvement in efficiency.

However, if such improvement were a continuing possibility as a function of increasing scale, there would be no limit to the size of firms. Our economy would be composed of giant monopolies, each supreme in its own field. Obviously, this eventuality has not occurred. The reason is that as a firm grows in size, the problems of organization, supervision, and coordination grow in complexity. Management becomes farther and farther removed from actual operations as the hierarchy of minor officialdom grows. As a consequence, beyond a certain size—which varies by industry—inefficiency develops, and the rate of increase in total product becomes less than proportionate to the increase in quantity of all factors used.

Another reason for the eventual decline in rate of growth of total output as size of firm grows is that beyond a certain point, it is not possible to increase entrepreneurship in the same proportion as other factors. Men who can efficiently manage million-dollar enterprises are few and far between. Consequently, as existing management finds it must itself coordinate larger quantities of labor and capital, inefficiency develops. This is simply a reflection of the operation of the law of diminishing returns—increasing amounts of labor and capital added to the unchanging factor of entrepreneurship result in diminishing returns in terms of total output.

Thus, the law of scale and the law of diminishing returns set important limitations on the proportion and amount of factors which will be used in individual firms. Were it not for the law of diminishing returns, there would be no limit to the output of a firm; were it not for the law of scale, there would be no limit to the amount of all factors which could profitably be combined under one management. These laws, therefore, play an important role in determining the physical environment in which labor will work and thereby influence the size of physical product which will be attributable to the efforts of particular workers.

MARGINAL PRODUCTIVITY CALCULATIONS

Few employers have ever heard of marginal productivity; yet they are called upon to apply the principles of this doctrine almost every day in the conduct of their business affairs. The question which is continually presented is: Will the purchase of additional units of a particular productive resource increase the revenue of the firm by an amount in excess of the addition in cost incidental to its employment? If the addition promises to augment profits so calculated, the resource will be acquired; if not, the opportunity to purchase or to employ will be foregone. Obviously, the calculation must ordinarily be approximate.

Determination of the anticipated marginal contribution to the firm attributable to the hiring of an additional worker would be facilitated if three conditions were satisfied: (1) if his employment did not require use of additional material or capital, so that his contribution would be net, without deduction for incidental expenses; (2) if the increment in output attributable to his employment could be measured in distinct, separable, completed physical units; and (3) if the price at which the increased output could be sold could be accurately forecast. In practice, these conditions are never realized, so that at best the employer's calculation of the marginal worth of an employee must remain in the realm of approximation.

In a Robinson Crusoe economy, where Crusoe had merely to evaluate the worth of the services of one man Friday, the marginal product of labor could be determined with fair precision. In a typical modern factory, however, where thousands of employees, aided by complex machinery, together pool their efforts to produce a joint product, the contribution of the individual employee becomes indistinct. Nevertheless, employers must make some estimate of the worth of additional employees. They do not go on hiring workers without limit.

Nature of Marginal Productivity Calculations

Table 10–1 is intended to clarify and elaborate the nature of short-hand calculation which the marginal productivity theory assumes employers make in determining the volume of employment in a firm. Few

TABLE 10–1

Marginal Productivity Calculations

(1) Units of Labor	(2) Total Product	(3) Marginal Physical Product	(4) Price per Unit (Dollars)	(5) Value of Marginal Physical Product (Dollars)	(6) Total Revenue (Dollars)	(7) Marginal Revenue Product (Dollars)
1	20	20	5.00	100	100	100
2	50	30	4.00	120	200	100
3	70	20	3.50	70	245	45
4	85	15	3.00	45	255	10
5	95	10	2.00	20	190	−65
6	100	5	1.00	5	100	−90

employers would have available such a detailed schedule as is here assumed, but the detailed figures will serve to illustrate more clearly the basic principles involved in marginal productivity determination.

Assume that our factory produces brooms and that the relationship between employment, physical product, and revenue is estimated by the employer to be as shown in Table 10–1. Consider first columns 1, 2, and 3 of Table 10–1. As additional units of labor are added to unchanging amounts of the other factors, the total physical product increases, at first more than in proportion to the increase in labor and subsequently less than in proportion to the increase in labor. Eventually, as more and more labor is hired, total product might actually decrease. This might be attributable to the fact that with, say, 10 men and a limited amount of machinery, the men would get in each other's way, with the result that total output would be curtailed. The variation in total product and marginal physical product shown in the table reflects the operation of the law of diminishing returns. If labor were paid in brooms and the rate of wages established in the market were 16 brooms, this employer could afford to hire only three workers. With three workers on his force, the employer gets production of 70 brooms, the third employee having increased production by 20 brooms. But the addition of a fourth worker would increase output only to 85 brooms. Fifteen brooms is therefore the marginal physical product attributable to the fourth worker, i.e., it is the increment in total physical production attributable to the employment of an additional unit of the variable factor. If wages are paid in brooms, the employer cannot afford to pay this man 16 brooms when he adds only 15 brooms to the output of the firm.

Value of the Marginal Physical Product of Labor

Since, in a modern capitalistic economy, labor is paid in money wages and not in physical product, employers must estimate the money value of the physical contribution made by additional units of labor. The value of the marginal physical product of labor is obtained by multiplying marginal physical product (column 3) by price per unit of product (column 4). This figure would be a fair index of the value to an employer of the additional output produced by additional units of labor if the additional output could be sold without any reduction in price as compared with a smaller output. In other words, if an employer assumed that he could market additional units of product at a constant price, he could afford to pay labor a wage just a trifle less than the price per unit of such additional output and still make a profit. This is the situation which exists in what economists call "perfect competition." In perfect competition, each firm is small and produces only a minor portion of the output in a particular industry. Furthermore, unlike monopolistic competition, the product of each firm in the industry is indistinguishable from the product of any other producer. As a consequence, the individual employer assumes that if he produces a little more, the addition to the total output of the entire industry will be so slight that it will not affect market price. This situation may exist in the case of farmers producing wheat. Each farmer feels that his output is so small relative to the total output of the industry that he can produce and sell almost any amount of wheat at the same price. In geometric terms, this would mean that the farmer assumes that his demand curve for wheat is horizontal, if we were to plot price of product along the Y axis and quantities expected to be sold along the X axis. In perfect competition the individual employer would hire workers until the wage was approximately equal to the value of marginal physical product added by the last worker hired.

The Marginal Revenue Product of Labor

However, under monopolistic competition the value of the marginal physical product of labor is not a fair index of the value to an employer of the additional units produced by added labor because the additional output can be sold only at a lower price, and this lowers not only the price for the additional units but also the price for all other units of the firm's production. Therefore, we must determine what is the net amount added to the revenue of the firm by the employment of the additional labor. This figure is supplied by the marginal revenue product (column 7). The marginal revenue product of labor is calculated either by finding the difference between total revenue obtained with a given amount of labor and that obtained with a smaller amount of labor or by subtracting from the value of the marginal physical product the loss in revenue, if any, on units of product produced without use of the additional units of the factor, when the loss is caused by a fall in price because of the augmented output.

If the wage rate for broommakers were established in the market at $30, this firm could afford to employ only three men. The marginal revenue product (column 7) for the fourth man is only $10. It would not be profitable for this firm to employ the fourth man, since his employment would cost the firm more than he adds to revenue. The employment of the third worker results in production of 20 extra units, which can be sold only by taking a reduction in price from $4 to $3.50. The value of the marginal physical product is $70 (column 4 multiplied by column 3). But the reduced price is applicable as well to the 50 units which could have been produced without the extra man, and therefore the loss of revenue on these units of $25 (50 multiplied by $0.50 equals $25) must be subtracted from $70, leaving $45 as the marginal revenue attributable to the use of the third worker. Thus, it is apparent that in monopolistic competition a worker cannot be paid the value of his marginal physical product, since this would exceed the amount of his marginal revenue contribution to the firm. It is therefore with reference to the marginal revenue product of labor that the employer will make his employment decisions.

CONDITIONS OF PROFIT MAXIMIZATION IN THE INDIVIDUAL FIRM

The principles of marginal productivity determination elucidated in the foregoing computations are illustrated in geometric form in Figure 10–2. The line marked *MRP* represents the marginal revenue product

FIGURE 10–2

Profit Maximization in the Individual Firm

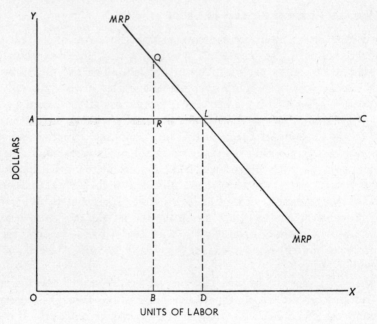

obtained from employment of varying amounts of labor. This curve therefore indicates the value to the employer of varying amounts of labor and is identical with his demand curve for labor. For *OB* units of labor the estimated marginal revenue product is *BQ;* as more labor is employed, marginal revenue product falls, so that for *OD* units of labor the marginal revenue product is equal to *DL*. Suppose, now, that a wage for this type of labor is established in the market of *OA* dollars. Suppose, further, that the employer can obtain any number of men he needs at this same wage level. The wage is therefore constant, regardless of the number of units of labor employed. This circumstance is shown by the horizontal line AC. This line is called the supply curve of labor because it indicates the amount of labor that will be supplied at a given wage. It also indicates the average cost to the employer of hiring additional units of labor. Since, in the present case, it has been assumed that each additional unit of labor can be obtained with no increase in price, the average cost and the marginal cost of each unit of labor are identical. The line AC therefore represents to the employer both the average cost and the marginal cost of hiring additional labor. At a later point in this discussion, we shall find that under different circumstances the average cost and marginal cost of labor may diverge.

Determination of Optimum Employment

With a demand curve and supply curve for labor as shown in Figure 10–2, what amount of labor will yield maximum profits for the employer? Suppose he employs only OB units. For this amount the marginal revenue product BQ is well above the cost RB, and it might therefore be thought that this amount would yield a maximum profit to the employer. But note that if the employer uses a little more labor, although marginal revenue product falls with each additional unit of labor utilized, he can nevertheless increase profits as long as the marginal revenue product of labor remains above its cost. This will be so until we come to the point of intersection of the marginal revenue curve and the wage. For any amount of labor less than OD the employer can increase his profit by using more labor; and for any amount of labor greater than OD the employer will be losing money, since he will be paying labor in wages more than it produces for him in revenue.

The point in equality of marginal revenue product and wage is therefore the point of maximum profit for the employer. Under the assumed circumstances of a horizontal supply curve for labor, the employer who is interested in obtaining the largest profit will seek to utilize that amount of labor for which the marginal revenue product of the last worker employed is approximately equal to his wage. If the employer follows this rule, ordinarily a reduction of wage rates will induce him to increase employment of labor, while an increase in wage rates will induce him to curtail employment of labor. This reaction is to be expected, however, only with a given marginal revenue product curve. If there should be an increase in wage rates concurrently with an increase in demand for labor (i.e., a shift to the right of the entire demand curve for labor), then it is quite possible that the wage increase will not produce any reduction in employment and, indeed, may even be associated with an increase in employment. This is frequently the case, as we shall see in our discussion in later chapters of wage changes during the business cycle. Increases in wage rates usually occur in periods when business is booming and the demand for labor is increasing. In such circumstances there is no immediate inducement for employers to curtail employment in response to the increased cost of labor. The marginal productivity theory, therefore, is quite consistent with the observed pattern of wage-employment relationships which develops over the period of the business cycle.

We have seen that maximum profits are obtained by the employer if he attempts to hire an amount of labor such that the marginal revenue product of the last man hired will approximate his wage. This principle is applicable to all factors of production which the employer utilizes. The marginal productivity theory assumes that wherever possible the employer will attempt to obtain maximum output at minimum cost. If he can do this by using more of one factor of production rather than another, he will do so. The decisive consideration in each case is the contribution to revenues in comparison with costs. For maximum profits the employer should utilize the various factors of production so that the ratio of the marginal revenue product of each factor to its cost will equal the ratio of marginal revenue product to cost of other factors. Of course, if the employer is able to use an amount of each factor such that its marginal revenue product is equal to cost, then the former condition of equality of ratios of respective marginal revenue products and costs will automatically be satisfied.[7]

EXPLOITATION OF LABOR

The marginal productivity theory assumes that there is a long-run tendency toward equality between the wage of labor and its marginal revenue product in the individual firm. Normally, the employer obtains his maximum profit by seeking to achieve this position. As we have seen, if the wage is below the marginal revenue product, it will pay him to increase output and employment to a point where this discrepancy is eliminated and the equality between wage and marginal revenue product is established. However, the marginal productivity theory recognizes that there may be certain situations in which a discrepancy can develop between marginal revenue product and wage which will be profitable for the employer to maintain, so that there will be no tendency to the normal equilibrium position of equality of wage and marginal revenue product. These exceptions from the general rule are referred to by economists as cases of exploitation of labor.

The term *exploitation* is used by economists simply to denote a condition in which labor will be paid a wage less than its marginal revenue product. It is a technical definition without social connotations. It has no necessary connection with the level of wage rates. The distressingly

---

[7] For a mathematical proof of the propositions stated in this section, see the Appendix at the end of this chapter.

low rates paid to labor in some marginal industries may present an acute labor problem, but the low rate is not itself any evidence of "exploitation" as the economist uses that term. Indeed, we shall see that exploitation of labor, as we have defined it, is as likely to be encountered where wages are high as where they are low.

Rising Supply Curve of Labor

Perhaps the most common source of exploitation is the lack of perfect elasticity in the supply curve for labor. In the preceding discussion, it was assumed that the supply curve for labor is horizontal (i.e., perfectly elastic); but frequently this will not be the case. For example, a firm may require such a substantial proportion of a particular type of labor in an area that it will have to offer higher wage rates when it wants additional labor, in order to attract workers away from other companies. This is particularly likely in cases of skilled labor which is in short supply. The type of exploitation here considered may therefore be more common where wage rates are high rather than low, as it is a result of scarcity in the labor market. In cases of such short supply a firm, in estimating its labor requirements, will take into account the fact that its demand for labor affects the market price of labor. The firm which is a large enough buyer of a particular class of labor so that its demand will affect the price of labor is termed a *monopsonist* by analogy to a monopolist who is a large enough seller of a commodity so that his supply will affect the price of a commodity. The monopsonist will assume that he is faced by a rising supply curve for labor, that is, that increasing amounts of labor can be obtained only at successively higher wage rates. This will affect his decision as to the amount of labor he will employ.

In our previous examples, we noted that if an employer can obtain additional workers at the same wage, the average cost of each additional worker and the marginal cost of each additional worker will be the same and will in each case be equal to the wage which is paid the worker. If, however, the employer has to pay higher wages to attract additional workers, the identity between average cost and marginal cost disappears. Suppose the prevailing wage paid by a firm has been $3 an hour, but in order to obtain additional workers, the employer finds he must increase the wage rate to $3.25 per hour. If he pays this rate to new workers, he will also be compelled to pay it to all other men of the same skill already in the firm, in order to avoid dissatisfaction among his employees. As a consequence, the addition to total wage cost (i.e., marginal cost) attributable to hiring an additional worker may under such circumstances be very great and considerably in excess of the wage, or average cost, of such a new man.

In Figure 10–3, units of labor hired by the firm are indicated along the X axis, while the cost of labor and its productivity in terms of dollars are indicated along the Y axis. The supply curve of labor (AC) is assumed to be rising to the firm. Each point on this line indicates the wage which will have to be paid to attract the amount of labor indicated along the X axis. The wage paid and the average cost of labor to the individual firm are therefore identical. However, when the average cost of labor is rising, the marginal cost will be greater, as has already been explained, since the marginal cost takes account not only of the higher wage paid

FIGURE 10–3

Exploitation: Upward Sloping Labor Supply Curve

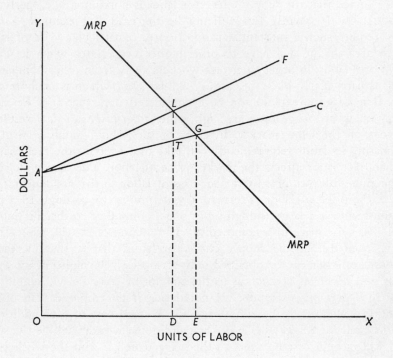

to a particular employee but also of the addition to payroll resulting from paying the same higher rate to all employees already employed by the firm. Marginal cost is indicated in Figure 10–3 by the line AF. Obviously, the employer has to take account of the expensive consequences in terms of his total payroll of paying higher rates for new men; and for this reason, he employs that amount of labor for which the marginal cost of labor and its marginal revenue product are equal. This equality is achieved if OD units of labor are employed. It will be recalled that in our previous example, where the supply curve of labor was constant, the employer also equated marginal cost of labor and marginal revenue product to maximize profits, since marginal cost of labor and the wage of labor were the same. However, in Figure 10–3, because the supply curve for labor is rising, for *OD* units of labor the marginal revenue product of labor (*DL*) will be above the wage paid to labor (*DT*). If the employer were to expand employment to *OE* units, which is the point where the wage and marginal revenue product are equal, he would, under the circumstances here set forth, reduce his profit. Here, then, is a case in which the wage will be less than marginal revenue product; therefore, exploitation will exist. Under the circumstances shown in Figure 10–3, the employer could not pay labor a wage equal to its marginal revenue product and still maximize profits.

Consequences of Exploitation

We have seen that if the wage of labor is approximately equated with its marginal revenue product, an increase in wage rates will lead the employer to reduce employment until at the smaller output the marginal revenue product of labor is raised to equal the now increased wage. In the case of exploitation attributable to a rising supply curve for labor, however, the effect of a wage increase upon employment will depend on whether there is a rise in the entire supply curve of labor or a change in its slope. If the entire marginal cost and average cost curves for labor shift upward but remain rising supply curves (as would be the case if there is a general increase in wage rates in the area), employment will be reduced in the individual firm, since there will have been a rise in the marginal cost of labor without a concomitant change in the marginal revenue productivity of labor. However, it is also possible that an increase in wage rates may be accompanied by a change in the shape of the supply curve of labor. For example, suppose a union enters the labor market and sets a uniform rate for labor, regardless of the number of workers required (within limits), which is equal to the former marginal cost of labor. In Figure 10–3, this would mean that the supply curve for labor would now be designated by a horizontal line drawn through point *L* on the marginal revenue product curve. If this were to occur, the employer would still find it profitable to employ the same number of employees (*OD*), since this amount would be indicated as most profitable by the intersection of the horizontal supply curve for labor and the demand curve for labor. The wage *DL* thus would be above the former wage *DT*, but because there would be no change in the marginal cost of labor, employment would be unaffected. All that would occur would be a reduction in profits of the firm. Here is a case in which workers would benefit from organization.

UNIONS AND MARGINAL PRODUCTIVITY THEORY

A rising supply curve for labor is most typical of skilled wage groups, but these are the very ones that are most likely to be highly unionized.

When a trade-union sets a minimum wage rate for work of a particular kind, regardless of the number of workers the employer hires to do it, the effect is to make the supply curve for labor to the employer horizontal or "perfectly elastic," as the economists say. This has the effect of eliminating exploitation attributable to a rising supply curve for labor. But union organization, by reason of its multifarious rules and regulations and restrictions on employer freedom of action, may also make it more difficult for employers to utilize the optimum amount of labor and thus may produce a discrepancy between marginal revenue product and wage.

The correspondence of a worker's wage with his individual contribution to the revenues of the firm depends in some degree upon the ability of the employer to determine the amount of such contribution. This presupposes that the employer can hire and fire at will, rearrange job classifications, change men from one position to another, substitute machinery for labor, and in general freely alter the combinations of labor and capital within the firm. Unions, however, have restricted many of these former prerogatives of management. Consequently, in firms where unions are strongly entrenched, workers are not freely substitutable, and the task of marginal productivity determination is undoubtedly made more difficult.

Effect of Union Rules

Union rules which limit the employer's ability to substitute machinery for labor and restrict the freedom of the employer to measure the contribution of labor to output of the firm may produce a range of indeterminateness in wage-employment relations. For example, many unions are now interested in requiring employers to pay dismissal wages to employees who are displaced as a result of technological change. Suppose that as a result of a wage increase an employer finds it is profitable to introduce a new machine which will displace 10 workers. If the union now compels the employer to pay these displaced workers dismissal wages for some period of time after they are laid off, the employer may decide it is no longer profitable to introduce the machine. The union insistence on a dismissal wage has obviously not increased the marginal revenue product of the labor involved; yet, it has had the practical effect of enabling the union to raise the wage rates of these workers without producing immediate technological unemployment.

In effect, union rules have produced a range of indeterminateness within which some changes in wage rates may be effected without altering employment. The range of indeterminateness, however, is much narrower than the short-run repercussions of employment would indicate. Any wage adjustment, whether it immediately alters employment or not, does affect profits and the inducement to invest. If these are adversely influenced by union wage demands, wage increases even within the "range of indeterminateness" may cause unemployment in the long run.

DEMAND FOR LABOR IN THE ECONOMY

As we have observed earlier in this chapter, the marginal productivity theory in its original form purported to explain the determination of wages in the economy as a whole. It laid down a long list of assumptions and emerged with a conclusion that in equilibrium the wage of labor in the economy as a whole would be equal to the marginal productivity of labor in its least profitable use. This conclusion—and the highly artificial assumptions upon which it was based—did much to bring the theory into disrepute. Moreover, proponents of the theory erroneously reasoned from the existence of unemployment in the labor market to the conclusion that wages were too high and that if wages were only reduced, unemployment could be eliminated.

We have seen that present-day labor economists do not look upon marginal productivity as a theory of wages, but rather as a theory of demand. But even here, limitations must be recognized. As a result of the work of John Maynard Keynes[8] in the field of general equilibrium analysis, it is generally accepted that the marginal productivity theory cannot serve as a general theory of employment and that the theory does not adequately explain the demand for labor in the economy as a whole. The demand curve for labor in the economy as a whole is not simply the sum of demand curves of all individual firms. The reason is that each individual demand curve for labor is drawn up under the assumption that wages and prices in other firms remain constant. Thus, when the individual employer considers what effect a reduction in wage rates will have on his labor requirements, he assumes that sales of his product will be unaffected by the reduction in wages. However, when we consider the economy as a whole, a reduction in the wages paid to all labor will affect the demand curve for all labor because wage earners are the principal purchasers of the product of industry. Whereas, for the individual firm, the demand curve for labor may be assumed to be independent of the supply curve for labor, this assumption cannot be made when we are considering the economy as a whole. Therefore, it is possible that a reduction in wage rates might not increase employment at all when the reduction is nationwide, even though increased employment would normally follow a wage reduction in the individual firm.

The demand for labor in the economy as a whole can only be understood by application of the aggregative analysis developed by Keynes,

---

[8] John Maynard Keynes, *The General Theory of Employment, Interest, and Money* (New York: Harcourt, Brace & Co., Inc., 1936).

in which attention is given to changes in savings, investment, and national income. However, the fact that marginal productivity analysis has proved inadequate to deal with the demand for labor in the economy as a whole does not necessarily mean that it cannot be used to advantage to explain the demand for labor in the individual firm. Exponents of this theory still contend that it gives a logical explanation of employer behavior in the individual firm.

Furthermore, even from the point of view of the economy as a whole, the marginal productivity theory helps us to understand why the level of wages is high in a country such as the United States and low in a country like India. The average level of wages in a particular economy will be determined by the scarcity of labor relative to other factors of production. In the United States, labor has always been in short supply relative to land and capital. As a consequence, the marginal product of labor has remained high. We have seen from previous examples in this chapter that as additional quantities of a factor of production are utilized, its marginal product declines. If labor were more plentiful in the United States, as it is in India, more labor would be used relative to capital, and its marginal product would be less. Employers have been ready to pay, and workers have been able to demand, a high level of wages in this country because the high ratio of land and labor to capital has made the incremental contribution of labor worth a high wage.

CRITIQUE OF THE MARGINAL PRODUCTIVITY THEORY

A number of criticisms have been leveled at the marginal productivity theory. Some of these have merit; others are based in part upon a lack of understanding of what the theory holds. The following are some of the major lines of attack against the marginal productivity theory.

1. Some economists object to the whole notion of marginality and marginal calculations on the ground that "businessmen don't think that way." It is all very well, they say, to draw up marginal revenue and marginal cost curves and sloping demand curves and rising supply curves, but the fact is that most employers have little or no idea of any points on these curves other than the point at which they are at the time. While businessmen know their existing prices, they do not know accurately how much their prices will have to be cut to sell additional units, or how much product can be sold at lower prices. Furthermore, factors of production are not easily divisible, so that, as a practical matter, businessmen cannot add one or two or three units of capital to determine how its marginal revenue productivity compares with that of labor. Capital is customarily embodied in "chunks" like machines and factories, and the employer cannot very well speculate on adding half a machine to his existing equipment. While this can be done to some extent in the long run when capital can be reinvested in various forms, the fact remains

that in the short run the indivisibility of units of the factors adds to the difficulties of determining marginal contributions.

This means that there are inevitably large areas of indeterminateness inherent in practical application of marginal productivity principles, assuming that employers try to apply them at all. Some economists doubt whether employers are even interested in marginal calculations. They point out that when labor costs rise, many businessmen talk about increasing output to reduce *average costs* per unit, whereas according to marginal productivity principles, they should be thinking in terms of decreasing output because of increased *marginal* costs. If businessmen are, in fact, more interested in the behavior of average rather than marginal costs, a substantial revision would be necessitated in marginal productivity doctrine.

Despite these criticisms, advocates of the marginal productivity theory maintain that marginalism still exemplifies the typical economic calculations of the average businessman. They point out that marginal-type calculations are really very simple and are practiced by employers in every aspect of business. For example, if an employer is asked why he does not take on another bookkeeper or purchase a particular machine, his answer will usually be that the added return or revenue or service would not justify the additional expense. Here is an example of the weighing of marginal contributions and marginal costs which the employer does in a rough sort of way, despite the admitted difficulties in making such calculations. This same sort of rough approximation is all that marginal productivity theorists claim is necessary to make their theory workable in practice.

2. Some economists claim that the market for labor does not function like the ordinary product market and that therefore the marginal productivity theory, which runs in conventional terms of supply and demand for labor, does not give a realistic picture of the labor market. We have already had occasion to consider some of the peculiarities of the labor market. Thus, there is typically no one price for a particular type of labor representing an equilibrium of supply and demand. On the contrary, many prices exist side by side, and there is little tendency for such differentials to disappear over time.

The contributions which have been made by labor economists in pointing out these characteristics of the labor market are important, but they do not invalidate supply and demand analysis. Both the volume of unemployment in a given labor market and the number of new job opportunities will have an effect on the whole structure of wage rates in a community, indicating that supply and demand considerations cannot be ignored. The fact that a union may set a wage in a particular market based upon a wage level established by some other union in a far distant city does not vitiate the usefulness of marginal productivity theory. Such a wage will probably differ from the wage which would be established in a free labor market; but whatever the wage which is established, it is still possible that the volume of employment at that wage will tend to be determined by the demand curve for labor, which reflects the marginal productivity of labor.

3. A major criticism directed against the marginal productivity theory stems from a fundamental disagreement as to the basic psychology and motivation of employers. Marginal productivity theorists, as we have seen, base their theory on the assumption that employers are motivated by a desire to *maximize* profits. But, as we have already observed, there is some evidence that management in certain companies may desire only a "fair return on investment," or may be motivated by considerations of community respect and other noneconomic objectives. It has even been suggested that the separation of management from ownership which typifies our large corporate business organizations may place management decisions in the hands of men who are more interested in such objectives as sales, power, prestige, and so forth, rather than maximum profits.[9] On the other hand, it can be argued that the increased professionalization of management and increased use by management of computers to obtain promptly the complex data necessary for accurate decision making will, if anything, tie business behavior closer to the theoretical goal of profit maximization.

Marginal productivity theorists, of course, recognize that all employers are not profit-minded to the same degree and that any decision in the labor market—as in any line of human endeavor—is the result of a complex of motivations, which may include considerations of prestige, family, security, power, and the like. However, they believe that most businessmen are normally concerned about how they are going to stay in business and that this involves keeping costs down and profits up. They contend, moreover, that managements in large corporations, whose balance sheets and profit and loss statements are made available to stockholders, are particularly interested in making a good showing relative to other large firms in the industry and in other industries. Management's reason for existing is to make profits for stockholder-owners, the usual measure of its success in earnings and dividends. Therefore, marginal productivity theorists state that as a general principle, it is fair to assume that maximization of profits is a dominant employer objective.

THE BARGAINING THEORY OF WAGES

Current interest in the peculiarities of the labor market and the dominant position of unions in shaping wage rates in many industries have led to a revival of interest in the bargaining theory of wages. The

---

[9] Fritz Machlup, "Theories of the Firm: Marginalist, Behavioral, Managerial," *American Economic Review*, Vol. 57 (March 1967), p. 5.

roots of this theory are found in the writings of early economists such as Adam Smith. The most complete recent expositions of a bargaining theory of wages are found in volumes by J. Pen[10] and John Cross.[11]

Basically, the bargaining theory holds that no single principle determines wage rates. In any labor market there may be a diversity of rates for the same type of labor. This diversity develops because of differences in the bargains made by various employers and their employees, or the unions representing the employees. Employers are conceived of as having upper limits above which they will not go in making a wage bargain. This upper limit will differ for various employers. Among the factors determining this upper limit are the productivity of the labor, the profitability of the business, the possibility of utilizing machinery as a substitute for labor, and the possibility that excessive labor costs might require the plant to shut down. The lower limit to the bargain is set by minimum wage rates established by state or federal governments, the possibility of labor moving to other firms or areas, community standards of what is a just wage, and similar considerations.

If the foregoing propositions are all that is involved in the bargaining theory of wages, that theory is quite consistent with the marginal productivity theory. For the latter merely holds that whatever the wage which is set—whether by government, collective bargaining, or market forces —the employer will attempt to adapt to it by employing an amount of labor such that its marginal revenue productivity will be equal to the wage. Some exponents of the bargaining theory overlook this and assume that because the exact level of the wage is indeterminate and may fall anywhere between the upper and the lower level above referred to, therefore the adaptation in terms of employment must also be indeterminate. Marginal productivity theorists deny this and have attempted to integrate the bargaining aspect of wage determination into the general structure of the marginal productivity theory.

For some economists, however, the bargaining theory is much more than just a theory of determination of wage levels. These economists extend bargaining principles to the relationship between wages and employment in the individual firm. They believe that this relationship is much more tenuous and indeterminate than the marginal productivity theory would lead one to believe. Thus, bargaining theorists maintain that a union, by superior bargaining power, may squeeze out monopoly profits for the benefit of organized employees without affecting the volume of employment in the firm. Likewise, they argue that organized labor may achieve wage increases at the expense of the remuneration

---

[10] J. Pen, *The Wage Rate Under Collective Bargaining* (Cambridge, Mass.: Harvard University Press, 1959).

[11] John Cross, *The Economics of Bargaining* (New York: Basic Books, Inc., Publishers, 1969).

going to other factors of production which are immobile or lack the benefit of organization to protect their interests.

These conclusions are also not necessarily inconsistent with marginal productivity theory. The latter has always recognized that in the short run, bargaining pressures may squeeze out monopoly profits or increase remuneration of one group at the expense of another, without affecting employment. In the long run, however, marginal productivity theorists contend that there is a tendency for adjustments to be made which do affect the volume of employment. While it may be true that we live in a world consisting of a continuous series of "short runs" and never clearly see the long-run effects of particular actions, nevertheless it would seem that any theory of the demand for labor must take account of the fact that short-run reactions to bargaining pressures are not the last word and that changes in location, size, and number of plants, investment in laborsaving machinery, and similar actions are part of the adjustment of employers to changed cost conditions, which take time to work themselves out.

SUMMARY

Theories of the demand for labor tend to evolve as our knowledge of the labor market improves and as the nature of the organization of industry and the labor market changes. The marginal productivity theory has held the center of the stage for many years as the accepted theory of labor demand, but recent criticisms indicate that it, too, is subject to revision and possible substitution by other theories. Whether its successor will be the bargaining theory or some other theory remains to be seen. At this point, no other theory has been elaborated in sufficient detail to constitute an adequate substitute.

In this and the preceding chapter, we have examined some of the factors which determine the supply and the demand of labor. We are now prepared to consider wage determination as it actually occurs in the labor market. This is the subject of the following chapter.

APPENDIX

The following analysis derives the marginal productivity theory from a general investigation of the theory of cost and production. Most of the following analysis applies irrespective of the elasticity of demand for the product of the firm under consideration (i.e., whether or not the industry is purely competitive). Although the analysis presented is restricted to two factors—capital and labor—it can be easily generalized to include any number of factors.

The maximum output of the product Q, which can be produced by the set of factors (K, L) is given by technical considerations and is represented by the production function.

$$Q = Q(K, L) \tag{1}$$

It is assumed that for each set of inputs there is a maximum output so that the function is single valued and has continuous partial derivatives of desired order. Further, neither marginal physical products can be negative, since otherwise production can be improved for the same input of one factor leaving the other idle, i.e.,

$$\frac{\delta Q}{\delta K}, \frac{\delta Q}{\delta L} \geq 0 \tag{2}$$

where the two partial derivatives are the marginal physical products of capital and labor respectively. By the assumption of perfect factor markets, unlimited amounts of each input can be purchased at the price r per unit of capital and w for each unit of labor

The total cost of the firm can be written as

$$C = F + rK + wL \tag{3}$$

where F represents the fixed costs which do not vary with the inputs and output (e.g., taxes). (In a particular case F may be zero.) In order to derive the total cost function for different levels of output, it is assumed that for given prices of the factors, and a given production function, the total cost is to be minimized. This will be a function as follows:

$$C = F + V(Q, r, w) . \tag{4}$$

If r and w are regarded as constant, the resulting relationship is the total cost curve.

Given the assumption of total cost minimization, there is an optimum combination of inputs so that the demand for each factor can be written as

$$\begin{aligned} K &= \phi_K(Q, w, r) \\ L &= \phi_L(Q, w, r) \end{aligned} \tag{5}$$

Substituting into (3), we have,

$$C = F + w\phi_K(Q, w, r) + r\phi_L(Q, w, r) = F + V(Q, w, r) \tag{6}$$

The problem is to minimize

$$C^{\cdot} = F + rK + wL \tag{7}$$

subject to

$$Q(K, L) = \bar{Q} = \text{constant.} \tag{8}$$

Mathematically, this is a constrained minimum problem which can be solved by the method of the Lagrangian multiplier. The Lagrangian function is written as

$$G = F + wL + rK - \lambda[Q(K, L) - \bar{Q}] \tag{9}$$

where $(-\lambda)$ is the Lagrangian multiplier whose economic interpretation will be furnished later. For a minimum,

$$\frac{\delta G}{\delta L} = 0 = w - \lambda \frac{\delta Q}{\delta L}$$
$$\frac{\delta G}{\delta K} = 0 = r - \lambda \frac{\delta Q}{\delta K} \tag{10}$$

which may be written as

$$\frac{1}{\lambda} = \frac{\delta Q/\delta L}{w} = \frac{\delta Q/\delta K}{r} \tag{11}$$

This is the economic law that *for total costs to be a minimum for a given output, the marginal productivity of the last unit of expenditure must be equal for all factors.* It must be noted that this condition is independent of the revenue curve of the firm and holds at every point on the cost curve.

For the optimum defined in (10) to be a proper constrained minimum, secondary necessary and sufficient conditions have to be satisfied.

Mathematically, the secondary conditions are that the bordered Hessian determinant and its principal minors alternate in sign, i.e.,

$$H = \begin{vmatrix} \dfrac{\delta^2 Q}{\delta K^2} & \dfrac{\delta^2 Q}{\delta K \delta L} & \dfrac{\delta Q}{\delta K} \\[2mm] \dfrac{\delta^2 Q}{\delta L \delta K} & \dfrac{\delta^2 Q}{\delta L^2} & \dfrac{\delta Q}{\delta L} \\[2mm] \dfrac{\delta Q}{\delta K} & \dfrac{\delta Q}{\delta L} & 0 \end{vmatrix} \tag{12}$$

Specifically

$$\frac{\delta^2 Q}{\delta K^2}\left(\frac{\delta Q}{\delta L}\right)^2 - 2\frac{\delta^2 Q}{\delta K \delta L}\frac{\delta Q}{\delta K}\frac{\delta Q}{\delta L} + \frac{\delta^2 Q}{\delta L^2}\left(\frac{\delta Q}{\delta K}\right)^2 < 0 \tag{13}$$

This condition is usually satisfied if the law of diminishing returns holds, i.e.,

$$\frac{\delta^2 Q}{\delta \Lambda^2} \quad \text{and} \quad \frac{\delta^2 Q}{\delta L^2} < 0$$

The economic significance of λ can be clarified by differentiating G in (9) with respect to Q, i.e.,

$$\frac{\delta G}{\delta Q} = \lambda \tag{14}$$

This suggests that λ may be a marginal cost. This can be demonstrated easily. Differentiating (7), we can write

$$dC = wdL + rdK \tag{15}$$

and the total differential of Q in (1) can be written as,

$$dQ = \frac{\delta Q}{\delta L} \, dL + \frac{\delta Q}{\delta K} \, dK. \tag{16}$$

Dividing (15) by (16), we obtain

$$\frac{\delta C}{\delta Q} = \frac{wdL + rdK}{\frac{\delta Q}{\delta L} \, dL + \frac{\delta Q}{\delta K} \, dK} \tag{17}$$

Substituting from (10) into (17)

$$\frac{\delta C}{\delta Q} = \frac{\lambda \left[\frac{\delta Q}{\delta L} \, dL + \frac{\delta Q}{\delta K} \, dK \right]}{\frac{\delta Q}{\delta L} \, dL + \frac{\delta Q}{\delta K} \, dK} \tag{18}$$

or

$$\frac{\delta C}{\delta Q} = \lambda$$

Substituting (18), (10) may be rewritten as

$$w = \frac{\delta C}{\delta Q} \cdot \frac{\delta Q}{\delta L} \tag{19}$$

$$r = \frac{\delta C}{\delta Q} \cdot \frac{\delta Q}{\delta K}$$

which may be stated as a theorem that *in order for total cost to be minimized for any given output, the price of each factor must be equal to the marginal physical product times marginal cost, irrespective of the revenue function.* Of course, profit maximization requires equality of marginal revenue and marginal cost. Therefore the theorem can also be stated that in the equilibrium position at which total cost will be minimized, the price of each factor must be equal to its marginal physical product times its marginal contribution to the revenue of the firm.

QUESTIONS FOR DISCUSSION

1. Explain what is meant by marginal productivity. What is the difference between the value of the marginal physical product of labor and the marginal revenue product of labor? Under what circumstances will they be the same?
2. Compare the marginal productivity theory with the bargaining theory of

wages. What points of similarity are there in the two theories? What are the merits and shortcomings of each?

3. What conditions may produce a rising supply curve for labor? Will employers apply marginal productivity principles when faced by a rising supply curve of labor? Discuss.

SUGGESTIONS FOR FURTHER READING

CROSS, JOHN. *The Economics of Bargaining.* New York: Basic Books, Inc., Publishers, 1969.

An exposition, with mathematical elaboration, of the impact of bargaining on the level of wages.

FLEISHER, BELTON M. *Labor Economics: Theory and Evidence,* chap. vi, "The Theory of the Demand for Labor: The Competitive Firm," pp. 119–40. Englewood Cliffs, N.J.: Prentice-Hall, Inc., 1970.

A concise mathematical explanation of the derivation of the short-run and long-run demand for labor.

HICKS, J. R. *The Theory of Wages,* chap. i, pp. 1–22. 2nd ed. London: Macmillan & Co., Ltd., 1963. (See also review of Chapter I by G. F. Shore, *ibid.,* pp. 249–67 and commentary on same by J. R. Hicks, pp. 321–27.)

A classic discussion of the demand for labor from the marginalist point of view with current commentaries on the theory.

McCONNELL, CAMPBELL, R. *Perspectives on Wage Determination,* pp. 7–23. New York: McGraw-Hill Book Co., 1970.

Excerpts from the writings of Ricardo, Mill, Marx, Walker, and Davidson setting forth the wage theories associated with those writers.

MACHLUP, FRITZ. "Theories of the Firm: Marginalist, Behavioral, Managerial," *American Economic Review,* Vol. LVII (March, 1967), pp. 1–33.

An excellent review and critique of various attacks which have been directed against marginal analysis, together with a bibliography of articles on this subject.

Chapter 11

WAGE DETERMINATION

UNDER TRADE UNIONISM

In the three preceding chapters, we have considered the supply of labor, the demand for labor, and the labor market in which these forces operate. Wage determination in the individual firm reflects the various economic forces and circumstances we have examined. Thus, *ceteris paribus*, the wage level in a particular firm will ordinarily be lower if the demand for labor is decreasing than if it is increasing. Wages will be higher when labor is in short supply than where there is a large body of unemployed labor available. Rates will tend to be lower in the South than in the North.

When union business agents and management representatives sit down to the conference table to negotiate a new contract, the foregoing circumstances set some limit to the range within which wage rates will finally be set. In this chapter, we shall examine the conditions which cause a particular schedule of rates to be agreed upon by union and management representatives in the individual firm. How are wage rates adjusted in the collective bargaining process? What is the relationship between rates in different firms in the same industry? What are the criteria and pertinent economic circumstances which union and management consider in determining wage rates? In discussing wage determination, we shall concentrate our attention on changes in money wage rates, but this should not lead the reader to underestimate the importance of fringe benefits. As we observed in Chapter 5, the practice in union negotiations in recent years has been for so-called "package" settlements which include improvements in various forms of supplementary compensation as well as basic pay.

THE INTERNAL WAGE STRUCTURE

In the typical large industrial establishment today, literally hundreds of individual wage rates or wage classifications have to be adjusted as part of a wage negotiation. In our theoretical discussion in earlier chapters, we have talked about "the wage rate in the individual firm." This is obviously a simplification. It would be more correct to talk about a wage structure. The wage structure is the whole complex of rates within the individual firm for all of the various jobs for which persons are employed. This wage structure does not necessarily move as a unit. There may be, of course, wage negotiations where a flat 10 cents an hour or a uniform percentage increase is given to all employees; but frequently, exceptions are made for particular groups of employees. There are always individual jobs which get out of line as a result of the passage of time and as a result of the impact of technological change. These require special treatment. Furthermore, there is the pressing problem of keeping a proper relationship between the skilled and the unskilled rates. As a result of these various factors, the wage structure may be compressed or stretched out from one negotiation to the next (viewing the wage structure in terms of the entire schedule of rates from the lowest to the highest paid employee).

While a great many rates must be altered in the course of a wage negotiation, labor and management do not normally make an issue of every individual rate. This would obviously take too much time. Instead, emphasis is placed upon the key rates in various job clusters. A job cluster may be defined as a stable group of job classifications or work assignments within a firm which are so linked together by technology, the administrative organization of the production process, or social custom that they have common wage-making characteristics.[1] Thus, in a factory, one job cluster may consist of various classes of lathe operators; another job cluster, of sweepers, janitors, etc.; another, of patternmakers, etc. Each cluster can be viewed as consisting of a key rate and associated rates. Key rates may be the highest rate in the particular cluster, the lowest, or sometimes the rate at which the greatest number of workers are employed. These are the rates on which union and management representatives focus in their bargaining negotiations, and once these rates are determined, the associated rates fall into line.

THE EXTERNAL WAGE STRUCTURE

Key rates in the individual firm are not determined in a vacuum. On the contrary, they are hammered out in a collective bargaining relationship where management attempts to safeguard its competitive position in the particular industry of which it is a part. Most company executives keep well informed as to the rates their competitors pay for comparable jobs. As one labor text puts it: "Wage level negotiation has been undertaken in the light of an increasingly refined and comprehensive knowl-

---

[1] John T. Dunlop, "The Task of Contemporary Wage Theory," in George W. Taylor and Frank C. Pierson (eds.), *New Concepts in Wage Discrimination* (New York: McGraw-Hill Book Co., 1957), p. 129.

edge of comparative wage rates."[2] Unless there are extenuating circumstances, management usually tries to keep its rates on par with its competitors', on the theory that if its rates are lower, it will lose employees, and if its rates are higher, it will lose business because of the higher costs.

One writer uses the concept of a "wage contour" to elucidate the relationship between the key rates of various individual firms or establishments. "A wage contour is a stable group of wage-determining units which are so linked together by (1) similarity of product markets, (2) resort to similar sources for a labor source, or (3) common labor-market organization (custom) that they have common wage-making characteristics."[3] For example, the basic steel contour for production jobs consists of basic steel producers throughout the nation. By contrast, newspapers in New York City constitute a separate wage contour not directly affected by rates in other cities. The wage contour normally contains one or, in some instances, several key settlements. The contour is composed of rates for a key firm(s) and a group of associated firms. The key settlement may be set by the largest firm, the price leader, or the firm which customarily plays the role of wage relations leader. As we shall see later in this chapter, leader-follower relationships in wage determination are extremely important in our basic industries. Some firms within a wage contour will follow the key settlement closely; others will follow it in varying degree. But this external relationship will have an important bearing on the decision which is made with respect to changes in the key rates in the various job clusters of each establishment's internal wage structure.

The concept of the wage contour helps to explain differences which prevail in rates for similar jobs in different industries. For example, a comparison of rates paid to motor truck drivers in Boston in a variety of industries indicated that the rates paid for teamsters in these essentially substitutable jobs were twice as high in magazine distribution as in scrap iron and metal.[4] The reason for the variation is that each rate was a reflection of conditions in its own wage contour. Each is a reflection of the product market. Magazine distributors were more concerned about the rates that their competitors *in that industry* had to pay for truck drivers than what the rate was in the scrap-iron business. Of course, in a perfect labor market, these differences could not prevail because teamsters would tend to move to the higher paying industry, and the lower paying industries would have to raise their rates in order to hold their employees. In actuality, these differences persist over long periods of time because of

---

[2] Sumner H. Slichter, J. J. Healy and E. R. Livernash, *The Impact of Collective Bargaining on Management* (Washington, D.C.: Brookings Institution, 1960), p. 592.

[3] Dunlop, *Task of Contemporary Wage Theory*, p. 131.

[4] *Ibid.*, p. 135.

the orientation of the wage rate determination process in terms of the product market and because of the differences in competitive conditions, profits, and demand conditions in the various industries using this similar type of labor.

In an important sense, the individual firm can be thought of as an internal labor market within which the pricing and allocation of labor is governed by a set of administrative rules and procedures. The internal market is connected to the external labor market by movement at certain job classifications which constitute "ports of entry and exit" to and from the internal labor market. In some industries, such as the garment industry, there will be many such ports of entry and a considerable flow of workers in and out of the firm at various occupational levels. On the other hand, in a steel plant, skills tend to be more highly specialized and may have to be acquired on the job, so that ports of entry are more limited.[5] The wage structure which develops within the firm, therefore, reflects the influence of the external labor market but also to an important degree depends upon the specific skills peculiar to the enterprise and differentials which develop from long-standing custom.

GENERAL WAGE INCREASES

Much of the friction which develops in collective bargaining involves the issue of "wage increases." What precisely do we mean by this phrase? General wage increases normally have little or no relation to merit. They are usually given to all workers, whether or not the employer is satisfied with their individual performance. The justification for the increase may be an increase in the cost of living or the high profits made by the employer. The performance of the company as a whole is always a consideration, but the performance of the individual worker is not usually at issue in such negotiations. The increases are often but not always uniform for all employees. Many industrial unions prefer to have uniform adjustments for all employees in terms of so many cents per hour because this tends to give the lower paid workers—who represent the bulk of the union membership—a larger percentage increase than higher paid workers.

In the 1930s and 1940s, when the advent of industrial unionism first made its impact felt on the wage structure, there was a strong trend for larger percentage wage adjustments for the lower paid employees. As a result, there was a definite narrowing of occupational differentials. By the early 1950s a slowing-down of this narrowing process was observable; and in recent years, there has been evidence of the maintenance of

---

[5] For an elaboration of this theory, see Peter B. Doeringer and Michael J. Piore, *Internal Labor Markets and Manpower Analysis* (Lexington, Mass.: D. C. Heath & Co., 1971), p. 2 ff.

reasonably stable differentials. This has been partly attributable to an increasing tendency to grant special increases for skilled workers.

What circumstances do unions and management take account of in determining the amount of a wage increase in an individual firm? Many arguments are used by ingenious union representatives to justify an increase in wage rates. Management representatives are equally adept at finding reasons why the increase cannot be made. In the following discussion, we shall consider some of the principal criteria which seem to play an important part in the determination of the size of general wage adjustments.

CRITERIA IN GENERAL WAGE ADJUSTMENTS

Intraindustry Comparative Standards

Perhaps the most common standard which is applied by both labor and management to determine whether a wage adjustment should be made in a particular firm is to compare its wage structure with those of other companies in the industry. Because of the importance of the standard of what the other fellow is doing, both union and management representatives usually come to the bargaining table armed with statistics, or at least a working knowledge, of what other firms in the industry are paying. In some industries, employers' associations make such data available; in others the employer may have to rely on telephone calls to the personnel directors of competing companies. Unions in many cases are able to obtain such data through their international office or through other locals.

Reliance on rates that other companies are paying would, at first glance, seem to put collective bargaining on a factual basis. "If a competitor can afford to pay given rates, why can't you?" is the question put by union agents to the employer. The trouble is that statistics—particularly when they are averages—may have little meaning because of shortcomings in their tabulation. Furthermore, job content of seemingly similar jobs varies considerably from firm to firm. The mere fact that a job classification calls for a stitcher, or a cutter, or a clerk, or a painter does not mean that the work or the skill required is identical or that the technical conditions will be similar for all employees having similar job descriptions. In the same industry or area the same job title may be used for dozens of dissimilar operations.

Actually, the criterion of intraindustry standards leaves ample room for bargaining. For example, the union may want to compare hourly rates in various plants, while the employer may want to compare weekly earnings. This is frequently the case where a company permits its employees to work some overtime each week at time and a half the regular rate, which gives its employees more take-home pay than workers in other plants. Nevertheless, the union will argue that hourly rates should be raised to bring them in line with rates in other plants in the industry.

Wage Leadership. In industries employing the most wage earners—steel, automotive bodies and parts, aircraft, rubber, baked goods, textiles, paper and paperboard, and others—the tendency is for the individual employer to keep his wage rates in line with rates paid by certain key firms in the industry, a policy which frequently results in an industrywide adjustment of wages whenever circumstances compel revision in such key companies.

The typical structure of an industry in the American economy is that four to eight companies will produce from one half to four fifths of the total output of the industry. Once wage scales have been set in the major companies, the pattern of wage adjustment for most employees in the industry has also been determined. Just as big companies influence small companies, so wage rates set in populous areas tend to affect rates in outlying areas. For example, building-trades negotiations in New York and Chicago are likely to be influential in local areas. The same situation will exist in printing industry negotiations in these two cities and in negotiations in the transit industry in Detroit and Boston.

Wage leadership does not depend upon the existence of national, regional, or other forms of industrywide bargaining. Key wage bargains are important whether wages are determined by collective bargaining or by unilateral company decision in the case of unorganized employees. In some industries, wage leadership existed prior to the advent of unions. For example, other steel companies have historically adjusted their wages to patterns set by the United States Steel Corporation. In this and other industries, wage leadership has often gone hand in hand with price leadership.

Although wage leadership has existed in the absence of union organization, union wage pressure has tended to spread and to make explicit uniformity in wage rates as a cardinal basis of management wage policy. There is now double pressure for meeting the other fellow's wage rates: from competitors and from labor itself. Union contracts requiring payment of wages on a par with rates prevailing for work of a similar kind in other firms in the industry hasten the spread of wage increases through an industry. At the same time, however, such pressure may produce a feeling among company executives that upward adjustments should not be made unless other firms in the industry are making them, or the union demands them; therefore, they make fewer, though larger, wage adjustments.

In some industries, there are not only wage leaders but also "high-wage firms." These companies try to pay more than the going rate for labor. Sometimes, such firms justify this policy on the ground that high wages attract better than average employees. In other cases, the reason for the policy may be to keep out a union. In any case, unions use such differentials to their advantage. In bargaining with other companies in the industry, they will argue that competitors of the high-wage firm should pay wages equal to those paid by the high-wage company. Then, after obtaining such an increase from the other firms, they will go back to the high-wage firm (once it has been organized) and contend that it should maintain its historical differential. Companies which have adopted a higher than average wage policy as a means of keeping out a union may thus find that they are stuck with the policy when the union organizes their employees.

Unions typically use such a leveling approach in their bargaining strategy. Rates for a particular class of employees may be relatively high in one firm, perhaps because of the length of service of these employees, or perhaps because of unusual conditions under which they have to work. The union will cite the example of these high rates to other firms in the industry, which are likely to be unaware of the special circumstances creating them, and will argue that they should meet these high rates. In the same way a "bad settlement" made by one employer in an industry who could not risk a strike for financial reasons can be used by a union as a lever to raise the rates of every other firm in the industry.

Union Attitudes toward Wage Uniformity. Most unions want uniformity in wage rates for similar jobs throughout an area of competitive production. Unions are dynamic organizations; but paradoxically, one of their major objectives is stability. Frequently, achievement of this aim is dependent upon elimination of competition between firms in the sphere of wage rates. The more competitive the industry, the smaller the units in the industry, and the less responsible the employers, the greater is the likelihood that union wage policy will seek competitive parity in labor cost as a measure to relieve pressure on the wage structure. In an industry in which there is considerable variation in the size and efficiency of the individual firms, a union must decide whether the welfare of its members can best be served by equalization of hourly rates, piece rates, or labor costs per unit in the various plants under union jurisdiction. In some circumstances, the policy of equalization of wage rates or hourly earnings will provide the maximum incentive to industrial efficiency. It may be adopted in the form of uniform wage scales, as in the building and printing industries, where jobs are skilled and occupational rungs clearly defined; or it may take the form of uniformity in plant average hourly earnings, as in the carpet and rug industry, where rapid technology and lack of standardization of operations and product make this the most expedient policy. Such a plan attempts to stabilize earnings while leaving costs to management. Since backward companies must pay as high rates as the most efficient firms, a policy of uniformity in hourly or day wage rates provides the maximum incentive to adoption of improved machinery by the less efficient companies in an industry.

If, on the other hand, the union decides to equalize piece rates or unit labor cost, the incentive afforded to employers to improve efficiency is reduced unless the union agrees to adjust rates downward as improvements in technique permit greater output. For if piece rates are fixed, introduction of improved machinery serves merely to increase output per worker, so that labor's earnings, not employers' profits, are augmented by technical advance. In the men's clothing industry, for example, the Amalgamated Clothing Workers, through its Market Stabilization Department, has attempted to standardize labor costs on a national scale. Standard labor costs are established for various grades of clothing, and conformity with the standards of quality and labor costs is enforced by union representatives. Since the labor cost on a given grade of clothing is fixed and cannot be reduced, the employer is deprived of virtually all incentive to improve his method of production and the quality of his garments. Since the stabilization program substantially reduces the employer's incentive to make improvements in technique, if it were strictly enforced it would deter technological progress in the unionized portion of the industry and provide a major opportunity for expansion of production and employment in nonunion shops. In practice, of course, strict enforcement of the stabilization plan has been impossible. Furthermore, the program does not apply to high-quality garments. Consequently, an area is still left in which an incentive is offered to the employer to improve methods of production. In this connection, it is important to realize that even if employers cannot reduce labor costs through mechanization, technological progress may still hold forth the prospect of savings in other costs, such as material, electricity, and so on.

The extent to which a strong union can introduce uniformity of wage rates in an industry is well illustrated by recent developments in the over-the-road trucking industry, where the Teamsters' Union substantially achieved national contracts. While local differentials still remain to some extent, the union has used the device of the long-term contract and common termination dates to achieve its goal of eliminating the great dispersion of rates which formerly existed in this industry. The trend toward wage standardization in the trucking industry has already gone far and is likely to continue.

On the whole, it seems likely that equalization of wage rates will come to be the dominant form of union wage policy. Of course, there must necessarily be variations from this to suit the peculiarities of individual industries, but the policy of uniformity will probably come to prevail in those industries in which it is practicable because it is best adapted to the political necessities of unionism. It is simple, and its aim of equality in a particularly obvious and just form commends it as a slogan for the rank and file. Its reasonableness is convincing. As one union leader puts it: "If Joe Smith goes into a store to buy a hat, he has to pay the same price for it whether he happens to be an employee of General Motors or American Motors. Then why shouldn't he be paid the same rate for his work?"

Union preference for uniformity in wage rates has already made its impact felt on various aspects of the wage structure of American industry. Within individual firms, unionism has generally eliminated personal differentials in rates or brought them into a formalized, controlled wage scale. Likewise, union organization has tended to reduce or eliminate interfirm differentials in the same product and labor market.[6]

Interindustry Comparative Standards

Wage determination in a particular firm may be affected not only by settlements made by key firms in the same industry but also by major companies in other industries. Some economists are of the opinion that we have reached the stage where a limited number of key wage bargains effectively influence the whole wage structure of the American economy. The concept of key wage bargains was a cornerstone of the Nixon administration's wage and price control plan which sought to regulate the advance of wages in general by focusing on wage adjustments in the largest firms in the economy. A study of wage changes made during the post–World War II period in 11 basic industries—steel, automotive, electrical, rubber, aluminum, aircraft, farm machinery, copper, petroleum refining, meat-packing, and shipbuilding—found a high degree of uniformity in the size of wage adjustments in these industries.[7]

Two other researchers have found a "contour group" consisting of the following industries: rubber, stone clay and glass, primary metals, fabricated metals, nonelectrical machinery, electrical machinery, transportation equipment, and instruments.[8] Wages in these industries were found to have moved almost identically since 1948. In the words of the investigators,

All of these industries are high-wage industries, have strong industrial unions, typically consist of large corporations that possess considerable market power, and are geographically centered in the Midwestern industrial heartland of the continent.[9]

How are these key wage bargains transmitted from one industry to another? According to one economist who has studied this phenomenon in detail, there are four important circumstances which help produce this uniformity in wage movement:[10]

---

[6] Clark Kerr, "Wage Relationships—The Comparative Impact of Market and Power Forces," in John T. Dunlop (ed.), *The Theory of Wage Determination* (London: Macmillan & Co., Ltd., 1957), p. 181.

[7] John E. Maher, "The Wage Pattern in the United States, 1946–1957," *Industrial and Labor Relations Review*, Vol. 16 (October 1961), p. 16.

[8] Otto Eckstein and Thomas A. Wilson, "The Determination of Money Wages in American Industry," *Quarterly Journal of Economics*, Vol. 76 (August 1962), pp. 384–85.

[9] *Ibid.* These trends are equally evident today.

[10] Maher, "Wage Pattern," pp. 5–6.

1. *The Input-Output Nexus.*   Many of these industries have close ties with each other because of a buyer-seller relationship. For example, the automotive industry is the largest consumer of rubber and electrical products; aircraft is the largest consumer of aluminum. Buyers and sellers have an understandable interest in the wage policies of each other, since a rise in labor costs and in prices of the supplier will ultimately affect the costs and prices of the buyer industry.

2. *Similar Technology.*   Most of these industries have a high capital-output and a high capital-labor ratio. Likewise, they are mass-production industries. Most produce capital goods or consumer durable goods. Therefore, they tend to react in similar fashion to current economic changes.

. 3. *Distribution of Participants.*   Most of these industries are clustered in particular geographical areas. Furthermore, the employees in these industries are represented for the most part by a relatively few large national unions.

4. *Institutional Channels of Communication.*   Most of the unions involved were originally CIO and most are now in the AFL–CIO. The leaders of the unions are important, nationally known figures in the labor movement, and there is considerable rivalry among them.

Such key wage bargains affect the thinking of unions and management in a variety of industries. Both tend to look to these key agreements as a barometer of the labor market, indicating what workers expect in the way of wage adjustments. In a very real sense, a handful of key negotiators representing management and labor can set trends which will affect the compensation of millions of workers in other industries. Faced with the need of resolving differences, management and union leaders find in key wage bargains a convenient figure upon which they can rationalize a contract. Moreover, union leaders find they must meet the increase obtained by a union leader in another industry, or their personal popularity will be affected. The size of the wage increase obtained by various labor leaders is as assiduously studied by their constituents as the batting averages of baseball players, and if a labor leader wants to stay at the top of the league, he has to keep pace with his rivals in other unions. Union leaders are alert to capitalize on new types of benefits which may have been incorporated in contracts in other industries. Although there are an estimated 150,000 collective bargaining agreements in effect in the United States, about 20 unions are responsible for three quarters of them, and there is a constant exchange of information among them.

The variation in wage adjustments among firms and industries reflects differences in profitability, as well as in the ability of management to pass along wage increases in the form of higher prices. The variations may also reflect the effect of union rivalries. Leaders of competing unions— whether they are competing for prestige within the labor movement or actually competing for membership—have to avoid falling into a "me, too" policy of simply following another union's lead. "Each policy has to give its followers benefits equal to those obtained under the rival's policies and at the same time must appear to differ from the rival's policy. This leads to a preference for minimum differentiations."[11] Such differentiations may be in the form of varying (1) the amount of the wage adjustment while following the cost of the total package of benefits, (2) the timing of the adjustments, or (3) the nature and extent of fringe benefits. Furthermore, variations from the key wage pattern are more common the smaller the company and the fewer the employees on its payroll. Nevertheless, even with small companies, there tends to be some spillover from the national trend.

Cost of Living

A criterion of major importance in wage negotiations—particularly during periods of rising prices such as we have experienced in recent years —is change in the cost of living. During periods of rising prices, wages typically lag behind prices. This lag is attributable in part to the fact that wages are much more "sticky" than prices. In fact, most wages of organized employees are fixed by contract for a given period, frequently a year. During the contract period, price increases may rob wage adjustments of much of their value. The extent to which inflation appears to neutralize wage increases is indicated in Table 11–1. Despite large wage gains achieved by labor in recent years, average spendable weekly earnings of workers with three dependents were no greater in 1971 than in 1965, using 1967 dollars as the base. It is understandable, then, that when union representatives sit down at the bargaining table, they naturally have in mind such figures as these and think in terms of a wage increase compensating for the rise in the cost of living as a minimum demand. Management, too, tends to be impressed by such general data and is anxious to provide its employees with some improvement in living standards.

Data of the type reported in Table 11–1 are often put on the bargaining table and supposedly put negotiations on a more concrete basis than would be true if such figures were not available. But what do such statistics really mean? Do they mean that the worker sitting across the table from the employer is no better off then he was in 1965 because the rise in cost of living has been eroding his earnings? Not necessarily so. A number of factors account for the apparent lack of improvement in real earnings, but the erosion cannot all be attributed to the rise in cost of living:

1. The data in Table 11–1 report weekly earnings. Weekly earnings

---

[11] Benson Soffer, "On Union Rivalries and the Minimum Differentiation of Wage Patterns," *Review of Economics and Statistics*, Vol. 41 (February 1959), p. 54.

TABLE 11-1

Average Weekly Earnings, Gross and Spendable, in Manufacturing Industries, in Current and 1967 Dollars, 1939–71

Year or month	Average gross weekly earnings		Average spendable weekly earnings [2]			
			Worker with no dependents		Worker with three dependents	
	Current dollars	1967 dollars [1]	Current dollars	1967 dollars [1]	Current dollars	1967 dollars [1]
1939	$23.64	$56.83	$23.37	$56.18	$23.40	$56.25
1940	24.96	59.43	24.46	58.24	24.71	58.83
1941	29.48	66.85	27.96	63.40	29.19	66.19
1942	36.68	75.16	31.80	65.16	36.31	74.41
1943	43.07	83.15	35.95	69.40	41.33	79.79
1944	45.70	86.72	37.99	72.09	43.76	83.04
1945	44.20	82.00	36.82	68.31	42.59	79.02
1946	43.32	74.05	37.31	63.78	42.79	73.15
1947	49.17	73.50	42.10	62.93	47.58	71.12
1948	53.12	73.68	46.57	64.59	52.31	72.55
1949	53.88	75.46	47.21	66.12	52.95	74.16
1950	58.32	80.89	50.26	69.71	56.36	78.17
1951	63.34	81.41	52.97	68.08	60.18	77.35
1952	67.16	84.48	55.04	69.23	62.98	79.22
1953	70.47	87.98	57.59	71.90	65.60	81.90
1954	70.49	87.57	58.45	72.61	65.65	81.55
1955	75.70	94.39	62.51	77.94	69.79	87.02
1956	78.78	96.78	64.92	79.75	72.25	88.76
1957	81.59	96.79	66.93	79.40	74.31	88.15
1958	82.71	95.51	67.82	78.31	75.23	86.87
1959	88.26	101.10	71.89	82.35	79.40	90.95
1960	89.72	101.15	72.57	81.82	80.11	90.32
1961	92.34	103.06	74.60	83.26	82.18	91.72
1962	96.56	106.58	77.86	85.94	85.53	94.40
1963	99.63	108.65	79.82	87.04	87.58	95.51
1964	102.97	110.84	84.40	90.85	92.18	99.22
1965	107.53	113.79	89.08	94.26	96.78	102.41
1966	112.34	115.58	91.57	94.21	99.45	102.31
1967	114.90	114.90	93.28	93.28	101.26	101.26
1968	122.51	117.57	97.70	93.76	106.75	102.45
1969	129.51	117.95	101.90	92.81	111.44	101.49
1970	133.73	114.99	106.62	91.68	115.90	99.66
1971 ᴾ	142.44	117.43	114.97	94.78	124.24	102.42
1970: Jan	131.60	116.15	105.03	92.70	114.17	100.77
Feb	130.94	114.96	104.53	91.77	113.69	99.82
Mar	132.40	115.63	105.63	92.25	114.85	100.31
Apr	131.47	114.12	104.93	91.09	114.06	99.01
May	132.93	114.89	106.02	91.63	115.27	99.63
June	134.74	115.86	107.38	92.33	116.71	100.35
July	134.46	115.22	107.17	91.83	116.48	99.81
Aug	134.13	114.74	106.92	91.46	116.22	99.42
Sept	135.43	115.26	107.90	91.83	117.25	99.79
Oct	133.45	113.00	106.41	90.10	115.68	97.95
Nov	134.58	113.57	107.26	90.51	116.58	98.38
Dec	138.45	116.25	110.16	92.49	119.66	100.47
1971: Jan	138.60	116.28	112.14	94.08	121.25	101.72
Feb	138.29	115.82	111.91	93.73	121.01	101.35
Mar	139.74	116.64	112.98	94.31	122.14	101.95
Apr	139.83	116.33	113.04	94.04	122.21	101.67
May	142.00	117.55	114.65	94.91	123.90	102.57
June	143.51	118.12	115.76	95.28	125.07	102.94
July	142.09	116.66	114.71	94.18	123.97	101.78
Aug	141.69	116.04	114.42	93.71	123.65	101.27
Sept	143.28	117.25	115.59	94.59	124.89	102.20
Oct	144.00	117.65	116.12	94.87	125.45	102.49
Nov ᴾ	144.72	118.04	116.65	95.15	126.01	102.78
Dec ᴾ	150.18	122.00	120.64	98.00	130.25	105.81

[1] Earnings in current dollars divided by the consumer price index.
[2] Average gross weekly earnings less social security and income taxes.
Source: Data, Department of Labor, Bureau of Labor Statistics; chart, *Economic Report of the President, 1972* (Washington, D.C.: U.S. Government Printing Office, 1972), Table B–33, p. 233.

are affected by a change in average hours worked. The average workweek in 1965 was over 41 hours whereas in 1971, due to the recession, it was only about 40 hours.[12]

2. Spendable earnings reflect changes in taxes. Increasing taxes are not the equivalent of lower wages because presumably higher taxes are accompanied by improved public services, including welfare and higher social security benefits.

3. Various indexes produce different measurements of the actual increase in the cost of living. For example, one economist[13] has found that the Consumer Price Index overstates increases in cost of living as compared with the deflator for personal consumption spending used in national income accounts by the federal government.

4. There has been a change in the employment mix in manufacturing because of the increasing employment of women and younger workers, which tended to bring down the level of average weekly earnings in 1971.

After taking account of these various changes, one economist found that in the period 1966 to 1970, there was a 12% difference between the official series on real spendable weekly earnings and what he considers a more realistic measure of real wages.[14] This analysis indicates that gross statistics must be used with care. Certainly, the matters referred to in paragraphs 1, 2, and 4 are unrelated to cost of living in the usual sense. Nevertheless, the union bargaining agent can still point to the fact that whatever the cause, the worker is no better off in terms of net cash in his pocket. Therefore, cost of living becomes a sort of crude slogan for labor to voice when it seeks to improve the net cash position of the employee, even though the lack of progress in net spendable earnings may not be attributable to increases in the cost of living per se..

Although union representatives place heavy reliance on increases in the cost of living as a justification for wage increases in times of rising prices, when the cost of living falls they shift their arguments with great facility to some less vulnerable criterion. At such times, they will usually argue in terms of the need to maintain purchasing power.

The cost of living many enter into wage negotiations in several ways. In most cases, it is simply another one of the key criteria which unions and management consider in arriving at a wage adjustment. In other situations the cost of living may affect wage determinations in a much more specific manner. This will be the case where unions and management have already incorporated in their collective bargaining agreements automatic cost-of-living adjustments or escalator clauses. These clauses

[12] U.S. Department of Labor, Bureau of Labor Statistics, *Employment and Earnings*, Vol. 18 (March 1972), Chart 12, p. 15.

[13] George L. Perry, economist for the Brookings Institution, cited in *New York Times*, May 9, 1971, Section F., p. 14.

[14] *Ibid.*

typically specify a precise relationship between changes in the cost of living and changes in the wage rates to be paid employees covered by the agreement. There is considerable variation in various contracts with respect to the ratio between cost-of-living changes and wage changes. Some contracts are adjustable only upward, but most make wages adjustable both upward and downward in response to changes in a specific cost-of-living index.

Development of Automatic Escalator Clauses. The development of automatic escalator clauses geared to changes in the cost of living may be said to have commenced with the General Motors contract of 1948. Prior to that time, cost-of-living provisions had been incorporated in various contracts; but in the aggregate, they covered relatively few workers. However, the General Motors settlement started a new trend. By 1950, approximately 2 million workers were covered by cost-of-living adjustments in labor contracts, and by 1960 the number had risen to 3.3 million.[15] During the early sixties, increases in the Consumer Price Index were quite modest, and cost of living was not a major factor in wage negotiations during this period. As a result, as of 1971 only about 3 million workers were covered by automatic cost-of-living adjustments in labor contracts. However, the sharp upturn in cost of living in the last few years has renewed labor's interest in such provisions. In 1972, it is estimated that more workers will be covered by such adjustments— about 4.3 million in all—than in any prior year.[16] The increase in coverage is mainly attributable to 1971 settlements in the steel industry, where such clauses were reinstituted after the parties had dropped them in 1962, and in the communications industry, where such clauses were negotiated for the first time.

Ability to Pay

One of the most important considerations affecting wage determination is the basic economic situation in the firm and industry which for convenience we can denominate as "ability to pay." When profits and sales are increasing, when the employer needs to hold and attract labor in order to fill a backlog of orders, when prospects for the year ahead are bright, it is not surprising that the employer will favorably consider demands for an upward wage adjustment. On the other hand, if profits have fallen, sales are off, idle capacity exists, unemployment prevails, and there is no immediate prospect of a change for the better in the economic situation of the firm, employers are understandably loathe to increase their costs by agreeing to wage increases.

Ability to pay, therefore, is undoubtedly a major consideration in

---

[15] *Monthly Labor Review*, Vol. 82 (December 1959), pp. 1324, 1327.

[16] *Monthly Labor Review*, Vol. 95 (January 1972), p. 7.

wage negotiations for most firms in good times and bad. Determination of ability to pay is, however, a highly controversial subject. Management, while often pleading inability to pay, is reluctant to make this an issue of fact and permit union representatives to "have a look at the books." Management fears in this regard are based on the belief that such a move would be a prelude to union interference in business operations and encroachment on the whole sphere of managerial prerogatives. The U.S. Supreme Court has ruled in the case of a dispute between the Truitt Manufacturing Company and a steelworkers' union that refusal by an employer to substantiate a claim of inability to pay increased wages *may* support a finding of failure to bargain in good faith.[17]

There is considerable difference of opinion between unions and management, and among economists as well, as to the extent to which differences in ability to pay should be reflected in differences in wage rates. On the one hand, union representatives frequently argue that workers have to pay the same price for their necessities of life whether they work for a profitable firm or a less profitable one and, therefore, should be paid the same wage in all companies for similar work. Yet, unions have withdrawn from this position where it appeared that such a policy would force marginal firms out of business and thus produce unemployment among union members.

Management representatives frequently use the ability-to-pay argument to obtain special concessions for their particular firms, particularly where for one reason or another, their cost of operation is higher than that of competitors. Obviously, the setting of different wage rates in an industry corresponding to the different level of profits in various firms would penalize initiative and good management, and would, in effect, offer a subsidy to the inefficient operators. On the other hand, a strict policy of wage uniformity based on the rates payable by the most efficient producer would force marginal firms out of business. Unions have had to choose between these two extremes and adapt their wage policies to the peculiar conditions existing in each industry. In most instances, they have made some concessions in the way of differentials for smaller, less profitable firms; but, as has been stated, their preference is for wage uniformity.

Other Criteria in Wage Determination

There are a number of other criteria which are frequently applied by both management and labor in the process of wage determination. For example, when unions seek a reduction in the workweek, the important criterion frequently becomes maintenance of take-home pay despite the reduction in hours worked. In some cases, the new hourly wage rate is

---

[17] *National Labor Relations Board* v. *Truitt Manufacturing Co.*, 351 U.S. 149 (1956).

simply the arithmetical result obtained by dividing the take-home pay prior to the reduction in hours by the reduced number of hours worked. Improvement in productivity is another circumstance which is receiving greater emphasis from labor in negotiations. We shall have occasion to examine the subject of productivity and wages in greater detail in Chapter 13. It is worthy of note, however, that while unions talk a great deal about productivity gains where it suits their purposes, there is no correlation between interindustry differences in productivity gains and wage increases. As a matter of fact, industries with the largest long-run productivity gains, such as chemicals, tobacco, lumber, and textiles, have not been characterized by particularly large wage gains.[18]

The criteria explored in the foregoing discussion play an important role in narrowing the range of possibilities in wage determination. In many cases, however, the wage which is finally agreed upon is a reflection of sheer bargaining power, and talk of intraindustry standards or cost-of-living changes is mere rationalization pressed into service to support demands or concessions which need justification. Even arbitrators write these criteria into their opinions to support decisions already arrived at for other reasons.

It is also important to remember that wage changes are typically arrived at in a series of "rounds." These frequently provide for subsequent wage changes to be made during the term of the contract one, two, or even three years in the future. The relevant criteria and considerations are those that existed at the time of negotiation of the round, not when the agreed upon wage adjustment takes effect.

The Influence of the Product Market on Wage Adjustments

The demand for labor is a derived demand. This proposition simply means that the employer hires labor, not just to utilize its services, but because labor will produce a product for which there is a demand in the market place. As we shall see in Chapter 12, where this concept will be more fully discussed, the characteristics of the product market can affect the elasticity of the employer's demand curve for labor and therefore can influence his decision as to the amount of labor he will utilize and the wages he will be prepared to pay.

In recent years, numerous statistical investigations have been undertaken to determine whether monopoly power in the product market tends to be correlated with larger wage adjustments in the labor market. The criterion of monopoly power frequently used in such studies—which is acknowledged to be subject to many shortcomings—is the so-called concentration ratio—the proportion of the volume of shipments accounted for by the four largest firms in an industry. If this index of monopoly

---

[18] Eckstein and Wilson, "Determination of Money Wages," p. 392.

power is accepted, then, there is considerable evidence that workers in "monopolistic" industries have enjoyed larger wage adjustments than those in competitive industries.[19] However, there is considerable disagreement as to whether this is a fortuitous or causal relationship.

On an a priori basis, it might be expected that monopolistic industries would offer a more favorable environment for union organizers than competitive industries and that therefore a higher degree of union organization would exist in the former than in the latter. From this it can be argued that the conjunction of union power in the labor market and monopoly power in the product market produce the phenomenon of higher wage adjustments. It is probably true that such concentrated industries are more fully organized. The reasons are obvious. Companies tend to be larger, and therefore in terms of money and time expended by union organizers per potential union member, they afford a more inviting target than a small firm. Secondly, barriers to entry into the industry make it easier for the union to maintain its control without worrying about the effect of nonunion competition.[20]

While it may be true that the less competitive an industry, the easier it is for the companies in the industry to pass along wage increases, this does not necessarily mean that monopolistic industries are easier targets for unions seeking large wage adjustments. The competitive nature of the product market affects the employer's ability to resist. Large companies in monopolistic industries are much readier to take a strike and to hold out for long periods against union demands than companies in more competitive industries. One would expect the highest wage adjustments to occur in relatively competitive industries with many small companies and a strong union, such as the trucking industry. Albert Rees has pointed out that in manufacturing it just so happens that almost all strong unions deal with concentrated industries, and so you get evidence of a correlation between "monopoly power" and size of wage adjustments, but in the economy as a whole, such correlation will not be apparent because there are many competitive industries—such as trucking, construction, and entertainment—which have very strong unions to deal with.[21]

UNION ATTITUDES IN WAGE DETERMINATION

Because strong unions dominate many of our major industries, union attitudes toward wage determination have a significant influence upon the

---

[19] See, for example, Bruce T. Allen, "Market Concentration and Wage Increases: U.S. Manufacturing, 1947–1964," *Industrial and Labor Relations Review*, Vol. 21 (April 1968), pp. 353–65.

[20] Adrian W. Throop, "The Union-Nonunion Wage Differential and Cost-Push Inflation," *American Economic Review*, Vol. 58 (March 1968), p. 83.

[21] Albert Rees, "Union Wage Gains and Enterprise Monopoly," *Essays on Industrial Relations Research* (Ann Arbor and Detroit, Mich.: University of Michigan–Wayne University, Institute of Industrial Relations, 1961), p. 133.

structure of wages in our economy. Union attitudes, as transmitted to management at the bargaining table, are a mixture of basic union needs filtered through and molded by the personalities of the union bargaining representatives. It is up to them properly to assess which of the many possible objectives of union wage policy are in the best interests of the union. They have to weigh the needs of the various groups who make up the membership—the older men and the younger men, the full-time workers and the part-time workers—and try to arrive at a "package" to present to management which will satisfy the divergent needs of these various groups. In any negotiations on behalf of a union a primary responsibility of a union representative is to set policies which will hold the union together and perpetuate it in the face of stresses within and attacks from without.

Union officials sense these needs and coordinate them with their own. Most union officials have come up through the ranks the hard way, and they do not like the idea of going back to the workbench or donning the apron. They have usually risen to positions of power by being fighters, and they know that the continued loyalty of the membership and the continued existence of their positions as officials depend upon their belligerence toward management and their success in achieving substantial gains for their membership. Their job is to sense the pulse of the members and to give them what they want.

What does the membership want? Or to put it more realistically, what might the union representative believe that the membership wants? There are various possible objectives of union wage policy.[22]

1. The largest wage bill, regardless of whether or not all union members are employed.
2. The largest wage bill, including funds from the public support of unemployed union members.
3. The largest private payroll to employed members, deducting from their wage income an amount to pay out-of-work benefits to unemployed members.
4. The largest possible amount of employment for union members.
5. The highest average wage income for each unit of labor affiliated with the union.

While union leaders can hardly be expected to formulate objectives in this precise fashion, they unquestionably take account of the alternatives of more money versus more unemployment, particularly in industries which are characterized by strong nonunion competition or the competition of substitutable products of other industries. The final wage

---

[22] John T. Dunlop, "Economic Model of a Trade Union," in Campbell R. McConnell (ed.), *Perspectives on Wage Determination* (New York: McGraw-Hill Book Co., 1970), pp. 98–107.

adjustment which union leaders fall back on as the minimum acceptable will be profoundly influenced by political influences within the union, by government pressures, by personal rivalries with other union leaders, and by similar noneconomic forces.

Union Attitudes toward Wage Cuts

Union leaders are elected to secure economic benefits for their constituents. In depressed times, however, they may be faced with demands for wage decreases. Generally, unions oppose such demands or only yield to them with the utmost reluctance when employer bargaining power is obviously overwhelming. There are many reasons for this attitude, both economic and political.

A basic reason for union opposition to wage reductions is that there is no assurance that a given change in wages will be associated with the corresponding change in labor cost or with any predictable change in costs or prices. Unit labor cost and wage rates or earnings do not necessarily move together; and in various industries, they have frequently moved in opposite directions.

Practically speaking, a union leader can ill afford the political repercussions of negotiating a wage cut avowedly to decrease or to prevent further unemployment, when neither he nor the employer can be at all certain that lower wages will have the hoped-for results. There is the further fact that most union leaders and the rank-and-file employees do not believe an employer when he pleads inability to pay. All too often, they have heard this complaint raised year after year during contract negotiations; yet, somehow, wage increases were granted, and the employer paid them. When a real crisis arises, the employer may have to take a strike to convince the union that this time he means business!

Unions resist employer demands for wage reductions in depressions because wage policy, by and large, is made by the employed rather than the unemployed union members. Even if there is reason on the part of the leadership to believe that the demand for the plant's labor is elastic, the employed members might prefer to pursue a wage policy of maximizing wage rates rather than employment. This is clearly the policy of the United Mine Workers and, generally, of most railway and building-trades unions.

Despite their firm opposition to wage cuts, unions have agreed to them on many occasions. There have been special reasons for such action in almost every case. Usually, the crucial factor is the presence of strong nonunion competition, which poses a threat to the continuance of plants under union contract. Another reason for unions accepting wage cuts is found in pressure from the unemployed. This makes itself felt in two ways. The unemployed members may believe that a wage reduction will increase their chances of employment. As their number grows, the pressure on the employed members to accede increases. In addition, the existence of unemployed reduces the union's bargaining power in negotiations. The fear that the unemployed will break a strike and that the employed will not hold out if a strike is called has impelled unions to agree to reductions.

Unemployment and Union Wage Policies

As has been pointed out, union leaders are extremely reluctant to accept a wage cut in the hope that it will increase employment. The wage cut means an immediate hardship to union members and to some extent constitutes a blot on the record of union leadership. The beneficial effects, if any, of the wage reduction may never become evident. Therefore, when a wage *cut* has to be weighed against the possibilities of increased unemployment at existing rates, most union leaders would argue in favor of maintenance of wages.

Is the same emphasis on wages and lack of recognition of employment reactions true when wage *increases* are under consideration? Under what circumstances is a limit set on wage increases by union recognition of the possibility that higher wages would endanger the competitive position of the firm and thereby create unemployment among union members?

There has been some controversy on this subject among economists in recent years. Some economists argue that the effect of a wage increase upon employment is unpredictable before the fact, and after the increase has been granted, it is impossible to determine what the effect of the increase has been on employment due to the constant fluctuation of business conditions. Therefore, it is argued, union leaders cannot normally take employment reactions into consideration in wage negotiations.

On the other hand, other economists contend that there are a number of industries where conditions exist which require that union leaders take account of possible employment reactions in making decisions as to wage policy. This is true where an industry is only partially unionized and imposition of excessive rates on organized firms will cause them to lose business to the nonunion sector of the industry. Similar concern with the employment effects of increased wage costs will also be found in industries characterized by strong competition in the product market and in industries where it is relatively easy for employers to move their plants to other areas.

Areas in which these conditions exist are by no means exceptional. About one out of every five workers in manufacturing is employed in industries where there is clearly no single-firm control of the product market and where competition among firms is keen—textiles, apparel, leather goods, furniture, and lumber. The textile and apparel industries have also been characterized by a movement of new capital into nonunion areas by reason of the high costs imposed by union wage pressure in organized areas. Industries in which union organization is only partial also are important in terms of workers employed. Probably less than 50% of the workers in the following manufacturing industries are covered by union agreements: baking; chemicals, excluding rayon yarn; flour and other grain products; furniture; hosiery; jewelry and silverware; knit goods; leather luggage; handbags; novelties; lumber; paper products; pottery, including chinaware; shoes; cut stock and findings; stone and clay products; and silk and rayon yarn. Industries which are between 80% and 100% organized today account for less than half of all gainfully employed workers. Therefore, there are many industries in which unions must take account of employment reactions simply because such consideration is essential to the continued existence and strength of the union.

Effect of Unions on Wage Adjustments

In Chapter 13, in our discussion of inflation, we shall consider in detail the question of whether or not unions accelerate the rate of wage increases in the American economy. For the purposes of the present discussion, however, it is pertinent to observe that union organization affects the nature, size, and frequency of wage changes in unionized firms. Unions have profoundly affected the *form* of wage adjustments in American industry. Supplementary unemployment benefits, cost-of-living adjustments, guaranteed annual wages, pay for employee birthdays, and all sorts of welfare plans—these are some of the diverse ways in which employees have expressed their preferences for wage adjustments through collective bargaining.

Unions also affect the frequency of wage adjustments. The timing of wage adjustments for nonunion workers is much less formalized than for unionized employees. Many nonunion factory workers do not receive wage increases each year;[23] on the other hand, many nonunion workers may have their rates increased at more frequent intervals. By contrast, most union factory workers do receive wage adjustments annually, either through annual negotiations or through deferred increases under contracts extending two or three years. Since nonunion workers are not tied by long-term labor contracts, it is understandable that when there are changes in the economic climate, nonunion plants will respond more quickly to such changes in terms of wage adjustments than organized firms. The nonunion response to an improvement in economic conditions is typically a change in the frequency of wage and benefit adjustments.[24]

The size of wage adjustments is also affected by the existence of

---

[23] William Davis and Lily Mary David, "Pattern Wage and Benefit Changes in Manufacturing," *Monthly Labor Review*, Vol. 91 (February 1968), p. 40.

[24] *Ibid.*

collective bargaining agreements. Nonunion wage adjustments will vary more in amount from year to year because of the fact that nonunion plants are more sensitive to changes in economic conditions. This is likely to be true both in a slack and in a tight labor market.[25] On the average, however, a worker in a union factory is likely to receive in any one year a smaller percentage but a larger cents-per-hour increase than the nonunion worker, and since the union employee receives increases more frequently, there is some evidence that over a period of years he gains proportionately more than a nonunion worker. Thus, one study found that over the period from 1959–66, general wage adjustments totaled approximately 25.8% in union establishments compared to 23.6% in nonunion factories.[26]

POWER ASPECTS OF WAGE DETERMINATION

Wage determination in unionized firms involves a balancing of power. Is it realistic to discuss power in economic terms—particularly with respect to union organizations—or are concepts from the political arena more relevant? On this basic issue, there is considerable disagreement among labor economists. The institutionalists contend that "among all the participants in economic life the trade union is least suited to purely economic analysis"[27] and that the union is an "essentially political rather than economic institution."[28] From this point of view, the union must be considered apart from its members. The union may "need" a strike to promote solidarity and loyalty, while from the point of view of any rational economic analysis, there is no economic justification for such action.

Other economists differ sharply with this point of view. John T. Dunlop, for example, concedes that emphasis upon political considerations may have some relevance in understanding the actions of newer unions in which there have been internal factional struggles. He maintains, however, that these situations constitute a minor portion of the spectrum of collective bargaining, and that, by and large, unions must make decisions which reflect economic realities in the long run.[29] Furthermore, the lack of objectives held in common by union leaders and union members cannot long endure without membership discontent leading to a change in leadership. On balance, therefore, it seems more meaningful to recog-

---

[25] U.S. Department of Labor, Bureau of Labor Statistics, *Trends in Labor Compensation in the United States, 1946–1966* (Washington, D.C.; 1967), p. 9.

[26] Davis and David, "Pattern Wage and Benefit Changes," p. 43.

[27] Arthur M. Ross, *Trade Union Wage Policy* (Berkeley: University of California Press, 1948), p. 7.

[28] Clark Kerr, "Economic Analysis and the Study of Industrial Relations," in McConnell, *Perspectives on Wage Determination*, p. 83.

[29] John T. Dunlop, "The Task of Contemporary Wage Theory," in *The Theory of Wage Determination* (London: Macmillan and Company Limited, 1957), pp. 3–29.

nize certain political and irrational elements in union decision making—just as these also exist in business decisions—but nevertheless to view union bargaining demands in an economic context.

Wage determination in unionized firms reflects the union's power to strike and to inflict damage by a strike, and the company's ability to withstand a strike and impose loss of earnings on employees. Even when a strike is not threatened, the power of a union to strike makes itself felt at the bargaining table.

Union bargaining power depends upon three basic elements: the right to strike, the ability to strike successfully, and the amount of loss which can be inflicted on the employer by a strike. The legal right to strike, of course, is a basic prerequisite to union power. If the union contract in question is a two-year contract with a wage reopening after one year and the contract contains a no-strike clause, the union may not be able to strike lawfully to enforce its wage demands during its term. A strike in violation of a contract may leave the union open to a suit by the employer for damages for breach of contract, or an injunction may be obtained to halt the unlawful work stoppage. Furthermore, when a union strike is unlawful, other unions frequently will not honor the picket line, and therefore the effectiveness of the strike is weakened. Obviously, when such circumstances exist, the union's bargaining power is limited.

If the union has the right to strike, the next consideration is its ability to strike successfully. This will depend upon such circumstances as the cohesiveness of the union, the degree of internal dissension, the possibility of raiding by rival unions, the amount of funds in the union treasury, the ability of the union to pay strike benefits, the extent to which strikers can obtain employment or compensation elsewhere, and, of course, the degree of support by the membership for the union demands. Even such circumstances as the time of year will affect the union's ability to strike successfully. Employees do not mind losing a few weeks' work on strike in the summertime, but they are loath to do so just before Christmas!

The third important factor which determines the bargaining power of the union is its ability to impose a substantial hardship on the employer by calling a strike. This will depend upon the nature of business of the employer, the position of the firm in the industry, its financial resources, and similar circumstances. If a company is engaged in retail trade, for example, it is extremely vulnerable to a strike because any business lost through a shutdown cannot be regained at a later date. People will not stop eating while a restaurant is on strike; they will simply eat their meals elsewhere. On the other hand, if an automobile company goes on strike, its permanent loss of business might be negligible. For a time, customers can be supplied out of inventory. Thereafter, many customers will wait for a particular make of car until production is resumed. Sometimes a strike may afford such companies a convenient excuse to curtail production and thus give dealers time to work down excessive inventories.

The power of the union to hurt the employer will depend upon the financial position and the profitability of the company. In some industries, companies work on narrow profit margins and have little working capital. They rely on continuing sales to enable them to meet their bills, and any interruption of production has to be avoided at all costs. In other cases, companies are financially strong and can stand a long strike. Frequently, large companies have a number of plants or branch operations, and if a strike shuts down only part of their operations, they can withstand a long strike by offsetting losses in one area with profits in another.

Just as a union's ability to strike successfully depends in part upon the time of year, so does its ability to impose losses on the employer. The threat of a strike is obviously most effective when the employer is going into his peak season. If contract negotiations break down during a slack season, the employer may not care about a strike, since he may have been thinking in terms of curtailing production and laying off employees anyhow. Both unions and management are keenly aware of the strategic importance of having contract negotiations occur at an advantageous time, and there is always a good deal of sparring over the issue of when a contract should expire or come up for renegotiation.

The loss which can be imposed upon a firm by a strike depends to some extent upon the class of labor involved and its importance in the entire scheme of production. It has long been recognized that the smaller the cost of a factor of production is relative to total costs, and the more essential it is to production, the higher its price can be pushed up without affecting the amount of the factor employers will utilize. In every plant or establishment, there are certain workers with relatively scarce skills who can paralyze production by a walkout. If their wages constitute only a small fraction of total costs of operation, it is understandable why an employer will frequently be willing to grant such workers large wage increases as the price of uninterrupted production. It was recognition of this principle which led the American Federation of Labor to organize skilled workers along craft lines.

Today, however, even a strike of unskilled workers can be as effective as a walkout of skilled craftsmen. This is the result of two developments: the refusal of other workers to cross a picket line and the decline in the use of strikebreakers. Today, a walkout of janitors and sweepers in a huge industrial establishment can, if it is a lawful strike, cause a complete shutdown and a forced layoff of thousands of workers. The right to strike has thus given great power even to unskilled groups, who are ready to use this power militantly.

All of the foregoing considerations must be weighed by the union representatives in presenting union demands at the bargaining table. They must estimate, too, just how long a strike might result, what is the possibility of government intervention, and what the chances are that employee dissatisfaction resulting from a long strike might endanger their own positions. Management must likewise consider the strength and weaknesses of its own bargaining position. The wage which is ultimately arrived at will reflect a balancing of these power considerations, the profitability of the firm, general supply and demand conditions, and the personalities of management and union representatives.

The Changing Balance of Power between Management and Unions

As we view the broad sweep of industrial relations in the American economy, it appears that there have been changing tides in the balance of power between unions and management. Prior to enactment of the Wagner Act in 1935, management clearly had the upper hand and unions found it difficult to organize in many industries. From the Wagner Act until 1947, when the Taft-Hartley Act was passed, union power grew rapidly; unions were able to use boycotts, picketing, secondary pressures on neutral employers, and other coercive actions in addition to the strike. With passage of the Taft-Hartley Act in 1947 and the Landrum-Griffin Act[30] in 1959, the pendulum again swung in the direction of management, as these two laws circumscribed many union bargaining weapons and weakened the ability of unions to organize effectively.

The changing fortunes of union and management from 1933 to 1959 were primarily influenced by the intervention of government in the labor market. In recent years, however, there is some evidence that economic influences and trends have altered the bargaining positions of the protagonists. These developments fall into three major categories:

1. *New Bargaining Techniques.* A major effort to alter the balance of power was mounted by the Industrial Union Department of the AFL–CIO during the decade of the sixties through the use of coalition bargaining. The campaign extended to a number of important industries: petroleum refining, nonferrous metals, metal products, chemicals, electrical equipment, and food processing. In each instance, the initial target situation was one in which a multiplant concern had been conducting separate negotiations with several different locals, frequently affiliated with more than one international union.[31] Although the record of coalition bargaining has thus far been spotty and unions have been unable to compel the enlargement of the scope of a bargaining unit when the employer has been opposed to the move, nevertheless maintenance of the status quo

---

[30] The content of the Taft-Hartley and Landrum-Griffin Acts will be considered in Chapters 19 and 20.

[31] George H. Hildebrand, "Bargaining Structure and Relative Power," in Richard L. Rowan (ed.), *Collective Bargaining: Survival in the 70's?* (Labor Relations and Public Policy Series, Report No. 5 [Philadelphia: Industrial Research Unit, Wharton School of Finance and Commerce, University of Pennsylvania, 1972]), p. 10.

has involved a cost to employers. The concept of coalition bargaining may ultimately erode some of the advantages which now accrue to an employer which has a number of geographically scattered plants with contracts with separate unions. In addition, as noted in earlier chapters, unions are attempting to bargain on a multinational basis as a means of coping with the multinational corporation.

Another bargaining technique with important implications for the balance of power is the recently judicially recognized right of the United Transportation Union to strike selectively against any of some 170 railroad carriers who are joined together for multiemployer bargaining.[32] The railroads are extremely vulnerable to whipsawing techniques; presumably the unions are shifting to this form of bargaining pressure because they believe that it will be more effective than industrywide bargaining with a group of employers.

2. *Inflation and Relative Bargaining Power.*   Although rapidly rising prices have deprived wage increases of much of their value in providing workers with additional purchasing power, the fact remains that an inflationary period with a tight labor market for skilled adult males tends to tip the balance of bargaining power in favor of unions. Despite the fact that in 1971 there were approximately 5 million unemployed persons in the United States, the unemployment rate for workers between the ages of 35 and 54 was only about 3%.[33] This meant that from the union point of view the threat of layoffs for a significant portion of the membership was reduced in consequence because such members could obtain jobs elsewhere. At the same time, rank-and-file militancy was fueled by the steady erosion of real earnings produced by the escalating cost of living. From the employer's point of view, the same inflation provided a mechanism to recoup higher wage costs in the form of higher prices, and therefore management resistance to strike threats was probably weakened. The economic atmosphere produced by inflation with expectations of a continuing rise in prices tends to assist unions in achieving larger settlements in wages and fringe benefits.

3. *Available Sources of Compensatory Income.*   The only justification for a strike as a technique in collective bargaining is that the costs imposed by a strike on both management and employees will eventually bring about a more reasonable attitude and lead to a compromise settlement. Recent trends, however, have weakened the effectiveness of strike action in achieving this objective. From the union standpoint, strikers have been able to find supplementary sources of income elsewhere, so that the costs to strikers of a prolonged shutdown have been reduced and the duration of strikes has therefore probably been lengthened. In recent

---

[32] *Ibid.,* p. 15.

[33] U.S. Department of Labor, *Manpower Report of the President, 1972* (Washington, D.C.: U.S. Government Printing Office, 1972), p. 177.

years, strikers have found such support from unemployment compensation payments (legal for strikers on the railroads and in two states), welfare payments, food stamps,[34] and, of course, strike funds. In addition, the increasing importance of part-time employment in our economy has provided an opportunity for strikers to obtain some earnings during plant shutdowns by driving cabs, working as clerks in retail establishments, and in other kinds of part-time employment.

At the same time as this trend has become evident, management has been increasing its ability to draw on earnings outside the area of labor conflict. In the case of management, this reserve of earning power is provided by ownership of businesses in a diversity of industries, some of which may be nonunion and/or overseas. Some multinational corporations derive as much as 50% of the total net profits from abroad. Obviously, a union in the United States would encounter greater difficulty in bringing effective economic pressure to bear upon such a multinational corporation than one whose total profit is dependent upon the production which unions can curtail through use of the strike. Little wonder that unions are staunch supporters of a strong antitrust policy against conglomerates!

From the union point of view, the multinational corporation poses the problem of production switching in the event of a strike in a particular plant and, in the long run, runaway plants on an international basis. Unions are today just beginning to attempt to develop strategies capable of dealing with such problems. The logical counterattack would involve internationally coordinated action by unions associated with subsidiaries of the same company in a number of countries. The practical difficulties facing unions attempting to implement such a strategy are obviously enormous. Nevertheless, in several instances, affiliated unions in various countries have coordinated their bargaining efforts against international corporations with multinational bargaining the aim.[35]

Whether on balance these trends have tipped the scales in favor of unionism or management depends to some extent upon the criteria which are used to judge success. Is a long strike evidence of the ability of management to resist or of the ability of unions to maintain concerted pressure of long duration? In any case, these trends need to be considered in any current evaluation of bargaining power as between unions and management. To the extent that both unions and management have strengthened their staying power, the public may be the loser, and this may shape public attitudes toward proposals to restrict the right to strike.

---

[34] See Armand J. Thieblot, Jr., and Ronald M. Cowin, *Welfare and Strikes: The Use of Public Funds To Support Strikes* (Labor Relations and Public Policy Series, Report No. 6 [Philadelphia: Industrial Research Unit, Wharton School of Finance and Commerce, University of Pennsylvania, 1972]).

[35] Based on research now in progress at the Industrial Research Unit of The Wharton School by Professor Richard L. Rowan.

EFFECTS OF WAGE OR PRICE FIXING BY GOVERNMENT

In Chapter 13, we shall consider in some detail governmental efforts to control wage adjustments through governmental pressures or legislation. However, it is pertinent to observe at this point that the existence of such governmental legislation may change the focus of union interest in collective bargaining. For example, as a result of the wage and price controls in effect at this writing, unions are demanding a return to one-year contracts, rather than continuing the trend to three-year contracts which was evidenced prior to wage controls. Some unions are requesting clauses which provide that any increases disallowed by the Pay Board will become effective as soon as the law and regulations permit, while others are insisting upon inclusion of a contract clause which states that an arbitrator shall determine how funds disallowed by the Pay Board may be assigned to areas outside the Pay Board's direct control. Since fringe benefits are partially exempt from the wage regulations, there is increasing interest by unions in this area—particularly in plans providing pensions, life insurance, health and welfare, and to some extent profit sharing.[36] Union leaders who can no longer direct their energies toward obtaining the highest wage possible may now focus on obtaining various changes in working rules and conditions. These changes in union policy indicate how governmental regulations designed to restrict one phase of the collective bargaining relationship can have unforseen—and perhaps costly repercussions—upon other aspects of the contractual relationship between management and labor.

SUMMARY

Wage determination in the American economy is a complex process. It reflects the influence of many forces. Thus if we were trying to explain why a production worker in a steel-fabricating company has a higher hourly wage rate than a production worker in a textile mill, the following are some of the major considerations which would require investigation:[37]

1. The monopoly power of the employer in the product market—Is it easy for the company to pass along to consumers the cost of higher wages?
2. The wage policy of the employer—Does it have a policy of paying wages equal to, or higher than, those of its competitors or of other firms in its local labor market area?
3. The state of union organization in the plant and industry—Is the employee a union member? What is the bargaining strength of the

---

[36] *AFL–CIO American Federationists*, March 1972, p. 12.

[37] Derived in part from the discussion in Leonard W. Weiss, "Concentration and Labor Earnings," *American Economic Review*, Vol. 56 (March 1966) pp. 96–117.

union, is its leadership aggressive, does it have to concern itself with nonunion competition? What is the extent of collective bargaining among firms with which the employer competes in the product market?

4. The trend of sales and employment in the respective industries—Are there unfilled job vacancies in the plant, is employment increasing and the demand for labor strong?

5. The supply of labor in the local labor market—Is there a large pool of qualified but unemployed labor available, or is labor in short supply?

6. The regularity of employment, both over the year and from year to year—Does the high wage rate in the steel company compensate in part for cyclical unemployment incident to the job?

7. The total package of compensation—What other benefits are received by the worker? To what extent can he expect overtime work? How do the two jobs compare when we look at weekly earnings or annual income?

8. Size of firm—Is this a small or large firm, a public corporation or a small family business?

9. Size of labor market—Is the plant located in a large metropolitan area or in a small town?

10. The overall labor force characteristics of the industry or firm—To what extent is the labor force in each firm composed of a high percentage of white, skilled, male workers?

11. Geographical location—Is the plant located in the South or in some other section of the country?

12. The personal characteristics of the employees in question—What is their respective age, race, education, health, etc.?

13. Profitability of the employer—How does profit of the employer compare with that of other firms in the particular industry? Was this a good year or a bad year? What is the trend in profits both in the firm and in the industry?

14. The job content—To what extent is a high degree of skill or training required to perform the particular job?

All of these considerations in varying degrees enter into the determination of wages. While we have placed considerable emphasis in this chapter on the role of unions in wage determination, it is important to recognize that the various factors enumerated above will shape and influence the impact which unions can exert upon the level and structure of wages.

QUESTIONS FOR DISCUSSION

1. Discuss the connection between the internal and external wage structure of a firm. What is the significance for collective bargaining of the concept of "wage clusters"?

2. Discuss the significance of key wage bargains in wage determination in the United States.

3. Discuss the interrelationship of monopoly power in the product market and union power in the labor market in terms of the effect of this interrelationship upon the wage level.

SUGGESTIONS FOR FURTHER READING

ALLEN, BRUCE T. "Market Concentration and Wage Increases: U.S. Manufacturing, 1947–1964," *Industrial and Labor Relations Review,* Vol. 21 (April 1968), pp. 353–65.

A discussion and empirical testing of the theory that those workers enjoy the most rapidly rising wages who are employed in partially monopolistic or oligopolistic industries.

BIERMAN, HAROLD, JR., *et al.,* "Game Theory and Bargaining," in McCONNELL, CAMPBELL R. (ed.), *Perspectives on Wage Determination.* pp. 142–49. New York: McGraw-Hill Book Co., 1970.

An attempt to elucidate the selection of strategies in bargaining between unions and management by use of a mathematical model and application of game theory.

EDELMAN, MURRAY, and FLEMING, R. W. *The Politics of Wage-Price Decisions.* Urbana, Ill.: University of Illinois Press, 1965.

An analysis of the gamut of interests, organizational influences, and political pressures that explain wage-price decisions in four countries.

LEVINSON, HAROLD. *Determining Forces in Collective Bargaining.* New York: John Wiley & Sons, Inc., 1966.

An examination of the impact of economic, political, and power variables on the determination of wages and fringe benefits in six Pacific Coast industries.

LEWIS, H. G. *Unionism and Relative Wages in the United States.* Chicago, Ill.: University of Chicago Press, 1963.

An empirical study of the impact of unions on relative wages in the United States.

MITCHELL, DANIEL. "Union Wage Policies: The Ross-Dunlop Debate Reopened," *Industrial Relations,* Vol. 4 (February 1972), pp. 46–61.

A review of the economic and political objectives of unions with reference to the Ross-Dunlop controversy.

Chapter 12

WAGE CHANGES AND

EMPLOYMENT

Union officials, in order to maintain their positions and retain the allegiance and interest of their membership, must constantly seek to obtain new benefits for their members. In view of the strength of organized labor in this country, it seems likely that over the long run the general trend of money wage rates in future years will be upward. What impact will such continuing wage pressure have upon employment?

The effect of wage changes upon employment constitutes one of the most controversial subjects in the field of labor economics. Most union leaders deny that there is any predictable relation between wage increases and employment in the *individual* firm in our dynamic economy. Orthodox economists generally take a contrary view. But when we come to the field of *general* wage adjustments occurring uniformly throughout the economy, we find that many economists argue that such wage adjustments need have no effect upon employment. What is the reason for this divergence in opinion? Under what circumstances will wage increases curtail employment? In this chapter, we shall inquire into the consequences of increases in wage rates upon employment, first from the point of view of the individual firm and secondly from the point of view of the economy at large. Finally, we shall examine some of the problems created by continuing union wage pressure.

WAGE CHANGES IN THE INDIVIDUAL FIRM

Short-Run Effect of Wage Increases

Assume that an increase occurs in the rate of wages which an employer is required to pay his labor force. This might be the result of a new union contract or of a minimum wage law or simply of increasing scarcity of labor in the labor market. Assume further that the demand for the product sold by the company remains unchanged, that there are no new inventions reducing costs of production in the firm, and that output in the company at the time the wage increase occurred was neither expanding nor contracting but was relatively stable. These various assumptions are generally taken care of by phrasing our inquiry in terms of the effect of a wage increase in the individual firm, "other things being equal."

Orthodox economists assume that the behavior of the employer under such circumstances will conform to the principles of marginal productivity determination, which we examined in Chapter 10. According to the marginal productivity theory, the employer endeavors to hire labor up to the point at which the marginal cost of labor is approximately equal to its marginal contribution to the revenue of the firm.

As we have seen in Chapter 10, if the supply of labor is perfectly elastic, the wage and marginal cost of labor are the same, and the employer will hire labor up to the point of approximate equality between marginal revenue product and wage. It will simplify our analysis if we ignore the complications produced by a rising supply curve for labor and, in the following discussion of employment policy in the individual firm, assume that the employer is faced by a perfectly elastic supply curve of labor so that marginal productivity determination will be made in terms of the wage of labor (which, under these conditions, will be equal to marginal cost of labor).

Under these circumstances, an employer who wishes to maximize profits will hire labor only up to the point where the last additional worker adds just enough revenue to compensate for the wage he receives. The lower the wage, the larger will be the size of the work force employed, since the employer can afford to keep on the payroll at such low wage rates those workers whose marginal contribution to the revenues of the firm is comparatively small. When wage costs rise, however, he will be compelled to lay off these men in order to achieve a new equilibrium in which the marginal revenue productivity of the least valuable man employed will be sufficiently great to equal the new higher wage level.

Wage Increases and Layoffs

The pressure on the employer to lay off workers when the wage rate rises comes about in two principal ways. In the first place, when wage costs rise, the employer generally finds it necessary to raise his price for his product in order to cover the increased labor costs. In some cases, he may find it inexpedient to raise prices but may achieve the same objective by lowering the quality of his product. In either case, whether the price be raised or quality impaired, he will ordinarily sell a smaller output, even though it is possible that his total sales receipts may increase or remain constant. With a smaller physical production, he will find that he needs fewer employees, and so he will be able to lay off some workers whose services are no longer required.

In the second place, when wage rates rise, the employer's profits will immediately be reduced. Therefore a strong incentive is provided for him to review his entire production setup in an effort to cut costs and save money. Even without a change in output, the employer may find it possible, by rescheduling output and rearranging work schedules, to eliminate some workers. Furthermore, if labor becomes more expensive, the employer may find that it is now economically profitable to utilize new laborsaving machinery in the plant which will also have the effect of displacing labor. Such substitution of machinery for labor usually takes some time to effect. The employer may have limited space in his plant, or perhaps he may have to defer substitution until his existing machinery is more fully depreciated. Substitution of machinery for labor, therefore, is ordinarily felt most as a long-run consequence of wage increases. It will be considered below in connection with our analysis of the long-run effects of wage pressure.

When labor becomes more expensive, employers are pressed to look over their labor force and decide whether certain jobs need to be performed at all, irrespective of whether they can be performed more cheaply by machines or automated devices. Thus, if labor is cheap, business establishments may employ a porter to clean floors and do odd jobs; but when this kind of labor becomes expensive, they may decide to eliminate this work and call in a contract cleaner on a periodic basis. This basic principle has important social implications. As we shall document in Chapter 16, with every rise in the minimum wage we have provided an incentive to employers to eliminate certain of the menial jobs at the lowest rung of the wage scale. This may be justified as part of a national effort to raise wage standards; yet it is quite probable that it is responsible for the creation of a substantial amount of hard-core unemployment. For in every society, there are persons whose education, training, and mental abilities are low, and these people can only find employment in jobs whose remuneration is low, corresponding to their low productivity.

Factors Affecting Elasticity of Demand for Labor

What determines the elasticity of the demand curve for labor in the short run? Or to put the question in another way: With a given increase in wage rates, what are the circumstances which determine whether the layoffs will be small (inelastic demand) or large (elastic demand)? Many years ago a famous economist, Alfred Marshall, formulated an answer to this question as part of his exposition of the laws of derived demand.[1] It was Marshall's theory that the demand for labor is a derived demand. Labor is not wanted for itself but for what it can produce. Therefore, if we want an explanation of the elasticity of demand for labor, we must

---

[1] Alfred Marshall, *Principles of Economics* (8th ed.; New York: Macmillan Co., 1920), pp. 383–86.

look to the demand for the final product and the supply of other factors of production, from which the demand for labor is derived.

According to Marshall:

'1. *The demand for labor will be the more inelastic the more essential the labor in question is in the production of the final product.* Obviously, the more skilled the worker is, the more likely that the employer will be highly dependent upon his services. Thus, the demand for labor for skilled patternmakers is more likely to be less elastic than for common laborers; and the patternmakers, if they were to go out on strike, would be better able to extract a higher wage from management without layoffs than could the common laborers. With the latter class of employee an employer may find that he can operate temporarily with supervisory help, or he can bring in nonunion employees. In today's labor market, essentiality can be the result either of a high degree of skill or of a tight control over entrancee into a trade exercised by a labor union.

' 2. *The demand for labor will be the more inelastic the more inelastic the demand for the final product.* The demand curve for the product will have a steep slope or be "inelastic" when increases in price of the product produce only a very small decrease in the quantity which consumers purchase of the product. A classic example of a product with an inelastic demand curve is salt. Even large increases in price would not materially affect sales of this product. If, however, the demand curve for the product is almost horizontal or "elastic," even a small increase in price will cause sales to fall off sharply, with the result that a large curtailment will be required in the labor force of the firm.

The range of possible reactions of employment to a wage increase may be crystallized by considering the difference in effect of wage increases under two extreme conditions of elasticity of demand for product—first, in a firm with a perfectly inelastic demand curve and, second, in a firm with a perfectly elastic demand curve. In the former case, the increase in costs resulting from a wage adjustment could be passed on completely to consumers in the form of a price rise without affecting sales volume at all. Therefore, there would be no unemployment caused by the price rise, although there could still be some unemployment resulting from substitution of factors within the firm. In the second case, at the other extreme, the firm with the elastic demand curve would be unable to pass any of the price increase on to consumers. The employer would find that to maximize profits, he would be better off selling a smaller volume at the same price and would therefore sharply curtail output and employment.

Firms in monopolistic positions are able to raise the price of their products without affecting sales materially, since consumers cannot shift easily to substitutes. On the basis of the foregoing theoretical analysis, therefore, we should expect that in firms which have an entrenched and protected position in the product market built up through advertising, patents, and sheer size and financial power, wage increases would produce relatively larger price increases and relatively less displacement of labor than in highly competitive companies.

When we are dealing with union wage adjustments on an industry-wide basis, and if the entire industry is well organized, then the demand curve for the product which is relevant is really the demand curve for the product of the entire industry. If, on the other hand, the union has organized only a part of the industry, then the demand curve which is significant is the demand curve for the product of the firms where wage adjustments are being made. The elasticity of demand for the product of these firms is likely to be greater than that for the product of the industry if there is a possibility that rates will not advance to the same extent in nonunion firms and that therefore nonunion product will be substituted by consumers for the product of the organized companies.

3. *The demand for labor will be the more inelastic the smaller the ratio of the labor cost in question to the total cost of product.* In some firms, labor costs constitute a relatively small proportion of total costs—frequently less than 10% of total costs. In such firms, if wage rates rise by, say, 5%, total costs would rise by only one half of 1%. If the full increase in total cost were reflected in a price increase, the rise in price would be so small that sales volume, and therefore employment, might not be affected to any significant degree.

But now, suppose that only a portion of the labor force is demanding an increase in wage rates. It is obvious that a small group of workers strategically placed in a company may be able to gain very large increases in rates for themselves, yet from the point of view of management the effect on overall costs may be minor. Of course, management must consider the effect of such wage changes upon the rates of other workers; but nevertheless, it still remains true that there are advantages to be gained in bargaining from being strong but small. From this point of view, small craft unions may well do a better job of wage bargaining for their membership than large industrial unions.

4. *The demand for labor will be the more inelastic the more inelastic the supply of other factors of production.* If the supply of other factors of production that are needed to work with the labor in question is inelastic, a small increase in demand will cause a large increase in the price of such factors. Conversely, a small reduction in demand will cause a sharp fall in the price of such factors. Two influences are seen at work in this relationship which can be illustrated by the following examples:

a) The "substitution effect." Suppose that a union of porters working for a company which cleans floors in various industrial and retail buildings demands a substantial wage increase. Management knows that if it purchases waxing and polishing machines it can speed up floor maintenance work and eliminate a number of porters. However, if the number of such machines available is limited so that any increase in demand will result in a sharp increase in the price asked for such machines, the bargaining power of the porters in demanding and obtaining wage increases will be improved. In other words, the inelasticity of the supply of this other factor of production will tend to make the demand for the porters' labor more inelastic. Management will then be prepared to pay more for this type of labor without substantially curtailing the amount of labor employed through increased mechanization.

b) *The "output effect."* The increase in costs resulting from the adjustment in wages given to the porters will necessitate an increase in price for services rendered by the floor-cleaning company. Therefore, it is likely that some of its customers will discontinue utilizing its services or will reduce their usage. Assume that the floor-cleaning company has been leasing polishing machines from another firm prior to the wage adjustment. Since the floor-cleaning company's business volume will be reduced as a result of the wage and price adjustments referred to above, it will have less need for polishing machines and may return some to the leasing firm. If the latter has no other place to use the machines and in effect is "stuck" with a fixed supply of them, it may be willing to accept a lower rental just to keep them busy. In other words, a relatively small reduction in demand for this factor of production might cause a substantial drop in its supply price. This is another way of saying that its supply curve is inelastic. If this were so, part of the wage increase gained by the porters could be achieved at the expense of the price paid for the other factor. In other words, an inelastic supply curve for a complementary factor of production would enable the porters to achieve a larger wage adjustment.

Circumstances in Which Wage Increases Do Not Reduce Employment

Suppose a union were to secure a substantial increase in wages from employers in a particular industry and the employers were then questioned as to the effect the wage adjustment would have on their employment policies. What would be the typical response? Chances are that most of the employers would say the wage increase would not cause them to cut their labor force; that, on the contrary, they intended to increase employment. They would explain that they had to give the wage increase in order to retain their present labor force and to attract additional workers.

Employers normally grant wage increases when times are good and prices are rising. They make wage changes in a dynamic business environment in which demand and supply conditions are in a continual state of flux. Against such a changing background, it is quite possible that wage increases will not be immediately associated with any diminution in employment. Let us consider briefly the various circumstances under which a wage increase need not have any adverse effect on employment.

1. *When output in the individual firm is increasing.* As we have observed, one avenue by which wage increases affect employment is through the reduction in output which is caused by the increase in product price made to cover the higher wage costs. If, however, output is increasing in the firm at the time the wage increase is made, the effect of employment in the firm may not be altered by the wage increase. Output may be increasing in a firm because of rising demand for its product attributable to a general business revival. During such a period, output, wages, profits, and prices all tend to rise together; and wage increases tend to be associated with increases, not decreases, in employment. Output may also be increasing in particular firms, even in periods of relative business stability, because the firm is growing, or the demand for the product of the industry is growing, or for similar reasons. Not only does expanding output normally carry with it additional job opportunities but also, in many industries—such as, for example, the steel industry—expanding output is associated with declining labor costs per unit of product. Therefore, if wage *rates* increase at a time when output is expanding in such industries, there may not even be any increase in unit labor costs, since the increase in wage rates may simply be offset by the decline in unit labor costs attributable to the expansion of output.

2. *When productivity is increasing.* As new and more productive machinery is introduced and changes are made in the organization of work, the productivity of labor tends to increase. This means that the employer will find that with a given number of workers, he can now produce a larger output than formerly. Such advance in productivity—which is a continuous process in our dynamic economy—has the effect of reducing labor costs per unit of product. Therefore, if money wage rates are raised at about the same rate that increasing productivity lowers unit labor costs, the two trends may offset each other; and on balance, there may be no net increase in unit labor costs. If the rate of increase in wage rates is no greater than the rate at which technological progress reduces unit labor costs, there will be no increase in unit labor cost, no increase in price, and no reduction in output and employment. However, although the wage increase under such circumstances does not produce unemployment, it may eliminate the possibility for any expansion of employment in the firm by preventing technological progress from being reflected in a reduction in price to consumers.

3. *When prices are inflexible.* There are certain situations in which a wage increase, even though it increases labor costs per unit, will not produce a change in the price charged by the individual firm. In such circumstances, the employer may calculate that even though his profits are being squeezed by failure to adjust prices, he would lose more if he tried to alter his price.

This condition may exist when there are only a few sellers in an industry. Such a situation is known as "oligopoly," and the demand curve of the individual firm, as seen by the employer, will often have a "kink" at the prevailing price. This is simply a geometric expression of the fact that each seller in the industry calculates that if he lowers his price, he will merely start a price war and therefore not appreciably increase his sales; whereas if he raises his price, his competitors may not follow suit, with the result that his sales will fall off sharply. Above the prevailing price the demand curve for the product of the individual firm approaches the horizontal, and below the prevailing price the demand curve approaches the vertical—thus producing the so-called "kink" at the prevailing price. Under such circumstances a rise in wage rates may not produce any change in prices or output. Consequently, employment will not be immediately affected. It must be borne in mind, however, that even when output remains constant, management may still find means of economizing on the use of labor which has become more expensive by reason of the wage increase. For example, in some industries, employers have sought to economize on the use of labor by resorting to the "stretch-out," i.e., a worker who formerly tended only one machine is required to operate two machines at the same rate of pay. Through this and similar devices a smaller labor force can be used more intensively, and some workers can be displaced, although output remains unchanged.

4. *When exploitation of labor exists.* As we observed in Chapter 10, a wage increase need not produce unemployment where a condition of exploitation of labor has previously existed. In other words, if an employer has been paying labor less than its marginal revenue product, and the effect of a wage adjustment is to increase the wage rate to the point of equivalence of marginal revenue product and wage, there will be no incentive for the employer to alter his price, output, and employment.

The foregoing analysis indicates that in the dynamic environment of the business world, the connection between wage changes and changes in employment is a very tenuous one. Wage increases do not necessarily produce increases in labor costs per unit of product—they may simply prevent reductions in labor costs attributable to technological change or increasing output from being reflected in price reductions to consumers. Even if the increase in wage rates increases labor costs per unit of product, it still may not affect prices where it is impracticable for the firm to raise prices because of competitive conditions; moreover, even if prices are raised, there need be no reduction in output or employment, if output was increasing anyway, or if the price increase is negligible because wages constitute such a small proportion of total costs.

Long-Run Effect of Wage Increases

As we have observed earlier in this chapter, the extent to which wage increases will produce unemployment in the individual firm in the long run can be summarized in the form of four laws:

If wages are raised, the resulting unemployment will be smaller in amount:

1. The less elastic the demand for the product.
2. The smaller the substitutability of labor in the process of production.
3. The smaller the portion which labor costs form of total costs.
4. The less elastic the supply schedules of the complementary factors.[2]

These "laws" are applicable in both the short run and the long run, but it is only in the long run that factors 2 and 4 can exercise their full effect. In essence, these two tendencies reduce to the degree of fluidity of capital. It is machinery that is ordinarily the complement of labor, as well as its most important substitute. In the long run, capital not only can be substituted for labor (factor 2), but it also may be removed to other industries, or the supply may be altered (factor 4).

At any moment of time, employers, if they have acted rationally, will have pushed their use of labor and capital to the point where they have reached a margin of indifference, i.e., it is immaterial to them whether they utilize a unit of capital or a unit of labor at the margin. From this it follows that if the price of labor rises, employers will find two actions profitable: (1) to substitute capital for labor by introducing laborsaving machinery; and (2) to shift from less capitalistic to more capitalistic industries, i.e., to industries where the ratio of labor to capital is smaller. These reactions both take time. A full adaptation to an increase in the wage of labor may take years to work itself out. As a consequence, the full effect of wage increases upon the volume of employment can be observed only in the long run.

WAGE PRESSURE AND MECHANIZATION

A major means of improving efficiency and saving labor in our industrial economy has been the machine. Machines, however, are costly, and businessmen will normally invest in laborsaving machinery only if the investment gives promise of paying for itself in a reasonable period of time. A laborsaving machine pays for itself in terms of manpower saved, reduction in spoilage, and so forth. The higher the wage rate of the labor which can be displaced by the machine, the larger the savings which the machine will effect, and the more attractive its purchase becomes.

Businessmen are not uniformly alert to the advantages of using labor-saving machinery. There are many laborsaving machines which are known today and which may be in use in some companies but which are not utilized by others, either because their labor costs are not high enough to warrant the expenditure on machinery or because management is

---

[2] A mathematical exposition of these four rules, which govern the derived demand for labor, is found in the appendix to this chapter.

inefficient and has not sufficient initiative to look around and find out how its costs might be lowered. Undoubtedly, a substantial improvement in the level of industrial efficiency could be obtained if inefficient employers were induced to bring their production methods into line with the best in the industry.

Wage pressure may exert this influence in certain circumstances. Wage increases are likely to be most effective as a stimulus to substitution of machinery for labor in firms where wages, prior to the wage increase, were low, and management relied on low wages rather than efficient methods to compete. For example, a study based upon an examination of Census of Manufacturing data found that among low-wage industries, firms affected by increased wage costs resulting from a rise in governmental minimum wage rates showed the greatest tendency to substitute nonwage inputs in the production process.[3] Employers are most likely to be sensitive to wage increases in firms where labor costs constitute a large proportion of total costs and where competition is keen and profit margins are slim.

In this connection, it should be observed that although in companies operating on low profit margins, wage increases frequently provide a spur to improved efficiency, an increase in material costs, or insurance rates, or general overhead may have precisely the same effect. The increase in costs compels management to look around in the industry and bring its own plant up to date with others.

Not all machinery is introduced because of an increase in labor costs. As a matter of fact, it is possible that in our dynamic economy, only a small part of the substitution of machinery for labor which occurs is attributable to changes in wage rates. The reason is that invention is continuously bringing onto the market new machines and devices which have a high laborsaving potential and which, in many cases, would be profitable to use even at a much lower wage rate. For example, when the "semiautomatics" were introduced in the bottle industry, the Glass Bottle Blowers Association attempted to compete with the machine by accepting a 45% reduction in the hand price on fruit jars, but this substantial wage cut proved ineffective, and the machine continued to be introduced. Here is an example of a machine which would have been profitable to use even at a wage level 45% lower than that which prevailed when it was introduced. Obviously, its introduction did not depend upon wage increases. Many other laborsaving machines fall in the same category. The point is that while wage increases accelerate the introduction of some machinery, a large part of the new machinery which is applied in industry depends upon research and invention which is not significantly influenced by changes in wage rates. The same is true of the modern

---

[3] David E. Kaun, "Minimum Wages, Factor Substitution, and the Marginal Producer," *Quarterly Journal of Economics*, Vol. 79 (August 1965), pp. 478–86.

development of automation, which was discussed in Chapter 6. The wide-spread application of automation in industry has depended upon our scientific know-how in the field of electronics and control mechanisms reaching a certain stage of development. On the other hand, a high wage level has been a factor in making application of automation practical.

Wage Pressure and Invention

We have seen that wage increases can affect the rate at which known mechanical improvements are applied by industry. Does the level of wages also affect the rate at which new methods are discovered? In other words, can wage pressure induce invention?

This is a subject upon which there is considerable theoretical discussion and controversy in the economic literature,[4] but very little substantiation in the form of empirical research. The theory of induced invention is usually associated with the name of J. R. Hicks,[5] who suggested that a rise in the rate of wages (the price of labor) relative to the rate of interest (the price of capital) would induce the discovery of methods of production which would save labor. This theory further postulates that the frequency of laborsaving inventions depends upon the rate of increase in wages relative to interest rates. Laborsaving inventions save labor, whereas capital-saving inventions save capital. According to this theory, if interest rates were to rise relative to wages, there would be a greater inducement to save capital; and as a result, the frequency of capital-saving inventions would increase.

Other economists, however, contend that because of the unpredictable nature of the process of invention, wage increases do not necessarily call forth any increase in the number of laborsaving discoveries. According to this view, most inventions will be laborsaving simply because of the continuing high cost of labor as an element of production and because most invention in our society is designed to lighten the arduousness of work.

However, William Fellner finds some statistical support for the concept of induced inventions. In a recent article he states:

A good general case can be made for the assumption that a tendency of labor income to rise relative to non-labor income—and hence a tendency for the weight of labor cost to rise in aggregate factor cost—places a premium

[4] See, for example, Syed Ahmad, "On the Theory of Induced Invention," *Economic Journal*, Vol. 76 (June 1966), pp. 344–57; William Fellner, "Profit Maximization, Utility Minimization, and the Rate and Direction of Innovation," Papers and Proceedings of the Seventy-eighth Annual Meeting of the American Economic Association, *American Economic Review Supplement*, Vol. 56 (May 1966), pp. 27–28.

[5] J. R. Hicks, *The Theory of Wages* (2d ed.; London: Macmillan & Co., Ltd. 1963), chap. vi, pp. 112–35. See also, for a critique of this theory, Gordon F. Bloom, "Note on Hicks' Theory of Invention," *American Economic Review*, Vol. 36, (March 1946), pp. 83–96.

on following through those research and innovative projects that are tilted more toward a proportionate reduction of labor costs than of capital costs.[6]

Is the increase in research expenditures in this country a response to continuing wage pressure? Funds spent on research and development performed by industry increased from $7.7 billion in 1957 to about $19 billion in 1970.[7] These were years characterized by a steady rise in money wages. On the other hand, research expenditures increased fivefold from 1920 to 1931, a period when wage rates were relatively stable. The great growth of research in this country cannot be attributed to wage pressure, although high wages, as one element of the cost-price structure, have undoubtedly produced an economic setting conducive to research and invention.

Does wage pressure influence the direction of industrial research projects? One would expect to find major emphasis in research to reduce costs in view of the continuing upward pressure of unions on wages, particularly in large companies which support most of the research activity in this country. However, a study conducted by one of the authors suggests that most research funds are allocated to research on new products and improvement of present products, rather than to new-process research.

This emphasis on product improvement is not entirely inconsistent with major interest on the part of management in reducing labor costs. Very often, a need arises in one industry for a machine to cut costs, and this idea filters back to a supplier, who then devises a new product or a new machine to help fill this need. A new computer is a new-product development from the point of view of the industry making it, yet can be a significant cost-saving development in the industry utilizing it.

Of course, not all invention occurs in the industrial laboratory. Every employer, every foreman—indeed, every employee—is a potential inventor. Anyone who designs a new way of arranging the flow of production, devises a new attachment for a machine which increases man-hour output, adds to the stream of invention. Wage pressure—like any other pressure on profits—tends to make employers look around for new avenues to save money and thus may stimulate some invention. However, it is doubtful that there is any close relationship between the rate of wages and the frequency of invention, as suggested by Hicks.

UNION WAGE MOVEMENTS AND INDUSTRIAL EFFICIENCY

In earlier chapters, we noted that union organization has tended to accelerate the adoption by management of two important wage practices.

---

[6] William Fellner, "Empirical Support for the Theory of Induced Invention," *Quarterly Journal of Economics*, Vol. 85 (1971), p. 603.

[7] *Business Week*, May 18, 1968, pp. 72–73. U.S. Department of Commerce, Bureau of the Census, *Pocket Data Book USA, 1971* (Washington, D.C.: U.S. Government Printing Office, 1971), p. 175.

The first is uniformity in wage rates. This is the result of the spread of multiunit bargaining and of union interest in the stabilization on an industrywide basis of hourly earnings, piece rates, or labor costs. There is now double pressure for uniformity in rates—from competitors and from labor itself. The second practice is simultaneity in wage adjustments. This is a by-product not only of multiunit bargaining but also of the growing importance of leader-follower relationships in wage policies. Company executives tend to feel that wage adjustments should not be given unless other companies are making them at more or less the same time. As a result of these two practices, wage increases tend to occur more or less simultaneously and of a fairly uniform amount in a large number of industries. Obviously, the effect of a wage increase upon efficiency may be quite different when the wage increase takes place in only one firm in an industry and when it occurs throughout an industry. What, then, is the likely effect of these union wage practices on industrial efficiency?

Favorable Effects on Efficiency

The policy of uniformity in wage rates in an industry may hasten the spread of improved methods of production from the more progressive firms to those that are less efficient. In most industries, there are three or four large companies that do the majority of the business and set the pace for the technological development of the industry. According to one study, the larger firms in an industry are generally quicker to introduce new techniques than their smaller competitors.[8] If unions compel the smaller firms to pay the same rates as the larger firms, the small companies will have to keep abreast of the latest developments if they are to survive.

Unfavorable Effects on Efficiency

While uniformity in wage rates probably contributes to an improved standard of industrial efficiency, simultaneity in wage increases probably lessens the effectiveness of the stimulus which normally is forthcoming from wage pressure. If wage rates are raised generally in an industry, the individual employer, knowing that his competitors are faced by the same rise in cost as he, is much more likely to attempt to pass on the increased labor costs in the form of higher prices to consumers, in the expectation that competitors will follow a similar course, than if he alone had been compelled to grant a wage increase. Price increases are more likely to follow industrywide changes in wage levels than changes within a single firm, because the average businessman, although he has a fair conception of the demand curve for his individual product, either has no

---

[8] Edwin Mansfield, "The Speed of Response of Firms to New Techniques," *Quarterly Journal of Economics*, Vol. 77 (May 1963), p. 310.

notion of a demand curve for the product of the industry or else assumes that it is inelastic within the relevant range. Thus, simultaneous union wage changes facilitate shifting the burden of higher labor costs to the consumer. To the extent that this is accomplished, the inducement afforded to management to increase its efficiency is lessened; and as a consequence, neither mechanization nor technological changes of other kinds may follow the wage increase. Profits may not be cut at all by the wage adjustment but merely be kept from rising as fast as they otherwise would have in good times.

WAGE CHANGES IN THE ECONOMY AS A WHOLE

We have seen that application of the marginal productivity theory to the problem of wage increases in the individual firm indicates that except in unusual cases of product demand and labor supply, the wage increase will result in a reduction of employment, *other things being equal.* The latter assumption is made to rule out the complications which might otherwise be produced by concurrent changes in the demand for the product or in the state of the arts. As mentioned, if a wage increase occurs in a firm at the same time as the demand for the product of the firm is growing and output is expanding, there need not be any immediate curtailment of employment. However, if other things remain equal— and if, in particular, we assume that the change in the supply curve for labor does not produce any change in the demand curve for labor—the wage increase will, according to orthodox economic theory, produce some reduction in employment in the individual firm.

When we come to analyze the effect of *general* changes in wage rates upon employment in the economy as a whole, we can no longer realistically assume that "other things will remain equal." The demand curve for labor in the economy as a whole is not independent of the supply curve for labor. Or to put the same proposition in a less technical way, changes in the amount of wages paid to labor as a whole are bound to affect the aggregate demand for labor. General wage adjustments affect the demand for labor because labor is industry's best customer, and if labor has more or less money to spend, the change in such expenditures may alter the total volume of employment in the economy. Furthermore, changes in wage levels throughout the economy will affect the profitability of investment, with the result that employers may increase or curtail their purchases of capital goods, This, too, will affect the total demand for labor in the economy.

Determinants of Aggregate Spending

What determines the volume of spending in the economy as a whole at any given time? Our understanding of this problem owes much to the theoretical analysis of John Maynard Keynes, a British economist, who developed a new approach to this problem in his famous work, *The General Theory of Employment, Interest, and Money*, which was published in 1936.[9] Keynes talks of total spending as "effective demand." Effective demand consists of two types of spending—spending by consumers, which is called consumption, and spending by businessmen for capital expenditures, which is called investment.

According to Keynes, as long as investment and consumption remain constant from one period of time to the next, output and employment also will be unchanged, and a stable level of income will be maintained from period to period, with no tendency to expand or contract. In order to maintain such a steady flow of income through the productive process, the amount of expenditure upon new investment must, according to Keynes, be equal to the amount which people are prepared to save out of their incomes.

For example, suppose that national income is $1,000 billion and that $800 billion of it is derived from the production of consumer goods, while $200 billion is derived from the production of capital goods. Assume further that consumers are prepared to spend annually $800 billion of their $1,000 billion income on consumer goods and to save the remainder. The total value of goods produced—both consumer goods and capital goods—is thus $1,000 billion, while consumers are ready to spend only $800 billion. Under such circumstances, in order to maintain national income at $1,000 billion in succeeding periods, businessmen must be prepared to spend $200 billion annually on new investment. If interest rates fall and make investment more attractive, businessmen would borrow money from the banks to undertake new investments; and as a result, income and employment would expand. The same reaction would occur if consumers were to increase their consumption. But if we assume that consumption and investment remain constant, then income and employment will remain constant from one period to the next.

Effect of a General Wage Adjustment: Special Case

Assume that unions obtain a general increase in wage rates throughout the economy. Assume further that the wage increase has no effect on interest rates or on businessmen's inclination to invest, and no effect on consumption. What effect would the wage increase have on employment? The answer is contained in the assumptions, for, as we have observed, if consumption or investment does not change, employment must also remain unchanged. Prices would rise, but output and employment would remain unchanged. A similar result would follow if there

[9] John Maynard Keynes, *The General Theory of Employment, Interest, and Money* (New York: Harcourt, Brace & Co., Inc., 1936).

were a reduction in wage rates under these restrictive assumptions. In the latter case, there would be a fall in prices, with no alteration in output or employment.

Effect of General Wage Increase upon Aggregate Spending

The foregoing examples of possible reactions to a general wage increase and a general wage reduction are admittedly special cases in the general Keynesian theoretical framework. Keynesian theorists do not maintain that a wage increase will not reduce employment, nor do they contend that a wage reduction will not increase employment. They merely attempt to show by the use of the foregoing type of example that a general wage adjustment need not affect employment at all and that if employment is affected, it is because of the reaction of the wage change upon the real determinants of the volume of employment—namely, the volume of investment and the amount of consumption expenditures. If these variables are affected favorably, so that total spending is maintained or increased, a wage reduction will increase employment, for there will now be the same or a larger aggregate demand to purchase goods whose cost, and presumably price, has been reduced by the wage cut. On the other hand, in the case of a wage increase, employment will increase only if total spending increases more than proportionately to the increase in prices produced by the higher level of costs.

Four possible reactions of total spending may be distinguished as resulting from a general increase in wage rates:

1. The wage increase may expand total spending more than it increases prices. This might be the case if a wage increase were made in times of business depression. Both businessmen and workers might take the wage increase as a signal that business revival was under way and so increase their expenditures. As industry increased its output from very low levels, labor costs per unit of output would tend to decline, and the economies in labor costs resulting from such increase in output might offset the increase in labor costs produced by the wage increase, so that there would be, on balance, little or no increase in unit labor costs or in prices. Under such circumstances the increase in total spending would buy a larger volume of goods and services and thus support a larger volume of employment.

The late Professor Sumner H. Slichter believed that this same result might occur during the upswing phase of a business cycle when general "pattern" wage settlements were involved. It was his belief that when general wage adjustments are made in various key industries at more or less the same time, employers are prone to raise prices because they know their competitors have been saddled with similar increases in cost and are likely to follow suit. Slichter contended that when all or most of the firms in an industry increased their prices, the total amount spent on the product of the industry would ordinarily increase because the demand for the product of most basic industries is inelastic. Therefore, in the short run, expenditures would be increased by customers for the product of the industry; and at the same time, the firms in the industry would be paying out more funds for labor. The combined effect of increased spending from these two sources—given a flexible credit system—might well increase the total amount of spending in the economy more than enough to sustain or increase production at the new higher level of prices.[10]

2. The wage increase may increase total spending no more than it increases prices. Such a situation might develop if a general wage increase were made throughout the economy at a time when output was at high levels and a point of full employment had been attained. Under such circumstances the wage increase would produce a sharp increase in costs and prices, and there would be little or no effect upon employment. The increased spending would, in effect, be dissipated in the form of higher prices.

3. The wage increase may increase total spending, but not as much as it increases prices. When a wage increase occurs during a period of inflation, it frequently causes price adjustments which are greater than the amount which would be required to compensate for the rise in labor costs. Businesses which have been looking for a pretext to raise prices now do so and blame the price rise on "higher labor costs." As a result, even if total spending increases, the rise in the general price level may be so great that the total volume of spending will be insufficient to purchase all of the goods and services offered at the higher price level, and output and employment may therefore decline in particular industries.

4. The wage increase may not increase total spending and may actually diminish it. This could happen if businessmen become alarmed by the rise in costs and prices, and decide to postpone making new investments until prices come down to a more reasonable level. Consumers also may take a similar view. If this attitude of "wait and see" becomes prevalent, total spending may decline despite the higher level of wages, and employment will be reduced as a consequence.

Effect of Wage Increase on Borrowing, Investment, and Consumption

How does a general wage increase bring about a change in total spending? Of primary importance to the Keynesian theorists is the effect of the wage increase upon the rate of interest. When wages rise, businessmen are compelled to increase their working capital to meet larger cash requirements for payment of wages. For a time, the banks will be willing to increase loans without raising the rate of interest; but as the volume of

---

[10] Sumner H. Slichter, "Labor Costs and Prices," in American Assembly, *Wages, Prices, Profits, and Productivity* (New York: Columbia University Press, 1959), p. 173.

outstanding loans increases, banks will ultimately raise interest rates and tend to become more selective in the borrowers to whom they will lend funds. At this point, the volume of spending will be affected in two ways. In the first place, the rise in interest rates will make certain investments unprofitable. Businessmen will curtail purchase of capital goods, and this will be reflected in smaller wage disbursements to employees in these industries. In the second place, refusal by the banks to loan to particular prospective borrowers because of the general tightening of the credit situation will mean that these businessmen will have to revise their plans and curtail contemplated expansion; and this, too, will be felt in the volume of aggregate spending.

The increase in wage rates may also affect the anticipated profit rate on investment. If the rise in wages increases labor costs, it may increase the number of business failures and produce reduction of output and unemployment in marginal firms. This may have a depressing effect on the business community. On the other hand, if the wage increase is viewed by businessmen as the beginning of a general upswing in wages and prices, the profitability of present investment will be increased, since presumably capital equipment will, in the future, be produced at even higher costs. Thus, businessmen may be induced to expand current expenditures upon investment.

A third possibility is that the wage increase will stimulate consumption. The initial effect of the wage increase may be to increase the size of the wage bill for industry at large. Furthermore, the rise in prices may tend to shift real income from fixed-income groups to wage earners who obtain wage adjustments. Some economists believe that as a result of such a shift, a larger portion of incomes will now be spent and a smaller portion saved than under the former distribution. If so, the wage increase will be felt in a higher level of spending in the market for consumers' goods. On the other hand, some investigations indicate that consumption expenditures are not likely to be significantly affected by shifts in income between various groups. On the whole, it must be admitted that very little is known about the effect of shifts in income on consumption habits of various groups in the community; and therefore it is premature to predict what effect wage increases would have on this variable.

It can be seen from the foregoing analysis that the net result of a wage increase upon the volume of spending and the volume of employment depends in large measure on the psychological effect which the wage increase has on the economy. If it is viewed as the beginning of or part of a sustained upward trend in business, the outcome is likely to be favorable to employment. On the other hand, if businessmen and consumers feel that costs have gotten out of line and defer purchases, the consequences of the wage increase upon employment will be adverse. Furthermore, the effect of the wage increase upon employment will be more favorable the earlier in a business upturn it occurs. As a boom wears on, the wage increase is more likely to be dissipated in the form of price increases and more likely to produce a rise in interest rates, with a consequent reduction in investment and employment.

Appraisal of Keynesian Approach

Although there is some feeling that the Keynesian theory and its advocates overemphasize the importance of changes in interest rates as a determinant of the volume of employment, there is no doubt that they have made an important contribution to clearer thinking in this field by directing attention to the effect of general wage adjustments upon the volume of total spending. Orthodox theorists tended tacitly to assume that aggregate demand would remain constant whether wage rates increased or decreased. Consequently, they were led to the conclusion that wage increases would produce price increases, reduced output, and contraction of employment. Keynes, however, demonstrated that aggregate demand is capable of expansion and that, as a consequence, it is possible that general wage increases will be reflected in a general increase in the price level, with no reduction in output or employment. Orthodox theorists tended to think in terms of an inelastic supply of money; Keynesian theorists reason in terms of an elastic money supply,[11] which is the product of our modern credit system.

The Keynesian theory and the modern marginal productivity theory are not inconsistent. Each gives us valuable analytical tools to approach the wage-employment relationship from a different point of view and under different circumstances. When we are dealing with macroeconomic problems involving the level of employment in the entire economy, we will find the Keynesian approach more useful, even if we differ with Keynes in his estimate of the effectiveness of the interest rate as a means of stimulating or curtailing investment and employment. On the other hand, when we are concerned with problems in particular firms or even in particular areas—as, for example, in analyzing the effect of minimum wage regulations on southern firms—we shall find the marginal productivity approach more helpful.

WAGE INCREASES AS A RECOVERY MEASURE IN DEPRESSION

An increase in wage rates in one firm will not ordinarily provide a basis for more jobs, since the rise in wage rates simply increases costs

---

[11] Although money as such does not figure directly in the basic equations of the Keynesian system, Keynes believed that the bank rate and the quantity of money influenced prices indirectly by their influence on the values of the terms in the fundamental equations linking savings, investment, and output. See R. Harrod, "Reassessment of Keynes's Views on Money," *Journal of Political Economy*, Vol. 78, No. 4, Part 1 (July/August 1970), pp. 617–25.

without measurably altering the demand for the output of this particular employer. But when wage rates are increased generally throughout the economy, the effect of these increased disbursements upon general consumer demand cannot be ignored. If there are no leakages, and if the banking system expands the quantity of money sufficiently to maintain a higher level of prices without a rise in interest rates, then the rise in wage cost need not reduce employment and may even increase it if the rise in wages and prices is taken as an indication of the end of the deflationary downturn.

In a depression period the existence of unused plant and equipment and the widespread operation of industry at less than optimum capacity may make possible a rise in money wages and employment with a less than proportionate increase in prices. This consideration was one of the motivating factors in the National Recovery Administration program of 1933, which sought to achieve recovery by expanding wage earners' buying power. This program achieved a small increase in real wages from June 1933 to June 1935; the index of weekly industrial earnings rose from 70 to 80, while the cost of living index rose from 96 to 107.5 Real wages thus rose from 72.9 to 74.3.[12]

Wage increases will not significantly enlarge consumption expenditures if the employed workers who receive wage adjustments simply save the additional income or use it to pay off indebtedness to banks. Moreover, even if the wage increases increase consumption, they may merely improve the short-term outlook for business without affecting the views of the business community concerning the profitability of long-term investment in heavy plant and equipment. Because wage increases tend to affect short-term rather than long-term expectations, any favorable reaction upon business expenditures is likely to be reflected in increased inventory accumulation, rather than in the purchase of fixed plant and equipment. Consequently, a recovery movement which is generated by increased wages is likely to be extremely susceptible to speculative influences. One reason that the speculative collapse of 1937 produced such a sharp curtailment in production and employment is the fact that long-term confidence had remained weak throughout the abortive boom, as evidenced by the tendency of businessmen to confine their buying of industrial equipment to replacement demands.

On the whole, relatively few economic theorists favor wage increases as a device to achieve recovery in depression. An exception is the school of underconsumptionists, who see in depression the cumulative effect of oversaving; in their view, wage increases are essential to eliminate the prime cause of the collapse of business, namely, the deficiency in consumer purchasing power. However, even granting their argument

---

[12] C. F. Roos, *NRA Economic Planning* (Cowles Commission Monograph No. 2 [Bloomington, Ind.: Principia Press, 1937]), p. 444.

that it is desirable—and even necessary—to raise *consumption* during depression, this in itself is not enough to assume recovery. It is the propensity to *spend*, not alone the propensity to *consume*, that is the crucial factor in the cyclical process. Spending must be stimulated by *all* groups in the community—by employers as well as by consumers. If every increase in expenditure by consumers were accompanied by a decrease in expenditure by employers, it is clear that no stimulus to business recovery would be imparted by wage increases.

Furthermore, in an economy which depends in part upon exporting to other countries, a general increase in labor costs at a time when other nations are undergoing the painful process of deflation may have a detrimental effect on employment in export industries. In our highly interrelated modern world, depressions tend to be worldwide, and recovery measures in one country must take account of conditions in other countries. If wages and prices are raised in this country at the same time as consumers in foreign countries find their incomes diminished and prices in their own countries reduced, our export industries will be less able to compete in foreign markets. The depressed condition of these industries will therefore be aggravated by the wage increase. In the absence of a concomitant increase in tariffs, our imports will be stimulated because domestic consumers will find that many articles can now be purchased cheaper abroad than at home. This may produce an unfavorable balance of payments which may require increased interest rates and a tightening in the money supply at the very time when credit restrictions should be relaxed.

WAGE REDUCTIONS AS A RECOVERY MEASURE IN DEPRESSION

Can a reduction in the general level of wages act as a stimulant to start an upturn of employment and investment in depression? Theoretically, a reduction in wage rates might reduce the rate of interest by diminishing the needs of business for cash. The reduction in rate of interest might induce increased investment on the part of businessmen. But if it were believed that all that was needed to achieve an increase in investment was a reduction in interest rates, it would obviously be sound policy to change such rates directly rather than to seek to influence such rates indirectly through a reduction of wage rates.

A reduction in wage rates in key industries may stimulate investment and employment, particularly where rates have gotten out of line in export industries so that such industries have difficulty in competing in the world market. In 1931 in Australia, wage levels were reduced 10% by order of the Commonwealth Arbitration Board, and this wage cut is generally credited with having contributed to Australia's recovery from the depression. Australia's economy is, of course, heavily dependent upon the prosperity of its export industries. To some extent something of the same nature may have occurred in 1921 in the United States when recovery seems to have been materially aided by wage and price reductions which brought our high wartime price structure into alignment with world levels.

However, by and large, wage reductions are not an effective recovery measure because of their tendency to produce anticipations of a further fall in wages and prices and because of their adverse effect upon effective demand. Since the immediate effect of a wage reduction is likely to be a decline in wage payments and consumer expenditures, there must be an immediate compensatory increase in spending by business on inventories or capital goods to prevent a shrinkage in total purchasing power. In periods of depression, however, businessmen typically are in a cautious mood and are unlikely to rush into new investment merely because of a wage reduction. Any savings effected by them in production costs as a result of the wage reduction may simply be used to pay off debt or to build up bank balances. Thus, wage reductions are likely to reduce effective demand yet hold forth little promise of stimulating the rate of investment.

APPRAISAL OF WAGE POLICY AS A RECOVERY MEASURE

This brief discussion serves to indicate that wage policy is not a very effective or convenient recovery measure. In those special situations where wage policy can be utilized, its effectiveness will depend upon the nature of the particular depression and the basic causes of the maladjustments existing in the economic situation. In 1929, for example, wage reductions could not halt the deflation due to bank failures, nor could they raise the depressed level of long-term expectations. On the other hand, in 1920–21, wage reductions did contribute to recovery because the high wages left over from the war inflation were *themselves* a cause of the ensuing depression.

The fact that there is no certainty that employment will be increased if wage rates are reduced or increased in periods of business recession strengthens the case for wage rigidity. Maintenance of wages may be the best way to maintain consumption expenditures. It is important to maintain consumption during depression because experience has demonstrated that new investment is not likely to revive until inventories have been used up, and this process of depletion takes time. In the three years 1933–35, it is estimated that business inventories declined nearly $4 billion[13] (measured in 1929 prices). This represents a considerable disinvestment and indicates the large amount of slack which needs to be taken up before investment is likely to resume. During the intervening period

---

[13] Simon Kuznets, *National Income and Capital Formation, 1919–1935* (New York: National Bureau of Economic Research, 1937), p. 40.

of adjustment, maintenance of wages is desirable to prevent cumulative contraction. The policy of maintaining wages during depression which was adopted by Sweden in the early 1930s enabled that country to make a quick recovery from the depression. Wages fell less than 5% in Sweden in the worst year of the depression.[14] On the other hand, no country made such drastic cuts in wages and other costs from 1930 to 1933 as the United States, yet no country suffered more intensely from that depression. In the United States, total payrolls in manufacturing, mining, and steam railroads fell by over half from 1929 to 1932.[15]

The severe wage deflation of the Great Depression is not likely to be repeated in the future unless the pattern of our industrial relations undergoes a sharp reversal. Unions characteristically think of wages as income rather than as a cost and consequently have little sympathy for proposals that wages be rendered "flexible" to assist recovery from depression. The experience of the recession in 1938, as well as during the post–World War II period, suggests that the wage rigidity produced by such union attitudes may produce a. cyclical pattern characterized by an extremely sharp fall in production and employment as declining demand impinges upon rigid wage costs. On the other hand, if consumer income is maintained by social security, relief, and supplementary unemployment benefit payments, a fairly rapid recovery can be achieved, since the relative stability of costs and prices attributable to maintenance of wage rates prevents the strengthening of deflationary forces.

APPENDIX

The derivation of the four rules referred to in the text, which determine the derived demand for labor, can be demonstrated as follows:

Consider a good that is produced by the use of two factors, capital K and labor L. The factors are compensated according to the value of their marginal revenue products (as explained in Chapter 10). Let Q be the quantity of the good produced according to its production function

$$Q = Q(K, L) \tag{1}$$

Also, let p be the price of the good per unit, w the wage rate per unit of labor input and r the interest rate per unit of capital input. We are interested in computing the derived elasticity of demand for labor λ given that η is the elasticity of demand for the good and μ is the elasticity of supply of capital.

Since the prices of the inputs are equal to their marginal revenue products by the assumption of profit maximization, we have

---

[14] A. Montgomery, *How Sweden Overcame the Depression, 1930–1933*, trans. L. B. Eyre (Stockholm: Alb. Bonniers Boktryckeri, 1938), p. 52.

[15] *Monthly Labor Review*, Vol. 57 (September 1940), p. 538.

$$w = p \frac{\delta Q}{\delta L} \qquad r = p \frac{\delta Q}{\delta K} \qquad (2)$$

By the definition of elasticity of demand and supply, we write

$$\eta = -\frac{dQ}{dp} \; \frac{Q}{p} \; ; \; \mu = \frac{dK}{dr} \; \frac{K}{r} \; ; \; \wedge = -\frac{dL}{dw} \; \frac{L}{w} \qquad (3)$$

If we equate total revenue and total costs, we have,

$$pQ = wL + rK \qquad (4)$$

Substituting from (2) into (4), we obtain,

$$Q = L \frac{\delta Q}{\delta L} + K \frac{\delta Q}{\delta K} \qquad (5)$$

If the industry under consideration has constant returns to scale, i.e., the production function is homogeneous of degree unity, (5) is an identity and can be differentiated partially with respect to K to yield,

$$\frac{\delta Q}{\delta K} = L \frac{\delta^2 Q}{\delta K \delta L} + K \frac{\delta^2 Q}{\delta K^2} + \frac{\delta Q}{\delta K} \qquad (6)$$

or

$$K \frac{\delta^2 Q}{\delta K^2} = -L \frac{\delta^2 Q}{\delta K \delta L} \qquad (6a)$$

The total differential of Q is written as

$$dQ = \frac{\delta Q}{\delta L} dL + \frac{\delta Q}{\delta K} dK \qquad (7)$$

which on substitution from (2) yields

$$pdQ = wdL + rdK \qquad (8)$$

By considering a change in the labor force by dL, we can rewrite the equality of revenue and costs in (4) in terms of derivatives as

$$pdQ + Qdp = wdL + Ldw + rdK + Kdr \qquad (9)$$

Substituting (8) into (9), we obtain

$$Qdp = Ldw + Kdr \qquad (10)$$

From the elasticity formulas in (3) and (10) above,

$$\frac{pdQ}{\eta} = \frac{wdL}{\lambda} - \frac{rdK}{\mu} \qquad (11)$$

From the definition of elasticity of supply of capital in (3), we can write

$$dK = \frac{K\mu}{r} dr = \frac{K\mu}{r} d\left(p \frac{\delta Q}{\delta K}\right) \qquad (12)$$

Substituting (6a) into (12), we can write

$$dK = \frac{K\mu}{r}\left\{ \frac{-rdQ}{Q\eta} + p\frac{\delta^2 Q}{\delta K \delta L}\left(dL - \frac{L}{K}dK \right) \right\}\tag{13}$$

Writing $\alpha = \dfrac{wr}{p^2 Q\dfrac{\delta^2 Q}{\delta K \delta L}}$ and $\beta = \dfrac{wL}{pQ}$, (11) after substitution from (13) can be

written as

$$\frac{pdQ}{\eta} = \frac{wdL}{\alpha} - \frac{rdK}{1-\beta}\left(\frac{1}{\mu} + \frac{\beta}{\alpha} \right)\tag{14}$$

Eliminating dQ, dL and dK from above, we have

$$\frac{\lambda - \alpha}{\eta - \lambda} = \left(\frac{\beta}{1-\beta} \right)\left(\frac{\mu + \alpha}{\mu + \eta} \right)\tag{15}$$

or

$$\lambda = \frac{\alpha(\eta + \mu) + \beta\mu(\eta - \alpha)}{\eta + \mu - \beta(\eta - \alpha)}$$

In this equation, η, β, μ correspond to statements 1, 3, and 4 of the formulation on p. 350 for the long run effects of wage increases, while α, being the elasticity of substitution, explains statement 2. $\dfrac{\delta^2 Q}{\delta K \delta L}$ gives the rate of change of the marginal product due to one input for a change in the other. If $\dfrac{\delta^2 Q}{\delta K \delta L}$ is infinite, $\alpha = 0$ and no substitution is possible, thus implying fixed coefficients of production of the Leontief type with the isoquants in Figure 12–1. If $\dfrac{\delta^2 Q}{\delta K \delta L}$ is zero, α is infinite and the

Figure 12–1

Production Isoquants for Leontief-Type Technology

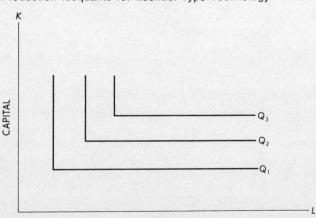

Figure 12–2

Production Isoquants Where Perfect
Substitutability Exists

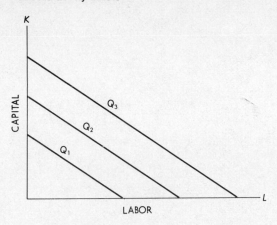

factors are perfect substitutes for each other with the production
isoquants being as shown in Figure 12–2. While $\dfrac{\delta^2 Q}{\delta K \delta L}$ is a rough measure
of the elasticity of substitution, it is not independent of the units of Q,
K and L. To make it independent of these units, we can multiply it by
$\dfrac{p^2 Q}{wr}$ and take its reciprocal to obtain a measure increasing with the possibility of substitution.

In order to derive the four rules set out, we differentiate the expression for λ with respect to the four variables η, a, β and μ.

$$\frac{\delta\lambda}{\delta\eta} = \beta \times \text{a square} \tag{16a}$$

$$\frac{\delta\lambda}{\delta\alpha} = (1 - \beta) \times \text{a square} \tag{16b}$$

$$\frac{\delta\lambda}{\delta\beta} = (\eta - \alpha)(\eta + \mu)(\mu + \alpha) \times \text{a square} \tag{16c}$$

$$\frac{\delta\lambda}{\delta\mu} = \beta(1 - \beta) \times \text{a square.} \tag{16d}$$

A square being always a positive quantity, the signs on the left-hand sides
in the above equations are the same as the quantities on the respective
right-hand sides.

Since β, the share of labor and total output, is always given by $0 \leq \beta$
≤ 1, the expressions in (16a), (16b), and (16d) are always positive. In
the case of (16c), we do not have a general rule. So long as μ. the elasticity

of supply of capital is positive and $\eta > a$, i.e., the elasticity of demand for the final product is greater than the elasticity of substitution, the third rule is valid. This is almost always true since supply elasticities are positive and the demand for the product is elastic while substitution is difficult.

QUESTIONS FOR DISCUSSION

1. Under what circumstances will a wage increase in a firm have little or no effect upon employment in that firm? Under what circumstances will a general increase throughout the economy have little or no effect on employment in the economy?
2. "The effect of a general wage increase upon employment in the economy as a whole is simply the sum of the effects of wage increases in all the individual firms in the economy." Discuss the validity of this statement.
3. Discuss the various possible effects of union wage pressure on the level of industrial efficiency. Are the consequences of union wage adjustments likely to differ from the effects of a wage increase in a single firm in an unorganized industry?

SUGGESTIONS FOR FURTHER READING

GATONS, PAUL K. and CEBULA, RICHARD J. "Wage-Rate Analysis: Differentials and Indeterminacy," *Industrial and Labor Relations Review*, Vol. 25 (January 1972), pp. 207–12.

An attempt to develop a simple model indicating that persistent interregional wage rate differentials are consistent with conventional wage theory and that the existence of a long-run supply range, rather than a curve, introduces an element of indeterminacy into wage rate analysis.

HICKS, J. R. *The Theory of Wages*, chap. vi, pp. 112–35. 2d ed. London: Macmillan & Co., Ltd. 1963.

Statement of the theory which gives major importance to wage pressure as a stimulus to labor saving invention.

KEYNES, JOHN MAYNARD. *The General Theory of Employment, Interest and Money*, chap. xix, pp. 257–71. New York: Harcourt Brace & Co., Inc., 1936.

Statement of the Keynesian theory of the effect of general wage changes.

LUCAS, ROBERT E., JR., and RAPPING, LEONARD A. "Real Wages, Employment, and Inflation," *Journal of Political Economy*, Vol. 77 (September/October 1969), pp. 721–54.

An attempt to construct and test an aggregative model of the United States labor market using marginal productivity concepts.

SATO, R., and KOIZUMI, T. "Substitutability, Complimentarity, and the Theory of Derived Demand," *The Review of Economic Studies*, Vol. 37 (June 1970), pp. 107–18.

A mathematical analysis and critique of Marshall's four rules of derived demand.

TOBIN, JAMES. "Inflation and Unemployment," *American Economic Review,* Vol. 62 (March 1972), pp. 1–18.

An excellent article showing the relevance of Keynesian analysis to current discussions of involuntary unemployment, Phillips curves, and inflation.

WILLIAMSON, J. "A Simple Neo-Keynesian Growth Model," *The Review of Economic Studies,* Vol. 37 (April 1970), pp. 157–71.

A mathematical statement of neo-Keynesian theory.

Chapter 13   WAGES, PRODUCTIVITY, AND INFLATION

The American economy faces a productivity crisis. The full impact and nature of this crisis is today becoming apparent to the policy makers of government, to business and union leaders, and to the public at large. The problem arises from the fact that the rate of increase in money wages, which over most of the decade of the sixties had advanced at a rate only slightly in excess of the rate of increase in man-hour output has now commenced to step ahead of productivity by such large increments as to threaten increases in unit labor costs in excess of 5% per annum.

As of spring 1972, governmental restrictions imposed upon wages and prices had slowed the upward movement of wage rates, but little had been done to accelerate the long-run upward movement of man-hour output. Although the rate of productivity advance normally quickens during a business recovery, in the first quarter of 1972 with rising output and climbing profits, the improvement registered by man-hour output in the private sector was only at a seasonally adjusted annual rate of 2.1% compared with the 3.6% rate for all of 1971. This poor performance led Secretary of Commerce Peter G. Peterson to urge that a "national crusade" was needed to boost productivity in order to lessen the upward march of unit labor costs and prices.[1]

The rate of annual improvement in productivity is no longer a matter of mere intellectual interest to labor economists. It has become a "hot" issue, both in labor negotiations and in decisions of public policy. The establishment by President Richard Nixon in June 1970 of a National Commission on Productivity to develop recommendations for programs and policies to improve productivity in the United States is simply one indication of the concern which public officials now share with respect to this vital issue. It is important, therefore, to understand what is meant by labor productivity and how it is measured. In this chapter, we shall consider in detail the nature of productivity, its interrelationship with wages and prices, and the impact of union wage pressure on inflation.

---

[1] *Wall Street Journal*, April 26, 1972, p. 5.

We shall also review various governmental efforts to deal with the problem of inflation.

CALCULATION OF PRODUCTIVITY INDEXES

Statistics of increased productivity are generally referred to as showing the increase in productivity of *labor*. This presentation tends to create the impression that in some way, labor is responsible for the increased output and so is entitled to a lion's share of the gains derived from increased productivity. Actually, productivity could just as easily be stated in terms of any other factor used in production, such as dollar of capital invested. Productivity is simply a ratio between output measured in specific units and any input factor, also measured in specific units. For example, most drivers are concerned with the number of miles per gallon they get from their automobiles. This is a simple illustration of output—in this case, mileage—measured in terms of a specific input— in this case, gasoline. The same output could be measured in terms of input of tires, or battery, or any of the money, materials, and factors which jointly are responsible for the final output of pleasurable driving. As a matter of custom and convenience, however, statistical series dealing with productivity are usually based upon a comparison over time of output in relation to labor input.[2] It is important to recognize that an index relating labor input and output, such as output per man-hour, reflects the combined influence of many variables, including changes in technology, capital investment, rate of plant utilization, managerial efficiency, and scale of operations as well as skill, quality, and effort of the labor force.

The most widely used statistics on productivity are those published by the Bureau of Labor Statistics of the U.S. Department of Labor. The Bureau makes available two series, one measuring productivity in terms of output per hour *paid* and the other in terms of output per hour *worked*. The hours-worked data are derived from a survey of households conducted each month by the Bureau of Census for the Bureau of Labor Statistics. The hours-paid data are based primarily on a monthly BLS survey of establishment payroll records. Theoretically, the difference between the two measures of labor input is equal to paid vacation time and other paid leave. Since the ratio of hours paid for relative to hours worked is continually rising as a result of the extension of fringe benefits, the productivity index based on hours paid will be lower than the index based on hours worked (i.e., the higher the hours input relative to output, the smaller will be the rise in the productivity index). Although

---

[2] For a clear and concise explanation of the various concepts and terms used in productivity measurement, it is recommended that the student read U.S. Department of Labor, Bureau of Labor Statistics, *The Meaning and Measurement of Productivity* (Bulletin No. 1714 [Washington, D.C.: U.S. Government Printing Office, 1971]).

most economists agree that hours worked is the more desirable measure for use in productivity calculations, because of lack of data most computations rely on hours paid.

As a result of the difficulty in obtaining and combining outputs of varied plants and industries, practically all statistics of productivity depend upon production data derived either by construction of an index of output or by deflation of a value series. The BLS generally adopts the latter technique and measures output in terms of the *constant dollar value of the goods and services produced* in the private sector of the economy. This means that an estimate must be made of the value of final goods and services produced by the economy, and this figure is then deflated by a price index so as to eliminate the effect of changing prices. The net result, therefore, after such deflation is a figure which, in theory, represents the "real" product of the economy.

Although statistics of labor productivity are frequently carried out to decimal points, they are at best only rough estimates. As one expert puts it: "A reliable growth rate of two significant digits is impossible to establish. Even the first digit is in grave doubt. . . ."[3] Yet, great significance is attached in public discussion to the first decimal point in productivity figures, which may indicate that the growth rate is, say, 3.5% rather than 3.1%. It is important to recognize that because of the complexity of our economy and the paucity of accurate statistical data concerning its operation, productivity calculations are from beginning to end based upon estimates, imputation, and intelligent guesswork. Nevertheless, over a long period of years, they give a fair indication of the degree of efficiency achieved relative to output in the utilization of labor.

PRODUCTIVITY TRENDS

If we take a long look back over the past 150 years, it appears that there has been a continuing acceleration in the rate of productivity improvement in our economy. It has been estimated that during the first half of the 19th century, productivity per man-hour increased about 25%. In the second half of the century, it may have doubled; and in the first half of the 20th century, it almost trebled.[4] Figure 13–1 shows the increasing rate of growth of output per man-hour from 1890 to 1965.

However, as can be seen from Table 13–1, man-hour output, which had grown at a rate of approximately 4% per annum from 1961 to 1966, commenced to decline in 1967, and in 1969 and 1970 grew at a rate of less that 1%—the poorest performance in 13 years. Some economists view this decline as evidence of a secular slowing in the rate of produc-

---

[3] Oskar Morgenstern, "Qui Numerare Incipit Errare Incipit," *Fortune*, Vol. 68 (October 1963), p. 173.

[4] Sumner H. Slichter, *Economic Growth in the United States*, ed. John T. Dunlop (Baltimore, Md.: J. H. Furst Co., 1961), p. 44.

FIGURE 13–1

Output per Man-Hour in Private Economy (1957–59 = 100)

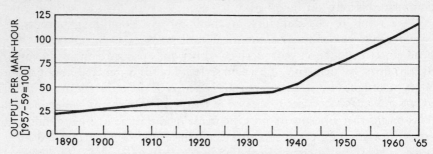

Source: Data, Bureau of Labor Statistics; National Bureau of Economic Research; chart, *Business Week*, October 15, 1966, p. 87. By permission of McGraw-Hill, Inc.

tivity improvement which could have serious implications in terms both of our ability to combat inflation here at home and our ability to compete effectively in the international marketplace. Other economists contend that the downturn is only cyclical and that with a resumption of business advance, the rate of increase in man-hour output will resume its historic path.

It is true that output per man-hour varies significantly from year to year and in manufacturing bears a close relationship to capacity utilization. Figure 13–2 indicates the close relationship which exists between

FIGURE 13–2

Output per Man-Hour and Output in the Private Economy, Quarterly Changes at Annual Rates, 1965–71

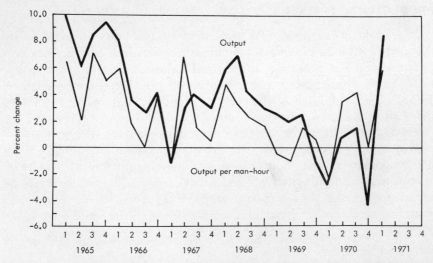

Source: U.S. Department of Labor, Bureau of Labor Statistics, *Productivity and the Economy* (Bulletin No. 1710 [Washington, D.C.: U.S. Government Printing Office, 1971]), p. 7.

Table 13–1

Indexes of Output per Man-Hour for the Private Economy and Year-to-Year Percent Change, 1947–71

Year	Indexes (1967=100)					Percent change over previous year				
	Total private	Farm	Nonfarm			Total private	Farm	Nonfarm		
			Total	Manu-facturing	Nonmanu-facturing			Total	Manu-facturing	Nonmanu-facturing
	Output per man-hour									
1947	51.3	29.2	57.1	54.8	58.2					
1948	53.6	34.0	58.8	57.9	59.2	4.5	16.3	3.0	5.6	1.8
1949	55.3	33.1	61.1	60.0	61.8	3.2	−2.5	4.0	3.7	4.4
1950	59.7	37.7	65.0	64.4	65.3	8.1	13.9	6.3	7.2	5.7
1951	61.5	37.9	66.3	65.9	66.4	3.0	.4	2.0	2.3	1.7
1952	62.7	41.2	66.9	66.2	67.2	1.9	8.8	.9	.4	1.2
1953	65.3	46.7	68.9	68.3	68.9	4.2	13.2	2.9	3.3	2.5
1954	66.9	49.1	70.5	69.5	71.0	2.4	5.1	2.3	1.7	3.0
1955	69.9	49.5	73.6	73.7	73.4	4.4	.9	4.4	6.0	3.5
1956	70.0	51.6	73.2	72.9	73.3	.2	4.3	−.6	−1.1	−.2
1957	72.0	54.7	74.8	74.4	75.0	2.9	6.0	2.2	2.0	2.4
1958	74.3	60.4	76.7	74.4	78.0	3.1	10.3	2.5	0	3.9
1959	76.9	61.5	79.3	78.5	79.8	3.6	1.8	3.4	5.6	2.3
1960	78.2	64.9	80.3	79.9	80.6	1.6	5.6	1.2	1.8	1.1
1961	80.9	70.0	82.7	81.8	83.3	3.5	7.9	3.0	2.4	3.3
1962	84.7	71.7	86.4	86.6	86.5	4.7	2.3	4.6	5.8	3.9
1963	87.7	78.1	89.1	90.1	88.7	3.6	9.0	3.1	4.0	2.6
1964	91.1	79.5	92.4	94.5	91.5	3.9	1.7	3.7	4.9	3.1
1965	94.2	86.9	95.1	98.3	93.5	3.4	9.3	2.9	4.1	2.2
1966	98.0	90.5	98.4	99.9	97.6	4.0	8.3	3.5	1.6	4.4
1967	100.0	100.0	100.0	100.0	100.0	2.1	6.3	1.6	.1	2.5
1968	102.9	100.2	102.9	104.7	101.9	2.9	.2	2.9	4.7	1.9
1969	103.4	110.7	102.7	106.1	101.1	.5	10.5	−.1	1.4	−.8
1970	104.3	115.6	103.5	107.7	101.7	.9	4.4	.7	1.5	.6
1971	108.1	125.6	107.0	111.6	105.3	3.6	8.6	3.4	3.6	3.6

Source: U.S. Department of Labor, *Manpower Report of the President, 1972.* (Washington, D.C.: U.S. Government Printing Office, 1972), Table G–1, p. 274.

percentage changes in output and output per man-hour. Typically, high rates of productivity gains are registered in early stages of cyclical recovery when unused human and capital resources are put into use. Thus, in the postwar period, productivity gains were the greatest in the recovery years of 1950 (8.1%), 1955 (4.4%), and 1962 (4.7%) (see Table 13–1). In 1971, output per man-hour of nonfarm workers rose 3.4% after advancing only 0.7% during 1970 (Table 13–1).

Diversity in Productivity Performance by Industry

The annual rate of productivity improvement represents an amalgam of many divergent component changes reflecting the different experience of various sectors and industries in the economy. The pace of productivity change has consistently been most rapid in agriculture, averaging about double the rate of change in nonfarm industries. As can be seen from Table 13–1, in 1969 farming registered an amazing 10.5% jump in man-hour output over the prior year (when gains were unusually low), while in the same year the nonfarm economy recorded an actual negative change in the rate of productivity advance. Likewise, individual industries follow quite different paths in terms of rate of growth in man-hour output. For example, from 1960 to 1970 petroleum pipelines showed an average annual percentage growth of 10%, petroleum refining 6%; tire manufacture 4%; glass containers 3%; cigarettes 1%; and footware practically none.[5]

Since the rate of man-hour output improvement varies among industries, changes in the industry mix can affect the overall rate of productivity change. As a matter of fact, the American economy may be entering a period in which sustaining a high rate of productivity growth will become more difficult than in the past. For several decades, the shift of workers out of agriculture, where productivity was below the average, contributed substantially to the increase in productivity in the economy as a whole. The number of workers left in agriculture is so small that this source can no longer be relied upon as significant. On the other hand, during the coming decade there will be a substantial increase in the proportion of the labor force employed in the service industries, where productivity and its rate of growth have been low relative to the national average. As a matter of fact, economists have calculated that the level of productivity in service industries is about half that of manufacturing and the rate of year-to-year increase has been 30% to 50% below that in manufacturing.[6]

As pointed out in Chapter 1, an increasing proportion of the American labor force has been employed in government. Some 18% of the civilian labor force already work for federal, state, and local governments, and the percentage is expected to rise further during the balance of the decade. This represents a major portion of the total civilian labor force, yet productivity concepts are difficult to apply to the "output" of such workers. As a consequence, the usual practice of the Bureau of Labor Statistics and the Department of Commerce in constructing overall productivity indexes for the economy is to assume zero productivity growth in government services. Obviously, this assumption has the effect of pulling down the overall rate of productivity growth for the economy as a whole as measured by such indexes.

A special task force funded by the National Commission on Productivity is now undertaking the task of devising a method to measure productivity in the governmental area. Plans call for the publication of a new federal productivity index which admittedly will cover only about 50% of the federal government's civilian employees but will nevertheless give some indication of productivity trends in the government sector. Preliminary estimates suggest that for the period 1967–71, the increases in productivity in the federal sector compared favorably with the lower-

---

[5] U.S. Department of Labor, Bureau of Labor Statistics, *Productivity and the Economy* (Bulletin No. 1710) [Washington, D.C.: U.S. Government Printing Office, 1971]), p. 21. The Bureau of Labor Statistics publishes output per man-hour for 40 industries, most of which involve manufacturing or processing.

[6] *Business Week*, May 13, 1972, p. 160.

then-usual 1.8% annual gain in the private sector. On the other hand, data for the U.S. Post Office—which is one of the few governmental agencies to maintain productivity data—indicate that output per man-hour rose at an annual rate of only 0.3% from 1965 to 1970—about one seventh the rate in private industry.[7]

Wages, Unit Labor Costs, Productivity, and Prices

During the decade of the sixties, average hourly earnings in the private nonfarm economy rose at an average annual rate of 5.2%, while productivity measured by man-hour output advanced by 2.8% per annum. The result was that unit labor costs rose by about 2.3% annually.[8] Labor cost is the single most important component of price and in recent years has constituted about 62½% to 65% of price.[9] In 1969, labor costs per unit of product rose 7%—the sharpest advance for employees in the private nonfarm sector since 1951[10]—while the Consumer Price Index rose 5.4%.[11] In 1970, unit labor costs rose 6.3% and in 1971, 3.4%.[12]

It is obvious that an acceleration in the rate of increase in unit labor costs can be transmitted into a spiraling price inflation of increasingly serious dimensions. When unit labor costs rise, profit margins are reduced unless businessmen raise prices. Thus, there is a strong incentive to offset rising unit labor costs with increased prices. This cannot always be done—competitive circumstances or depressed industry or general economic conditions may delay the adjustment. Eventually, however, the adjustment must be made if industry is to remain profitable. As a consequence there is a fairly close correlation over time between changes in unit labor costs and changes in prices. Thus, years of large increases in unit labor costs such as 1948, 1951, 1956, and 1969 were also years of large increases in prices.

The sharp breakout in unit labor costs which occurred in 1969 reflected the influence of two trends. On the one hand, there has been a steady escalation in the rate of increase of employee compensation since 1965. From 1960 to 1965, the annual increment in hourly compensation of workers in the private nonfarm economy averaged about 4.3%.[13] Median first-year wage adjustments negotiated in collective bargaining fluctuated in a narrow range, between annual increases of 2.8% and

---

[7] *Ibid.*

[8] U.S. Department of Labor data.

[9] *Economic Report of the President, 1970* (Washington, D.C.: U.S. Government Printing Office, 1970), p. 53.

[10] *Ibid.,* p. 51.

[11] *Ibid.,* p. 56.

[12] U.S. Department of Labor data.

[13] *Report to the National Commission on Productivity by the Council of Economic Advisers,* (Washington, D.C., August 7, 1970), p. II-9.

3.2%.[14] In recent years, however, there has been a sharp escalation in the size of the annual increment in employee wages under union agreements. In 1970, median first-year increases in wages under major collective bargaining agreements amounted to 12% compared to 10.9% in 1969 and 8.1% in 1968. In 1971, despite wage restraints in the latter part of the year, median first-year increases amounted to 13.9%.[15] First-year increases have generally exceeded in percentage change the amount of

FIGURE 13–3

Increases under Major Agreements (average* annual rate of increase negotiated)

Annual Rates of Wage Increases* Negotiated in 1971† (3,271,800 workers)

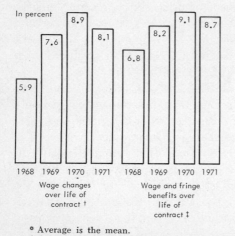

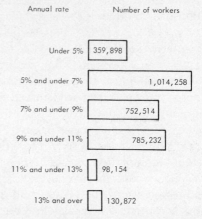

* Average is the mean.
† Agreements covering 1,000 or more workers.
‡ Agreements covering 5,000 or more workers.

* Average rate of wage increase excluding cost-of-living escalator clauses.
† Agreements covering 1,000 or more workers.

Source: Data, Bureau of Labor Statistics, Department of Labor; chart, *AFL–CIO American Federationist*, Vol. 79, (March 1972), p. 15.

the wage adjustment over the life of the contract. Nevertheless, as can be seen from Figure 13–3, increases in wages averaged over 8% in 1970 and 1971. To this must be added the cost of fringe benefits which also enter into the determination of unit labor costs. Figure 13–3 shows that the cost of such benefits has been growing at a rapid rate.

At the same time as these large wage and benefit adjustments have been raising unit costs, productivity change—which could produce an offsetting decline in unit costs—has tended to slacken. Even if the return of business recovery raises the rate of productivity advance, the U.S. Department of Labor has estimated rate of growth in man-hour output in

---

[14] *Ibid.*
[15] U.S. Department of Labor data.

the private sector for the decade of the seventies at only 3%—a slightly slower pace than that registered in the sixties.[16] If this prediction should prove to be valid, the nation is confronted with a serious challenge of continuing inflation for the years ahead. For we are faced on the one hand with a wage explosion which wage and price controls have thus far been able only to blunt but not to halt, and on the other hand by changing economic and social conditions in our economy which may make for a slower, rather than a more rapid, rise in man-hour output in the future. A clean environment, consumerism, and improvement of the quality of life are all important goals in the American economy; but

TABLE 13–2

Average Annual Percentage Change in Manufacturing Industries, 1965–70; Output per Man-Hour, Compensation per Man-Hour and Unit Labor Costs

Country	Output per Man-Hour	Compensation per Man-Hour	Unit Labor Costs	
			National Currency	*U.S. Dollars*
United States..........	2.1	6.0	3.9	3.9
Belgium...............	6.8	8.4	1.4	1.4
Canada...............	3.5	8.3	4.6	5.1
France...............	6.6	9.5	2.7	0.6
Germany.............	5.3	8.7	3.2	4.7
Italy.................	5.1	9.1	3.8	3.8
Japan................	14.2	15.1	0.8	0.8
Netherlands..........	8.5	11.1	2.5	2.5
Sweden..............	7.9	10.6	2.5	2.5
Switzerland..........	6.2	6.2	0.0	0.0
United Kingdom.......	3.6	7.6	3.8	−0.2

Source: U.S. Department of Labor, *Productivity and the Economy*, p. 30.

clean water and clean air do not enter into the calculation of productivity data, and their achievement may well raise unit labor costs rather than lower them.

The American economy can absorb wage increases of the dimensions recorded in recent years only if it achieves an accelerated rate of increase in man-hour output. As Table 13–3 indicates, Japan has the dubious distinction of the most rapidly rising level of money wages of any industrial country—an average annual rate of over 15% from 1965 to 1970—but because it also achieved an astounding annual increment in man-hour output of 14.2%, unit labor costs rose hardly at all. Because of our slower productivity growth, unit labor costs rose more sharply in the United States during the decade of the sixties than in any other

[16] U.S. Department of Labor, *The U.S. Economy in 1980* (Bulletin No. 1673 [Washington, D.C.: U.S. Government Printing Office, 1970]), p. 1.

country except Canada and Germany. The balance between wage changes and productivity growth is important not only because of its impact on inflation within the United States but also because of its influence upon our competitive relation to other industrial nations in the world market. Although a rapid rate of productivity improvement is desirable if we as a nation are to succeed in controlling inflation, it must also be recognized that rapid increase in man-hour output can produce serious problems of unemployment.

The Relation of Productivity and Employment

Increasing productivity is, of course, a manifestation of the dynamic influence of technological change in our economy which over the long run has created more jobs than it has displaced. On the other hand, the year-to-year improvement in productivity has a definite relation to employment which has important implications for governmental policy.

The volume of unemployment in our economy depends upon three major factors:

1. The growth in the labor force.
2. The increase in output per man-hour.
3. The growth of total demand for goods and services.

Changes in the average hours of work are also relevant, though quantitatively less important than the three factors enumerated above. As productivity rises, less labor is required per dollar of total output, or more goods and services can be produced with the same number of man-hours. Consequently, if output does not grow, employment will decline; if output increases more rapidly than productivity (less any decline in average hours worked), employment will rise. But we must also take account of the fact that the labor force is growing each year too. So unless gross national product (the total expenditure for goods and services in the economy, corrected for price changes) rises more rapidly than the sum of productivity increases and labor force growth (modified by the change in hours of work), the increase in employment will be inadequate to absorb the growth in the labor force, and the rate of unemployment will increase. Only when total production expands faster than the rate of labor force growth *plus* the rate of productivity increase and *minus* the rate at which average annual hours fall will the rate of unemployment be reduced.[17]

What does all this mean in concrete terms? The challenge is well stated by Garth L. Mangum:

[17] *Technology and the American Economy* (Report of the National Commission on Technology, Automation, and Economic Progress [Washington, D.C.: U.S. Government Printing Office, 1966]), Vol. I, p. 10.

For the next 15 years the average annual growth of the labor force will be about 1¾ percent. The average annual rate of increase in output per manhour has been 2.8 percent over the postwar period. Leaving aside any question of acceleration in the latter rate, the sum is 4½ percent per year, the rate at which jobs must be created just to keep unemployment from rising above the already excessive level of unemployment. These numbers represent an unprecedented challenge. An economy with a 3% historical growth rate and a 3.5% record for the past two decades must suddenly and permanently begin creating jobs at a rate of 4½% and above.[18]

In the following chapter, in our discussion of unemployment, we shall consider further implications of this quotation.

FACTORS AFFECTING GROWTH IN OUTPUT PER MAN-HOUR

In the long run, improvement in output per man-hour comes primarily from three sources: (1) an increase in the amount of capital per worker; (2) an improvement in the quality of the work force; and (3) the impact of research and development. How have these factors influenced productivity in the past and what is the outlook for the future?

Capital per Worker

Contrary to popular conception, productivity does not depend primarily on human effort. The main reason for increased productivity in the United States is the increased efficiency of machine technology. Not only is the machinery which a worker uses today far more efficient than the machinery in use 50 or 100 years ago, but also the amount of capital used per worker has increased enormously over the years. For example, during the period from 1939 to 1963, capital per worker in manufacturing rose from $5,188 to $21,498.[19] From 1947 to 1968, the stock of fixed capital per employed person in the private economy increased at an annual average rate of 2.6%.[20] In the past two decades, the amount of horsepower utilized in factories has practically doubled.[21]

Although these statistics appear impressive, the fact is that relative to other industrialized nations the United States is falling behind in its rate of input of capital in the productive process. During the period

---

[18] Garth L. Mangum, "The Role of 'Job Creation' Programs," in *Unemployment in a Prosperous Economy*, ed. William G. Bowen and Frederick H. Harbison (Princeton University Research Report Series No. 108 [Princeton, N.J., 1965]), p. 107.

[19] National Industrial Conference Board, *Economic Almanac, 1967–68* (New York, 1967), p. 276.

[20] U.S. Department of Commerce, *Statistical Abstract of the United States, 1971* (Washington, D.C.: U.S. Government Printing Office, 1971), p. 469.

[21] U.S. Department of Commerce, Bureau of the Census, *Pocket Data Book USA, 1971* (Washington, D.C.: U.S. Government Printing Office, 1971). p. 299.

1960 to 1969, capital spending in the United States amounted on the average to about 13% of gross national product per annum compared to 27% for Japan, 20% in Germany and the Netherlands, and 18% in Sweden and France. From 1970 to 1972, reinvestment dropped further in the United States to annual rates of only 8% of GNP.[22] If we are to accelerate the rate of productivity advance in the future, business will have to invest far more in capital, plant, and equipment than is presently the case.

Quality of Labor

We have seen that there has been a marked reduction in the utilization of unskilled common labor in our modern economy and, on the other hand, a sharp increase in semiskilled, skilled, and professional and technical jobs. Employment of professional and technical workers, who have been the fastest growing occupational group during the past decade, will increase about twice as fast as total employment during the decade of the seventies, according to estimates of the U.S. Department of Labor.[23] A further measure of progress in quality of labor is the rising level of educational attainment. Each upcoming generation remains in school longer. For example, in 1950 about 18% of men 30 to 34 years of age had some college experience; by 1970, the ratio had increased to 33%; and by 1990, it is expected to exceed 38%. At present about 23% of women aged 30–34 have been to college; by 1990, the proportion will exceed 37%.[24] Equally significant has been the tremendous increase in scientists, engineers, and other professional workers with advanced degrees—the brainpower of our economy. In 1965, 539,000 Bachelor's and first professional degrees were awarded—more than 250,000 above the number awarded just 10 years earlier. By 1975, the number of such degrees is expected to reach 900,000![25]

Research and Development

We observed in Chapter 12 that there has been a steady rise in research and development expenditures over the years. This has undoubtedly contributed to the rise in productivity and has enabled our nation to maintain a favorable balance of trade with respect to the products of high-technology industries. However, in recent years an

---

[22] *Wall Street Journal*, December 28, 1971, p. 1.

[23] U.S. Department of Labor, *Manpower Report of the President, 1972* (Washington, D.C.: U.S. Government Printing Office, 1972), p. 111.

[24] National Industrial Conference Board, *The U.S. Economy in 1990* (New York, 1972), p. 30

[25] *Manpower Report, 1967*, pp. 167–68.

undesirable trend has developed. Although total research and development expenditures in current dollars are estimated to have risen from just over $5 billion in 1953 to $25.7 billion in 1970, when these costs are deflated by a price indicator it appears that our research and development expenditures in real terms reached their peak in 1967 at about $25.4 billion in 1968 dollars and have decreased since then to less than $22 billion in 1968 dollars.[26] The continuation of such a downward trend would make an acceleration of productivity advance in the years ahead quite unlikely and would pose serious problems even to maintenance of past rates of increase.

ALTERNATE MEANS OF DISTRIBUTING PRODUCTIVITY BENEFITS

Should the gains of increasing productivity be distributed through falling prices or rising money wages? On the whole, reduction in commodity prices would seem by all odds to be the *fairest* method of distributing the benefits of increasing productivity. In large measure, the increasing productivity of labor reflects the combined efforts of the whole community—of savers who contribute the capital equipment, of scientists who pioneer new methods, of entrepreneurs who combine the factors into new and more efficient working teams, and of workers who contribute the skill and brawn to make the technological advances a physical reality. Therefore, if these groups are all to be treated equitably, the increase in productivity representing their joint efforts should be reflected in falling prices, since only in this way can all groups share alike.

Does labor as a group have any special claim to the gains of technological advance that its needs should be given precedence over those of the rest of the community? Labor, as a group, may bear the major share of the inconveniences and dislocations produced by technological change, so that a preferential right to the benefits might be claimed as compensation. However, the particular workers who would get preferential treatment would be those who remain employed at the higher wages, while the ones who actually suffer the "inconveniences and dislocations" would find that the buying power of their relief checks would be reduced by the preferential treatment accorded their more fortunate employed brethren. Moreover, labor is not the only group affected by the incidence of technological change. Innovation in one firm may produce bankruptcy in competitors, compelling entrepreneurs to move to other areas to seek new businesses. Similarly, stockholders and bondholders may suffer losses as a result of improved processes in competing firms. Are

---

[26] Patrick E. Haggerty, "Technology and the American Standard of Living," Charles M. Schwab Memorial Lecture, American Iron and Steel Institute, May 27, 1970, p. 18.

savers and entrepreneurs also entitled to compensation for the dislocations caused by technological change?

While it is difficult to prove that labor has any special right to the gains of productivity, some defense of distribution in the form of higher money wages is possible on the ground that unless this method is adopted, the full potentialities of technological progress will not be realized. Some economists believe that the greatest stimulus is afforded to new investment, and adjustment to technological progress is facilitated, when the price level remains relatively stable. Such stability of prices could be achieved by raising money wages as productivity increases. Union leaders recommend this policy, arguing that increased wage payments are necessary to stimulate effective demand and to provide a market for the increased abundance of industrial production.

On the other hand, other economists maintain that a slowly falling price level is best designed to increase employment and production. They stress the distinction between *productivity* and *production*. Productivity may increase in an industry, yet production can decrease. This occurred in the coal industry, for example, where labor costs were driven up so high as to act as a deterrent to increased production and employment, until recent demands of utilities altered the pattern. Some economists fear that this situation may be duplicated in our economy, with the result that production is not increasing fast enough to absorb the workers displaced by technological advance.

Actually, when the problem of distributing the gains of increased productivity is viewed as part of the larger problem of maintaining full employment, there may not be a "best way" of distributing the gains of technological progress. A policy that worked well during the decade of the twenties may not produce the same result during the sixties, account being taken of the rigidities in our labor market resulting from union organization and a possible increase in the importance of administered pricing. In this complex area of economic analysis, it must be recognized that the effect of reduction in prices or of rising wages upon production and employment will depend upon the stage of the business cycle, businessmen's anticipations, and other circumstances which vary from time to time.

It should also be mentioned that from the practical point of view, little enthusiasm is generated for the policy of falling prices among the general public. Employees, of course, prefer more money in their pay envelope. To trade this for an expectation that prices may fall in the future is to trade a real and present benefit for something which is conjectural and of indeterminate magnitude. Employers also prefer to do business in an economy which has a slight inflationary bias. Such an economic environment is much more propitious for expansion and for taking risks; falling prices have too often been associated with periods of recession and therefore unconsciously dampen business expectations.

HOW GAINS OF INCREASING PRODUCTIVITY HAVE BEEN DISTRIBUTED

Over the last hundred years the typical adjustment of the American economy to technological advance reflected in rising man-hour output has been in the form of rising money wages rather than through a falling price level. No other price series has risen as rapidly as hourly earnings of labor.

The Long-Term Trend in Real Wages

Real wages have risen more or less continuously in this country for over one hundred years; during most of this time, union organization was either nonexistent or of negligible importance. As Table 13–3 indicates, in the 57 years from 1914 to 1971 average hourly earnings of production workers in manufacturing rose from 22 cents to $3.19 while real average hourly earnings almost quadrupled. Since 1967 the rate of advance in real hourly earnings has slowed as the rate of increase in the price level has escalated. Indeed, as can be seen from Table 13–3, real average hourly earnings were actually lower in 1971 than in 1962. It should be cautioned, however, that the figures for hourly earnings are averages and are influenced by the change in the mix of workers which occurred over the period of years in question. The decline noted in real hourly earnings in the table does not necessarily imply that a typical worker in manufacturing experienced such a diminution. Furthermore, if a price index other than the Consumer Price Index were used to correct money earnings for intervening changes in the price level, a different result might be obtained.

It will be observed that the improvement in real weekly earnings recorded in Table 13–3 is somewhat less on a percentage basis than for real hourly earnings. This undoubtedly reflects the influence of a shorter workweek and the fact that workers have chosen to take some of the gains of increasing productivity in the form of leisure time.

Since 1900, real hourly compensation of production workers in manufacturing (average hourly earnings plus fringe benefits deflated by the change in consumer prices) has risen at approximately the same average rate as the average hourly productivity of manufacturing labor. However, the gains of labor extend beyond the increase in purchasing power of hourly earnings; for, concomitant with the rise in earnings, there has been a substantial reduction in working time. Furthermore, the average number of days worked in a year has declined substantially through longer vacations and more frequent holidays.

The U.S. Bureau of Labor Statistics now publishes four different series commencing with the year 1964 indicating trends in real earnings of labor. The content of these various series differs, and their relative

TABLE 13–3

"Real" and Gross Average Hourly and Weekly Earnings of Production Workers in Manufacturing Industries, Selected Years, 1914–71

Year	In Current Dollars			In 1967 Dollars	
	Hourly Earnings	Weekly Earnings	CPI* 1967 = 100	Hourly Earnings	Weekly Earnings
1914............	0.22	10.92	30.1	0.73	36.27
1919............	0.47	21.84	51.8	0.91	42.16
1929............	0.56	24.76	51.3	1.09	48.27
1933............	0.44	16.65	38.8	1.13	42.91
1939............	0.63	23.64	41.6	1.51	56.83
1947............	1.22	49.17	66.9	1.82	73.50
1948............	1.33	53.12	72.1	1.84	73.68
1949............	1.34	53.88	71.4	1.87	75.46
1950............	1.44	58.32	72.1	1.99	80.89
1951............	1.56	63.34	77.8	2.00	81.41
1952............	1.65	67.16	79.5	2.07	84.48
1953............	1.74	70.47	80.1	2.17	87.98
1954............	1.78	70.49	80.5	2.21	87.57
1955............	1.86	75.70	80.2	2.31	94.39
1956............	1.95	78.78	81.4	2.39	96.78
1957............	2.05	81.59	84.3	2.43	96.79
1958............	2.11	82.71	86.6	2.43	95.51
1959............	2.19	88.26	87.3	2.50	101.10
1960............	2.26	89.72	88.7	2.54	101.15
1961............	2.32	92.34	89.6	2.58	103.06
1962............	2.39	96.56	90.6	2.63	106.58
1963............	2.46	99.63	91.7	2.68	108.65
1964............	2.53	102.97	92.9	2.72	110.84
1965............	2.61	107.53	94.5	2.76	113.79
1966............	2.72	112.34	97.2	2.79	115.58
1967............	2.83	114.90	100.0	2.83	114.90
1968............	3.01	122.51	104.2	2.88	117.57
1969............	3.19	129.51	109.8	2.90	117.95
1970............	3.36	133.73	116.3	2.88	114.99
1971............	3.19	129.51	121.3	2.62	106.77

* Consumer price index of the U.S. Bureau of Labor Statistics.
  Source: Data for 1914–66 adapted from National Industrial Conference Board, *Economic Almanac,* 1967–1968 (New York: Macmillan Co., 1967), p. 53; subsequent data provided by The Conference Board.

movements can vary from year to year (see Figure 13–4). These series are as follows:[27]

1. *Real adjusted average hourly earnings.* This is a monthly series based on average hourly earnings for production and nonsupervisory workers in the private nonfarm economy. The series is adjusted for changes in overtime (in manufacturing only) and shifts in employment among narrowly defined industries. When deflated by the Consumer Price Index, it provides the best measure of changes in real *wage rates.* This is the proper series to use if a comparison is to be made between

---

[27] For a discussion of these series, see Thomas W. Gavett, "Measures of Change in Real Wages and Earnings, "*Monthly Labor Review,* Vol. 95 (February 1972), pp. 48–53.

real wages and productivity, since the data are conceptually and technically consistent with published productivity data.

2. *Real average weekly earnings.* This is a measure of weekly earnings of all production and nonsupervisory workers in the nonfarm private economy deflated by a price index. It is affected both by employment and overtime shifts as well as by the average number of hours worked per week. The number of hours could change because of a shift in the overall industrial mix of employment, a change in the number of over-

FIGURE 13–4

Four-Quarter Rates of Change in Real Earnings and Compensation, 1965–71

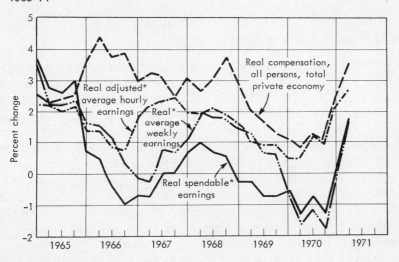

* Private nonfarm economy.
   Source: Thomas W. Gavett, "Measures of Change in Real Wages and Earnings, *Monthly Labor Review*, Vol. 95 (February 1972), p. 51.

time hours worked, or an increase in the number of part-time workers. This series does not, therefore, measure real earnings of the average worker but only the *average earnings for all workers.*

3. *Real compensation all persons total private economy.* This is a measure of real labor payments per hour, but includes supervisory or nonproduction workers, self-employed persons, farm employees, and private household workers. In addition, fringe benefits are included. Unlike series (1), this series is affected by shifts in employment among industries and changes in the amount of overtime worked.

4. *Real spendable earnings.* This is a measure of take-home pay which assumes that the worker has either no dependents or three dependents and is based upon real gross weekly earnings data adjusted for federal income tax and social security tax deductions. The result is affected by

the changing mix of workers in the labor force as well as by a change in actual earnings. Therefore, the series does not purport to measure the spendable earnings of the average worker, but only the *average real spendable earnings of all workers.*

The variance among these series is indicated by the fact that from 1964 to 1970, real compensation per man-hour rose 16.4%; real adjusted average hourly earnings rose 9.3%; real gross weekly earnings rose 4.6%; and real spendable earnings rose only 1.2%. If the span 1965 to 1970 is used, real spendable earnings declined by 1.5%![28] This analysis indicates how it is possible to secure a series to substantiate almost any position in economics, particularly when a change in the base period can materially alter the end result!

Labor's Relative Share in National Income

Has the rise in the price of labor given labor as a group a larger share than other groups in the increased national income? Some economists answer in the negative. They claim that the percentage of national income going to labor has remained relatively constant over a long period of years, except in deep depression. This statistical record has led some economists to conclude that for the material prosperity of labor as a whole, it makes no great difference whether money wages rise swiftly or slowly, or whether labor is organized or unorganized; for—according to these economists—without regard to these factors, labor's distributive share tends to remain fairly constant over time.[29]

Presumably, the mechanism that would produce this result would follow one or the other of the following avenues: (1) Money wages are pushed up and are followed by price increases, with the result that labor does not succeed in improving its position relative to other factors of production. (2) Money wages are pushed up; other prices are not raised correspondingly; and employers suffer a reduction in profits, curtail the use of labor, and substitute capital, with the same result as in (1) above.

Upon analysis, however, it will be found that the statement that labor's distributive share has remained fairly constant is both ambiguous and inaccurate. In the first place, what is meant by "labor's distributive share"? We can compare the share of compensation of employees as a percentage of national income, as a percentage of privately produced income, or as a percentage of income originating in corporate business, to cite only a few possibilities. As can be seen from Table 13–4, the results

---

[28] *Ibid.,* pp. 49–50.

[29] For example, in an article appropriately called "A Law That Cannot Be Repealed," Professor Sidney Weintraub presents statistics purporting to prove that since 1900, American business enterprises have spent roughly 50 cents of each dollar of sales revenue on wages and the remainder on interest, rent, profits, and taxes. See *Challenge,* April 1962, p. 18.

TABLE 13-4

Share of Compensation of Employees in Various Income Totals, 1929-70

Year	As Percent of National Income	As Percent of Income Originating in Corporate Business	As Percent of Income Originating in Private Industry
1929	58.2	74.2	55.6
1930	61.9	78.5	59.0
1931	66.6	87.9	63.2
1932	73.0	101.1	69.3
1933	73.6	101.6	69.5
1934	70.0	88.1	65.6
1935	65.4	83.3	60.8
1936	66.1	79.7	61.3
1937	65.1	79.7	61.0
1938	66.6	82.3	61.8
1939	66.1	80.5	61.6
1940	63.9	75.8	59.5
1941	61.9	72.4	57.6
1942	61.9	71.5	56.8
1943	64.3	72.0	57.6
1944	66.4	73.6	58.8
1945	68.0	76.8	59.8
1946	65.1	79.5	60.1
1947	65.0	77.0	61.3
1948	63.1	74.3	59.5
1949	64.7	75.4	60.7
1950	63.7	73.1	59.8
1951	64.6	73.3	60.3
1952	66.7	76.2	62.3
1953	68.3	77.9	64.2
1954	68.8	79.2	64.6
1955	67.8	76.5	63.6
1956	69.1	78.5	65.1
1957	69.6	79.4	65.6
1958	70.0	80.7	65.6
1959	69.5	78.4	65.3
1960	70.8	80.2	66.6
1961	70.9	80.6	66.5
1962	71.2	80.5	66.7
1963	70.8	80.0	65.4
1964	70.6	79.2	65.2
1965	69.8	75.1	64.6
1966	70.2	77.9	65.2
1967	71.5	79.6	65.8
1968	72.4	79.9	66.7
1969	74.0	82.3	68.6
1970	75.6	84.5	70.1

Source: Gertrude Deutsch, *Relative National Accounts* (Technical Paper No. 4 [New York: National Conference Board, 1964]), pp. 19–22; *Economic Report of the President, 1972,* Table B–12, p. 209; *Survey of Current Business,* Tables on National Income, 1964–72.

shown by the various series are not the same. In the second place, analysis of the two most comprehensive series—relating employee compensation to national income and to privately produced income—indicates that there has been a definite shift in distribution of income to labor over the period studied.

The Council of Economic Advisers has analyzed various series relating to distributive shares going to labor from 1947 to 1969. Employee compensation as a share of GNP rose from 55.7% in 1947 to 58.4% in 1960 and 60.6% in 1969. Employee compensation as a share of national income rose from 64.8% in 1947 to 71.0% in 1960 and 73.3% in 1969. Labor's share of gross product originating in nonfinancial corporations fell from 65.9% in 1947 to 65.5% in 1960[30] and fell still further to 65.1% in 1969, although the figures for the entire period are remarkably constant.

It is obvious that judgments with respect to the constancy or the change in share of national product going to labor have to be made with caution and depend in part upon the particular series of data which is being analyzed. As has been indicated, the movement of broad series for the economy as a whole tend to suggest that there has been some shift over the years to labor at the expense of other recipients. When national income data are examined, some of the apparent shift to employees is illusory and attributable to the transfer from self-employment. Thus when there is a shift from self-employment and proprietorship, as from independent farming to industrial employment, the resultant figures will show a decline in proprietor's income and a rise in employees' income, even though some of the proprietors' income is labor income.

However, there is also a sound theoretical reason for expecting some shift over time to labor in distributive share. One writer has explained this shift as follows:

One important factor has been the change in the relative supplies of labor and capital. The number of man-hours worked has not expanded as fast as population despite the great rise in real hourly earnings, while reproducible capital (in constant prices) has nearly doubled in relation to manhours. The greater responsiveness of the supply of capital to the demands of a growing economy has led to price-induced substitution with existing techniques and probably also to capital-using innovations. The opportunity for factor substitution in this historical rather than in a static sense has been of great practical importance as a built-in stabilizer of relative shares. Aside from relative factor supplies, shifts in the structure of industry, particularly those involving a diminution in the relative importance of agriculture, have probably operated to favor the labor share. Rising prices, by adversely affecting the income of rentiers, may also have contributed to the increase in the relative share of labor.[31]

It should also be observed that even if labor received only a constant share in national income, it would be gaining materially relative to other groups, for no other group has achieved greater gains in leisure time than

---

[30] Council of Economic Advisers, *Report to The National Commission on Productivity, Inflation Alert*, August 7, 1970, p. A–3 and PA–15.

[31] Irving B. Kravis, "Relative Income Shares in Fact and Theory," *American Economic Review*, Vol. 49 (December 1959), p. 918.

has labor in the past 50 years. It is possible that union organization has proved effective in accelerating the rate at which increasing productivity is converted into leisure as well as in securing for employees various benefits, such as paid vacations, which are not fully reflected in statistics of national income payments.

Effect of Union Organization upon Income Shares

While labor as a group may have increased its share in national income, this does not mean that all groups within labor have fared equally well. If strong unions such as the Steelworkers and the Automobile Workers win large wage increases which set off an inflationary spiral, while bank clerks, for example, obtain only small wage increases, the effect may be to redistribute real income from the latter to the former. However, some investigations suggest that labor's share of income, industry by industry, has fared no more favorably in unionized industries than in nonunion industries. As a matter of fact, there is some evidence that labor's share of income originating in manufacturing, mining, and public utility industries, where union organization is very strong, has tended to decline over the past 25 years, while the labor share of income originating in finance and services, where unions have made few inroads, has risen.[32] However, the evidence on impact of unions on labor's relative share is inconclusive. Very often, results depend upon the base year used, the selection of industries studied, and similar statistical conditions.

WAGE POLICY AND PRODUCTIVITY CHANGES

What is the "best" relationship between wages and productivity, taking account of the institutional rigidities in our economic system and the objective of avoiding inflation? In 1962, the Council of Economic Advisers adopted so-called "wage-price guideposts" as a standard for the public to use in judging the extent to which private price and wage decisions were consistent with the public interest in a noninflationary economy. From 1962 to 1967—when the Council ceased recommending a specific percentage figure and simply called for "restraint" in wage changes—the Council suggested a norm for wage adjustments approximating the trend rate for productivity in the economy as a whole, or about 3.2% per annum. The Council recognized that productivity changes vary substantially from year to year and therefore recommended that the trend rate over a number of years be used as the guide for labor and business to follow in their wage negotiations.

In the words of the President's Council of Economic Advisers:

----

[32] See Allan M. Cartter, *Theory of Wages and Employment* (Homewood, Ill.: Richard D. Irwin, Inc., 1959), p. 167.

The general guide for noninflationary wage behavior is that the rate of increase in wage rates (including fringe benefits) in each industry be equal to the trend rate of overall productivity increase. . . . The general guide for noninflationary price behavior calls for price reduction if the industry's rate of productivity increase exceeds the overall rate, for this would mean declining unit labor costs; it calls for an appropriate increase in price if the opposite relationship prevails; and it calls for stable prices if the two rates of productivity increase are equal.[33]

Any guide to wage policy, however, must recognize that wages are not only a cost and therefore a determinant of prices, but also a price reflecting the influence of supply and demand in the labor market. The Council of Economic Advisers recognizes this ambivalent role of wages and spells out two circumstances in which variations should be permitted in the general guide in order to permit adjustments in the labor market:

1. Wage rate increases should exceed the general guide rate in an industry which would otherwise be unable to attract sufficient labor or where wage rates have been exceptionally low.
2. Wage rate increases should be less than the general guide rate in an industry which could not provide jobs for its entire labor force even in times of generally full employment, or where wage rates have been exceptionally high.[34]

The rate of productivity change does not bear any necessary relationship to the rate of expansion or contraction in an industry. Therefore a further modification of the general guide is suggested by the Council to take account of movements of capital into or out of an industry:

1. Prices should rise more rapidly or fall more slowly than indicated by the general wage guide in an industry where the level of profits has been insufficient to attract capital required to finance a needed expansion in capacity, or in which costs other than labor costs have risen.
2. Prices should rise more slowly or fall more rapidly than indicated by the general guide in an industry in which the relation of productive capacity to full-employment demand shows the desirability of an out-flow of capital, or in which costs other than labor costs have fallen, or where excessive market power created a higher rate of profit than can be earned elsewhere on an investment of comparable risk.[35]

It should perhaps be observed that the statement that wage rates should rise at the same pace as man-hour output does not mean that the

---

[33] *Economic Report of the President, January, 1962* (Washington, D.C.: U.S. Government Printing Office, 1962), p. 189. The "trend rate" is the annual average percentage change in output per man-hour during the latest five years. A mathematical exposition of the theory upon which the guideposts rest is set forth in the appendix to this chapter.

[34] *Ibid.*

[35] *Ibid.*

entire increase in man-hour output should go to labor. If this result were to follow, nothing would be left over to pay a return on the increased amount of capital used to produce the increased output. An example will make this clear. Suppose that employee compensation for the economy as a whole averages $2 per hour and that the value of output per hour averages $3. Suppose that over a period of years, average output per hour rises to $4. If wages are to rise at the same rate as man-hour output, they should rise by one third—from $2 to $2.67 per hour. If wages rose by $1 an hour, equal to the full value of the increase in output per hour, the dollar amount of profits and interest per hour's work would be unchanged. This would mean that the return of capital per unit would actually fall, since the amount of capital used per hour has tended to increase over time and is perhaps the major factor responsible for increasing productivity. It is obvious, therefore, that if labor were to attempt to appropriate for itself the entire increase in man-hour output, there would be little point in investing additional capital in business. Capital formation would be discouraged, and the ultimate result would be a decline in investment and a diminution in job opportunities.

The experience with the wage-price guideposts indicate the difficulty in controlling wages through voluntary restraints as pressures build up in the latter part of a boom period. From 1962 to 1964, unemployment in the nation averaged close to 4 million persons. Against this backdrop, the guideposts, together with White House pressure, had some success in holding down the rate of advance in wage rates. Thus, in 1965 the United Steelworkers, after a call from the President, settled their wage dispute for about 3.5%, or very close to the wage-price guideline. In 1966, however, unemployment dropped below 3 million, and the pressures in the labor market blew the lid off voluntary restraints. A succession of strikes resulted in settlements substantially in excess of the guidelines, with the railroad shopcrafts, for example, winning adjustments of 5.6%. By 1967, the Council of Economic Advisers ceased recommending any specific figure and merely called for restraint, but the plea fell on deaf ears. In that year the United Auto Workers scored a 6% gain in wages, and in 1968 the target was even higher, with the Communication Workers of America gaining wage increases averaging about 6.5% over three years.

The value of the wage-price guideposts is a much debated issue among economists, labor leaders, and businessmen. Some believe that popularization of the notion that wages should advance in line with productivity simply established a minimum for wage demands, while strong unions were able to build upon this and bargain additional amounts above the minimum to which they felt their membership was entitled. However, as Robert Solow has pointed out, "For every employer who complains that unions take the guidepost figure for a floor, there is a union leader who complains that employers take it for a ceiling."[36] Other observers, more favorably impressed by the guideposts, feel that they focused public attention and discussion on a crucial issue and may have led both management and labor to temper wage and price decisions made during this period. Still others contend that the guideposts were never expressed in terms that were meaningful to negotiators at the bargaining table and that the complexities of "package" bargaining cannot be contained in a single overall percentage figure.

GOVERNMENTAL WAGE STABILIZATION

If governmental persuasion and governmental wage guidelines do not suffice to temper the size of wage adjustments, can governmental regulation control the movement of wages and prices? The United States and a number of foreign nations have attempted this route to stabilization. The problems encountered are discussed in the following section.

World War II Wage Stabilization

In 1939, the United States possessed a relatively large volume of unused resources. The Bureau of Labor Statistics estimated unemployment in 1939 at almost 9.5 million. The steel industry was operating at only about five-eighths capacity, the textile industry at three-quarters capacity. This unused capacity was typical of the potential of war industry in general.

Under these circumstances, the country was able to commence war production without serious inflation at the outset. Nevertheless, new purchasing power created by increased employment in war industry caused purchasing power to expand at a more rapid rate than output of civilian goods. This, plus shortages of key skills, products, and equipment, tended to push prices up before unused resources of men and machines were fully employed.

At the time of the Japanese attack on Pearl Harbor on December 7, 1941, there had already been established an agency, the National Defense Mediation Board, to deal with strikes which interfered with defense production. This agency, however, was threatening to fall apart. President Franklin D. Roosevelt therefore convened a special Labor-Management Conference, 'which resulted in the establishment of the National War Labor Board (WLB).

Until October 1942, the WLB had no authority over voluntary wage

---

[36] Robert M. Solow, "The Case against the Case against the Guideposts," in George P. Shultz and Robert Z. Aliber, *Guidelines, Informal Controls and the Market Place* (Chicago: University of Chicago Press, 1966), p. 45. This book contains a series of articles presenting favorable and unfavorable opinions concerning the guideposts.

adjustments. During the first nine months of its existence, however, when its sole concern was with cases involving disputes between labor and management, the WLB developed its basic stabilization program, which was later applied both to voluntary requests for wage adjustments (submitted either from management alone in nonunion plants or jointly from union and management in union plants) and to cases in which the WLB decided disputes between unions and management.

The core of this program was the so-called "Little Steel Formula." Basically, this formula provided that establishments which had not had an increase of 15% in average straight-time hourly earnings since January 1941 (equivalent to the rise in living costs between January 1941, and May 1942), should be permitted to increase wages to this amount. It is noteworthy that wages were thus stabilized at this level without regard to increases in the cost of living which followed after May 1942.

Wages are, however, almost never, in the strict sense of the word, stabilized. Rather, wages are restrained. Thus, although the WLB stabilized basic wage rates in accordance with the Little Steel Formula, wages continued to rise throughout the World War II period. This happened because workers received wage increases on account of promotions, by changing jobs, by receiving merit or length-of-service increases, or by alteration of piece rates. Then, too, workers increased their earnings (without altering wage rates) by working overtime and by working evening or night shifts, for which a bonus or "shift differential" was paid. Finally, although wage rates were stabilized, the WLB permitted the institution and liberalization of fringe benefits, such as vacations, holidays, or health and welfare plans; and the WLB granted wage adjustments to eliminate inequities and substandards, and to aid in war production.

Dispute Cases versus Stabilization

To stabilize wages and settle labor disputes at the same time is both conflicting and complementary. It is conflicting in that frequently a dispute could most easily be settled by ignoring stabilization. "Quickie" strikes during World War II frequently were strikes against stabilization rather than against the employer, who was often willing to pay higher wages but was not permitted to do so. If, however, stabilization is ignored in order to settle a dispute, obviously the way would be clear to circumvent stabilization simply by invoking a dispute.

Effects of World War II Stabilization

The rise in the cost of living between January 1941 and July 1945 was approximately 33.3%. During the same period, basic wage rates increased about 24%; straight-time hourly earnings, adjusted for employment shifts, 40.5%; gross hourly earnings, 51.2%; and gross weekly earnings, 70.5%.[37]

In terms of spendable earnings, the increases were much less. Inflation control involves use of taxes and credit controls as well as of wage and price controls. The average worker supporting a wife and two children had increases in spendable earnings (real earnings less federal taxes) between January 1941 and July 1945 of 24%; the average single worker saw his spendable earnings increase only 11.6%.

On the basis of these data, a good case can be made that wages during World War II were stabilized about as well as could be expected. Partially, perhaps, because wages and prices were controlled well and decontrolled too fast, a dramatic wage-price spiral featured the immediate postwar years, pushing consumer prices up at a rapid rate. When it appeared that wages and prices were approaching stability, the Korean War began, and a new wage-price spiral commenced.

WAGE STABILIZATION DURING THE KOREAN WAR

When the Korean War started in June 1950, the United States had been experiencing a decade of war and postwar prosperity of unprecedented magnitude, and full employment of manpower and equipment. The inflationary impact of the Korean War was immediate—but immediate more because of psychological than because of basic economic factors. For despite full employment, war expenditures in bulk did not occur until *after* the greatest price increases.

Immediately, everyone—consumer and producer alike—seemed to act as if he had played the role before. Goods were snapped up off the shelves, labor agreements were voluntarily reopened to grant wage increases, factories worked overtime trying to fill the accelerated demands, and prices shot up. Here was inflation resulting not from a shortage of supply relative to demand but because people *expected* shortages to occur and because they *expected* prices and wages to be stabilized. Everyone seemed busy buying against a shortage which never occurred, and raising wages and prices to get ahead of wage and price control which came too late.

Although wage and price control legislation was enacted soon after the Communists invaded South Korea, President Harry S Truman's administration did not invoke it until a serious wage-price spiral had already occurred. Once price and wage controls were invoked, the inflation halted its runaway course. In view of the psychological character of the inflation and the lack of any genuine supply shortage relative to demand, it is logical to assume that the slowness to invoke controls was a costly

---

[37] National War Labor Board, *Termination Report* (Washington, D.C.: U.S. Government Printing Office, n.d.), Vol. I, p. 55.

mistake. Once controls were invoked, however, they worked quite differently from those of World War II.

The Wage Stabilization Board

Wage stabilization during the Korean War was administered by the Wage Stabilization Board. Whereas the War Labor Board of World War II was created as an agency with power to act only in dispute cases and then later was granted authority over voluntary wage adjustments, the Wage Stabilization Board was created to control voluntary wage adjustments and then later was given limited control over dispute cases. Although a dispute case—the Steelworkers–Big Steel controversy—just about put the finishing touches on the work of the Wage Stabilization Board, most of the controversies before the WSB were cases in which employers and unions joined forces in an endeavor to obtain special consideration.

The approach of the War Labor Board of World War II, in general, was to set policy on the basis of its decision in individual cases, particularly dispute cases. Thus, we have already noted that the basic stabilization doctrine—the Little Steel Formula—was arrived at in that fashion. The approach of the Wage Stabilization Board was quite different. After wages and prices were temporarily frozen on January 25, 1951, the WSB began promulgating regulations governing the conditions under which such increases as merit, length of service, promotion, inequity, etc., could be granted without specific WSB approval. Unions and managements which wanted permission for larger increases than allowed by the general regulations then had to request specific permission from the WSB. As requests were granted, general regulations were changed, so that although *initial* policy was set by general regulation, specific cases modified the regulations and resulted in new ones.

In a real sense, the wage stabilization picture during the Korean War resembled a game of leapfrog. A general regulation, which set a permissive wage increase ceiling, was laid down. A special case came up, and the increase permitted jumping the ceiling. Soon after the price-wage freeze on January 25, 1951, these "leaps" proceeded rapidly; then, for a while, they slowed down. In the end, they took one big leap—the steel case—and then, wage stabilization virtually collapsed. Wage controls were anything but a conspicuous success during the Korean War.

ANALYSIS OF WAGE CONTROLS OF WORLD WAR II AND OF THE KOREAN WAR

Why did wage controls work quite differently during World War II than during the Korean War? There are several reasons, grounded in the different character of the times and of unions and employers during those times.

Different Economic and Psychological Conditions

We have already noted some of the different economic and psychological conditions of the two periods. The slow start of the defense program in 1939, the background of a depression decade, and the lack of personal and business income savings and borrowing capacity all prevented inflation from getting a running start. In contrast was the Korean War period: a background of a prosperity decade, with plenty of personal and business income savings and borrowing capacity, all of which could be (and seemingly was) put to use to bid prices up.

Equally as important as, if not more important than, economic conditions were the different psychological conditions of the two periods. World War II was an all-out effort psychologically. Contributing to inflation was unpatriotic. Nearly everyone was involved emotionally in the war effort.

The Korean War was a partial effort, psychologically and emotionally as well as economically and militarily, especially as soon as the hopes for easy victory faded. Under those conditions, concern with the general problem of inflation was decidedly secondary in most peoples' minds. The psychological reaction to the outbreak of the Korean War—buying and bidding up prices and wages so as to be in the best possible economic position when controls were imposed—is the best indicator of the public's (including businesses' and unions') reaction to controls at that time.

The Changing Character of Labor and Management

As different as were economic and psychological conditions during World War II and the Korean War, they were no more different than were the attitudes of management and labor. During World War II, management still fought unions on the prime issues of wages, fringes, and union security. Indeed, management of the early 1940s can truly be said not to have accepted unions as a permanent institution. Consequently, management fought unions hard on the crucial issues of wages. *It appears quite clear in retrospect that wage stabilization succeeded so well during World War II because employers feared that wage increases would be ruinous to them and therefore supported stabilization.*

Management's fight on the wage front during World War II was strengthened by the belief among employers that they could not expect to obtain a fair profit from a price control agency and the Democratic administration. Consequently, if they yielded on wages, employers expected that price lids would be maintained, and they would be caught in a price-wage squeeze.

By the time the Korean War broke out, managements, especially of large companies, had found that they could live with unions, even with large wage increases, fringes, and the granting of union security. Consequently, these employers were more interested in labor peace than in wage stabilization. The president of General Motors argued before the Wage Stabilization Board against freezing the cost-of-living and annual improvement increases in his agreement with the United Automobile Workers at least as vehemently as did the president of the UAW.

Moreover, experience had convinced employers that the government would give them a square deal on prices, even if the government was not of their political choice. By the time of the Korean War, there was little fear of a price-wage squeeze in business circles.

The unions of the Korean War had changed since the beginning of World War II as much as employers. At the start of World War II, unions were new in most industries, insecure and unaccepted. They gladly accepted union security in place of wage increases, and then fringes to keep wage rates stable. During World War II, unions were feeling their way and gaining acceptance.

By the time the Korean War began, unions had gained acceptance, security, fringes, and large wage increases after surviving the postwar labor strife rather handily. Being responsive to their membership, unions saw no answer but wage increases to offset the effects of rising prices on union members. With management anxious to cooperate, the unions obtained what they wanted.

"Stabilization" by Big Bargains

During World War II the government, acting through the War Labor Board, a tripartite agency, composed equally of labor, management, and public representatives, established its stabilization norm—the Little Steel Formula—and stuck to it, with some yielding on the fringes. The then current war, the economic and psychological situations, and the prevailing character of labor and management relations made that possible.

During the Korean War the government adopted no such independent position. Essentially, what the Wage Stabilization Board did was "to take the top national bargains [especially the UAW–General Motors agreement] and turn them into governmental policy."[38] When a bargain exceeded such policy it was sometimes turned down; but often, it was approved as a special case. The then current war, the economic and psychological situations, and the prevailing character of labor and management relations again made that possible.

---

[38] Clark Kerr, "Governmental Wage Restraints: Their Limitations and Uses in a Mobilized Economy," *Proceedings of the Fourth Annual Meeting,* Industrial Relations Research Association, Boston, 1951, pp. 14–30.

The effect of stabilizing at "big bargain" levels, as the Korean War WSB did, is undoubtedly to push wages of some companies higher than would otherwise have occurred. For once the top limits are set, unions, in response to the membership, push for the limit. It would probably be accurate to state that the Korean War stabilization program was not only started too late but was also maintained too late. For after the institution of controls stopped the psychological inflation, they tended more, in the absence of serious supply-demand disequilibria, to push wages up to the big bargains than to keep them stabilized.

THE NIXON ADMINISTRATION WAGE AND PRICE CONTROLS

The comparative experience of wage controls during World War II and the Korean War sheds much light on the difficulties faced by an economy which attempts to control wages. Without the economic similarity of World War II conditions, and lacking also the patriotic and psychological factors therein involved, one could predict great problems in any attempt to control—or, more accurately, to restrain—wages. Yet, by the end of the summer of 1971, it was apparent that some strong action needed to be taken by government to check the escalation of expectations with respect to wages and prices. Each round of wages was becoming larger than the preceding one, and despite large money wage adjustments, weekly spendable earnings of employees were no higher than in 1965. Against this background, George Meany, president of the AFL–CIO publicly stated that organized labor would accept wage and price controls provided that controls covered profits, rents, interests, and all prices.

The second quarter of 1971 brought with it a rapid deterioration in the U.S. balance-of-payments position. The trade balance, which had improved briefly in the first quarter fell sharply in the spring. There was a strong outflow of funds from the United States, and speculation was rife that there would be devaluation. The nation was faced by a deteriorating position in world markets, a 6% unemployment rate, and a mounting level of wages and prices.

On August 15, 1971, President Nixon—who had heretofore been an outspoken critic of governmental wage and price regulation—announced a dramatic change in policy. The United States suspended the convertability of the dollar into gold or other reserve assets for the first time since 1934. It imposed a temporary surcharge on dutiable imports. Prices, wages, and rents were frozen for 90 days. The international measures and the wage-price controls were both designed to create conditions in which a more expansive budget policy would be safer and more effective in dealing with the persistent problem of unemployment. The imposition of such controls represented a unique chapter in American economic policy, since the action was taken when the nation was not formally at war and the economy was operating at significantly less than full capacity in both the product and labor markets.

At the end of the 90-day period, the President unveiled the outlines of the continuing wage and price control procedure, which became known as "Phase II." The administration sought to control wages and prices in the economy primarily through stringent controls on large companies.[39] A major reason for this emphasis was the desire to avoid establishment of a huge governmental bureaucracy. Responsibility for price controls was delegated to a 7-member Commission composed wholly of public members, while wage controls were to be administered by a 15-member tripartite Pay Board consisting of representatives of labor, business, and the public.

The announced goal of the administration was to reduce inflation to about a 2½% per annum price rise by the end of 1972. With this rate of permissible price increases and with an assumed rate of productivity advance of 3%, the Pay Board initially set its standard for permissible wage adjustments at 5.5%. Recognizing that it would be presented with some hardship cases, the Board further decreed that it would, in special cases, permit wage adjustments in excess of 5.5% but not more than 7% if such adjustments were necessary to bring the cumulative increase during the last three years to 7% per year, or to preserve certain limited traditional relationships with wages in other trades or industries, or to attract labor in shortage situations.

The problem raised by fringe benefits caused a further modification of the Pay Board's goals. Congress gave the Board a mandate to exclude contributions to fringe benefit plans that were not "unreasonably inconsistent" with the 5.5% standard. The Board interpreted this to permit fringe benefits contributions of up to 0.7% of total compensation. Therefore, as a practical matter, this allowance must be added to the 5.5% wage standard; the Pay Board's standard for permissible increases in total compensation is, therefore, at this writing 6.2%.

At the very outset of its operation, the Pay Board was faced with the thorny issue as to what to do about wage adjustments which were to have gone into effect under collective agreements but were halted during the 90-day freeze period. Should these increases now be permitted retroactively? The Board, with the five labor members dissenting, ruled in November 1971 that such payments could not be made, bringing charges from the labor members that the Board was abrogating valid contracts. However, Congress in adopting amendments to the Economic Stabilization Act in December 1971, specifically incorporated provisions in law which made possible the payment of the majority of retroactive wages due under such clauses.

---

[39] At the end of six months of operation under Phase II, the Cost of Living Council lifted controls from 5 million small businesses leaving only 1.5 million large companies subject to wage and price constraints (*Business Week*, May 6, 1972, p. 23).

The Board soon found that the only hope for its continued existence was to play the law of averages. Some contracts would have to be approved even though they violated the standards, but it was hoped that there would be a sufficient number of contracts below the standard so that the overall goals of stabilization could be achieved. Thus, the Board approved a 16% single year wage-fringe increase under the bituminous coal contract. In January 1972, the Board vetoed 12% increases requested under aerospace contracts but approved 8.3% first-year increases and further agreed that the unpaid balance could be added to second-year adjustments provided for under the contract. A major stumbling block was presented by the West Coast Longshoremen's contract which provided for a 20.9% increase in wages. After much controversy, the Board disallowed the amount requested but agreed to approve 14.9%, even though this was far in excess of the standards set by the Board.

Organized Labor and Phase II Stabilization

From the day the Pay Board was established, it was involved in acrimonious conflict with organized labor. At first the labor members refused to serve at all, until President Nixon, in a memorandum to George Meany, AFL–CIO President, agreed that the Pay Board would be autonomous and that the Cost of Living Council, appointed by the President to supervise the stabilization effort, would not "approve, revise, veto, or revoke standards of criteria developed by the Pay Board." Once the Board was in operation, the labor members found themselves frequently outvoted by the combination of public and business members of the Board. Finally, on March 22, 1972, all of the labor members except Frank Fitzsimmons, president of the Teamsters' Union, resigned from the Board. In leaving the Board, Meany charged that the Board was not really tripartite and represented a coalition of business and political interests. He further criticized the entire stabilization program as a one-sided affair in which profits were permitted to increase, interest rates were not regulated, and workers found their wages controlled while the prices they paid for necessities continued to rise. President Nixon then reconstituted the Pay Board with a corresponding reduction of business members and stated that it would continue to function as a public Board, consisting of five public members, one labor representative, and one business member.

Appraisal of the Phase II Wage Stabilization

It is still too early to make any judgments as to the impact which the Pay Board's action will have on the upward trend of money wages. At the outset, the Board recognized that it had to contend with a backlog of cases where bargains had been made in an uncontrolled environment or where wage adjustments were due to be made and bore a historical relationship to large adjustments made in the period before the freeze. However, it was the Board's hope that by scaling down some of the large bargains which had been agreed upon, it would lower expectations for the future and ultimately induce a more moderate level of wage adjustments. In April 1972, the Board claimed that the total weighted average of increases cleared by the Board to that date averaged about 5%, but it estimated that the average for the year might inch up to 6%.[40] If adjustments could be held within this range, it would represent a substantial reduction from 1971. Although, for the first quarter of 1972, wage adjustments under major collective bargaining agreements approved by the Pay Board averaged 7.8% on an annual basis, as compared with 8.1% in 1971,[41] by August 1972, the average was close to 5.5%.

A major criticism directed against the Board has been that its decisions have been political and that it has been ready to make exceptions when threatened by strike action from powerful unions. As a result, it appears that a mine union or a longshore union can count on doing substantially better than the 7% maximum, while the company with nonunion employees is frozen at 5.5%. Likewise the Board's regulations with respect to merit increases have tended to favor employees working under formal labor contracts as contrasted with those in nonunion shops where merit raise policies are less formalized. It is obvious that a Board of this nature must consider each decision in the light of the need for its own survival. Furthermore, the power of the labor unions in Congress has not been lost on the Board. As has already been mentioned, when the unions could not get retroactivity through the Pay Board, they succeeded in getting Congress to write it into law. As a consequence, whether or not union members are actively represented in the decision-making process of the Pay Board, it seems likely that the Board will continue to bend to union power in fashioning its decisions.

Unions whose members are subject to control of the Pay Board also object to the favored treatment which appears to be given to construction industry employees under the existing stabilization policy. Prior to establishment of the Pay Board, a Construction Industry Stabilization Committee (CISC) was already functioning and attempting to damp down the rate of wage increases in that industry. After the Pay Board was established, the CISC continued its work as a semiautonomous board. In early 1972, wage increases approved by this Committee were averaging 14.6% for the first year of contracts.[42] Criticism of such favoritism and expansion of nonunion construction sharply reduced these increases by mid-1972.

---

[40] 79 LRR 335, April 17, 1972.
[41] *Business Week*, May 6, 1972, p. 16.
[42] *Business Week*, May 6, 1972, p. 23.

Is the present wage stabilization effort a temporary phase or are we witnessing the first stage of a continuing process of governmental regulation of the labor market? Those who argue that wage controls need only be temporary argue that inflation was already beginning to slacken in late 1971 and that the primary purpose of the wage and price stabilization program was to reduce the level of expectations. According to this argument, there is no longer any large excess of demand, so that after a period of stability, controls will no longer be necessary. Other spokesmen are less sanguine about the outlook. For example, Henry B. Schacht, president of Cummins Engine Corporation, sees wage and price controls as part of a continuing "new franchise that society is writing for the corporation."[43] One of the dangers is that unions will find ways, through escrow funds and other devices, to reserve for the future the part of negotiated wage adjustments which the Pay Board disallows. Such increases in cost will overhang the market and make both business and government reluctant to relinquish controls.

Perhaps the critical factor which will determine the continuation of wage and price controls will be their ability to achieve the announced goals. In this respect, the stabilization program has certain advantages which were not true during the Korean conflict. Unemployment is high, there is considerable excess capacity, and productivity should increase as the recovery continues. However, the impact of devaluation on the prices of imports, the lack of control on agricultural prices, and the continuing high level of governmental deficits all have an inflationary potential.

THE LABOR DILEMMA

The American economy faces a dilemma. As a nation we have as objectives two goals which may not be compatible: full employment and price stability. In 1971, there were about 5 million persons unemployed in the United States. Furthermore, millions more were underemployed or were denied the benefits of full employment. Any massive governmental efforts to reduce unemployment, to cut down the idleness of our teenagers, and to lessen the poverty and despair in our slums can only be accomplished through the expenditures of vast sums of money which will add fuel to the fires of inflation. On the other hand, primary emphasis upon controlling inflation would require continuing wage and price controls and restrictive fiscal and monetary policy which would hamper efforts to stimulate business recovery and increase employment opportunities.

---

[43] Lewis Beman, "The Emerging Debate about Inflation," *Fortune* Vol. 85 (March 1972), p. 53.

The Concept of the Phillips Curve[44]

Theoretically there is a "trade-off" relationship between a given rate of price increase and the rate of unemployment. It has become customary to speak of this relationship in terms of the "Phillips curve." The latter is an analytical tool first used by Professor A. W. Phillips, who applied it to relate changes in money wages to the level of unemployment in the British economy.[45] Other studies have expanded upon this work and have derived a modified application indicating the trade-off relationship between unemployment and changes in the price level.[46] Obviously, the relationship or lack thereof may depend upon the particular index used to measure changes in the "price level," since all such indexes do not necessarily move uniformly together over time.

One economist[47] has derived a regression equation based upon percentage changes in quarterly values of the Consumer Price Index (P) as the dependent variable and the inverse of the quarterly value of the unemployment rate (UR^{-1}) as the independent variable. The resultant equation $P = -.828 + 6.371 \ UR^{-1}$ yields a curve shown in Figure 13–5. Based on this relationship, in order to have a 4% unemployment rate on an annual basis the economy would have to accept at least a 3% annual rise in the Consumer Price Index.

The most significant fact which emerges from discussions of Phillips curves is that the trade-off between unemployment and inflation seems to have worsened. According to most of the Phillips curves drawn in the 1960s, a 6% rate of unemployment should have "bought" an inflation rate of about 1%. As one economist has recently stated:

Five years ago no one drew a Phillips curve through the almost 6% inflation at 6% unemployment that we have lately experienced . . . there is the possibility of "structural change" or permanent upward shift of the curve. . . .[48]

Has the Phillips curve shifted to the right over time? Such a shift would mean that to reduce unemployment to any given rate, a higher

---

[44] A mathematical analysis of the concept of the Phillips curve is set forth in the appendix to this chapter.

[45] A. W. Phillips, "The Relation Between Unemployment and the Rate of Change of Money Wage Rates in the United Kingdom, 1861–1957," *Economica*, Vol. 25 (November 1958), pp. 283–99.

[46] See George L. Perry, *Unemployment, Money Wage Rates and Inflation* (Cambridge, M.I.T. Press, 1966). Perry explains quarterly changes in the money wage level in terms of changes in the unemployment rate, the cost-of-living index, the level of profits, and the change in profits from one quarter to the next.

[47] Jerome C. Darnell, "Another Look at the Trade-Off between Inflation and Unemployment," *Conference Board Record*, Vol. 7 (January 1970), pp. 18–19.

[48] Martin J. Bailey, "The 1971 Report of the President's Council of Economic Advisers: Inflation and Recession," *American Economic Review*, Vol. 61 (September 1971), p. 519.

FIGURE 13–5

Modified Phillips Curve

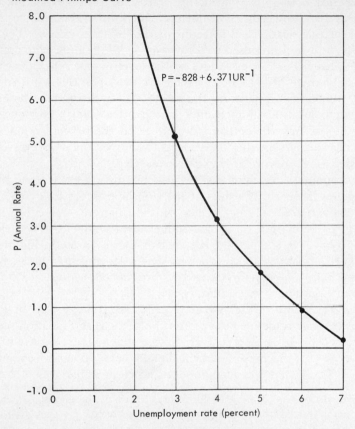

$$P = -828 + 6.371UR^{-1}$$

Source: Jerome C. Darnell, "Another Look at the Trade-Off between Inflation and Unemployment," *Conference Board Record*, Vol. 7 (January 1970), p. 21.

rate of inflation would have to be tolerated. In February 1972, a confidential study prepared for the Nixon administration declared that reducing the unemployment rate to 4% of the labor force would risk an inflation rate of 4% or higher.[49] The study claims that it is now more difficult than in years past to reduce unemployment because of the changing nature of the labor force. According to the study, the central economic dilemma facing the nation is that when a general stimulus is used to reduce unemployment that is mainly concentrated among the young, women, and disadvantaged groups, manpower shortages rapidly develop in the skilled-male-over-25-year-old category, which eventually

---

[49] *Wall Street Journal*, February 18, 1972, p. 3.

puts "pressure in the inflation boiler."[50] We shall discuss in more detail in the next chapter the changing nature of unemployment in this nation and its relevance to the concept of "normal" unemployment.

Discussions of the so-called Phillips curve raise two fundamental issues. In the first place, there is nothing immutable about the relationship which the curve illustrates. Presumably, it can be altered through proper application of public policy. The objective of national policy should be to reduce the job-price trade-off so that more progress can be made in reducing unemployment with a minimum increase in price. Such an objective, which would move the Phillips curve to the left, calls for elimination of structural imperfections in the labor market, improving the mobility of labor, providing better training for new additions to the labor force, and for similar constructive measures.

In the second place, it is important to recognize that a stable price level, though desirable, is not an end in itself. The costs of achieving this goal should be measured by the loss of output and real income which the economy must suffer because it is working at less than full capacity. Erosion of purchasing power is to be lamented—but so is unemployment and lost output.

UNIONS AND WAGE INFLATION

Much of the discussion on the wage-price-inflation issue tends to cast unions as villains of the piece. The reasoning is that if it were not for union bargaining strength and their "exorbitant" wage demands, wage rates would not be pushed up as fast, and therefore the dilemma with its unpalatable consequences would never have to be faced. There are really two logical steps in this reasoning which require examination. First, is it true that unions make wage rates higher than they would otherwise be? Second, to what extent is price inflation the result primarily of cost-push or of demand-pull factors?

Do Unions Accelerate the Rise in Wage Levels? Negative View

Those who contend that unions have not caused wage rates generally to rise any faster than they would have in the absence of union organization emphasize that changes in wage rates, like changes in prices, are simply the reflection of more fundamental developments in the underlying forces which determine supply and demand in the marketplace. They claim that the sharp increases in money wage rates which occurred in the post–World War II period and are recurring now are the result of the increase in the supply and velocity of money which made itself felt through an expanding demand for goods of all kinds. The growth of

---
[50] *Ibid.*

consumer credit, large expenditures upon plant and equipment, high farm incomes, rising governmental expenditures, and similar circumstances contributed to the inflation, which in turn produced a shortage of labor and high wage rates.

This viewpoint has been succinctly expressed by Charls Walker:

Cost-push pressures, spurred on by excessive wage increases relative to productivity gains, are the result, not the cause, of the inflationary process. If this were not the case, the stability in unit labor costs between 1960 and 1965 could not be explained. It was not until after 1965 when demand-pull inflation overwhelmed the economy that increases in labor compensation began to outstrip gains in productivity.[51]

Wage Gains among Unorganized Workers

We have spoken earlier of unions being mere avenues through which inflationary forces transmit their impact to wages and prices. In support of this position, it may be observed that money wage rates seem to have risen as fast, if not faster, in previous periods of inflation, when union organization was a negligible factor in the labor market. For example, in the period from 1917 to 1921, organized labor represented less than 12% of the labor force, as contrasted with 25% in the post–World War II period. Yet increases in money wage rates generally in these two postwar periods of inflation were strikingly similar.

Another illuminating comparison is provided by the steel industry. Workers in this industry actually made larger percentage gains in money and real hourly earnings during the period 1914–20, when union organization was negligible, than during the period 1939–48, when the CIO United Steelworkers spearheaded a drive for wage increases in the industry.[52]

That union organization is not necessary to give workers large increases in money wages if the necessary factors are present—high demand for labor and/or shortage of labor supply—is illustrated by comparing gains in wages and salaries in largely organized and largely unorganized sectors of the economy. For example, average hourly earnings of employees (production or nonsupervisory) in manufacturing, a highly organized sector of the economy, increased from $2.53 in 1964 to $3.71 in 1972, or an increase of 47%. During the same period, average hourly earnings in services increased from $1.94 to $3.08 or 59%; in wholesale and retail trade, from $1.96 to $2.98, or 52%; and in finance, insurance, and real estate from $2.30 to $3.39, or 47%.[53] Employees in the latter three

---

[51] Charls Walker, "Cost-Push Inflation: What It Is and What Not To Do About It," *Conference Board Record*, Vol. 7 (April 1970), p. 25.

[52] Albert Rees, "Postwar Wage Determination in the Basic Steel Industry," *American Economic Review*, Vol 41 (June 1951), p. 400.

[53] U.S. Department of Labor, *Employment and Earnings*, Vol. 18 (March 1972), p. 79.

largely unorganized sectors of the economy have done as well or better than their counterparts in heavily organized manufacturing industries.

Anyone who has sought to hire a maid or someone to perform house-work can attest to the fact that without the aid of union organization, domestic servants have probably achieved greater gains in hourly earnings during the past decade than members of the United Automobile Workers! Indeed, it can be argued that rather than accelerating increases in the wage level, union organization has inhibited such increases, relative to nonunion employees, primarily because of the lag produced by the term of existing wage contracts. Union wage adjustments, as a consequence, tend to follow rather than to lead nonunion wage adjustments during an inflationary period in the economy.

Do Unions Accelerate the Rise in Wage Levels? Affirmative View

A number of economists have concluded that unions do push up money wages to a level higher than that which would exist in a nonunion economy. Most of the empirical studies which have been conducted with respect to this problem concern the immediate post–World War II era, but the conclusions would seem to hold for our more recent experience. H. Gregg Lewis, for example, concludes that the average union/nonunion relative wage was approximately 10%–15% higher than it would have been in the absence of union organization.[54] Albert Rees concludes that "strong American unions seem to be able to raise the relative earnings of their members by 15 to 25 per cent."[55] These and other economists argue that it would be surprising if unions did not have this effect in view of the fact that the principal purpose of the trade-union movement is to influence the level of money wage rates. Unions have compelled many companies to accept conditions which management opposed, such as the union shop and the closed shop. It would seem strange if their bargaining power could not also compel management to accept wage levels above those that management would voluntarily establish for nonunion em-ployees.[56] Evidence of the ability of unions to force such high wage levels on employers is found in the history of the many employers in the coal, hosiery, cotton textile, garment, and shoe industries who were forced out of business because the union compelled them to pay wages above the nonunion scale.

Have wages simply been chasing prices up, or have wages been pushing

---

[54] H. Gregg Lewis, *Unionism and Relative Wages in the United States* (Chicago: University of Chicago Press, 1963), p. 5.

[55] Albert Rees, *The Economics of Trade Unions* (Chicago: University of Chicago Press, 1962), p. 77.

[56] Sumner H. Slichter, "Do the Wage-Fixing Arrangements in the American Labor Market Have an Inflationary Bias?" in Richard L. Rowan and Herbert R. Northrup (eds.), *Readings in Labor Economics and Labor Relations* (Homewood, Ill.: Richard D. Irwin, Inc., 1968), p. 460.

prices up? A number of economists contend that given conditions in the market favorable to the exercise of union bargaining power, union organization results in a greater inflation in wages and prices than would occur in a nonunion economy. The following are some of the reasons advanced in support of this contention:

1. First and foremost is the dominant position of labor unions in our key industries. Between 80% and 100% of employees are under union contracts in the aluminum, steel, coal and metal-mining, automobile and automobile parts, agricultural equipment, rubber products, shipbuilding, building construction, longshoring, railroad, and trucking industries. With such complete control of the labor force in these industries, unions are in a position to exact higher rates than would be the case in a free labor market. Furthermore, since bargaining tends to be on a multiunit basis, all or most of the employers of the industry have their labor costs raised more or less simultaneously. As a result, there is a natural inclination to raise prices, since each producer knows that his competitor "is in the same boat" and will welcome a chance to pass on increased costs to consumers.

It is significant, too, that the industries in which unions are strongest are key industries from which wage and price changes fan out rapidly in the entire economy. As one writer has put it: "Strong textile unionism and weak auto unionism would produce a different wage atmosphere."[57] Economists who believe that unions create an inflationary bias in wage changes stress the fact that a comparison of the size of wage changes in union and nonunion companies will not reveal a significant differential, because it is well known that nonunion companies, in order to avoid union organization, keep their wages abreast of, and frequently exceed, wage adjustments being made in organized firms in their particular industry.

2. In the second place, in a highly unionized economy, key wage bargains are spread rapidly from one industry to another, even though supply and demand conditions within the "follower" industries may not justify the same increase as that granted in the "leader" industry. Union workers are strong believers in uniformity of wages—that is, uniformity with the highest wage rate paid. This is particularly true where members of one international union may be employed in a number of industries. If a profitable firm in one industry employing members of a particular union gives a large wage adjustment, the cry immediately goes up from the membership to obtain the same increase for all members of the union. Whereas, in a nonunion economy, wage adjustments are likely to spread gradually by affecting local supply and demand conditions, and to vary in size depending upon the profitability of the particular firm and local conditions, in a unionized economy key wage adjustments jump rapidly

---

[57] Lloyd G. Reynolds, "Structural Determinants of Cost Inflation and Remedial Measures," *Monthly Labor Review*, Vol. 82 (August 1959), p. 873.

from one industry to another. Thus, it is possible that wage increases may spread more rapidly and may be more likely to produce price increases in a unionized economy than in a free labor market.

3. Events indicate that unions will press for further advances in wage rates even when profits are declining and unemployment is growing in the economy or in an industry. Wages rose in each of the years 1949, 1954, and 1958, despite falling demand for labor and relatively high unemployment. There is considerable evidence that wage increases under trade-unions are less sensitive to the existence of high unemployment than under nonunion conditions.[58] One investigator found that the relation of wage changes to varying levels of unemployment was stronger in the period prior to 1930 than in the last 20 years. Inasmuch as unionism has played a more important role since World War II than before 1930, "trade unions would appear to have made wage increases less sensitive to unemployment than under the essentially nonunion conditions during the first 30 years of the century."[59] While there is room for disagreement as to the influence of unions on the level of money wage rates in periods of rapid expansion, there seems to be little doubt that unions hold up wages in periods of severe contraction and, in fact, tend to push up wages in the early stages of business contractions.

4. The existence of union contractual arrangements with employers was until recently a factor which on the whole retarded the wage-price spiral by producing a minimum time lag during which wage rates could not be negotiated. The stabilizing effect of such contracts has, however, been offset by two developments. The first is the inclusion in union contracts of cost-of-living escalator provisions. Whereas, previously, the cost of living had been merely one of the many factors which entered into wage negotiations, under escalator provisions, there is a direct and automatic relationship between wage rates and the cost of living. The second is incorporation of an "annual improvement factor" in union contracts, guaranteeing the members of the bargaining unit a minimum increase based upon supposed increases in productivity. The combined effect of these two developments tends to make union contracts into inflation-producing documents.

The Effect of Cost-of-Living Provisions in Union Contracts

As we mentioned in Chapter 11, the sharp upturn in prices in recent years has renewed organized labor's interest in automatic cost-of-living

[58] See, for example, Robert R. France, "Wages, Unemployment and Prices in the United States, 1890–1932, 1947–1957," *Industrial and Labor Relations Review*, Vol. 15 (January 1962), pp. 171–90; and Kenneth M. McCaffree, "A Further Consideration of Wages, Unemployment, and Prices in the U.S., 1948–1958," *Industrial and Labor Relations Review*, Vol 17 (October 1963), pp. 60–74.

[59] McCaffree, "Wages, Unemployment, and Prices," p. 60.

adjustment provisions. It is estimated that in 1972 about 4.3 million employees will be covered by such clauses.[60] Do escalator clauses in union contracts *cause* inflation? The answer would seem to be no. Considered alone, cost-of-living adjustment clauses do not initiate inflation, but they can *intensify* an inflationary trend attributable to other factors. As one economist puts it: "Escalator clauses appear more likely to feed a monetary or fiscal inflation than to initiate one. There seems to be little question, however, that wage escalation would act to aggravate an existing inflation due to these forces. By reducing or eliminating the normal time lag in making wage adjustments, a barrier to spiraling incomes and labor costs would be lowered."[61] Whereas wage rates are most commonly negotiated annually in the absence of long-term agreements, wages are frequently adjusted quarterly pursuant to cost-of-living clauses in long-term contracts. Furthermore, the very existence of escalator clauses in labor contracts in key industries may increase the inflationary expectations of employers and labor in other sectors of the economy, and thus result in larger wage settlements than might otherwise be arrived at.

Assume, for example, that the cost-of-living index goes up as a result of an increase in farm prices. The result may be a wage increase for a million workers. This wage increase can, in turn, result in widespread price increases. Then, by the time the next quarter comes around again, a sufficient round of price increases may have been created so that another cost-of-living wage adjustment will be justified under the contract. This cumulative relationship proceeds on a quarterly basis and offsets the tendency of many businesses to let prices alone except when they are jolted by large increases in cost, such as may be produced by a large wage adjustment. To put the matter another way, frequent cost-of-living adjustments jar industry into frequent price increases, which intensify the upward wage-price spiral.

Wage increases resulting from escalator clauses generally take place in manufacturing industries and therefore affect the prices of manufactured goods. When such prices rise, the cost of goods purchased by the farmer tends to rise, which in turn produces an increase in the price for farm products. To the extent that farm prices rise as a result, there will be a tendency for the consumer price index to rise, since food accounts for about one third of the index. And once the consumer price index rises, the stage has been set for another increase in wages under escalator provisions in industry.

The inflationary potential of escalator clauses has been recognized by many foreign countries since the end of World War II, and many governments—among them Chile, France, Australia, Austria, Belgium, Nor-

---

[60] *Monthly Labor Review*, Vol. 95 (January 1972), p. 7.

[61] Jules Backman, "Wage Escalation and Inflation," *Industrial and Labor Relations Review*, Vol. 13 (April 1960), p. 405.

way, Denmark, Sweden, and Finland—have taken steps either to prohibit this type of automatic adjustment or to restrict it in order to lessen its tendency to feed inflationary forces. In this country, limitations on escalator clauses have been introduced primarily at the insistence of management in collective bargaining agreements. Business must have known costs in order to project prices and production for the future. An open-end escalator clause introduces an element of uncertainty into management planning which businessmen have been trying to avoid by placing ceilings or other limitations on cost-of-living adjustments in labor contracts.

APPRAISAL OF THE DILEMMA

Continuing inflation—particularly at an accelerated rate—is intolerable, since it would erode the standard of living of fixed-income groups, endanger the stability of the dollar in international commerce, and might eventually lead to coercive controls in our society. Inflation in the United States is a policy packed with political dynamite; for if the middle-class citizens of America rightly or wrongly come to conclude that wage pressure by organized labor is responsible for the erosion of their savings, then they might be led to sponsor and support restrictive measures which would spell the end of a free labor market as we know it.

On the other hand, a high rate of unemployment is also an intolerable condition for our society. But this depends upon who is unemployed: Is it the male breadwinner of the family? Or is it the part-timer, the youth, the married woman who is anxious to reenter the labor force? If the present 6% unemployment rate were concentrated among male breadwinners, there might be a different focus of public policy today. However, the nature of our unemployment has changed substantially in recent years. In the next chapter, we shall consider the significance of this change which explains why continuing emphasis will probably be placed upon control of inflation in this country.

APPENDIX: INFLATION, UNEMPLOYMENT AND THE PHILLIPS CURVE

The Wage, Price and Productivity Relationship:

The equilibrium in the labor market is determined by the interaction of the demand and supply of labor, which are represented by the following equations:

$$\text{Demand}: w = f(L) \text{ or } W = P \cdot f(L) \tag{1}$$

$$\text{Supply}: \quad w = g(L) \text{ or } W = P \cdot g(L) \tag{2}$$

where w is the real wage rate, W is the money wage rate, P is the price level, $f(L)$ and $g(L)$ are the functional forms of the demand and supply equations for labor. (Recall that the demand for labor is obtained by setting the marginal productivity of labor equal to the wage rate while the supply of labor is determined by the aggregate tradeoff between work and leisure.) Equating demand to supply gives the labor market equilibrium

$$f(L) = g(L) \text{ or } P \cdot f(L) = P \cdot g(L) \tag{3}$$

The basic wage-price-productivity relationship can be derived from a version of the labor market equilibrium condition in (1). For any given L, the price level is given by

$$P = \frac{W}{f(L)} \tag{4}$$

FIGURE 13–6

Equilibrium in the Labor Market

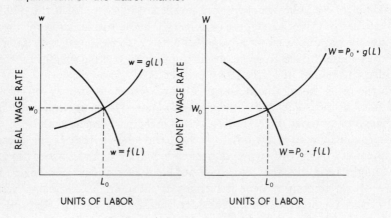

If the money wage rate W and the marginal productivity of labor grow at the same rate, there will be no change in the equilibrium price level P. For example, if the initial price level P_1 is given by

$$P_1 = \frac{W}{[f(L)]_1}$$

and both W and $f(L)$ grow at $a\%$ annually, the wage and marginal productivity after one year are $W_2 = W_1[1 + a/100]$ and $[f(L)]_2 = [f(L)]_1[1 + a/100]$ respectively. In logarithmic terms, (4) can be written as

$$\log_e P = \log_e W - \log_e [f(L)] \tag{5}$$

Differentiating with respect to time, we obtain

$$\dot{P} = \dot{W} - [f\dot{(}L)] \tag{6}$$

where dots denote percentage rates of growth of the respective variables for small changes. Thus

$$\dot{P} = \frac{dP/dt}{P}$$

Equation (6) indicates that if W and $f(L)$ grow at the same rate so that $\dot{W} = [f\dot{(}L)]$, $\dot{P}$ will be 0, i.e., the equilibrium price level will remain unchanged. Alternatively, since the real wage w is just W/P, the growth rate in real wage is given by

$$\dot{w} = \dot{W} - \dot{P} \tag{7}$$

If money wages grow as fast as productivity and P remains unchanged so that $\dot{P} = 0$, (7) combined with (6) yields

$$\dot{w} = \dot{W} - \dot{P} = [f\dot{(}L)] \tag{8}$$

The noninflationary rule for wages states that *the real wage rate can grow as fast as productivity with no change in the equilibrium price level.*

The analysis can be extended to consider the unit labor cost and the labor share of output. The labor cost per unit of real output c can be written as

$$c = \frac{WL}{Q} = \frac{W}{Q/L} \tag{9}$$

where L is the total labor force employed. Taking logarithms we obtain,

$$\log_e c = \log_e W - \log_e (Q/L) \tag{10}$$

or differentiating,

$$\dot{c} = \dot{W} - (Q\dot{/}L)$$

This implies that unit labor cost remains constant if the money wage rate and labor productivity increase at the same rate.

The labor share of total output can be written as

$$S_L = \frac{WL}{PQ} = \frac{w}{Q/L} \tag{11}$$

As demonstrated earlier, if the real wage w and the productivity Q/L change by the same percentage, the equilibrium price level remains unchanged. Taking logarithms and differentiating,

$$\dot{S}_L = \dot{w} - (Q\dot{/}L) \tag{12}$$

Hence, if w and Q/L change by the same rate, the labor share of output remains constant—$\dot{S}_L = 0$.

The wage-price-productivity analysis above forms the basis for the Council of Economic Advisers' wage-price guideposts referred to in Chapter 13. According to the general guidepost, in industries where productivity increased more than average, prices should fall and in other industries where the productivity change was relatively slow, prices should rise, maintaining overall price stability. This implies that all wages grow at about the same rate. With bars indicating economy-wide averages, the wage guidepost says

$$\dot{W}_i = \overline{(\dot{Q}/L)} \tag{13}$$

By this criterion, wages in every industry i should grow as fast as the average labor productivity. Unit labor costs in industry i will grow at the rate

$$\dot{c}_i = \dot{W}_i - (\dot{Q}/L)_i = \overline{(\dot{Q}/L)} - (\dot{Q}/L)_i \tag{14}$$

Hence, if industry i has productivity growing faster than average, its labor costs fall and according to the guidepost its prices should fall to preserve constant relative shares of labor and capital. Conversely, for industries with slower than average productivity growth, the guidepost recommends a price rise. Thus, on the average, a constant price level would be maintained.

The Phillips Curve: The Relation of Wage Changes to Unemployment

In the previous discussion of wages, prices and productivity, it was assumed that the labor supply curve shifts up through time and the conditions for noninflationary wage increases were derived. In order to understand why the money wage rate moves upward, a discussion of the Phillips curve relating unemployment u to the percentage rate of increase in money wages $\dot{W}$, is important.

An outward shift of the demand curve for labor causes an increase in the wage rate due to the creation of excess demand in the labor market. Thus, at the wage rate W_o, (which was initially the equilibrium wage rate and hence labor supply and demand were equated), there is excess demand for labor given by $L_o^d - L_o^s$. This excess demand for labor causes a rise in the money wage rate from W_o. Assuming that the percentage rate of change in the money rate $\dot{W}$ depends on the excess demand for labor, we can write

$$\dot{W} = \phi(L^d - L^s); \ \phi' > 0 \tag{15}$$

FIGURE 13–7

Excess Demand in the Labor Market

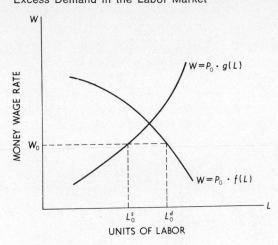

The motivation for deriving the Phillips curve relationship was to estimate a wage adjustment equation independently of the demand and supply curves in the labor market, which are difficult to estimate empirically.

The excess supply in the labor market is just the negative of the excess demand and equation (15) can be rewritten as

$$\dot{W} = -\phi(L^s - L^d); \ \phi' > 0 \tag{16}$$

The unemployment rate u can be introduced as a proxy for excess supply since as excess supply increases, the unemployment rate increases. (It should be noted that even when the labor market is in equilibrium, i.e., excess supply is zero, positive unemployment exists, as shown in Figure 13–8).

Substituting the unemployment rate for excess supply, equation (16) becomes

$$\dot{W} = \psi(u); \ \psi' < 0 \tag{17}$$

Thus, as unemployment increases, the rate of increase of wages falls and vice versa. Equation (17) is the basic Phillips curve relation represented in Figure 13–9.

The curve is shown to have a convex shape since as unemployment is reduced by constant amounts, the wage rate rises more than proportionately with $\dot{W} \to \infty$ as $u \to 0$ since the unemployment rate cannot become negative. On the other hand, there must be some institutional

FIGURE 13–8

Relation of Excess Supply and Rate of Unemployment

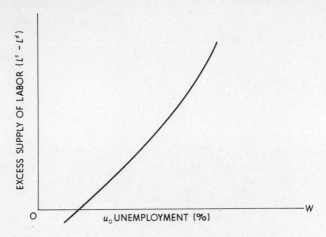

lower boundary below which $\dot{W}$ cannot fall. It is not possible to reduce $\dot{W}$ to approach $-\infty$ with growing unemployment, but a stable rate of wage decrease will be reached. As $u \rightarrow 100\%$, the lower bound of $\dot{W}$ is reached as shown in the figure above. While these arguments are merely hypothetical, the empirical estimates seem to confirm the convexity proposition. The convex shape implies that if unemployment is fluctuating

FIGURE 13–9

The Phillips Curve

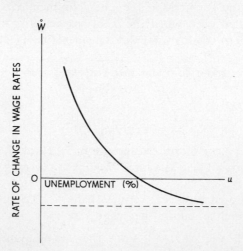

symmetrically about a particular level, say $\bar{u}$, the average pressure on wages goes up more below $\bar{u}$ than it goes down above $\bar{u}$, because of the convexity of the curve. Thus, the broader the fluctuation in unemployment rate (for the same average unemployment rate), the greater will be the inflationary pressures.

Given that the relative shares of labor and capital are constant, the percentage rate of change of prices is given by

$$\dot{P} = \dot{W} - \frac{\dot{Q}}{L} \tag{18}$$

Thus, there is a link between inflation in prices and wage increases so that the Phillips curve can be stated in terms of both prices and wages. With a 3% annual increase in productivity for instance, a zero increase in prices corresponds to a 3% annual wage increase. Hence, the Phillips curve in Figure 13–9 can be restated in price terms by shifting it downwards by 3%. From a study of the increase in labor productivity, P. A. Samuelson and R. M. Solow suggested that the level of unemployment and rate of wage increase that maintain price stability in the United States are 4.5% and 3% per annum respectively.

One of the best empirical studies of the Phillips curve in the United States has been made by George Perry who added several explanatory variables to the basic relationship. The general form of the Perry wage change function is

$$\dot{W} = \psi(u, \dot{P}, R, \Delta R) \tag{19}$$

where $\dot{P}$ is the rate of price change in percentage terms, R is the net profit rate and ΔR is the change in the net profit rate. According to theory, $\delta\psi/\delta u < 0$ and $\delta\psi/\delta\dot{P}$, $\delta\psi/\delta R$ and $\delta\psi/\delta\Delta R$ are all positive. The reason for including $\dot{P}$ is that a price increase in the previous period shifts the labor supply curve in the present period so that the wage increase is even higher. Perry's argument for including corporate profit rates is that higher corporate profit rates cause greater bargaining by unions so that wages rise more. However, the argument can be made that greater profits allow companies to hold out longer against union demands for wage increases. The argument for including ΔR is that recent increases in R cause unions to expect higher future profits thus increasing wage demands. The empirical estimate of the linear form of the function in (19) is

$$\dot{W}_t = -4.3 + 0.4\dot{P}_{t-1} + 14.7\frac{1}{u_t} + 0.4R_t + 0.8\Delta R_t \tag{20}$$

If the $\dot{P}$ term is eliminated using $\dot{P} = \dot{W} - (\dot{Q}/L)$, when the relative shares are constant, we obtain,

$$\dot{W}_t = -4.3 + 0.4(\dot{W} - (\dot{Q}/L)_{t-1} + 14.7\frac{1}{u_t} + 0.4R_{t-1} \qquad (21)$$

In the long run steady state situation, $\dot{W}_t \simeq \dot{W}_{t-1}$, so that equation (21) can be solved to obtain

$$\dot{W} = -7.2 - 0.7(\dot{Q}/L) + 24.5\frac{1}{u} + 0.7R \qquad (22)$$

Taking the labor productivity Q/L to be growing at about 3% annually, a family of Perry-Phillips curves can be drawn for the U.S. economy for various profit rates as shown in Figure 13–10.

FIGURE 13–10

The Phillips Curves

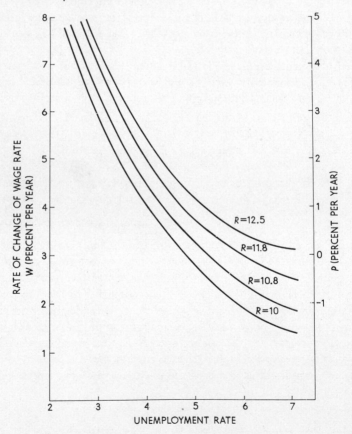

Adapted from G. L. Perry, *Unemployment, Money Wage Rates and Inflation* (Cambridge, Mass.: M.I.T. Press, 1966), p. 63.

QUESTIONS FOR DISCUSSION

1. How have the gains of increased productivity been distributed in the post-war years? From the point of view of achieving maximum employment in our economy, what is the "best" method of distributing such gains?

2. What is meant by "labor productivity"? How does this concept differ from "labor efficiency"? What are the factors which have produced the increase in output per manhour in American industry?

3. Are union organization, full employment, and price stability compatible in a free labor market? Discuss the economic and political implications of this question.

4. Union leaders maintain that cost-of-living escalator clauses in union contracts are beneficial to the economy because they help to maintain the real purchasing power of the workingman's dollar. Discuss the validity of this statement with particular relation to the problem of inflation.

5. Do you think it is possible for government to hold annual price increases to 2.5% and wage increases to 5.5%? Explain your answer.

SUGGESTIONS FOR FURTHER READING

BURCK, GILBERT.   "Union Power and the New Inflation," *Fortune*, Vol. 83 (February 1971), pp. 65–9, 119–20.

A discussion of the significance of the worldwide wage explosion now affecting all industrialized economies.

DARNELL, JEROME C. "Another Look at the Trade-Off between Inflation and Unemployment," *Conference Board Record*, Vol. 7 (January 1970), pp. 17–23.

A concise analysis of the relationship between price changes and unemployment rates which examines the change in the Phillips curve over time.

ECKSTEIN, OTTO and BRENNER, ROGER. *The Inflation Process in the United States and the Alternatives before Us.* Supplementary Paper No. 13. New York: Committee for Economic Development, 1962.

A major statistical and analytical treatise on the various sources of economic growth, including an appraisal of the contribution made by the various factors of production,

ECKSTEIN, OTTO and BRENNER, ROGER. *The Inflation Process in the United States.* Study prepared for the Joint Economic Committee, 92nd Congress, 2nd Session (Washington: Government Printing Office, 1972).

A study which seeks to identify the process which produced the recent combination of rapid inflation and unemployment. ›

KENDRICK, JOHN W. "The Productivity Factor in Phase 2," *Conference Board Record*, Vol 9 (March 1972), pp. 28–35.

An explanation of how to calculate productivity gains on an individual firm basis.

SOLOW, ROBERT M. "The Wage-Price Issue and the Guideposts," in HARBISON, F. H. and MOONEY, J. D. (eds.), *Critical Issues in Employment Policy*, pp.

57–74. Princeton University Research Report Series No. 109. Princeton, N.J., 1966.

An appraisal of the contribution made by the wage-price guideposts in damping down the inflationary spiral.

ULMAN, LLOYD, and FLANAGAN, ROBERT J.   *Wage Restraint: A Study of Income Policies in Western Europe*. Berkeley: University of California Press, 1971.

An excellent study of attempts to restrain increases in wages and prices in the United Kingdom, Netherlands, Sweden, Denmark, France, West Germany, and Italy.

Chapter 14

UNEMPLOYMENT AND POVERTY IN A HIGH-EMPLOYMENT ECONOMY

In the previous and earlier chapters of this text, we have referred to the paradoxical problem which faces this nation, namely that at the same time as total employment and gross national product continue to record annual increases, we are also faced with continuing high levels of unemployment and persistent poverty in our midst affecting millions of our citizens. In this chapter, we shall examine these two problems—unemployment and poverty—and shall consider their nature, extent, and probable causes.

THE EXTENT OF UNEMPLOYMENT

Unemployment of some amount is a normal concomitant of a free labor market. Irregularity of employment is, in a sense, one of the costs which a system of free enterprise exacts in return for the privileges it bestows. Thus, the American worker has greater liberty than a worker anywhere else in the world to shift his place of employment in order to benefit his economic welfare. This is no idle gift—indeed, as we have seen from our discussion of the labor market, it is a privilege frequently exercised by the American worker. But the freedom of the worker to quit and to move is balanced by the freedom of the employer to fire, with the result that the individual employee is subjected to the vicissitudes of his current employer's business fortunes. Similarly, the absence of a central planning board integrating the production and employment policies of various firms means that in certain industries, there may be a temporary surplus of labor while, at the same time, there can be shortages of labor in others.

Thus, employment and unemployment typically fluctuate over time. A major determinant of the volume of unemployment is the level of business activity. At the depth of the Great Depression in 1933, one in every four persons was unemployed. On the other hand, in 1953 only about 1.8 million persons were unemployed out of a total civilian labor force of 63 million, or about 2.9% of the labor force.[1]

---

[1] U.S. Department of Labor, *Manpower Report of the President, 1971* (Washington, D.C.: U.S. Government Printing Office, 1971). Table A–1, p. 203.

In 1971, the number of unemployed averaged about 5 million, representing an unemployment rate of about 6%; yet the number of jobholders actually rose by more than 1 million during the year. Of those unemployed in 1971, 4 million were looking for full-time jobs and 1 million for part-time work.[2] Persons who have involuntarily lost their jobs make up only about one half of the unemployed. The balance is made up of voluntary quits, persons who have recently reentered the labor force, and new entrants to the labor force.[3]

The labor force and the rolls of the employed and unemployed are in a state of constant flux. For example, there is a tremendous influx of young people into the labor market in June of each year after the school year ends. Between May and June of 1971, the labor force showed a net increase of nearly 1.9 million persons with 1.1 million persons initially unsuccessful in their job search.[4] Thus, unemployment rates typically fluctuate over the year.

The number of persons who experience some unemployment during a given year is roughly three to four times the average number unemployed over the year. Thus, in recent years as many as 15 million persons experienced some unemployment.[5] During 1971, about 45% of the workers who experienced some unemployment were out of work less than five weeks.[6] Presumably unemployment for this group resulted largely from voluntary job changes, some delay in finding new jobs, and the usual seasonal layoffs.

MEASUREMENT OF UNEMPLOYMENT

Although unemployment represents a serious problem facing our economy, our knowledge of the actual dimensions of the problem leave much to be desired. As was pointed out in Chapter 1, our statistics on unemployment are based upon a monthly survey of 35,000 households, the results of which are extrapolated for the economy as a whole. As a result of data made available by the 1970 census, this survey procedure is now in process of being improved. The changes include redesignation of primary sampling units, new sample selection and design, reweighting of the sample, and introduction of new population controls. Preliminary figures indicate that the 1970 census will increase the estimates of civilian noninstitutional population 16 years old and over by approximately

---

[2] G. P. Green and J. F. Stinson, "Employment and Unemployment in 1971," *Monthly Labor Review*, Vol. 95 (February 1972), p. 25.

[3] *Monthly Labor Review*, Vol. 95 (February 1972), Table 6, p. 100.

[4] John E. Bregger, "Unemployment Statistics and What They Mean," *Monthly Labor Review*, Vol. 94 (November 1971), p. 23.

[5] *Ibid.*, p. 25.

[6] *Economic Report of the President, 1972* (Washington, D.C.: U.S. Government Printing Office, 1972), p. 224.

775,000 and of the civilian labor force and total employment levels by a little over 300,000 compared to prior estimates. Estimates of unemployment levels will be virtually unchanged, and there will be no effect upon percent distributions within age groups or on labor force participation and unemployment rates of individual groups.[7] Although the 1970 census seems to confirm prior estimates of unemployment rates in the economy, some economists nevertheless maintain that sample-based statistics are inadequate for the purpose and should be supplemented with a biennial Census of Unemployment.

A further criticism directed at the statistics is that the particular definitions adopted in the survey understate the true volume of unemployment in the nation by failing to take account of the so-called "invisible unemployed" who are not counted in official unemployment statistics. The invisible unemployed fall into four major categories:

1. Persons who are working part time but would like full-time work if they could find it. The extra hours these men and women would work if they could find full-time employment represent a surplus of labor which is not reflected in official statistics. The reason is that the government figures include in the "employed" category anyone who has worked at least one hour for pay in the week preceding the survey. In 1971, there were almost 2.5 million workers on part time for economic reasons, of whom about 1.2 million normally work full time but were unable to find full-time employment.[8]

2. Seasonal workers who would like year-round employment if they could get it. The Bureau of Census does not even include in the labor force seasonal workers who were neither working nor seeking work in the survey week. While many in this group may desire employment only on a seasonal basis, there are undoubtedly many others who would prefer year-round employment but do not even bother to look for it because of their belief, based on past experience, that there are no job opportunities for their particular skills.

3. A broader group of persons (including some seasonal workers) who are often referred to as "discouraged workers." These persons are outside the labor force primarily because they believe that it would be futile to look for a job, but they are available for, and would like, work now. However, since such persons would answer in a survey that they are not looking for a job, they would normally be excluded from total labor force statistics.

---

[7] *Monthly Labor Review,* Vol. 95 (February 1972), p. 97.

[8] U.S. Department of Labor, *Manpower Report, of the President, 1972* (Washington, D.C.: U.S. Government Printing Office, 1972), p. 190. Persons on part-time work for economic reasons include those who worked less than 35 hours during the survey week because of slack work, job changing during the week, material shortages, or inability to find full-time work.

FIGURE 14–1

Trends in Total Unemployment and Discouraged Workers, 1967–71 (seasonally adjusted)

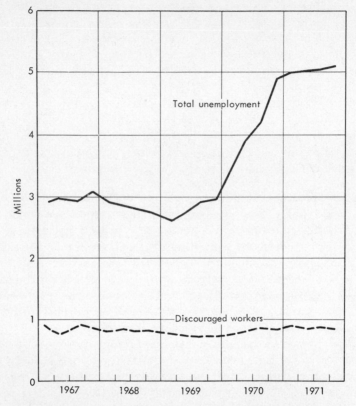

Source: Gloria P. Green and John F. Stinson, "Employment and Unemployment in 1971," *Monthly Labor Review*, Vol. 95 (February 1972), p. 26.

The U.S. Department of Labor maintains a series which purports to measure the number of such "discouraged workers." Although the number of persons in this category has risen in recent years, averaging 775,000 in 1971,[9] the number has tended to fall as a percentage of the total amount of unemployment (see Figure 14–1). This is rather surprising because one would have expected that the sharp increase in unemployment which characterized the 1970–71 recession would have led many persons temporarily to give up looking for a job. Most discouraged workers are women and teen-agers who may be under less economic pressure than adult males to persist in a seemingly futile job hunt. In 1971, these two groups constituted three quarters of all discouraged workers.[10] Also included in this group are retired persons who

---

[9] *Manpower Report, 1972,* p. 38.
[10] *Ibid.*

might take jobs if the right kind of employment were available and persons with limited education or skills who come into the labor market only when jobs are so abundant that their handicaps are overlooked.

4. Persons with physical handicaps. These persons are treated as unemployable rather than unemployed and are excluded from the labor force figure. Experience during World War II, however, taught employers that there is a definite place in industry for the blind, the maimed, and the crippled. The U.S. Department of Labor has estimated that there are about 5 to 7 million handicapped workers who could be placed in industrial occupations. In considering statistics of unemployment, it is important to bear in mind that concepts of employability alter with the changing needs of the economy and that tomorrow we may consider persons to be unemployed who today are deemed unemployable.

It is apparent that inclusion of some or all of the so-called "invisible unemployed" in unemployment statistics would give an entirely different picture of our needs for the future in terms of providing new jobs. To this number we could also add those who are "unemployed" on a *qualitative* basis—i.e., a person with a college degree who for one reason or another may be compelled to take a job which does not utilize his skills. Undoubtedly there are great numbers of our workers—white and nonwhite —who fall in this category which might better be called "underemployment."

The existence of the invisible unemployed complicates the problem of devising a policy to reduce unemployment. As we have mentioned, in 1971, 5 million persons were classified as unemployed under the official statistics. As government moves through appropriate monetary, fiscal, and manpower policy to reduce this figure, it finds that it is to some extent on a treadmill. For the more successful it is in expanding the demand for jobs and reducing the supply of unemployed labor, the more likely are the members of the invisible unemployed to seek jobs in the labor market. Another way of saying this is that the labor force participation rate tends to increase when jobs are plentiful and wages are high. Furthermore, employment of the invisible unemployed may further accelerate the rise in unit labor costs which currently faces the economy, since it is likely that members of this group, because of lack of training and job experience, are less productive than members of the regular labor force.

THE CHANGING INCIDENCE OF UNEMPLOYMENT

Although at this writing the economy is experiencing the highest unemployment rate in the past 10 years, the impact of unemployment upon the economy has been far different from its impact in earlier years. If we compare 1971 with 1961—the last previous year in which unemployment climbed over 6%—we find that in 1971 men 25 years and over accounted for 29% of the unemployed, whereas in 1961 men in this age group accounted for 44% of total unemployment. Table 14–1 indicates how the changing composition of the labor force has been associated with changes in unemployment rates between 1961 and 1971. The larger proportion of women and teen-age unemployment and the smaller ratio of adult male unemployment results from structural changes which have occurred in the labor force, primarily the coming of age of the "baby boom" offspring, the increase in the participation of women in the labor

TABLE 14–1

Composition of the Civilian Labor Force and Unemployment by Sex and Age, Annual Averages, 1961 and 1971 (numbers in thousands)

Sex and age	Civilian labor force		Unemployment		
	Number	Percent distri- bution	Number	Percent distri- bution	Rate
1961					
Total 16 years and over__	70,460	100.0	4,714	100.0	6.7
Men 20 years and over___	43,860	62.2	2,518	53.4	5.7
20–24 years_____	4,253	6.0	458	9.7	10.8
25 years and over___	39,605	56.2	2,061	43.7	5.2
Women 20 years and over_	21,664	30.7	1,368	29.0	6.3
20–24 years_____	2,697	3.8	265	5.6	9.8
25 years and over___	18,967	26.9	1,103	23.4	5.8
Both sexes, 16–19 years__	4,936	7.0	828	17.6	16.8
Married men_____	36,259	51.5	1,676	35.5	4.6
1971					
Total 16 years and over__	84,113	100.0	4,993	100.0	5.9
Men 20 years and over___	47,861	56.9	2,086	41.8	4.4
20–24 years_____	6,194	7.4	635	12.7	10.3
25 years and over___	41,666	49.5	1,451	29.1	3.5
Women 20 years and over_	28,799	34.2	1,650	33.0	5.7
20–24 years_____	5,071	6.0	486	9.7	9.6
25 years and over___	23,728	28.2	1,164	23.3	4.9
Both sexes, 16–19 years__	7,453	8.9	1,257	25.2	16.9
Married men_____	39,183	46.6	1,251	25.1	3.2

Source: *Monthly Labor Review*, Vol. 95 (February 1972), p. 27.

force, and the increase in the number of students seeking part-time work. Particularly striking is the fact that whereas in 1961 teen-agers accounted for only one of every six unemployed, by 1971 their ratio had risen to one out of every four unemployed.[11]

Another significant change in the incidence of unemployment can be observed in its impact by occupation and industry. In 1971, workers in blue-collar occupations accounted for 44% of total unemployment, compared to 51% in 1961. This decline is in part a reflection of the contraction in the numbers of blue-collar employees over the decade. However, it is also true that the unemployment rate for the blue-collar workers as a

[11] *Manpower Report, 1972*, p. 40.

group was significantly lower in 1971 than in 1961, although still above the jobless rate for all workers.[12] The 1971 recession bore especially hard upon professional and technical personnel, particularly those employed in aerospace and defense-related companies. For example, the 1971 jobless rate for professional workers, although only 2.9%, was up nearly a full percentage point from 1970 and was at the highest level ever recorded by the U.S. Bureau of Labor Statistics.[13]

The industrial composition of unemployment in 1971 also differed somewhat from that in 1961. Workers who held their last jobs in service-producing industries, including government, represented a larger proportion of the unemployed in 1971 than in 1961, reflecting the rapid expansion of employment in these industries over the intervening decade. However, manufacturing and construction workers still bore the brunt of unemployment in 1971, although to a lesser extent than in 1961.[14]

The change which has occurred in the structure of employment and unemployment over the past decade has had an effect upon the volume of long-term joblessness in the American economy. In 1971, there were 1.2 million persons unemployed 15 weeks or longer out of total unemployment of about 5 million, or 24%. In 1961, there were 1.5 million unemployed for over 15 weeks out of total unemployment of 4.8 million, or 31%.[15] A major reason for this decline is the increasing importance of young workers and women in the labor force. These two groups typically have high job turnover, high mobility, and relatively short durations of unemployment. As these two groups have come to represent a larger segment of the labor force, there has been an increase in the relative number of workers who experience unemployment for short periods of time, and thus the proportion which long-term jobless represent of all unemployed workers has declined.

In summary, the structural shifts in the labor force during the past decade—toward more women and teen-agers and a lower proportion of adult male workers—have altered the composition of unemployment and also affected its duration and overall rate. It has been estimated that if the age-sex distribution of the labor force had been the same in 1971 as it was in 1961, the overall unemployment rate would have been 5.5% in 1971, rather than 5.9% (assuming that the rates for each age-sex group were the same as those actually recorded in 1971).[16]

To put the matter a different way, the changing composition of the labor force can produce a gradually increasing rate of unemployment *even though business activity is maintained at a high level.* One estimate concludes that the unemployment rate would have risen from 4.1% in

---

[12] *Ibid.,* p. 42.

[13] *Wall Street Journal,* January 17, 1972, p. 1.

[14] *Manpower Report, 1972,* p. 42.

[15] Data derived from *ibid.,* Table A–23, p. 187, and Table A–22, p. 185.

[16] *Ibid.,* p. 43.

1956 to 4.5% in 1971 even if the rate of unemployment had stayed constant at its 1956 level[17] (1956 was selected as a base year because it was a peacetime year with almost normal—4.1%—unemployment).

The changing composition of the work force which can produce this "creeping unemployment" can obviously make our national goal to reduce unemployment much more difficult to achieve in the future. Much will depend upon the trend in labor force participation by women. It is possible that movements such as "women's lib," a continuing rise in the median age at which women marry, the decline in the birthrate and the increased educational attainment of women will lead to a continuation of existing trends toward the participation by women in the labor force. On the other hand, the U.S. Bureau of Labor Statistics projects a slightly lower participation rate for women in 1975 than in 1970.[18] Furthermore, lengthening periods of education for youth may tend to reduce their participation in the labor force. The Council of Economic Advisers has concluded that by 1985 these factors and further changes in the age stratification of the population will produce changes in the composition of the labor force which will operate in the direction of reducing overall unemployment rates.[19]

Unemployment amid Labor Shortages

One of the paradoxes of the labor market today is that despite a 6% unemployment rate it is still difficult to hire a good plumber or repairman or painter. One has only to look at the jobs advertised in newspapers which appear day after day to realize that there is a lack of balance between the kinds of workers who are looking for jobs and the kinds of jobs that are available. The nature of this imbalance can be better understood by looking again at the composition of unemployment.

In December 1971, there were 5,216,000 persons unemployed in the American economy. These persons can be classified in age-sex groups as follows:[20]

> Males, 20 years and over..................... 2,141,000
> Females, 20 years and over.................. 1,710,000
> All teen-agers (16–19 years)................ 1,365,000

As can be seen from these data, teen-agers and females account for 59% of the total volume of unemployment. The significant fact about unemployment for these two groups is that to some extent it represents a state of mind, whereas for the adult male it usually represents a harsh fact.

---

[17] *Economic Report of the President, 1972*, Table 25, p. 115.

[18] U.S. Department of Labor, Bureau of Labor Statistics, *The U.S. Labor Force: Projections to 1985* (Special Labor Force Report 119 [Washington, D.C., February 1970]), p. A–4..

[19] *Economic Report of the President, 1972*, p. 115.

[20] Green and Stinson, "Employment and Unemployment, 1971," p. 25.

Unemployment for the adult male normally means that he has been employed and lost his job. On the other hand, for teen-agers and females, unemployment, as recorded in the official statistics, may simply indicate a change in state of mind. Thus, if a married woman who has not been working decides that she would like to get a part-time job, this decision converts her from a person who formerly was outside of the labor force to one who is now unemployed (assuming that the change in state of mind was also associated with some specific job-seeking activity).

This is not to minimize the importance of finding jobs for teen-agers and females. Lack of employment may compel the teen-ager to leave college and may impose real hardships on the woman who is the sole source of support for her family. The significant fact, however, is that unemployment among these two groups is represented to a large degree by persons who are merely seeking jobs and may never have worked before. For example, in November 1971, 44% of the jobless adult women had actually been out of the labor market for some time and had only recently decided to work again, but had been unable to find jobs to their liking.[21] The teen-ager who is looking for a part-time job after school is counted with the same weight in the unemployment statistics as the adult male who has lost his job. The December 1971 jobless rate for teen-agers was over 17%; the rate for adult males was only 4.4% and for married men only 3.3%[22]—yet official statistics in effect average all these rates together to compile the overall rate. Such a procedure obviously gives to the high teen-age unemployment rate an impact quite out of line with the true significance of this group in the labor market.

This analysis indicates that the labor market employment situation is actually considerably tighter than overall statistics would seem to indicate. Unemployment is concentrated among groups who to a large extent are new entrants and therefore lack skills and training which match the needs of the marketplace. This growing disparity has developed despite the fact that new entrants are better educated than ever before in our history. Unfortunately, education is not the equivalent of job training. As a matter of fact, the U.S. Department of Labor has warned that "the job mix and education mix are . . . out of balance" and that new kinds of jobs will be needed in order to provide employment for the growing numbers of high school graduates.[23] It is apparent that manpower training and manpower policy will be of increasing importance in the years ahead if we are to achieve any substantial success in reducing overall unemployment rates. Current efforts of the federal government in this area will be discussed in Chapter 15.

---

[21] *Wall Street Journal*, January 17, 1972, p. 1.

[22] *Ibid.*

[23] U.S. Department of Labor, Bureau of Labor Statistics, *Educational Attainment of Workers, March 1969 and 1970* (Washington, D.C., October 1970), p. 15.

WHO ARE THE UNEMPLOYED?

Statistics of unemployment are made by individuals. Who are the unemployed? Who is the typical unemployed person? What are the conditions or circumstances which typify the bulk of our unemployment?

Unskilled Workers

The unemployed person is likely to be unskilled. As can be seen from Table 14–2, the unemployment rate for nonfarm laborers is greater than for any other group in the labor market. This is true year after year without variation. The second highest rate is usually that of operatives and kindred semiskilled workers. By contrast, the rate for professional, technical, and managerial personnel has until recently generally averaged less than 1.5%. The composition of unemployment since 1970 has been unique because of the high rate of unemployment among professional and technical personnel. This rate rose from 1.3% in 1969 to 2.0% in 1970 to 2.9% in 1971, the latter being the highest level ever recorded for this group.[24] The high rate of unemployment reflected sharp cutbacks in defense and aerospace production and in government-financed research.

Youth

Unemployment has always been substantially higher among young persons than among adults. Teen-agers, for example, include a large proportion of new entrants into the labor market, and they customarily have a period of unemployment associated with "shopping around" for satisfactory positions. Frequently they begin their working careers by taking part-time jobs which may be temporary or seasonal. Young people, since they have fewer family commitments than older workers, change their jobs more frequently in search for the "right" job. Furthermore, they tend to be more vulnerable to layoffs because of inexperience and lack of seniority.

In the past few years, however, the sharp increase in the incidence of unemployment among this group has created a problem of grave concern to our nation. The rate of unemployment among men and women 16–19 years of age has risen from 12.2% in 1969 to 15.3% in 1970 to 16.9% in 1971.[25] During the same period, the unemployment rate among Negro males and females aged 16–19 (and those of other races) increased from 24% to 31.7%.[26] With one out of every three black youth unemployed,

---

[24] Green and Stinson, "Employment and Unemployment, 1971," p. 25.

[25] *Ibid.*, Table 2, p. 23.

[26] *Ibid.*

TABLE 14-2

Unemployment Rates by Industry and Occupational Groups, 1969-71

Industry and occupational groups	Annual averages			Seasonally adjusted quarterly averages								
				1969	1970				1971			
	1969	1970	1971	4th	1st	2d	3d	4th	1st	2d	3d	4th
INDUSTRY												
Private, nonagricultural wage and salary workers [1]	3.5	5.2	6.2	3.7	4.3	5.0	5.6	6.3	6.3	6.3	6.2	6.2
Construction	6.0	9.7	10.4	6.4	7.8	10.3	11.7	10.9	11.0	10.4	9.9	10.2
Manufacturing	3.3	5.6	6.8	3.7	4.4	5.1	5.9	7.2	7.0	6.8	6.8	6.7
Durable goods	3.0	5.7	7.0	3.6	4.4	5.0	5.9	7.8	7.2	7.2	6.8	6.9
Nondurable goods	3.7	5.4	6.5	4.0	4.3	5.2	5.9	6.4	6.6	6.2	6.8	6.4
Transportation and public utilities	2.2	3.2	3.8	2.5	2.8	3.3	3.2	3.7	4.0	3.9	3.2	4.3
Wholesale and retail trade	4.1	5.3	6.4	4.1	4.6	5.3	5.5	6.2	6.3	6.7	6.3	6.4
Finance and service industries	3.2	4.2	5.1	3.1	3.4	4.0	4.6	4.8	5.0	5.0	5.3	5.0
Government wage and salary	1.9	2.2	2.9	2.1	2.1	2.1	2.1	2.8	2.8	2.8	3.0	3.3
Agricultural wage and salary	6.1	7.5	7.9	6.2	6.4	7.0	8.3	9.0	8.3	6.5	8.8	8.0
OCCUPATION												
White-collar workers	2.1	2.8	3.5	2.2	2.4	2.8	2.9	3.5	3.6	3.5	3.5	3.5
Professional and technical	1.3	2.0	2.9	1.5	1.8	1.9	2.0	2.5	3.2	2.9	2.8	3.0
Managers and administrators except farm	.9	1.3	1.6	1.0	1.0	1.3	1.5	1.6	1.6	1.6	1.6	1.8
Clerical workers	3.0	4.0	4.8	3.1	3.3	4.0	4.1	4.9	4.8	4.9	4.8	4.8
Sales workers	2.9	3.9	4.4	2.8	3.2	3.9	3.9	4.7	4.2	4.7	4.4	4.0
Blue-collar workers	3.9	6.2	7.4	4.3	5.0	6.0	6.9	7.5	7.5	7.3	7.6	7.4
Craftsmen and foremen	2.2	3.8	4.7	2.3	2.7	3.8	4.7	4.5	4.5	4.1	5.5	4.6
Operatives	4.4	7.1	8.3	5.0	5.7	6.6	7.5	8.7	8.5	8.5	8.2	8.2
Nonfarm laborers	6.7	9.5	10.8	7.1	7.9	9.3	10.3	10.8	10.7	10.3	10.4	11.4
Service workers	4.2	5.3	6.3	4.7	4.7	5.0	5.0	6.0	6.1	6.3	6.6	6.4
Farm workers	1.9	2.6	2.6	2.0	2.1	2.5	3.0	3.0	2.9	2.0	2.8	2.7

1 Includes mining, not shown separately.

Source: G. P. Green and J. F. Stinson, "Employment and Unemployment in 1971," *Monthly Labor Review*, Vol. 95 (February 1972), Table 4, p. 25.

the potential for violence and juvenile delinquency in our central cities is greatly magnified. Because of a bulge in the curve of population growth, the number of young blacks aged 14 to 24 is increasing about twice as fast as the total black population of our central cities.[27] At the same time, the reduced calls for the draft will make the surplus of youth in the civilian labor market even more acute. It is indeed paradoxical that the United States keeps larger proportions of its children in school longer than does any other nation to insure their preparation for productive lifetime activity, yet the unemployment rate among youth is far higher in the United States than in any other industrial nation.

Unless productive employment can be found for the youth of our nation, we shall reap a bitter social harvest of unrest and delinquency. Alleviation of this problem may require revision of our minimum wage laws to provide exemptions for youth and increased emphasis upon vocational education in our high schools, as discussed in Chapter 16.

A special category of young worker deserving of our attention is the Vietnam veteran returning to civilian life. In February 1972, about 4.1 million Vietnam veterans were in the labor force; 3.7 million held jobs and 400,000 were unemployed.[28] The unemployment rate among young veterans aged 20–29 years was 9.7% compared to 8.7% for nonveterans of the same age group.[29] This 1% differential represents an improvement over the situation which existed in February 1971, when the unemployment rate for the same age group of veterans was 11.1% versus 8.7% for non-veterans.[30]

It would be expected that unemployment rates for veterans would exceed those for nonveterans. In the first place, most nonveterans already had jobs, while the young veterans were entering the civilian labor force just as jobs were becoming harder to find during the business slowdown. Furthermore, Vietnam veterans may receive unemployment insurance payments regardless of their prior work experience, and this cushion may influence them to continue searching until they find the right job. On the other hand, many young nonveterans may not have enough wage credits to obtain unemployment compensation while they look for work, and therefore they may be more inclined to take any job available. Despite the improvement in veteran employment, there is still a need for continuation of training and placement efforts to insure that these men and women can take a productive place in the civilian labor market.

---

[27] *Report of the National Advisory Commission on Civil Disorders* (New York: Bantam Books, Inc., Publishers, 1968), p. 269.

[28] U.S. Department of Labor, *Employment and Earnings*, Vol. 18 (March 1972), p. 3.

[29] *Ibid.*

[30] *Ibid.*

The Uneducated

The relationship between education and unemployment must be approached with caution because apparent correlations may in fact be attributable to causes other than the lack of education. For example, data for 1969 indicate that the rate of unemployment for workers 18 years and over with 9 years or less of education was only 3.8% while the rate for those with 1–3 years of high school was 4.9%.[31] Does this mean that the more education a worker has, the more likely he is to be unemployed? The answer is no. The comparison actually involves two quite different groups of workers. Persons in the former category tend to be more mature older workers who completed their formal education 10 years or more ago and have since acquired the skills and experience necessary to maintain stable jobs. The latter group includes the high school dropouts who have neither the education, the skills, and possibly not even the motivation, to find permanent jobs in the labor market.

In general, however, broad statistical comparisons of unemployed and employed tend to show higher unemployment rates for the group with lesser educational attainment. One reason is that workers with minimum educational achievements tend to be employed as blue-collar workers, laborers, and in various occupations which are more exposed to the vicissitudes of the business cycle. Over the past decade, however, the relative advantage of education as insurance against unemployment has tended to diminish. For example, in 1959 the median education of the employed was 12 years and of the unemployed 9.9 years. Since then, the average education of the unemployed has risen, so that by 1971 the difference between the median education of the employed (12.4) and the unemployed (12.2) no longer had statistical significance.[32] The increase in the unemployment rate for well-educated persons in recent years reflects, on the one hand, the high jobless rate among engineers, technical personnel, and other white-collar workers associated with aerospace and defense industries and, on the other hand, the high rate of unemployment among young high school graduates.

The college graduate in our society can still look forward to a career marked by less unemployment than the high school graduate, primarily because of the difference in occupations to which the two groups will gravitate. Nevertheless, recent trends lend support to the thesis that the education mix and the job mix may be out of balance. Today, the history major with a Ph.D may have as much difficulty in finding a job as the high school dropout!

---

[31] U.S. Department of Labor, *Educational Attainment of Workers*, p. 13.

[32] William V. Deutermann, "Educational Attainment of Workers, March 1971," *Monthly Labor Review*, Vol. 94 (November 1971), p. 31.

Older Workers

Unemployment among older workers poses a special problem. The difficulty is not so much in the rate of unemployment as in its duration once it occurs. In 1970, men aged 45–54 had a lower unemployment rate than any other age group.[33] Older workers are less likely to lose their jobs than younger employees because they are protected by seniority rights, but when they do become unemployed, they have a serious problem in finding a new job. Frequently they are the victims of a plant shutdown and find that their only skill has become obsolete. Long-time ties to family and community render them less mobile than younger workers, so they often stay on in depressed areas, even though there is little likelihood of finding a new job there. As a result, their average duration of unemployment once it occurs tends to be long. In 1970, the average duration of unemployment for men 45 years of age and over was nearly double that of young men under 25 years of age. About 28 of every 100 unemployed men over 45 had been looking for work for 15 weeks or longer, compared to 19 of every 100 unemployed men aged 20 to 24. The longest duration of unemployment characterizes men over 65, who in 1970 had an average duration of unemployment of 17.4 weeks compared to the average for men over 16 of 9.5 weeks.[34] Many older workers, still short of retirement, may simply stop looking for work after a time and therefore do not even get counted as unemployed under the Bureau of Census definitions.

Black Workers

The unemployment rate for whites and nonwhites declined continually during the decade of the 1960s. In 1970 and 1971, rates again turned upward. However, black unemployment did not increase as rapidly as white unemployment, and therefore in 1970—for the first time since 1953—the ratio of black to white unemployment fell below the 2 to 1 ratio. Although the rate of unemployment for black adult workers has fallen since 1960, the rate for black teen-agers is higher than it was a decade earlier (see Table 14.3).

A number of factors have played a role in the narrowing of the black-white unemployment rate. The 1970–71 slowdown in employment growth hit particularly hard at sophisticated aerospace and other technically oriented companies, where white employment was disproportionately high. Relatively few layoffs occurred in government and service industries where black employment is concentrated. Secondly, labor force participation rates for black youth between the ages of 16 and 24

---

[33] U.S. Department of Labor, Bureau of Labor Statistics, *The Employment Problems of Older Workers* (Bulletin No. 1721 [Washington, D.C., 1971], p. 6.
[34] *Ibid.*

fell at the same time that rates for white young persons were rising.[35] This decline was probably an indication that a disproportionate number of young black workers were becoming discouraged over job prospects as a result of the high rate of unemployment among their age group and were leaving the labor force.

In attempting to determine the full incidence of unemployment on the black population, it is important to remember, as we indicated in our earlier discussion in this chapter, that conventional definitions and surveys used for measurement of unemployment may tend to underestimate

TABLE 14–3

Unemployment Rates, by Sex and Age: 1960 and 1968 to 1970 (annual averages)

Subject	Negro and Other Races				White			
	1960	1968	1969	1970	1960	1968	1969	1970
Total.............	10.2	6.7	6.5	8.2	4.9	3.2	3.2	4.5
Adult men..............	9.6	3.9	3.7	5.6	4.2	2.0	1.9	3.2
Adult women............	8.3	6.3	5.8	6.9	4.6	3.4	3.4	4.4
Teen-agers*.............	24.4	25.0	24.4	29.1	13.4	11.0	10.8	13.5

° "Teen-agers" include persons 16 to 19 years old.
Source: U.S. Department of Labor, Bureau of Labor Statistics, *The Social and Economic Status of Negroes in the United States, 1970*, (BLS Report No. 394 (Washington, D.C., July 1971), p. 49.

the true amount of black unemployment. As a matter of fact, the Census Bureau estimates that its Current Population Survey misses about 13% of the nonwhite population of working age compared with about 2% of the white. The Bureau estimates that the undercount is greatest among nonwhite men in the prime working years. If unemployment rates for the undercounted are twice those for the counted, the undercount could change the total unemployment rate for nonwhites by about one half of 1%.[36] Likewise, since the Census Survey lists anyone who worked *at all* during the survey week as being "employed," official estimates undoubtedly understate the real impact of underemployment on blacks, many of whom are compelled to take part-time work even though they would prefer full-time employment.

The proportion of persons of working age who neither work nor look for work is another indication of inequality of opportunity, since discouragement in finding jobs is an important reason given by blacks for remaining outside the labor force. Discouragement over job prospects

[35] U.S. Department of Labor, Bureau of Labor Statistics, *The Negro Employment Situation* (Report No. 391 [Washington, D.C., 1971]), p. 5.

[36] U.S. Department of Labor, Bureau of Labor Statistics, *Social and Economic Conditions of Negroes in the United States* (Report No. 332 [Washington, D.C., 1967]), p. 38.

TABLE 14–4

Negro and Other Races as a Percent of All Workers in Selected Occupations: 1960 and 1970

Occupation	*1960*	*1970*
Total, employed....................	11	11
Professional and technical..................	4	7
Medical and other health.................	4	8
Teachers, except college.................	7	10
Managers, officials, and proprietors..........	3	4
Clerical...............................	5	8
Sales..................................	2	4
Craftsmen and foremen....................	5	7
Construction craftsmen..................	7	7
Machinists, jobsetters, and other metal craftsmen.........................	4	6
Foremen.............................	2	5
Operatives.............................	12	14
Durable goods.........................	10	14
Nondurable goods......................	9	15
Nonfarm laborers........................	27	23
Private household workers..................	50	42
Other service workers.....................	20	19
Protective services.....................	5	8
Waiters, cooks, and bartenders............	15	13
Farmers and farm workers.................	16	11

Source: U.S. Department of Labor, Bureau of Labor Statistics, *The
Social and Economic Status of Negroes in the United States, 1970*
(BLS Report No. 394 [Washington, D.C., July 1971]), Table 49, p. 61.

is typically more marked among blacks than whites. In 1971, blacks who
constitute about 11% of the civilian labor force made up about one
fourth of all discouraged workers.[37]

A number of reasons have been advanced for the high unemployment
rate among nonwhite workers. A major cause is their heavy concentration in occupations such as unskilled farm and nonfarm labor, semiskilled
production jobs, and service work where there is typically a great deal
of unemployment. Today blacks hold 23% of all nonfarm laboring jobs
but only 8% of clerical jobs (see Table 14–4). Despite considerable
progress during the past decade, almost two fifths of black men and almost one half of black women in 1970 were employed in service, laboring, or farm jobs.[38] Furthermore, within each broad occupational group,
unemployment is substantially higher for nonwhite workers because
they tend to be near the bottom of the ladder in terms of skill and
seniority.

[37] Green and Stinson, "Employment and Unemployment, 1971," p. 26.

[38] U.S. Department of Labor, Bureau of Labor Statistics, *The Social and Economic
Status of Negroes in the United States, 1970* (BLS Report No. 394 [Washington,
D.C., July 1971]), Table 48, p. 60.

Lack of education is another major cause for the high incidence of unemployment among nonwhites. The nonwhite worker frequently comes from a poor family and is compelled to leave school early in order to supplement family income. Lack of skills plus discriminatory hiring practices then force him into unskilled low-paying jobs which fluctuate most with the business cycle. Fortunately, substantial improvement has been made in educational attainments of nonwhite workers in the past decade. The median education of black workers in October 1952 was 7.6 years compared to 11.4 years of white workers. By March 1970, the median for blacks had advanced to 11.7 years and stood only 0.7 years behind whites.[39] The educational gap is most apparent among older workers. Therefore, as young, better-educated entrants to the labor force take their place in industry, the differential in years of education—although not necessarily in quality of education—will tend to narrow further.

However, statistics of years in school are not a very meaningful index of educational achievement when comparisons are being made between inner city and suburban schools. Public schools in the slum areas of large cities typically lag behind national educational norms. Many black graduates or inner city high schools have major deficiencies in the three R's—as do white graduates as well. However, education has much more of a payoff for whites who come from slum areas than for blacks. A recent study indicated that the weekly wage of white high school graduates in slum areas was nearly $25 higher than that of whites who had not attended high school; for blacks the difference was only $8. In terms of median salaries, a high school education was found to have three times as high a payoff for whites as for blacks.[40]

There is no simple answer to the problem of black unemployment. It must be attached on a broad front. Success in reducing the rate of unemployment depends upon the degree of cooperation forthcoming from both business and organized labor, both of whom have been guilty of discriminatory practices. It is apparent that even if all blacks who want to work were given jobs, their rate of unemployment would be disproportionately high as long as they were concentrated in industries and occupations which have the least stability over the business cycle. Better education and improved training, therefore, are essential to any real solution of this problem.

OCCUPATIONAL CHARACTERISTICS OF THE UNEMPLOYED

In some occupations, unemployment is part of the normal routine of the ebb and flow of work. Take, for example, the construction industry,

---

[39] U.S. Department of Labor, *Educational Attainment of Workers*, p. 11.

[40] *Manpower Report, 1971*, p. 93.

which has an unemployment rate almost twice the rate for all workers (see Table 14–2). Construction is subject to sharp seasonal swings; projects are short term, and the worker has only a passing attachment to any particular employer. The high hourly rates paid in this industry are intended to compensate workers—in part, at least—for the loss of income they regularly suffer in the intervals between jobs.

On the other hand, the high rate of unemployment among mine workers reflects a long-term reduction in jobs attributable to mechanization and competition from other products. Many mine workers are reluctant to leave their communities when they lose their jobs; as a result, they become part of a long-term unemployed hard core clustered in depressed areas.

In manufacturing, fluctuations in employment are closely tied to the level of activity in the particular industry and to the stage of the general business cycle. The automobile industry is an example of an industry which is subject to major swings in demand by consumers and in which employment fluctuates from month to month and from year to year.

In Chapter 1, we commented on the shift in employment that is occurring between goods-producing and service-producing industries. As service-oriented employment grows in our economy, it will tend to introduce a greater degree of employment stability over the cycle than formerly existed when a greater proportion of persons were employed as production workers in goods-producing industries. Industries such as construction, mining, and nondurable goods manufacturing had unemployment rates in 1971 higher than the average for the entire private economy.

Furthermore, as can be seen from Table 14–2, white-collar workers have unemployment rates about half that of blue-collar workers. The shift in employment from blue- to white-collar workers should also tend to stabilize employment.

THE LOCATION OF UNEMPLOYMENT

One of the characteristics of our unemployment problem is pockets of unemployment that persist in various depressed areas of the country. For example, Appalachia comes to mind as a region which continues to have persistent unemployment reflecting the effects of the migration from the area of coal-mining and the lack of any other industry to take up the slack in manpower. While Appalachia is more than half rural, many urban areas are also trouble spots. As of January 1972, there were 863 areas in the United States classified by the U.S. Department of Labor as areas of "substantial or persistent unemployment."[41]

---

[41] U.S. Department of Labor, Manpower Administration, *Area Trends in Employment and Unemployment* (January 1972), p. 2.

Classification by the Labor Department of areas with respect to their degree of unemployment is based upon the following technical definitions:

Substantial Unemployment: An area is placed in this category when:
1. Unemployment in the area is equal to 6% or more of its work force, discounting seasonal or temporary factors, and
2. It is anticipated that the rate of unemployment during the next two months will remain at 6% or more, discounting seasonal or temporary factors.

Persistent Unemployment: An area is placed in this category when:
1. Unemployment in the area is equal to 6% or more of its work force and has been at least 50% above the national average for 3 of the preceding 4 calendar years; or
2. Unemployment is 6% or more and has been at least 75% above the national average for 2 of 3 preceding calendar years; or
3. Unemployment is 6% or more and has been at least 100% above the national average for 1 of the 2 preceding calendar years.[42]

Persistent unemployment areas are potentially eligible for all types of assistance under the Public Works and Economic Development Act. The number of areas included in the persistent unemployment class, as of early 1972, attests to the difficulty the nation faces in achieving a major reduction in unemployment levels.

Unemployment in the Cities

In the last few years, Americans have suddenly become aware that their large central cities are literally decaying. Poverty, crime, disease, inadequate housing, and unemployment—all of these seem to have crowded into the central cities. The problem of the central cities has been further complicated by the gravitation of large numbers of blacks to these areas, while white workers and their families moved to the suburbs. In 1960, 53% of blacks and only 32% of whites lived in central cities. By 1970, the percentage of the black population which lives in central cities had risen to 58%, while that for whites fell to 28%.[43] Within metropolitan areas, the degree of concentration is even higher. In such areas, about 60% of all whites live in suburbs while close to 80% of the blacks live in central cities.[44]

The great majority of the nation's unemployed are concentrated in metropolitan areas (see Figure 14–2) with high rates of unemployment among Negroes, among youth, and above all among Negro youth. The unemployment rate for Negro teen-agers in central cities was 32% in

[42] See *Ibid.,* p. 5.
[43] *Social and Economic Status of Negroes,* Table 7, p. 13.
[44] *Manpower Report, 1971,* p. 84.

1970, more than six times the national average.[45] Nearly three fourths of all Negro unemployed are concentrated in metropolitan areas, with the great majority in the central cities. (see Figure 14–2).

Unemployment rates characteristically rise as one moves from the suburbs to the central city to urban poverty neighborhoods. In 1970, the relationship between unemployment rates in these three subdivisions of metropolitan areas was as shown in the following table.

	White	Negro
Suburbs	4.5	7.4
Central cities	4.9	8.3
Poverty neighborhoods*	6.3	9.5

* The poverty neighborhood classification adopted by the U.S. Bureau of Labor Statistics is based on a ranking of census tracts according to 1960 data on income, education, skills, housing, and proportion of broken families. The poorest one fifth of these tracts in the nation's 100 largest metropolitan areas are considered poverty neighborhoods.
Source: *Manpower Report of the President, 1971,* Table 2, p. 87.

Negroes, Puerto Ricans, and other minority groups are heavily concentrated in poverty neighborhoods of our central cities. In New York City, for example, the latest census data indicate that about 82% of the Negro population in 1970 lived in the 26 officially designated poverty areas. During the decade of the sixties, there was an outflow of 1 million non-Puerto Rican whites from these poverty areas, while at the same time the black population of such depressed neighborhoods grew by more than 380,000.[46]

Why is unemployment higher in our central cities than in our suburban areas. The answer is not to be found in a numerical lack of jobs. The fact is that most central cities have a larger total number of jobs than the rest of the metropolitan area in which they are located. Furthermore, the percentage of jobs located in central cities is generally greater than the percentage of the area's population living there. Many suburban residents commute to jobs in the central city, but there is little reverse commutation to the expanding employment centers in the suburbs.

The primary problem of the job market in the central city is the lack of correspondence between the job requirements and the skills available among central city residents. The businesses which have been growing in the central cities—finance, insurance, real estate, business service, etc.— require a preponderance of white-collar employees, professional, administrative, and clerical. At the same time, there has been little growth in

[45] *Ibid.,* p. 85.
[46] *New York Times,* March 6, 1972, p. 22.

FIGURE 14–2

Metropolitan Areas Contain More than Two Thirds of the Nation's Unemployed and Nearly Three Fourths of the Negro
Unemployed.

Percent of total unemployed, 1970

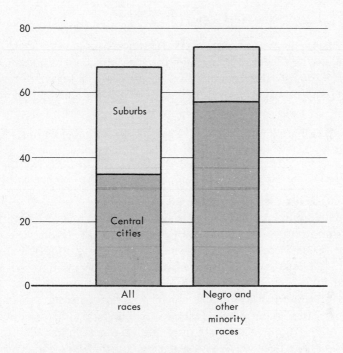

Source: *Manpower Report of the President, 1971* (Washington, D.C.:
U.S. Government Printing Office, 1971), Chart 12, p. 87.

blue-collar employment, and in some cities an actual decline has manifested itself in this category. Unfortunately, a high proportion of central
city residents lack the necessary education and training to qualify for
such white-collar jobs, while blue-collar opportunities are declining or
offer work only on a sporadic basis at low wages.

We have seen from an earlier discussion in this chapter that a change
in the composition of the work force can itself produce an increase in
the rate of unemployment. This same development can be seen at work
in the central city. The labor force of the central city contains a high
proportion of nonwhite workers who traditionally have a higher incidence of unemployment. Likewise, the central city has a high proportion of newcomers—from other regions and often from other countries

—who usually experience more difficulty in obtaining jobs. In poverty neighborhoods, a high proportion of households have women heads, who frequently can accept only part-time or casual employment. For these and other reasons which have been discussed in Chapter 8, central city residents may be cut off from the primary labor market and are subjected to the vicissitudes and high unemployment rates of the secondary labor market.

POVERTY AND UNEMPLOYMENT

How many poor are there in the American economy? What are the causes of poverty? Are we making progress in eliminating it? The answers to these questions would not in any case be easy, but they are further complicated by the difficulty in adequately defining the concept of poverty. As one writer has aptly put it:

Depending upon how poverty is defined, one can conclude that it is not a serious problem in the United States, that it is an insoluble problem, that we now are making great strides toward eliminating it, that we are not making any progress at all—or almost anything in between these extreme alternatives.[47]

Most statistics used by governmental agencies are based upon a so-called "poverty index" which was developed by the Social Security Administration in 1964. For families of three or more persons, the poverty level was set at three times the cost of an economy food plan designed by the U.S. Department of Agriculture to provide minimum nutritional needs for "emergency or temporary use when funds are low." Annual revisions of the poverty income cutoff for various sized family groups and for various geographical areas were formerly based upon price changes of the items in the economy food budget. Since 1969, the poverty cutoffs have been revised to reflect upward movements in the over-all Consumer Price Index.[48]

In 1970, the poverty threshold, based upon this definition, was $3,968 for an urban family of four.[49] There were 25.5 million persons who fell below this threshold, representing an increase of 1.2 million over the previous year. This was the first year-to-year increase in absolute number

---

[47] Victor R. Fuchs, Redefining Poverty and Redistributing Income," *The Public Interest*, No. 8 (Summer 1967), p. 88. One difficulty with conventional definitions of poverty is that they are based upon income and do not take account of assets which an individual may own. Thus, a retired farmer who owns his farm mortgage-free and owns stocks and bonds may be a member of the "poverty" group, yet be living quite comfortably.

[48] U.S. Department of Commerce, Bureau of Census, *Revision in Poverty Statistics, 1959 to 1968*, Current Population Reports, Special Studies, Series P–23, No. 28 (August 12, 1969), p. 1.

[49] U.S. Department of Commerce, Bureau of Census, *Consumer Income*, Current Population Reports, Series P–60, No. 77 (May 7, 1971), p. 1.

of the poor since 1959.[50] Despite this increase, the number of poor persons as well as their proportion of the population have fallen substantially since 1959. As Table 14–5 indicates, the proportion of poor in the population fell from 22.4% in 1959 to 12.2% in 1969; the percentage increased slightly to about 13% in 1970.[51]

Thus, use of conventional indexes for measuring poverty gives hope that eventually poverty can be totally eliminated as living standards rise

TABLE 14–5

Persons Below Poverty Level by Status and Race, 1959 and 1969 (in millions)

	1959			1969		
		Below poverty level			Below poverty level	
Status and race	Total	Number	Percent	Total	Number	**Percent**
All persons	176.6	39.5	22.4	199.8	24.3	**12.2**
In families	165.9	34.6	20.8	185.4	19.4	**10.5**
Head	45.1	8.3	18.5	51.2	5.0	**9.7**
Male	40.6	6.4	15.8	45.7	3.1	**6.9**
Female	4.5	1.9	42.6	5.6	1.8	**32.3**
Members under age 18 [1]	64.0	17.2	26.9	69.8	9.8	**14.1**
Other members	56.8	9.0	15.9	64.4	4.7	**7.3**
Unrelated individuals [2]	10.7	4.9	46.1	14.5	4.9	**33.6**
White	157.0	28.5	18.1	175.4	16.7	**9.5**
In families	147.8	24.4	16.5	162.9	12.7	**7.8**
With male head	137.3	20.2	14.7	150.4	9.1	**6.1**
With female head	10.5	4.2	40.2	12.5	3.6	**28.9**
Unrelated individuals [2]	9.2	4.0	44.1	12.5	4.0	**31.8**
Negro and other	19.6	11.0	56.2	24.5	7.6	**31.1**
Percent of total	11.1	27.8	(X)	12.3	31.3	**(X)**
In families	18.1	10.1	56.0	22.5	6.7	**29.9**
With male head	14.4	7.3	51.0	16.6	3.3	**20.0**
With female head	3.7	2.8	75.6	5.9	3.4	**57.9**
Unrelated individuals [2]	1.5	0.9	57.4	2.0	0.9	**44.9**

(X) Not applicable.
[1] Other than head or wife.
[2] Age 14 and over.
Source: Adapted from U.S. Department of Commerce, Bureau of Census, *Pocket Data Book USA, 1971* (Washington, D.C.: U.S. Government Printing Office, 1971), Table 279, p. 203.

in the economy as a whole. Of course, if we used a fixed-income standard in terms of dollars without annual revision to take account of changes in the Consumer Price Index, poverty would tend to "disappear" with the upward escalation in prices.

It is probable that a more meaningful definition of poverty can be given in relative terms. In other words, in any given society at any point of time, the "poor" can be thought of as those at the bottom of the income distribution pattern. Some economists would focus attention on how far those at the bottom are from the median income group. Using the definition of the poor as "any family whose income is less than half

---

[50] *New York Times,* November 14, 1971, p. 41.
[51] U.S. Bureau of Census, *Consumer Income,* p. 1.

TABLE 14-6

Persons Below Poverty Level by Residence, 1959 and 1969

Item	Number (millions)			Percent		
	U.S.	Metro-politan areas	Nonmetro-politan areas	U.S.	Metro-politan areas	Nonmetro-politan areas
1959						
Total	38.8	17.0	21.7	22.0	15.3	33.2
Under 25 years	20.0	8.8	11.2	25.3	18.1	36.8
65 years and over	5.5	2.5	3.0	35.2	26.9	47.0
White	28.3	11.8	16.5	18.1	12.0	28.2
Negro	9.9	5.0	4.9	55.1	42.8	77.7
1969						
Total	24.3	12.3	12.0	12.2	9.5	17.1
Under 25 years	12.2	6.4	5.8	13.2	10.7	17.9
65 years and over	4.8	2.3	2.5	25.3	20.2	33.3
White	16.7	8.2	8.5	9.5	7.3	13.5
Negro	7.2	3.9	3.4	32.3	24.4	51.5

Source: Adapted from U.S. Department of Commerce, Bureau of Census, *Pocket Data Book USA, 1971* (Washington, D.C.: U.S. Government Printing Office, 1971), Table 280, p. 203.

of the median family income," Victor Fuchs has found that the proportion of families with less than half the median income has remained constant at about 20% throughout the postwar period.[52]

As a matter of fact, it appears that despite our efforts as a nation to effect some income transference from the wealthy to the poor, there has been relatively little change in the proportions of national income received by various income groups. The accompanying table shows the percentages of income that went to various categories of families during the period 1950–70.

Group	*1970*	*1965*	*1950*
Lowest fifth	5.5%	5.3%	4.5%
Second fifth	12.0	12.1	12.0
Middle fifth	17.4	17.7	17.4
Fourth fifth	23.5	23.7	23.5
Highest fifth	41.6	41.3	42.6

Source: Federal Reserve Board data; from *Wall Street Journal*, February 28, 1972, p. 1.

The Profile of Poverty

New Census Bureau data indicate in dramatic fashion the changes which are occurring in the composition and location of poverty in the United States.

---

[52] Fuchs, "Redefining Poverty," p. 89.

Location. Poverty is increasingly becoming a phenomenon of our large metropolitan areas. Whereas in 1960 only about 43% of the poor lived in metropolitan areas, by 1970 over half of all poor persons lived in such areas (see Table 14–6). In 1970, the South region had 46% of all of the nation's poor persons, almost the same percentage as in 1959,[53] indicating that despite that region's rapid growth in employment and production in recent years, poverty remains a persistent problem. The incidence of poverty is particularly high among southern blacks—they are over three times as likely to be poor as southern whites. Nevertheless, there are more than a million more poor whites in the South than poor blacks.[54] Furthermore, poverty in the South is much more a rural phenomenon than it is in the North and West. For example, in 1970 about 65% of the black poor and 63% of the white poor in the South lived in nonmetropolitan areas. In contrast, outside the South, 94% of the black poor and 56% of the white poor lived in metropolitan areas.[55] As might be expected, within metropolitan areas, the central cities are tending to become repositories of the poor. In 1970, about 50% of poor white families living in metropolitan areas and 80% of poor black families were central city residents.[56] From 1969 to 1970 alone, the poor population of central cities grew by about 400,000.[57]

Family Composition. In 1970, persons in households headed by a woman constituted only 14% of all persons in the population but about 44% of poor persons.[58] Poverty in the United States is particularly an affliction of the young. In 1970, children under 18 years accounted for about 36% of all white persons below the poverty level and 54% of all blacks who were poor.[59] Between 1959 and 1970, there has been a striking change in the number of poor children in fatherless families. In 1959, 24% of all poor children were in female-headed households; by 1970 the figure had jumped to 46%.[60] The aged also are heavily represented in the poverty population. Almost 20% of poor persons are over 65.[61] With a high percentage of our poverty population consisting of the young, the aged, and women who head households, it is apparent that poverty cannot simply be eradicated by providing training and employment.

Racial Composition. In 1970, the poverty rate for blacks was more

---

[53] Ray Marshall, "Some Rural Economic Development Problems in the South," *Monthly Labor Review*, Vol. 95 (February 1972), p. 28.

[54] *Ibid.*

[55] *Ibid.*

[56] U.S. Bureau of Census, *Consumer Income*, p. 1.

[57] *New York Times*, November 14, 1971, p. 41.

[58] U.S. Bureau of Census, *Consumer Income*, p. 1.

[59] *Ibid.*

[60] *New York Times*, November 14, 1971, p. 41.

[61] *Ibid.*

than three times that for whites.[62] Of the 25.5 million people in poverty in 1970, 30% were black and about 9% were of Spanish-speaking background. Among all blacks, 34% are poor; among all persons of Spanish-Speaking origin, 24% are poor.[63] It is obvious that racial discrimination is closely associated with poverty in the United States.

Relation to Labor Force.   In 1933, at the depths of the Great Depres-

FIGURE 14–3

Poverty and Employment (many peope remain poor despite employment.

Proportion of all poor families with:

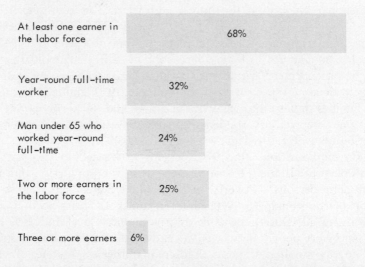

At least one earner in the labor force	68%
Year-round full-time worker	32%
Man under 65 who worked year-round full-time	24%
Two or more earners in the labor force	25%
Three or more earners	6%

Source: Data, U.S. Department of Health, Education and Welfare; chart, Chase Manhattan Bank, *Business in Brief,* No. 88 (October 1969), p. 3.

sion there was a close relationship between poverty and unemployment. This relationship no longer holds. Although the increase in unemployment during the past few years has tended to cloud the relationship, it is clear that from 1962 to 1968 the unemployment rate declined substantially—the unemployment rate for men 20 years and over fell from 5.7% to about 2%, while at the same time there was an enormous increase in the welfare case load under Aid to Families with Dependent Children (AFDC), from less than 400,000 cases in 1962 to over 700,000 in 1968.[64] Contrary to popular impression, a large proportion of the per-

---

[62] U.S. Bureau of Census, *Consumer Income,* p. 1.

[63] *New York Times,* November 14, 1971, p. 41.

[64] Chase Manhattan Bank, *Business in Brief,* No. 88 (October 1969), p. 2. From fiscal 1960 to fiscal 1970, federal and state welfare costs more than tripled—from $2.8 billion to $8.7 billion. The number of recipients rose from 5.8 million to 14.3 million. (Data from U.S. Department of Health, Education and Welfare.)

sons classified as poor are actually employed. As a matter of fact, 68% of all poor families have at least one wage earner (see Figure 14–3), and it is estimated that over half of those classified as poor are employed.[65] In 1970, out of 5,214,000 families classified as being below the poverty minimum, only 270,000 were headed by a person who considered himself or herself unemployed.[66] Over half of the family heads were not in the labor force at all;[67] those that were employed tended to be working in occupations with very low wages. For example, of 2.8 million poor families whose head worked in 1970, about 50% were employed as farmers and farm laborers, nonfarm laborers, and service, including private households.[68] These occupations characteristically provide irregular employment at low wages.

Programs to Eliminate Poverty

Efforts to reduce and ultimately to eliminate poverty have followed three general courses of action.

The first involves the stimulation of economic growth in the hope that as production and employment rise, the poor and the disadvantaged will benefit along with all other members of our society. This policy has in fact had considerable effect if we measure progress by the number of poor households or poor persons falling within the conventional definition of poverty as prescribed by the Social Security Administration. The Council of Economic Advisers estimated that if the rate of reduction in poverty achieved during the period 1959–67 could be continued, poverty would be eliminated in about 10 years.[69] Actually, it is doubtful that this rate of improvement could be continued because as poverty declines numerically, an increasing fraction of the remaining poor are members of households whose economic status is least affected by prosperity. For example, households headed by women with children, disabled persons, or elderly persons account for about 60% of all poor households,[70] and they are not too likely to be helped by improvement in the labor market.

The second avenue involves training programs to enable members of poverty groups to obtain gainful employment. Obviously, such programs cannot be very helpful to mothers who must stay at home, the aged, disabled, and children. Although only a small percentage of the total

---

[65] Robert E. Klitgaard, "The Dual Labor Market and Manpower Policy," *Monthly Labor Review*, Vol. 94 (November 1971), p. 45.

[66] U.S. Bureau of Census, *Consumer Income*, p. 5.

[67] *Ibid.*

[68] *Ibid.*

[69] *Economic Report of the President, January 1969* (Washington, D.C.: U.S. Government Printing Office, 1969), p. 159.

[70] *Ibid.*

number of persons on welfare are employable males (in New York about 4%–5%), provision of adequate jobs for such men could have a multiplier effect by removing their families from the welfare rolls. This has been estimated at 20%–25% of all welfare recipients in New York.[71]

Thus, training programs can be meaningful as an avenue to reduce poverty, particularly with respect to those poor persons with actual or potential attachment to the labor force. This group consists largely of the poorly educated, the less skilled, and the persons who are exposed to discrimination because of their race. Their number was estimated to be about 7.9 million in 1966, with a projected decline to about a little more than 5 million in 1975.[72] It is noteworthy that in 1970 about 31% of poverty families were headed by persons with less than eight years of elementary school education.[73] Although manpower training would seem to be a useful type of assistance to this group of poor persons, in actuality only about 5% of funds for the poor have been directed to training programs. The bulk of assistance has been in the form of cash grants.[74]

The third possible avenue to reduce poverty involves various forms of income transference payments in which funds are in effect taken by taxation from the more well-to-do and given to the poor as outright grants. It has been calculated that in 1970 it would have taken $11.4 billion to raise the incomes of all poor families and unrelated individuals above the poverty line.[75] While the nation is unlikely to undertake such a massive effort at income distribution, less ambitious proposals are being put forward with increasing frequency. The so-called "negative income tax," for example, would use the federal income tax system as a means for redistributing income. Filing an income tax return, for the poor, would take the place of the current means test. Persons with incomes higher than the minimum support levels would pay a tax, while persons with incomes below this figure would receive a benefit payment through the tax system.

The welfare programs proposed by the Nixon administration combine income supplements for poor families with a large role assigned to job training and child care services for heads of poor families. Under the so-called "Workfare Plan," the basic benefit for families without any income would be $500 each for the first two members and $300 for each additional member up to a total of seven. A family of four would thus receive $1,600 a year. Recipients who work would be permitted to keep the first $60 a month 'and would forgo only 50 cents in benefits for each

[71] Chase Manhattan Bank, *Business in Brief*, p. 4.

[72] Leonard A. Lecht, *Poor Persons in the Labor Force: A Universe of Need* (Report Prepared for the U.S. Department of Labor, Manpower Administration, [October 1970]), p. I–5.

[73] U.S. Bureau of Census, *Consumer Income*, p. 5.

[74] Lecht, *Poor Persons in the Labor Force*, p. VI–3.

[75] U.S. Bureau of Census, *Consumer Income*, p. 1.

$1 earned above that. Those who accepted job training would get a bonus of $30 per month. Employable recipients, except for mothers of pre-school-age children, would be required to accept suitable jobs or training. Those who refused would lose their benefits, but their family would continue to be assisted.

A controversial aspect of such support programs has been the question of their effect upon the incentive to work. It is difficult to devise an adequate income transfer program with basic income guarantees which are adequate and at the same time to assure that persons with earnings from work will receive a higher total income than those who do not work. Income support programs therefore usually include some formula to provide an incentive for earning additional income. Preliminary findings of an experimental project which was designed to test out the impact of income support programs on incentives to work suggest that the danger that withdrawal from the labor force would be encouraged is probably minimal.[76]

How can we win the battle against poverty? Substantial progress has already been made in reducing the number of poor, both white and non-white. But more work and effort is needed, not only from the government but also from business, labor, and various social and philanthropic agencies. Fortunately, we are not dealing with a problem of mass poverty, such as that which typifies many underdeveloped countries, nor are we faced by poverty resulting from large-scale unemployment. Poverty in this country is a problem of certain specific people whose personal, social, demographic, and environmental characteristics must be changed in order to enable them to escape from poverty.

It is obvious that mere financial assistance to needy families is not enough. We must improve the "employability" of these underprivileged groups so that they can raise their incomes through productive work. This calls for expansion of employment opportunities in depressed areas and strengthening of federal, state, and local programs of training. These same programs are also necessary to reduce hard-core unemployment and upgrade the skills of our substandard employed. A number of federal programs have made an encouraging start in these directions. Manpower programs will be discussed in detail in Chapter 15.

TYPES OF UNEMPLOYMENT

Unemployment can be classified into various types, either from the point of view of the individuals concerned or from the point of view of economists who look at the phenomenon of unemployment as it affects the economy as a whole.

---

[76] "Can Handouts Make Better Wage Earners?" *Business Week*, February 28, 1970, pp. 80–82.

Unemployment from the Worker's Point of View

Table 14–7 classifies the total amount of unemployment which existed in February 1971 and February 1972 on the basis of reasons given by unemployed persons to the survey interviewer. The term "job losers" used in the table includes persons on layoff, whether temporary or indefinite, as well as those who lose their jobs permanently. Persons who voluntarily leave their jobs and immediately start to look for other work are termed "job leavers." The relative proportions of these two groups and new job seekers will vary over the year. For example, as might be expected, the number of unemployed who are new entrants to the labor market rises sharply in June of each year when the school year ends. As can be seen from the table, in February 1972 only about half of the unemployed had actually lost jobs. Inability of new entrants to find jobs accounted for 40% of total unemployment.

Economic Classifications of Unemployment

Economists customarily classify unemployment into various types, such as cyclical, technological, seasonal, and other categories, which we shall consider in the following discussion. Obviously, any such categorization is arbitrary. For example, technological unemployment—the displacement of labor attributable to mechanization and automation—is frequently distinguished from cyclical unemployment—the unemployment associated with the rise and fall of business activity over the cycle. In actuality, it is almost impossible to separate these two kinds of unemployment, for the typical unemployment problem is the complex result of a number of diverse factors. Nevertheless, such classification is useful in pointing out a direction for public policy and in enabling economists, trade-union officials, and other persons concerned with the problem of unemployment to attach this complex phenomenon in an orderly manner.

CYCLICAL UNEMPLOYMENT

The outstanding source of unemployment in our modern economy is the recurrent fluctuation in business which has been called the business cycle. While the business cycle has characterized American industrial development almost since its inception, mass unemployment of a cyclical nature is a comparatively recent problem. Prior to 1929, the number of unemployed in industry did not exceed 5 million per annum. Yet, in 1933, it is estimated that approximately 13 million workers were unemployed. The figure of 13 million understates the tragedy of unemployment, for another 25 million persons were directly or indirectly dependent upon these unemployed.

TABLE 14-7

Unemployed Persons by Reasons for Unemployment, Sex, Age, and Color

Reason for Unemployment	Total Unemployed		Male, 20 Years and Over		Female, 20 Years and Over		Both Sexes, 16 to 19 Years		White		Negro and Other Races	
	Feb. 1972	Feb. 1971	Feb. 1972	Feb. 1971	Feb. 1972	Feb. 1971	Feb. 1972	Feb. 1971	Feb. 1972	Feb. 1971	Feb. 1972	Feb. 1971
Unemployment level												
Total unemployed, in thousands	5,412	5,442	2,461	2,582	1,595	1,733	1,356	1,127	4,383	4,511	1,028	931
Lost last job	2,677	2,958	1,641	1,795	705	857	331	306	2,227	2,467	451	491
Left last job	611	644	249	282	234	231	129	131	509	542	102	102
Reentered labor force	1,557	1,372	515	448	593	581	449	343	1,223	1,106	334	266
Never worked before	566	468	55	57	63	64	448	347	424	396	142	72
Total unemployed, percent distribution	100.0	100.0	100.0	100.0	100.0	100.0	100.0	100.0	100.0	100.0	100.0	100.0
Lost last job	49.5	54.3	66.7	69.5	44.3	49.5	24.4	27.1	50.8	54.7	43.9	52.8
Left last job	11.3	11.8	10.1	10.9	14.6	13.3	9.5	11.6	11.6	12.0	9.9	11.0
Reentered labor force	28.8	25.2	20.9	17.3	37.2	33.5	33.1	30.5	27.9	24.5	32.5	28.6
Never worked before	10.5	8.6	2.3	2.2	4.0	3.7	33.0	30.8	9.7	8.8	13.8	7.7
Unemployment rate												
Total unemployment rate	6.4	6.6	5.1	5.5	5.4	6.0	19.0	17.0	5.8	6.1	11.0	10.2
Job-loser rate*	3.1	3.6	3.4	3.8	2.4	2.9	4.7	4.6	3.0	3.4	4.8	5.4
Job-leaver rate*	0.7	0.8	0.5	0.6	0.8	0.8	1.8	2.0	0.7	0.7	1.1	1.1
Reentrant rate*	1.8	1.7	1.1	0.9	2.0	2.0	6.3	5.2	1.6	1.5	3.6	2.9
New entrant rate*	0.7	0.6	0.1	0.1	0.2	0.2	6.3	5.2	0.6	0.5	1.5	0.8

* Unemployment rates are calculated as a percent of the civilian labor force.
Source: U.S. Department of Labor, *Employment and Earnings*, Vol. 18 (March 1972), Table A–12, p. 31.

Characteristics of Cyclical Unemployment

The causes of the business cycle constitute a separate field of study which is outside the scope of our immediate inquiry in this book. It is pertinent to this discussion, however, to observe certain definite characteristics in the fluctuation of employment which customarily develop in boom and depression. Thus, for example, it is well established that the durable-goods-producing industries experience more extreme variations in output and employment over the cycle than those producing nondurable goods. The construction industry is particularly hard hit during depression, the reason being that investment in homes or business plants is the type of expenditure which can easily be postponed when income declines.

The burden of cyclical unemployment is not spread evenly. Some industries and occupations fare reasonably well, while others are subject to extreme variations in demand. Employment in manufacturing has proved to be one of the most volatile in the nonagricultural group. Since employment in the service industries is much more stable over the cycle than in manufacturing, the shift in employment from the latter to the former will have a stabilizing effect upon employment over the cycle. While the economy has seemed less susceptible in recent years to the extreme depression-boom cycle of the 1920s and 1930s, nevertheless a cyclical pattern in employment and unemployment still persists.

SECULAR TRENDS IN EMPLOYMENT

Secular trends are long-term trends which may perhaps take 50 years to run their course. They are distinguishable from cyclical movements, which on the average do not exceed 10 years in duration. Secular trends in employment within an industry are due to the influence of technological change, population growth, and competition from other industries.

Secular trends are at work not only in particular industries but also in the economy as a whole, and perhaps also in the world at large. Thus, changes in gold supply, wars, changes in the pattern of consumer demand, and population shift will all affect employment trends.

TECHNOLOGICAL UNEMPLOYMENT

Technological unemployment is that displacement of labor by machinery and improved methods of production which is attributable to advances of the arts and sciences or to improvements in the technique of management. This definition does not make technological unemployment synonymous with all kinds of displacement of labor by machinery. For example, suppose that a minimum wage is imposed on an industry, doubling the wage rates it has to pay. Employers would now find it profitable to introduce machines already known and in use in other industries but which hitherto had not been profitable to utilize in this particular industry operating at a low wage rate. Some labor will be displaced by the introduction of the machines, but it would be misleading to attribute this to technological change. The unemployment in this case is attributable to the rise in the price of labor and would have occurred even in a stationary state where technological progress was absent. Thus, for the purpose of precise analytical reasoning, it is important to distinguish "substitution" unemployment from "technological" unemployment. In actual practice, however, it is usually impossible to separate the two, so that any figures for technological unemployment are likely to contain a substantial amount of substitution unemployment as well.

Possibility of Permanent Technological Unemployment

Can laborsaving machinery produce permanent technological unemployment? The answer to this question will depend upon whether we are considering a particular firm or industry, on the one hand, or the economy as a whole, on the other. In a particular firm or industry, the effect of a laborsaving machine upon employment will depend upon the rate of introduction of the machine, the laborsaving capacity of the machine, the extent to which the skills of the old workers are still useful under the new method of production, and the elasticity of demand for the product.

Whether laborsaving machinery can produce permanent technological unemployment in the economy as a whole has long been the subject of controversy in the literature. According to economic theory, the effect of a laborsaving invention is to raise the marginal product of capital relative to labor and thus reduce the relative share of labor in the national income. Some writers have seized on this possibility to argue that a decline in the relative share of labor in the national income will mean a shift of income from those classes which save little to those which save more, with the result that consumer purchasing power will be diminished, a deflationary influence will be exerted on the consumption goods industries, and the equilibrium level of employment will therefore be reduced.[77] This conclusion, however, rests on an erroneous major premise and is not borne out by historical evidence. While most inventions are laborsaving, there has been no long-run trend toward a reduced share for labor in the national income. The effect of a laborsaving invention in reducing the relative share of labor in the national income is only temporary. Since the invention also increases the marginal productivity of capital, and therefore the expectation of profits, investment will increase and thereby raise the marginal productivity of labor and the level of employment.

---

[77] Joan Robinson, *Essays in the Theory of Employment* (New York: Macmillan Co., 1937), p. 135.

Technological Progress and Employment Opportunities

The kind of technological progress we have experienced in the past has expanded employment opportunities for two reasons. In the first place, the production of laborsaving machinery has itself constituted a major form of new investment and has contributed directly to a rise in employment in the durable goods industries. In the second place, the invention of a laborsaving device such as the gasoline engine ushering in the automobile age has created a tremendous tide of secondary investment in road construction, gas stations, tire plants, motels, etc. Therefore, even though technological change as we have known it has produced serious problems of dislocation of communities, obsolescence of skills, and large-scale unemployment, it also has at the same time opened up extensive new job opportunities.

What about automation? Is this just a new version of laborsaving invention—or is it something different which may therefore have quite different repercussions upon employment? Automation means continuous automatic production, linking together more than one already mechanized operation, with the product automatically transferred between two or among several operations. Automation has reduced the number of workers required in many offices and plants, but it has created many new jobs in industries which manufacture and assemble the intricate machines and complicated controls which make automation possible.

On the other hand, it is possible that automation does not create as much secondary investment as some of the earlier developments in technology, because it involves not so much a substitution of machinery for labor as a linking and integration of already mechanized operations and the application of electronic controls. Furthermore, the immediate impact of automation can be serious in an economy striving to reduce already high levels of unemployment; for automation can render whole plants obsolete and substantially alter the skill requirements of the job market.

Despite the fact that automation presents acute and peculiar problems with respect to the level of employment, it seems likely that in the long run—as one aspect of the stream of technological progress—automation will provide a net benefit to the economy both in terms of employment and in terms of standard of living. It is well to remember that 30 years ago, nuclear fission was an abstract theory; today, several hundred thousand workers are employed in the production and application of nuclear products. Who is to say what new products, what new avenues of production and distribution, the new frontier of automation will open up?

SEASONAL UNEMPLOYMENT

Seasonal unemployment is due to variations in business during the year caused by climatic or other seasonal changes in supply and by changing seasonal demands reflecting custom, habit, and style factors. On the supply side, seasonal variations result in a fluctuating flow of materials or seasonal alteration in production techniques. Agriculture, for example, reflects the direct influence of the weather and therefore is peculiarly susceptible to seasonal variation in output and employment. Moreover, the various industries which process agricultural products are likewise subject to seasonal fluctuation in employment due to the availability or nonavailability of the raw material upon which their operation depends. On the demand side, seasonal variations are particularly marked in those industries which produce unstandardized consumption goods with relatively elastic demands. The Easter bonnet and the Christmas card are two illustrations of commodities in the demand for which seasonality plays a dominant role. To a lesser extent, seasonal variations attributable to either supply or demand conditions characterize the manufacture of agricultural equipment and the fertilizer, construction, and mining industries.

The seasonal variation in employment in particular industries takes on such a definite pattern that it can be forecast with considerable exactitude. Within any large state or area—if industry is diversified—opposite seasonal variations tend to counteract one another, so that the net seasonal fluctuations in total employment may be relatively small in consequence. For the country as a whole, such a balancing will always occur; but because of the distance involved and the insufficient mobility of labor, a substantial amount of seasonal unemployment may remain. Statistical techniques have been developed to eliminate the influence of seasonality from data of employment, production, and sales, so as to permit analysis of such statistics free from the distortion of seasonal variations, which tend to obscure long-term trends.

In agriculture, the problem of seasonal unemployment is even more acute. The seasonality of the pattern of demand for labor has given rise to a migratory labor force, moving from one area to another, following the cycle of the crops. These people, generally in the very low income brackets, unable to form fixed associations or community ties, present a serious political and sociological problem with which no relief agency has been able to cope.

FRICTIONAL UNEMPLOYMENT

Frictional unemployment is attributable to time lost in changing jobs rather than to a lack of job opportunities. Frictional unemployment, defined broadly enough, could encompass almost all types of unemployment, since the cyclical unemployed, the seasonal worker, and the victim of declining demand in a particular industry must all take time to find new jobs. Frictional unemployment, however, is generally associated with joblessness of relatively short duration. Some idea of the magnitude of frictional unemployment can be gained from examination of the duration-of-unemployment data published by the U.S. Bureau of Labor Statistics. These reveal that in 1971 a total of 3,812,000 persons were unemployed for periods of less than 15 weeks. Over 2 million persons were unemployed for periods of less than five weeks.[78] It seems likely that with a labor force of about 85 million persons, there can be expected to be a changing pool of about 3 million or 4 million employees who are in process of changing jobs.

The volume of frictional unemployment to some extent reflects the ability of workers to withstand some unemployment while they are looking around for a job. The high wages earned by our employees while they are at work and the unemployment compensation benefits those involuntarily unemployed receive while out of work enable them to take more time while looking for a new job and to find an opening which will improve their ultimate income, rather than being compelled to take the first job opening available.

Frictional unemployment is a reflection of freedom of movement in the labor market coupled with some degree of immobility. John Doe quits his job in Cleveland to go to work in Detroit, but it may be several months at the earliest before he can move his family and start work in the new location. Such friction exists even with regard to changes of jobs within a given city or state. Public employment exchanges tend to reduce time lost by giving better publicity to job openings. Unions may also perform the same function. As we noted in our discussion of labor mobility in Chapter 8, the search for work is still pursued on a rather haphazard basis by most workers. There is much that can be done in this area by government and business to improve information about job vacancies. Any such improvement would tend to lower frictional unemployment.

Demand versus Structural Unemployment

Definition and classification of types of unemployment constitute more than a useful exercise in orderly thinking. The classification of unemployment as one type or another can have important ramifications in terms of policy decisions, for a remedy which is applicable to one kind of unemployment may not be appropriate if the unemployment is attributable to other causes.

Because of the difficulty in classifying the unemployment which exists from time to time, discussions by economists and public officials have proceeded primarily on the basis of the comparative effectiveness of reducing total unemployment by (1) measures to raise aggregate demand, via tax policy, expenditure increase, or monetary expansion; or (2) measures to improve the employability of the unemployed via retraining,

---

[78] *Manpower Report, 1972,* Table A–20, p. 181.

education, placement, and other labor market policies. Those emphasizing
the former represent the "inadequate demand" school; those stressing the
latter represent the "structural" point of view. It should be emphasized
that adherents of these two points of view recognize that this is not an
all-black or all-white situation and that there must be a judicious mixture
of the two policies.

Walter W. Heller, former Chairman of the Council of Economic
Advisers, has been a strong proponent of the inadequate demand point of
view. He has contended that hard-core unemployment represents only an
insignificant part of total unemployment and that a large part of it—due
to such factors as obsolescence, automation, changes in demand, and the
like—would disappear if proper tax, spending, and credit policies
produced an expansion of demand.[79] Economists holding this position do
not discount the worth of retraining programs but emphasize that jobs
are created only by the spending of money. As one writer puts it: "Education does not create jobs, retraining does not create jobs; placement
does not create jobs . . . jobs are created only by the purchase of goods
and services."[80] Likewise, adherents of this position are inclined to minimize the difficulty of employing various disadvantaged groups in the
marketplace. As Arthur Okun, a former member of the Council puts it,
". . . the teenage worker and the Negro worker pose a hard problem,
but not a hard-core problem. Quite the contrary, their job opportunities
are especially sensitive to over-all economic conditions."[81] In summary,
the aggregate demand proponents in effect contend that practically any
desired employment level could be attained by aggregate means alone if
we would or could accept the consequences in terms of inflation.

The opposing view, propounded by such economic authorities as
William McChesney Martin, Jr., former Chairman of the Federal Reserve Board and Martin R. Gainsbrugh, Chief Economist for the Conference Board, hold that structural unemployment has become indefinitely persistent even in periods of tight labor markets and that
elimination of the unemployment which continues to plague certain
groups in the labor market through good times and bad will require
special programs tailored to the needs of these disadvantaged groups.
Gainsbrugh contends that structural changes in the character of unemployment call for structural changes in the techniques to be applied
to combat it. He recommends consideration of the following special
programs:

---

[79] See, for example, *Economic Report of the President, 1964* (Washington, D.C.:
U.S. Government Printing Office, 1964), pp. 166–90.

[80] Garth Mangum, "The Role of 'Job' Creation Programs," in William G. Bowen
and Frederick H. Harbison (eds.), *Unemployment in a Prosperous Economy* (Princeton University Research Report Series No. 108 [Princeton, N.J., 1965]), p. 108.

[81] Arthur M. Okun, "The Role of Aggregate Demand in Alleviating Unemployment," in Bowen and Harbison, *Unemployment in a Prosperous Economy*, p. 76.

1. A lower minimum wage rate for the young.
2. Special tax or other incentives to stimulate and expand research activity by industry.
3. Retraining and relocation grants to help move unemployed professionals into such new areas of opportunity as environmental control.
4. Special training subsidies to stimulate employers to hire the unskilled or hard core unemployed.[82]

Structuralists as a group stress the needs for such special programs and fear that if we try to solve structural unemployment by a massive monetary and fiscal stimulation of overall demand, we shall have to carry this program to such lengths as to create serious new problems of an inflationary character.

Although the debate between aggregate demand theorists and the structuralists continues, recent events have tended to buttress the structuralists' position. The apparent shifting of the Phillips curve, as discussed in Chapter 13, has placed new constraints on monetary policy designed to eliminate unemployment through aggregate demand changes. Furthermore the persistence of unemployment among particular groups has dramatized the need for special programs. In the words of President Nixon's Council of Economic Advisers:

In 1971 the unemployment rate for 16–19 year olds was 16.9 percent compared to a rate of 3.2 percent for married males; in 1969, a year of very tight labor markets, the rate for teenagers was 12.2 percent, compared to 1.5 percent for married males. The persistence of this large differential in both good times and bad suggests that factors other than the lack of aggregate demand cause the differential.[83]

THE CHALLENGE OF A HIGH-EMPLOYMENT ECONOMY

In 1946, Congress enacted the Employment Act of 1946. This stature provides:

It is the continuing policy and responsibility of the federal government to use all practicable means consistent with its needs and obligations and other essential considerations of national policy, with the assistance and cooperation of industry, agriculture, labor and state and local governments, to coordinate and utilize all its plans, functions, and resources, for the purpose of creating and maintaining, in a manner calculated to foster and promote free competitive enterprise and the general welfare, conditions under which there will be afforded useful employment opportunities including self-employment, for those able, willing and seeking to work and to promote maximum employment, production and purchasing power.

Under this act the President is charged with the responsibility of formulating a program to achieve the objectives stated in the statute. To

---

[82] *Wall Street Journal*, January 18, 1972, p. 9.
[83] *Economic Report of the President, 1972*, p. 114.

assist the President in carrying out this responsibility, a Council of Economic Advisers was created in the Executive Office of the President. The Council prepares for the President annually, for submission by him to Congress, an Economic Report, which includes relevant data on current levels of employment, purchasing power, and production, and recommendations for such legislative actions as may best effectuate the purposes of the act.

The Employment Act of 1946 is not a *full*-employment act. Its aim has been interpreted to be *high-level* employment, and the content of that concept has tended to change over time, reflecting what appears to be a growing difficulty in reducing the volume of unemployment. For many years, the accepted goal was a 4% norm. Recently, however, administration spokesmen, such as former Treasury Secretary John Connally, have labeled 4% unemployment as a peacetime norm a mere "myth,"[84] while economist Walter W. Heller, former Chairman of the Council of Economic Advisers, concedes that a 4% unemployment rate is a "tougher target now" than when he broached it back in 1961 as an interim goal for the Kennedy administration.[85]

The fact is that except in periods of wartime activity, the percentage of unemployment relative to the civilian labor force has not fallen below 4%. If we exclude from consideration the years 1951–53, which marked large-scale participation by the United States in the Korean War and the years 1966–69 during which we were heavily involved in the Vietnam conflict, it can be seen that in times of normal peacetime activity, unemployment rates have generally exceeded 4% (see Table 14–7).

In view of recent changes in the composition of labor force, achievement of even a 4.5% unemployment rate over the next few years will be extremely difficult. In order to bring unemployment down from the current level of 6% to a 4.5% goal, we must provide new jobs not only for those presently in the labor force who are unemployed, but also for the new job seekers who will enter the labor market in the next few years. The number of such new entrants will depend upon the existing age structure of the population and upon changing participation rates. The latter factor is especially difficult to forecast, since participation rates are themselves influenced by economic conditions. Thus, the tighter the labor market becomes, the higher participation rates rise, and the greater the increase which is required in the number of jobs to achieve the 4.5% goal.

One recent study bases its forecasts of future unemployment rates upon a "high-growth" and a "low-growth" projection of increases in the labor force. Under the former, in order to reduce unemployment to 4.5% by the fourth quarter of 1973, there would have to be an increase of 7.1

---

[84] *Wall Street Journal*, January 21, 1972, p. 30.
[85] *Ibid.*

TABLE 14-8

Selected Unemployment Rates, 1948-71 (percent)

Year or month	All work-ers	By sex and age			By color		By selected groups				Labor force time lost [4]
		Both sexes 16-19 years	Men 20 years and over	Wom-en 20 years and over	White	Negro and other races	Expe-rienced wage and salary workers	Mar-ried men [1]	Full-time work-ers [2]	Blue-collar work-ers [3]	
1948	3.8	9.2	3.2	3.6	3.5	5.9	4.3			4.2	
1949	5.9	13.4	5.4	5.3	5.6	8.9	6.8	3.5	5.4	8.0	
1950	5.3	12.2	4.7	5.1	4.9	9.0	6.0	4.6	5.0	7.2	
1951	3.3	8.2	2.5	4.0	3.1	5.3	3.7	1.5	2.6	3.9	
1952	3.0	8.5	2.4	3.2	2.8	5.4	3.3	1.4	2.5	3.6	
1953	2.9	7.6	2.5	2.9	2.7	4.5	3.2	1.7		3.4	
1954	5.5	12.6	4.9	5.5	5.0	9.9	6.2	4.0	5.2	7.2	
1955	4.4	11.0	3.8	4.4	3.9	8.7	4.8	2.8	3.8	5.8	
1956	4.1	11.1	3.4	4.2	3.6	8.3	4.4	2.6	3.7	5.1	5.1
1957	4.3	11.6	3.6	4.1	3.8	7.9	4.6	2.8	4.0	6.2	5.3
1958	6.8	15.9	6.2	6.1	6.1	12.6	7.2	5.1	7.2	10.2	8.1
1959	5.5	14.6	4.7	5.2	4.8	10.7	5.7	3.6		7.6	6.6
1960	5.5	14.7	4.7	5.1	4.9	10.2	5.7	3.7		7.8	6.7
1961	6.7	16.8	5.7	6.3	6.0	12.4	6.8	4.6	6.7	9.2	8.0
1962	5.5	14.7	4.6	5.4	4.9	10.9	5.6	3.6		7.4	6.7
1963	5.7	17.2	4.5	5.4	5.0	10.8	5.5	3.4	5.4	7.3	6.4
1964	5.2	16.2	3.9	5.2	4.6	9.6	5.0	2.8	4.8	6.3	5.8
1965	4.5	14.8	3.2	4.5	4.1	8.1	4.3	2.4	4.2	5.3	5.0
1966	3.8	12.8	2.5	3.8	3.4	7.3	3.5	1.9	3.4	4.2	4.2
1967	3.8	12.8	2.3	4.2	3.4	7.4	3.6	1.8	3.5	4.4	4.2
1968	3.6	12.7	2.2	3.8	3.2	6.7	3.4	1.6	3.1	4.1	4.0
1969	3.5	12.2	2.1	3.7	3.1	6.4	3.3	1.5	3.1	3.9	3.9
1970	4.9	15.2	3.5	4.8	4.5	8.2	4.8	2.6	4.5	6.2	5.4
1971	5.9	16.9	4.4	5.7	5.4	9.9	5.7	3.2	5.5	7.4	6.4

[1] Married men living with their wives. Data for 1949 and 1951-54 are for April; 1950, for March.

[2] Data for 1949-61 are for May.

[3] Includes craftsmen, operatives, and nonfarm laborers. Data for 1948-57 are based on data for January, April, July, and October.

[4] Man-hours lost by the unemployed and persons on part time for economic reasons as a percent of potentially available labor force man-hours.

Source: *Economic Report of the President, 1972* (Washington, D.C.: U.S. Government Printing Office, 1972), Table B-24, p. 223.

million jobs, while under the low-growth projection the required job increase would have to be 5.9 million.[86] Employment increases of this magnitude over such a short period are likely to be achieved and indeed would be without precedent in recent postwar years.

Over a longer period of years, the task of achieving a 4.5% unemployment rate is made difficult by a number of significant trends affecting the labor market. As has been pointed out, women are becoming an ever-increasing portion of the labor force, and they have characteristically exhibited a higher rate of employment than men. The continuing trend

---

[86] T. Aldrich Finegan, "Labor Force Growth and the Return to Full Employment," *Monthly Labor Review*, Vol. 95 (February 1972), p. 33.

from farm and rural to urban pursuits tends to convert what may have been underemployment to unemployment visible in the official statistics. The curtailment of unemployment in ordinance and aerospace industries is likely to produce unemployment which is unusually persistent because of the highly specialized skills of the personnel involved. The education industry, which had supplied thousands of new job opportunities in the decade of the sixties, is now in a state of contraction. These and other changes which have occurred and are occurring in our economy will make it difficult to reduce unemployment rates to the 4.5% level.

Perhaps of most significance is the fact that the elasticity of the labor force with respect to the availability of job opportunities may have risen in recent years. There has been a substantial increase in the fraction of the potential labor force (i.e., those persons already in the labor force plus those not in the labor force, but having previous work experience) consisting of married women, students, retired persons, and others, all of whom have more flexibility than heads of families in determining when and on what basis they will work. Because of the existence of this growing reserve of potential workers, some observers[87] believe that in any future expansion of business activity, there will be a relatively larger growth of the labor force than in previous recovery periods. If this should occur, as the economy runs "faster" in terms of employment expansion, it may in fact seem to "stand still" in terms of official unemployment rates.

In view of the foregoing, perhaps more attention needs to be given to the "quality" of unemployment than to the quantity. While the right to productive employment should be afforded to all members of the labor force regardless of age, color, or sex, nevertheless the impact of unemployment upon our society may be quite different if it falls most heavily upon teen-age students and part-time female employees than if it is concentrated among adult married men. Rather than seeking to achieve an overall aggregate rate of 4% or 4.5%, government should address itself to realistic goals with respect to various subgroups of workers within the labor force. Such differentiation of goals is more likely to be rewarded with success and furthermore would emphasize the need for specially tailored programs to meet the particular needs of the various subgroups in the labor market.

QUESTIONS FOR DISCUSSION

1. How has the incidence of unemployment changed in the American economy from 1961 to 1971?
2. "Hard-core unemployment is not made of rock, but of ice, and melts when total demand expands." Discuss the validity of this quotation.

---

[87] *Ibid.,* p. 37.

3. Discuss the merits and deficiencies of the definition of unemployment used by the Bureau of the Census. In your opinion, what groups are excluded by this definition who should be counted among the unemployed?

4. Discuss the meaning of the following concepts: poverty; invisible unemployment; persistent unemployment; frictional unemployment.

5. Discuss the characteristics of the typical unemployed person. Of what significance is the shift in employment from goods-producing to service industries?

SUGGESTIONS FOR FURTHER READING

GREEN, GLORIA P, and STINSON, JOHN F. "Employment and Unemployment in 1971," *Monthly Labor Review,* Vol. 95 (February 1972), pp. 20–28.

A concise up-to-date discussion of the characteristics of unemployment in 1971 as contrasted with earlier years.

MACNAMEE, HOLLY. "Adding Up the Problems of the Poor,"; Heineman, Ben W., "Guaranteed Annual Income: A Placebo or a Cure?"; Fitzhugh, G. W., "The Economic Impact of Income Maintenance," *Conference Board Record* (May 1969), pp. 22–36.

A series of articles dealing with the incidence of poverty and the merits and drawbacks of various proposals to eliminate it.

NORTHRUP, HERBERT R., et al. *Negro Employment in Basic Industry.* Studies of Negro Employment, Vol. 1. Philadelphia: Industrial Research Unit, Wharton School of Finance and Commerce, University of Pennsylvania, 1970.

A series of studies which discuss hiring practices and other aspects of the Negro employment problem in six basic industries in the United States.

Chapter 15

MANPOWER PLANNING BY

BUSINESS AND GOVERNMENT

"Manpower planning" as a concept is both new and old. It is new in both its micro and macro aspects in the emphasis placed upon it as an urgent function of business and government; it is old in that business and government have long engaged in manpower planning, both formally and informally. In recent years, however, rapid technological advancement, the changing nature of the business environment, increased competitive pressures from abroad, and the continued scarcity of some skilled personnel in the face of persistent unemployment have led companies to attempt to do a more effective job of forecasting company manpower requirements and the potential sources and means of fulfilling these needs.

Government interest in manpower planning historically has been concerned with providing for educational needs—until recently very largely local and state functions—and with encouraging particular types of manpower development—vocational and agricultural education, military officer training, and particularly obvious technical needs, for example, meteorologists for airports. In addition, the Armed Forces have effectively trained personnel requiring many types of skills, such as airplane pilots, mechanics of all description, cooks, and many other types of workers. Also, through the Bureau of Apprentice Training, U.S. Department of Labor, formal apprenticeship training has been encouraged, and through the Office of Education, U.S. Department of Health, Education and Welfare, educational activities have been furthered generally.

The 1960s saw government enter the manpower planning field massively. The persistence of structural unemployment, the civil rights movement, and the desire to eliminate poverty spurred great interest in the need to fit persons for jobs. The employment services of the states and the federal government were obviously inadequate to perform this function. A myriad of agencies came into being, and billions of dollars have been spent on manpower development, planning, upgrading and associated programs. Yet, as Chapter 14 emphasized, the structural aspects of unemployment are far from overcome. This chapter analyzes business and federal government manpower planning and assesses their capability to ameliorate manpower problems, and particularly unemployment.

MANPOWER PLANNING AT THE FIRM

A management publication defines manpower planning as "a process intended to assure an organization that it will have the proper number of properly qualified and motivated employees in its work force at some specified future time to carry on the work that will have to be done."[1]

Since firms engage in manpower planning for a variety of objectives, and because their manpower needs vary, their manpower planning activities vary considerably. In general, however, manpower planning at the firm, or micro level, may be said to have four aspects: (1) forecasting, (2) inventorying, (3) determining problem areas, and (4) planning for future needs.

Forecasting. To do planning of any type, it is necessary to estimate future requirements. This, in turn, involves judgments concerning matters both internal and external to the firm's control. The general state of business, industrial developments, and other factors affecting a firm's product demand must be estimated and projected in terms of the quantity and quality of labor required for a firm's production and sales. Obviously, the farther into the future the firm projects, the less precise are likely to be the results. To aid in these projects, companies develop mathematical models of future production based on different assumptions, often using general economic models, such as the Wharton Econometric Model, and project manpower on the basis of various assumptions as future business conditions.

Inventorying. The second step involves essentially an examination of existing human resources in order to determine whether they are employed optimally and to assess the extent to which they can meet the firm's future needs. The most comprehensive manner in which this is accomplished is by use of sophisticated data processing systems. Characteristics, capabilities, experience, educational attainment, and such pertinent aspects for the future as age, supervisory ratings, and so on, can all be put on tape and retrieved by modern computers in any part or form desired. Such inventorying received a strong impetus in the early 1960s, when companies were reexamining their black and other minority race employees, hoping to discover educational backgrounds and/or skills which had heretofore been ignored. As labor markets tightened in the 1960s while business expanded, the need to know the potential for skill development and expansion in the firm's own labor force greatly increased, and manpower inventorying became more common.

Determining Problem Areas. The third basic step involves a comparison of projected future manpower needs with resources estimated to be available from current manpower. To the extent that this comparison is accurate, it can demonstrate where shortages of numbers or skills are

---

[1] Walter S. Wilkstrom, *Manpower Planning: Evolving Systems* (Report No. 521 [New York: The Conference Board, 1971]), p. 1.

likely to exist in the future. It will, of course, be obvious to the reader that the longer the projection, the more risky in terms of accuracy becomes the comparative projection.

Planning for Future Needs. With the scarcities estimated, a planning program is required to overcome problems. Such programs can include training of existing or newly recruited manpower, intensive recruitment of persons with particular skills or educational backgrounds, transfer of key personnel from one sector of the firm to another where the need is greater, or new programs of compensation and motivation in order to increase employee interest in upgrading or personnel development.

The New Emphasis

All the activities summarized above have, as already noted, been practiced by personnel departments for years, as they strove to overcome labor shortages or attempted to insure an adequate manpower supply. What differentiates the situation today from previous eras is (1) the pressure to employ minorities and women; (2) the changing demographic composition of the labor force, and in many labor markets, the changing racial mix as well; and (3) the impact on the labor force of rapid technological developments.

Government Civil Rights Impact. To comply with government directives about minority labor force utilization, employers must have considerable knowledge about such workers—their availability, their relative size in the labor force and population, the degree of training they will have to be given to make them eligible for work or promotion—and plot this knowledge against the firm's projected labor force requirements.[2] In order to provide this information to governmental authorities and to defend their practices, many firms have been compelled to develop more detailed manpower and training programs than they would otherwise have done. The increased emphasis on female manpower utilization will also expand the need for effective planning of labor resources.

For the first time, many companies now incorporate manpower planning in all future planning, whereas in the past the assumption was made (not always correctly) that manpower would be available for future needs. Nevertheless, such manpower planning, despite pressure from government involving minority and female utilization, remains relatively undeveloped. A survey by The Conference Board in 1971 stated:

---

[2] We shall discuss government equal employment opportunity programs in Chapter 23. It should be noted here that government contractors, which include almost every concern of large size, must go beyond open doors to take "affirmative action" in employing minorities and women. This is often construed as a virtual requirement to train unqualified persons in order to qualify them.

In the course of this study line managers and personnel specialists in 84 companies were interviewed concerning their manpower planning priorities. Only 24 companies reported anything that they considered to be a manpower planning system. Most of these firms were larger organizations selected for the study because it was known that they had recognized and responded to a need for more effective manpower planning. And, in most of those cases, their manpower planning systems were only about five years old [as of 1971].[3]

One reason why even the threat of sanctions concerning the utilization of minorities and women has not spurred greater efforts to plan manpower is that the imponderables loom so large. The needs for manpower in the future depend upon so much that is extraneous to the firm: the general state of politics within the country and throughout the world; the general state of business; the character and quality of the labor force in the firm's plant areas; technology bearing upon the firm's products; changes in the character of demand by the overall population; and many others. Such plans as are made must, by the nature of the problem, be flexible—but flexible or not, such planning seems essential if manpower is not to be a major constraint of effective firm success not only for reasons of civil rights policy but also because of the changing labor force and technological developments.

Changing Labor Force Supply. Western Electric Company, the manufacturing arm of American Telephone and Telegraph Company, has major plants located in the areas of Newark, New Jersey, and Chicago. These plants were once surrounded by enclaves of European immigrants and their families. Many such workers brought with them to this country skills acquired in their European training, and they encouraged their sons and daughters to seek employment at Western's plants. The company could count on a labor supply that was imbued with mechanical interest and background.

Now the areas around these plants are peopled by black migrants from the rural South or second-generation urban blacks. Schools have deteriorated, family mechanical background is largely absent, family structure and motivation weaker. Obviously, the type, degree, intensity, and scope of training required to create a labor force out of the current supply is far different and undoubtedly much more expensive and lengthy than was the case 20 years ago. To be successful, manpower planning must integrate such training with the nature of jobs required in the future. Perhaps jobs can be altered to fit more nearly the background of the labor force.[4] Certainly, however, a company in similar

---

[3] Wikstrom, *Manpower Planning*, p. 5. Our debt to this excellent study is heavy.

[4] On Western Electric's racial policies, see Theodore V. Purcell and Daniel P. Mulvey, *The Negro in the Electrical Manufacturing Industry* (Racial Policies of American Industry, Report No. 27 [Philadelphia: Industrial Research Unit, Wharton School of Finance and Commerce, University of Pennsylvania, 1971]), esp. pp. 105–6.

circumstances can meet neither its own manpower needs nor government imposed civil rights requirements unless it plans in terms of the changed labor force now available to it.

The demographic factors in the labor force also require careful planning. General Motors opened a new facility at Lordstown, Ohio, to produce its subcompact "Vega." It found the labor force was composed almost exclusively of young people—under 30 years and for the most part, under 25. In view of the labor force characteristics resulting from birthrates of past decades (as described in Chapter 1), this should not have been surprising. General Motors found the young employees less inclined to accept management direction, demanding of lax work habits (10 minutes break each hour!), and quick to strike. The character of the labor force, lacking an older-worker mix, upset production goals. Perhaps a better integration of work methods, manpower planning, and production planning could have averted some of the problems.[5]

Technology and Planning.   The rapidly changing technology of recent years has been both an incentive for and a hindrance to manpower planning at the firm level. The incentive comes from the need for knowledge and skills required in new technology which may involve exotic metals, advanced electronic, mechanical, hydraulic, or pneumatic skills, or various combinations of all these. How to plan for the acquisition of these skills, and to what extent, involves much careful thought. At the same time, constant changes in technology and its varied usage with different product combinations can discourage any long-range forecasts.

Such problems are typical of the aerospace industry, which is frequently requested to build products, or to incorporate systems into products, which have never before even been designed. Such, in effect, was the job of the companies that prepared the hardware and systems for the Apollo moon landing program. They were required to develop the capacity to handle metals and plastics especially designed for the project. This meant extensive, worldwide recruiting of specialists, plus intensive training. Indeed, because of its constant work at the frontier of knowledge and the tremendous fluctuations of employment which results from the awarding and completion of government contracts, the aerospace industry is without peer in training. Manpower planning in this industry must include reliance on training departments that can impart knowledge of all kinds quickly and effectively.

Unfortunately, training in this industry frequently brings skills to a high level and then discards them. Thus, when building the C–5A, the world's largest airplane, which also has one of the most advanced radar, control, and navigational systems of any airplane, Lockheed Aircraft

---

[5] *New York Times*, April 2, 1972; *Business Week*, March 4, 1972, pp. 69–70 and April 1, 1972, pp. 22–23.

Company discovered it could find no electromechanical mechanics sufficiently capable of maintaining the equipment utilized in the manufacturing process. Sixty especially well-qualified mechanics were given two years of on-the-job training plus 1,000 hours of classroom instruction. Two years after this expensive but necessary program was completed, their work on the 81 planes ordered by the Air Force was completed, and they had to be laid off. If a new order is received, the company may have to go through the whole process again.

FIRM MANPOWER PLANNING AND UNEMPLOYMENT

To what extent can manpower planning at the firm level alleviate unemployment? The answer would seem to depend on the character of the unemployment. Seasonal unemployment has been an early and reasonably successful target of manpower planning by companies. Part of the reason has been union pressure. Requirements to lay off by seniority, with attendant high costs of "bumping" (as described in Chapter 6), has induced many companies to plan their production in a manner that will smooth out seasonal peaks and valleys. Where that cannot be accomplished, other companies have employed special seasonal workers. For example, one construction concern utilizes college students to handle its peak summer needs and maintains a permanent force year around. Companies with peak Christmas or Easter businesses employ part-time workers to meet the load. The need for such workers and their usefulness in manpower plannings is attested by the number of successful concerns in the business of supplying part-time labor. In the automobile industry, "short-week" pay, under supplemental unemployment benefit plans, has induced companies to plan manpower with shutdowns of assembly lines for a few days per week instead of layoffs. This is a form of division of work, as noted in Chapter 5, that avoids reassignment of worker schedules and duties.

Insofar as unemployment is attributable to long-term business declines, company manpower planning, by proper forecasting, can contribute to handling of the problem by allowing the labor force to decline by attrition, but it cannot solve the problem. The cure is new business, and manpower planning can basically aid by training employees to handle new duties. If, however, the sales are not forthcoming, manpower planning cannot solve the problem, except to give advance warning and some retraining to the individuals affected.

Much the same is true of cyclical unemployment. The real problem is to avoid the downturns by a product mix or other such program; manpower planning is the dependent variable geared to business needs; it is not an end in itself.

Business manpower planning has done its best service against unemployment in structural unemployment matters; spurred by government pressure and the civil rights revolution, industry alone, or in combination with government, has devised programs which have brought into the labor market thousands of employees whose prior education and skill had heretofore marked them as unfit for all but the most menial work. This involves a shift in the prior training role of industry. Historically, private industry has built upon the employee's past education by training, motivating and developing him on the job and throughout his working life.[6] Partly as a result of the increasing complexity of industrial jobs and partly because of the failure of the American educational system to provide large numbers of our society with appropriate tools for work—particularly, effective communications, arithmetic, and work habit skills—industry has also increasingly assumed the pretraining educational role. In turn, this has been done to provide firms an effective labor force and to meet their affirmative action requirements in minority employment. Training of the disadvantaged is a new, but growing, aspect of manpower planning.

A major problem in industry training of the disadvantaged to meet manpower requirements is that it is necessarily cyclical. Thus, Chrysler Corporation was compelled to curtail a major program when car sales declined in 1970; it had no jobs available for trainees and so it could not in good conscience train them. Similarly, the extraordinary training capacity of the aerospace industry which was beginning to show excellent results in training the hard core, ceased to be utilized when the industry's employment fell by 50% after 1969.

An effective attack on structural unemployment obviously involves both private and public manpower planning and attendant training. We therefore turn to a review of the manpower planning activities of the federal government.

FEDERAL MANPOWER PROGRAMS[7]

For more than 10 years, the federal government has been involved in manpower training through a number of programs having a diversity of sponsors—public and private corporations, states, counties, and cities. The prime responsibility for the administration of federal manpower training programs rests with the Department of Labor, but both the Office of Economic Opportunity (OEO) and the Department of Health, Education, and Welfare (HEW) are also involved in varying degrees.

---

[6] See Charles A. Myers, *The Role of the Private Sector in Manpower Development* (Policy Studies in Employment and Welfare, No. 10 [Baltimore: Johns Hopkins Press, 1971]).

[7] This section draws heavily on recent analysis completed by the Comptroller General of the United States, entitled *Federal Manpower Training Programs—GAO Conclusions and Observations* (Report to the Committee on Appropriations, U.S. Senate [Washington, D.C.: U.S. Department of Labor; Department of Health, Education, and Welfare; and Office of Economic Opportunity, February 17, 1972]).

Manpower training as a distinct program at the federal level came into being in the 1960s and received its initial recognition in the Area Redevelopment Act of 1961, which provided job-oriented training programs for unemployed and underemployed persons. In 1962, Congress enacted the Manpower Development and Training Act (MDTA), which has been continually broadened and extended through subsequent amendment. This act provides institutional and on-the-job training for unemployed, disadvantaged youth, and older workers; experimental and demonstration programs; and various supportive services. In 1964, the second major enabling legislation for manpower programs was passed by Congress. Under the title of the Equal Opportunity Act (EOA), the legislation created a range of programs for poverty communities, including Job Corps, Neighborhood Youth Corps, and Work Experience and Training Program for welfare recipients.

The next major manpower bill was enacted in 1968. It authorized the so-called "WIN" program to provide intensive "employability development" services for selected recipients in the Aid to Families with Dependent Children (AFDC) category. Finally, in July 1971, the Emergency Employment Act was passed by Congress, providing funding for public service employment for unemployed persons during periods of high unemployment.

Manpower Programs: Enrollment and Costs

Enrollments in federally assisted work and training programs have continued to rise each year. In fiscal 1971, new enrollments exceeded 2.1 million, a 15% increase over the 1970 level. During fiscal 1972, enrollments are expected to total over 2.3 million[8] (see Table 15–1). The 1972 increase reflects hirings under the Public Employment Program (PEP) authorized by the Emergency Employment Act.

The great majority of enrollees in manpower programs—about 93% in fiscal 1971—are poor or otherwise disadvantaged.[9] For manpower purposes a disadvantaged person is defined as a poor person who does not have suitable employment and who is either (1) a school dropout; (2) a member of a minority group; (3) under 22 years of age; (4) 45 years of age or over; or (5) handicapped. About 34% of enrollees are members of families on public assistance. Women represent 43% of the 1971 enrollees; Negroes 52%; Spanish-speaking people 16%; youth under 22 73%; and school dropouts 62%.[10]

Over a million youths 16 to 21 years of age were first-time enrollees in federal manpower programs during fiscal 1971. About two thirds were in the Neighborhood Youth Corps' in-school and summer programs,

---

[8] U.S. Department of Labor, *Manpower Report of the President, 1972* (Washington, D.C.: U.S. Government Printing Office, 1972), p. 56.

[9] *Ibid.*, p. 59.

[10] *Ibid.*

TABLE 15–1

New Enrollments* in Federally Assisted Work and Training Programs, Fiscal Years 1964 and 1970–73 (thousands)

			Fiscal Year		
Program	1964	1970	1971	1972 (Estimated)	1973 (Projected)
Total...........................	278	1,830	2,109	2,318	2,292
Institutional training under the MDTA....	69	130	156	166	166
JOBS (federally financed) and other OJT†	9	177	184	136	131
Neighborhood Youth Corps:					
In-school and summer...................	...	436	562	583	567
Out-of-school.........................	...	46	53	49	49
Operation Mainstream....................	...	12	22	22	22
Public Service Careers....................	...	4	45	32	29
Concentrated Employment Program........	...	110	77	69	69
Job Corps...............................	...	43	50	53	55
Work Incentive Program..................	...‗	93	96	112	133
Public Employment Program..............	...	...	...	160	92
Veterans programs.......................	‡	83	86	83	83
Vocational rehabilitation.................	179	411	468	517	558
Other programs§.......................	21	285	311	335	339

  * Generally larger than the number of training or work opportunities programmed because turnover or short-term training results in more than one individual in a given enrollment opportunity. Persons served by more than one program are counted only once. Therefore, totals for some programs differ from those for first-time enrollments in appendix table F–1.
  † Includes the MDTA–OJT program which ended with fiscal 1970 (except for national contracts) and the JOBS–Optional Program which began with fiscal 1971; also Apprenticeship Outreach, with 27,500 enrollees in fiscal 1971.
  ‡ Included with "other programs."
  § Includes a wide variety of programs, some quite small—for example, Foster Grandparents and vocational training for Indians provided by the Department of the Interior. Data for some programs are estimated.
  Note: Detail may not add to totals because of rounding.
  Source: Data, Office of Management and Budget, *Special Analysis, Budget of the United States Government, Fiscal Year 1973*, pp. 140 and 142; chart, U.S. Department of Labor, *Manpower Report of the President, 1972* (Washington, D.C.: U.S. Government Printing Office, 1972), p. 56.

holding part-time or vacation jobs designed to give poor youths much-needed income and help them stay in school or return there in the fall.[11] These programs had a measurable effect upon unemployment. For example, in July 1971, there were 499,000 unemployed black youths in the labor market aged 16 to 21, representing an unemployment rate of 28%. At the same time, more than 415,000 black youths were enrolled in manpower programs. It is not known whether all of these young people would have been active job seekers, but if the manpower programs represented an alternative to unsuccessful job seeking for only two thirds of the enrollees, the jobless rate for young blacks would have been 43% in July 1971 without these programs![12] These startling statistics need to be borne in mind when criticism of the manpower programs are considered later in this chapter.

---

[11] *Ibid.*, p. 95.
[12] *Ibid.*

Manpower training is expensive, whether undertaken by government or industry. From fiscal 1963 to fiscal 1971, the Department of Labor obligated over $6 billion for manpower training programs. For fiscal 1972, the planned Department of Labor funding for such programs is about $2.6 billion, including $1 billion for programs under the Emergency Employment Act. In addition, HEW and OEO have budgeted

TABLE 15–2

Estimated Funding for Major Manpower Training Programs Administered by the Department of Labor (fiscal 1972)

	Estimated Fiscal Year 1972 Funding (000 omitted)
Manpower Development and Training Act—institutional training	$ 324,800
On-the-job training	60,500
Job Corps	197,200
NYC	362,500
Operation Mainstream	38,800
CEP	172,800
JOBS program	200,000
Public Service Careers program	125,800
WIN program	197,100
Emergency Employment Act	1,000,000
	$2,679,500

Source: Comptroller General of the United States, *Federal Manpower Training Programs—GAO Conclusions and Observations* (Report to the Committee on Appropriations, U.S. Senate, [Washington, D.C.: U.S. Department of Labor; Department of Health, Education, and Welfare; and Office of Economic Opportunity, February 17, 1972]), p. 13.

millions of dollars for programs under their supervision.[13] The estimated fiscal year 1972 funding for major training programs administered by the U.S. Department of Labor is set forth in Table 15–2. The total estimated outlay in 1972 for manpower and related programs is $4.3 billion. President Nixon's budget request for 1973 will raise this sum to over $5 billion.[14]

Scope and Purpose of Manpower Programs

The major objective, for which purpose these vast sums are spent, is

. . . to develop job skills and thereby help the unemployed and underemployed, particularly welfare recipients and other disadvantaged persons, to make the transition to better jobs, better pay, and higher skill levels.[15]

[13] Comptroller General, *Federal Manpower Training Programs*, p. 13.

[14] *Manpower Report, 1972*, p. 57.

[15] Comptroller General, *Federal Manpower Training Programs*, p. 6.

The manpower activities encompassed by the various programs referred to include:

1. Recruitment, counseling, testing, placement, and follow-up services.
2. Classroom instruction in both remedial education and occupational skills.
3. Training on-the-job with both public and private employers aided by manpower subsidies.
4. Work experience and short-term employment for special age groups and those temporarily unemployed and transitional public service employment at all levels of government.
5. Ancillary or supportive services, such as child-care assistance, relocation assistance, and minor health care or treatment.

The Parade of Programs

The proliferation of manpower agencies continues at an unbroken pace each year. The following are brief descriptions of some of the major programs.

MDTA Institutional Training. Provides classroom occupational training and related supportive services for unemployed persons 16 years of age and older who cannot reasonably be expected to obtain full-time employment with their present skills, and for underemployed persons who are working but who, with training, could obtain higher level employment. Training relevant to the local labor market, as determined by the state employment service, usually is provided in skills centers or in public or private vocational schools.

MDTA On-the-Job Training. Provides occupational training for unemployed and underemployed persons who cannot reasonably obtain appropriate full-time employment without MDTA assistance. Such training generally is conducted through private industry—local employers, national groups, such as union organizations, or nonprofit organizations —in the regular work environment. The private firms are reimbursed by the federal government either directly or through the states for costs of instruction, and the trainees are on the payrolls of the employers.

Job Corps. Provides special services for disadvantaged young men and women aged 14 to 21 to train them to become productive citizens and to assist them in finding jobs, entering college, or enrolling in the Armed Services. The program utilizes residential urban and rural conservation centers and nonresidential centers which serve as skill-training centers but permit the youths to remain near or in their home communities. Job Corps centers are run by state and federal agencies, private industry, and public or nonprofit agencies. As of October 1971, there were 34 civilian conservation centers, 16 urban centers, and 15 residential manpower and residential support centers in operation.[16]

---

[16] *Ibid.*, p. 15.

National Youth Corps (*NYC*). Provides opportunities to students of low-income families to earn sufficient funds to remain in school while receiving useful work experience and some supportive services; it also provides work experience training and supportive services for youths from low-income families who have dropped out of school. As can be seen from Table 15–2, more federal funds are planned to be expended on this program in fiscal 1972 than any other manpower program except for the Emergency Employment Act. Enrollees work an average of 26 hours a week during the summer and 8 to 15 hours a week during the school year at a minimum wage of $1.60 per hour.

Operation Mainstream. Provides work training and employment activities, with necessary supportive services, for chronically unemployed needy adults who have poor employment prospects and who are unable —because of age, lack of employment opportunity, or otherwise—to secure appropriate employment or training assistance under other programs. Participants must be 22 years or older; however, 40% of the enrollment must be adults 55 years of age and older.

Concentrated Employment Program (*CEP*). Provides a system of packaging and delivering manpower services to disadvantaged residents of a locally defined CEP area. The Manpower Administration works through a single contract with a single sponsor (usually a Community Action Agency) to provide counseling, basic education, training, job development and placement, and other sources.

The JOBS Program. This program[17] provides training and employment for disadvantaged persons. The Department of Labor administers this program in cooperation with the National Alliance of Businessmen. The program consists of a contract component and a noncontract, or voluntary, component. Under the former, private employers enter into contracts with the Department of Labor, either individually or in groups, for the employment and training of disadvantaged persons. The contracts provide for reimbursement by government of the extraordinary costs in hiring, training, and retaining disadvantaged persons. Under the noncontract component, private employers pledge to hire specific numbers of disadvantaged persons without cost to the government.

The Work Incentive Program (*WIN*). Provides recipients of aid under the AFDC program with training and supportive services with the objective of moving them from welfare dependency to economic self-sufficiency. At the federal level, this program is administered jointly by the Department of Labor and HEW. At the state level, the state employment services, under contract with the Department of Labor, sponsor the program.

The Opportunities Industrialization Centers Program (*OIC*). Provides motivational and basic work orientation, basic education, skills

---

[17] Not to be confused with the Jobs Corps, which is a separate program.

training, and job placement assistance to unemployed and underemployed persons who have not been attracted to public-agency-sponsored manpower programs. OIC is unique in that it was started by a group of private citizens without federal funding. The program emphasizes minority-group leadership. At present the program is funded largely by the Department of Labor, HEW, and OEO. As of July 1971, 68 centers were in operation of which 62 were federally funded.[18]

The Emergency Employment Act of 1971. Provides funds to state and local governments in a two-year program to hire an estimated 150,000 to 200,000 unemployed or underemployed persons for public service jobs. The program envisages that these jobs are to be transitional in nature and that the participants are to move on to regular jobs as soon as practicable. The federal government pays 90% of this program. Unlike most of the other programs enumerated, its primary emphasis is not on minority groups or those who need basic education or skills training in order to hold any job. A major objective of the program was to provide transitional employment for engineers and other highly skilled persons who lost their jobs as a result of the scaling down of defense and aerospace work.

The foregoing discussion does not cover all of the federal manpower programs. Others which have attracted considerable attention are Operation Mainstream, aimed at the chronically unemployed poor, 22 years and over, primarily from rural areas, and New Careers, which provides work experience and training in the human service field for disadvantaged adults and out-of-school youths. The federal government is also heavily involved in vocational education and vocational rehabilitation. Expenditures for the former in 1970 amounted to about $285 million and for the latter about $478 million.[19]

Appraisal of Federal Manpower Programs

The manpower efforts of the federal government have been unique in that an integral part of these programs has been an attempt to measure and evaluate performance. For example, in fiscal 1969, $21 million was spent for special experimental and demonstration projects, $5 million for government funded research, and $4 million for internal evaluation.[20] Furthermore, many private efforts have been made by labor economists and others interested in the manpower field to evaluate the effectiveness of these programs. As a result, there is a considerable body of information concerning the performance of federal manpower programs. However,

---

[18] Comptroller General, *Federal Manpower Training Programs*, p. 18.

[19] Sar A. Levitan and Robert Taggart, III, *Social Experimentation and Manpower Policy: The Rhetoric and the Reality* (Policy Studies in Employment and Welfare No. 9 [Baltimore: Johns Hopkins Press, 1971]), pp. 110–11.

[20] *Ibid.*, p. 2.

it must be conceded at the outset that performance and effectiveness in the social area are difficult to measure and, therefore, despite impressive statistical compilations, which purport to support or to negate the effectiveness of specific manpower programs, there still remains differences of opinion as to the accomplishments of such programs.

A number of criticisms have been directed against the operation of federal manpower programs. Most frequently voiced are the following.

1. The proliferation of specific manpower programs[21] has built in rigidities that frustrate efforts to allocate limited resources and to utilize them most effectively. The existence of special category programs inhibits the ability of local communities to design manpower programs tailored to the needs of the local situation. Furthermore, although each program is supposed to serve a distinct client group, many persons in need of training could qualify under several programs because of similar conditions of eligibility. This creates a problem for the individual, because he probably is not familiar enough with any of the programs to decide which is best suited to his needs, and therefore the programs' intake personnel make that decision for him. Unfortunately, there is evidence that such personnel have an overriding concern to fill available slots in particular programs rather than to develop a mix of services that the applicant needs to become a productive member of the labor force.[22]

2. Costs of particular programs have been excessively high in relationship to expected benefits. The Job Corps has been a special target for this kind of criticism, after it was revealed that the costs of training a participant in a resident camp amounted to about $8,000 in the early years of the program. Attempts to justify this high cost by a showing of benefits in terms of increased earning power of "graduates" were not very convincing. As one study puts it: ". . . on the basis of widely varying estimates of educational gains, the Job Corps benefit-cost ratio might range from 1.69 to .53, permitting the conclusion that the Corps could be either a fairly worthwhile investment or a waste of money."[23]

3. The training provided under a number of the programs has been ineffective. Some critics contend that the training provided by employers under the Jobs Program, for example, was little more than would normally be provided without the program. In some cases, large subsidies may have been paid, more for hiring than for training; for instance, $3,600 was given for training janitors in one case; $3,900 for laborers, and $3,400 for office boys![24] Although many companies undertook substantial costs to provide adequate training and consultative services to disad-

---

[21] An investigation in a large eastern city revealed that there were 18 different organizations involved in job development and placement services. See Comptroller General, *Federal Manpower Training Programs*, p. 4.

[22] *Ibid.*, p. 49.

[23] Levitan and Taggart, *Social Experimentation and Manpower Policy*, p. 22.

[24] *Ibid.*, pp. 49–50.

vantaged hires, others "creamed the market" or hired persons they would have hired anyway.

A common criticism of the training offered under most federal programs has been that it has not been sufficiently geared to employer needs; therefore, participants take training in one field and end up being employed, if at all, in others. For example, a recent study of job training programs in urban poverty areas found that while the training offered prepared men for employment in the more highly skilled, better paying crafts, such as plumbing or carpentry, the bulk of the jobs actually held by poverty area men were in semiskilled occupations, such as local delivery truck driving, assembly line work, and general service station work.[25] It would be unfair, however, to fault the Manpower Administration entirely for this result, because obviously such factors as racial discrimination, union entrance requirments, and other institutional barriers may have impeded the hiring of trainees in jobs for which they had acquired skills. However, there is some evidence that a number of federal programs have been expanded faster than government's ability to staff competently has permitted. As a result, there has been some decline in the quality of training offered and a deterioration in lines of communication with prospective employers.

4. The federal manpower programs have failed to adapt to the changing economic conditions by altering the direction and nature of their programs. From 1964 to 1969, when federal manpower programs scored their most rapid growth, the nation was experiencing a period of business expansion and a tight labor market. From 1966 to 1969, unemployment averaged less than 3 million persons on an annual basis. Against this economic backdrop, it was obviously easier to place disadvantaged persons in industry.

In 1972, however, conditions had changed markedly: 5 million men and women were employed, many of them with excellent educational backgrounds and superior skills. With high levels of unemployment, not only do increasing numbers of persons need manpower services but also there is a change in the nature of clients. Furthermore, business has a pool of competent unemployed workers to choose from and therefore is less interested in participating in programs to assist the disadvantaged. In these circumstances, public sector training programs are practically imperative. To continue to process disadvantaged persons through so-called training programs with no jobs in prospect can only result in more embitterment and disillusionment.

Manpower programs can change in response to altered circumstances. The Manpower Development and Training Act of 1962 was originally passed to deal with the problem of technological unemployment, par-

---

[25] Roberta V. McKay, "Job Training Programs in Urban Poverty Areas," *Monthly Labor Review,* Vol. 94 (August 1971), p. 39.

ticularly among skilled workers. Subsequent amendments adopted it to cope with the disadvantaged members of the labor force. The question is whether similar revision in direction and outlook is now possible in current manpower programs or whether entrenched bureaucracy will inhibit change.

The Emerging Role of Federal Manpower Policy

After 10 years of experimentation, the broad outlines are now emerging of a new comprehensive federal manpower policy. This policy will attempt to integrate the fragmented patchwork of earlier programs into a unified, consistent overall policy and to link it more closely to broad economic policy over the business cycle. Key elements in such a policy are likely to be the following.

1. Emphasis will swing away from helping primarily the disadvantaged to covering the entire labor force. The unemployed engineer, the apprentice plumber, and the disadvantaged youth in the ghetto will all be included in the program.

2. The nation will move closer to acceptance of the concept of government as "the employer of last resort." A key feature of the Emergency Employment Act is the linkage of funds to the level of unemployment. When the unemployment rate rises above 4.5%, funds are turned on; when the rate falls below 4.5% for three successive months, funds are turned off. Although the Emergency Employment Act provides only for a two-year transitional program, the Manpower Revenue Sharing Bill, which the Nixon administration has introduced in Congress, incorporates a permanent program of this type.

3. There will be a major focus on specialized programs to upgrade the skills of the unemployed and of employees on the lower rungs of career ladders in order to break labor-market bottlenecks and improve productivity. Basic to this program emphasis is the notion that structural changes in the functioning of the labor market can move the Phillips curve to the left and thus favorably influence the trade-off relationship between unemployment and inflation.[26]

4. Federal spending on manpower programs will continue to grow. Manpower training is growth industry. Table 15–3 shows the growth in expenditures and in training slots from 1963 to 1971. The expenditures for 1973, as has been mentioned, will probably exceed $5 billion. This sum, although large, represents a smaller proportional national commitment than is found in some foreign countries.

5. Efforts will be made to cut, prune, and consolidate various programs which now overlap and to delegate increasing responsibility for

---

[26] See, for an example of this viewpoint, Charles C. Holt et al., *The Unemployment-Inflation Dilemma: A Manpower Solution* (Washington, D.C.: The Urban Institute, 1971).

administration to state and local agencies. The Manpower Administration now operates under a contract system that requires it to deal with as many as 10,000 local governmental units, businesses, foundations, and other groups that operate manpower programs at the community level. Some simplification of this structure would undoubtedly lead to better and less costly administration and supervision by the federal government.

Legislation designed to achieve this objective was introduced in Congress in 1972 under the title of the Manpower Revenue Sharing Act. This measure proposes that the present direct federal support of training and work-experience programs under the Manpower Development and

TABLE 15–3

Growth of Federal Spending and Training Efforts in Manpower Programs, 1963–71

Fiscal year	Federal spending* Millions of dollars	Training slots
1963	$ 56	59,200
1964	142	125,800
1965	433	510,200
1966	615	808,800
1967	796	808,400
1968	802	823,800
1969	1,030	910,700
1970	1,429	966,400
1971	1,637	1,187,200

° Funds obligated under MDTA, EOA, & Social Security Act
Source: Data, Manpower Administration; chart, *Business Week*, August 7, 1971, p. 48.

Training Act and the Economic Opportunity Act be replaced by federal grants to state and local governments, which would plan and administer their manpower programs in accordance with local needs. The bill would authorize $2 billion in appropriations for the first full year, of which 85% would be apportioned among state and local government units and 15% would be used by the Secretary of Labor for labor-market information programs, job banks, research and development, evaluation, technical assistance, and special projects. The concept of decentralization embodied in this bill does not find support in all circles. The AFL–CIO opposes the Nixon administration proposals on the grounds that they represent an abdication of federal responsibility to state and local governments in the administration and development of manpower programs.[27] The Committee for Economic Development approves the con-

---

[27] AFL–CIO Convention Statement on Manpower, *AFL–CIO American Federationist*, Vol. 79 (January 1972), p. 11.

cept of decentralization but argues that in view of the fact many state and local governments lack capacity either for planning or for vigorous administration, the federal government should retain responsibility for reviewing and approving state and local manpower plans which are federally funded, and of monitoring the effectiveness of ongoing programs.[28]

6. Increasing efforts will be made to get employable persons off the welfare rolls and into jobs. As has already been mentioned in Chapter 14, the Nixon Administration in 1971 proposed a major reform of the welfare laws. A major element of this program—which requires 1.5 million welfare recipients under AFDC to register for work and take jobs, or possibly lose their benefits—slipped through Congress in December 1971 as a rider to the 1971 tax bill. At the same time, as part of the new work incentive program (WIN), employers were granted tax incentives to hire welfare recipients. According to Assistant Labor Secretary Malcolm R. Lovell, Jr., the hiring incentives are equal to about 40% of first year wage costs.[29] Although some doubt has been expressed with respect to the effectiveness of the tax incentive program—employers have to keep employees for 12 months beyond the 12 months for which they get the tax credit—the WIN program is a response to a rising public demand "to do something about welfare."

Manpower Policy and Public Employment

Manpower training fails in its purpose if it does not place trainees in productive jobs. But with a continuing high level of unemployment in the private sector, the prospect of placement for most trainees is dim. In this circumstance, attention has turned to the public sector as a possible avenue for the creation of jobs. As mentioned, a step in this direction has been taken with the enactment of the Emergency Employment Act. The concept of using the public sector to provide jobs has always been viewed with suspicion in this country but has been established practice in many European nations. For example, in Sweden government contracts for construction are adjusted as to amount, timing, and geographical location as unemployment deepens. In February–March 1968, it was estimated that about 125,000 Swedish workers were saved from unemployment by such measures—a number roughly equivalent to 2.5 million workers in the United States, which has a labor force 20 times larger than Sweden.[30]

In the United States, the concept of using the public sector to provide

[28] Committee for Economic Development, *Training and Jobs for the Urban Poor* (New York: Committee for Economic Development, 1970), p. 16.

[29] *Business Week*, July 8, 1972, p. 20.

[30] Beatrice G. Reubens, *The Hard-To-Employ: European Programs* (New York: Columbia University Press, 1970), p. 386.

jobs is still a highly controversial issue. Opponents fear another WPA and a multitude of make-work, "leaf-raking" jobs. Others, while agreeing that involvement of the public sector in manpower training is desirable, disagree with the notion that manpower funds should be used to finance mere job creation. They would prefer that Congress determine whether additional federal financial support is required to provide an adequate level of public services, recognizing that the funding of additional services would automatically generate additional employment opportunities.[31] The AFL–CIO chooses to meet the critical issue squarely. In the words of Andrew J. Bremiller, Director of the Department of Legislation, AFL–CIO:

> For those who remain unemployed or seriously underemployed, a federally financed public-service employment program is the only logical answer. The Government should be the employer of last resort.[32]

It is unlikely that in the foreseeable future government will in fact serve as the employer of last resort in the sense of providing a job for everyone who wants to work. Our ventures into this area are likely to be on a much more modest scale. The Emergency Employment Act envisages the hiring of only about 145,000 workers in fiscal 1972 by various state and local governments. Even a doubling or tripling of this program would not make much impact on the total unemployment rolls of 5 million. Furthermore, while local government needs people to provide additional services, the needs are often for particular skills which may not be readily available among the unemployed. Nevertheless, despite these and other problems, it seems likely that the American economy will see a gradual extension of the principles incorporated in the Emergency Employment Act. Local governments are faced by budgetary restraints and taxpayer revolts which will require a retrenchment in services rendered. At the same time, the federal government is becoming increasingly aware of the inability of the private sector to absorb the unemployed. Greater use of federal funding to enlarge job opportunities in public employment appears to be a logical way of resolving the problems faced by government at the federal and local levels.

The Problem of Aspirations

As we have observed, manpower training without a provision of jobs is not enough. It is now gradually becoming evident that there is still another obstacle to hurdle: the mere provision of jobs is not enough either! It is apparent that many jobs with low status and little oppor-

---

[31] See Minority Report, Senate Committee on Labor and Public Welfare, accompanying S. 3867, the Employment and Training Opportunities Act of 1970, *Congressional Digest*, Vol. 50 (March 1971), p. 81.

[32] *Ibid.*, p. 94.

tunity for advancement are simply not deemed acceptable by large segments of our unemployed. We are therefore faced by the unique problem that even though there are millions of employed Americans working at such jobs, our unemployed—many of them poor, disadvantaged, and from minority races—will not accept such employment.

This startling fact was forcefully brought out in a recent study of participants in a CEP program in Columbus, Ohio. In the words of the investigators:

> The major conclusion arising from the data collected in this study is that most of the young men who participated in the Columbus CEP were unemployed because they were unwilling to take the kinds of jobs that were normally available to them. . . . The young men who were interviewed for this study knew they could get low level dead-end jobs any time they wanted to. They simply did not care to work in such jobs and there is no reason to believe that any amount of coaching, job guidance, or orientation programs could convince them that they should take such jobs. A CEP-type program, to be successful with the unemployed who have this attitude, would have to offer jobs paying at least the average wage for the local labor market.[33]

If this condition is widespread, then it is obvious that manpower programs must place greater emphasis upon upgrading. Furthermore, it raises serious problems as to the attraction of jobs which might be provided in state and local government through federal funding; for if such jobs are also viewed as dead-end without real opportunities for advancement, trainees may place them in the same category as jobs for dishwashers and elevator operators.

QUESTIONS FOR DISCUSSION

1. Why do some firms engage in manpower planning and others not at all? If you were managing an aerospace concern, would you spend funds on manpower planning? Explain your answer.
2. To what extent can private firms solve unemployment by effective manpower planning?
3. How does the stage of the business cycle affect the need for and the nature of manpower training programs? Can manpower training be an effective anticyclical device?
4. How can manpower planning affect the trade-off relationship between inflation and unemployment?
5. Discuss the pros and cons of the federal government becoming the "Employer of Last Resort."

---

[33] Morgan V. Lewis, Elchanan Cohn, and David Hughes, *Recruiting, Placing, and Retaining the Hard-to-Employ* (Institute for Research in Human Resources, University Park, Pa.: Pennsylvania State University, 1971), p. 2.

SUGGESTIONS FOR FURTHER READING

COMPTROLLER GENERAL OF THE UNITED STATES. Report to the Committee on Appropriations, U.S. Senate, *Federal Manpower Training Programs—GAO Conclusions and Observations*. Washington, D.C.: Department of Labor; Department of Health, Education and Welfare; Office of Economic Opportunity, February 17, 1972.

This report contains background information on the principal manpower programs and a critical review of their performance.

LEVITAN, SAR A., and TAGGART, ROBERT, III. *Social Experimentation and Manpower Policy: The Rhetoric and the Reality*. Policy Studies in Employment and Welfare, No. 9. Baltimore: Johns Hopkins Press, 1971.

A study, in the form of a concise monograph, of the problems involved in attempting to apply measurement, evaluation, and cost-benefit analysis to manpower programs.

MYERS, CHARLES A. *The Role of the Private Sector in Manpower Development*. Policy Studies in Employment and Welfare, No. 10. Baltimore: Johns Hopkins Press, 1971.

An examination of what business does and can do to upgrade the labor force and the planning necessary to do this. Also analyzed is the role of the business-government cooperative effort to aid the disadvantaged.

REUBENS, BEATRICE G. *The Hard-To-Employ: European Programs*. New York: Columbia University Press, 1970.

A study of the manpower experiences of nine European countries.

U.S. DEPARTMENT OF LABOR. *Manpower Report of the President*. Washington, D.C.: U.S. Government Printing Office, annually.

Each annual report normally contains a summary of major manpower developments as well as an analysis of the objectives and operations of particular programs.

WIKSTROM, WALTER S. *Manpower Planning: Evolving Systems*. Report No. 521. New York: The Conference Board, 1971.

A detailed study of manpower planning by companies with numerous instructive case studies.

PART V

Minimum Wages, Maximum Hours, and Governmental Security Programs

Chapter

16

MINIMUM WAGES AND

MAXIMUM HOURS

The establishment of minimum wages and maximum hours for the work force has long been a function of government. The rationale is both humanitarian and economic. This chapter examines the movements for ever higher minimum wages and for limiting hours of work, and discusses the economic consequences of such legislation.

THE FEDERAL FAIR LABOR STANDARDS ACT

The basic minimum wage law, the Fair Labor Standards Act, often termed the wage and hour law, was first enacted in 1938 and has since been amended several times. The original minimum wage was set at 25 cents per hour. In 1972, Congress was debating the establishment of a minimum above $2.00, with lower minima for special work groups. The history of the act is summarized in Figure 16–1. Since its passage, the act has also regulated hours of work by requiring that all work over a standard workweek, set since 1940 at 40 hours, be paid for at the rate of time and one half the regular wage.

The Fair Labor Standards Act never covered all employees. As a result of amendments of the last decade, the U.S. Department of Labor estimates that approximately 45.4 million workers are covered by the act. An additional 5.6 million are covered by similar state legislation. Those outside the law's purview include principally employees of small farms and small or intrastate businesses; some government employees largely covered by other and often more generous laws; and managerial, supervisory, professional, and outside sales personnel whose compensation generally would in any case be unaffected by minimum wage legislation. Table 16–1 summarizes the coverage of the Fair Labor Standards Act and of state minimum wage legislation by industrial groups.

Superminimum and Prevailing Wages

In addition to the FLSA, there are special *super minimum*, or prevailing wage laws which govern wages of particular groups. Thus, under a

FIGURE 16–1

Federal Minimum Wage History

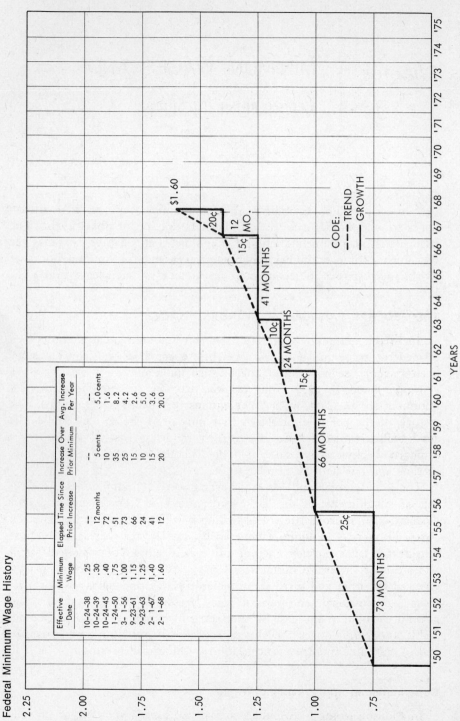

Effective Date	Minimum Wage	Elapsed Time Since Prior Increase	Increase Over Prior Minimum	Avg. Increase Per Year
10-24-38	.25	--	--	--
10-24-39	.30	12 months	5 cents	5.0 cents
10-24-45	.40	72	10	1.6
1-24-50	.75	51	35	8.2
3- 1-56	1.00	73	25	4.2
9-23-61	1.15	66	15	2.6
9-23-63	1.25	24	10	5.0
2- 1-67	1.40	41	15	3.6
2- 1-68	1.60	12	20	20.0

CODE:

---- TREND

—— GROWTH

YEARS

'50 '51 '52 '53 '54 '55 '56 '57 '58 '59 '60 '61 '62 '63 '64 '65 '66 '67 '68 '69 '70 '71 '72 '73 '74 '75

complex formula, airline pilots are guaranteed wages in excess of $15,000 (some earn more than $50,000), and their hours may not exceed 85 per month.

A second superminimum wage law, known as the Davis-Bacon Act, was first passed in 1931. As later amended, it requires contractors engaged in construction work valued at $2,000 or more, and paid for by federal funds, to compensate employees on the basis of "prevailing wages." In 1965, by the O'Hara-McNamara Services Act, the Davis-Bacon type of regulation was extended to government-contract on-site services other than construction—for example, machinery installation.[1]

The Secretary of Labor determines prevailing minimum rates for the various crafts under the Davis-Bacon Act procedure. As interpreted by Secretaries since 1931, "prevailing" is usually synonymous with "union." Building-trades unions have found the Davis-Bacon Act a valuable tool to prevent undercutting of their wages and to assist the extension of the union rate to a wider area. For, not infrequently, the union rate has been determined to be prevailing in a locality not even unionized but in addition paying considerably less than the union rate which actually prevails in a large city some miles away.

A third superminimum wage law is the Public Contracts or Walsh-Healey Act, which was enacted in 1936, two years prior to the passage of the Fair Labor Standards Act, as a means of filling part of the gap left by the demise of the NRA. The Walsh-Healey Act provided, among other things, that for all government in-plant contracts in excess of $10,000, wages should not be less than the "prevailing minimum" as established by the Secretary of Labor. The wage-setting mechanisms of this law were rendered inoperative in 1964 by a court decision,[2] thus ending a very controversial government activity.[3]

State Minimum Wage Laws

State minimum wage laws were originally enacted to cover employment of women and children only, but since World War II, states have increasingly enacted laws of general application. Only the latter type

---

[1] Some 35 states have laws similar to the Davis-Bacon Act.

[2] The Secretary used data collected by the U.S. Bureau of Labor Statistics to determine prevailing wages. Since these data were gathered for other BLS purposes on promise to cooperating employers that no individual company would be identified, their source could not be given to those who wanted to check them, thus denying due process in a proceeding. See *Wirtz* v. *Baldor Electric Co.*, 16 WH Cases 551 (1964).

[3] Two studies shed much light on the Walsh-Healey Act and its procedure: Herbert C. Morton, *Public Contracts and Private Wages: Experience under the Walsh-Healey Act* (Washington, D.C.: Brookings Institution, 1965); and Carroll L. Christensen and Richard A. Myren, *Wage Policy under the Walsh-Healey Public Contracts Act: A Critical Review* (Bloomington, Ind.: University of Indiana Press, 1966).

TABLE 16–1

Estimated Number of Employed Wage and Salary Workers in the Civilian Labor Force Classified by Their Status under the *Minimum Wage* Provisions of the Fair Labor Standards Act, by Industry Division, United States, September 1971 (in thousands)

Industry Division	Number of Employed Wage and Salary Workers in the Civilian Labor Force				Number of Nonsupervisory Employees Subject to the Minimum Wage Provisions of the FLSA			Number of Nonsupervisory Employees Not Subject to the Minimum Wage Provisions of the FLSA		
	Total	Exempt under Section 13(a)(1) of FLSA[1]		Nonsupervisory Employees excluding Outside Salesmen	Total	Subject Prior to the 1966 Amendments[2]	Subject as a Result of the 1966 Amendments	Total Exempt from or Not Covered by FLSA	Subject to State Laws or Orders Only[3]	Not Subject to FLSA or State Laws or Orders
		Executive, Administrative, and Professional Personnel	Outside Salesmen							
All industries	75,126	13,015	2,015	60,096	45,383	34,057	11,326	16,728	5,649	11,079
Private sector	62,029	8,172	2,015	51,842	42,056	34,057	7,999	11,801	4,451	7,350
Agriculture[4]	1,306	70	...	1,236	495	...	495	741	110	631
Mining	623	66	...	557	552	552	...	5	1	4
Contract construction	3,471	279	2	3,190	3,175	2,636	539	17	7	10
Manufacturing	18,840	1,895	449	16,496	16,389	16,323	66	556	103	453
Transportation, communications, utilities	4,509	464	9	4,036	3,962	3,859	103	83	35	48
Wholesale trade	3,880	563	787	2,530	2,522	2,404	118	795	88	707
Retail trade	11,362	1,040	98	10,224	6,222	3,489	2,723	4,100	2,493	1,607
Finance, insurance, real estate	3,829	544	646	2,639	2,490	2,405	85	795	143	652

Services (excluding domestic service)[5]	12,095	3,251	24	8,820	6,249	2,379	3,870	...	2,595	1,471	1,124
Domestic service	2,114	...	...	2,114	...	...	...	...	2,114	...	2,114
Public sector	13,097	4,843	...	8,254	3,327	...	3,327	...	4,927	1,198	3,729
Federal government	2,666	299	...	2,367	641	...	641	...	1,726	...	1,726
State and local government	10,431	4,544	...	5,887	2,686	...	2,686	...	3,201	1,198	2,003

[1] Section 13(a)(1) exempts from the minimum wage and overtime provisions of the Fair Labor Standards Act "any employee employed in a bona fide executive, administrative, or professional capacity (including any employee employed in the capacity of academic administrative personnel, or teacher in elementary or secondary schools), or in the capacity of outside salesman . . ."

[2] Relates to currently employed workers who would have been subject under criteria in effect prior to the 1966 amendments.

[3] Number of employees subject to state minimum wage laws or orders only relate to states with minimum wage laws or orders that were enacted or revised between January 1962 and January 1972. No estimates were made for State law coverage of domestic service employees.

[4] Estimates for agriculture relate to May 1971.

[5] Estimates for educational services relate to October 1971.

Note: In 1972, Congress was considering extending coverage of the Fair Labor Standards Act to domestic servants and to employees of small units of chain stores.

Source: U.S. Department of Labor, *Minimum Wage and Maximum Hours Standards under the Fair Labor Standards Act*, January 1972, pp. 37, 38.

would now appear operative, since the Civil Rights Act of 1964, by outlawing sex as well as race discrimination, prohibits such distinctions. In 1972, 42 states, Puerto Rico, the District of Columbia, and Guam had minimum wage laws. In two of these states,[4] the minima are set too low to be effective. The data in Table 16–1 shows that approximately 16.7 million persons are covered by state laws other than the obsolete ones and that 11 million are under both federal and state laws. In the latter case, the higher minimum applies.

Table 16–2 lists the states which have minimum wage laws and gives the rates currently in effect. Some of these laws set a statutory minimum; others permit the rates to be adjusted by administrative procedures which allow the establishment of different rates for different industries, and within limits, raising rates without new legislative sanction. Still other laws establish rates by reference to the federal Fair Labor Standards Act.

Minimum Wages and Employment—the Theory

Minimum wage legislation means higher wage costs to the individual employer affected by such legislation. Economic theory tells us that if an employer finds that labor has become more expensive, he will try to economize in its use or to get more work out of his labor force. There may be some workers who can be dropped from the payroll simply by rescheduling work or changing assignment of duties. In some cases, it may be possible to eliminate jobs which no longer "pay" at the higher wage rate. The most effective way of reducing labor costs is, of course, through substituting machinery for labor. The lower the wage paid prior to the establishment of the minimum wage, and the greater the increase in costs imposed by such legislation, the greater the incentive to the employer to introduce laborsaving machinery.

In many cases, the process of mechanization will involve purchase of machinery which was already known and in use in the industry but which was not adopted at the low-wage level. Sometimes, however, the wage increase will cause employers to introduce machinery which would have been profitable to introduce even at a lower wage level but which management failed to adopt because of inefficiency and reliance on payment of substandard wages as a means of competition. In other words, imposition of a minimum wage may provide the "shock" which compels inefficient management to look around in the industry and bring its production methods in line with more efficient firms in order to survive. This will involve not only adoption of laborsaving machinery but also methods and layouts which will reduce overhead, material costs, insurance expense, and other expenditures. It should be remembered that introduction of laborsaving machinery is sometimes a long-term process.

---

[4] Kansas and Louisiana.

TABLE 16–2

Basic Minimum Wage and Overtime Premium Pay Provisions Applicable to Non-agricultural Employment under State Laws,[1] September 1, 1972

Jurisdiction (State)	Basic Minimum Rate[2] (Per Hour)	Premium Pay After Designated Hours[3] Daily	Premium Pay After Designated Hours[3] Weekly
Alaska	$2.10	8	40
Arizona[4]	...	...	...
Arkansas (Applicable to employers of 5 or more)	1.20	8 (W)[5]	7th day (W)[5]
California	1.65	8 12 d.t. During first 8 on 7th day. After 8 on 7th day d.t.	40 on 6th day.
Colorado	1.00 to 1.25		40–42
Connecticut	1.85[6]		40
Delaware	1.60		
District of Columbia	1.60 to 2.25		40
Georgia (Applicable to employers of 6 or more, or employers with annual sales of $40,000 or more)	1.25		
Guam	1.90		40
	2.05		40
Hawaii	1.60		40
Idaho	1.40	8 (W)[5]	48 (W)[5]
	1.60	8 (W)[5]	48 (W)[5]
Illinois (Applicable to employers of 5 or more full-time employees)	1.40		
	1.60		
Indiana (Applicable to employers of 4 or more in any workweek)	1.25		
North Dakota	1.00 to 1.45		
Ohio (W)	75¢ to 1.25		
Oklahoma (Applicable to employers of 10 or more full-time employees at any one location, or to employer with gross annual business of $100,000 or more regardless of number of employees)	1.40		
Oregon	1.25		40
Pennsylvania	1.60		40
Puerto Rico	65¢ to 1.60	8 d.t. statutory rest day d.t.	48 d.t.
Rhode Island	1.60		48 (W)[5]
South Dakota	1.00		
Texas	1.40	9 (W)[5]	
Utah	1.20 to 1.35		
Vermont (Applicable to employers of 2 or more)	1.60[6]		40
Washington	1.60		
West Virginia (Applicable to employers of 6 or more in any calendar week at one location)	1.20		48
	1.40		48
	1.60		48

TABLE 16–2 *(Continued)*

Jurisdiction (State)	Basic Minimum Rate[2] (Per Hour)	Premium Pay After Designated Hours[3] Daily	Premium Pay After Designated Hours[3] Weekly
Wisconsin (W)	1.45	9[5]	48[5]
Wyoming	1.50	8 (W)[5]	
	1.60	8 (W)[5]	
Kentucky[1]	65¢ to 75¢		44–48 m.r.
Maine (*Except* hospital and nursing home employees; and *except* employers of less than 4)	1.80[6]		40
	1.60		40
	1.80		40
	1.40		40
	1.60		40
	1.80		40
Maryland[8]	1.60		40
Massachusetts	1.75[7]		40
Michigan (Applicable to employers of 4 or more at any one time within any calendar year. If employer has 4 or more at any one time, he is covered by the law for remainder of such calendar year)	1.60		
Minnesota	75¢ to 1.60		
Montana	1.60		40
Nebraska (Applicable to employers of 4 or more at any one time)	1.00		
Nevada	1.60	8[9]	48[9]
New Hampshire	1.60[6]		
New Jersey	1.50		40
New Mexico (*Except* service employees, as defined) (Applicable to employers of 4 or more at any one time)	1.60		48 (W)[5]
	1.30		48 (W)[5]
New York	1.85[6]		40 m.r.
North Carolina (Applicable to employers of 4 or more at any one time)	1.45		
	1.60		

[1] In general the laws apply to men, women, and minors, except for entries designated (W) which indicates the provisions apply only to women, or to females, or to women and minors. In Kentucky, although the law applies to "employees," current wage orders are enforced only for women and minors. Not shown are additional details on coverage and rates, such as exemptions from coverage of minors under the age of 16 or 18 in a few states, lower rates for minors under 18 in several states, and other variations, including lower rates for agricultural workers.

[2] Rates listed are those of general application. Rates shown in a range indicate variations established by wage orders on the basis of industry, occupation, population zone, or other factors.

[3] The premium rate is 1½ times the employee's regular rate, except where indicated by "m.r.," meaning 1½ times the minimum rate, or by "d.t.," meaning double time, i.e., 2 times the employee's regular rate. Hours shown in a range indicate variations established by different wage orders.

[4] *Arizona:* The Laundry and Drycleaning Order sets $21.60 a week in drycleaning and $18.72 in laundry work for a workweek of 36 to 40 hours; the Retail Trade Order sets $26.40 for a standard workweek, i.e., 48 a week (8 a day, 6 days) or 42 a week (6 a day, 7 days).

[5] In the following seven states, the premium pay provision is included in a specific women's law rather than the minimum wage law. In *Arkansas, Idaho, Wisconsin,* and *Wyoming,* it is in a women's overtime pay law; in *Texas,* in a former maximum hours law for women converted to a voluntary overtime law, under which daily overtime is paid if the employee works more than 40 hours a week; in *Rhode Island,* in a women's maximum hours and overtime pay provision which, under an Attorney General Opinion, is in effect being applied as a voluntary overtime provision. In *New Mexico,* it is included in a female hours law which fixes a maximum 8-hour day, 48-hour week but permits emergency overtime in excess of 8 hours a day up to 50 hours a week. In addition, an exemption from this law is available to females who sign an agreement to work more

TABLE 16–2 (Concluded)

than 8 hours a day or 40 hours a week, provided the agreement calls for time and one-half pay after 40 hours a week. Coverages of these premium pay provisions differ from that of the minimum wage laws.

6 Connecticut, Maine, New Hampshire, New York, and Vermont have provided for automatic upward adjustment if the federal rate is increased. *Connecticut's* rate will be one half of 1% more than any changed federal rate; *Maine* and *New York* will match a Federal increase up to $2; *New Hampshire* deleted the dollar rate in its law and adopted the federal rate by reference; and *Vermont's* rate will equal any federal increase.

7 *Connecticut:* Law is inapplicable to individuals employed in manufacturing establishments subject to FLSA. *Massachusetts:* The 1971 amendment increasing the rate from $1.60 to $1.75 postponed the effective date in manufacturing, whether interstate or intrastate, until the FLSA rate equals or exceeds the state rate.

8 *Maryland:* A Baltimore city Ordinance, applicable to employers of three or more, sets a rate of $1.65 an hour. The maximum tip allowance is 50%.

9 *Nevada:* Not applicable to males whose overtime rates are established by or who are specifically exempt from FLSA. Overtime pay for females is derived from a female hours provision in the wage-hour law which fixes a maximum 8-hour day, 48-hour week but which permits females to work up to 12 hours a day, 56 a week, in prescribed circumstances.

Note: Some States have rate differentials for all service (tipped) occupations or for all such occupations in restaurants and/or hotels.

Source: U.S. Department of Labor, Employment Standards Administration.

Some employers may not be able to utilize the newest machinery in an antiquated plant and may have to delay purchase of machinery until they can move to a new location; other employers may try to get a few more years out of old equipment before making the large capital expenditure required for modern machinery. As a result, the displacement of labor through the introduction of laborsaving machinery may not occur until several years after the imposition of the minimum wage; and if business meanwhile increases, there may be no unemployment observable at all.

Another avenue by which a minimum wage may react upon employment is through the effect of the wage increase on price. Large companies frequently have big advertising budgets and are able to obtain a higher price for their products by building up the idea of quality in consumers' minds. Small companies, on the other hand, must often compete primarily on the basis of price. If a minimum wage raises the labor costs of smaller concerns, it puts them at a substantial competitive disadvantage. If they raise prices to compensate for the increase in costs, some part of their business will tend to shift to their larger competitors, and they may eventually be forced out of business. If this result occurs, the total volume of employment in the industry may be lowered after the shift of business is effected, even though some labor displaced in small companies is employed by larger ones. The reason is that the larger concerns are likely to be more mechanized, and a dollar's sales in such companies will require employment of a smaller amount of labor than in the smaller, low-wage plants.

It should be noted that if a minimum wage law produces unemployment, the incidence of unemployment may be expected to fall most heavily upon those with the least skills—that is, upon those employees whose wages have been below the legal minimum and who have the most difficulty in finding jobs. It will be recalled that in our analysis of unemployment in Chapter 14, it was pointed out that a disproportionate share of the persistent unemployment in recent years has fallen upon the unskilled group. Our succeeding analysis will attempt to determine whether this unemployment has been partially a result of minimum wage legislation.

Minimum wage legislation affects not only employer efficiency but employee efficiency as well. Workers who in 1938 received less than the minimum of 25 cents per hour obviously had difficulties in making ends meet. Similarly, in 1968, workers who earned less than the $1.60-an-hour minimum, or $64, for a 40-hour week, had difficulty in providing adequate food, clothing, shelter, and medical care for themselves and their families. Establishment of a minimum wage which eliminates sub-standard wages is likely to have some beneficial effect on the health, efficiency, and morale of workers which may be reflected in improved man-hour production. Also, the higher cost of labor makes employers more labor-conscious and is likely to cause management to devote more time and effort to training workers and selecting new employees more carefully. The net result may be better productivity, which will tend, in part, to offset the higher wage costs, so that the rise in unit labor costs will be less than the rise in wage rates. To the extent that this is true, the effect of the wage increase on employment will be lessened.

In general, economic theorists conclude that imposition of a minimum wage will tend to produce some unemployment in the individual firm affected by such legislation. The amount of the unemployment will vary from firm to firm, depending upon the magnitude of the wage increase, the importance of labor costs relative to total costs, the ability of the employer to reduce costs other than labor costs, the extent to which business of the firm falls off if it increases prices, the effect of the wage increase on man-hour output, and the extent to which the company introduces laborsaving machinery. As has already been mentioned, however, the tendency to reduction of employment may not be observable because of counteracting changes in the business scene.

Empirical Studies—The 25-Cent Minimum of 1938

Fortunately, we can do more than theorize about the imposition of a minimum wage. We have empirical studies which shed light on what actually occurred when minimum wage laws were imposed, starting with the imposition of the 25-cent-per-hour minimum in 1938.

Two weeks after the 25-cent-an-hour minimum went into effect (this was the initial requirement of the Fair Labor Standards Act of 1938), the administrator of the act reported to the President that, in all, between 30,000 and 50,000 persons, or less than 0.05% of the workers affected by the law, lost their employment for reasons probably traceable to the act.

Of these workers, about 90% were concentrated in a few industries in the South, such as pecan shelling, tobacco stemming, lumbering, and bagging. Other industries which were seriously affected by the minimum wage included cottonseed crushing, seamless hosiery, and cotton garment manufacture.[5]

Many firms in these industries reacted to the wage increase by substituting machinery for labor, but other reactions included:

1. Narrowing differentials between the high-paid and the low-paid workers by not granting increases to high-paid workers equal to those required to bring the lowest paid within the law.
2. Carefully weeding out inefficient employees.
3. Establishing higher standards of efficiency for new personnel and improving selection techniques to put these standards into effect.
4. Increasing attention to working conditions and other personnel problems in order to improve the general efficiency of the labor force.

Management had almost complete freedom to make these adjustments, since in industries which were directly affected by the 1938 legislation, unionization was largely absent.

The net effect of these adjustments upon employment is not entirely clear, but it appears that in a few industries the substitution of machinery for low-paid hand labor created substantial technological unemployment. In such industries as tobacco stemming and cottonseed crushing, an average of from 3 to 10 workers were displaced by a single machine. In these industries, extremely low wages made labor so cheap that basic mechanical improvements had previously never been seriously considered.

Hardship engendered by this technological unemployment was, however, offset by the fact that the Fair Labor Standards Act of 1938 was inaugurated at the depth of the 1937–38 recession, and business conditions and employment generally improved immediately thereafter. Moreover, in 1940 the defense boom inaugurated a period of prosperity which more than took up any slack in employment caused by technological developments.

Besides creating some technological unemployment, the Fair Labor Standards Act also upset the competitive equilibrium in many industries. High-wage firms often were required to make little or no adjustment in order to conform with the act; low-wage firms, on the other hand, faced a serious situation. A study of 26 plants in the seamless hosiery industry

---

[5] See, for example, U.S. Bureau of Labor Statistics, *Hours and Earnings of Employees of Independent Tobacco Stemmeries* (Serial No. 1388 [Washington, D.C.: U.S. Government Printing Office, 1941]); and J. F. Moloney, "Some Effects of the Fair Labor Standards Act upon Southern Industry," *Southern Economic Journal*, Vol. 9 (July 1942), pp. 5–23.

indicated that the 12 high-wage plants made few wage adjustments between 1938 and 1939, while the 11 low-wage plants were forced to raise
wages 35%. In many instances, these low-wage companies also made
large expenditures in capital equipment in order to maintain a sound cost
position. In this same industry, employment in the high-wage firms increased between 1938 and 1940 by 7.5%, while employment in the low-
wage group decreased 12.8%.[6]

The Effects of the 75-Cent Minimum of 1949

The situation at the time of the establishment of the 75-cent minimum
in 1950 was similar to that in 1938 when the initial 25-cent minimum became effective. Unionization was still largely absent from the industries
directly affected, which were largely the same ones affected in 1938, so
that management had pretty much of a free hand to adjust to the higher
minimum. And once again, the effect of the higher minimum was
obscured by an economic upswing resulting from military action—this
time the Korean War, which began six months after the 75-cent minimum went into effect.

The $1 Minimum of 1956

The $1 minimum wage had a more severe and direct effect on em-
ployment than did previous legislation. Employment in industries which
had substantial employment at rates under $1 declined even in 1956–57
when the economy was strong. Sixteen of the so-called "high-impact"
industries suffered a drop in employment from 10% to 25%, with unskilled workers especially hard hit.[7] Because lower rated employees received increases required by law, but lesser or no increases were granted
to higher rated jobs, wage schedules were compressed.[8]

---

[6] A. F. Hinrichs, "Effects of the 25 Cent Minimum Wage on Employment in
the Seamless Hosiery Industry," *Journal of the American Statistical Association,* Vol.
35 (March 1940), pp. 13–23; and H. M. Douty, "Minimum Wage Regulation in
the Seamless Hosiery Industry," *Southern Economic Journal,* Vol. 15 (October
1948), pp. 176–89.

[7] U.S. Department of Labor, Wage and Public Contracts Division, *Studies of
the Effects of the $1.00 Minimum Wage* (Washington, D.C.: U.S. Government
Printing Office, 1959). See also Harry M. Douty, "Some Effects of the $1.00 Minimum
Wage in the United States," *Economica,* Vol. 27 (May 1960), pp. 137–47. For a
critique of the Department of Labor studies, see George Macesich and Charles T.
Stewart, Jr., "Recent Department of Labor Studies of Minimum Wage Effects,"
Southern Economic Journal, Vol. 26 (April 1960), pp. 281–90.

[8] *Ibid.,* and David E. Kaun, "Economics of the Minimum Wage: The Effects
of the Fair Labor Standards Act, 1945–1960" (unpublished doctoral dissertation, Stanford University, 1963).

The 1961 Amendments

In 1961, Congress raised the minimum for previously covered workers to $1.15 as of September 1, 1961, and $1.25 as of September 1, 1963. In addition, the act was extended to 3.6 million additional workers, mostly in retail trade. For those newly covered, overtime payments were waived for three years, and minima were set at $1 as of September 1, 1961; $1.15 four years later; and $1.25 as of September 1, 1966. As a result, approximately 15% of those covered in 1961 received wage increases, but this included nearly 67% of those in the 15 southern industries which have been affected by every change in the Fair Labor Standards Act since 1938. In 1963, the increase in the minimum of $1.25 affected directly an estimated additional 2.6 million workers, again including those in these 15 southern industries. In October 1960, for example, average hourly earnings in the southern lumber industry were $1.18 per hour; by June 1962, these earnings had risen to $1.27 under the impact of the minimum, with 63% of the employees receiving wage increases. Employment in this industry continued on a downward trend, dropping from 173,000 to 141,000 between October 1960, and June 1962.[9]

The 1961 and 1963 increases in the minimum wage law brought under the act low-wage retail employees who had not been covered since the 1949 amendments. Employment in retailing continued its expansion; but in nonmetropolitan areas of the South, employment in covered retail trade declined from 160,000 in June 1961 to 143,000 in June 1962, while employment in retail trade in these areas in establishments *not* covered by the FLSA rose from 549,000 to 574,000.[10]

The 1965 Amendments

The 1965 amendments, which raised the minimum wage to $1.60 per hour in two steps for those already within the purview of the law and in several steps for those newly brought within its coverage, was enacted in a period of great prosperity and rising employment. Government sponsors of higher minimum wage laws hailed the results as contributing to the fight against poverty without substantially affecting employment. A more careful examination of the available data indicate that the effects of

---

[9] U.S. Department of Labor, *Report Submitted to the Congress in Accordance with the Requirements of Section 4(d) of the Fair Labor Standards Act* (Washington, D.C.: U.S. Government Printing Office, January 1963), pp. vii, 35, and 40.

[10] U.S. Department of Labor, *Effects of Minimum Wage Rates Established under the Fair Labor Standards Act in Retail Trade in the United States and Puerto Rico: A Study of Changes in Wage Structure of a Matched Sample of Retail Establishments, 1961–1962* (Washington, D.C.: U.S. Government Printing Office, November 1963), p. 5.

the 1965 amendments are those which one might expect in a period of economic expansion:

—employment in some of the newly covered sectors, such as laundries and agriculture declined, with the latter continuing, and perhaps accelerating a long-term trend;[11]

—some industries, such as motels and hotels, restaurants and hospitals continued to expand, but these sectors of the economy also experienced considerable price increases. Drug stores accommodated to the situation by eliminating lunch counters, and reducing employment by 12 percent, thus throwing out of work many marginal employees, including large numbers of blacks.[12]

—the same industries in the South, which have been directly affected by every rise in the minimum wage were again affected, but as during World War II and the Korean War, the impact was obscured for several years by the rising level of sales and prosperity.

The impact of the changes in minimum wage legislation in the 1960s, like that in previous prosperous times was often more likely to be felt after some time lag, rather than immediately. Mechanization takes time. Equipment installed as a result of higher minima may not be in place until a year or more after the effective date of the change in the law. Moreover, the impact is often delayed when the law becomes effective because times are prosperous and business is expanding. When the business cycle turns downward, then marginal employees are let go, or not hired. Moreover, the impact is likely to be especially hard on the young, the black, the disadvantaged, and the untrained—often one and the same. Empirical studies not only of the federal law effects, but also of those of state laws[13] amply support the theoretical economic expectation that increased unemployment is a likely result of raising minimum wages.[14]

---

[11] Agricultural employment was also affected by the cutting-off of "Bracero" or imported Mexican labor. Reducing supply is, of course, another way to raise minimum wages.

[12] See F. Marion Fletcher, *The Negro in the Drug Store Industry* (Racial Policies of American Industry, Report No. 24 [Philadelphia: Industrial Research Unit, Wharton School of Finance and Commerce, University of Pennsylvania, 1971]), pp. 17–18.

[13] A good summary of studies and their findings in regard to minimum wages and employment, including studies of state legislation, is found in John M. Peterson and Charles T. Stewart, Jr., *Employment Effects of Minimum Wage Rates* (Washington, D.C.: American Enterprise Institute for Public Policy Research, 1969). See also Patrick M. Lenihan, "The Economic Affects of Minimum Wage Orders" [in Wisconsin] (unpublished Ph.D. dissertation, University of Wisconsin, 1967); James E. Estes, *The Minimum Wage and Its Impact on South Carolina* (Bureau of Business and Economic Research, Report No. 18 [Columbia: College of Business Administration, University of South Carolina, 1968]); and M. Z. Wolfson, "A Reexamination of the Wage and Employment Effects of the Minimum Wage on the Southern Pine Industry" (unpublished Ph.D. dissertation, University of Illinois, 1971).

[14] Many studies of the U.S. Department of Labor have ignored these employment effects. In the words of one critic, "The actual statistics of Labor Department industry studies have, in the great bulk of postwar cases, shown declines in employment in the wake of minimum wage increases—though the *stated conclusion* of

Minimum Wages, Poverty, and Youth

The U.S. Department of Labor reported that the $1.60 minimum wage meant that "for the first time in the history of the Fair Labor Standards Act, the statutory minimum wage will yield an above-poverty wage."[15] This is perhaps a correct statement for those who receive the wage, but it ignores the possible impact on employment, not only of the marginal employees already on industry's rolls, but perhaps of a more important group, the submarginal population which even in prosperity finds great difficulty in obtaining work. Moreover, this statement ignores the potential impact of the minimum wage on youth employment.

A subsequent study of the U.S. Bureau of Labor Statistics found that both higher minimum wages and the extension of minimum wage coverage to retail trade, services, and agriculture had probably contributed to an unemployment rate of 16–17-year-olds five times that of those 25 years of age and older, and also to an unemployment rate of 18–19-year-olds higher than the average. One reason for this is that a higher proportion of youngsters work in the newly covered industries than in the labor force as a whole. Often they are marginal employees, easily replaced by other, more productive workers at higher minimum wage rates or by machines. In some cases, such as the already noted phasing out of drug-store soda fountains, "youth work" has simply been eliminated. The study concluded that a youth differential in the minimum wage would greatly aid employment of young persons.[16] Such a differential exists in various forms in 39 state minimum wage laws and has been advocated for any changes in the federal law by the Nixon administration.

There is also considerable evidence that increases in minimum wages have had adverse effects not only on the volume of employment of youths and of other marginal employees, for example, blacks and other minorities with poor educational backgrounds, but also on the vulner-

---

these same studies has usually been that there is no evidence of unemployment caused by the minimum wage." (Thomas Sowell, "Discussion, the Shorter Work-week Controversy," *Industrial and Labor Relations Review*, Vol. 18 [January 1965], p. 243). For further criticisms of the Department of Labor's studies, and defenses by Department analysts, see Macesich and Stewart, note 7, above; H. M. Douty and Max Schiferl, comment on Macesich and Stewart article, *Southern Economic Journal*, Vol. 27 (January 1961), pp. 239–42), and reply by former, *ibid.*, pp. 243–44. For further criticisms of Department of Labor findings, see William J. Shkurti and Belton M. Fleisher, "Employment and Wage Rates in Retail Trade Subsequent to the 1961 Amendments to the Fair Labor Standards Act," *Southern Economic Journal*, Vol. 35 (July 1968), pp. 37–48.

[15] U.S. Department of Labor, Wage and Hour and Public Contracts Divisions, *Minimum Wages and Maximum Hours Standards under the Fair Labor Standards Act* (Washington, D.C.: 1968), p. 2.

[16] Thomas W. Gavett, "Youth Unemployment and Minimum Wages," *Monthly Labor Review*, Vol. 93 (March 1970), pp. 3–15. See also T. G. Moore, "The Effect of Minimum Wages on Teenage Unemployment Rates," *Journal of Political Economy*, Vol. 79 (July–August 1971), pp. 897–902.

ability of such groups to cyclical unemployment. As a result, teen-agers are now able to obtain less employment even when employment is growing at a reasonably good pace, and they are more likely to suffer unemployment in periods of short-term employment changes.[17] The persistence of the high unemployment rate among teen-agers, noted in Chapter 14, is, of course, indicative of the sensitivity of teen-agers to unemployment. In that chapter, as well as in several others, we have noted that the unemployment rate of blacks has consistently been twice that of whites, the unemployment rate of black teen-agers, four to five times that of white adult males.

A youth differential has been opposed particularly by the AFL–CIO, which is on record "that the minimum wage represents a floor under wages and that no one—young, old, black or white, male or female—should be asked to work for less than the wage floor."[18] The AFL–CIO is also a stronger supporter of an ever higher minimum and of an extension of the act's coverage to all workers not now within its purview. The federation's reasoning relies heavily upon the minimum wage as a cure for poverty, while at the same time denying any causal relationship between rising minimum wages and unemployment in general, or youth unemployment in particular.

In future years, as we have noted throughout this text, the greatest employment opportunities will occur among professional and technical occupations. Among the manual occupations, the need for skilled mechanics will also increase. But the number of unskilled jobs will remain relatively stationary, despite a tremendous increase in unskilled additions to the labor market. It seems, therefore, ever more apparent that the higher the wage minimum, the greater will be the effort to substitute machinery for unskilled work or to recast methods somehow so as to make the unskilled increasingly unnecessary, particularly in manufacturing enterprises. To push for even higher minimums in spite of these labor market facts, as Congress and various state legislatures continue to do, is likely to make unemployed victims of those who are supposed to become higher paid beneficiaries of a minimum wage law.

There is another concern about raising the minimum wage which is of great significance. Although the imposition of a higher minimum does tend to narrow differentials, it also tends to exert an upward pressure on

---

[17] Marvin Kosters and Finis Welch, "The Effects of Minimum Wages on the Distribution of Changes in Aggregate Employment," *American Economic Review,* Vol. 62 (June 1972), p. 320. A mathematical model designed by these authors as the basis for their analysis is set forth in the appendix to this chapter.

[18] *Fair Labor Standards Amendments of 1971* (Hearings before the Subcommittee on Labor of the Committee on Labor and Public Welfare, U.S. Senate, 92nd Cong., 1st sess., on S. 1861 and S. 2259, 1971 [Washington, D.C.: U.S. Government Printing Office, 1971]), Part 1, p. 70. A complete statement of the AFL–CIO's position is found in pp. 75–116 of these Hearings.

wages above the minimum, both in industries directly affected and in all other industries competing for labor. This adds still another inflationary push to the economy, in which inflationary tendencies are already so strong. To the extent that an upward revision in the minimum wage results in price increases, it will again hurt most the low-wage groups for whom the minimum is urged as a benefit.

Our concern with poverty is therefore very likely in conflict with the policy of a steadily rising minimum wage. Perhaps minimum wages should continue to rise and the resulting unemployment should be tolerated. In such case, it should be understood that one of the costs of minimum wage legislation is increased public welfare, training, rehabilitation, and subsidy payments to those who are priced out of the labor market.

THE SHORTER WORKWEEK

From colonial days to 1950, the average workweek gradually declined to a norm of 40 hours. This is required by the Fair Labor Standards Act unless the employer pays time and one half the regular rate. The normal workday has become 8 hours, with time and one half required by most union contracts and by the Public Contracts (Walsh-Healey) Act, but not by the FLSA for work beyond 8 (unless it brings the weekly total over 40). State laws which limited the hours of women, or denied them access to nightwork or hazardous jobs, are no longer applicable if, as is generally true, the work is covered by the Civil Rights Act of 1964, because that law forbids such distinctions on the basis of sex as well as of race. Figure 16–2 demonstrates that the workweek has remained at 40 hours since World War II.

FIGURE 16–2

Average Weekly Hours, 1850–1971

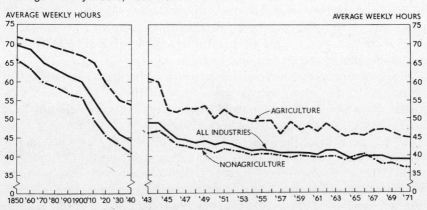

Source: U.S. Bureau of Labor Statistics.

THE ARGUMENTS FOR SHORTER HOURS

Legislation and union bargaining power have been the principal forces in the history of hours reduction. More recently, other factors, such as the need for a reduction in commuting time in large metropolitan areas, have become significant, particularly in arguments, discussed below, to restructure the workweek from five 8-hour days to four 10-hour ones.

The traditional arguments of the proponents of a shorter workweek are: (1) The health of the population will be improved by a shorter workweek; (2) shorter hours mean increased leisure, which is not only good in itself but also will permit workers to purchase and enjoy the products of industry; (3) shorter hours will increase worker efficiency enough to offset the loss in work time; and (4) shorter hours are necessary to insure full employment. Today, only the last is argued in depth, with the second point utilized as a support for the employment argument.

Health and Leisure

Shorter hours have frequently been advocated as a health measure. It is on this basis, for example, that the regulation of hours for women and the regulation of hours in dangerous trades primarily rest. Regulation of hours in transportation is also partly based on this argument, although here it is the health and safety of the consumer as well as that of the worker which is protected. Since these arguments are more applicable to a longer workweek than 40 hours, they are infrequently used today except in dangerous or very strenuous occupations.

Purchasing Power Theory

Organized labor has traditionally put forth the argument that increased leisure with earnings maintained would permit workers the time to spend more as consumers and thus would bolster the economy. Other proponents of a shorter workweek support this argument and also maintain that more leisure would be helpful in encouraging citizens to participate in political and civil affairs.

During recent years, it has been customary for union leadership to overemphasize the purchasing power theory of the business cycle. Obviously, if workers were employed 12 hours a day, they would not have much time to do anything else besides eat and sleep, and they would not make very good customers for that part of the industry which does not produce absolute necessities. Since only a very small portion of industry produces these absolute necessities, it is also obvious that demand must exist for the miscellaneous luxuries, semiluxuries, and other things which make up America's high living standard. Shortening the working day, so long as it does not impair earnings, may make workers better customers for these essentials and nonessentials of modern capitalistic production.

Certainly, the five-day week and shorter working hours have greatly expanded spending for leisure. Moreover, the employee who works shorter hours receives a greater exposure to advertising over radio, television, and other media, and this may make him more desirous of spending to "keep up" or to enjoy the latest conveniences or luxuries.

But how much more the average worker's family will spend on consumption goods if his hours are reduced below 40 is not easy to determine. This leisure argument assumes that the increased costs resulting from decreasing the hours will not adversely affect employment and therefore, in turn, adversely affect consumer expenditures, which, as we shall point out, is likely to occur; and it also assumes the shorter hour movement will not be simply a device to increase overtime pay. Where actual hours are not reduced but merely made more expensive by penalty overtime payments, the increased leisure argument is irrelevant; for here, the workers' take-home pay, not the workers' leisure, is increased.

Efficiency and Productivity

Historically, the reduction in hours of work has been accompanied by increases in productivity. As a result, the increased costs occasioned by shorter hours have not led to higher prices—at least over long periods of time. The fact that shorter hours and increased productivity have marched hand in hand has given birth to the argument that reduced hours increase efficiency and/or productivity and hence absorb the increased costs of shorter hours, even if the shorter hours are accompanied by wage adjustments sufficient to maintain weekly earnings.

Productivity and worker efficiency are not necessarily synonymous terms. Productivity is not a measurement of the man alone but of the man and his equipment. It is a statistic commonly measured by dividing output by man-hours worked. As already noted, rising labor productivity is largely a manifestation of the joint contribution of increasing capital, improved managerial technique, and scientific advance.

On the other hand, labor efficiency, as defined here, refers to changes in output resulting solely from changes in labor effort or input, other factors being held constant. Hence an increase in labor efficiency will result in an increase in productivity, but an increase in productivity does not necessarily mean that labor efficiency has increased.

Shorter Hours and Efficiency. Unfortunately, there have been few studies made of the effect of hours on labor efficiency, and those which are available deal mainly with increases in hours above rather than reductions below 40. In addition, most of the more important studies which attempt to relate efficiency and hours of work were made during World

War II, when conditions were quite abnormal. Moreover, such factors as changing attitudes toward work and the affluent workforce make one hesitant to draw conclusions applicable to today from results of World War II experiences.

Nevertheless, the studies did show that a seven-day workweek caused output to fall as worker fatigue accumulated from continued overtime, with spoilage, accidents, and absenteeism rising as time went on. On the other hand, an increase to a six-day from a five-day week resulted in rising output despite increased absenteeism. The study by the U.S. Bureau of Labor Statistics concluded that "the addition of the sixth day had no disadvantageous effect on output, provided daily hours were held to eight."[19] Other studies support the conclusion that the 48-hour week was best for war production and that adding the sixth day had no ill effect unless the daily hours were excessive. It should be noted again, however, that different results might occur if the six-day week were inaugurated in peacetime.

After the war, many of the plants covered by the BLS survey resumed a normal five-day week. Although the increase in hours by the addition of a sixth day had resulted in an almost proportionate increase in weekly output in most cases, a decrease in hours was accompanied by a less than proportionate decrease in production. As in the increase of the workweek, so, too, in the decrease—absenteeism among men was little affected by the shift. Women's absences increased after both changes, in the latter instance probably because they lost interest in the work and were preparing for a resumption of household duties. The most logical explanation advanced for the observed improvement in efficiency as hours of work were reduced was that workers who were paid on an incentive basis wished to make up lost take-home pay brought about by the elimination of time and a half for the sixth day.

The 36-Hour Week Experience in Akron

As we have noted, large segments of the rubber tire industry, especially in Akron, Ohio, have worked on a six-hour day, six-day week schedule since the 1930s. The results have been relatively unsatisfactory to both employees and companies, both in terms of earnings and productivity, so that only a few plants are left operating these hours. Moreover, tire manufacturing is now no longer concentrated in Akron, but rather often in newer plants, particularly in the South, where the eight-hour day persists.

One of the authors has been interviewing a company official over the last 25 years on the effects of the six-hour day. His company has always

---

[19] U.S. Bureau of Labor Statistics, *Hours of Work and Output* (Bulletin No. 917 [Washington: Government Printing Office, 1947]).

been disappointed with results of the six-hour day insofar as improved efficiency is concerned; but he also noted that wage rates are higher and plants are older in Akron than in other areas, and that therefore comparisons between the six-hour day in Akron and the eight-hour day in other rubber tire plants are difficult to make. The last plant of this company which was on the six-hour schedule converted to eight hours in 1967. A few years later, the last tire plants outside of Akron changed from the 36-hour week to the standard 40 one, and in 1972, Firestone also converted. It is likely that the 36-hour week will shortly disappear from the industry.

A striking development of short work schedules, such as have existed in Akron, is their propensity to encourage moonlighting. According to one study: "In Akron the best guesses hold that 16 to 20 percent of the rubber workers hold a second job, not a *part*-time job but a *full*-time job. About another 40 percent hold down a second, merely part-time employment."[20]

A second study found that "the incidence of dual wage or job holding is significantly higher for . . . 36-hour Akron rubber workers than for . . . 40-hour rubber workers located outside of Akron," and that "total multijobholding is significantly related to the length of the primary job workweek."[21] Actually, the desire of members of the United Rubber Workers to hold on to the 36-hour week has been a direct function of moonlighting. The leaders of the United Rubber Workers made a determined attempt at the 1956 convention to eliminate the six-hour day and go back to the 40-hour week. They were defeated precisely because the Akron workers did not want to give up the extra income they gained from holding two jobs and working many hours over 40 per week. In the last several years, however, the plants have hired thousands of young employees who desire more opportunity for earnings on their primary job and who have not as yet developed outside income interests. The votes of these new employees are tipping the balance in favor of the 8-hour day, 40-hour week. In 1972, when the Firestone local of the United Rubber Workers voted 2,356 to 977 to give up the 36-hour week, one supporter of the change commented, "A lot of the guys in the shop who were talking down . . . [the 40-hour week] were the ones who had two jobs. They'll just have to give one up now."[22]

As of now only the Goodyear Tire and Rubber, General Tire, and Mohawk Rubber companies remain on the six-day week. Goodyear finds some advantages as well as disadvantages. It can expand shifts from six to eight without paying overtime during heavy vacation schedules; and it

---

[20] Sebastian de Grazia, *Of Time, Work and Leisure.* (New York: Twentieth Century Fund, 1962), p. 71.

[21] John C. Deiter, *MultiJobHolding and the Short Workweek Issue.* (Ann Arbor, Mich.: University Microfilms, Inc., 1965), p. 81.

[22] *Business Week*, March 18, 1972, p. 67.

can cut down to 30 hours when orders decline. On the other hand, the six-hour shifts mean additional fringe costs, since fringe costs, as noted in Chapter 5, are largely a function of number of employees, not hours worked. In addition, six-hour day shifts may well be less efficient because of the larger number of start-up and readying-to-quit periods in which production is usually low.

The high fringe costs to employers and the potential higher earnings of employees on 8-hour shifts have led to the gradual abandonment of the rubber industry's 6-hour day, 36-hour week. The experience under it is not conclusive as to the shorter workweek; it does, however, point up some of the basic economic problems involved.

Construction Industry

The powerful unions in the construction industry have pushed their standard workweek below 40 and their workday to seven hours or less. In fact, however, this is largely a method of increasing compensation by making additional employment available at penalty overtime—time and one half or double time. The extreme case was that of the New York City electricians who won a 25-hour week—but a guarantee of at least five hours overtime. In a real sense, this is not hours reduction but rather one aspect of union wage policy. It has not been emulated significantly in other industries where unions have less than the enormous power which they have exhibited in construction. Undoubtedly, such policies have contributed to the expansion of nonunion construction which the Building Trades Department of the AFL–CIO has acknowledged to be occurring.[23]

Moonlighting

A workweek of less than 40 per week is not likely to yield discernible improvements in efficiency. It does seem to encourage people to make productive use of their time by seeking other work. Such moonlighting is not new, but it seems to be a regular phenomenon. In May 1971, a total of 4 million persons, 5.1% of all employed workers, were counted as moonlighters—that is, they held two jobs or more.[24] Since, however, in order to avoid taxes, union, or employer censure, many moonlighters do not report their second activity, the actual number of moonlighters is probably considerably greater.[25] A majority of moonlighters is found

---

[23] See, for example, the comments at the 1972 convention of the Operating Engineers' Union, *Construction Labor Report*, No. 865 (April 26, 1972), pp. A–13–A–17.

[24] Howard V. Hayghe and Kopp Michelotti, "Multiple Jobholding in 1970 and 1971." *Monthly Labor Review*, Vol. 94 (October 1971), pp. 38–45.

[25] *Ibid.;* and de Grazia, *op. cit.,* pp. 71–72.

among professional, self-employed, government-employed, education, and farming groups, but more recently the number of those from blue-collar workers has been increasing.

In times of unemployment, moonlighting is often attacked as a contributor to that unemployment. The studies of moonlighters which have been made, however, do not bear this out. The largest segment of moonlighters are those with a special skill which is in demand or those who have a strong desire to enhance their incomes. Their moonlighting activity supplements their basic income from the primary job but is usually insufficient as a primary means of support. Moonlighting does not vary with employment or unemployment trends.[26]

Moonlighting is a further indication of the preference of many persons for additional income rather than additional leisure. The grievances in nearly any company inevitably include complaints from some workers that they did not receive a fair share of overtime work—"the golden hours" at time and one half or double time. The following comment of a then union research director, which was delivered almost two decades ago, is still relevant:

Aside from the workers' desire for their paid holidays and paid vacations there is no evidence in recent experience that workers want shorter *daily* or *weekly* hours. The evidence is all on the other side. Hundreds of local and national officials have testified that the most numerous and persistent grievances are disputes over the sharing of overtime work. The issue usually is not that someone has been made to work, but that he has been deprived of a chance to make overtime pay.[27]

HOURS REDUCTION AND EMPLOYMENT

There are two points of view from which reduction in hours of work per day or per week can be examined as a remedy for unemployment. The first is a reduction in hours without a change in the basic wage rate, so that the workers previously employed now receive fewer hours of work and correspondingly reduced earnings. The second is the effect of a shortening of hours with compensatory increases in basic rates, so that earnings for the shorter working time remain undiminished. No one now seriously advocates the first approach. Nevertheless, a short analysis of the possible effects on unemployment of a reduction in hours without compensatory overtime will point up the economic relationships between hours reduction and employment, and will also help to clarify those relationships where compensatory wage adjustments are involved.

---

[26] Hayghe and Michelotti, *loc. cit.*

[27] George Brooks, "The History of Organized Labor's Drive for Shorter Hours of Work," *AFL–CIO Conference on Shorter Hours of Work*, published in Special Report No. 1, *Daily Labor Report*, No. 177 (September 11, 1956), p. 13.

Shorter Hours with Unchanged Basic Wage Rates

It is not unusual for persons to assume logic and correctness in the statement attributed to Samuel Gompers that "if anyone is out of work, the hours of work are too long." The idea is that if hours are only reduced sufficiently, unemployment can be automatically eliminated.

A realistic look at the supply factors shows that the effect of shortening hours, even without the compensatory adjustments in wage rates which unions demand, cannot be assessed by a mere arithmetical calculation. For example, it might be thought that as long as basic rates are unchanged, unit labor costs should likewise remain constant. But employers will have to add new workers who will require training and who may be less skilled than those already employed, so that the immediate effect of the plan is probably to produce some decline in the efficiency of labor. Moreover, in some industries, work sharing produces technical difficulties. The balance of operations may not be workable with two 6-hour shifts instead of one 8-hour shift—or, for that matter, there just might not be enough demand for two shifts of 32 or 35 hours where one of 40 hours now suffices.

Even if unit labor costs do not change, capital costs per unit of output will be increased in those plants which operate fewer hours per week after the shorter hour program is inaugurated. The rise in fixed costs per unit will force marginal firms out of business and thus add to the amount of unemployment. Moreover, the reduction in profits in all plants will make entrepreneurs somewhat more reluctant to invest; and therefore, in the long run the level of employment may be further reduced.

On the demand side the shortening of hours of work of employed labor may provide job opportunities for persons formerly on relief or receiving unemployment benefits. Where there are no compensatory wage adjustments, the earnings of those formerly employed full time will be reduced, and therefore an increase in consumer demand can only follow if the newly employed workers greatly expand purchases over what they had consumed while receiving unemployment benefits or on relief to an extent greater than the drop in expenditures by those formerly employed 40 hours and now working and earning less.

Reduction in Hours with Compensatory Wage Increases

On the whole, a program of shorter hours is unacceptable to labor unless it is accompanied by compensatory wage adjustments, so that labor income is maintained. In advocating such a policy to reduce unemployment, organized labor has shown its customary bias in emphasizing the role of demand conditions and ignoring the more immediate repercussions of the increased hourly price of labor on costs and business profits.

Employers, by and large, can be expected to react to a program of reduced hours with compensatory hourly wage increases as they would react to any increase in marginal cost. Prices will tend to rise; a smaller output will be demanded; and ultimately, a new equilibrium will be established at a lower level of output. In order to think this through, let us assume that the demand for labor under these circumstances in a particular firm has an elasticity of unity. If the union raises hourly rates 5% and reduces hours of work by 5%, it will have duplicated the readjustment that the employer himself would have made to the changed cost conditions. But since a new equilibrium has been established at the higher unit price of labor, there is no incentive to hire any additional labor. It is therefore clear that if the demand curve for labor in a particular firm has an elasticity of unity or greater, the reemployment objective of the shorter hour movement must fail of accomplishment.

The precise value to be assigned to the elasticity of demand for labor has been the subject of some controversy among economists. On the whole, it seems likely that in depression periods, when management is extremely sensitive to cost increases of any kind, the demand for labor is elastic, at least in an upward direction. That is, a given percentage increase in wage rates will produce a more than proportional reduction in employment. Although there is room for disagreement as to the precise value of the elasticity of demand for labor, it seems likely that the reduction in hours must be substantially greater than the percentage increase in hourly wage rates if the immediate effect of the institution of the shorter working week is not to increase the volume of employment. The effect of the shorter hours of work with compensatory wage adjustments will depend upon the relation between three factors: (1) the percentage decrease in the hours of work, (2) the percentage increase in hourly rates, and (3) the elasticity of demand for labor. Thus, if the elasticity of demand for labor were equal to minus two (i.e., the volume of employment diminishes 2% with each increase of 1% in wage rates), and if the increase in hourly rates were 5%, then the percentage reduction in hours would have to be more than 10% if more workers were to be hired.

Effect of Increasing the Number of Shifts

More promising as a means of converting unemployment into leisure is the six-hour shift, provided that the six-hour shift means the use of two or more shifts per day. Suppose, for example, that a plant in a continuous-process industry has been accustomed to run continuously for five days a week, using three eight-hour shifts. If this plant were to change to four shifts of six hours each, it would appear that employment would be increased. However, if each worker, now employed a shorter number of hours, wishes to keep his pay undiminished, it is evident that there will be a rise in labor cost per unit, despite the fact that the number of shifts has increased. The increased labor costs will be reflected in higher prices and a reduced total output, so that ultimately no permanent increase in employment may result from this changeover.

But there are circumstances in which the addition of another shift may tend to increase employment. The substitution of two six-hour shifts for a previous eight-hour day, or perhaps for a longer day including some employment at overtime, will tend to reduce capital costs per unit by allowing management to work capital longer while labor works shorter hours. The decrease in total unit costs attributable to this influence will tend to offset the increase in unit labor costs occasioned by shortening the hours of work with compensatory wage increases, so that, on balance, profits may be unimpaired.

While it may be conceded that the more intensive use of capital is a favorable factor, it should be recognized that if the increase in the number of shifts does increase employment, it will have this effect only after a series of highly complicated long-run influences are set in motion. The spreading of overhead will not affect marginal costs, while the reduction of hours with increases in basic hourly rates will raise marginal costs. Hence, as far as immediate price and output reactions are concerned, the change in the number of shifts does not alter the picture. Some plants will be forced out of business, while other plants, in which the proportion of labor costs is relatively low and overhead costs relatively high, will find their profits increased by the changeover to additional shifts. Ultimately, the number of plants in the industry undergoing the change will diminish, with a larger volume of business concentrated in a smaller number of firms, each using capital more intensively than was true before the shorter-hour program was inaugurated.

The ability to inaugurate an additional shift will vary considerably from industry to industry; and in those firms attempting it, the benefits obtained will vary, depending upon the importance of overhead costs. In some plants where equipment is antiquated, working additional shifts may mean increasingly frequent breakdowns without adequate time for repairs. In industries which do not operate continuously, the amount of reemployment which can be provided by a shortening of hours of work will depend in part upon the availability of unused machinery and equipment. To the extent that less efficient equipment is brought into use, the upward pressure on costs is intensified.

Interindustry Shifts

A program of shorter hours with undiminished take-home pay would produce important changes in the demand for particular industries. The increased availability of leisure would probably be reflected in an increased demand for sporting goods and other recreational goods by which leisure can be made more enjoyable. Likewise, the effect of the increased wage disbursements—assuming that there were some initial reemployment—would operate to stimulate the consumer goods industries. At the same time, however, the nondurable consumer goods industries would experience the greatest increases of cost relative to the rest of the economy, since it appears that the nondurable consumer goods industries have higher ratios of wages to value added than do the capital goods industries. Thus, insofar as the effect on costs is concerned, the former industries would be hardest hit by the combination of shorter hours and increased wage rates; while the capital goods industries, having a higher ratio of capital costs, would be the ones to benefit most from the addition of extra shifts.

This combination of altered cost and demand positions would ultimately produce some readjustment in the disposition of the total labor force among the various industries in the economy. The net effect upon employment can only be conjectural. If wage disbursements increase initially as a result of the shorter hours of work with compensatory wage rate increases, it appears that a larger proportion of the national income would be spent on nondurable consumer goods than before the hours program was instituted. Two factors will contribute to this result. On the one hand, the total income of wage earners will increase if there is some reemployment; and the income of workingpeople, particularly during periods of large-scale unemployment, is likely to be spent upon nondurable consumer goods. But as we have seen, these are the very industries which will feel most of the impact of the shorter-hour program. Therefore, prices will rise in these industries relative to the general price level; but because of the relatively inelastic demand typical of these industries, the total receipts of the nondurable consumer goods industries will probably increase. This augmented volume of expenditure concentrated in these industries will probably support a larger volume of employment than it would under its previous distribution, since the nondurable consumer goods are likely to be more labor-employing than other industries. At the same time, since the proportion of labor costs to total costs is less in the capital goods industries than in the nondurable consumer goods industries, and since the adjustments resulting from the changeover to more shifts with shorter hours per employee may lead to a more efficient allocation of output concentrated in fewer plants, prices of machines should rise less than in proportion to consumer goods. This would stimulate the demand for laborsaving machinery and thus increase the volume of investment and employment.

Shortages of Skilled Labor

Any general uniform reduction in hours per week is likely to increase the number of bottlenecks which develop in production and therefore raise a barrier to full employment. A shortage of skilled workers in a key industry can have repercussions which produce unemployment throughout the economy. If the shorter hour program is applied to skilled workers, management is faced by three alternatives, all of which are likely to react unfavorably upon employment generally. Management can, of course, employ the same skilled workers as before, but now pay them additional overtime because of the shortening of the basic workweek. This would have the same effect as a wage increase and would therefore raise costs and prices. On the other hand, management can attempt to hire other workers and train them to fill these jobs; but these men will, on the average, be less experienced and make more mistakes, so that labor cost per unit will tend to rise through their employment. Lastly, if management is unwilling or unable to find additional skilled help, bottlenecks and shortages will develop which will cause stoppages, depriving even the unskilled of their jobs.

The shortage of skilled labor is often a regional or local problem. It can be especially severe in small towns having available only a limited pool of labor. Thus a program of shorter hours must be undertaken with caution. On the other hand, in some industries, it is conceivable that a reasonable shortening of hours, even if it does produce some rise in costs, could be accomplished without too difficult a readjustment. An appreciation of the various possible repercussions of a shorter hour program indicates the danger of any general uniform shortening of hours accomplished by legislative decree.

NATURE OF UNEMPLOYMENT

Any attempt to utilize shortening of hours as a means of curbing unemployment must also consider the nature of the unemployment. That of the early 1970s has been overwhelmingly structural—the young, the unskilled, and the Negro, disabilities often found in one person. Certainly, merely reducing hours of work cannot accomplish the miracle of finding jobs for those who do not have the background, education, training, means, or motivation to accept even unskilled jobs in industry. Nor will reducing hours transfer people from the high unemployment inner cores of the cities to the new manufacturing plants in the suburbs and rural areas.

To the extent, therefore, that unemployment is structural, a decrease in hours will not solve such unemployment problems unless it is accompanied by an extraordinarily successful retraining and integration program, together with greater improvement in the mobility of labor. But the costs of such programs, combined with the burden imposed by the shorter workweek (as noted below) could easily discourage rather than encourage employment. Dividing up work—and raising its costs—is not likely to improve the matching of jobs and men.

COSTS OF THE SHORTER-HOUR PROGRAM

Figure 16–3 shows the hourly increases required to maintain weekly pay as a 40-hour schedule drops to 32. Approximately a 14% increase is needed to offset a five-hour decline, and more than a 25% increase to accomplish an eight-hour decline.

FIGURE 16–3

Rising Cost of a Shorter Workweek

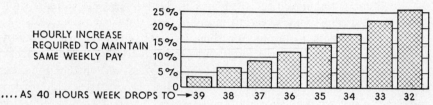

Source: Reprinted by special permission from *Business Week,* October 20, 1962. Copyright, 1962, by McGraw-Hill, Inc.

Even this is not the whole story. Suppose the workweek is reduced to 35 hours, but the business requires 40 hours of work to meet its commitments. Then, five hours must be worked at time and one half. As calculated in Table 16–3, this would mean an increase not of 14% but of

TABLE 16–3

Cost of Reduction in Workweek

> Cost of reduction in workweek:
> 1. No loss of pay for employee
> 2. No loss of production for employer
>
> Assume rate of pay = $3 per hour; for 40-hour week, weekly pay = $120
> 1. If workweek is lowered to 35 hours:
>   No loss of pay for employee; hourly rate now raised to $3.43 to equal $120 weekly take-home pay
>   Increase in weekly rate 14.3%.
> 2. If employer requires 40-hour week:
>   Five hours must be worked overtime; time and one half of $3.43 = $5.15; 35 hours @ $3.43 plus 5 hours @ $5.15 = $145.80.
>   Increase in weekly rate 21.5%.

21.5%! Obviously, such wage increases cannot be borne by a significant segment of American industry—and equally obviously, such wage increases therefore would be likely to create unemployment, not employment.

AUTOMATION AND HOURS

In the early 1960s, when unemployment ranged from 5% to 7.5% of the labor force, union officials particularly, but many other persons as well, argued that automation was rapidly reducing the number of jobs, so that hours reduction would be necessary to offset resultant unemployment, while on the other hand, increased productivity gained from automation would permit the increased costs of the hours reductions to be absorbed by industry.

Actually, this has proved both an incorrect analysis and an oversimplification. Automation has actually tended to increase overall the number of jobs. To be sure, changes effected by automation have helped to create or accentuate unemployment problems in some areas and among some labor force groups while creating industries and jobs for other areas and groups. The effects of automation thus vary considerably from industry to industry, from area to area, and from one labor force group to another.

Moreover, the advent of technological progress and automation does not proceed smoothly throughout industry, but rather varies widely from industry to industry in its extent and character. A general hours reduction would therefore fall on both heavily and lightly automated industries, on the industries for which technological unemployment is a problem, and on those growing as a result of changing technology. It would give a bonus to the fully employed—or threaten their employment. It would seek, against heavy economic odds, to help those not fully employed.

To succeed in creating employment, a reduction in hours from 40 to 35, with pay maintained, would require a minimum productivity increase of 15%—a most unlikely development. But even if such an increase in productivity occurred, it would probably be insufficient because the substantial investment in expensive equipment required by automation greatly increases fixed costs. To the extent that a shorter workweek keeps this equipment idle, fixed costs per unit during operating periods increase and tend to offset decreases in costs resulting from increases in productivity.

A shorter workweek, with take-home pay maintained, would so increase costs that automation could well be discouraged except for the larger, wealthier firms. This could accelerate a trend toward economic concentration and possibly increase rather than diminish technological unemployment.

The most desirable manner of attaining full employment is by high-volume production, so that labor is fully employed 40 hours a week and the community benefits from technological progress in the form of a rising level of real income. From the point of view of maximizing national welfare, increasing leisure for labor, obtained by reducing hours of work below 40 a week, can hardly be preferred to rising real income for the whole community. Moreover, it must be reiterated again that there is no guarantee that a reduction in the workweek will increase employment. The crux of the problem is whether full employment could in fact be attained at the 35-hour level or whether the rise in costs attributable to the program of shorter hours with less work would not so depress business confidence that investment would be discouraged and unemployment would prevail even with the shorter workweek.

OVERTIME AND EMPLOYMENT

From time to time, when unemployment has been serious, proposals have been made to increase overtime pay under the Fair Labor Standards Act from time and one half to double time. The rationale is that it is sometimes cheaper to pay workers time and one half than to employ additional workers, and therefore by making overtime more expensive, unemployment would be reduced. In 1964, President Lyndon B. Johnson proposed this to Congress. The idea had the strong backing of organized labor, but did not reach a congressional vote.

Fringes, Overtime, and Turnover Costs

We noted in Chapter 5 that fringe benefit costs have risen rapidly and substantially. Moreover, fringe benefits such as hospitalization, and many governmental benefits such as social security, are employee-related, not hours-related. In addition, state unemployment benefit systems, as will be explained in Chapter 17, penalize companies with excessive turnover and hence favor long hours, not more employees.[28]

On the other hand, overtime costs have risen, too, because the base by which time and one half is figured has risen sharply. In other words, if a wage is increased from $2 to $2.50 per hour, overtime increases from $3 to $3.75. Overtime's expense has therefore tended to keep pace with the rise in fringe costs in many industries.

Such an analysis is, however, unrealistic because (1) it assumes the employer is certain that he knows how long he will need a new employee (or overtime), and (2) it ignores training and layoff costs. The average employer often hesitates to add to the labor force until he feels reasonable assurance that he has need of an employee for a longer period. In the meantime, he will usually use overtime work to fill his needs.

The basic reason for the hesitation to hire is not only the high cost of fringes, but also the high cost of employing and laying off workers. Finding, interviewing, processing, and training people can often cost several hundred dollars per employee. Then, if a layoff occurs, new expenses mount. In a large New England plant studied by one of the authors, each time one person was laid off, three to five "bumps" occurred as a result of the working of the plant seniority system. The plant management estimated that each layoff cost $600–$900 because of the upset, retraining, and lost time involved! Naturally, in such a situation, management will prefer to utilize overtime rather than hire new employees if it is uncertain as to the length of time for which additional work hours are needed.

---

[28] On this subject, in general, see Joseph W. Garbarino, "Fringe Benefits and Overtime as Barriers to Expanding Employment," *Industrial and Labor Relations Review*, Vol. 17 (April 1964), pp. 426–42; and particularly the comment thereon by Robert M. MacDonald and reply by Professor Garbarino, *ibid.*, Vol. 19 (July 1966), pp. 562–72.

There is evidence that the amount of overtime utilized in industry has been increasing.[29] Whether this is a function of increased fringe benefit costs is not known. If, however, it is related to the increased costs of hiring and laying off employees, making it more expensive to utilize overtime is a dubious remedy. The net effect would be an increase in labor cost, either because of utilizing the more expensive overtime or because of hiring more employees instead of using overtime, which, if our assumptions are correct, would be an additional cost over the former use of overtime at time and one half. This, of course, assumes that the company or industry would not offset the new costs by a decrease in labor utilization, which is by far the most likely impact. Obviously, the relation of fringe benefits, overtime, and employment is complex, and employment would not easily be generated by altering this relationship.

THE 4-DAY, 40-HOUR WEEK

A number of small concerns in industry, plus several large insurance companies and banks, instituted the 4-day, 40-hour week in the early 1970s by having their employees work 10 hours per day instead of the traditional 8. Although given wide publicity, this "movement" has not spread into the industrial mainstream.

The four-day week has much initial allure. The prospects of a three-day weekend, and to the urban area dweller, of one less day to commute, are pleasant to contemplate indeed. Many employers also have visions of a happier and more productive labor force, and where labor shortages exist, of greater ease in manpower procurement. Closer examination, however, reveals many problems.

Often management and workers or unions are thinking quite differently in contemplating the four-day week. Management sees greater utilization of capital by having an expanded work force employed 10 hours, 5 days per week, but each employee working only 4 days. Thus, an employee works Monday-Thursday one week, Tuesday-Friday another, Wednesday-Friday and the following Monday, a third week, and so on. The three-day weekend does not occur for an individual regularly, because the plant or office is working, with the fifth day a "swing" one. This is how insurance companies are operating a four-day week.

Where a two- or three-shift operation is already in effect, the restructured workweek does not fit well. On a 3-shift operation, or on continuously operated facilities, it is complicated and difficult to work other than 8-hour shifts—8 not 10 divides evenly into 24 hours per day and 168 per week. For two shifts, shifts would run 7 A.M. to 3 P.M., and 3 P.M. to 11 P.M. for an 8-hour arrangement, but 7 A.M. to 5 P.M. and 5 P.M. to 3 A.M. for a 10-hour one; few would want the latter hours.

The main blocks to an expansion of the 10-hour, 4-day, or another

---

[29] See the MacDonald comment for details of this point.

type of restructured workweek, may be legislation and union opposition. The Public Contracts (Walsh-Healey) Act, as noted previously, requires that time and one half the regular wage rate be paid for all work in excess of eight hours in a day for virtually all work on government contracts. It is not practical for companies to segregate government and nongovernment work and, since government is very pervasive, this is an effective bar to change.

Union contracts usually provide for similar daily penalty overtime. Unions have been generally opposed to a workweek restructuring because they believe it will block hours reduction without loss of weekly pay. Nearly all companies which have adopted the 4-day, 40-hour week are nonunion.

Proponents of the restructured workweek claim that it has, or will, increase efficiency and reduce absenteeism. They point to less commuting loss of time and less start-up and "getting-ready-to-leave" time in a week. Whether such alleged gains will continue once employees become accustomed to the new schedules remains to be seen. What impact the longer day will have on efficiency and accidents also remains to be determined. In any case, union opposition and legal constraints are likely to keep the restructured week from spreading unless a breakthrough occurs in a major industry.

On the other hand, the 4-day week—without 40-hours—may be closer than seems apparent. In 1971, a new federal law required the celebration of five holidays on Mondays, thus assuring five additional four-day weeks. Since employees generally receive holiday pay, this legislation assures 40 hours pay for 4 days' work for millions of Americans several times per year.

Perhaps more important is the remarkable increase in absenteeism that plagues American industry. One analysis figured that the absentee rate had increased 77% between 1961 and 1969.[30] The great bulk of such absenteeism occurs on Mondays and Fridays. Workers may be opting for leisure and three-day weekends more than previous studies—including our own—have ascertained.

CONCLUDING REMARKS

Whenever unemployment becomes a serious problem, the question of shorter hours will come to the fore. Nevertheless, a reduction of the workweek seems at best a poor remedy for the problem of unemployment, and certainly no solution for the disadvantaged in our society who are without jobs. If our society decides to take improvement in productivity in the form of reduced hours of work rather than in disposable income, economic growth can be impaired. Hence a further reduction in hours could well curtail rather than expand employment. It remains to be

[30] *Morgan Guaranty Survey*, April 1970, p. 10.

seen whether daily hours will increase in the future to accommodate new demands for leisure without reducing the workweek.

APPENDIX[31]

The model [designed by Drs. Kosters and Welsch to demonstrate that minimum wages make teen-agers and blacks more vulnerable to cyclical unemployment and less likely to gain in the upward cycle movement of employment] is estimated one equation at a time without imposing the constraints of internal consistency, $\Sigma_i \beta_{it} = \Sigma \gamma_{it} = 1$ and $\Sigma_i \eta_{pi} \gamma_{it} = \Sigma \eta_{ri} \beta_{it} = 0$. The estimation technique is nonlinear. We simply iterate over values of η_p and η_r to minimize the residual sum of squares. The typical equation (omitting subscript, i) is

$$E_t = \gamma_0 Z_{1t} + \beta_0 Z_{2t} + U_t$$

where Z_1 and Z_2 are constructs that are respectively proportional to E_{pt} and E_{rt}, where the factors of proportionality are of the form

$$log\,(Z_{1t}/E_{pt}) = \eta_p\,log\,M_t + t\,log\,(1 + r)$$
$$log\,(Z_{2t}/E_{rt}) = \eta_r\,log\,M_t + t\,log\,(1 + r)$$

There are 60 observations and 4 parameters, γ_0, β_0, η_{pi}, η_{ri} are estimated. For particular values of η_p and η_r, Z_1, and Z_2 are computed and the *OLS* regression of E_{it} on Z_1 and Z_2 is then calculated. Iterating over η_p and η_r, that solution is selected to minimize the residual sum of squares.

The standard errors of $\hat{\gamma}_0$ and $\hat{\beta}_0$ are computed as though the regression of E_i on Z_1 and Z_2 were of the standard form except that degrees of freedom are 56 instead of 58. The standard errors of η_{pi} and η_{ri} are computed heuristically to measure the sensitivity of the residual sum of squares to the constraints $\eta_{pi} = 0$ and $\eta_{ri} = 0$. Specifically, to compute the standard error of $\hat{\eta}_p$ we first estimate the equation as described above and then impose the constraint, $\eta_{pi} = 0$ and iterate on η_{ri} to minimize the residual sum of squares. Let Q_0 represent the unconstrained residual sum of squares and let Q_1 represent the constrained sum of squares. Then compute

$$``F_{1.56}" = \frac{Q_1 - Q_0}{Q_0/56},$$
$$``t_{56}" = (``F_{1.56}")^{1/2},$$

and

$$\sigma(\hat{\eta}_p) = \frac{\hat{\eta}_p}{``t_{56}"}$$

The standard error of $\hat{\eta}_r$ is computed the same way.

[31] Reproduced by permission from Marvin Kosters and Finis Welch, "The Effects of Minimum Wages on the Distribution of Changes in Aggregate Employment," *American Economic Review*, Vol. 62 (June 1972), pp. 330–33.

The employment data are quarterly averages computed from seasonally adjusted monthly data reported in *Employment and Earnings*. The minimum wage and coverage data were provided by the U.S. Department of Labor and supplied to us by Thomas G. Moore. The minimum wage data are reported in Kosters and Welch.[32]

The quarterly growth rates in employment for each of the groups are computed as observed growth rates between the years 1956-III to 1957-II and one decade later, 1966-III to 1967-II. This period was chosen because overall unemployment rates were similar in both years. The relative growth rate, r_i, is the quarterly growth rate of employment in this group relative to that of aggregate employment over the decade. They are:

	White Males	Nonwhite Males	White Females	Nonwhite Females
Adults............	−.0023	−.0003	.0023	.0027
Teenagers........	.0077	.0029	.0071	.0063

Quarterly growth rate in aggregate employment = .0035.

QUESTIONS FOR DISCUSSION

1. Is there a competitive tendency toward reduction of hours of work? Evaluate the importance of governmental legislation and union organization in shortening hours of work.

2. Discuss the relationship of hours reduction and efficiency. What are the advantages and disadvantages of a six-hour shift? The 4-day, 10-hour week?

3. Do you favor a minimum wage differential for teen-agers? Explain your answer.

4. Evaluate minimum wages as a poverty cure.

SUGGESTIONS FOR FURTHER READING

BARTH, PETER S. "The Minimum Wage and Teen-Age Unemployment," *Proceedings of the Twenty-Second Annual Winter Meeting. Industrial Relations Research Association*, pp. 296–310. New York, 1969.

A careful analysis of the impact of minimum wages on teen age employment.

DANKERT, CLYDE E. et al. (eds.). *Hours of Work*. Industrial Relations Research Association, Publication No. 32. New York: Harper & Row, Publishers, 1965.

A series of articles by 12 social scientists on various aspects of the workweek and hours controversy.

---

[32] M. Kosters and F. Welch, *The Effects of Minimum Wages on the Distribution of Changes in Aggregate Employment*, RM-6273-OEO, The RAND Corp., Santa Monica, Calif., September 1970.

HAYGHE, HOWARD V., and MICHELOTTI, KOPP. "Multiple Jobholding in 1970–1971." Also HEDGES, JANICE N. "A Look at the 4-Day Workweek," *Monthly Labor Review,* Vol. XCIV (October 1971), pp. 33–45.

Two articles on aspects of the workweek question.

PETERSON, JOHN M., and STEWART, CHARLES T. *Employment Effects of Minimum Wage Rates.* Washington, D.C.: American Enterprise Institute for Public Policy Research, 1969.

A careful analysis of the literature and issues involving the impact of minimum wages on jobs.

Chapter 17

GOVERNMENT PROGRAMS FOR SECURITY AGAINST OLD AGE, UNEMPLOYMENT, AND ACCIDENT OR ILLNESS

In Chapter 5, we discussed those "fringe benefits" designed to protect employees against the expenses or loss of income occasioned by old age, unemployment, or ill health. Self-help and private means were the traditional methods employed by Americans to guard against such eventualities. Even today, after 25 years of accelerated growth of public welfare and social insurance, private means cover a significant proportion of the population.

The depression which began in 1929 forcefully called attention to the need for an overall, national, or social approach to the problems caused by loss of income to the family. To be sure, some attack had already been begun prior to 1929 on the need to supply an income to the family when the breadwinner no longer could produce a paycheck, but the pre-1929 approach was confined largely to compensating the worker for loss sustained in accidents suffered at the place of work—workmen's compensation. It was not until 1935, with the passage of the Social Security Act, that an overall program was begun to deal with loss of income because of old age, death of the breadwinner, or unemployment. In almost every election year, beginning with 1950, significant amendments have been enacted. Despite the many changes, the double-pronged "insurance-assistance" approach to the alleviation of economic security which was originally adopted remains in effect.

Table 17–1 summarizes the American social security system and illustrates the complicated nature and administration of the various laws. A detailed analysis of all facets of this vast program would involve another book the size of this one. Here, rather, we shall concentrate on the principal "insurance" features and the key economic and industrial relations issues involved. It must be noted, however, that the burgeoning welfare load (see Figure 17–1) has a profound impact on the social insurances if only to exert pressure to expand the latter in order to relieve the former. It therefore remains to be seen whether in the future the historic distinctions between "insurance" and "welfare" can be maintained. The former specifies with precision the conditions governing eligibility and the amount of benefits to which the individual meeting these conditions is

529

TABLE 17–1

A Summary of the American Social Security System

Administered directly by the federal government:
"Social Security" (old-age, survivors, disability, and health insurance—OASDHI).
Railroad programs, including retirement, unemployment, and disability insurance.
Veterans programs providing pensions, compensation, annuities and burial awards.
Administered under state laws:
Unemployment insurance, including programs for federal employees and ex-servicemen.
Workmen's compensation and state temporary disability insurance.
Public Aid: Included here are welfare programs which provide money payments and
    services to needy families financed from general revenues. Means tests are generally
    required. The following programs are included:
Administered under state laws, usually in conformance to some federal standards:
Food Stamps (administered under Department of Agriculture)
Surplus food distributions (administered under Department of Agriculture)
Aid to Families with Dependent Children
Aid to the Blind
Old-Age Assistance
Emergency Aid
Aid to the Permanently and Totally Disabled
Work Relief
Work Incentive program (administered under Department of Labor)
Administered by the states and localities without federal funds:
Public assistance and general assistance (sometimes called "relief").

---

entitled; the latter provides for means tests to determine eligibility and
benefit amounts. President Nixon's welfare reform proposals would provide automatic welfare for those with low incomes, thus eliminating
means tests and much discretionary administrative authority.

THE OLD AGE, SURVIVORS, DISABILITY, AND HEALTH INSURANCE PROGRAM (OASDHI)

OASDHI is an all federally administered program, covering over 90%
of all employed persons and providing the following types of benefits:

Retirement benefits:
Primary monthly benefit to retired worker (reduced benefit, ages 62–
    64; full benefit, age 65).
Monthly benefit to his wife if 62 or older (reduced if claimed before
    age 65).
Monthly benefit to his dependent children under 18 or disabled.
Monthly benefit to wife, whatever age, if caring for child.
Monthly benefit to dependent husband, if 62 or over (reduced if claimed
    before age 65).
Survivors' benefits:
Monthly benefit to widow, 60 or older.

FIGURE 17–1

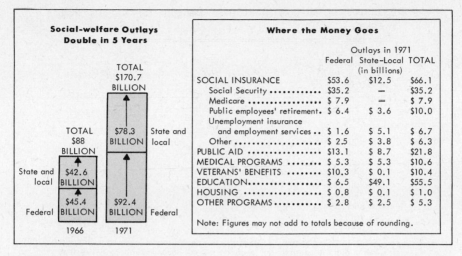

Source: Data, U.S. Department of Health, Education, and Welfare; chart reproduced from *U.S. News & World Report*, January 3, 1972, p. 43, with permission. Copyright © 1971, U.S. News & World Report, Inc.

Monthly benefit to widow or divorced wife, whatever age, if caring for dependent children.

Monthly benefit to child under 18 or disabled.

Monthly benefit to dependent widower 62 or older.

Monthly benefit to dependent parent 62 or over.

Burial benefit in lump sum to widow or widower, or to person who paid burial expenses.

Disability benefits:

Monthly benefit to worker if totally disabled for work.

Monthly benefits for same dependents as under retirement benefits.

Monthly benefit to disabled widows and widowers between ages 50 and 62.

Medical benefits:

Hospital, nursing, and outpatient service.

Voluntary supplementary coverage.

OASDHI is thus designed to provide a pension for those retired or disabled; survivorship benefits to those who lose their breadwinner or primary social security recipient; and medical benefits to the aged. These benefits are not limited by life insurance, private pensions, or other private arrangements, except that those who earn stipulated amounts as employees or self-employed persons cannot collect full social security until they reach their 70's.

All benefits are based upon the monthly payment to the worker who retires at age 65 or over, which is called the primary insurance amount.

TABLE 17–2

Examples of Monthly Retirement Benefits for Various Pay Brackets—OASDHI

Average Monthly Pay Subject to Social SecurityTaxes in Working Years	*For Workers Retired at 65*	*For Married Couples Retired at 65*
$ 76 or less	$ 85	$127
100	109	163
200	154	232
300	193	290
400	233	350
500	270	405
600	310	465
700	343	514
750	355	532
800	365	547
900	385	577
1,000	405	607

Note: Benefits figures are rounded to the nearest dollar. Retirement benefits in the upper classifications will not be paid for several years. As workers pay taxes on higher earnings—up to $10,800 in 1973, and to $12,000 beginning in 1974—maximum benefits will approach $405 for a worker retiring at 65. Benefits and taxes are also subject to automatic cost of living increases.
Source: Social Security Administration

This, in turn, is determined by the worker's average monthly wage. While there is more than one method of computing the average monthly wage, it will usually be figured as follows: The total of creditable earnings in covered employment and self-employment after 1950, or age 21 if later, and until age 65 (62, if a woman) is divided by the number of months elapsing in this period, except that the five years of lowest earnings are omitted, as well as any years for which a disability freeze was in effect. Retired workers who start collecting benefits at 62, 63, or 64 receive less than the primary insurance amount. The full amount, however, is payable to eligible disabled workers, regardless of age.

The monthly benefits for dependents of a retired or disabled worker, the survivors of a deceased worker, or the disabled widow or widower of a deceased worker are equal to specified fractions of the primary insurance amount. Table 17–2 shows the benefit schedules as of 1973. Congress has increased benefits every two years, on election years, and has recently moved to provide automatic cost-of-living increases as well.

Financing

The OASDHI program is paid for by equal contributions from both employer and employee in covered employment. Self-employed persons covered by the program pay three quarters as much as the total of employer and employee contributions on the same amount of earnings. The tax rate keeps growing (see Table 17–3). Initially, the employee tax was 1% on the first $3,000 of earnings. By 2011, with Medicare added to the benefits, as discussed below, the tax for employee, and the cost to the employer for each employee is scheduled to be $876, with all earnings up to a $12,000 base subject to tax. If past actions are a guide, this could be increased further in order to pay for still more benefits. In any case, benefits and taxes can be automatically increased pursuant to a new cost-of-living provision enacted in 1972.

The OASDHI taxes are collected by the payroll deduction method for the employed, and with income taxes for the self-employed, under the administration of the Internal Revenue Service. The bulk of the taxes collected are deposited in the OASI Trust Fund of the U.S. Treasury. The balance goes into separate Disability Insurance, Health Insurance, and Supplementary Medical Insurance Trust funds. All expenses and benefits of the program come from these tax receipts. The reserve portions of the trust funds are invested in interest-bearing U.S. government securities. As of January 1973, the reserves in these trust funds approximated $35 billion, with about $25 billion in the OASI Fund.

TABLE 17–3

Social Security Taxes

Yearly Pay	Maximum Tax on Each Worker, with Employers Paying a Matching Amount					
	1972	1973	1974–77	1978–80	1981–85	By 2011
$ 3,000.................	$156	$176	$176	$182	$185	$219
4,000.................	208	234	234	242	246	292
5,000.................	260	293	293	303	308	365
6,000.................	312	351	351	363	369	438
7,500.................	390	439	439	454	461	548
8,000.................	416	468	468	484	492	584
9,000.................	468	527	527	545	554	657
10,000.................	468	585	585	605	615	730
11,000.................	468	632	644	666	677	803
12,000 and over.........	468	632	702	726	738	876

Yearly Self-Employment Earnings	Maximum Tax on Self-Employed Person					
	1972	1973	1974–77	1978–80	1981–85	1986 and After
$ 3,000.................	$225	$240	$240	$248	$ 251	$ 254
4,000.................	300	320	320	330	334	338
5,000.................	375	400	400	413	418	423
6,000.................	450	480	480	495	501	507
7,000.................	525	560	560	578	585	592
8,000.................	600	640	640	660	668	676
9,000.................	675	720	720	743	752	761
10,000.................	675	800	800	825	835	845
11,000.................	675	864	880	908	919	930
12,000 and over.........	675	864	960	990	1,002	1,014

Source: Social Security Administration
Note: Tax figures shown above make no allowance for automatic cost-of-living increases required by 1972 amendments to Social Security Act.

Administration

The OASDHI is a wholly federal government-administered program, with the exceptions that initial determinations of disability are made by state agencies and that medical expense benefits are administered through fiscal intermediaries such as Blue Cross and private insurance carriers. Two departments of the federal government share these administrative functions—the Treasury and the Department of Health, Education, and Welfare. The Internal Revenue Service of the Treasury collects the taxes, and the Secretary of the Treasury is the managing trustee of the trust funds. The Treasury also issues benefit checks, and appropriations are made from the fund to cover administrative expenses.

All other administrative functions are handled by the Social Security Administration, which is now a division of the Department of Health, Education, and Welfare. Centralized records are kept in Baltimore, Maryland, and field offices are located throughout the United States. In addition, research and actuarial divisions are attached to the Social Security Administration in Washington as is an appeals council which hears cases involving claimants who are dissatisfied with interpretations of eligibility or amount of benefits due.

OLD AGE ASSISTANCE (OAA)

The Social Security inaugurated an assistance program for those over 65 years of age, in need, and not covered, or sufficiently provided for by OASDHI. The number of persons so situated declined between 1955 and 1970 by 440,000, leaving 2.1 million still receiving OAA, undoubtedly because of the increase in OASDHI benefits. Nevertheless, because of increases in the size of assistance payments, the total cost of OAA in that 15-year period rose from $1.6 billion to $1.9 billion.[1] Such funds are taken from general federal and state revenues, with states administering the program under federal guidelines and with benefits varying from state to state.

CURRENT OASDHI ISSUES

Most students of social security favor, in principle, the widest possible coverage of an insurance program and the narrowest possible coverage of an assistance program. This preference is based upon both social and economic grounds. The social reasons are grounded in the democratic belief that older persons have a right to spend their final years in dignity, with an income based upon right rather than an income secured on the basis of demonstrated need. Under an insurance system, the worker and his employer, or the self-employed person, contribute during his working

[1] *U.S. News and World Report,* February 8, 1971, p. 33.

life a given amount of earnings, which is then used to finance an income after retirement. By complying with the published rules of the insurance system, the retirement income is earned. Need is not a factor.

In contrast, assistance is based upon need, which means that need has to be defined. Even with the best of intentions, different administrators will define need differently. In other instances, favoritism or political pressure may determine who receives assistance and who does not. In Louisiana, a change in administrations brought with it a twofold increase in the number of old-age assistance recipients. The aged are a significant group worth pleasing to the ambitious politician, sometimes without proper consideration for the general welfare. Under such circumstances, need can be redefined in terms of political regularity, with consequent degradation of the older person in real need.

The economic grounds for preferring an insurance program to an assistance program are closely related to the social ones. Insurance is paid for by the beneficiaries or their employers under a system of taxation that is clearly earmarked for a specific purpose. Assistance comes out of general taxation, which permits liberality without tying costs to benefits, or costs to responsibilities. In the long run, assistance is likely to be found to be less efficient and more expensive, with those employed burdened with the care of an increasing older population that has not provided for its own retirement by insurance.

Because Old Age Assistance has refused to "go away" as posited by the framers of the Social Security Act, despite the great expansion of coverage and benefits of OASDHI, and mindful also of the burgeoning welfare load involved in another aid program, Aid to Dependent Children,[2] there has developed a strong movement to commingle insurance and aid, either by paying the latter out of revenues designed for the former, or by paying for all benefits out of general revenues. Neither seems advisable.

The present method of financing old-age and survivor benefits is actually a practical compromise between two extremes: pay as you go and level premium. The latter would require a uniform contribution rate at all times, much higher to meet current outlays in earlier years and lower than necessary for the same purposes in later years. Because of enormous reserve fund with its potential deflationary impact, which level-premium financing would require building up, it has not been adopted. Rather, the plan has been to set taxes on an increasing basis which will divide costs over the years and build up a large but not enormous (for the job to be done) reserve. The fund can then absorb short-term fluctuations in

---

[2] AFDC grew from $625 million paid out to 2.2 million persons in 1955 to $4.1 billions paid to 9.1 million persons in 1970—a sevenfold increase during the most prosperous years in our history. (Data, U.S. Department of Health, Education, and Welfare.)

benefits and at the same time grow to such a size that its interest earnings can be a significant aid in overall financing.

Proponents of the pay-as-you-go method argue that we are actually paying as we go now, since, when current contributions are exceeded by costs, we shall have to convert the government securities in the Trust Fund into cash by taxation or borrowing. Hence, they believe that it would be better to meet benefit costs as they arise.

There are several objections to this viewpoint. One very practical one is that it jumps costs too high at a later date after keeping them low initially, so that employees and employers become conditioned to a large benefit for a low cost and resist future increases which must become effective if pay as you go is not to be dropped in favor of meeting costs either from general taxation or by deficit financing. Another objection along these same lines is that short-term fluctuations in benefits can occur and thus cause erratic and uncertain tax changes if strict pay-as-you-go financing is to be maintained.

The contention that we are already on a pay-as-you-go plan, since the assets of the Trust Fund are invested in government securities, is open to serious question. The securities purchased for the Trust Fund are not created for that purpose. If they were not sold to the Trust Fund, they would be sold elsewhere to permit the government to borrow the funds it needs. So long as there are government bonds or securities outstanding, it makes no difference whether they are in the hands of private banks or public trust funds insofar as costs are concerned. It therefore follows that we are not now on a pay-as-you-go plan because government taxation or borrowing to redeem the securities in the Trust Fund pays the cost of the services or projects for which the bonds were issued, not the costs of old-age and survivor benefits. It is no more an unusual procedure for the OASI Trust Fund to invest in government securities than for a private insurance company's reserve fund to do the same with its current surpluses.

Pay as you go is based upon a very dangerous assumption, for it assumes that future generations and Congresses will be willing to levy special taxes at a much higher rate than present ones. The cost of retirement is both a present one and a future one. By levying all the cost of those retired at the time of retirement, pay-as-you-go adherents would have us, in effect, live off our depreciation. What we would be doing would be analogous to the factory owner who takes no heed of machine depreciation until the machine wears out. Then he must charge the cost of a new machine against the profits of a single year, instead of spreading the cost over many years. Proper provision for the aged requires that the costs of retirement be divided between the future and the present.

On the other hand, the larger the Trust Fund surpluses become, the more is the temptation to raise benefits or to use those benefits for other purposes. Essentially, those who would utilize the OASI Trust Fund for

Old Age Assistance want to throw the burden of caring for needy aged entirely on employers and employees who are taxed to provide the various OASDHI benefits for insured retirees under that system. This not only seems unfair but it would also increase the desire to abandon the present method of financing from "earmarked" taxes to general revenue sources.

"Earmarked" Taxes versus General Revenues

Regardless of OAA financing, the question is repeatedly raised whether OASHDI benefits should be financed from general revenues rather than by means of an "earmarked" tax as is presently the situation. Those who favor the use of general revenues point out that the present OASDHI tax is regressive in nature in that lower income and middle-income families pay a higher proportion of their incomes than do families with higher incomes. They also point out that the use of general revenues would permit a greater degree of fiscal flexibility in that taxes or benefits could be raised or lowered independently. On a more immediate and short-term basis, this could permit the financing of substantial increases in benefits that have been contemplated by several members of Congress.

On the other hand, proponents of our present system of an earmarked tax argue that the use of general revenues would remove the restraints inherent in a program where taxes and benefits are directly tied together. Removal of these restraints could permit an escalation of benefits and taxes. Moreover, proponents argue that it would be difficult to draw a logical line as to how much of the program should be financed from general revenues; that pressures would mount for the increased use of general revenues; and that ultimately, the entire program would be financed on this basis.

Early Retirement

The cost of a retirement program now and in the future is going to depend considerably on how many persons past 65 continue to work. The more that do work, the less will be the cost. A large number of persons— almost 15% of the total—who are eligible for OASDHI benefits continue to work instead. If all eligible persons were to retire and take benefits at age 65, or if limits on income were removed as a condition of receiving benefits, long-range costs of OASDHI would greatly increase.

Because many persons over 65 prefer work to retirement, forced retirement increases the cost of an adequate retirement program. Yet public policy, as noted in Chapter 5, is moving toward earlier and more liberalized retirement without meeting the hard questions of whether this is the wisest course in terms of alternative use of resources. It does seem incongruous, however, that as medical science extends useful working

FIGURE 17–2

Medicare—What It Means

PART A BASIC COVERAGE	PART B SUPPLEMENTARY COVERAGE
(Financed by increased Social Security taxes.)	(Voluntary insurance financed by individual monthly premiums of $5.80 and federal funds from general revenues; individual pays first $50 of his total annual costs and 20% of the cost of all services totaling more than $50.)

Hospital Care
Full coverage after the first $68 for up to 60 days in each period of illness;* coverage up to 30 additional days, for which the patient pays $17 a day. "Lifetime reserve" of 60 days toward which patient pays $34 a day. Psychiatric care is included for up to 60 days in each period of illness with a lifetime limit of 190 days.

Physician's Care
Physicians' and surgeons' (including certain dental surgeons') fees. (100% reimbursement for radiological or pathological services by physicians to patients in hospitals.)

Nursing Home Care

Posthospital care for 20 days in each period of illness at no cost to patient, plus 80 additional days, for which patient pays $8.50 per day.

Home Nursing Care
Up to 100 home health visits each year in addition to those allowed under the basic plan, without any requirement for prior hospitalization.

Home Nursing Care
Up to 100 visits by nurses or technicians in each period of illness at no cost to patient.

Other Health Services and Supplies
Coverage includes cost of outpatient charges, X rays and other diagnostic tests, radiological treatments, casts, splints, artificial limbs, and ambulance service.

Out-of-Hospital Benefits
Yearly limits for treatment of mental, psychoneurotic, and personality disorders is $250.

* A period of illness, as defined by the bill, normally starts with the first day of hospitalization and ends whenever the patient has spent 60 consecutive days without hospital or nursing home care.
Source: U.S. Department of Health, Education and Welfare.

life, public and private pensions systems are moving to shorten it. Given the costs involved, as noted in Chapter 5, one must question this trend.

MEDICARE

Medicare is a hospital and medical insurance program for the aged which is composed of two parts, as set forth in Figure 17–2 Part A, the "basic coverage," is financed by payroll taxes added to the basic social security taxes. Part B, the "supplementary coverage," is paid for by contributions from beneficiaries and federal funds from general revenues as noted in Figure 17–2. Eligibility is basically the same as for the social security system. The payroll taxes for the Medicare program are included in the tabulations depicted in Table 17–3.

Considering the magnitude of this program at its inception (19 million people became covered on July 1, 1966, and by the end of the first year about 18 million had signed up), Medicare got off to a surprisingly smooth start. There have been, of course, a number of administrative problems—notably delays in processing bills from hospitals and doctors. However, when one considers that during its first year, hospital services to elderly Americans increased by 15% to 20% and the program involved some 6,500 hospitals, 250,000 physicians, 1,200 home health agencies, 74 Blue Cross organizations, 33 Blue Shield plans, 15 insurance companies, 100 group practice prepayment plans, and numerous other agencies (and in 1967, when the posthospital extended care benefits became available, 2,800 extended care facilities were added), the early administration problems seem relatively inconsequential.

One of the most controversial aspects of the Medicare program is its costs. Partially because estimates were based on existing utilization prior to its enactment despite the generally known propensity for the availability of prepaid medical care to enhance its usage, costs have greatly exceeded any forecasts, with $7.9 billion paid out in 1971 (see Figure 17–1), and the trend moving upward rapidly. Overutilization and malingering undoubtedly have contributed to this problem, but the most significant item has been the rising cost of medical services and hospital labor costs. The cost of medical care has been advancing faster than other elements of living expense and, with the advent of Medicare, rose quite sharply, as the demand for services increased.

Still another issue of the federal government's program for providing health care is the cost of Medicaid—provided for under Title 19 of the Social Security Act. Under this program, the federal government provides financial assistance to the states that provide medical assistance for individuals who are on welfare or who are "medically needy." As of 1970, Medicaid was in effect in all states except Alaska and Arizona. The cost of Medicaid was originally expected to involve a federal outlay of under $1 billion per year, but by 1970 it had quickly exceeded that amount and was expected to be in excess of $3 billion per year by the end of 1972. Part of the difficulty is due to the fact that the states were allowed to establish their own standards as to who would be considered as "medically needy." Liberal state standards greatly expanded the number of potential beneficiaries, until the federal government restricted beneficiaries to persons whose income is no more than 133% of the maximum welfare payment in the state.

UNEMPLOYMENT COMPENSATION

Unemployment compensation (or "insurance": both terms are used) is part of the broad spectrum of social insurance programs, and provides cash benefits to regularly employed members of the labor force who become involuntarily unemployed and who are able and willing to accept suitable jobs. Although unemployment compensation was established by the Social Security Act of 1935, the federal government does not exert great influence over either the administration or the funding of the program. Funding is not raised from general revenues but rather from a tax imposed on employers.

Administration

Unemployment compensation is primarily a state-administered program. The federal act provided an incentive to the states to establish their own unemployment insurance plans by imposing a federal tax, 90% of which could be offset by employer taxes paid under state laws meeting certain general standards. The tax, of 3.0% on the first $3,000 of annual wages of an employee, was originally imposed on all employers having eight or more employees in covered employment in 20 weeks of the year. All of these conditions have by now changed, but the principles remain the same.

All of the states have approved unemployment insurance programs, and because it is a state program, there is wide variation among the states with respect to specific provisions. Employers who are subject to these programs pay their state tax and receive credit against their federal tax. The remaining federal tax (about 0.4% of the covered payroll) is used by the federal government for federal and state administration (including the operation of public employment offices) and to bolster the reserves of the state programs. The state taxes are deposited in the unemployment trust fund in the federal treasury, and from these funds the states make weekly payments to unemployed persons covered by the state laws. Separate accounts are maintained for each state.

Operations

The Social Security Act did not establish or make mandatory unemployment compensation laws. It was enabling legislation allowing the states to do so, imposing a tax structure which greatly encouraged them to do so, and establishing minimum conditions for their programs if they participated. Each state determines specific qualifications for benefits (for example, allowable reasons for job separation), specific interpretation of terms (for example, "able to work," "available for work") and other conditions, such as allowable earnings when unemployed.

The federal act does stipulate situations where a state cannot deny aid to an otherwise eligible applicant, particularly if he refuses to accept new work because:

1. The job opening is available because of a strike or lockout.
2. The wages or conditions are substantially less favorable than those prevailing for similar work in the locality.
3. The job requires an individual to join, resign from, or refrain from joining a bona fide labor organization.

When a worker is unemployed, he reports to the local employment office, where, if the office cannot place him in a suitable job, he may file a claim for benefits. These are paid to the worker on a weekly basis in an amount and for a period determined by state law. Generally, the amount is about 50% of past earnings, subject to a maximum, which varies among the states from $45 to $130 per week as of January 1972.[3]

The state agencies which administer this program are generally either part of state departments of labor or an independent department or board. They operate through approximately 2,000 local employment offices, which not only handle the unemployment claims but provide job-finding and other services. Federal functions are mostly handled by the U.S. Department of Labor, although the Treasury Department maintains and invests the trust fund. Separate funds and programs now exist for railroad employees, ex-servicemen and federal civilian employees.

Subject to these and other federal requirements, the states have considerable discretion in deciding who shall be covered, the amount and duration of benefits, the taxes to be paid, and the procedures to be used for handling claims. For example, a state may include in its own program a provision whereby an employer with low-unemployment history may pay a lower tax, or it may adopt a standard tax rate which is different (higher) than the federal rate of 2.7%.

Coverage

Unemployment insurance is provided for only covered employment. This historically included primarily industrial and commercial workers in private industry, and excluded from coverage agricultural workers, domestics, certain casual labor, employees in some governmental and nonprofit organizations, the self-employed, and employees in small firms. Over the years, however, the states added coverage on employers with only a single worker, domestics or agricultural workers, and other excluded groups. Then in 1970, Congress enacted the Employment Security Amendments (Public Law 91–373), which required almost all states to

---

[3] Joseph A. Hickey, "A Report on State Compensation Laws," *Monthly Labor Review,* Vol. 95 (January 1972), pp. 42–45.

amend their laws in 1971 to conform to federal standards as to coverage. As a result of this legislation a sizable segment of state government employment, nonprofit organizations, and small business establishments were brought within the scope of the various state laws, adding about 4.75 million additional jobs to those covered.[4] In total, about 85% of all those employed are now within the purview of state or federal unemployment insurance legislation.

Eligibility

Eligibility conditions, like all other aspects of the individual state provisions, vary greatly, but there are usually these four:

1. The period of unemployment must be longer than some waiting period (usually one week).
2. The claimant must have qualified for benefits by having worked some minimum time or earned a minimum amount in covered jobs. (Usually 15 weeks or $500, sometimes in more than one fiscal quarter.)
3. The individual must have a continuing attachment to the labor force indicated by registration for work at an employment office (and sometimes be "actively seeking work" or show "willingness to accept suitable work").
4. Most states refuse benefits to those who terminate their employment under specified conditions.

The general purpose of these qualifications is to restrict benefits to those who become unemployed through no fault of their own. It is generally held that an employee who voluntarily leaves his job or is terminated through his own fault should take the consequences. The series of disqualifying reasons includes: discharge for misconduct or cause, dishonesty or criminal acts, voluntarily leaving without good cause, refusal of suitable work, participation or involvement in a labor dispute, pregnancy, customary layoffs of short and known duration, quitting to attend school or become self-employed, and fraudulent misrepresentation. All of these disqualifications are subject to greatly different conditions under state laws. The eligibility conditions relating to disqualification of strikers is discussed below.

Financing

Not all states actually charge employers at the legal maximum rate, and most states reduce the rates charged employers who have good un-

---

[4] *Ibid.*, p. 40.

employment histories. This is known as "experience rating," and is designed to encourage employment stabilizing practices. The tax is imposed entirely on the employer in all states except the following, where the additional rates indicated are charged the employees:

Alaska........0.3%–0.9%	Puerto Rico....0.5%
California......1.0%	Rhode Island....1.0%
New Jersey....1.0%	

Employee contributions are usually earmarked for disability insurance, which is discussed later in this chapter.

As a result of the Employment Security Amendments of 1970, which increased the federal taxable wage base to $4,200 per employee, more than one half the states followed suit and increased their wage base. In most cases, this was the first amendment of this aspect of the law since it was established.[5]

The federal share of the unemployment compensation tax (0.4%) is first used for annual appropriations to the states to cover the costs of administration of the unemployment compensation laws. The entire cost of administration is covered by these grants because all funds collected from taxes on employers or employees must be used for payment of benefits. Federal grants are also made to the states for the cost of administering the state employment offices, through which unemployment compensation benefits are handled. Since the costs of administration prior to the 1950s proved to be less than anticipated, the federal government developed a substantial surplus from its tax share. The Administrative Financing Act of 1954 utilized these surpluses to protect the solvency of the insurance funds. It provides for the automatic appropriation to the Federal Unemployment Trust Fund of the annual excess of federal unemployment tax collections over employment security administrative expenses. These excess collections were used first to establish and maintain a $550 million fund in the federal unemployment account available for noninterest-bearing loans to state agencies with depleted reserves. The excess collections beyond $550 million are used to establish a $250 million reserve for administrative expenses. Finally, any excess tax collections are returned to the states.

During the recession of 1958, the federal funds were insufficient to provide adequate loan facilities when unemployment severely drained state reserves. As a result, several states were eligible for loans for which there were no funds.[6] Whether the 0.4% federal tax will yield enough funds to pay even for administration in the future remains to be seen.

---

[5] *Ibid.*

[6] *Hearings before the Committee on Wages and Means on Unemployment Compensation* (House of Representatives, 86th Cong., 1st sess. [Washington, D.C.: U.S. Government Printing Office, April, 1959]), pp. 8–9.

Benefit Duration

Benefits become available in all states except four after a one-week waiting period. In Connecticut, Delaware, Maryland, and Nevada (and under the railroad program), there is no waiting period. The traditional maximum period for benefit duration was 26 weeks, with several states providing longer periods. Beginning in 1958, however, Congress passed a series of acts which permitted the states to extend benefits for up to 13 weeks for those who exhausted unemployment benefits and to borrow from the federal government for that purpose. The Employment Security Amendments of 1971 included a permanent program for extending the duration of benefits when a claimant has exhausted regular benefits and high unemployment makes it difficult to find a job. Financed jointly by the federal and state governments, this provision extends benefit duration by a maximum of 13 weeks on top of the regular period up to a total benefit duration of 39 weeks. Extended benefits became payable in all states as of January 1, 1972, when the national insured unemployment rate[7] is 4.5% for three consecutive months and they continue until the rate drops below 4.5% for a like period.[8]

The 1971 legislation also provides for extended benefits for individual states that adopt the program when the insured unemployment rate averages 4% for any 13 consecutive week period and exceeds 120% of the average of the rates for the same 13-week periods in each of the two preceding years. As of January 1972, 26 states had adopted this program.[9]

Unemployment Compensation and Strikers

Of particular significance to the study of labor relations and labor economics is the impact of unemployment compensation on strikes. As in other aspects of the program, there is considerable variation among the states. The railroad program is the most liberal in this regard, paying compensation to strikers, and those otherwise involved in strikes, from the moment of the strike regardless of the circumstances. Some $53.8 million was thus expended between 1953 and 1971 (as set forth in Table 17–4), by the railroads to finance strikes against themselves.

Among the states, New York and Rhode Island pay benefits after waiting periods of seven and eight weeks respectively, 14 states pay benefits if the employer locks out his employees,[10] and other states pro-

---

[7] "Insured unemployment rate" is the rate of unemployment among workers covered by unemployment compensation.

[8] Hickey, "Report on State Compensation Laws," pp. 42, 46.

[9] *Ibid.*, p. 46.

[10] The difference between a strike and a lockout is sometimes a matter of semantics, and the definitional distinction between the two in unemployment compensation laws leads to deliberate misuse or misapplication. After a 155-day strike at Westinghouse in 1956, the state unemployment compensation director in Pennsyl-

TABLE 17–4

Benefit Costs of Strikes in Railroad Industry 1953–71

Calendar Year	Benefits Paid		
	Strikers	Nonstrikers*	Total
1953.	$ 596,300	$ 77,900†	$ 674,200
1954.	8,100	140,500†	148,600
1955.	4,342,100	1,715,000	6,957,100
1956.	81,395	49,493	130,888
1957.	870,262	2,582,123	3,452,385
1958.	12,000	49,400	61,400
1959.	1,190	7,800	8,990
1960.	1,961,000	5,066,100	7,027,100
1961.	122,143	1,043,874	1,166,017
1962.	371,623	3,257,924	3,629,547
1963.	2,566,280	1,373,400	3,939,680
1964.	2,050,836	977,484	3,028,320
1965.	510,780	926,942	1,437,722
1966.	176,679	1,180,351	1,357,030
1967.	930,530	1,176,547	2,107,077
1968.	519,066	1,015,840	1,534,906
1969.	308,090	663,640	971,730
1970.	12,300	824,975	837,275
1971.	4,626,600	11,569,435	16,196,035
Totals.	$20,067,274	$33,698,728	$53,766,002

° "Nonstrikers" idled during labor disputes by refusing to cross picket lines.
† Figures of nonstrikers in these years are incomplete.
Source: Figures compiled by Railroad Retirement Board and provided by the National Railway Labor Conference.

vide benefits where the employee may be actively involved but technically not striking (see Table 17–5). Such a situation occurs, as in the 1970 General Motors strike in which the United Automobile Workers did not call out its members in several GM parts plants, despite its general strike against the corporation, because these plants supplied parts to other automobile companies. The UAW wished to maintain operations at these companies in order to reduce expenses to itself and to increase pressure on General Motors. Since, however, production at these plants was largely for General Motors operations, large numbers of workers were laid off for the duration of the strike and received unemployment benefits despite their participation in the union tactics and strategy.

In Chapter 7, we discussed the questionable public policy of supporting strikers by public aid and the potential consequences thereof on the collective bargaining system. Paying unemployment compensation to

vania termed the stoppage a "lockout," and thus the strikers were eligible for compensation. Westinghouse took the matter to the courts and won a reversal. See, *Westinghouse Electric Corp.* v. *Unemployment Compensation Bd. of Review,* 144 A.2d 852 (Pa., 1958).

TABLE 17–5

State Unemployment Insurance Laws Regulating Eligibility of Strikers

State (1)	During stoppage of work due to dispute (29 states) (2)	While dispute in active progress (12 states) (3)	Other (11 states) (4)	Disputes excluded if due to— Employer's failure to conform to— Contract (4 states) (5)	Labor law (4 states) (6)	Lock-out (14 states) (7)	Individuals are excluded if neither they nor any of the same grade or class are—* Participating in dispute (42 states) (8)	Financing dispute (30 states) (9)	Directly interested in dispute (41 states) (10)
Alabama		X							
Alaska	X			X	X		X		X
Arizona			X	X	X		X	X	X
Arkansas			X			X	X		X
California	X					X			
Colorado			X			X	X	X	X
Connecticut			X			X	X	X	X
Delaware	X								
District of Columbia		X					X		X
Florida		X					X	X	X
Georgia	X						X	X	X
Hawaii	X						X		
Idaho			X				X	X	X
Illinois	X						X	X	X
Indiana	X						X	X	X
Iowa	X						X	X	X
Kansas	X						X	X	X
Kentucky		X				X			
Louisiana		X							X
Maine	X						X	X	X
Maryland	X					X	X	X	X
Massachusetts	X						X	X	X
Michigan			X			X	X	X	X
Minnesota		X				X			
Mississippi	X					X	X	X	X
Missouri	X						X	X	X
Montana	X				X		X	X	X
Nebraska	X						X	X	X
Nevada		X					X	X	X
New Hampshire	X			X		X	X	X	X
New Jersey	X						X	X	X
New Mexico	X						X		X
New York			X						
North Carolina			X						
North Dakota	X						X		X
Ohio			X			X			X
Oklahoma	X						X		X
Oregon		X					X	X	X
Pennsylvania	X					X	X		X
Puerto Rico	X						X		X
Rhode Island			X				X	X	X
South Carolina		X					X	X	X
South Dakota	X						X	X	X
Tennessee		X					X		X
Texas	X						X	X	X
Utah	X				X	X			
Vermont	X						X	X	X
Virginia			X				X	X	X
Washington	X						X	X	X
West Virginia	X			X		X	X	X	X
Wisconsin		X							
Wyoming	X						X	X	X

* Various additional restrictions are found in state laws relating to striker eligibility.

Source: U.S. Department of Labor.

strikers requires the employer to finance strikes against himself because the taxes to support the program are paid almost exclusively by employers. As the *New York Times* aptly noted after a long telephone repairmen strike in that state:

The New York Telephone Co. had $41 million credited to its insurance reserve account when the first strike benefits were paid last September. By the end of last week every dollar in the account had been drained and the company was $500,000 in the red in its payments into the fund. Quite apart from these payments, the Bell System strikers received an estimated $11 million in union emergency strike benefits, plus an uncalculated additional amount in government welfare and Medicaid payments.

To replenish its unemployment insurance account, the telephone company's taxes—geared to the volume of joblessness it throws on the fund—will go up from $3 million in 1971 to $11.6 million this year and $12.7 million next year. In a real sense, the extra money will come not from the Bell System but from telephone users, who will now find the higher costs in wages and taxes reflected in the company's rate base.[11]

Other Unemployment Compensation Issues

Closely related to the use (or misuse) of unemployment compensation is that of eligibility in general. Since the purpose of unemployment insurance is to protect persons who are genuinely attached to the labor force from hardships incurred when temporarily unemployed and seeking other work, eligibility conditions must be set. As these conditions have steadily become less stringent, and benefits have become both more liberal and more widely supplemented, abuses have become more widespread. Not working at public expense in effect becomes more nearly equated with working.

The problem arises because we are witnessing two parallel revolutions which affect unemployment insurance. There is steady pressure and a noticeable trend toward payment of higher benefits for longer periods of more uniform duration. At the same time, as noted in Chapter 1, an extraordinary growth in part-time secondary workers in the labor force has occurred. For persons with only marginal attachment to the labor force, the temptation presented by larger benefits paid for as long as 39 weeks can lead to an increase in malingering and other undesirable practices, which, in the past, have never been problems of any magnitude in the system. The federal-state system will have to balance protection against fraud and malingering against requirements of fairness.

Since eligibility is related to employment within a particular state, workers would lose rights by moving from one state to another if it were not for the existence of an Interstate Benefit Plan whereby workers who qualify for benefits in one state may draw their benefits in another.

---

[11] *New York Times*, February 18, 1972, editorial, p. 32M.

The original home state pays the benefits, and the state in which the worker then dwells acts as the agent for the transaction. All 50 states cooperate in this plan. The Interstate Benefit Plan, however, does not help a worker who would qualify for benefits only if his credits in both states were totaled. As a result, a "basic plan for combining wages" has been subscribed to by the states. This plan provides for the totaling of credits where that is necessary to make determinations for eligibility. Still another problem arises when a worker is eligible for benefits but would be eligible for the maximum benefits only by combining wages in the states. The Extended Interstate Benefit Plan for Combining Wages, adopted by the states, is specifically designed to handle this problem.

Again, however, as the services provided by unemployment compensation laws are expanded, so is the opportunity to benefit without seriously looking for work. A New York housewife, laid off, finds it pleasant to collect benefits while enjoying the Florida sun, and her working husband is on a four weeks vacation from his job. Attachment to the labor force is now often loosely enough defined to permit such perversions of the intent of the law.

Vacation and retirement also give rise to troublesome questions. Several states permit benefits to be paid if the worker is on vacation without pay, through no fault of his own. On the other hand, a state may refuse payment on the ground that the employment relation still continues during vacation or that the worker on vacation is not available for work.

Another abuse affects those who retire but claim they are looking for work. In many states, workers and executives collect 26 weeks of unemployment insurance after retirement—and never return to the labor market.

Unemployment compensation remains, nonetheless, a reasonably effective program for the relief of temporary unemployment. Since benefits cease after 26 or 39 weeks, it cannot offset longer range or permanent job loss. By confining its use to its principal purpose, it could be made even more effective.

WORKMEN'S COMPENSATION

Workmen's compensation was the first type of social insurance to be developed extensively in the United States. It is designed to assure prompt payment of benefits to employees injured on the job or afflicted by occupational diseases; or in the case of a fatality in industry, to pay benefits to dependents. Workmen's compensation does not cover accident or injury outside of working hours, but only such accidents as occur on or pertain to the job.

The Development of Workmen's Compensation

Before workmen's compensation laws were passed, an employee injured on the job had little recourse. To be sure, under the common law the employer was required to provide a reasonably safe place for his employees to work. If, however, an employee was injured and the employer did not voluntarily pay some compensation, then the employee had to take his case to court for redress.

Besides the fact that employees rarely had the funds to hire sufficient legal assistance to pursue a case of this character in court, the employer had certain defenses which made it difficult for the employee to collect damages. In the first place, an employer might plead contributory negligence: that is, that the victim was also at fault to some degree. Or the employer might attempt to prove that the real fault was lodged with a fellow worker. This was known as the "doctrine of common employment" or the "fellow-servant doctrine." If these defenses were not available, the employer might plead a third one—the "doctrine of assumption of risk." Under this doctrine the employee was assumed to have had knowledge that he was engaged in a dangerous occupation and, therefore, if he still chose to work in that occupation, he had to assume the known risks of being injured.

In the latter part of the 19th and the early 20th centuries, the federal government and several states passed legislation designed to modify some of these common-law doctrines. It was not, however, until the lawmakers ruled out the question of blame in industrial accidents by passing workmen's compensation laws that progress was really made in providing compensation for injuries incurred on the job. These laws made the employer liable for work injuries, without regard to who was at fault. Hence, the injured employee could be compensated (1) even if the employer's negligence did not cause the accident and (2) even if the employee himself was negligent. Compensation laws were based on the theory that work injuries were inevitable and that the problem was to provide restitution rather than fix blame.

The Nature of Workmen's Compensation Laws

The first state workmen's compensation law was passed in New York in 1909. By 1948, workmen's compensation legislation had been enacted by all of the states, as well as by Puerto Rico. Special federal compensation laws cover civilian government employees, longshoremen and harbor workers, private employees in the District of Columbia, and since 1969, coal miners.

Workmen's compensation legislation, however, does not completely cover the American work force. Some states fail to provide coverage for certain types of accidents or diseases; and agricultural, domestic, and certain other workers are usually excluded from coverage of these laws. In 18 jurisdictions, workmen's compensation acts are elective rather than compulsory. In such states, employers may refuse to operate under the compensation act if they prefer to risk suit for damages by injured workers. In a few states, the laws are compulsory as to some employments and elective in others. When employers elect not to come under a compensation act, employees are remitted to their old remedies at common law, and must prove that the employer was negligent. In such circumstances, however, the employer loses his common-law defenses—contributory negligence, the fellow-servant doctrine, and assumption of the risk.

Besides agricultural and domestic workers, compensation laws usually exclude casual employment. In addition, railway employees come under the Federal Employers' Liability Act (FELA) rather than under workmen's compensation. And maritime employees come under the Jones Act, which gives them the same rights that railroad workers have under the FELA. These two employee groups claim that they are able to collect more compensation by negligence suits than by compensation laws because of the fact that juries are generally sympathetic to them and unsympathetic to railroad and shipping concerns. As of January 1972, in 25 jurisdictions, private employers who have less than a specified number of employees, varying from 2 to 15, are excluded from compulsory coverage of compensation legislation.[12]

Compensation laws are limited not only as to persons and employers included but also as to injuries covered. For example, some states exclude coverage if the employee is under the influence of alcohol or drugs, or if the accident is caused by willful misconduct, or gross negligence. In addition, a large number of states restrict coverage, to some extent, for occupational disease.

Nature of Benefits

Workmen's compensation laws provide two basic types of benefits: (1) cash payments for loss of income or death and (2) medical services, including rehabilitation, or cash payments for these services.

Most of the acts provide cash benefits based upon a percentage of the worker's wage up to a specified maximum. A few states vary the payments with the worker's marital status and number of dependents. The periods during which the compensation is paid vary tremendously, and the maximum weekly payments range from $40 to $150.

Death benefits also vary considerably. In some states, in the District of

---

[12] Most basic data on workmen's compensation in this chapter is taken from U.S. Chamber of Commerce, *Analysis of Workmen's Compensation Laws* (1972 ed.; Washington, D.C.).

Columbia, and under the federal compensation acts, payments are made to the widow for an unemployed period which is until remarriage, and to children until they reach a specified age. In others, death benefits are limited to payments for periods ranging from 300 to 1,000 weeks, but these states can continue to pay to children until they reach a specified age. Death benefits are usually based upon a percentage of the average weekly wage of the deceased workman; but Oklahoma pays a lump sum, and Kansas pays a flat pension.

Twenty-seven states, the District of Columbia, and the federal acts make permanent total disability payments for life or for the entire period of the disability. The remaining jurisdictions limit the time from 330 weeks to 550 weeks or limit the total amount of payments. Payments also vary in some states according to the number of dependents.

Sixteen states, the District of Columbia, and the federal acts make temporary total disability payments for the entire period of disability. In the other states, the payments are limited from 208 to 1,000 weeks and in various amounts. Some temporary total disability recipients also are paid additional benefits for dependent children.

Most compensation laws provide payments for permanent partial disability. Two categories of such injuries are generally recognized— scheduled and nonscheduled. The former includes specific injuries such as the loss of use of an arm or a leg; the latter includes more general injuries such as an injury to the head or back. Most states provide specific payments for scheduled injuries, and the maximum payable for such injuries varies considerably. For example, for the loss of an arm at the shoulder, a specified amount is payable. Payments for nonscheduled injuries are generally related to the loss of earning power; and, in many cases, they exceed payments for scheduled injuries.

In all the compensation acts, medical aid is required to be furnished to the injured employee. Approximately half of the states confine medical benefits for occupational diseases and accidents as to duration or cost, or both. In addition, all acts require the employer to furnish artificial limbs and other necessary appliances.

Before any cash payments are made, nearly all states require a waiting period of one week after the injury. Medical benefits begin immediately, however, and compensation may be retroactive to the date of injury if the disability continues beyond the waiting period.

Administration

To make certain that benefit payments will be paid when due, the states require that the covered employer obtain insurance or give proof of his qualifications to carry his own risk, which is known as self-insurance. In most of the states, the employer is permitted to insure with private insurance companies. State insurance systems exist in 18 states and Puerto

Rico. In six of these states and in Puerto Rico, the system is called "exclusive," because employers are required to insure in the monopolistic state fund. Competitive state funds exist in 12 states, where employers may choose whether they will insure their risks in the state fund or with private insurance companies, or qualify as "self-insurers" with the privilege of carrying their own risks.

In most states, a specific agency has been established to administer the act. In five states, however, there is no administrative agency empowered to supervise the compensation law, and injured workers can look only to the courts to enforce their claims. In states where the law is administered by a commission or board, the state agency usually has exclusive jurisdiction over the determination of facts, with appeals to the courts limited to questions of law. In a few states, however, the courts can consider the issues anew.

Second-Injury Funds and Special Provisions

A second injury to an employee who has already sustained an injury —such as the loss of a limb—may cause an employee to be totally disabled. If an employer were held responsible for the resulting total disability, this would encourage hiring discrimination against the handicapped. Therefore, nearly all states had second-injury funds which limit the employer's liability to the disability caused by the second injury alone. The difference between the disability for the loss as a whole, and what the loss would have been in the absence of a prior injury, is made up from the fund.

Financing

Unlike the situation for other social insurances, the funds for workmen's compensation are not provided for by specific taxes levied upon employer or employee, or both. There is no central fund from which compensation is payable to eligible injured workers. Rather, the employee's compensation claim is against his employer, who must insure the risk. In nearly all jurisdictions, workers make no direct contributions to costs.

Analysis of Workmen's Compensation

A careful scholar of the social insurances pointed out as early as 1949 that workmen's compensation:

. . . bears the scars of the fact that it was a pioneer social insurance program. . . . Restricted coverage, limitation of risks recognized . . . dollar limitations to amounts payable, the presence of private insurance techniques and self-insurance—all stem from the early and understandable desire to proceed with caution and to hedge the program with various safeguards designed to secure public acceptance and to allay misgivings on the part of employers.[13]

The complicated benefit system, the costly and inefficient overlapping between compensation and other insurance programs and inadequate coverage because of the large numbers of excluded categories, the failure to make provision for all occupational diseases and the number of laws which are elective, all have been criticized for many years.

Administration is perhaps the weakest phase of workmen's compensation. There is tremendous variation from state to state in the caliber of administration. Some states make an excellent effort to see that claims are promptly paid, that workers know their rights, and that final reports are received from insurance companies on benefits paid, how benefits were computed, and the nature of the injury for which benefits were paid. Unfortunately, such good administration is apparently relatively uncommon. Many states collect little pertinent information. The majority of employed workers apparently do not know their rights, and state administrators make no real effort to correct this lack of information. Only a few states attempt to find out how promptly workers are paid, how much is paid for medical expenses, how adequate benefits are to take the place of lost wages, and for what purpose benefits are paid. Moreover, inordinately expensive administration is the rule rather than the exception. It has been estimated that a large percentage of the cost of workmen's compensation goes for administration.

Since both insurance companies and employers have an interest in keeping costs at a minimum, and since most workers are not too well informed of their rights, the pressure to keep benefits down, to avoid expansion of coverage, and to pay the very least allowable in compensation is dominant in most state legislatures and most state administrative agencies. Moreover, since the individual is usually left to obtain his own benefits, he frequently becomes involved in litigation and lawyers' fees, if he is to protect his rights, or else faces loss of benefits because of ignorance of his rights. In other instances, benefits have been held up by attempts of insurance companies to transfer doubtful jurisdictional cases to the state jurisdiction which pays the least benefit. On the other hand, sometimes compensation costs can get out of line because of excessive liberality of state administrations, or because of intense pressure from unions in behalf of their members.

There are, however, sturdy pressures for reform. The passage of the Federal Coal Mine Health and Safety Act of 1969 and the subsequent creation of the National Commission on State Workmen's Compensation Acts, which made a very thorough study of all aspects of such laws, were clear warnings to states to improve their laws or face federal pre-

[13] Eveline M. Burns, *The American Social Security System* (Boston: Houghton Mifflin Co., 1949), p. 186.

emption. In 1971, the legislatures of 49 states and Puerto Rico enacted about 300 improvements to existing laws, about double the usual number.[14] Moreover, the existence and administration of the Williams-Steiger Occupational Safety and Health Act of 1970 should act as a continuing spur to state workmen's compensation legislation.

THE OCCUPATIONAL HEALTH AND SAFETY ACT OF 1970

The prime objective of workmen's compensation legislation is, of course, the payment of benefits to those injured on the job. If, however, the social purpose of workmen's compensation is to be achieved, it should encourage safe working practices which will prevent injuries before they occur; and it must provide the means to rehabilitate workers who have been injured so that they can, insofar as possible, become self-supporting once more.

There can be no doubt that workmen's compensation has encouraged safe working practices. The insurance rate which is charged to the employer is determined by the accident frequency and severity record of his factory. Substantial savings in insurance costs accrue to the employer whose plant safety record is of high quality. The larger insurance companies in the compensation field provide safety counseling as part of their services. In addition, most states provide for safety inspections. Many employers have found that they can regain all of their costs spent on safety by reduced costs in compensation through fewer work injuries.

Unfortunately, relatively few plants have had adequate safety programs. Estimates of the Bureau of Labor Statistics indicate that only one third of all workers were subject to planned, organized safety efforts prior to 1970. Consequently, American industry averaged 2 million disabling injuries and 14,000 deaths, with an estimated direct economic loss of 250 million man-days of work—representing full-time employment of about 1 million persons for one year, despite the fact that the severity and the frequency of injuries per man-hour worked have, for the most part, declined over the years.

Although accident prevention is obviously socially more desirable than compensation after injury, most workmen's compensation administrators either have had no authority to enforce safety regulations or no funds to spend on safety, or no interest in the subject. In some states, industrial health and safety programs and law enforcement are assigned to one department, workmen's compensation administration to another. Workmen's compensation legislation has been less a stimulation to

---

[14] Florence C. Johnson, "Changes in Workmen's Compensation in 1971," *Monthly Labor Review,* Vol. 95 (January 1972), p. 51.

rehabilitation than to accident prevention. Only about one third of the state laws contain specific provisions for tiding permanently impaired workers over a period of vocational rehabilitation. A few other states make liberal provisions for the same purpose, although not unlimited ones. Usually, however, the awards for rehabilitation are meager, and insufficient to accomplish the task.

This need to improve plant safety practices led Congress to enact the Occupational Health and Safety Act of 1970 (OHSA) "to assure so far as possible every working man and woman in the Nation safe and healthful working conditions and to preserve our human resources." It covers virtually all industry and employment in the country not covered by special laws, such as the Coal Mine Health and Safety Act. Employers are charged with maintaining safe and healthful places of work and with complying with safety and health standards under the act; employees likewise have the duty to comply with such standards and rules. The Secretary of Labor is responsible for promulgating and enforcing health and safety standards; if any employer is cited for a violation, he may contest it before a new three-man quasi-judicial body, the Occupational Safety and Health Review Commission. Orders of the Commission are reviewable in the U.S. Court of Appeals.

OHSA has virtually created a new right for workers—the right of a safe and healthful place of employment. Failure of employers to comply can mean fines or business shutdowns. Moreover, inspections must be made upon employee complaints, and plants are subject to unannounced inspections at any time by a new force of federal inspectors. Representatives of employees—usually union representatives—have the right to accompany inspectors on their rounds.

A controversial aspect of this new law is the potential for it to become a tool of industrial warfare.[15] As noted in Chapter 6, it is an old tactic of unions to use safety as a defense of featherbedding or as a means of harassing an employer. On the other hand, many union complaints about health and safety are genuine. An examination of union and company publications since mid-1970[16] clearly demonstrates that unions believe that OHSA provides a mechanism to increase their interest in health and safety and to enhance their right for an effective voice in working conditions affecting health and safety, whereas employers fear that this interest will be used as a wedge to increase union penetration into managerial functions and to force additional wage and benefit concessions.

One certain effect of OHSA is a greater interest in health and safety

---

[15] Legislation designed to effectuate noise abatement and to protect hearing, as well as various state and federal environmental laws, can have similar impacts on labor relations.

[16] By one of the authors.

standards. Safety practices, plant housekeeping, and top-management interest in accident prevention have all been enhanced. Hopefully, this will continue, and OHSA's great contribution will be its prime purpose—less accidents and more lives saved.

DISABILITY LEGISLATION

Disability legislation is of two types: permanent and total, and temporary. Permanent and total disability legislation is, as discussed above, part of the old-age, survivors, disability, and health insurance (OASDHI) legislation. Essentially it involves the payment of old-age benefits earlier than they would otherwise be due, without reduction of benefits, when the covered employee has become disabled and is no longer able to work. The OASDHI program also provides the same disability benefits for dependents as they would receive under retirement benefits and for benefits to disabled widows and widowers between ages 50 and 62.

Temporary disability insurance is payable for a fixed period, for example, 26 weeks. Whereas workmen's compensation pays compensation for occupational injuries and illnesses, temporary disability insurance is designed to provide compensation for injuries and illnesses contracted away from, and not related to, the job. Finally, although every state has a workmen's compensation law, only four states have enacted temporary disability insurance laws—California, New Jersey, New York, and Rhode Island. The Railroad Unemployment Insurance Act also provides temporary disability benefits for nonoccupational as well as occupational disability. Thus, nearly all temporary disability insurance is covered by private welfare programs, including union-management rules.

Development of Disability Insurance

In 1942, Rhode Island enacted the first disability insurance law. At that time, Rhode Island imposed a tax of 1.5% of payroll on employees, in addition to taxes upon employers, for support of unemployment compensation. This employee payroll tax was reduced to 0.5% in 1942, but the 1% reduction in employee payroll tax on the first $3,000 of wages was shifted to support the disability legislation.

In 1946, Congress amended the Social Security Act to permit states which had levied taxes upon employees in support of unemployment compensation to use an amount equal to the total employee contributions to the unemployment trust fund for cash disability payments. On the basis of this legislation, which affected nine states, Rhode Island discontinued its 0.5% tax on employees for unemployment compensation but continued its 1% disability tax, and California and New Jersey enacted a disability insurance law wholly separate and distinct from unemployment compensation.

Analysis of State Disability Legislation

The four state disability insurance laws are of three distinct kinds. The oldest of the state laws, that of Rhode Island, provides for a single state fund which collects all contributions and pays all benefits. No private plans can be substituted for the Rhode Island state fund, nor is any cognizance taken of any benefits that may be provided under a private plan. Like the other states, Rhode Island and New Jersey provide a seven-day waiting period before benefits are paid; but whereas the other three states require a waiting period before each separate disability is compensated, Rhode Island requires only one waiting period each benefit year.

The laws of Rhode Island, California, and New Jersey are administered by the state unemployment compensation agencies in these states. These three disability laws follow the unemployment compensation system in regard to eligibility requirements. Temporary disability is defined, in general, to mean physical or mental illness incapacitating a person so that he cannot perform his work. By administering the disability legislation with existing unemployment compensation agencies, the records of unemployment insurance can be utilized and administrative savings effected.

In California, New Jersey, and New York, employers may self-insure or insure with a private carrier or the state fund. In California and New Jersey, workers are automatically covered by the state plan unless the employer takes affirmative action to institute a private plan. Both California and New Jersey attempt to safeguard the state funds against adverse selection of risks, for example, by requiring that private plans do not discriminate against any class of risks, such as plants which hire a large portion of women (since women generally lose more time because of illness than men). In California, the requirements have been such that most private insurers have withdrawn from this market, thus leaving the state plan as the primary method by which most workers are covered.

The New York law differs radically from the other three, in that it is wholly divorced from unemployment compensation and in that there is no limitation upon rights to establish private plans. New York's law is administered by the State Workmen's Compensation Commission, and the administration of the law is modeled upon the state workmen's compensation administration. New York's law, like those of the other three states, has a 26-week benefit duration.

The failure of temporary disability legislation to spread beyond the four state and railroad jurisdictions is not a result of a political deadlock on the merits of providing protection against nonoccupational disabilities. Rather, it is a result of a conflict over methods, particularly the following: (1) the degree of federal versus state participation; (2) private insurance versus public financing; and (3) administrative tie-up with unemployment compensation versus administrative tie-up with workmen's compensation. Until these issues are resolved or compromises are reached, temporary disability legislation is not likely to spread. In the state of Washington, for example, an act of the legislature was nullified in a state referendum because opponents of any law were joined by opponents of the type of law enacted. Since this occurred, in 1950, no new law has been enacted by any state, and private plans have filled the void.

THE HEALTH INSURANCE ISSUE

The plethora of social insurance and welfare programs still find, after a quarter of a century of agitation, no all-inclusive health insurance program. Older persons are covered by Medicare and Medicaid, with the burgeoning welfare load made more costly by the latter. An ever-increasing number of the persons are covered by private health insurance, but proposals before Congress in 1972 indicate quite clearly the increased likelihood that millions of Americans not now covered by federal programs will be brought within their purview in the near future. Two proposals indicate the scope of what the future may hold, one by President Richard M. Nixon, the other by Senator Edward M. Kennedy.

The President's State of the Union Message in January 1971 proposed to abolish Medicaid and to substitute therefor, a subsidized private insurance program under which a limited range of medical services would be available to the poor. Catastrophic illness or accident insurance would be established for all families, and increased aid to medical schools would be furnished together with incentives designed to extend medical care and services to areas now poorly served, such as rural sectors and inner urban districts.

The Kennedy plan was originally developed by a committee established by Walter Reuther, the late United Automobile Workers' president, and is backed by the AFL–CIO, among others. It would pay virtually all medical expenses for everyone. The Nixon plan would be financed by increased taxes, plus individual insurance premiums. The Kennedy plan would require greatly increased social security taxes, plus revenues from general taxes. What may be conservative estimates of costs for the Nixon plan are about $2 billion–$3 billion; for the Kennedy plan, $40 billion–$77 billion.[17]

The basic issue before the American people regarding health expenditures can be stated in terms of opportunity cost: What does one wish to give up to improve health care. Burgeoning medical costs are illustrated in Figure 17–3. Although proponents of new federal health insurance programs claim that the costs involved with their proposals are substantially substitutes for existing costs, this is not too likely, because the very availability of prepaid medical programs creates an enlarged demand

---

[17] *U.S. News and World Report*, February 8, 1971, p. 35.

FIGURE 17–3

Soaring Medical Costs—and No End in Sight

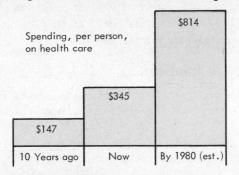

Spending, per person, on health care

$814

$345

$147

| 10 Years ago | Now | By 1980 (est.) |

TODAY, outlays for health take 7 cents out of every dollar spent in the U.S. for goods and services.

BY 1980, health care will take almost 11 cents of each dollar.

EXAMPLES OF HOW
HEALTH CHARGES ARE SKYROCKETING

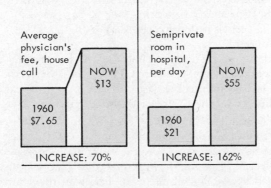

Average physician's fee, house call

NOW $13

1960 $7.65

INCREASE: 70%

Semiprivate room in hospital, per day

NOW $55

1960 $21

INCREASE: 162%

Source: Data, U.S. Social Security Administration; U.S. Dept. of Labor; chart, *U.S. News & World Report*, February 8, 1971, p. 35. Copyright © 1971, U.S. News & World Report, Inc.

for the services. Consequently, any new program creates a supply shortage and increased costs. A very real question is whether the facilities and medical personnel should not be built up before dramatic new programs are incorporated into the system. Most of all, basic decisions should be made as to the extent of our national resources that we should divert to health care instead of economic growth, housing, old-age benefits, or other equally praiseworthy and sound economic ventures and programs.

In the final analysis, of course, political pressures will probably determine the nature of future health insurance programs as has been the case in the past. The American social security system is a rare blend of public and private, federal and state, generous and meager. Whether, if carefully planned, it would be more satisfactory remains a question. Unless, however, some hard decisions are made as to priorities, it could prove more burdensome than supportive.

QUESTIONS FOR DISCUSSION

1. Do you believe that OASDHI should continue to be financed by payroll taxes? Should such taxes also pay for Old-Age Assistance? Explain your answers.
2. What is the role of unemployment compensation? Should the program be federalized? Should strikers ever receive benefits? Explain your answers.
3. What are the shortcomings and strong features of workmen's compensation? What will be the likely impact of the Occupational, Safety and Health Act of 1970 on workmen's compensation laws?
4. Are you in favor of national health insurance? If so, what "insurance package" do you advocate? How do you defend your position when it is alleged that such insurance would be too costly?

SUGGESTIONS FOR FURTHER READING

NATIONAL COMMISSION ON STATE WORKMEN'S COMPENSATION LAWS. *Compendium on Workmen's Compensation; Report to the President and the Congress;* and various technical papers. Washington, D.C.: U.S. Government Printing Office, 1972.

These studies are without doubt the most complete available for all aspects of workmen's compensation. They will provide the basic source of knowledge on the subject for years to come and are expected to have a significant impact on the future of the state system of laws.

"The Nation's Health—Some Issues," *Annals of the American Academy of Political and Social Science*, Vol. 399 (January 1972), entire issue.

Contributors discuss the poor, the sick, and the student; hospital and physician costs and charges; the experience with medical insurance programs in the United States; and problems of health in the United States in perspective.

"Occupational Health and Safety," in RICHARD L. ROWAN (ed.). *Collective Bargaining: Survival in the '70's?* pp. 393–424. Philadelphia: Industrial Research Unit, Wharton School of Finance and Commerce, University of Pennsylvania, 1972.

The chairman of the Occupational Health and Safety Review Commission, a leading labor official and a management spokesman discuss the impact of OHSA on collective bargaining.

U.S. DEPARTMENT OF HEALTH, EDUCATION, AND WELFARE. *Social Security Programs in the United States.* Social Security Administration, various years.

A detailed explanation of social security and unemployment compensation programs, issued whenever the laws are modified.

PART VI

Government Control of
Labor Relations

Chapter 18

GOVERNMENTAL CONTROL

OF THE WEAPONS OF

CONFLICT

Americans pride themselves on having maintained free collective bargaining and a free labor market in a world which is becoming increasingly regimented and collectivized. But the degree of freedom in our collective bargaining is relative. It is relatively unrestricted when compared with labor relations in the Soviet Union and other countries in the Communist bloc. On the other hand, an appraisal of the development of labor relations in this country reveals a patchwork of judicial decisions, laws, and regulations which have continually eroded and narrowed the field of individual action. In this chapter, we shall examine in detail some of the major weapons of conflict in the struggle for power between unions and management and shall consider how governmental and judicial controls have attempted to curtail their use.

LABOR AND THE COURTS IN EARLY AMERICA

The basic economic and social environment in the United States has, on the whole, been hostile to the development of union organization. In a land of opportunity, rich in natural resources and capable of providing a high standard of living to its wage earners, trade-unions have been unable to draw their membership from a proletariat with strong class allegiance, as in most European nations. On the contrary, class lines have been fluid; and even among wage earners, there has been continuing respect and support for the institution of private property. Union leaders have come to recognize this difference in outlook among our workers and have had to adopt a new kind of unionism—antisocialistic and business oriented— in order to attract and retain membership.

This same strength of private property rights which is a product of the free enterprise of the American environment is reflected in the attitude of both employers and courts toward union organization. In their struggle for recognition of the right to organize, unions have had to combat not only antagonistic employers, vehemently committed to defend their right to run their own businesses without interference from their employees, but also an unfriendly judiciary and an inimical common

563

law. Members of the judiciary tended to be selected from the propertied classes of the community and therefore reflected a conservative attitude in their opinion in labor disputes. But even had their personal predilections been liberal, the fact remains that the controlling precedents of common law were generally restrictive of organized labor's actions.

Our common law, which is based upon the customs of the land as reflected in the accumulated decisions of the judiciary, has its roots in English history. In the 18th century, English courts outlawed labor combinations which exerted pressure to increase wages or to secure the closed shop as a means toward that end. British courts and statesmen considered such combinations among workmen to be inimical to the public interest because they interfered with the free working of market forces. In the famous *Philadelphia Cordwainers* case of 1906, and in numerous others during the next 30 years, American state courts adopted this same viewpoint and held that concerted action by combinations of workmen to better their wages and working conditions represented an illegal conspiracy against the public and against employers.

Then in 1842, in the case of *Commonwealth* v. *Hunt*,[1] the Supreme Judicial Court of Massachusetts decided that a strike in support of a closed shop was not, per se, illegal; and that unless it could also be shown that the workers' objectives were bad, the conspiracy doctrine did not apply. Although the conspiracy doctrine continued to be utilized occasionally for some years to break up strikes, the decision in *Commonwealth* v. *Hunt* dealt it a blow from which it never recovered.

Judicial Tests of Legality

After the decision in *Commonwealth* v. *Hunt*, many courts tended to judge the legality of union activity on the basis of "motive" and "intent." This proved to be a highly subjective standard, which frequently reflected the prejudices of the individual judge rather than the facts of the case. Equally unsatisfactory was the so-called "means" test, which attempted to draw the line between permissible and unlawful union activity on the basis of whether or not the union action involved peaceful persuasion or unlawful intimidation. A further theory utilized by courts in labor cases in these early years was the doctrine of restraint of trade. This doctrine assumed much greater importance in judicial decisions with the subsequent enactment of the Sherman Antitrust Act, which will be discussed later. The doctrine of restraint of trade, however, also existed in common law. In general, the common-law doctrine was based on the premise that everyone should have equal access to the market and that when two or more persons combined to block access to the market and thereby inflicted injury upon the public, a conspiracy in restraint of

---

[1] 4 Metcalf 111 (1842).

trade existed. All restraints, whether inspired by labor or industry, were not considered illegal per se. The legality of such restraints was held to depend upon their "reasonableness," which was determined by the courts by weighing the extent of coercion exercised, if any, and the effect of the restraint on the volume of business and access to the market.

The Injunction

By the late part of the 19th century, the courts had generally recognized the right of employees to organize in unions without civil or criminal liability. However, the use of concerted economic weapons—the strike, the boycott, and picketing—was generally held unlawful on the basis of one of the theories referred to above. The most effective weapon management was able to utilize to restrain such action by unions was the injunction.

The major objective of organized labor in the latter part of the 19th and the early part of the 20th century was to free itself from the shackles of the injunction. The injunction is a legal technique developed in equity courts to provide relief against continuing injury where recovery in the form of monetary damages does not suffice. Upon a showing that "irreparable damage" might occur to the party requesting the relief unless certain acts of the defendant are stopped, the judge may issue an order forbidding the defendant to do such acts. If the defendant disobeys the court order, he may be fined or imprisoned for contempt of court.

The effectiveness of the injunction was based upon the speed with which it could be secured and the manner in which it could be applied. An employer could go into court and secure what is known as an ex parte injunction by alleging that grave and irreparable damage would occur to his business or property if the injunction were not granted. Such an ex parte injunction could be obtaineed by the employer or his attorney appearing before a single judge, without notice to the union and giving the judge only his side of the story. If the judge granted the request for an injunction—as he usually did—he would issue an order of the court forbidding the union officers and members to do a long list of prohibited acts. Such an order would completely tie up union organizational activities, and at the same time leave the employer free to discharge union members and otherwise act to destroy union organization in his plant before the union could be heard in court. By the time the case was brought to a hearing to determine whether the injunction should be dissolved or made permanent, the employer could often whip the union. If union officials violated any part of the injunction, they could be held in contempt of court and fined or jailed by the court, without trial by jury. This was true whether or not the injunction was made permanent.

The application of injunctions to labor disputes developed rapidly after the *Debs* case of 1895.[2] In that case, Eugene Debs, leader of the Pullman strike,[3] was enjoined by an order obtained by the U.S. government from continuing a boycott of Pullman cars which, the government alleged, interfered with interstate commerce and the transportation of the mail. Although injunctions had been used in labor disputes prior to this time, the case focused nationwide attention on the injunction technique as a weapon against union organizational activities.

A further development which contributed to the popularity of the injunction as a management tool in labor disputes was the so-called "yellow-dog" contract. This is a contract which an employer requires a worker to sign, stating that as a condition of employment, he agrees not to join a union. The phrase "yellow dog" was applied by unionists at an early date to workers who signed such contracts, and the contracts have been known by that appellation ever since.

In practice, employers made no real attempt to enforce such contracts against the individual workers who signed them. The importance of the contracts was that if they were legal, then attempts by union organizers to compel workers who had signed such contracts to join a union were deliberate efforts to cause a breach of such contracts, and such action could be enjoined by the courts. Unionists maintained that because workers had no choice but to sign such agreements, they were without force or effect. The majority of state courts rejected this view, holding that inequality of bargaining power did not preclude enforcement of contracts. The New York courts, however, accepted labor's point of view.

Because of the general antagonistic attitude of the courts, labor unions attempted at an early date to secure passage of legislation which would outlaw yellow-dog contracts and thus curb the use of this effective antiunion organization weapon. Between 1890 and 1914, no less than 14 states enacted legislation making it a misdemeanor or otherwise unlawful for employers (1) to exact yellow-dog contracts from their employees and (2) to interfere with the right of the employees to join or otherwise belong to a legitimate union. In addition, in 1898, Congress passed the Erdman Act, which contained similar provisions for the benefit of operating employees of the railroads.

The courts, however, declined to view with favor this legislation, which contained the principles of the Wagner Act 40 years before that law was conceived. The Supreme Court found that both the state laws and the pertinent section of the Erdman Act were unconstitutional because the 5th and 14th amendments to the Constitution guarantee freedom

---

[2] *In re Debs,* 158 U.S. 654, 15 S. Ct. 900 (1895).

[3] The strike involved an abortive attempt to establish industrial unionism on the railroads.

of contract as a property right.[4] According to the courts, an employer had a constitutional right to request his employees to sign yellow-dog contracts and to enforce such contracts, and also to discharge his employees because of union activities. In short, the courts held that furthering union activities or even preventing interference therewith was not a sufficient promotion of the general welfare to permit interference with the sanctity of contracts, not even if they were yellow-dog contracts. Furthermore, in 1917, in the *Hitchman Coal and Coke* case,[5] the U.S. Supreme Court completely supported the enforceability of yellow-dog contracts. It ruled that a court of equity could issue an injunction restraining attempts to organize employees bound by contracts with their employer not to join a labor union. Needless to say, these decisions caused unionists to take an extremely jaundiced view of the judiciary and to redouble their efforts to curb judicial interference in labor-management relations.

THE APPLICATION OF THE ANTITRUST LAWS TO ORGANIZED LABOR

Section I of the Sherman Act of 1890 states: "Every contract, combination in the form of trust, or otherwise, or conspiracy in restraint of trade or commerce among the several States, or with foreign nations, is hereby declared to be illegal." For some years after this act was passed, there was speculation as to whether or not this broad statutory language applied to labor. Finally, in 1908, in the case of *Loewe* v. *Lawlor*,[6] commonly known as the *Danbury Hatters* case, the U.S. Supreme Court ruled that a nationwide boycott organized by the union to persuade wholesalers and retailers to refrain from buying the company's products was an illegal restraint on commerce. The Court interpreted the statutory phrase, "restraint of trade or commerce," to apply to interference by a union with the interstate shipment of goods. The Court ordered the union to pay treble damages amounting to over half a million dollars, and individual members of the union were held responsible for their share of such damages.

Labor leaders were justifiably concerned about this result and immediately commenced pressure for exemption of labor from the antitrust laws. This drive culminated in the passage of the Clayton Act of 1914. Section 6 of that act declared:

. . . nothing contained in the antitrust laws shall be construed to forbid the existence and operation of labor . . . organizations, instituted for the purposes of

---

[4] *Coppage* v. *Kansas*, 236 U.S. 1, 35 S. Ct. 240 (1915), which nullified the state laws; and *Adair* v. *United States*, 208 U.S. 161, 28 S. Ct. 277 (1908), which nullified Section 10 of the Erdman Act.

[5] *Hitchman Coal and Coke Co.* v. *Mitchell*, 245 U.S. 229, 38 S. Ct 65 (1917).

[6] 208 U.S. 274, 28 S. Ct 301 (1908).

mutual help, and not having capital stock or conducted for profits, or to forbid or restrain individual members of such organizations from lawfully carrying out the legitimate objects thereof; nor shall such organizations, or the members thereof, be held or construed to be illegal combinations or conspiracies in restraint of trade under the antitrust laws.

Section 20 of the Clayton Act barred issuance of federal injunctions prohibiting activities such as strikes, boycotts, or picketing "in any case between an employer and employees, or between employers and employees, or between employees, or between persons employed and persons seeking employment, involving or growing out of, a dispute concerning terms or conditions of employment." This same section concludes with a broad statement that none of the acts specified in this paragraph shall be considered violations "of any law of the United States."

Despite this broad language, the U.S. Supreme Court in 1921 in the case of *Duplex Printing Company* v. *Deering*[7] held that the Clayton Act did not give labor unions a complete exemption from the antitrust laws. The case involved a secondary boycott of products of Duplex carried out for the most part by persons who did not stand in a direct employment relationship with Duplex. Construing the language of Section 20 of the Clayton Act narrowly, the Court held that the defendants were not entitled to exemption from the Sherman Act. As a result of this decision, which appeared to nullify congressional intent, employers stepped up their use of the injunction as a weapon to curb labor's organizing efforts.

OTHER LEGAL IMPEDIMENTS TO ORGANIZATION

Another major impediment to organization provided by the common law was the freedom of an employer to refuse employment to workers because of union activity. Employers thus could maintain what might be called an "antiunion closed shop." In furtherance of antiunion activities, employers were, in the absence of legislation, free to engage in blacklisting of union members and to utilize labor spies to ferret out union sympathizers. The common law did provide that a worker may not be hounded or libeled in order to prevent him from seeking security or maintaining employment, but this protection proved of little value because the employer also had the right to advise other employers that he had discharged a man because of his union or "radical" sympathies or activities.

More than one half of the states now have laws which outlaw the blacklist, and six states require employers, upon demand, to give discharged employees a truthful statement of the reasons for discharge.

---

[7] 254 U.S. 443, 41 S. Ct. 172 (1921).

These state laws against blacklisting, however, have not been easily enforced, although in at least one case, such a law was used by workers to secure an injunction against the use of the blacklist.[8] It was almost impossible to prevent one employer from telling another over the telephone that Jones, Smith, and Brown were "radical unionists," so that when these three applied for employment to the second employer, they were refused a job on the ground that no vacancies were available. It was not until the passage of the National Labor Relations Act in 1935 that effective protection against blacklisting was finally achieved.

STRIKES, BOYCOTTS, AND PICKETING AND THE COURTS BEFORE 1932

As has been pointed out in the discussion thus far, the courts (in years prior to 1932) tended to interpret both the common law and the statutory law in a manner unfavorable to the development of organized labor. The practical effect of such an antagonistic attitude on the part of the judiciary can best be appreciated by examining its impact on the major weapons a union can utilize to achieve its objectives—the strike, the boycott, and picketing. From the point of view of federal law, it is convenient to consider judicial interpretation prior to 1932 and after 1932, since in that year the Congress enacted the Norris–La Guardia Act, which drastically altered the power of federal courts to intervene in labor disputes.

Strikes

Workers on strike do not ordinarily regard themselves as having terminated their employment relationship. They have left their work temporarily, and in concert, in order to secure more favorable terms of employment. But they regard themselves as having a vested or property right in their jobs. The courts, however, have not recognized this right until very recently—and then only in a modified form. On the whole, courts have been more ready to accept ideas concerning employer property rights than employee property rights—at least until recently.

As we pointed out at the beginning of this chapter, after the courts abandoned the theory of conspiracy, they continued to regulate union conduct by looking into the motives or intent of union conduct. In the case of strikes, this involved an analysis of the purpose or objective of the walkout.

Courts have frequently enjoined the continuance of a strike where the purpose of the strike was to force the employer to cooperate in committing an illegal act. They have also taken similar action in cases

---

[8] E. E. Witte, *The Government in Labor Disputes* (New York: McGraw-Hill Book Co., 1932), pp. 212–20.

where, after weighing the damage done by a strike against the objective sought to be accomplished, they have concluded that the strike was "unjustified." This is, of course, a highly subjective criterion, but it has been widely applied in a variety of circumstances. For example, prior to 1932, judges frequently found sympathetic strikes unlawful. These are strikes by one group of workers in support of another, such as a strike of plumbers out of sympathy for striking gravediggers. Judges have found no possible justification for inflicting loss on the employers of plumbers merely because of a dispute between gravediggers and their employers. Likewise, despite the pathbreaking case of *Commonwealth* v. *Hunt*, many state courts, if not the majority, have condemned strikes to obtain a closed shop. The reason is that the closed shop is regarded as monopolistic and attaching a condition to the right of a worker to obtain employment.

On the other hand, in the case of strikes against technological change and jurisdictional strikes, courts have usually adopted a "hands off" attitude. Although most courts have indicated that they regard strikes aimed at preventing technological advance as harmful to society, they have recognized the problem that such progress often creates for workers and have usually not interfered, in the absence of legislative enactment, with the attempts of unions to retard technological change. Likewise, in the case of jurisdictional strikes—which are contests between unions over which group of workers shall perform a specified piece of work—most courts have declined to enjoin strikes per se. They have regarded jurisdictional strikes as a matter for regulation by the legislative branch of the government.

Lockouts

A lockout is an act by an employer or employers locking out employees from their jobs in an effort to compel them to accede to the terms of employment desired by management. In contrast to the strike, where numbers and relationships may under the conspiracy doctrine make a difference, a lockout under common law may be practiced without legal restriction, whether by a single employer or by employers in combination. What one employer may do, all may do. There is, however, one exception to this common-law principle, and that is that a lockout in violation of a collective agreement may be enjoined. On the other hand, an employer who is a member of an association and obligated thereby to cooperate with his fellow employers may be sued if he fails to cooperate in the lockout activities.

Boycotts

Economic pressure by unions can be exerted in other ways than by strikes. One of the most familiar of labor's weapons has always been the boycott. In a certain sense, all strikes are boycotts. For when workers are on strike, they are "boycotting" their employer and urging all others to do likewise. Such a strike would thus qualify as a "primary" boycott —primary because the strikers are exerting pressure directly on the employer on whom they are making their demands.

Generally, however, strikes are not considered as coming within the meaning of boycotts. In public discussions, the term *boycott* is used almost exclusively to mean an organized refusal to deal with someone in order to induce him to change some practice he follows. Such a boycott may be in the form of a "we do not patronize" list or in other forms of pressure designed to prevent sales of particular products, or it may be a refusal to handle certain goods.

Illustrations of such pressures are readily found in everyday union activity. For example, the United Automobile Workers resorted to a nationwide boycott of Kohler products in a long drawn-out battle against this manufacturer of plumbing wares. In another case, this same union asked its members not to use fishing tackle manufactured by a firm which allegedly had locked out members of the United Steelworkers. Union building-trades men have usually refused to handle materials manufactured under nonunion conditions.

Boycotts of these types are not as simple as strikes because they can involve pressure on third parties. For example, if the United Automobile Workers picketed a store which was selling fishing tackle purchased from the aforementioned firm, it would be engaging in a "secondary boycott"—that is, it would be applying pressure on a third party in order to aid the Steelworkers' fight the manufacturer directly involved in the dispute.

Before 1932, a majority of American courts held secondary boycotts unlawful per se—"as if it were a separate category of tort liability."[9] Other courts, however, recognized that labor had an interest in maintaining standards and therefore had a right to engage in boycotts for this purpose. For example, some courts have upheld labor's rights to boycott nonunion products on the ground that the distribution of goods produced under nonunion conditions will depress standards won by the union.

Picketing before the Norris–La Guardia Act

One of the most controversial questions of public policy in the field of labor relations today concerns the extent to which picketing by labor unions should be regulated. A companion question upon which conflicting views are found in the field of labor law involves the extent to which such limitations on the right to picket are constitutionally permissible.

Picketing is a familiar form of pressure utilized by unions which has

---

[9] Charles O. Gregory, *Labor and the Law* (2d rev. ed.; New York: W. W. Norton & Co.; Inc., 1961), p. 122.

become an indispensable adjunct of the strike. Picketing usually involves the patrolling of a struck establishment by one or more persons bearing signs of placards stating that the workers are on strike or that the employer is unfair to organized labor, or words of similar effect. The average worker will not pass a picket line. This is based partly on the fear of social ostracism; partly on the feeling that unless he supports the group on strike, they may not support him some day when his union is out on the street; partly on fear of physical violence; sometimes because of fear of sanctions contained in the constitution of his own union. Whatever the motivations, it is clear that the picket line is a most effective weapon. In our highly unionized economy a picket line, manned even by a small group in a large company, can completely paralyze a plant or establishment because other union men who work in the plant, or deliver it supplies, will not cross the picket line.

Picketing may be thought of in two ways. It is a form of expression, letting the public and labor supporters know that a controversy exists and giving labor's side of that controversy. It is also a form of pressure intended to dissuade persons from patronizing or entering a place of business.

At first, the courts took the view that picketing per se was illegal. Later, they grudgingly conceded that picketing was legal as long as it was peacefully conducted and did not bar entrance to and exit from the plant, and as long as it did not obstruct traffic on a public thoroughfare. But while the courts conceded the legality of picketing, they also severely regulated it, often limiting the number of pickets permitted and generally outlawing "stranger picketing"—that is, picketing by persons not employees of the plant. The attitude of the courts on stranger picketing was conditioned by their belief that workers had no interest in a labor controversy unless they were employees of the plant itself, a theory which ignores the relation of labor conditions in one plant with those in another.

Those who believed in labor's right to picket freely did not generally support picketing which prevented entrance and exit into a plant, or picketing which obstructed ordinary commerce on a public thoroughfare. They took the view, however, that picketing was a form of expression and hence, if peacefully conducted, was protected by the first amendment, as are other forms of communication. That viewpoint, however, was almost unanimously rejected by the courts prior to 1932. Indeed, the tendency right up to the passage of the Norris–La Guardia Act was to limit rather than to expand the right of labor to picket in support of its interests.

THE NORRIS–LA GUARDIA ACT

In 1932, when the membership of the American Federation of Labor was the lowest in 20 years, the AFL achieved its greatest legislative triumph to date. After almost 50 years of sustained effort, the AFL succeeded in making the federal judiciary "neutral" in labor disputes. The law which accomplished this result was the Norris–La Guardia Anti-injunction Act, passed by a Democratic-controlled House of Representatives and a Republican Senate, and signed by the then Republican President, Herbert Hoover.

We have seen how labor had been frustrated in its aim to secure passage of legislation which would effectively make lawful the use of union tactics deemed necessary by labor for its survival and successful growth. The Norris–La Guardia Act represented a new approach to this problem. It did not legalize union action; it simply deprived the federal courts of jurisdiction in most situations involving labor disputes. It reflected essentially a laissez-faire philosophy. The law should intervene only to prevent damage to tangible property and to preserve public order; otherwise, the disputants should be left to their own resources to work out their problems. Both labor and business would now be free to promote their own interests in the field of labor policy through self-help, without interference from the courts. The act thus represented a reaction to judicial policy making, which had produced the anomalous result of the same action being enjoinable in one state and not in another. Henceforth, all federal courts were barred from passing judgment as to the lawfulness or unlawfulness of the objectives of labor's actions. This same principle was soon extended to many state courts, for the federal act was immediately copied by a dozen or more state legislatures.

The Norris–La Guardia Act commences with a statement of public policy which affirms the right of workers to engage in collective bargaining through unions of their own choosing. Yellow-dog contracts are declared to be against this public policy, and the federal courts are instructed not to enforce such contracts. Then, Section 4 of the act states that:

No court of the United States shall have jurisdiction to issue any restraining order or temporary or permanent injunction in any case involving or growing out of any labor dispute. . . .

The act defines "labor dispute" in the broadest possible way so as to preclude judicial constructions, such as occurred in the Clayton Act, which whittled away the effect of the latter law:

The term "labor dispute" includes any controversy concerning terms or conditions of employment, or concerning the association or representation of persons in negotiating, fixing, maintaining, changing or seeking to arrange terms or conditions of employment, regardless of whether or not the disputants stand in the proximate relation of employer and employee."

It will be observed that Congress specifically took account of the fact that organized labor had a valid interest in conditions of employment even where it did not represent a single employee and that although such a situation did not involve a dispute technically between "an employer" and its "employees," nevertheless the protection afforded by the Norris–La Guardia Act was applicable.

The Norris–La Guardia Act has been aptly called "the last monument to the spirit of complete free enterprise for unions."[10] It left unions pretty much free to use their tactical weapons without judicial inter-. ference. As we shall see, a "liberalized" Supreme Court interpreted the statute broadly so as to confer almost complete immunity on labor leaders in labor disputes. The act, in effect, outlawed injunctions in labor disputes except where violence was involved. As long as violence was not used, unions could resort to threats, coercion, boycotts, picketing, strikes, and so on, without fear of federal court action. Moreover, even where violence was involved, the granting of injunctions was severely restricted by statutory prohibitions. Some labor critics say that the act went too far in freeing unions from court intervention and that the problems we face today in terms of abuse of union tactics would not have resulted had the Norris–La Guardia Act attempted to make a distinction between lawful and unlawful union objectives, as did the Clayton Act. This is a debatable issue which we shall better understand after discussing the Norris–La Guardia Act and its aftermath.

The Norris–La Guardia Act and the Courts

With a single piece of legislation, Congress thus repealed a century of judicial interpretation and created laissez-faire, or economic free enterprise, for organized labor as well as for business. Henceforth the courts were not to interfere with strikes, boycotts, and picketing which were conducted peacefully and otherwise within the law. Moreover, by defining "labor dispute" in a broad fashion, Congress insured labor's right to engage in sympathy strikes, secondary boycotts, stranger picketing, and other activities where nonemployees of a concern come to the aid of the concern's employees in labor disputes directly or by applying pressure upon third parties.

Reversal of Sherman Act Decisions

The combined effect of the Norris–La Guardia Act and the liberalized view of labor disputes which the Supreme Court adopted after 1937 resulted in a revision of precedents on the application of the Sherman Act to organized labor. Commencing in 1940, the Supreme Court handed down a group of landmark decisions which seemed to delineate the legal status of unions under the antitrust laws. Three leading cases—*Apex Hosiery Co.* v. *Leader*,[11] *United States* v. *Hutcheson*,[12] and *Allen-Bradley*

---

[10] Gregory, *Labor and the Law*, p. 197.

[11] 310 U.S. 469, 60 S. Ct. 982 (1940).

[12] 312 U.S. 219, 61 S. Ct. 463 (1941).

Co. v. *Local 3, International Brotherhood of Electrical Workers*[13]— broadly defined the permissible limits of concerted union activity, and suggested that unions are subject to the antitrust laws under existing legislation only.

1. Where the union intends to achieve some commercial restraint primarily and not as a by-product of its essential intent to advance its own cause.
2. Where union activity is not in the course of a labor dispute as broadly defined by the Norris–La Guardia Act.
3. Where a union combines with some nonlabor group to achieve some direct commercial restraint.

The extended immunity granted to labor from the antitrust laws and the injunction was followed to its logical conclusion in other decisions, to which we have already referred in Chapter 7. Their combined effect was to permit unions to perform many acts which the law classifies as illegal when done by other groups or organizations within the community. It is not surprising, therefore, that this line of decisions, together with the tremendous growth in economic power of organized labor in the past few decades, produced a demand in some circles for new legislation which would "subject labor to the antitrust laws."

Then on June 7, 1965, the U.S. Supreme Court handed down two landmark decisions which seemed to indicate that unions might not be as immune from antitrust liability as was generally thought. Both of these cases were brought by employers against unions alleging violations of Sections 1 and 2 of the Sherman Antitrust Act. In the so-called *Pennington* case,[14] the employer alleged that the United Mine Workers had conspired with large coal operators to force smaller operators, including the plaintiff, out of business by raising wage rates and fringe benefits in the big companies and then forcing these rates on the smaller companies with the knowledge that the latter would have to close down. Although the case was remanded for a new trial because of an error in the instruction given to the jury by the trial judge, the Supreme Court held that if the United Mine Workers had in fact conspired with the major coal operators to drive the smaller operators out of business by requiring them to sign wage agreements which they could not afford, they would be guilty of a violation of the Sherman Act.

The *Pennington* case is of paramount importance for two reasons. In the first place, it reversed the generally accepted assumption which prevailed until that time that any union action relating to wage agreements

---

[13] 325 U.S. 797, 65 S. Ct. 1533 (1945).

[14] *United Mine Workers* v. *Pennington*, 59 LRRM 2369, 381 U.S. 657 (1965). In subsequent decisions since this case, federal courts relying on the *Pennington* precedent have found the United Mine Workers in violation of the Sherman Act and have assessed treble damages.

with employers was exempt from the antitrust laws. The *Pennington* decision indicates that a union agreement with one employer or group of employers with respect to wages, hours, or working conditions that the union will seek to negotiate with *other* employers is not exempt from prosecution. In the second place, the trial court left it to the jury to determine as a *question of fact* whether there was a purpose among the alleged conspirators to impose a national contract upon the small producers with the intent of restraining trade and driving them out of business or whether the purpose was to improve working conditions, compensation, and other legitimate union objectives. This sounds very much like the old judicial tests of legality of union action which sought to determine "motive" and "intent."

In the *Jewel Tea* case,[15] decided on the same day, the company claimed that the Meat Cutters Union had violated the Sherman Act by negotiating agreements with Chicago food stores which provided that meat could not be sold before 9 A.M. or after 6 P.M., even if there were no butchers in the store. Jewel maintained that the union's insistence on the marketing-hours provision was part of a conspiracy between the union and the Associated Food Retailers of Greater Chicago, which represents the independent food stores and meat dealers. Although the company lost its case before the High Court, the actual decision represented a loss for organized labor; for the Court's opinion made it clear that if the trial judge had not found, as a question of fact, that there was an intimate connection between hours of work and hours of sale, the agreement negotiated by the union might well have been a violation of the Sherman Act. Here again, as in the *Pennington* case, the Supreme Court has indicated that findings of fact arrived at in a courtroom by a jury or by a trial judge sitting without a jury can impose liability on unions under the antitrust laws, even though the subject matter involves an issue which unions can reasonably believe is a proper subject for collective bargaining.

While critics of organized labor may draw comfort from these cases, the decisions will do little to curb the abuses of which most businessmen complain, yet will add an additional element of uncertainty into the collective bargaining process. "Bringing labor under the antitrust laws" is not really a satisfactory solution for labor problems. Our existing antitrust laws have not been particularly successful in preventing monopoly in industry, and court decisions have been notably unsuccessful in clarifying in businessmen's minds what is lawful and unlawful in this complicated field of law. To inject the courts into this area would simply add confusion rather than solve the problem. What is needed is specific legislation aimed at eliminating particular abuses upon which there is

---

[15] *Local 189, Amalgamated Meat Cutters* v. *Jewel Tea Co.*, 59 LRRM 2376, 381 U.S. 674 (1965).

general agreement that governmental action must taken. For example, consideration should be given to a comprehensive review of the Norris–La Guardia Act to adapt it to the current labor scene. It should be remembered that when that act was passed, there was no Wagner Act or Taft-Hartley Act; and furthermore, organized labor had not achieved its present position of strength in industry at large. Many labor experts agree that the original purpose of the Norris–La Guardia Act has long since been fulfilled and that the statute is in many respects obsolete.

PICKETING AFTER THE NORRIS–LA GUARDIA ACT

As we have seen, the enactment of the Norris–La Guardia Act in 1932 substantially limited the power of the federal courts to issue injunctions in labor disputes. State courts, however, continued to enjoin picketing under a variety of circumstances and for a variety of reasons, except where the power of state courts had been circumscribed by the enactment of state "little Norris–La Guardia acts," modeled after the federal statute.

In passing judgment on the legality of strikes, courts sometimes made a distinction between organizational picketing and recognition picketing. The former is said to involve picketing by a minority union directed to the employees of an employer in order to persuade them to become union members or to win their adherence to the union cause. The latter is directed to the employer in order to compel him to recognize the minority union; in effect, it brings pressure on the employer to force the employees to join the picketing union. In practice, it is difficult to make a valid distinction between the two forms of picketing, for either type, if effective, will bring economic pressure to bear upon both employer and employees, with the objective of compelling recognition of the minority union as the bargaining representative for the employees.

Before considering the attitude of the courts toward picketing since enactment of the Norris–La Guardia Act, it may be helpful to explore the conflicting arguments, pro and con, advanced by union and management spokesmen on the subject of picketing. Should recognition picketing be permitted, prohibited, or restricted, and under what circumstances? For the purpose of this discussion, we shall consider organizational and recognition picketing as being substantially the same, since the same arguments are in general applicable to the two types of picketing.

Arguments Favoring Unrestricted Recognition Picketing

Union spokesmen argue that the picket line is labor's most effective organizing device. They contend that many employers are still extremely hostile to labor and can prevent employees from really expressing their desires unless the union can apply economic pressure. They argue further

that unions must have the right to picket even after dismissal of a representation case or loss of an election because employers sometimes
maneuver unions into an election proceeding before the union is really
ready, and therefore the union must be able to continue to try to get its
message across to employees. Finally, union spokesmen contend that they
have a basic right to try to cure conditions which threaten the maintenance of wages and other working conditions in organized companies.
If most of an industry is organized, for example, but a few employers
are nonunion, pay low rates, and cut prices, they can demoralize the
entire industry. Unions maintain that under such circumstances, they
must have the right to continue to picket and bring pressure on the nonunion employer until he has been organized. If attaining this objective
requires some employees to join the union against their will, union
spokesmen feel that this is still in accord with democratic procedures
because the union must look to the wishes of the majority of workers
in the industry, not in an individual plant.

Arguments Favoring Restriction of Recognition Picketing

Management spokesmen who contend that recognition picketing
should be prohibited usually begin with the Taft-Hartley Act itself (or
similar state labor relations acts) as the basis for their argument. That act
and its predecessor (the Wagner Act) were intended to reduce the many
industrial disputes arising out of the problem of selection of a collective
bargaining representative. Furthermore, it was made clear in the Taft-
Hartley Act that employees were to be free *not* to join a union if they
did not want to. In view of these acts, the argument runs, recognition
picketing should be prohibited. Union organizers can still distribute
literature at plant gates and hold meetings to explain their position to
employees. Beyond that, the peaceful machinery of the National Labor
Relations Board and state labor relations boards should be substituted for
the economic pressure and violence generated by the picket line. This
argument is particularly forceful when the peaceful machinery has been
used and the union has lost. The management viewpoint is put cogently
by former NLRB member Joseph A. Jenkins, who, in his concurring
opinion in the *Curtis* case, said: "I do not believe that Congress intended
to or did write a statute providing for elections conducted at public
expense which are to be considered binding if the union wins, but not
binding if the union loses."[16]

If recognition picketing can continue indefinitely even after a union
has been decisively rejected by employees in an NLRB election, a small
employer cannot possibly withstand the pressures which can be applied
by a powerful union. Opponents of unrestricted picketing emphasize the
coercive aspects in picketing and the tremendous power this weapon

---

[16] *Curtis Brothers, Inc.,* 41 LRRM 1025, 1033.

confers on union leaders, who can break many businesses at their whim. They question whether the picket line, as an organizing device, is entitled to the same protection today, when organized labor numbers 18 million, as when its membership was a weak 3 million.

Picketing and Free Speech

Commencing in 1937, a series of cases was brought before the U.S. Supreme Court involving the question whether picketing could be restricted by state legislatures and courts or whether it was protected from such regulation as a form of free speech guaranteed by the first amendment of the federal Constitution. These cases are of major interest to students of labor problems not only because they concern a major union weapon—picketing—but also because they indicate how the changing views of the Supreme Court may influence the pattern of state legislative and judicial control of labor relations and thus profoundly affect the evolution of collective bargaining in our society. As will appear more fully in the following discussion, it seems in retrospect that the Supreme Court first became intrigued with the idea of treating picketing as a form of free speech entitled to constitutional protection and then retreated from this position when it recognized the coercive elements present in picketing and the legitimate right of the states to limit picketing in certain instances to protect the public interest.

In 1937, in a case which affirmed the right of a state to enact a "little Norris–La Guardia Act," Justice Louis D. Brandeis remarked: "Members of a union might without special statutory authorization by a State make known the facts of a labor dispute, for freedom of speech is guaranteed by the Federal Constitution."[17] This statement was misconstrued by many lawyers and judges to mean that picketing was a form of free speech guaranteed by the Constitution. Actually, Justice Brandeis merely said that union members might make known the facts of a dispute, without stating what means they might use for this purpose. He did not say that union members had a constitutional right to make known facts by means of a picket line. Nevertheless, three years later, in the case of *Thronhill* v. *Alabama*,[18] the Supreme Court completely accepted the doctrine that picketing was a form of free speech. An Alabama law, which termed picketing a form of loitering and made it a misdemeanor, was held unconstitutional on the ground that picketing is a form of speech protected by the first amendment and that a penal statute which makes picketing a misdemeanor without regard to the manner in which it is conducted is unconstitutional on its face. In the companion case of *Carlson* v. *California*[19] the Supreme Court elaborated the doctrine of

---

[17] *Senn* v. *Tile Layers' Protective Union*, 301 U.S. 468. 57 S. Ct. 857 (1937).

[18] 310 U.S. 88, 60 S. Ct. 736 (1940).

[19] 310 U.S. 106, 113; 60 S. Ct. 746, 749 (1940).

picketing as a form of speech in the following words: "Publicizing the facts of a labor dispute in a peaceful way through appropriate means, whether by pamphlet, by word of mouth or by banner, must now be regarded as within that liberty of communication which is secured to every person by the Fourteenth Amendment against abridgement by a State." And in 1941, in *American Federation of Labor* v. *Swing*,[20] the U.S. Supreme Court held unconstitutional the decision of the Illinois Supreme Court enjoining peaceful stranger picketing of a beauty parlor when none of the employees of the beauty parlor were members of the union conducting the picketing.

However, the notion that picketing is merely a form of free speech did not prove very satisfactory, in view of the coercive elements usually present in picketing. As a result, the U.S. Supreme Court slowly began to modify its views. In 1941, the Supreme Court refused to set aside an Illinois injunction which forebade all picketing by a milk drivers' union where there had been a background of previous violence.[21] In three important cases handed down in 1950, the Supreme Court held that the state courts could constitutionally restrict picketing which had as its objective action which violated a state statute or was deemed contrary to public policy.[22]

Finally, in *Vogt* v. *Teamsters*,[23] the Supreme Court upheld the action of a Wisconsin court in enjoining simple stranger picketing, thus fully acknowledging the retreat from the Thornhill doctrine and amounting, as the dissenters observed, to "formal surrender." Speaking for a majority of the Supreme Court, Justice Felix Frankfurter stated that picketing is fully subject to the right of the states to balance the social interests between employers and unions, provided only that the states' policies are rational. Although Justice Frankfurther noted that the states could not, under the Thornhill doctrine, proscribe all picketing per se, he made it clear that state courts and legislatures are free to decide whether to permit or suppress any particular picket line for any reason other than a blanket policy against picketing.[24]

---

[20] 312 U.S. 321, 61 S. Ct. 568 (1941).

[21] *Milk Wagon Drivers* v. *Meadowmoor Dairies, Inc.*, 312 U.S. 287, 61 S. Ct. 552 (1941).

[22] *Building Service International Union* v. *Gazzam*, 339 U.S. 532, 70 S. Ct. 784 (1950); *Hughes* v. *Superior Court of State of California*, 339 U.S. 460, 70 S. Ct. 718 (1950); *International Brotherhood of Teamsters* v. *Hanke*, 339 U.S. 470, 70 S. Ct. 773 (1950).

[23] 354 U.S. 284, 77 S. Ct. 31 (1956).

[24] However, states cannot enact laws restricting peaceful picketing in a manner which deprives workers of rights guaranteed under the Taft-Hartley Act. Thus, for example, the U.S. Supreme Court has held unlawful a Virginia statute which imposed a fine on any person participating in picketing who was not a "bona fide" employee of the business or industry being picketed. Such a law against stranger picketing would be inconsistent with the Taft-Hartley Act, which makes no distinction as to whether a person picketing is an employee or not. See *Waxman* v. *Commonwealth of Virginia*, 51 LRRM 2221 (October 8, 1962).

In May 1968, in the *Logan Valley Plaza* case,[25] the Supreme Court, again expressly equating picketing with the right of free speech under the first amendment, voided an injunction by a state court against picketing carried on in a shopping center on private property. In this case, a union which was attempting to organize a supermarket located in a shopping center carried on peaceful picketing in the parking lot and on the sidewalks and parcel pickup area of the market. The state court had issued an injunction against such picketing and compelled the union to picket out on the highway, which was obviously much less effective. In a divided opinion, the Court held that because the shopping center serves as the community business block and is freely accessible and open to people in the area, the state court could not, through the use of the doctrine of trespass, infringe on the privilege of persons to exercise their rights of free speech. The Court went on to say, however, that the fact that it was invalidating a blanket injunction against *all* picketing in the center did not mean that the owners could not prescribe reasonable regulations as to where the picketing could be carried on within the shopping center.

This decision not only frees unions from what had been a major handicap in carrying out effective picketing as part of organizing drives in the retail business but also raises some disturbing questions as to how far the right of free speech can be exercised at the expense of the equally protected constitutional right of private property.

The cases referred to above all arose as the result of efforts of state courts and legislatures to prohibit or restrict picketing. The federal government has also passed legislation restricting labor's right to picket. These restrictions are embodied in the Taft-Hartley Act and in the Landrum-Griffin Act, which we shall consider in detail in Chapters 19 and 20. In 1951, the Supreme Court, in a decision consistent with its changed viewpoint toward picketing, held that the provisions of the Taft-Hartley Act banning certain types of picketing in connection with secondary boycotts did not violate constitutional guarantees of free speech.[26]

Present Status of Picketing

As far as federal law is concerned, picketing by unions for either organizational or recognitional purposes is now subject to major limitations imposed by the Landrum-Griffin Act in 1959. We shall examine

---

[25] *Amalgamated Food Employees Local 590* v. *Logan Valley Plaza*, 68 LRRM 2209, 88 Sup. Ct. 1601 (1968).

[26] *International Brotherhood of Electrical Workers* v. *National Labor Relations Board,* 341 U.S. 694, 71 S. Ct. 954 (1951). As this book is going to press, the Supreme Court, with four new appointees by President Nixon, appears to be moving farther away from equating picketing with free speech, and more toward permitting restraints on picketing. Thus a 1972 case would seem particularly to limit the doctrine set forth in the case cited in note 25 above.

these provisions in detail in Chapter 20. The Congress, in adopting these restrictive provisions, attempted to make a distinction between picketing which is coercive in effect and that which is designed solely to inform the public of a labor dispute and does not have the effect of interfering with deliveries to a business establishment. As we shall learn from our analysis of these statutory provisions, such a distinction is extremely difficult to apply in practice. Decisions of the NLRB on this subject have been so confusing that neither labor nor management today can be wholly certain as to the legality of a picket line.

BOYCOTTS AFTER THE NORRIS–LA GUARDIA ACT

We have seen that the Norris–La Guardia Act deprived the federal courts of jurisdiction in most cases involving labor disputes. However, its effect upon such union tactics as boycotts was even broader, for the U.S. Supreme Court interpreted the Norris–La Guardia Act as not only depriving the federal courts of jurisdiction to enjoin labor tactics enumerated in Section 4 of that act but also as making such acts lawful for all purposes under federal law. This momentous decision was enunciated by the Court in the *Hutcheson* case,[27] which involved a secondary boycott organized by a carpenters' union against the Anheuser-Busch Brewing Company. The Court held that because of the intervention of the Norris–La Guardia Act, which had "infused new spirit" into the Clayton Act, such union conduct did not violate the Sherman Act, even though in 1908 it had reached a contrary conclusion on similar facts in the *Danbury Hatters* case.

As a result of a more liberal judicial attitude reflecting the spirit of the Norris–La Guardia and Wagner acts, by the late 1930s and early 1940s union boycotts were no longer repressed by federal courts. The result was a major expansion in the use of the secondary boycott by organized labor. Strategically placed unions, particularly in the field of distribution, were able to expand their sphere of organization by bringing pressure on persons whose only relation to the dispute was that they did business with the particular employer involved. The Teamsters exerted additional pressure on nonunion employers by obtaining "hot cargo" agreements, in which employers agreed not to deal with nonunion employers.

The abuses which arose from the widespread use of such tactics by organized labor, together with the rash of strikes in 1947, led to a demand for restrictive labor legislation. The Taft-Hartley Act, passed in that year, had as one of its prime objectives the outlawing of all secondary boycotts. As we shall observe in our discussion of this act in Chapter 19, the provisions directed against secondary boycotts were poorly drawn

---

[27] *United States* v. *Hutcheson.* 312 U.S. 219, 61 S. Ct. 463 (1941).

and left many loopholes. Additional statutory restrictions aimed at closing these loopholes were incorporated in the Landrum-Griffin Act, which will be analyzed in Chapter 20.

LIMITATIONS ON THE RIGHT TO STRIKE

Writers are often prone to equate the right to strike with democracy and a free labor market. It has been said that preservation of the right to strike is what distinguishes our economy from those of Communist nations and that if this right is compromised, then other individual rights will also suffer. Actually, however, the right to strike has been limited in a number of important respects by the Taft-Hartley and Landrum-Griffin Acts, and yet economic democracy still flourishes in our country. The change from the era of uninhibited union action under the Norris–La Guardia Act is a rather remarkable one and is deserving of closer scrutiny.

Strike action can be divided into two general categories—primary and secondary. A primary strike is a strike which occurs in connection with a labor dispute and directly involves the employer of the striking workers. A secondary strike is a strike which is aimed at an employer other than the employer of the striking workers. Suppose the carpenters on a construction job strike for higher wages. This is a primary strike directed against their employer, who, let us say, is the general contractor on the job. Now, a nonunion flooring subcontractor brings in nonunion men to put down asphalt tile flooring in the building. The carpenters go on strike in protest against the use of nonunion workers on the job. This is a secondary strike.

While it is difficult to generalize in such a complicated field, it can be said that the law generally permits primary strike activity and prohibits secondary strike activity. A similar rule applies to picketing. There are, however, important exceptions. All secondary strike activity is not unlawful; and on the other hand, there are many kinds of primary strike activity which are either prohibited or subject to limitations under our statutes. Let us examine some of the major types of primary strike activity which are restricted by federal law.

Strikes against Public Policy as Set Forth in Federal Statutes

In this category would fall strikes which directly violate or compel an employer to violate restrictive provisions contained in labor laws such as the Taft-Hartley law. Thus, for example, it is unlawful for a union to strike to compel an employer to recognize one union when another union has already been certified as the collective bargaining agency by the NLRB. The NLRB has held that it is unlawful for a union to strike to compel an employer to sign a "hot cargo" contract in the construction industry, even though the statute expressly permits such contracts if voluntarily made. A strike for a closed shop is unlawful under the Taft-Hartley Act, and it is also unlawful in many states under common law.

Strikes Arising out of Jurisdictional Disputes

The Taft-Hartley Act makes it an unfair labor practice for a union to engage in a strike to force or require any employer to assign particular work to employees in a particular labor organization or in a particular trade, craft, or class rather than to employees in another labor organization or in another trade, craft, or class, unless such employer is failing to conform to an order or certification of the Board determining the bargaining representative for employees performing such work. The law further provides that whenever it is charged that there has been a violation of this section, "the Board is empowered and directed to hear and determine the dispute out of which such unfair labor practice shall have arisen." The U.S. Supreme Court has held that this provision means that the Board must inquire into the merits of the dispute and then make a binding award of the work.[28] The Board has discretionary authority to seek an injunction against jurisdictional strikes in violation of the statute. As a result of these statutory provisions, the NLRB is now required to determine jurisdictional disputes by what amounts to compulsory arbitration.

Strikes during the Term of a Valid Collective Bargaining Agreement

The Taft-Hartley Act specifically prohibits strikes called before the end of a 60-day-notice period prior to the expiration of collective bargaining agreements. This provision was included in the law in order to give conciliation agencies sufficient time to meet with the parties and attempt to resolve disputes before a walkout occurs. Quite apart from this provision, a strike to compel a change in the terms of a contract prior to the expiration date of the contract has been held to be unlawful under the Taft-Hartley Act. This is true whether or not the contract contains a no-strike agreement. A strike in violation of a collective bargaining agreement is not protected concerted activity under the Taft-Hartley Act and may constitute an unfair labor practice.[29] A strike during the term of a contract over grievances or in protest over employer unfair labor practices is not, however, unlawful (unless in violation of a no-strike clause).

---

[28] *National Labor Relations Board* v. *Radio Engineers Union*, 47 LRRM 2332, 364 U.S. 578 (1961).

[29] *United Mine Workers of America* (Boone County Coal Corp.), 117 NLRB 1095 (1957); enforcement denied, 257 F. (2d) 211 (D.C. Cir. 1958). Cf. *Boeing Airplane Co.* v. *National Labor Relations Board*, 174 F. (2d) 988 (D.C. Cir. 1949).

Suppose that a collective bargaining agreement contains both a no-strike agreement on the part of the union and a commitment by union and management to submit certain types of disputes to binding arbitration. Suppose further that such a dispute arises, goes to arbitration, and the union loses. The union then strikes. What are the employer's rights? Section 301 of the Taft-Hartley Act provides that suits for violation of contracts between an employer and a union may be brought in any district court of the United States. The remedy of the employer in such a suit would be for damages for breach of contract, but a victory in such a suit might represent a hollow triumph if the union were permitted to continue its strike. However, the blanket prohibitions of the Norris–La Guardia Act against use of injunctions in labor disputes seemed to bar the injunction as a remedy available in federal court to employers caught in such an impasse. This was the conclusion which the U.S. Supreme Court reached in 1962 in the leading case of *Sinclair Refining Co.* v. *Atkinson.*[30]

In a strong dissent, Justice Brennan warned that:

. . . this decision deals a crippling blow to the cause of grievance arbitration itself. . . . since unions cannot be enjoined by a federal court from striking in open defiance of their undertakings to arbitrate, employers will pause long before committing themselves to obligations enforceable against them but not against their unions.[31]

The one-sided doctrine embodied in the Sinclair decision did not stand for long. Eight years later, Justice Brennan delivered the majority opinion in the *Boys Markets* case,[32] expressly overruling the Sinclair decision. Thus, the injunction is now available to employers in federal court under the circumstances above outlined. Still unclear is the effect of this decision (which by its express terms applies to federal courts) in states having little Norris–La Guardia laws, of which some 14 prohibit injunctions for breach of no-strike obligations.[33]

Strikes against the Government as Employer

Most governmental bodies—federal, state, and municipal—forbid strikes by employees on the ground that such strikes are against the sovereign and therefore against the public interest. Section 305 of the Taft-Hartley Act makes it unlawful for any individual employed by the United States or any agency thereof, including wholly owned govern-

---

[30] 370 U.S. 195, 45 LC Para 17,674 (1962).

[31] 370 U.S. 195, 227.

[32] *Boys Markets, Inc.* v. *Retail Clerks, Local 770*, 26 L. Ed 2d 199, 62 LC Para 10, 902 (1970).

[33] See Robert M. Cassel, "The Labor Injunction to Enforce No-Strike Provisions, *Labor Law Journal*, Vol. 22 (March 1971), pp. 229–36. See also Chapter 21.

ment corporations, to participate in any strike. The problem of government employees and the right to strike will be more fully explored in Chapter 22.

National Emergency Strikes

The Taft-Hartley Act contains provisions enabling the government to obtain a temporary injunction in cases involving strikes which imperil or threaten to endanger the national health or safety. After such an injunction is obtained, the strike action becomes unlawful. These provisions will be discussed in Chapter 21.

The foregoing brief outline describes the status of strikes in interstate commerce where federal labor laws are applicable. Where state law is applicable to a local dispute, the results will depend upon the provisions of that state statute, or upon common law in the absence of an applicable statute. Basically, courts, in the absence of statutes to guide them, still apply the old rule of ends and means. If the ends are illegal, the court is likely to enjoin the strike, no matter how peaceful the means used may be. This result reflects the historical judicial attitude that a strike is fundamentally an intentional tortious interference with an advantageous business relationship and therefore should only be permitted if it is carried on for a proper purpose. Strikes to improve working conditions are generally held to be for a valid purpose, but a strike for a closed shop may still be held lawful in one state and illegal in another.

LIMITATIONS ON THE RIGHT TO LOCK OUT

Labor legislation in this country has gradually deprived employers of most of the effective tactical weapons which they used in the past to combat efforts of unions to organize their employees. We have seen how the Norris–La Guardia Act outlawed the yellow-dog contract and barred injunctions against unions in federal court—thus eliminating two devices which had been widely used to discourage union organizing efforts. Likewise, the unfair labor practice provisions of the Wagner and Taft-Hartley laws restricted other tactics frequently utilized by antiunion employers, such as discriminatory hiring and firing practices, spying on employees, antiunion speeches, and so forth. While this restrictive legislation was primarily intended to prevent employers from obstructing the efforts of employees to organize and bargain through representatives of their own choosing, it also had the effect of weakening the tactical position of employers who reach an impasse in bargaining with unions over economic issues. For example, the Norris–La Guardia Act and the state statutes patterned after it have made it extremely difficult to halt mass picketing, vandalism, and other violence which sometimes results from efforts of management to bring employees through a picket line into a struck plant. As a consequence, most employers are reluctant to run a plant with strikebreakers, even though they have a legal right to do so. The Norris–La Guardia Act, therefore, tends to make the picket line a more effective weapon for imposing economic losses upon the employer and consequently gives the union a strategic advantage in collective bargaining.

There is another effective employer tactical weapon which is relatively little used and about which little has been written. That is the right to lock out. In some respects, the employer's right to lock out his employees may be thought of as paralleling the employees' right to withhold their services through strike action. Just as the right to strike has been subjected to restrictions where it contravenes certain purposes, so the employer's right to shut down operations has been held to be a limited managerial prerogative. Although, with minor exceptions,[34] there are no statutory prohibitions against use of the lockout, nevertheless, as a result of decisions of the NLRB and the courts, the lockout has been so circumscribed by restrictions that an employer involved in a labor dispute would be ill advised to shut down his plant without first obtaining competent legal advice.

In the first place, it is clear that an employer cannot use the lockout as a device to avoid union organization. The Taft-Hartley Act prohibits discharges of employees where the purpose is to discourage membership in a labor organization. Since an employer cannot discharge individual employees in order to deter unionization, it is not surprising that both the NLRB and the courts have held that he cannot shut down an entire plant and lay off all employees in order to accomplish the same result. Of course, employers will generally point to some economic reason for the shutdown, while union spokesmen will claim that the action was taken to break the union. Cases which come before the NLRB on this issue usually involve complex factual situations susceptible to either interpretation, which tends to complicate the problem presented to the Board for determination.

In the second place, the rule has been established that an employer cannot seek to avoid his commitment under an existing union contract or to wrest bargaining concessions from a union by shutting down his plant and moving to another area. In such cases, the NLRB has usually required the employer to offer employment to the former employees at the new location, to pay their moving expenses to such new location, and, in addition, to make the employees whole for the loss they may have suffered by reason of the unlawful discharge.

---

[34] The Taft-Hartley Act prohibits lockouts (and strikes) for a period of 60 days after notice is given of a proposed modification or expiration of a collective bargaining agreement (Section 8 [*d*] [4]). In addition, lockouts (and strikes) which imperil the national health and safety are subject to injunction for a limited period of time during the fact-finding procedure prescribed by Section 206 of the Taft-Hartley Act.

In the third place, the NLRB for many years looked upon the lockout as a lawful employer weapon only where unusual economic circumstances justified it as a *defensive* measure against a threatened strike. The Board condemned lockouts by individual employers undertaken in the course of collective bargaining negotiations to bring pressure on the union for a satisfactory settlement. Although the union can strike to enforce its demands, the NLRB had generally taken the position that a lockout in such circumstances would interfere with the protected concerted activities of the employees. For example, in the *American Brake Shoe*[35] case, the Board said that if an anticipatory lockout were to be permitted as lawful, the employer would be immunized from effective strike action and the employees' right to strike would be rendered virtually meaningless.

However, in 1965, in the *American Shipbuilding*[36] case, the U.S. Supreme Court held that a company did not violate the Taft-Hartley Act when, after an impasse had been reached in contract negotiations, it shut down its plant and laid off employees for the purpose of bringing pressure to bear on the union which was threatening to strike during the company's busiest season. In subsequent decisions, the NLRB has stated that it views this decision as obliterating any distinction between offensive and defensive lockouts. Nevertheless, it seems that some significant differences still remain. If a lockout is defensive, i.e., invoked either by a multiemployer group in response to a whipsawing strike against one member of the group or by an individual employer in anticipation of a threatened strike, employers may continue to operate by using replacements for locked-out employees. However, if the lockout is offensive, i.e., invoked in support of a bargaining position without regard to a strike or threatened strike, then the employer is probably in violation of the Taft-Hartley Act if he continues to operate by using replacements for locked-out employees.

Because of the uncertainty which still surrounds the law of lockout, it is used infrequently by employers, and then only rarely do employers seek to operate with replacements. Therefore, much of the fear which the NLRB apparently shares with respect to an unrestricted lockout policy seems to be unwarranted; for a lockout still deprives the employer of the opportunity to carry on business. It precipitates what the employer normally hopes to avoid and therefore is not likely to be widely used regardless of a more liberal trend in the decisions. It is most likely to be resorted to in multiemployer bargaining situations and in cases where an individual employer wishes to forestall a union which is prone to resort to quickie strikes and violence.

---

[35] 116 NLRB 832.
[36] 58 LRRM 2672, 380 U.S. 300 (1965).

ARBITRATION OR GOVERNMENT PROCESS

There are two principal avenues through which disputes between labor and management can be resolved. The first involves resort to arbitration procedures, which to an increasing extent are being included in collective bargaining agreements as the final step in the orderly resolution of disputes arising under the contract. The second avenue involves an appeal to the National Labor Relations Board and ultimately to the courts.

There are a number of compelling reasons for favoring the first alternative as a matter of public policy. As will be pointed out in the next chapter, the NLRB is faced with a mounting load of cases, which makes prompt resolution of disputes difficult to achieve. Arbitrators develop a special expertise with relation to particular industries and firms and can frequently make a more satisfactory decision with respect to complex issues than the NLRB. Finally, there is the danger that continual resort to government to resolve problems in the field of labor relations will erode the process of collective bargaining. Voluntary arbitration appears to be a much more salutary, prompt, and effective way of settling many disputes which do not threaten the existence of the union itself.

In recent years, in a succession of cases, both the courts and the NLRB have spoken out in favor of deferral to the private arbitration system where there appears to be an overlap between that system and the applicable labor law. Thus in *United Steelworkers* v. *Warrior & Gulf Navigation Co.*,[37] the Supreme Court held that when a party sought to compel arbitration in a suit under Section 301 of the Labor-Management Relations Act, the courts should resolve questions of interpretation of the arbitration clause by applying a strong presumption in favor of arbitrability. As we observed in the earlier discussion in this chapter, the Supreme Court's decision in the *Boys Markets* case will also strengthen the process of arbitration. The National Labor Relations Board has set forth four criteria to guide it in determining when to defer to private arbitration. The Board will defer to arbitration when:

1. The contract provides grievance and arbitration machinery.
2. There is no showing that the alleged unilateral action has been taken to undermine the union.
3. There is a claim of privilege under the contract by the respondent.
4. It appears that an arbitrator's interpretation of the contract would resolve the controversy as well as the Board's.[38]

---

[37] 363 U.S. 574 (1960).

[38] *Joseph Schlitz Brewing Co.*, 175 NLRB No. 23. These criteria were affirmed in *Collyer Insulated Wire*, 192 NLRB No. 150, in which the NLRB stated that these guidelines would set the Board's policy in similar cases in the future.

The Board's action in this regard seems to be on firm ground. A number of commentators contend that deferral should be further broadened so that a broad range of discipline cases could be handled through the arbitration procedure.[39] Most labor economists would agree with the statement of Board Chairman Miller who expressed the opinion:

I think that when parties have voluntarily agreed upon a mechanism for the adjustment of their disputes, then to the widest extent possible we ought to permit that machinery to operate and not complicate the situation by permitting either party to side-step those processes and instead look to government in the form of this Board to decide the merits of their disputes.[40]

QUESTIONS FOR DISCUSSION

1. What is meant by the term *injunction?* Discuss the manner in which the injunction has been used to impede labor's organizational efforts. To what extent can employers still use the injunction in labor disputes?
2. Should all picketing be treated as a form of free speech? Discuss the changing attitude of the U.S. Supreme Court on this issue.
3. What are the points of similarity between the strike and the lockout? In what way do the two actions differ? Should employers have the same freedom to lockout as unions have to strike?
4. Should unions be subject to the antitrust laws? Discuss the validity of the tests established by the *Pennington* and *Jewel Tea* cases as criteria for determining whether or not the Sherman Act prohibitions are applicable to concerted action by employees.

SUGGESTIONS FOR FURTHER READING

ABODEELY, JOHN E.   "Injunctive Powers under the National Labor Relations Act," pp. 106–26, in ROWAN, RICHARD L. (ed.), *Collective Bargaining: Survival in the 70's?* Philadelphia: Industrial Research Unit, Wharton School of Finance and Commerce, University of Pennsylvania, 1972.

   A discussion of the merits and demerits of broadened use of the injunction in labor relations, with particular reference to the power of the NLRB to seek injunctive relief under Sections 10 (j) and 10 (l) of the Taft-Hartley Act.

LEV, EDWARD R.   "Suggestions for Management: The Lockout," *Labor Law Journal*, Vol. 19 (February 1968), pp. 80–111.

   A review of cases on employer lockouts at the NLRB and court level by a writer critical of the Board's approach.

---

[39] See, for example, Albeon G. Anderson, Jr., "Concurrent Jurisdiction—NLRB and Private Arbitration: A Pragmatic Analysis," *Boston College Industrial and Commercial Law Review*, Vol. 12 (December 1970), pp. 179–202.

[40] Remarks at the Conference of Western States Employer Association Executives, 167 D.L.R. D-1 (1971).

Rosen, Samuel D.   "Area Standards Picketing," *Labor Law Journal*, Vol. 23 (February 1972), pp. 67–79.

A discussion which, although primarily concerned with the problems posed by area standards picketing, provides an excellent classification of the various types of picketing.

Unkovic, Nicholas.   "Enforcing the No-Strike Clause," *Labor Law Journal*, Vol. 21 (July 1970), pp. 387–96.

An analysis of the significance of the action of the U.S. Supreme Court in the *Boys Markets* case overruling Sinclair Refining.

Chapter

19

THE TAFT-HARTLEY ACT

Since its enactment in 1947, the Labor-Management Relations Act of 1947—more popularly known as the Taft-Hartley Act—has been the subject of controversy. Although at its inception it was most criticized by labor leaders, who characterized it as a "slave labor law," it is now widely condemned by businessmen, who argue that the NLRB has interpreted the act in a manner inconsistent with the intent of Congress. In this chapter, we shall consider in detail various provisions of this act and its effect upon employers, unions, individual employees, and the general public. Since the Taft-Hartley Act is, in form, an amendment of the earlier National Labor Relations Act, or Wagner Act, as it is commonly known, we shall commence our discussion with a brief consideration of the Wagner Act.

THE WAGNER ACT

Legislative Background and Statutory Policy

The Wagner Act was enacted largely because of the failure on the part of American employers to modernize their concepts of industrial relations by giving employees an opportunity to participate in the determination of wages, hours, and working conditions. The failure of industry to alter its long-standing policies and voluntarily to recognize unions of its employees was all the more remarkable in view of the ample warnings that if industry did not act, government would be compelled to do so. Commencing in 1885, a long list of government commissions, agencies, and (in later years) statutes contained governmental endorsement of the principle of collective bargaining. In 1898, Congress passed the Erdman Act, which contained provisions making discrimination against union activity on the railroads a misdemeanor. Although this provision was declared unconstitutional, later railway legislation, including the Railway Labor Act of 1926, endorsed unionism and collective bargaining. Between 1890 and 1914, no less than 14 states enacted legislation similar to the Erdman Act, only to have the courts declare such laws unconstitutional. Both the

Norris–La Guardia Act of 1932 and the National Industrial Recovery Act of 1933 contained statements of policy endorsing the right of employees to bargain through representatives of their own choosing, but neither act contained effective penalties in case of employer disinclination to conform to these statutory purposes.

In 1935, Congress passed the Wagner Act, which, in retrospect, appears to be the most significant labor law ever enacted in the United States. Congress virtually ordered employers to stop interfering with the efforts of unions to organize their employees. It put the power of the federal government behind the union organizer, assuring him that employees could make the choice whether or not to join a union without fear of employer interference. Moreover, in contrast to earlier legislation, the Wagner Act provided an effective mechanism to secure compliance by employers. The Wagner Act, therefore, required a completely new orientation of employer industrial relations policies.

The heart of the substantive provisions of the Wagner Act is contained in Section 7, which states the statutory policy in these words: "Employees shall have the right to self-organization, to form, join, or assist labor organizations, to bargain collectively through representatives of their own choosing, and to engage in concerted activities, for the purpose of collective bargaining or other mutual aid or protection."

The administration of the Wagner Act was given to a three-man National Labor Relations Board. The NLRB developed a large staff to enable it to carry on its work, including attorneys, investigators, hearing officers, review officers, and the many clerical personnel required to perform the detailed work in a nationwide administrative agency. The NLRB had jurisdiction only over employers engaged in interstate commerce. The Supreme Court has given the phrase *interstate commerce* an elastic definition, so that the jurisdiction of the Board has been held to apply not only to companies actively engaged in shipping products across state lines, but also to intrastate businesses which use a substantial quantity of raw materials shipped across state lines or sell products a substantial portion of which are destined for shipment across state lines.

UNFAIR LABOR PRACTICES

Enactment of the Wagner Act occurred at a time when the labor market was vastly different from that which exists in industry today. Organized labor numbered only 4 million union members, primarily concentrated in the construction trades, transportation, mining, and needle trades. The great basic industries of the country were either unorganized or were characterized by bargaining with company unions dominated by management. In 1935, for example, industries such as basic steel, agricultural implements, petroleum refining, rubber products, electrical machinery, and meat-packing had from 50% to 80% of their employees covered by company unions.[1] Employers were openly hostile to unions and used every weapon at their command to prevent union organization. Lockouts, intimidation, blacklists, yellow-dog contracts, spying, and discrimination were commonplace.

In drafting the Wagner Act, Congress recognized that business hostility to unions was a fact to be reckoned with and that pious pronouncements of policy in favor of union organization, unbuttressed by sanctions against violators of congressional policy, would achieve nothing. The act therefore enumerated so-called "employer unfair practices" and made such conduct unlawful. Furthermore, it empowered the NLRB to issue cease and desist orders against such illegal conduct, and to enforce such orders in the courts. During the 12 years of the Wagner Act administration until its amendment in 1947, employees and their representatives filed more than 45,000 charges of unfair labor practices against employers with the NLRB. It is therefore apparent that protection of employees against management unfair labor practices constituted a major function of the Board.

The unfair labor practices prohibited by the Wagner Act (in each case directed against employers) are the following:

1. *To interfere with, restrain, or coerce employees in the exercise of rights guaranteed in Section 7.* This is an all-inclusive provision which actually covers all of the more specific unfair labor practices enumerated below. However, it was aimed at such employer practices as spying on unions, questioning employees about their union affiliation, using blacklists or yellow-dog contracts, or favoring one union over another.

A major problem which arose under this section involved the question of freedom of speech. Since unions were weak during the early years of the Wagner Act, the NLRB considered the effect of antiunion speeches by employers as an important part of a totality of conduct which might interfere with the rights of employees under the act. Employers complained that the NLRB went too far in its zeal to protect employees and actually deprived employers of rights of free speech guaranteed by the Constitution.

2. *To dominate or interfere with the formation or administration of any labor organization or contribute financial or other support to it.* This section was designed to prevent the formation or use of company unions which were supported by and subservient to the employer. As has been mentioned, company unions were commonly used by employers in the early 1930s as a device to deter legitimate independent unionism; but as a result of the effective enforcement of this provision, employer-controlled company unions gradually disappeared from the labor scene.

3. *By discrimination in regard to hire or tenure of employment or*

---

[1] H. A. Millis and E. C. Brown, *From the Wagner Act to Taft-Hartley* (Chicago: University of Chicago Press, 1950), p. 110.

*any term or condition of employment to encourage or discourage mem-
bership in any labor organization.* This section was designed to make it
unlawful for employers to use blacklists, yellow-dog contracts, or other
devices to discourage membership in unions. Employers were forbidden
to inquire of job applicants whether they were union members or favored
unions, and employers could not fire employees because of union membership or lawful concerted activities protected under the act.

A proviso was included in this section permitting an employer who
had entered into an agreement with a union duly representing his employees to require membership in the union as a condition of employment.
This was the so-called "closed-shop" proviso, which was amended by the
Taft-Hartley Act.

*4. To discharge or otherwise discriminate against an employee be-
cause he has filed charges or given testimony under the act.* This section
was deemed necessary by Congress in order to assure protection to
employees who invoked the provisions of the act against employers.

*5. To refuse to bargain collectively with the representatives of his
employees duly chosen pursuant to other provisions of the act.* This
section of the law was inserted to require employers to meet and negotiate
with representatives of their employees. It is clear from the legislative
history of the act that Congress did not intend to compel employers to
agree to anything; it did want to assure that they would at least sit
down and bargain. The language of this section aroused violent criticism
from management spokesmen, who objected to the fact that the obligation to bargain was imposed only on them and not on unions. Furthermore, they criticized the manner in which the NLRB established criteria
as to what was "good-faith" bargaining, claiming that such rules, in effect,
required employers to come to an agreement contrary to the original
statutory purpose.

The prohibition of specific unfair labor practices in the Wagner Act
ushered in a new era in labor relations. Whereas, in earlier years labor
leaders found the power of the courts interfering with their organizing
activities, with the advent of the Wagner Act the courts, in effect, became
an ally of labor, standing ready to enforce valid orders of the NLRB in
cases where the Board found an employer guilty of unfair labor practices
and the employer ignored the Board's cease and desist order. Despite its
shortcomings, and despite the delays attendant upon its enforcement, the
unfair labor practice procedure contained in the act represented such an
improvement from organized labor's point of view over pre–Wagner Act
conditions that organizing activity was greatly enhanced.

In a typical unfair labor practice case under the Wagner Act, the
NLRB received a complaint from the union in behalf of an individual
worker alleging some violation of the act. A field examiner of the Board
investigated the case, and if the Board found that there was sufficient
evidence to warrant a hearing, it set down the case for hearing and, if

necessary, issued such subpoenas as were needed for the appearances of records and persons. In more than three quarters of the cases, however, settlement was achieved by informal methods before the hearing actually took place.

Hearings under the Wagner Act were conducted under the best accepted methods of administrative process. The NLRB was always careful to give all interested parties due notice and the right of hearing. However, the Board did act as both judge and prosecutor, which to some critics seemed unfair. Criticism of this feature of administration of the law ultimately led to establishment of the position of independent General Counsel under the Taft-Hartley Act, whose job it is to initiate complaints and bring them before the Board.

In enforcing unfair labor practice cases, the Board could issue certain orders. For example, it might require the employer to "cease and desist" from activities which it found in violation of the law. More important, it might require the employer to take affirmative action—for example, the reinstatement with back pay of employees who had been discharged or discriminated against because of union activity, or even the employment of workers who were never hired but who were refused employment because of their union affiliation. In addition, the Board could order the employer to disestablish a company union and withdraw recognition from any union which was recognized or with which he bargained if that union had been aided by the employer. Finally, in cases in which the employer was found to have refused to bargain with a union which was the duly chosen representative of his employees, the NLRB would order him to bargain upon request of that union.

REPRESENTATION CASES

Equally as important as unfair labor practice cases in the work of the NLRB, and every bit as controversial as a result of the split in the American labor movement which existed until 1955, have been representation cases. Section 9(a) of the Wagner Act provided that "Representatives . . . selected for the purposes of collective bargaining by the majority of the employees in a unit appropriate for such purposes, shall be the exclusive representatives of all the employees in such unit for the purposes of collective bargaining. . . ." This provision, with important additions which we shall consider at a later point in this discussion, was carried over into the Taft-Hartley Act.

Congress adopted the majority rule principle basically because experience had shown that it was the only practical method. The representative of the majority is thus the representative of all the employees in the bargaining unit, whether or not they are union members, just as a congressman represents all persons in his district regardless of whether they are members of his party or whether they voted for him or his opponent in the last election. If minority representation were permitted in collective bargaining, the employer would be constantly faced with demands from one group or another desirous of attracting support. Obviously, under such a setup, neither collective bargaining nor a business would stand much chance of survival. The NLRB has further determined that majority means a majority of the employees voting, not a majority of those eligible. This compels all interested groups to vie in getting out the vote. As a result, votes cast in NLRB elections averaged 80%–90% of those eligible, as compared with the average of 50%–65% of those eligible who vote in national elections.

In order to determine whether or not a particular union was the representative of workers in a plant, the NLRB held elections by secret ballot among the employees. The names of the union or unions seeking certification were placed on the ballot along with "no union." If a union won a majority of the votes cast, it was certified as the collective bargaining agent with which the employer had to bargain as the exclusive representative of the employees involved. If "no union" received a majority, no certification was made.

BARGAINING UNIT PROBLEMS

One of the most difficult kinds of problems faced by the NLRB involved deciding which employees were eligible to vote in an election to determine the bargaining agent and which groups of employees should have the right to separate choice of bargaining agents. Congress delegated these problems, known as questions of the "appropriate bargaining unit," to the NLRB, giving it almost unlimited authority[2] in Section 9(*b*) of the Wagner Act, which stated that "the Board shall decide in each case whether, in order to insure to employees the full benefit of their right to self-organization and to collective bargaining, and otherwise to effectuate the policies of this Act, the unit appropriate for the purposes of collective bargaining shall be the employer unit, craft unit, plant unit, or subdivision thereof." This wide authority was given to the NLRB in the belief, based on experience of the National Recovery Administration labor boards, that the various problems which arose were not foreseeable and could best be determined by the NLRB.

Although the Board decided each case on the merits, it grouped the facts determining its bargaining unit decisions around two basic criteria —the history of collective bargaining, if any, and the mutuality of interests of the employees. A typical bargaining unit was composed of production and maintenance employees in a single plant. Foremen and supervisors were excluded from the production workers' unit because of

---

[2] This authority has been restricted to some extent in the Taft-Hartley Act with respect to craft units, guards, and professional employees. See subsequent discussion in this chapter.

their peculiar relation to management. Likewise, office, clerical, and white-collar workers were separated from production and maintenance employees, as were professional employees. In addition, guards and watchmen were placed in separate units because of their unique position, and temporary employees were often deemed outside the bargaining unit because they had no permanent status in the plant. All these decisions were based on the fact that production and maintenance employees have a basic common denominator which was lacking among other plant groups, especially since many of the latter have a special and different relation to the employer.

Effect of AFL–CIO Rivalry

Determination of the bargaining unit was complicated by the rivalry between the AFL and the CIO. The struggle between these two groups was bitterly fought in cases involving the question whether employees should be represented on a craft or on an industrial basis. During the early years of the Wagner Act, the CIO concentrated organizing drives in the great basic industries of the country—steel, automobile, electrical, chemical, oil, etc.—and sought to organize companies on an industrial basis. This drive brought it into conflict with the AFL, which frequently represented strategically placed craft groups in such industries. In resolving the issue of the appropriate bargaining unit, where both an industrial union and a craft union claimed the right to represent a particular group of workers, the NLRB would consider the claims of both parties; and if it found, upon the basis of all the circumstances, that the craft could logically lay claim to consideration as a separate bargaining unit, and if there was reasonable doubt as to whether the majority of this craft preferred representation by the craft union or the industrial union, the Board permitted the workers in the craft to determine the issue for themselves. The Board accomplished this by providing that the workers in the craft would have a choice in an election of voting for the craft union, the industrial union, or no union, whereas the other production workers could vote only for the industrial union or no union.

When Congress passed the Wagner Act, it did not, of course, foresee the split in the labor movement. Therefore, it anticipated that in those situations where employees wanted to be represented by a union, a petition for an election would be filed with the Board by the union (normally an AFL affiliate), and a prompt, peaceful determination of the question of the representation would be made through the administrative procedures of the Board.

This procedure broke down when AFL and CIO unions engaged in a bitter struggle with each other over the right to represent employees in given bargaining units. Instead, the plant became a battleground, with both employer and employees as casualties. If one union felt confident enough to move for an early election, the other union would use all sorts of pressures to defer it. If it appeared that one union was successfully signing up members in a plant, the other might institute a boycott of the products of the company, picket the premises, threaten workers, or use similar pressures to weaken the hold of the rival union. The employer could do nothing to protect his business or employees against such tactics, for the Norris–La Guardia Act had deprived employers of their most effective weapon—the injunction. Since the Wagner Act imposed no prohibition on the activities of unions similar to the unfair labor practices proscribed for employers, employees had no way to protect themselves against such union pressures.

Even after one union was certified as the exclusive bargaining agent, there was nothing in the Wagner Act which prohibited a rival union from continuing its organizing and harassing activities, including picketing and boycotting. Employers were bound by the results of an NLRB election; but a rival union which lost an election was not bound by such results as a practical matter, since it could still attempt to achieve through economic pressure what it could not accomplish through peaceful procedures under the act.

WAGNER ACT, UNION GROWTH, AND STRIKES

That the Wagner Act achieved its basic purpose in compelling a change in employer policy toward unions cannot be doubted. In 1935, when the act became law, union membership stood at 3.9 million. In 1947, when the Wagner Act was amended, union membership exceeded 15 million. Although this union growth must be attributed to many factors, it was without a doubt substantially hastened by the Wagner Act. If the Wagner Act is judged in terms of fulfillment of its stated policy of "encouraging the practice and procedure of collective bargaining," it was eminently successful.

On the other hand, the Wagner Act cannot be said to have minimized the causes of industrial disputes except in one important respect. The representation procedure of the act provided a peaceful and democratic means of determining whether a union had the right to represent a group of employees. The substitution of NLRB procedure for the use of force in determining this question was one of the great contributions of the act.

Insofar as strikes generally are concerned, however, the Wagner Act had little contribution to make. Congress gave the NLRB no authority to interfere in disputes over terms and conditions of employment. Once the union was certified as bargaining agent and the employer's conduct was purged of unfair labor practices, the Wagner Act left matters to the parties themselves. But since the protection of the act spurred union activity, the period 1935–41 saw a great surge of union growth. A combination of immature unions and managements inexperienced in industrial relations resulted in numerous strikes which more mature and experienced parties might have avoided. Critics of the Wagner Act blamed either the act or its administration by the NLRB as the cause of the strife. Proponents of the act blamed management opposition to both the act and unions as the cause. Perhaps a more accurate analysis would place the blame mainly on the growing pains of unions and the learning pains of management.

THE TAFT-HARTLEY ACT

The Wagner Act was under severe public criticism from its enactment in 1935 until its amendment 12 years later. Repeated attempts to modify the Wagner Act were bottled up in congressional committees, but finally, in 1946, the stage was set for new labor legislation by an unprecedented wave of strikes. In that year, time lost through strikes reached an all-time high of 116 million man-days—a figure three times higher than in the previous year or in 1937, the two worst years up to that time for which such statistics are available. Then followed the congressional elections of November 1946, which reflected strong public dissatisfaction with current labor policies and which were interpreted by Congress as a mandate for corrective labor legislation. On June 23, 1947, the Labor-Management Relations Act—more popularly known as the Taft-Hartley Act—was passed by Congress over President Truman's veto.

Thus ended an important stage in the development of national labor policy in this country. The attitude of government toward collective bargaining by employees had passed through a succession of stages from active hostility in the early 1800s, when labor organizations were prosecuted as conspiracies, to active encouragement of union organization under the Wagner Act. Enactment of the Taft-Hartley law represented a new stage in government treatment of both management and labor. The metamorphosis which had occurred in public thinking on the subject of collective bargaining is well exemplified by a comparison of the original phraseology of Section 7 of the Wagner Act with its revised wording in the Taft-Hartley Act: "Employees shall have the right to self-organization . . . for the purpose of collective bargaining or other mutual aid or protection, *and shall also have the right to refrain from any or all of such activities.* . . ." Whereas, formerly, the weight of government influence had been placed behind union organization activities, the Taft-Hartley Act appeared to place the government in the position of a neutral, recognizing the right of employees to organize or not to organize. In theory, the government was to be not a partisan but a policeman, protecting both management and labor from unfair labor practices. However, as we shall observe in the later discussion, critics have alleged that the actual administration of the act has deviated from this apparent statutory policy.

The Taft-Hartley Act also qualified the principle that organized labor should be free to use its economic weapons without restriction. Secondary boycotts, strikes, and picketing for certain purposes were all subjected to regulation by the act. In this and other respects which will be discussed in the text, the Taft-Hartley Act established the principle that law, protecting the interest of management, labor, and the public, plays a necessary role in labor relations.

Scope and Administration of the Act

The Labor-Management Relations Act of 1947 was, in form, an amendment of the Wagner Act. Title I incorporated the text of the Wagner Act—with, however, a number of major modifications and additions. Title II, which dealt with conciliation of labor disputes and national emergency strikes, is discussed in Chapter 21. Title III authorized suits by and against unions, and Title IV created a joint committee to study and report on basic problems affecting friendly labor relations and productivity. Administration of the act remained under the National Labor Relations Board, but a number of important changes were made in the composition and power of the NLRB. Section 3 of the act enlarged the Board from three to five members. To remedy the oft-repeated charge made against the Board under the Wagner Act that it was both judge and prosecutor, the prosecuting function was removed from the Board and vested in a General Counsel who in this respect was made completely independent of the Board. In the handling of cases the General Counsel has final authority, subject neither to appeal to the Board nor to appeal to the courts, both as to institution of formal unfair labor practice proceedings and as to dismissal of charges. However, the General Counsel is subject to the Board's direction in matters of basic policy, such as determination of what categories of employers and employees are subject to coverage of the act. The General Counsel is responsible for the administration of the Board's field offices and field personnel, but not the staff of trial examiners who hear unfair practice cases.

Although collective bargaining is today firmly established in American industry, the total case load handled by the Board continues to mount year after year. In the fiscal year ending June 30, 1970, there were 33,581 cases filed with the Board, including 21,038 unfair labor practice charges.[3] Figure 19–1 shows the division of the Board's case load as between unfair labor practice charges and representation elections over the past decade. Unfair labor practice charges which in 1961 constituted about 52% of the Board's incoming cases had by 1970 risen to about 62%. The 21,038 unfair labor practice charges filed in 1970 represented

---

[3] *Thirty-Fifth Annual Report of the National Labor Relations Board* for the fiscal year ending June 30, 1970 (Washington, D.C.: U.S. Government Printing Office, 1971), p. 1.

FIGURE 19–1

Case Intake of NLRB by Unfair Labor Practice Changes and Representation Petitions (1961–1970)

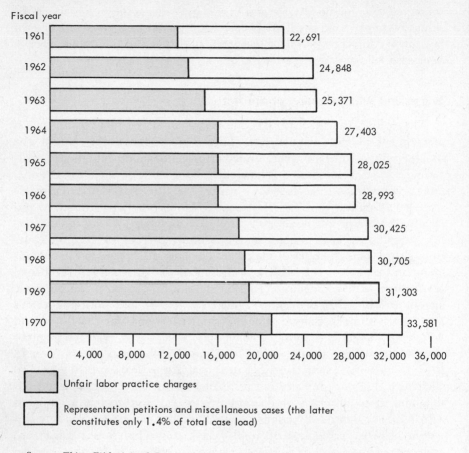

Fiscal year

1961	22,691
1962	24,848
1963	25,371
1964	27,403
1965	28,025
1966	28,993
1967	30,425
1968	30,705
1969	31,303
1970	33,581

0   4,000   8,000   12,000   16,000   20,000   24,000   28,000   32,000   36,000

Unfair labor practice charges

Representation petitions and miscellaneous cases (the latter constitutes only 1.4% of total case load)

Source: *Thirty-Fifth Annual Report of the National Labor Relations Board,* p. 2.

an 85% increase over the number filed 10 years earlier.[4] Of the unfair labor practice charges filed, 13,601 alleged violations by employers while 7,330 alleged unlawful conduct on the part of unions.[5]

The NLRB closed a total of 32,353 cases in 1970 of which 19,851 involved unfair labor practice charges. Significantly, about 92% of these cases were closed by regional offices, making formal decisions by the Board unnecessary.[6] The Board has sought to speed up its handling of cases by delegating decision-making authority to the Board's 31 regional

[4] *Ibid.*
[5] *Ibid.,* p. 11.
[6] *Ibid., p.* 1.

directors in representation cases, pursuant to authority given the Board by Congress in 1959 amendments to the act. Congress has refused, however, to authorize such delegation of authority in the handling of unfair labor practice charges. Therefore, in such cases the Board has had to rely on voluntary processes to speed up handling and settlement. A major reason why case loads continue to rise is the tendency, particularly of unions, to file charges as a bargaining tactic.

Extent of Coverage of the Act

Although the coverage of the Taft-Hartley Act is extremely broad, nevertheless certain employers, employees, and types of business are excluded from its application either by statutory definition or administrative determination.[7]

Local Business. Under both the original Wagner Act and the Taft-Hartley Act, the NLRB was granted jurisdiction extending to any business "affecting commerce." Because of its limited budget, however, the Board has never exercised fully the powers granted to it by Congress. In 1950, 1954, and 1958, the Board laid down general standards intended to exclude "local businesses" from the Board's jurisdiction. These standards, based upon sales volume and similar criteria, were intended to keep the Board from being inundated with a flood of cases involving small companies with relatively few employees. For example, under the present standards the Board will not take jurisdiction of cases involving retail concerns unless they do a gross volume of business in excess of $500,000. Nonretail concerns must show at least $50,000 "outflow or inflow, direct or indirect."[8] Other standards are established for office buildings, public utilities, radio stations, and other enterprises.

The action of the Board in thus limiting its jurisdiction nullified in practice certain aspects of the protection which the act attempted to afford to small employers. For example, the Taft-Hartley Act makes it an unfair labor practice to coerce an employer or self-employed person to join a union. Obviously, this provision is most meaningful in the case of

---

[7] Judicial interpretation is a further determinant of coverage. For example, in 1971, the U.S. Supreme Court decided that retired employees are not "employees" under the act, and therefore unions have no right to bargain over retirees' rights under a health insurance plan. *Allied Chemical Workers, Local 1.* v. *Pittsburgh Plate Glass Co.,* 404 U.S. 157 (1971).

[8] Direct outflow refers to goods shipped or services furnished by the employer outside the state. Indirect outflow includes sales within the state to users meeting any standard except solely an indirect inflow or indirect outflow standard. Direct inflow refers to goods or services furnished directly to the employer from outside the state in which the employer is located. Indirect inflow refers to the purchase of goods or services which originated outside the employer's state but which he purchased from a seller within the state. Direct and indirect outflow may be combined, and direct and indirect inflow may also be combined to meet the $50,000 requirement. However, outflow and inflow may *not* be combined.

small employers or self-employed persons working without hired help; yet the Board would not ordinarily take jurisdiction of such cases because the business involved would not normally meet the Board's jurisdictional requirements. To make matters worse, the U.S. Supreme Court held in a series of decisions that state labor relations boards had no power to act in cases involving interstate commerce where the National Labor Relations Board had refused to assert jurisdiction. The High Court reasoned that Congress, by vesting in the NLRB jurisdiction over labor relations matters affecting interstate commerce, had completely displaced state power to act. The net result of NLRB policy and the Supreme Court's interpretation of the law was the creation of a no-man's land in the field of labor relations where the small employer was without a forum to hear his case. This serious defect in the administration of the Taft-Hartley Act was not remedied until enactment of the Landrum-Griffin Act in 1959.

Supervisors. The Taft-Hartley Act made important changes in the definition of the word *employee,* as this term was used in the Wagner Act, with the result that supervisors were excluded from the protective coverage of the act. Under the Wagner Act the NLRB vacillated as to whether or not that act protected the right of supervisors to form unions and engage in collective bargaining, but it consistently held that the act protected supervisors as employees from discriminatory practices by employers. Under the Taft-Hartley Act, however, supervisors were deprived of both of these protections and were therefore compelled to rely solely on economic weapons to achieve their objectives. Supervisors could still join unions, but employers were free to use any means to intimidate and forestall such organization. In practice, the Taft-Hartley Act dealt unions of supervisors a hard blow. After its enactment, contracts of the Foreman's Association of America with Ford Motor Company and other important firms were not renewed. However, the act has had little effect in printing and other industries in which it was customary to include foremen in unions of employees. In the years since the Taft-Hartley Act was passed, management has done much to upgrade foremen, so that some writers contend that the once controversial issue of excluding foremen from protection of the Act is now largely moot.[9]

Agricultural Workers. The term *employee* is defined in the act to exclude "any individual employed as an agricultural laborer." Therefore, there is no governmental protection afforded to agricultural employees who may wish to form unions. In the late 1960s, Cesar Chavez made headlines with his United Farmworkers Organizing Committee (UFWOC) by using picketing, boycotts, and similar tactics to organize workers in the California grape and lettuce fields. Chavez's organizing activities

---

[9] For a discussion of the effect of the act on foremen, see J. E. Moore, "The National Labor Relations Board and Supervisors," *Labor Law Journal,* Vol. 21 (April 1970), pp. 190–205.

focused attention on the glaring deficiencies in existing law as far as agricultural workers are concerned and gave rise to a demand for a new labor law to cover such workers. For example, UFWOC attempted to organize employees in the lettuce industry even though their employers had valid contracts with the Teamsters' Union. Growers found that they were caught in the cross fire between the two organizations with no means to determine the true wishes of the employees. Since UFWOC was not technically a labor organization as defined under the Taft-Hartley Act, it was not barred from utilizing the secondary boycott, secondary picketing, and other coercive tactics denied to conventional unions. However, in early 1972, some wine-processing employees signed up as members of UFWOC. Since these were not agricultural workers but industrial employees, UFWOC technically became classified as a labor organization![10] The NLRB General Counsel filed a complaint to halt UFWOC's actions in organizing a boycott of retail stores which were selling wine produced by a company it was seeking to organize. Thus although UFWOC may at times be subject to the restrictive prohibitions of the Taft-Hartley Act, the employees whom it seeks to organize in agricultural enterprises still are denied the right to NLRB-conducted elections. The UFWOC, on the other hand, has had immunity in some boycotts that it would not have had if it came fully within the purview of Taft-Hartley. Bills are presently being considered in Congress which would establish a separate labor law for agricultural employees or bring them under the coverage of the Taft-Hartley Act.

Government Employees.   The term *employer* in the law excludes "the United States or any wholly owned government corporation, or any Federal Reserve Bank, or any State or political subdivision thereof." Employees working for such employers are not covered by the act. Collective bargaining by government employees is a relatively new development; its present rapid development could not have been foreseen in 1947.[11] As far as state and local government employees are concerned, their bargaining rights vary from one jurisdiction to another. Some observers believe that this diversity is sound in view of the newness of the movement and our lack of experience in understanding how effectively to deal with it. However, some unions of state and local government employees have been pushing for a standardized federal law. As in the case of agricultural employees, there is no unanimity as to how this should be done. One group of public employees, led by the Coalition of Employee Organizations, supports passage of a separate federal law for nonfederal public employees, while another group supports a bill which would amend the Taft-Hartley Act by eliminating the exclusion from the

---

[10] 79 LRR 303, April 3, 1972. Under the act, for an organization to qualify as a "labor organization," its members must be "employees" as defined in the law.

[11] See Chapter 22 for a discussion of the problems raised by collective bargaining on behalf of government employees.

definition of "employer" of the words "any state or political subdivision thereof."[12]

HOW THE EMPLOYER WAS AFFECTED

In form, the Taft-Hartley Act retained the five unfair labor practices specified in the Wagner Act; and therefore, to a casual reader, it might appear that the employer is still subject to the same restrictions as under the Wagner Act. Actually, however, newly added provisions in the law were intended to afford the employer important new freedoms.

Free Speech

The Taft-Hartley Act accepted in principle employers' complaints on the "free speech" issue. Under the original Wagner Act the employer was prohibited from interfering with employee organization activities. This was so construed that practically any opinion expressed by an employer against union organization was held to be an unfair labor practice. In the years immediately prior to enactment of the Taft-Hartley Act, however, the Board modified its views so as to permit some employer opinions to be stated in the interest of preserving the right of free speech. During the time of the Wagner Act, NLRB policy toward employer free speech went through three distinct phases:

The first was characterized by the requirement that the employer maintain strict neutrality by remaining silent; the second, by the concession that the employer could express his antiunion views, so long as they were not accompanied by threats or promises, and so long as employees were not required to listen; and the third, by the refinement that the employer could make non-coercive antiunion speeches to compulsory audiences of his employees, provided that similar opportunities were afforded union representatives to express their views.[13]

The Taft-Hartley Act attempted to clarify employer rights of free speech by specifically providing in Section 8(c) that the expression of any views, arguments, or opinions could not be considered evidence of an unfair labor practice unless there was an actual threat of reprisal or force or promise of benefit.

Although a literal application of the words of this section could have seriously deterred union organizing activity in those areas, such as parts of the South, where unions are not yet entrenched, in actual practice the benefit derived by employers from this particular provision has depended

---

[12] 79 LRR 290, March 27, 1972. See Chapter 22 for a further discussion of governmental employee relations and public policy.

[13] Joseph Shister, Benjamin Aaron, and C. W. Summers (eds.), *Public Policy and Collective Bargaining* (Industrial Relations Research Association Publication No. 27 [New York: Harper & Row, Publishers, 1962]), p. 35.

upon whether or not the majority of the Board members represented the views of a Republican or Democratic administration. In recent years the Board's implementation of this statutory language has been criticized more by employers than by union spokesmen. The NLRB has restricted the application of Section 8(c) by holding that it applies only to unfair labor practice cases and not to representation elections. In March 1970, the majority report of the Senate Subcommittee on Separation of Powers, which had held extensive hearings with respect to NLRB policy, concluded that:

the present Board has initiated a trend toward ever increasing restrictions on employer speech and has gone to the limit and beyond in finding a coercive impact in isolated and relatively innocuous remarks by employers.[14]

Designation of Union as Bargaining Agent through Authorization Cards

One of the most controversial issues of the Board's administration of the act involves its use of union authorization cards as a means of determining the collective bargaining representative. Under the Wagner Act the Board was authorized to hold secret ballot elections "or utilize any other suitable method" to determine the representative of the employees. The Taft-Hartley amendments deleted the quoted phrase, which led most management spokesmen to believe that the secret ballot election was the only permissible method of determining the bargaining representative. However, the Board maintains that in cases where the employer's unfair conduct has made the secret ballot a nullity, it is useless to hold a runoff election, since presumably the same unfair conduct will have vitiated the results of this election. Therefore, the Board relies on authorization cards solicited by the union from employees in which employees are to indicate their consent to the union acting as their bargaining representative.

In theory the Board is correct, since it would seem that Congress must have intended that the Board have some alternative method of determining the wishes of employees in cases of flagrant violations of the act by an employer. The problem lies in the great number of cases where the conduct of the employer does not go this far, but simply represents a doubt as to the majority status of the union and opposition to the union being designated as bargaining agent. Under these circumstances union agents have now found a procedure whereby they can get two chances to win representation. First, the organizing union solicits signatures from employees. Sometimes threats, misrepresentations, and arm-twisting of various sorts will be involved, and frequently employees may think they are simply authorizing a secret election at which they can then vote

---

[14] 73 LRR Analysis 34 (March 2, 1970). As the NLRB has become more dominated by President Nixon's appointees, this trend has been declining.

against the union without fear of reprisal. Once the union agents have a majority of signatures, they notify the employer of this fact and request formal bargaining. The union usually offers to prove its majority status by submitting the cards to an independent third party. The union petitions the Board for an election either at the same time or within a short time thereafter.

If the employer voluntarily bargains with the union, the petition for the election is withdrawn and the plant has been organized. If the employer refuses recognition, the union may still succeed in organizing the plant without an election. This depends upon whether the Board finds that the employer had a "good-faith" doubt as to the majority status of the union as evidenced by the authorization cards. If the Board finds that the employer did not have such doubt but simply sought to delay action by seeking an election, it may deny him an election and order him to bargain with the union. Even if the Board finds that there was good-faith doubt, the election may never be held if the employer commits an unfair labor practice before the election. The union can then withdraw the election petition, alleging that the unfair practice eliminates the possibility of a fair election, and under appropriate circumstances, the Board may then order the employer to bargain with the union. Finally, even if the union loses the election, it may then allege that employer preelection conduct constituted an unfair labor practice, and again the Board may compel the employer to bargain.

Are authorization cards a valid indication of employee preference? The Fourth Circuit has declared that they are "inherently unreliable" and that "an employer could not help but doubt the results of a card check."[15] There seems to be little doubt that signature cards are inferior to an election and that employees frequently change their minds after signing an authorization card, the significance of which may not have been fully understood by them. The Board itself has expressed its reservations concerning authorization cards but, on the other hand, has felt that this device was necessary where a secret ballot could no longer reflect employee free choice because of unfair conduct on the part of the employer.

The Supreme Court in the *Gissel Packing* case[16] affirmed the Board's right to use authorization cards. The Court stated that use of a bargaining order based upon signature cards was appropriate:

1. In exceptional cases marked by outrageous and pervasive unfair labor practices of such a nature that their coercive effects cannot be eliminated by the application of traditional remedies.
2. In cases such as *Gissel Packing*, marked by less pervasive practices which nevertheless still have the tendency to undermine majority strength and impede the election process. The Board's use of cards in

---

[15] *Logan Packing*, 66 LRRM 2596.
[16] *NLRB* v. *Gissel Packing Co.*, 395 U.S. 575 (1969).

such instances is appropriate if there is a showing that at one point the union had a majority representation in the bargaining unit.

Despite the *Gissel* case, the controversy over the Board's use of authorization cards and the basic issue of the Board's determination as to when such use is appropriate still are subject to continuing criticism. Although employers attack the Board for having gone too far, the fact is that the Board has elected not to go the authorization card route in a number of cases where there was substantial evidence of coercion and threats by management personnel.[17] Moreover, the tendency of President Nixon's appointees is to utilize authorization cards to a much less degree than did their predecessors.

Fortunately, bargaining orders based on authorization cards represent only a minority of representation decisions handled by the Board. Nevertheless, the minor importance of such cases in the overall case load of the Board is no consolation to the employer who finds himself faced with an order to bargain with a union which, rightly or wrongly, he believes does not represent a majority of workers in the bargaining unit. Nor is it any consolation to employees who find themselves represented by a union that was opposed by a majority of the bargaining unit.

Reinstatement

Section 10(*c*) of the act prohibited the Board from ordering reinstatement or back pay in any case where the discharge was made "for cause." This provision was included, according to the majority report of the House Labor Committee, in order to "put an end to the belief, now widely held and certainly justified by the Board's decisions, that engaging in union activities carries with it a license to loaf, wander about the plant, refuse to work, waste time, break rules and engage in incivilities and other disorders and misconduct." The basis for this charge does not appear to have been factual.

The NLRB has continued to order reinstatement where circumstances warrant this remedy for workers illegally discharged. Unfortunately, there are still more violations of the act involving a discriminatory discharge by an employer than any other type of unfair labor practice.[18] In the fiscal year ending June 30, 1970, the Board awarded back pay to 6,828 workers, amounting to $2.7 million; 3,779 employees were offered reinstatement and about 72% accepted.[19]

In September 1962, the Board for the first time commenced adding 6% interest to back-pay awards granted to employees who were illegally

[17] See, for example, *Stoutco, Inc.*, 73 LRRM 1107 (1969) and *Schrementi Bros, Inc.*, 72 LRRM 1481 (1969).

[18] See *Thirty-Fifth Annual Report of the NLRB*, p. 11.

[19] *Ibid.*, p. 14.

discharged. While there was no specific authorization in the Taft-Hartley Act for such action, the Board relied on "accepted legal and equitable principles" as justification for adding interest to back-pay awards.[20] Some writers now question whether the addition of 6% is sufficient to make a worker "whole" in view of the fact that if during the interim he had found it necessary to take a loan from a bank or installment loan company, he would have had to pay 18% per year. It has been suggested that raising the rate of interest on back-pay awards might make employers more interested in complying expeditiously with the terms of a back-pay award,[21] but there is no evidence to support this assertion.

Union spokesmen complain that the remedial powers available to the Board to deal with unlawful discharge cases are wholly inadequate. It is unlikely that a hostile employer is dissuaded from firing a union organizer by the knowledge that two or three years in the future he may have to reinstate the worker with back pay plus 6%. The Board, however, has announced its conclusion in the *Ex-Cell-O Corporation* case[22] that the awarding of compensatory or punitive damages is precluded by Section 8(*d*) of the Taft-Hartley Act, which prohibits the Board from imposing contract terms on the parties to a labor dispute.

Procedural Privileges

Employers were also granted important procedural rights. Whereas, previously, employers could petition for an election only when confronted with demands for bargaining rights by two or more competing unions, they could now seek an election whenever a union made a demand for recognition. The grant of this privilege to the employer restrained premature claims of representation by unions attempting to organize a plant; for if the union failed to secure a majority vote in an election called by the employer, the act prohibited the holding of another election for 12 months. The right to request an election has been frequently utilized by employers. During the fiscal year ended June 30, 1970, employers petitioned for elections in 317 cases.[23]

Another important right provided in the Taft-Hartley Act is the privilege to sue unions in federal court for breach of contract. Section 301(*a*) of the act provides:

Suits for violation of contracts between an employer and a labor organization representing employees in an industry affecting commerce as defined in

---

[20] *NLRB Press Release*, September 21, 1962.

[21] See Dell B. Johannesen, "Continuing Controversy: New Remedies for Old Unfair Labor Practices," *Labor Law Journal*, Vol. 23 (February 1972), p. 101.

[22] *Ex-Cell-O Corp.*, 185 NLRB No. 20, 74 LRRM 1740 (August 25, 1970); rev'd. per curiam sub. nom *UAW* v. *NLRB*, No. 24,577, 76 LRRM 2753 (D.C. Cir., March 19, 1971).

[23] *Thirty-Fifth Annual Report of the NLRB*, p. 180.

this Act, or between any such labor organizations, may be brought in any district court of the United States having jurisdiction of the parties without respect to the amount in controversy or without regard to the citizenship of the parties.[24]

Furthermore, Section 303 of the act provides that whoever is injured in his business or property by reason of certain enumerated unfair labor practices of a labor organization may sue in federal district court "and shall recover the damages by him sustained and the cost of the suit." Although contrary to the grim prognostications of union leaders, there has been no rush by employers to sue unions[25] in federal court, nevertheless, this section of the act carries with it implications of great significance for the development of labor relations in this country.

One direct result of the inclusion of Section 301(*a*) in the Taft-Hartley Act has been an increase in frequency of clauses in labor contracts protecting the union against financial liability in the event of unauthorized strikes. Contrary to expectations, however, there appears to have been no reduction in the frequency of no-strike clauses in labor agreements negotiated since enactment of the Taft-Hartley amendments.

, important

Good-Faith Bargaining

It will be recalled that the Wagner Act provided that it was an unfair labor practice for an employer to refuse to bargain collectively with representatives of his employees. The statute did not set forth the requirements of bargaining in good faith, but the NLRB gradually developed a series of rules which, in the eyes of employers, erroneously interpreted the statute and required the employer to make counterproposals and thereby accede to union demands. The Taft-Hartley amendments added a new provision, Section 8(*d*), which defined the obligation to bargain and stated further that the obligation "does not compel either party to agree to a proposal or require the making of a concession." Despite this statutory instruction, the NLRB has nevertheless tended to view a refusal to make a counterproposal as evidence of bad faith.

A classic test of the meaning of the statutory language was posed by the 1960 case involving negotiations between the International Union of Electrical Workers and the General Electric Company. The company, in accordance with a long-standing policy which has become known as

---

[24] While Section 301(*a*) is considered above in connection with employer procedural rights, it should be noted that equal rights are accorded to unions to bring suits against employers.

[25] The Landrum-Griffin Act amendments to the Taft-Hartley Act broadened this provision so that today an employer can sue a union for damages sustained as the result of any activity or conduct defined as an unfair labor practice in Section 8(*b*) (4) of the Taft-Hartley Act, as amended.

"Boulwarism,"[26] offered a complete package of benefits to the union and then, except for minor modifications, sought to stand by this offer. IUE, after a short strike, finally signed a contract with GE, but then filed a charge with the NLRB alleging that the company had not bargained in good faith. Four and one-half years after the 1960 three-year agreement was signed and 18 months after GE, the IUE, and 100 other unions had peacefully arrived at successor three-year contracts, the NLRB ruled that GE was guilty of bargaining in bad faith![27]

In finding a violation of Section 8(*a*)(5) of the Taft-Hartley Act, the NLRB rested its conclusion upon an alleged "totality of conduct" by the company which in its opinion tended to "freeze" its bargaining stance, even though admittedly the company had made certain concessions from its first offer and even though the Board found that the company was at all times willing and anxious to sign a new contract. This case raised serious questions in the minds of employers, management consultants, and lawyers as to whether it is any longer possible for employers to engage in so-called "tough" bargaining with unions.

The Board has attempted to use the good-faith bargaining provisions of the act to compel an employer to sign a contract containing a provision which it strongly objected to. In the *H. K. Porter* case,[28] the Board found that an employer had failed to bargain in good faith when it refused to sign a contract containing a union dues checkoff. Significantly, the union had insisted just as adamantly that it would not sign a contract *unless* it contained a checkoff; yet this apparently did not constitute a violation of the good-faith bargaining requirements of the act. In a subsequent hearing on this case[29] before the circuit court, the issue was raised as to whether or not the company could be forced to grant the checkoff clause, and the court held that the Board had the authority to order the company to do so. The NLRB then ordered the company to grant the checkoff. Such action would bring us very close to compulsory arbitration. However, upon appeal, the U.S. Supreme Court held that the Board was without power to enter such an order.[30] The Court stated that while the Board does have the power to require employers and unions to negotiate, it is without power to compel a company or a union to agree

---

[26] See Herbert R. Northrup, *Boulwarism* (Ann Arbor, Mich.: Bureau of Industrial Relations, University of Michigan, 1964).

[27] *General Electric Company*, 150 NLRB 192 (1964). The decision of the Board was subsequently upheld by the U.S. Circuit Court of Appeals and the U.S. Supreme Court denied review (*NLRB* v. *General Electric Co.*, CA 2d [1969], 72 LRRM 2530, cert. denied U.S. Sup. Ct. [1970] 73 LRRM 2600).

[28] *NLRB* v. *H. K. Porter Company, Inc.*, 153 NLRB 1370 (1965), enf. 363 F.2d 272 (D.C. Circ. 1966).

[29] *Steelworkers* v. *NLRB*, 66 LRRM 2761 (D.C. Circ., December 1967).

[30] *H. K. Porter* v. *NLRB*, 397 U.S. 99 (1970) reversing 414 F.2d 1123 (C.A.D.C.) enfcg. 172 NLRB No. 72.

to any substantive contractual provision of a collective bargaining agreement.

Although the H. K. Porter case stands as a brake on the authority of the Board to write collective bargaining agreements for the parties, the line between dictating the substance of contracts and merely requiring the parties to negotiate is a fine one. Relying on the good-faith bargaining requirements of the act, the Board not only tells employers and unions when they must make concessions but also has set up a complicated set of rules as to what they can and cannot bargain about. First, the parties have a mandatory obligation to bargain about rates of pay, wages, hours, or other conditions of employment. This language has been broadly construed by the Board and the courts to include such matters as Christmas bonuses,[31] employee-stock purchase plans,[32] and employee discounts on purchase of the employer's product.[33] Perhaps most significant is the fact that the U.S. Supreme Court supported the contention of the Board that a company has a mandatory obligation under the Taft-Hartley Act to bargain with union representatives concerning an economically motivated decision to subcontract out work which had theretofore been performed by the employees in the bargaining unit. In the now-famous *Fibreboard Paper Products* case,[34] the Court affirmed the order of the Board requiring the company to resume the subcontracted operation and to reinstate the displaced employees with back pay. This decision was greeted with dismay by employers on the grounds that the requirement to bargain about what they considered to be vital management decisions with respect to operation of the business would result in endless delays and deprive business of flexibility in an era when change and prompt reaction to change are the keynotes of business. On the other hand, the Board contends that where subcontracting impinges upon work which the bargaining unit is qualified to do, the union should have an opportunity to discuss with the employer the proposed decision to give this work to others.

A second class of bargaining subjects falls in a prohibited category. These are items, such as the closed shop, which Congress has declared contrary to public policy. Finally, there are matters which may be classified as "nonmandatory subjects," such as, for example, an employer demand that the union contract contain a clause calling for a prestrike secret vote of the employees as to the employer's last offer. The Supreme Court has held that the parties can talk about such subjects, but if either party

---

[31] *General Telephone*, 54 LRRM 1055, *affd.* CA 5(1964), 57 LRRM 1055.

[32] *NLRB* v. *Richford Oil Corp.*, CA D.C. (1956), 37 LRRM 2327; cert. denied S. Ct. (1956), 37 LRRM 2837.

[33] *Central Illinois Public Service Co.*, 51 LRRM 1508, affd. CA 7(1963), 54 LRRM 2586.

[34] *Fibreboard Paper Products Corp.* v. *NLRB*, 57 LRRM 2609, 379 U.S. 203 (1964).

insists upon inclusion of such matters in a contract, it violates the good-faith bargaining requirement of the law![35]

The good-faith bargaining requirement of the Taft-Hartley Act has been the subject of so much litigation, has resulted in so many controversial decisions, and has caused so much delay in collective bargaining negotiations that employers, unions, and the Board alike agree that a change is desirable. As to what that change should be, however, there is no agreement. Many economists believe that the distinctions between mandatory and nonmandatory bargaining are satisfactory for the courtroom but not for the smoke-filled conference room, and that collective bargaining would benefit if the Section 8(a)(5) provision were scrapped. Employers would like to eliminate the power of the Board in this area, which they believe infringes on the right to manage their business. Employer opposition also stems from the fact that the Board has used this section of the law to require bargaining with a union even where it may have lost an election, as we observed in our earlier discussion.

On the other hand, unions and the Board are concerned by the fact that the simple order to bargain is not effective in compelling a truly recalcitrant employer to deal with the union, except after what may be years of litigation. Numerous study commissions, beginning with the Senate Advisory Panel on Labor-Management Relations Law in 1960, have taken note of the inadequacy of the Board's power under Section 8(a)(5) and have observed that the resultant delays have frequently been injurious to the rights of employees. Some labor experts believe that new remedies need to be fashioned, such as, for example, making the benefits of a contract retroactive to the date of the first refusal by the employer to bargain in good faith. This, however, would be an extreme remedy which, again, would take us a long way down the road to compulsory arbitration; for it would put the Board in the position of writing a contract for labor and management which the parties had never mutually agreed to. Thus far, the Board has declined to take such drastic action and has relied primarily on cease and desist orders.

HOW UNIONS WERE AFFECTED

Unfair Labor Practices

The Wagner Act sought to overcome the disparity of bargaining power between employers and employees which existed at the time of its enactment. Therefore, its restrictive provisions were all directed at employers, while unions were left free to engage in strikes, picketing, and various forms of coercion short of violence, in order to achieve organiza-

---

[35] *National Labor Relations Board* v. *Wooster Division of Borg-Warner Corp.*, 356 U.S. 342, 78 S. Ct. 718 (1958).

tion of the workers. For this reason the Wagner Act was criticized as being a one-sided law. The Taft-Hartley Act was designed to remedy this one-sidedness. It proceeded on the assumption that substantial equality of bargaining power had been achieved and that therefore both union and management should be subject to similar prohibitions regarding unfair practices.[36] The bulk of unfair labor practice cases handled by the Board continue to be brought against employers, but a substantial number now involve complaints against unions. In the fiscal year ended June 30, 1970, a total of 7,330 unfair labor practice charges were filed against unions.[37]

The unfair labor practices to which unions are subject are six in number, enumerated in Section 8(*b*) of the act:

1. *Restraint or Coercion.* It was made an unfair labor practice for a union to restrain or coerce employees in the exercise of the rights guaranteed them in Section 7. The latter guarantees the right to bargain collectively through representatives of the employees' own choosing and also the right to refrain from such activity (except where a union shop has been authorized by law). Most of the unfair labor practice charges filed against unions involve alleged violation of this section of the law. In fiscal 1970, 4,055 charges were filed alleging illegal restraint and coercion of employees by unions.[38] Among the union activities which have been found violative of this section of the act are mass picketing, the blocking of ingress to and egress from struck plants, and threatened physical violence toward employees. Recently, the statutory language has been construed to impose an obligation upon a labor organization, when acting as exclusive bargaining agent, to refrain from taking any "unfair" action against employees in matters affecting their employment. The NLRB has held that a union was guilty of an unfair labor practice where it unfairly reduced an employee's seniority classification.[39] On the other hand, the Supreme Court, by a divided vote, sustained the Board's holding that a union did not violate this section of the act when it imposed and subsequently instituted court proceedings to enforce fines against members who crossed a lawful picket line in support of the union's authorized strike.[40]

2. *Illegal Demands for Union Security.* It was made an unfair labor practice for a union to cause an employer to discriminate against an employee for nonmembership in a union unless there was a union security contract with the employer which was recognized under the act. The closed shop was prohibited, even though both employer and employees

---

[36] Despite this change in emphasis, more than 80% of the Board's time under the Taft-Hartley Act has been spent in handling cases submitted by unions, not employers.

[37] *Thirty-Fifth Annual Report, of the NLRB*, p. 11.

[38] *Ibid.*

[39] *Miranda Fuel Company, Inc.,* 51 LRRM 1585.

[40] *NLRB* v. *Allis Chalmers Manufacturing Company,* 338 U.S. 175.

were satisfied with its operation. This prohibition, if enforced, could have had far-reaching effects upon labor relations in view of the fact that prior to enactment of the Taft-Hartley law, in the neighborhood of 4.8 million employees worked under closed-shop arrangements.[41] However, on the whole, closed-shop industries have either ignored the prohibition or circumvented it. This part of the law imposes no penalties and therefore is not brought into operation unless an individual employee charges an unfair labor practice.

A union-shop provision in a collective agreement was recognized under the act if it allowed at least 30 days after hiring before new employees were required to become members of the union. However, before a union could negotiate such a security provision, it was required to fulfill a number of conditions: (*a*) file all required reports and affidavits, (*b*) receive designation as bargaining representative by a majority of the employees, (*c*) show that at least 30% of the employees in the bargaining unit wish to authorize the union to make a union security agreement, and (*d*) secure a majority vote of all employees in the unit in favor of such a clause, in a specially conducted NLRB election. The requirement of a special election proved to be a time-consuming and costly formality. In October 1951, after a period of four years in which the NLRB held 46,146 union-shop elections, of which 97% authorized the union shop, the act was amended by the so-called "Taft-Humphrey amendments" so as to permit voluntary union-shop contracts without elections.

Even if a union satisfied all the requirements enumerated above and even if an employer engaged in interstate commerce was willing to grant the union shop, its inclusion in a collective bargaining contract was prohibited under the act if the particular state in which the business was located imposed more drastic conditions on union security clauses or forbade them entirely. Despite dire predictions by labor leaders, there is no evidence that this latter provision seriously weakened the labor movement, although it did accelerate enactment of "right-to-work" laws by a number of states. As of January 1972, the union shop was prohibited in 19 states.

As was pointed out in Chapter 6, the Taft-Hartley Act makes it illegal for a union or an employer to enforce a union security clause against anyone for any reason other than nonpayment of dues or initiation fees. The inclusion of this clause in the act is evidence of the concern of Congress that the union shop, by giving the union a monopoly of job opportunities in the particular establishment, might be used as a club to intimidate workers who disagreed with the policies of union officials.

3. *Refusal to Bargain.* It was made an unfair practice for a union to refuse to bargain collectively with an employer. This provision was

---
[41] *Monthly Labor Review,* Vol. 64 (May 1947), p. 766.

apparently directed at those unions which had become so powerful that their "bargaining" activities consisted of presenting demands with a "take it or leave it" attitude. It is doubtful, however, that this provision has brought about any change of attitude by unions in negotiations, since the act makes it clear that the obligation to bargain in good faith does not compel a union (or an employer) to "agree to a proposal or require the making of a concession." Furthermore, bargaining by ultimatum by unions seems to have been sanctioned by the NLRB under certain circumstances, yet denied to employers. (See *GE* case, *supra*.)

For example, in one recent case,[42] the Board held that the unions involved did not refuse to bargain in good faith by giving the employer an ultimatum backed by a strike threat to sign certain contract proposals immediately, without any further opportunity to consult with its bargaining agent. The ultimatum was the culmination of protracted bargaining which had extended over a period of five months and resulted in an impasse.

4. *Illegal Strikes and Boycotts.* Section $8(b)(4)$ of the act made it an unfair labor practice for a union to engage in or to encourage any strike[43] or refusal by employees to use, manufacture, transport, work, or handle goods if an object of such action was one of the following:

a) To require an employer or self-employed person to join a union or an employer organization. The purpose of this clause was to prevent unions from forcing independent businessmen, such as plumbers, bakery deliverymen, and others, to join a union. Congress believed that the economic independence of these groups should be protected, even though their hours of work and earnings might affect the standard of employees who work for hire in the same occupation.

b) To force the employer or any other person to cease dealing in the products of another employer or to cease doing business with any other person. This clause was directed at the so-called "secondary boycott." If employees in plant A strike to compel employer A to grant higher wages or to grant a union shop, this involves direct action against the employer primarily involved in the dispute; but if the employees, having a grievance against employer A, picket or induce a strike in company B, which uses the products of plant A, then a secondary boycott or secondary action is involved. Congress not only made the secondary boycott an unfair labor practice but it also directed the NLRB to seek federal court injunctions against its continuance under certain circumstances and, furthermore, authorized damage suits to be brought in federal court by employers against unions which engage in secondary boycotts. Congress thus condemned secondary boycotts because they unduly widen

---

[42] *Lumber and Sawmill Workers' Union,* 47 LRRM 1287.

[43] The act defined "strike" to include a concerted stoppage or slowdown.

the area of industrial disputes by interrupting the operations of employers only remotely connected with the chief cause of the controversy.

Congress may also have been concerned about the secondary boycott because it had become a potent weapon in the hands of strong labor unions to force union membership on unwilling employees. Since the national labor policy now stated that employees should have the right to join or to refrain from joining a union (unless there was a compulsory union-shop provision in effect), it is not surprising that Congress found it necessary to restrict boycotts in order to make employee rights of self-determination effective.

Union leaders objected vehemently to these provisions of the act. They pointed out that the act even outlawed such traditional union action as a concerted refusal to handle "scab" products made in a nonunion shop or in a shop in which a strike was in progress. Even where one nonunion employer threatened the working standards of an otherwise fully organized industry, a refusal on the part of employees in the organized plants to handle or process goods intended for or coming from the nonunion plant would violate the act.

While it is clear from the foregoing discussion that the Taft-Hartley Act effectively curtailed many forms of union secondary boycott activity, nevertheless, it also left major loopholes. Thus, if a Teamster business agent attempted to persuade X's employees not to handle the goods manufactured by Y, this was unlawful; yet the act did not prohibit the business agent from warning X directly that he had better not handle Y's product! Likewise, the act permitted boycott action applied through inducement of employees individually, instead of in concert, and inducement of employees of railroads, municipalities, and governmental agencies. Inducement of supervisors was also not barred by the original Taft-Hartley language, because the statute referred to inducements to the "employees of any employer," and the definition of "employee" in the act excluded supervisory personnel. One other loophole resulted from NLRB rulings on "hot cargo" agreements. After some vacillation the Board held that "hot cargo" agreements could validly be included in collective bargaining agreements and presumably could be enforced by appropriate court action. The fact that they were sanctioned as a subject of collective bargaining and were included in contracts enforceable in law strengthened the hands of unions in making secondary boycott action effective.

One of the most difficult problems arising in connection with the ban on secondary boycotts was the determination as to where primary action ended and secondary action began. For example, if a picket line around plant A in which a labor dispute existed prevented drivers from employer B from entering and picking up merchandise, was the picket line unlawful because of its effect on employees of employer B? The NLRB has answered no, since the strike against A is privileged activity, and the repercussions on B are only incidental. But suppose the primary dispute is with a trucking company. Can the employees of that company picket the trucks they are loading and unloading on the premises of employer A? This raises the question of the so-called "ambulatory situs" —the trucks are in a sense an extension of the employer's business site. The Board has ruled that such picketing is permissible where it is confined to one employer and conducted at the only place where the union could picket effectively.[44]

In the subsequent *Moore Drydock* case,[45] the Board developed a set of standards in which picketing of the secondary employer's premises is permissible if:

1. The picketing is strictly limited to times when the *situs* of dispute is located on the secondary employer's premises;
2. At the time of the picketing the primary employer is engaged in its normal business at the situs;
3. The picketing is limited to places reasonably close to the location of the *situs;* and
4. The picketing discloses clearly that the dispute is with the primary employer.[46]

These standards sought to balance the conflicting interests of union and the neutral employer. However, in subsequent decisions the Board has seemed to move away from the Moore standards and has permitted secondary picketing under circumstances seemingly in conflict with the Moore doctrine.[47]

Another situation in which the line between primary and secondary action is blurred is the so-called "common situs" problem, which has been a major source of friction in the construction industry, where it is customary for a general contractor and various subcontractors to work on the same premises. Suppose employees of the general contractor or union subcontractors picket the premises in protest over another subcontractor using nonunion labor. Under the Board and court interpretations of Section 8(*b*)(4)(*A*), such action has been held to be a secondary boycott. It is not surprising that the building-trades unions are the most frequent users of the secondary boycott technique. For the fiscal year 1970, *NLRB* records show that 2,290 secondary boycott charges were filed with the Board.[48] Unions in the building and construction field were involved in a large number of such complaints. The building-trades unions

---

[44] *Schultz Refrigerated Service, Inc.,* 87 NLRB 502 (1949).

[45] *Sailors' Union* (Moore Drydock Co.), 92 NLRB 547 (1950).

[46] 92 NLRB at 549.

[47] For a discussion of this subject, see Ralph M. Dereshinsky, *The NLRB and Secondary Boycotts* (Labor Relations and Public Policy Series, Report No. 4 [Philadelphia: Industrial Research Unit, Wharton School of Finance and Commerce, University of Pennsylvania, 1972]), particularly pp. 5–49.

[48] *Thirty-Fifth Annual Report of the NLRB,* p. 11.

contend there is no secondary boycott action involved because there is really only one employer—the general contractor—and all of the subcontractors are so related to him by the nature of the work that they cannot be considered to be "neutrals" so far as picketing is concerned. The Supreme Court, however, has held that the subcontractors are to be treated as independent employers in considering the applicability of Section 8(*b*)(4)(*A*).[49]

c) *To force or require an employer (including the employer of the strikers) to recognize or bargain with one union if another union is the certified bargaining agent, or to force another employer (not the employer of the strikers) to recognize an uncertified union.* This clause was intended to protect employers from strikes by an uncertified union, aimed at compelling the employer to deal with it rather than with another union already certified. Under the Wagner Act, many companies found themselves in a disastrous dilemma as a result of rivalry between CIO and AFL unions. If the employer yielded to the pressure of the uncertified union, he violated the Wagner Act and was subject to sanctions for so doing. If he did not yield, his business could be destroyed. He could get no injunction or court relief against the picketing because of the anti-injunction provisions of the Norris-La Guardia Act. The dilemma to the employees was as real. Because they had exercised their right of free choice, they stood to lose their jobs through the efforts of the union which they had rejected.

The attempts on the part of unions to nullify the right of workers to join unions of their own choosing were indefensible and completely at variance with the basic principles of the Wagner Act. Such activities were also, of course, part of the basic conflict between the principle of exclusive jurisdiction upon which American unionism had been built and the principle of self-determined organization which the Wagner Act made law.

The Taft-Hartley Act made such strikes illegal and made it mandatory for the NLRB to seek injunctive relief in the courts, if, after a preliminary investigation, there was reason to believe that the union was engaging in a strike prohibited by this section.

d) *To force or require an employer to assign particular work to employees in one union or craft rather than to employees in another union or craft.* This clause was intended to outlaw the so-called "jurisdictional" strike. Such strikes, growing out of controversies as to which craft has the right to perform a particular job, were particularly common in the construction industry and evoked widespread public criticism. As a direct result of the enactment of the Taft-Hartley law, the building-trades unions set up machinery to adjust jurisdictional disputes among the various crafts.

---

[49] *NLRB* v. *Denver Bldg Trades Council,* 341 U.S. 675 (1950).

A union which engaged in any of the activities banned in the above four situations committed an unfair labor practice and rendered itself liable in damages to anyone whose business or property was injured as a result of the strike. Moreover, when a charge was filed alleging that a union was engaging in activities under (*a*), (*b*), or (*c*) above, it was made mandatory that the Board seek an injunction against the union, if the Board had reasonable cause to believe the charge was true. In the case of jurisdictional disputes, however, the Board had to hear and decide such cases itself unless, within 10 days after the charge was filed, the parties agreed to voluntary adjustment. The mandatory injunction provision mentioned above did not apply to jurisdictional disputes, but the NLRB could seek an injunction in situations where such relief was appropriate.

In the fiscal year ended June 30, 1970, injunctions were granted in 31 cases involving jurisdictional disputes, most of them in the building and construction industry.[50] It is obvious from this record that the machinery set up by the building trades to handle their disputes is not fully effective.

Although the Board has often been attacked for injecting itself into the substance of collective bargaining, it religiously refrained from making determinations of work assignments in jurisdictional dispute cases coming before it. In 1961, however, in the *Columbia Broadcasting* case,[51] which involved a dispute between a union of television technicians and a union of stage employees over which union would control the work of providing electric lighting for television shows, the Supreme Court held that the NLRB could not "duck" this responsibility imposed upon it by Congress and that it must make an affirmative award of disputed work in such cases. The assumption by the Board of the role of arbiter in such disputes will add pressure on unions to settle such controversies through their own dispute machinery.

5. *Excessive Initiation Fees.* It was made an unfair labor practice for a union which had a union-shop agreement to charge membership fees in an amount which the Board found excessive or discriminatory under all the circumstances. In a number of cases, the Board has ordered a union to reduce its admission fees, but the total effect of this provision has been minor.

6. *Featherbedding.* It was made an unfair labor practice for a union to "cause or attempt to cause an employer to pay or deliver or agree to pay or deliver any money or other thing of value, in the nature of an exaction, for services which are not performed or not to be performed." This clause is sometimes referred to as the "antifeatherbedding" provision; but actually, its scope is much more limited than the practice of

---

[50] *Thirty-Fifth Annual Report of the NLRB*, p. 131.

[51] *National Labor Relations Board* v. *Radio and Television Broadcast Engineers' Union*, 364 U.S. 573, 81 S. Ct. 330 (1961).

make-work rules which is ordinarily encompassed within the term "featherbedding." If some work is performed in return for the compensation—even though it is mere standing around during a recorded broadcast—then the statutory requirement of "services which are not performed" is not satisfied, and the provision is not applicable. Thus, the Supreme Court ruled that the practice of the International Typographical Union in requiring pay for setting so-called "bogus" type which is not used and the practice of the American Federation of Musicians of requiring pay for "standby orchestras" when outside bands play in local theaters were both lawful under this provision.

Loyalty Affidavit

One of the most controversial provisions of the act was directed at Communist officers who have been in power in a few American unions. Section 9(b) of the act disqualified a labor organization both as a bargaining agency and as a complainant under the act unless there was on file with the Board an affidavit executed

by each officer of such labor organization and the officers of any national or international labor organization of which it is an affiliate or constituent unit that he is not a member of the Communist Party or affiliated with such party, and that he does not believe in, and is not a member of or supports any organization that believes in or teaches the overthrow of the United States Government by force or by any illegal or unconstitutional methods.

This provision evoked considerable criticism, from both unions and other sources, on the ground that it was unconstitutional to discriminate on the basis of membership in the Communist party when that party was a legal organization entitled to a place on our electoral ballots. However, the Supreme Court settled this issue in 1950 by ruling that Congress had a right to require the oaths to protect the public against the "evils of conduct." Union spokesmen also argued against the one-sided nature of the affidavit provision, which required the loyalty oath from union officers but not from employers.

Noncompliance by many Communist-dominated unions did, however, prove very detrimental to these organizations, and severe membership losses were suffered by many of them. Today, as noted in Chapter 2, only two significant Communist-dominated unions remain—the International Longshoremen's and Warehousemen's Union and the United Electrical, Radio and Machine Workers of America. Although these results derived in part from causes other than the Taft-Hartley Act, there is no question but that the act strengthened the hand of non-Communist elements in unions and paved the way for the decline of Communist influence in the labor movement.

Reports and Financial Accounts

The act also required unions to file with the Secretary of Labor copies of their constitutions, bylaws, reports showing salaries of officers above $5,000, initiation fees, and annual financial statements. The only sanction applied for failure to file reports was denial of use of the machinery of the NLRB. Unfortunately, the unions which did not voluntarily file financial reports were concentrated in the buildings and amusement trades; they were so well entrenched that they had little need to use the NLRB and therefore did not have to comply with such provisions. The reporting provisions of the act were repealed by the Landrum-Griffin Act (see Chapter 20).

Restrictions on Political Contributions

The act made it unlawful for any labor union to make a contribution or expenditure in connection with any election to any federal political office. The prohibition as to contributions corresponded to a similar prohibition applicable to corporations under the Corrupt Practices Act. Addition of the broad term "expenditures," however, in the restriction applicable to unions, raised doubts as to the constitutionality of the provisions. The Supreme Court has held that the ban of this section does not apply to expenditure of union funds in publishing the *CIO News*, which advised members to vote for certain candidates in a congressional election.[52]

Contributions to Union Welfare Funds

In recent years, health and welfare funds supported in whole or in part by employer contributions have become increasingly popular as a subject of union-management negotiation. Such funds require the collection of very large sums of money. Consequently, Congress felt the need for legislation which would hold union leaders to strict accountability in the administration of such sums. Section 302 of the act attempted to accomplish this purpose by permitting welfare funds maintained by employer contributions only when the payments are held in trust and the fund is administered jointly by employer and employee representatives, with neutral persons available to settle possible disputes. However, funds in existence prior to January 1946 were exempted. Furthermore, experience demonstrated that employers evidence little interest in the administration of such joint funds, with the result that in some industries, corrupt union officials have been able to utilize to their own personal gain the tremendous sums which build up in such funds over a period of time. Congressional investigation of the handling of

---

[52] *U.S.* v. *CIO*, 22 LRRM 2194.

certain of these welfare funds led to such shocking disclosures that it became clear that further legislation would be required in order to conserve and protect such funds against possible abuses. The Teller Act of 1958 and the Landrum-Griffin Act were direct results of such investigations.

HOW THE INDIVIDUAL WORKER WAS AFFECTED

A major objective claimed by the framers of the Taft-Hartley Act was to protect individual employees from the arbitrary power wielded by some labor leaders. Consequently, a number of important new privileges were granted to employees, with corresponding limitations on unions, on the theory that the actions of the latter have not always been truly representative of the will of the workers in the collective bargaining unit.

Elections

The Taft-Hartley Act made a number of important changes in election procedure. Under the original Wagner Act procedure, if two or more unions were on the ballot in an election to choose a bargaining representative, the employees voting in a "runoff" election did not have an opportunity to cast a negative vote (i.e., "no union") in the runoff, unless the no-union choice had received a plurality of votes cast in the first election. In other words, the employees were limited in the runoff election to a choice between two unions, even though one of these unions might have run in third place. Later the NLRB changed this procedure by requiring the two highest choices to be placed on the runoff ballot, so that the no-union choice could appear on the runoff ballot even if it had not received a plurality of votes in the first election. The Taft-Hartley Act made this procedure a matter of law.

The act also gave employees the right to seek elections to decertify a bargaining representative which no longer represented th majority of workers. In decertification elections held under the act, the bargaining representative has been decertified in about two out of every three elections, indicating that in many cases unions in the course of time cease to represent the will of the workers.

Representation elections still require a major portion of the Board's time. In fiscal 1970, the Board conducted 8074 secret ballot representation elections of which 80% were arranged by agreement of the parties as to the appropriate unit, date, and place of election.[53] Table 19–1 indicates how the number of elections held annually has risen steadily over the years, while the percentage won by unions has tended to decline.

---

[53] *Thirty-Fifth Annual Report of the NLRB*, p. 7.

TABLE 19–1

Results of NLRB Representation Elections
(selected years 1936–70)

	Elections		Employees Involved	
Fiscal Year	Total	Percent Won by Unions	Total Eligible	Total Valid Votes Cast
1936.........	31	81	9,512	7,572
1940.........	1,192	77	595,075	532,955
1945.........	4,919	83	1,087,177	893,758
1950.........	5,619	74	890,374	786,382
1955.........	4,215	68	515,995	453,442
1960.........	6,380	59	483,964	436,723
1965.........	7,576	61	531,971	480,280
1967.........	7,882	60	611,006	542,999
1970.........	8,074	55	608,558	531,402

Source: National Labor Relations Board data.

The Taft-Hartley Act also made an important change in the rule governing the right of employees on strike to vote in representation elections. Under the Wagner Act the Board had ruled that in a strike caused by employer unfair labor practices, only strikers were eligible to vote, since they were entitled to reinstatement; whereas in a strike over economic issues, both replacements and strikers were eligible to vote. The Taft-Hartley Act, however, contained a specific provision that "employees on strike who are not entitled to reinstatement shall not be eligible to vote." In an economic strike the employer has the legal right to fill jobs of strikers with permanent replacements. Therefore, in an economic strike, strikers who are replaced could lose the right to vote in a representation election. This provision was attacked by union spokesmen, who claimed that it would enable antiunion employers to provoke a strike, recruit nonunion replacements, and then call for an election. The strikebreakers could elect "representatives," and this would bar an independent, effective union from calling an election for a year, or they might vote for decertification of the existing union. This provision, which became known as a "union-busting" provision, was amended by the Landrum-Griffin Act, as explained in Chapter 20.

Ban on Compulsory Checkoff

The act prohibited the compulsory checkoff, the method by which union dues are deducted by the employer from the worker's wages and paid directly to the union treasury. The checkoff of membership dues was made lawful only where individual employees execute a written assignment of wages for not longer than one year or for the duration of the applicable union contract, whichever is shorter.

Bargaining Unit Problems

Under the Taft-Hartley Act, as under the Wagner Act, the NLRB continued to be vested with authority to determine the appropriate bargaining unit. This authority, however, was limited in the case of professional employees, craft workers, and guards.

Craft-Industrial Problems. As we have noted in our discussion of the Wagner Act, one of the most difficult problems faced by the NLRB was the contest between AFL and CIO unions as to whether the appropriate bargaining unit should be a craft or an industrial unit. Congress, of course, had been concerned primarily with the question whether employees wanted *any* union to represent them, rather than *which* union. This highly explosive issue was dumped into the lap of the NLRB with little statutory guidance to assist it in its determination. Section 9(*b*) of the Wagner Act simply directed the Board to "decide in each case whether, in order to insure to employees the full benefit of their right to self-organization, and otherwise to effectuate the policies of the Act, the unit appropriate for the purposes of collective bargaining shall be the employer unit, craft unit, plant unit, or subdivision thereof."

In making such determinations, the NLRB found that it had to weigh and balance two often conflicting objectives of labor policy: self-determination and stability in industrial relations. Self-determination, which favored craft severance, could, if carried to an extreme, result in the fragmentation of collective bargaining into a myriad of small, ineffective units. Moreover, it raised the problem of multiplicity of negotiations, more jurisdictional disputes, and possible weakening of industrial unions. On the other hand, the policy of stability, which was frequently synonymous with favored treatment for industrial unions, could mean that individual crafts would be submerged in a large union without regard to their peculiar problems. Moreover, preference for larger industrial unions could lead to dissatisfaction among substantial groups of employees within the union.

The Board wrestled with this problem throughout the Wagner Act period. In the early years, it tended to favor large industrial unions as most conducive to effective collective bargaining. Then, in 1937, this trend was reversed, and the Globe doctrine[54] evolved, which in most instances allowed craftworkers in initial representation elections to determine whether they wanted to be in a plantwide union or have a separate

---

[54] The *Globe* doctrine, which involves the principle of self-determination by a particular group of employees as to their bargaining unit, is so called because it was first enunciated in the case of the *Globe Machine and Stamping Co.*, 3 NLRB 294 (1937).

craft. The Board was for a time more reluctant to allow craft severance where craftsmen had already been included in a large industrial union; but in 1942 the Board's policy shifted, and severance was permitted where a "true" craft was involved.

However, the Board's policies on bargaining units did not satisfy either the CIO or the AFL. The Taft-Hartley Act sought to settle this issue by writing into law the restriction that the Board may not decide that a craft unit is inappropriate on the ground that an industrial unit had already been established by a prior Board determination, unless a majority of employees in the proposed craft unit voted against the craft unit. This clause was criticized by CIO officials, who argue that it could be used to permit various splinter craft groups to break off from established industrial unions. These fears proved groundless, however; and in actual practice, this provision produced little change in NLRB procedure with regard to representation of skilled crafts. The NLRB wisely interpreted this provision as prohibiting it from using a prior unit determination as the sole ground for decision as to the appropriateness of a craft union, but as still giving it discretion to include skilled workers in a larger industrial union where the work of the skilled group is so integrated with that of the production workers that a separate unit would be inappropriate.

Under its present practice, the Board now considers all relevant factors to determine a severance issue, such as whether the employees sought are skilled journeymen craftsmen or constitute a functionally distinct department; bargaining history at the plant and in the industry; the extent to which the employees have established or maintained their separate identity; the integration of the production process; and the qualifications of the union seeking severance.[55]

Extent of Bargaining Unit. The power of the Board to determine the appropriate bargaining unit can have a material effect upon the ability of unions to organize the unit in question. Generally, the smaller the unit, the easier it is for the union to obtain a majority of the employees, but fragmentation of bargaining units would create a difficult problem for employers, who might find that they have to bargain with many different unions in a multiunit organization. In both the retail industry and the insurance industry, the Board originally believed that wider geographic units were appropriate, but after finding that a large unit inhibited organization, it changed its policy to approve smaller units. Thus, in the retail chain store field, prior to 1961, the Board's policy was to make bargaining units coextensive with the employer's administrative division or the geographic area involved. However, this policy was abandoned in the *Sav-on Drug* case,[56] which involved a group of chain drugstores. Under

---

[55] These criteria were enunciated in *Mallinckrodt Chemical Works*, 64 LRRM 1011.

[56] *Sav-on Drugs, Inc.*, 51 LRRM 1152.

the Board's present practice in the retail chain store field, the individual store will be found to be an appropriate unit where there is substantial autonomy in each store and no material interchange of employees. Similarly, in the insurance industry, the Board originally concluded that statewide units were appropriate,[57] but after years of experimentation it changed its policy and found the district office to be more appropriate.[58]

Critics of the Board have accused it of going too far in the direction of atomizing bargaining units, so that in department store units, for example, there may be separate bargaining units for selling and non-selling personnel. However, in appraising the administration by the Board of its duty to determine the appropriate bargaining unit, it is important to realize that the Board has had no clear guide as to congressional intent and that the Taft-Hartley Act actually contains conflicting statements of statutory policy. It was, in a sense, a political instrument which attempted in one law to appease critics of the Wagner Act yet not wholly alienate organized labor. Although the Taft-Hartley Act added many provisions apparently intended to restrict actions of the Board which, under the Wagner Act, had seemed to favor labor unduly or had neglected the rights of individual workers who did not want to be represented by unions, nevertheless Section 1 of the act, which contains the general statement of statutory policy, retains language clearly affirming it to be the policy of the United States to encourage "the practice and procedure of collective bargaining." Since the determination of the appropriate bargaining unit is a typical kind of administrative decision involving the application of expertise, the Board can exercise wide discretion in its weighing of the relevant issues and can obviously consider the impact of the unit determination on collective bargaining, as long as the extent to which employees have organized is not controlling.

The power of the Board in this area is particularly impressive because it is normally not subject to court review. Although Section 10 of the act provides for court review in the case of any person "aggrieved by a final order of the Board," the Supreme Court has decided that certifications of a bargaining agent are not "final orders" in this sense and therefore cannot be appealed to the courts.[59] Normally, the only way an employer can obtain judicial review of an NLRB order in an election case is to refuse to bargain with the union certified by the Board. When the union brings an unfair labor practice charge, the NLRB's order to bargain can be appealed, and at such time the certification of the bargaining agent and the record of the election are subject to review by the

---

[57] *Metropolitan Life Insurance Company*, 56 NLRB 1635.

[58] *Quaker State Life Insurance Company*, 134 NLRB 960.

[59] If, however, a Board certification violates an express provision of the statute such as improperly grouping together professional and nonprofessional employees in the same bargaining unit, the courts will set aside the action of the Board (*Leedom* v. *Kyne*, 358 U.S. 184, 79 S. Ct. 180 [1958]).

court. However, this process is not open to a union that wishes to challenge an election ruling.

Discrimination against Minority Groups

Section 8 (*a*) (3) of the act provided that an employer was not justified in discriminating against an employee for nonmembership in a labor organization if he had reasonable ground for believing that such membership was not available to the employee on the same terms and conditions generally applicable to other members. At first glance, this appears to mean that a union-shop contract could not be applied to black employees unless blacks were fully and equally admitted with whites to union membership. However, another section (8[*b*][1]) provided that a union shall have the right to prescribe its own rules with respect to the acquisition or retention of membership. Moreover, the Senate-House Conference Report expressly declared that the act did not disturb arrangements in which Negroes were relegated to an auxiliary local.[60]

For many years the Taft-Hartley Act had little or no effect upon discrimination against blacks practiced by unions. However, as public opinion focused more and more on this problem, the NLRB gradually evolved the doctrine that a bargaining agent certified by a public authority had a duty to represent all members of the bargaining unit fairly. Thus, in *Pioneer Bus Company*,[61] the Board stated that execution of a contract that discriminates on the basis of race would endanger a union's certification as exclusive bargaining agent and would not bar an election sought by another union. In *Hughes Tool Company*,[62] the Board found a union guilty of unfair labor practices and stripped it of its certification as bargaining agent because of its racial discrimination practices. And in *International Longshoremen's Association, Local 1367*,[63] the Board found a union local guilty of unfair labor practices where it had established separate all-white and all-black locals and divided work unfairly.

A federal court has held that the prohibitions in the Taft-Hartley Act against unfair labor practices also ban discrimination on the basis of race. In *United Packinghouse, Food and Allied Workers* v. *NLRB*[64] the Court of Appeals for the District of Columbia Circuit ruled that a policy and practice of discrimination by an employer against employees on account of race or national origin would constitute a violation of Section 8(*a*)(1).

---

[60] The Conference Report refers specifically to the case of *Larus and Brother Co.*, 62 NLRB 1075 (1945), as an example of an arrangement not disturbed by the act. Any other interpretation would have alienated southern Democrats, who were among the Taft-Hartley Act's most ardent supporters.

[61] 51 LRRM 1546.

[62] 56 LRRM 1289.

[63] 148 NLRB No. 44.

[64] 70 LRRM 2489 (D.C. Cir., February 7, 1969).

There is perhaps a more understandable relationship between the grant of an exclusive bargaining power to a union and its duty to represent all employees in the unit fairly than the relationship between the employer's duty not to discriminate to deter unionization and the obligation to treat all races equally. Nevertheless, the Court found that the latter obligation was consistent with the purposes of the Taft-Hartley Act because racial discrimination would create industrial unrest and induce apathy on the part of minority employees which would deter them from asserting their full rights under the act. If this interpretation is sustained by the Supreme Court, the Taft-Hartley Act and the Board may become the focal point for a flood of cases alleging that employers are parties to racial discrimination, despite the fact that Congress has provided another remedy for such cases under Title VII of the Civil Rights Act of 1964 (see Chapter 23).

Other Procedural Safeguards

Among other important rights given to individual employees to strengthen their positions relative to the union was the power to sue the union for damages resulting from an illegal strike. Also, the employee was given the right to present grievances directly to his empoyer and to have such grievances adjusted without the intervention of the union representative. The adjustment could not be inconsistent with the terms of the collective bargaining agreement, and the union was given the right to have its representative present at the adjustment.

HOW THE PUBLIC WAS AFFECTED BY THE LAW

One of the major reasons for enactment of the Taft-Hartley Act was the general recognition on the part of the public and lawmakers that some means had to be devised to protect the community from stoppages of the flow of essential commodities and services such as characterized the wave of strikes in 1946. The Wagner Act itself had contained no prohibition against strikes of any kind; instead, it provided a peaceful alternative to the costly strikes which had been fought over the denial of basic rights of union recognition. In 1937, 60% of the workers on strike were involved in organizational disputes. In 1945, only 22% of the strikers were out on organizational strikes.[65] Thus, the Wagner Act was successful in reducing this particular form of work stoppage. At the same time, however, strikes over economic issues—wages, hours, and working conditions—increased in importance. Moreover, industrywide bargaining led to walkouts involving an entire industry instead of merely one

---

[65] National Labor Relations Board, *Eleventh Annual Report* (Washington, D.C.: U.S. Government Printing Office, 1946), p. 2, n. 1.

plant. Thus, the same number of strikes in 1946 as in 1937 produced four times as many man-days lost in the later year. The Taft-Hartley Act attempted by a number of procedures and prohibitions to narrow and restrict the use by organized labor of the strike weapon.

Prohibited Strikes

Certain types of strikes deemed unduly oppressive to employers and the public were outlawed. These have been considered earlier in this chapter and included secondary strikes and boycotts, jurisdictional disputes, and strikes to upset the certification of a rival union. Any person injured in his business or property as a result of such unlawful strikes could bring suit for damages against the offending union.

Strikes against the federal government were likewise forbidden, and any individual employed by the United States who went on strike was subject to immediate discharge and loss of civil service status. We shall discuss this section in Chapter 22.

Strikes called in violation of no-strike clauses in collective bargaining agreements were not prohibited, but the act provided a procedure whereby the union could be sued by the employer in federal court for damages due to breach of contract. It was hoped that the act, by facilitating the bringing of suits against unions, would make for stricter observance of such clauses and thus lessen the number of work stoppages.

National Emergency Strikes

Finally, the Taft-Hartley Act established procedures to govern so-called "national emergency" strikes. This procedure, which is discussed in Chapter 21, did not, however, forbid such strikes but merely provided for their postponement.

APPRAISAL OF THE TAFT-HARTLEY ACT

Whether the Taft-Hartley Act is a "good" or a "bad" law depends in large measure upon the standard by which it is judged. If it is deemed desirable to afford greater freedom and privileges of self-determination to the individual worker, then it would seem that the act constituted a rather hesitant advance in labor legislation. On the other hand, if one believes that progressive social policy requires strengthening labor organizations on the theory that all but a few unions are still at a disadvantage in bargaining with employers, then the various restrictions imposed upon the activities of unions appear less desirable.

Standards, therefore, affect one's view of the act, and such standards frequently reflect the social bias of the individual. However, one standard is at hand which lends itself to a fairly objective appraisal. That is the extent to which the act facilitated the process of effective collective bargaining.

Ways in Which the Act Encouraged Effective Collective Bargaining

Effective collective bargaining may be defined as bargaining which in general represents the will of the majority of workers. The decertification procedure provided by the Taft-Hartley Act enabled employees to rid themselves of a union which because of corrupt leadership or other causes no longer represented the majority of workers. Likewise, the Communist affidavit requirements may have served to lessen industrial disputes which reflected, not the bona fide grievances of workers, but rather the planned intrigues of Communist officials. The prohibition against the closed shop and restrictions on the union shop were intended to eliminate practices such as the selling of jobs through issuance of work permits which benefited the union bosses rather than the union membership; but these provisions were largely ineffective.

Effective collective bargaining assumes also a balance of power between labor and management. Under the Wagner Act, however, the balance of power in some industries had been so turned in labor's favor that individual employers had no choice but to accept the union's demands. The Taft-Hartley Act sought to remedy this situation by imposing an obligation to bargain upon both the union and the employer. Moreover, on the premise that effective collective bargaining requires responsible parties to the agreement, the act made unions subject to court actions for breach of contract. But this premise ignored the fact that sound industrial relations are not built by running to the courts. Furthermore, as we have already observed in the prior discussion, the plethora of Board and Court decisions on what constitutes good-faith bargaining has probably been detrimental to the establishment of sound voluntary bargaining relations.

Effective collective bargaining assumes that the democratic privilege of self-determination of wages, hours, and working conditions will be reasonably exercised so as not to inconvenience the public by widespread work stoppages. Such union devices as the secondary boycott, jurisdictional strikes, and industrywide strikes in essential industries unnecessarily burden the public. Therefore, the Taft-Hartley Act narrowed the use of the strike weapon within limits deemed consistent with the public interest.

Ways in Which the Act Impeded Effective Collective Bargaining

The act enabled employers to delay peaceful determination of a bargaining representative through the NLRB machinery and therefore encouraged unions to strike to obtain recognition. An employer bent on delaying an election for certification of a bargaining representative could delay proceedings by charging the union with unfair labor practices, and since most organizing campaigns usually involve some "high-pressure" salesmanship by union advocates, a prima facie case of coercion frequently could be made out. On the other hand, recent NLRB rulings have all gone far to eliminate the employers' right of free speech.

The act used as a sanction in a number of provisions the deprivation of rights under the act. Thus, for example, employees who struck in violation of the cooling-off period provisions and unions which failed to sign non-Communist affidavits were forbidden to use the machinery of the Board. Obviously, however, these men and these unions would continue to take part in industrial relations, and their unprotected status only invited attacks by antiunion employers. If the objective of the act was equality between management and unions in collective bargaining, sanctions for enforcement should not have been put in the hands of employers. Such a policy invites industrial unrest rather than compliance with the act.

The act was intended to restore the balance of power in collective bargaining relations. But Congress had in mind the circumstances which exist in highly organized industries, without fully recognizing that in some areas, organization is still in an incipient state and that in such areas the act gave an antiunion employer power to prevent the emergence of effective collective bargaining. Particularly potent in this respect were the provisions which guaranteed the employer "free speech" and enabled him to sue a union in federal court (and thus weaken it financially) and to charge it with unfair labor practices in organizing. Under other provisions of the act an employer could provoke a walkout over economic issues and then be free to replace the strikers with nonunion men. The act stated that the strikers could not vote in an election, but the strikebreakers were given this privilege. Antiunion employers could thus use a strike over wages to change the bargaining representative in their plants. Again recent administration of the act has re-altered this power balance and particularly left small employers with little recourse to resist large unions.

The Taft-Hartley Act represented a step in the direction of government dictation of the content of collective bargaining agreements. The act told employers and unions what they could and what they could not include in contracts with respect to welfare plans, union security clauses, and checkoff of dues. While this approach is probably unavoidable if the purpose of the act to protect employees is to be made effective, in the long run this trend may prove detrimental to continuation of voluntary collective bargaining. As we shall see in the next chapter, the Landrum-Griffin Act takes an even bigger step in this direction and subjects the internal affairs of union organizations to governmental regulation.

Effect of Taft-Hartley Act on Growth of Union Organization

There is no question that the rate of growth of unions has slowed down in recent years and that from 1947 to the present, contrary to experience in prior years, unions have grown at a slower rate than the labor force. It is not clear, however, whether the full blame for labor's organizing woes can be put on the Taft-Hartley Act, although labor leaders find this legislation a convenient excuse for lack of progress. As we observed in Chapter 2, it seems likely that more fundamental developments may be responsible for the decline of union membership, among them the shift in employment from manufacturing to service industries; the tremendous growth in white-collar employment; the geographical shift of industry to the Midwest and to the South, where public opinion has been more hostile to union organization than in other sections; the lack of aggressive leadership in unions; and the increasing difficulty of union organization now that most large companies are organized and it is in the smaller companies that unions must seek new members.

Criticism of Administration of the Act by the NLRB

Many critics of our present labor policy have aimed their attack, not against the Taft-Hartley Act, but rather against the manner in which the NLRB has administered it. It should be recognized that the NLRB is more than an administrative body carrying out the mandate of Congress. It is also a policy-making body, and almost necessarily so; for the Taft-Hartley Act merely sets forth rules in general terms, and it is the function of the Board to amplify this language so that it is applicable to the multitude of diverse cases which present themselves to it for decision.

In recent years the Board, as administered by appointees of the Kennedy and Johnson administrations, has been subject to sharp attack by management spokesmen for alleged bias in favor of labor. The record shows that various Board decisions have restricted management prerogatives and favored unions in a number of critical areas:

1. Blunting restrictions on union tactical weapons, such as the picket line.
2. Restricting employer counterweapons, such as employer free speech.
3. Defining the bargaining unit to facilitate organizing efforts of unions.
4. Relying on card checks as opposed to secret ballot elections in cases where employers have been accused of unfair labor practices.

Although it is true that the Board has seemingly tipped the balance in favor of organized labor in the above described areas, it is also true that, in general, its views on these controversial issues have been upheld by the U.S. Supreme Court.

There is no question that the composition of the Board, as changed by

Presidential appointments from time to time, has made a difference in its attitude toward labor and management. In some ways, this makes the evolution of labor policy more responsive to changing public attitudes, as evidenced by changing national administrations. On the other hand, Board members are called upon to carry out quasi-judicial functions, and therefore many critics contend that they should be appointed for life so that they are not subject to political influences.

The lack of regard for *stare decisis* by the Board has made it difficult for management and labor leaders alike to make policy decisions with any assurance that they will comply with what the Board considers lawful practice. Many lawyers argue that if the Board wishes to change a long-standing policy, it should do so by utilizing the process of the Administrative Procedures Act, which requires due notice and an opportunity to argue the merits of the new policy. The Board, on the contrary, simply uses a particular case as a vehicle to change its policy, which can be obviously unfair to the participants in that case.

Suggestions for Reform

Proposals for changing both the act and the Board have been forthcoming in increasing numbers in recent years from labor, management, members of the bar, labor economists, and from members of the NLRB itself. Board Chairman Edward B. Miller has openly admitted that the Board as presently constituted cannot cope with the steadily rising case load which threatens to engulf it.[66]

Many of the suggested reform measures which have been proposed make a distinction between the two basic functions of the Board. The first is the determination by secret ballot elections (and occasionally by card checks) whether employees in an appropriate bargaining unit wish to have unions represent them in collective bargaining negotiations with employers. This is a typical administrative function in which the Board has developed considerable expertise. The Board conducts about 8,000 elections every year, and most are run without incident. Since its inception, the NLRB has conducted more than 200,000 elections in which more than 26 million voters have cast their ballots for or against representation. Today about four out of every five elections are conducted on an amicable basis by agreement between the employer and union.[67]

Although the Board's decisions on appropriate bargaining units have frequently been attacked and its use of card checks rather than secret

---

[66] See Address by Edward B. Miller to Labor Law Conference, Louisiana State University, Baton Rouge, La., January 22, 1971, reported in 76 LRR 89.

[67] John H. Fanning, "The Viability of NLRB Regulation in the Future," in Richard L. Rowan (ed.), *Collective Bargaining: Survival in the 70's?* (Philadelphia: Industrial Research Unit, Wharton School of Finance and Commerce. University of Pennsylvania, 1972), p. 29.

ballot elections in limited cases has raised the ire of employers, the fact remains that it has handled the overall election procedure with reasonable efficiency. The median time from filing a representation petition to the date of the election has averaged about 49 days—certainly a creditable performance for an administrative agency. By contrast, in unfair labor practice cases, the median time from the filing of a charge to the date of the Board decision has averaged 319 days.[68] It is doubtful that a labor court would improve on the Board's performance in representation matters.

A second function of the Board is to prevent and to remedy unfair labor practices whether committed by unions or employers. It is in this area that the Board is particularly vulnerable. The accusation has continually been made that the Board, with a membership which changes with shifts in political power on a national scene, cannot be judicial; yet in the unfair labor practice area, it in effect must make judicial decisions. Suggestions for reform run the gamut from formation of a Labor Court to giving jurisdiction of unfair labor practice cases to federal courts.[69]

Justice must be timely or it is not justice. This aphorism is as true in labor relations as it is in the courts of law. Reinstatement which comes three years later to an employee who has been wrongfully discharged may be an empty victory. Yet in Section $8(a)(3)$ unfair labor practice discharge cases, the total median days elapsed from filing of the charge to issuance of a circuit court enforcement order has been about 855 days![70] The Board itself has recognized that new procedures are needed to expedite unfair labor practice case handling. Member Fanning recommends a certiorari type of review procedure in unfair labor practice cases which would permit the Board to delegate any of its functions to its Trial Examiners, with the Board retaining a discretionary right of review in the nature of a certiorari proceeding with two Members possessing the power to grant Board Review. It has been estimated that between 100 and 140 days could be saved through implementation of this concept.[71] Although it is true that such procedures may save time, this delegation of judicial functions would hardly answer the criticism of those who wish to eliminate all Board action of this kind because of the alleged political bias of Board members.

One way that the Board could expedite cases, and thus provide greater justice where a real need exists, is to resist expanding its jurisdiction and to establish priorities among types of cases. Thus, in recent years, despite its expanding backlog, it has asserted jurisdiction over univer-

---

[68] Fritz Lyne, "The National Labor Relations Board and Suggested Alternatives," *Labor Law Journal*, Vol. 23 (July 1971), p. 411.

[69] *Ibid.*

[70] Charles J. Morris, "The Need for New and Coherent Regulatory Mechanisms," in Rowan, *Collective Bargaining*, p. 44.

[71] Fanning, "Viability of NLRB Regulation," pp. 37–38.

sities and nursing homes, adding thereby to its case load. Many of the cases filed under Sections 8(a)5, and (b)3, the "bargaining in good faith" sections, are merely tactical bargaining techniques. Dr. Bernard Samoff, director of the NLRB's Fourth Regional Office, has suggested that the Board establish a priority list of cases and place 8(a)5 and (b)3 cases at the bottom to discourage their use.[72] Professor George W. Taylor has long advocated that, except for the initial contract between unions and companies, Board jurisdiction in "good-faith" bargaining cases be eliminated. Many other authorities not only agree but would eliminate these sections entirely, not only to reduce the Board's backlog, but also to block its propensity to insert into the substantive areas of collective bargaining.[73]

Union spokesmen argue that the best way to expedite the handling of unfair labor practice cases is to reduce the case load and that this will only happen when the Board is given the power to assess sufficiently stringent penalties so as to deter unfair labor practices on the part of employers. The AFL–CIO, for example, recommends that the Board should have the power to disqualify from federal government contracts or orders employers who deliberately and repeatedly violate the Act.[74] Union spokesmen have also argued that the Board should have the power to assess double or treble damages against employers in flagrant discharge cases.

Another frequent suggestion is that the Board be given power to grant injunctive relief. At present, if a party violates a Board order, the Board must seek to enforce it in a federal court of appeals. It is at this stage that the longest delays occur, since it requires on the average an additional 396 days before a court of appeals renders its decision in such cases.[75]

Although a number of recent proposals[76] as well as legislation introduced in Congress incorporate the concept of a labor court to handle labor cases, it is doubtful that the NLRB will be scrapped for such an alternative. Even the Ervin Committee—which certainly was not a friend

---

[72] See Bernard Samoff, "The Case of the Burgeoning Load of the NLRB," and "Coping with the NLRB's Growing Caseload," *Labor Law Journal,* Vol. 22 (October 1971), pp. 611–30; and (December 1971), pp. 739–62.

[73] See George W. Taylor, "Collective Bargaining in Transition," in Arthur Weber (ed.), *The Structure of Collective Bargaining* (New York: Free Press, 1961), pp. 343, 347–48. See also *The Public Interest in Collective Bargaining* (New York: Committee for Economic Development, 1961), pp. 81–82; William Gomberg, "Government Participation in Union Regulation and Collective Bargaining," *Labor Law Journal,* Vol. 13 (November 1962), pp. 941, 946–47; Herbert R. Northrup, *Compulsory Arbitration and Government Intervention in Labor Disputes.* (Washington, D.C.: Labor Policy Association, 1966), pp. 103–5; and Samoff, "Case of the Burgeoning Load," pp. 611–30.

[74] *AFL–CIO American Federationist,* Vol. 78 (December 1971), p. 23.

[75] 84 Harv. L. Rev. 1670, 1673.

[76] See, for example, Morris, "Need for New Mechanisms," pp. 42–76.

of the Board—concluded after long hearings that a labor court would merely freeze labor law doctrine rather than improve it and would ac-centuate the undesirable reliance on adjudication rather than rule-making in cases where discretion exists.[77]

QUESTIONS FOR DISCUSSION

1. What is meant by the term "unfair labor practice"? How are charges of unfair labor practices handled by the NLRB? How does the Taft-Hartley Act differ from the Wagner Act in its approach toward unfair labor practices?
2. What is meant by "mandatory" and "nonmandatory" subjects of collective bargaining? Give examples of each. Does this distinction make sense in practical collective bargaining? Do you think that the "good-faith" bar-gaining provisions of the Taft-Hartley Act should be repealed?
3. In what way have recent decisions by the NLRB tended to facilitate union organization? Is this action consistent with the statutory purposes set forth in the Taft-Hartley Act?
4. Discuss the actual and potential effects of the Taft-Hartley Act upon collective bargaining.
5. In what respects, if any, do you think the Taft-Hartley Act should be changed. How would you implement your decision?

SUGGESTIONS FOR FURTHER READING

ABODEELY, JOHN E. *The NLRB and the Appropriate Bargaining Unit.* Labor Relations and Public Policy Series, Report No. 3. Philadelphia: Industrial Research Unit, Wharton School of Finance and Commerce, University of Pennsylvania, 1971.

A detailed analysis of NLRB bargaining unit policy and its evolvement over the years.

HERMAN, EDWARD E., and SKINNER, GORDON S. *Labor Law: Cases, Text, and Legislation.* New York: Random House, Inc. 1972.

A convenient source book for some of the leading cases in labor law.

LYNE, FRITZ L. "The National Labor Relations Board and Suggested Al-ternatives," *Labor Law Journal,* Vol. 22 (July 1971), pp. 408–23.

A review and appraisal of various proposals to abolish the Board and to substitute for it a new system to carry out its functions.

MOORE, JOSEPH E. "The National Labor Relations Board and Supervisors," *Labor Law Journal,* Vol. 21 (April 1970), pp. 195–205.

A discussion of the impact of the Taft-Hartley provisions on unioniza-tion of foremen.

MORRIS, CHARLES J. "The Need for New and Coherent Regulatory Mecha-nisms," in ROWAN, RICHARD L (ed.), *Collective Bargaining: Survival in the*

---

[77] 73 LRR Anal 36 (March 2, 1970).

70's? Philadelphia: Industrial Research Unit, Wharton School of Finance and Commerce, University of Pennsylvania, 1972, pp. 42–76.

A review of the inadequacies in present NLRB administration and a proposal for a labor court.

NATIONAL LABOR RELATIONS BOARD. *Annual Report.* Washington, D.C.: U.S. Government Printing Office.

The annual reports of the Board, covering operations of the fiscal year ended June 30, are excellent sources for statistics as well as providing a summary of action taken by the NLRB on key issues.

"NLRB Power to Award Damages in Unfair Labor Practice Cases," *Harvard Law Review,* Vol. 84 (May 1971), pp. 1670–1701.

A note discussing the inadequacy of remedies available to the Board and the legality of assessment of punitive or compensatory damages.

Chapter 20

THE LANDRUM-GRIFFIN ACT

In the preceding chapters, we have seen how the role of law and government has evolved in the field of union-management relations. The Norris–La Guardia Act was essentially laissez faire in attitude. The purpose of the statute was to prevent law—in the form of the court injunction—from interfering with union-management relations. Then came the Wagner Act, in which the force of law was used to assist organized labor. Government power was committed to protect the right to organize and to restrict employer interference with such rights. Union tactics were left virtually unregulated. As a result of its favored position, organized labor grew so strong that abuses developed, and the need was recognized for restrictions on the power of unions. The Taft-Hartley Act was enacted, with government now placed in the role of policing certain actions of both labor and management. However, abuses continued to come to light in the internal administration of unions. Since much of the power wielded by unions over individual workers stems from union monopoly over job opportunities provided under both the Wagner and the Taft-Hartley Acts, government has felt a responsibility to safeguard the rights of individual union members. As a result, the conduct of internal union affairs has come to be viewed as a federal problem.

Regulation of internal union procedures is a major purpose of the Labor-Management Reporting and Disclosure Act of 1959, more popularly known as the Landrum-Griffin Act. Passage of this law marked the culmination of the well-publicized hearings of the Senate Select Committee on Improper activities in the Labor or Management Field (McClellan Committee), which revealed that many union officials were guilty of coercion, violence, and denial to union members of basic rights; that small employers were being victimized through use of secondary boycotts, extortion, picketing, and similar techniques; and that employers were guilty of interfering with employee rights through use of "sweetheart" contracts and bribery of union officials by hired consultants.

SCOPE AND COVERAGE OF THE ACT

The Landrum-Griffin Act comprises seven different sections, called "titles," each of which deals with a different phase of the act's coverage. Title I contains a bill of rights for members of labor organizations. Title II requires unions and employers to file various reports[1] with the Secretary of Labor. Title III requires unions to file reports relating to so-called "trusteeships" over other labor organizations. Title IV contains detailed provisions with respect to the term of office of union officials, election procedures, and procedures for removal of union officers. Title V contains provisions relating to the fiduciary responsibility of union officials, requires the bonding of such officials, prohibits loans by unions to employees of such organizations resulting in a total indebtedness in excess of $2,000, and prohibits certain classes of persons with records of crime or Communist affiliation from holding union office. Title VI contains a number of miscellaneous provisions, among them a prohibition against extortionate picketing and a grant of power to the Secretary of Labor to investigate violations of the act.

Title VII contains a number of amendments to the Taft-Hartley Act relating to federal-state jurisdiction, voting rights of economic strikers, and secondary boycotts and recognition picketing. Many congressmen believed that the Landrum-Griffin Act should stand on its own feet and deal only with new areas of regulation, leaving to later enactments the complex task of amending the Taft-Hartley Act. However, so much pressure was brought to bear upon Congress, particularly with respect to the inadequacies of the Taft-Hartley Act prohibitions against secondary boycotts and picketing, that Title VII, embodying such amendments, was finally incorporated in the law as passed.

The act grants to the Secretary of Labor broad powers to investigate possible violations of the law and to institute appropriate civil or criminal action. This authorization does not, however, apply to the bill-of-rights section or to the amendments of the Taft-Hartley Act. In the case of violations of the former section, union members must bring their own civil actions in the U.S. district courts. As to the latter category, enforcement is the responsibility of the National Labor Relations Board. A Bureau of Labor-Management Reports—now called the Office of Labor-Management and Welfare-Pension Reports (LMWP)—was established in

---

[1] None of the above-described reports relate directly to the operation of employee welfare and pension plans. Reporting on the operation of such funds is covered by a different statute—the Welfare and Pension Plans Disclosure Act of 1958, as amended in 1962, more commonly known as the Teller Act. This act requires that a description of every plan covered by the act be filed with the Secretary of Labor; and thereafter, annual reports must be filed, giving details of operation of the funds. Broad powers of investigation and enforcement are granted to the Secretary of Labor; but as noted in previous chapters, major abuses in this area are still extant, and much more money is involved in welfare and pension funds than in union treasuries.

the U.S. Department of Labor to handle the day-to-day administration of the act. This office reported about 51,000 active disclosure files as of June 30, 1970.[2]

Like its predecessor, the Taft-Hartley Act, the Landrum-Griffin Act relates to employers and labor organizations in industries "affecting commerce." However, the scope of the latter is broadened by the fact that many of its provisions are applicable to employees and employers covered by the Railway Labor Act, who were expressly excluded from the Taft-Hartley provisions. The definition of "employer" includes anyone considered an employer under any federal law. The definition is thus the most comprehensive to be found in federal law.

HOW THE EMPLOYER WAS AFFECTED

The Landrum-Griffin Act imposes new obligations as well as new benefits upon employers.

Restrictions on Employers

Although the McClellan Committee devoted most of its attention to abuses of labor organizations, it uncovered a number of examples of malpractice by employers in their dealings with employees and unions. Thus, some companies paid union officials in order to obtain so-called "sweetheart" contracts, which permitted continuation of substandard working conditions; or companies conspired with officials of a "friendly" union to permit organizing of the company's workers to the exclusion of other more belligerent unions. The committee also found evidence that some companies were interfering with the rights of employees to organize by using so-called "labor consultants." The committee noted that the Taft-Hartley Act could not deal effectively with such activity because the NLRB had no power to act against independent contractors serving as labor consultants.

Title II of the Landrum-Griffin Act requires employers to file annual reports with the Secretary of Labor disclosing payments and loans to unions, union officers, shop stewards, and employees of unions. The reporting requirement applies to payments and loans, whether direct or indirect, whether in cash or other things of value, but excludes deductions of union dues pursuant to a checkoff and certain other classes of "valid" employer payments. Other subsections require reports by employers of payments to employees, employee committees, or labor consultants which

---

[2] U.S. Department of Labor, Labor-Management Services Administration, *Compliance, Enforcement and Reporting in 1970 under the Labor-Management Reporting and Disclosure Act.* (Washington, D.C.: U.S. Government Printing Office, 1971), p. 2.

might affect the free choice of employees to exercise their right to organize and bargain collectively. Labor consultants who, pursuant to an arrangement with an employer, undertake to persuade employees in the exercise of their organizing or bargaining rights, or to supply information to the employer concerning employee or union activity in connection with a labor dispute, except information solely for use in legal or arbitration proceedings, must also file detailed reports.

Title V of the law expands Section 302 of the Taft-Hartley Act by broadening the types of payments which are criminal offenses. Payments are now unlawful, for example, if they are made by an employer or his agent to:

1. Any representative of his employees.
2. A union, or its officers or employees, which is seeking to represent or represents or would admit to membership employees of the employer.
3. Employees or committees of employees of the employer in excess of their normal compensation for the purpose of causing them to influence other employees in the exercise of their organizing or bargaining rights.
4. Any officer or employee of a union with intent to influence him with respect to his actions or duties as a union representative or official.

Lawyers have expressed concern that these criminal provisions are very broad—in fact, broader than the corresponding reporting provisions contained in Title II, so that, technically, certain payments which need not be reported may actually be criminal offenses! Furthermore, since certain acts which must be reported are subject to criminal penalties, there is some question as to the constitutionality of these reporting requirements in view of the protection against self-incrimination guaranteed under the fifth amendment. From the date of passage of the act to June 30, 1970, only 2,059 employer reports had been filed with the LMWP.[3] The low incidence in reporting is undoubtedly attributable in large measure to the fact that the clearest examples of reportable activities are often those which constitute a violation of section $8(a)$ of the Taft-Hartley Act, with the result that persons so involved are understandably reluctant to make a full disclosure.

Benefits of Landrum-Griffin Act to Employers

Although the reporting requirements of the Landrum-Griffin Act are onerous to employers already burdened by reporting requirements of many other federal agencies, nevertheless the benefits to employers conferred by the new law far outweigh its disadvantages. Despite some weakening of the provisions of the act by NLRB and court decisions, the

---

[3] *Ibid.*

sections of the act further restricting secondary boycotts and organizational picketing by unions are of substantial importance to employers. So also are the sections aimed at eliminating the so-called "no-man's land" in NLRB jurisdiction.

Restrictions on Union Secondary Boycotts

We observed in the preceding chapter that although the Taft-Hartley Act purported to outlaw secondary boycotts, many loopholes developed in practice. Thus, if a Teamster business agent attempted to persuade X's employees not to handle the goods manufactured by Y, this was unlawful; yet the Taft-Hartley Act did not prohibit the business agent from warning X directly that he had better not handle Y's product! Likewise, the former law permitted boycott action applied through inducement of employees individually, instead of in concert, and inducement of employees of railroads, municipalities, and governmental agencies. The Landrum-Griffin Act closed all of these loopholes.

Under the Taft-Hartley Act, it was common practice for unions to induce employers to sign collective bargaining agreements which contained a so-called "hot cargo" clause. In accepting this provision, the employer agreed that his employees would not handle the goods of anyone with whom the union was having a labor dispute. The act makes it an unfair labor practice for any labor organization and any employer to enter into such agreements. Two exceptions are provided in the statute: agreements in the construction industry relating to contracting or subcontracting of work done at the construction site and agreements relating to jobbers, subcontractors, and the like in the apparel and clothing industry.

Despite the legislative history of the Landrum-Griffin restrictions on "hot cargo" and secondary boycott action by unions, the U.S. Supreme Court in 1967 held that a union did not violate the "hot cargo" or secondary boycott provisions by maintaining and enforcing contract provisions that (1) gave union members the right to refuse to install prefabricated doors at a construction project and (2) specified that an employer would not subcontract certain construction work. The majority of the Court—with four justices dissenting—said that even if such conduct comes within the broad language of the statutory prohibitions, it was not congressional intent to ban traditional primary activity of unions. In the view of the majority, the action of the union was not "secondary" action but was rather designed to preserve work traditionally done by the union members with the primary employer.[4]

The effect of the statutory restrictions against secondary boycotts

---

[4] *National Woodwork Manufacturers Assoc.* v. *NLRB*, 64 LRRM 2801, 386 U.S. 612 (1967).

has also been weakened by interpretations of the Board and the courts of the so-called "publicity proviso." This proviso appears in the amended Section 8(b)(4) of the National Labor Relations Act after enumeration of prohibitions on various forms of strikes and boycotts. The proviso states:

Provided further, that for the purposes of this paragraph (4) only, nothing contained in such paragraph shall be construed to prohibit publicity, other than picketing, for the purpose of truthfully advising the public, including consumers and members of a labor organization, that a product or products are produced by an employer with whom the labor organization has a primary dispute and are distributed by another employer, as long as such publicity does not have the effect of inducing any individual employed by any person other than the primary employer in the course of his employment to refuse to pick up, deliver, or transport any goods, or not to perform any services, at the establishment of the employer engaged in such distribution.

Since the above-mentioned proviso specifically excludes "picketing" from protected union activity, it was generally assumed that picketing in connection with secondary boycott action was unlawful even when directed to the public. However, in a decision handed down by a divided Court, the Supreme Court has indicated that this is not so. In the case before the Court, a Teamsters' union, which had a primary dispute with an organization of fruit packers, set up picket lines in front of retail stores which sold fruit purchased from the packers. The picket signs advised consumers not to buy the fruit because it was nonunion. Pickets were instructed not to patrol delivery entrances or exits, and other precautions were taken not to interfere with the flow of merchandise in and out of the stores. No employees stopped work, and deliveries were not affected. Nevertheless, the NLRB found that the union action was unlawful secondary boycott action intended to force the stores to cease doing business with the packers. However, when the case reached the Supreme Court, the Court reversed the Board and held that so-called "consumer picketing" at neutral stores for the purpose of persuading customers to cease buying *products* of a struck primary employer does not violate the law, even though it may cause economic loss to the stores of the neutral third party.[5] The Court concluded that Congress had not intended to ban all consumer picketing and that it was necessary to distinguish between a union appeal to the public not to trade with the secondary employer (presumably unlawful) and what the Court found existed in the present case—a union appeal to the public not to buy the merchandise of the primary employer.

Although the *Tree Fruits* decision was greeted with dismay by management spokesmen, who argued that it emasculated the proviso of

_____
[5] *National Labor Relations Board* v. *Fruit Packers Local 760,* 55 LRRM 2961 (1964).

Section 8 (*b*)(4), the loophole so opened has been a narrow one and has been restricted by subsequent decisions. For example, in a case involving the Teamsters' Union, picket signs at a restaurant stated: "To the consumer: Sunshine Bread is sold here. Do not buy Sunshine Bread." The restaurant did not retail bread but served it with meals. The NLRB found that this picketing was illegal on the ground that it was conducted for the purpose of inducing customers not to eat at all at the restaurant rather than merely not to eat Sunshine Bread. The Board did not think it realistic that customers could select the brand of bread they wanted in a restaurant, and therefore sympathizers with the union's message would probably go elsewhere.[6]

The *Tree Fruits* decision has not advanced the cause of generalized union label picketing. In *Bedding, Curtain and Drapery Workers Union Local 140* v. *NLRB*,[7] the union picketed three retail furniture stores in connection with its disputes against one of their suppliers, a bedding manufacturer. The picket signs stated: "Appeal to the public. Please do not buy nonunion furniture, upholstery and bedding. Look for this union label when buying furniture, upholstery and bedding. (Union Label) United Furniture Workers of America, AFL–CIO." The Court upheld the NLRB's cease and desist order under Section 8 (*b*)(4). It distinguished *Tree Fruits* on the basis that the picket signs did not specify the company or its product in its message to consumers. It stated that the union's appeal to "look for the label" was not specific enough identification of the boycotted product or company and that the appeal to forgo purchases of nonunion furniture, upholstery, and bedding was too broad, since the primary employer manufactured only bedding. The court concluded that the consumer picketing had failed to isolate the dispute and was closer to an appeal to shut off all trade with the secondary employer than to picketing which only persuades customers not to buy the struck product.

It is apparent from the foregoing discussion that while the Landrum-Griffin amendments further tightened restrictions on secondary boycotts, the new language apparently contains its own "loopholes," but only a case-by-case clarification will determine precisely what they are. There will undoubtedly be many years of litigation and possible further congressional legislation before limitations on secondary boycotts are clearly defined.

Restrictions on Picketing

The same can be said of the Landrum-Griffin restrictions on picketing. The act makes extortionate picketing—picketing intended to "shake

---

[6] *American Bread Company*, 170 NLRB 91.

[7] 390 F 2d 495 (2d Cir. 1968).

down" an employer for the personal profit of a union agent rather than for the benefit of employees—a federal offense. Furthermore, in perhaps the most controversial section of the law, major restrictions are imposed upon recognition and organizational picketing. The new law makes it an unfair labor practice for a labor organization to picket or threaten to picket an employer where an object thereof is forcing or requiring an employer to recognize or bargain with a labor organization as the representative of his employees, or forcing or requiring the employees of an employer to accept or select such labor organization as their collective bargaining representative, unless such labor organization is currently certified as the representative of such employees, under any of the following circumstances:

(A) Where an employer has lawfully recognized another union and the question of representation may not be legally raised at this time.
(B) Where a Taft-Hartley Act election has been held within the past 12 months.
(C) Where the picketing has been conducted without a petition for a representation election being filed within a reasonable period of time, not to exceed 30 days from commencement of the picketing.

The application of these provisions is made subject to a so-called "consumer picketing" proviso, which has been the source of much controversy. It states, in substance, that nothing in subparagraph (C), quoted above,

. . . shall be construed to prohibit any picketing or other publicity for the purpose of truthfully advising the public (including consumers) that an employer does not employ members of, or have a contract with, a labor organization, unless an effect of such picketing is to induce any individual employed by any other person in the course of his employment, not to pick up, deliver or transport any goods or not to perform any services.

The scope and meaning of these provisions is by no means clear, and a definitive interpretation of the foregoing language must await determination by the Supreme Court. Meanwhile, the National Labor Relations Board, in a series of influential decisions, has laid out these guidelines based upon its construction of the statutory language:

1. *Informational Picketing.* If the sole object of the picketing is to inform the public, and recognition of the union is not an objective of the picketing, the picketing is lawful and is not barred by any of the subsections enumerated above. Furthermore, even if such picketing interferes with deliveries or pickups, it is lawful nontheless.[8]

2. *Dual-Purpose Picketing.* A picket line frequently has as its purpose both informing the public and securing recognition by an employer. Such picketing is presumably unlawful where the circumstances set out

---

[8] *Crown Cafeteria*, 49 LRRM 1648, reversing 47 LRRM 1321.

in subsections (A) and (B) above prevail. If (A) or (B) is not applicable, such picketing is entitled to the protection of the proviso to subsection (C) unless it interferes with deliveries, etc.[9] The NLRB has further held that mere isolated interferences with deliveries are not enough to make the picketing illegal. Despite the fact that the consumer picketing proviso expressly refers to "*an* effect" and "*any* individual" (italics added), the NLRB has read the language as if Congress were concerned only with a "substantial" effect and has held that there is a violation of the law only if picketing has "disrupted, interfered with or curtailed the employer's business."[10]

3. *Recognition Picketing.*   Picketing intended to compel the employer to recognize the union as bargaining representative for his employees is subject to the prohibitions of subsection (C), and the picketing will be enjoined if it continues more than 30 days without a petition for an election being filed.[11] The Board has held, however, that so-called "union standards" picketing is not recognition picketing. Therefore, even if an employer has signed a contract with another certified labor organization, it is not unlawful, according to the NLRB, for another union to picket where the signs carried by the pickets merely state that the employer pays wages lower than the standards set by the picketing union, and there is no attempt by the union to obtain recognition from the employer.[12]

It is apparent from the foregoing brief outline that the NLRB has greatly narrowed the scope of the restrictive provisions contained in the Landrum-Griffin Act as they apply to picketing. Under the present Board, if the evidence shows that a union pickets an employer to protest against wage rates, unfair labor practices, working conditions, or discharge of employees, the NLRB will not interfere with the union action, even if deliveries to the employer are disrupted.

Many of the key decisions have been handed down by a divided Board. The application of the statute is obviously not clear to the members of the Board, and it is even more uncertain for the average union member. Gone are the simple days when the Norris–La Guardia Act granted automatic immunity to such action. By contrast, a union leader who today determines to place a picket line around a plant needs a lawyer at his side to guide him. The legality of the picketing may depend upon the wording of placards which the pickets carry and how people react to them. It may depend upon the relationship between the employer and

---

[9] *Ibid.*

[10] *Barker Bros. Corp. and Golds, Inc.,* 51 LRRM 1053.

[11] The statutory criterion is a "reasonable period of time not to exceed thirty days." The NLRB has held 17 days is a reasonable time in which to file in one case (*International Brotherhood of Teamsters,* 127 NLRB 958, enf. 289 F. [2d] 41) and 18 days in another (*Sapulpa Typographical Union,* 45 LRRM 2400).

[12] *Claude Everett Construction Co.,* 49 LRRM 1757.

the union, between the employer and a rival union, or between the employer and other employers with whom the union has a dispute. Most of all, the lawfulness of the picket line may hinge upon what the NLRB interprets the objective and purpose of the picket line to be.[13] To the average laboring man, such examination of motives and objectives seems like a return to the old doctrine of lawful and unlawful objectives, motives, and other mystical criteria which courts found so convenient in the past to justify injunctions against union activity.

Elimination of Jurisdictional No-Man's Land

Another important employer benefit conferred by the Labor Reform Act is the elimination of the so-called "no-man's land" created by the refusal of the National Labor Relations Board to assert jurisdiction over certain labor disputes which did not meet its jurisdictional standards. Under the Taft-Hartley Act the NLRB found it had neither the time nor the money required to handle the great number of labor disputes involving small employers; therefore, it imposed certain jurisdictional limitations on itself, stating in effect that it would not become involved in a dispute if the employer's sales volume was less than a certain prescribed figure. But when the small employer then went to the state court for relief, the U.S. Supreme Court ruled that the state court had no right to hear the case if the NLRB *could* have taken jurisdiction, even if it *did* not! As a consequence, small employers were denied a forum to give them relief from union coercive tactics, even though their larger competitors were protected by the NLRB.

The Landrum-Griffin Act seeks to solve this problem by amending the Taft-Hartley Act so as to permit the states to assert jurisdiction over labor disputes in interstate commerce over which the NLRB declines to take jurisdiction. The law authorizes the NLRB to decline to assert jurisdiction over any labor disputes which it determines would have only a slight impact upon interstate commerce, but it cannot reduce its jurisdiction below the standards prevailing on August 1, 1959. The Board is

---

[13] The *Crown Cafeteria* case is a good illustration of how subjective judgments —which reflect the particular bias of the Board member or judge—now determine the lawfulness or unlawfulness of a picket line. In that case a union picketed a new cafeteria which had refused to hire through a union hiring hall or to sign a contract. The picket signs were addressed to "members of organized labor and their friends," stated that the cafeteria was "nonunion," and asked them not to patronize it. No stoppage of deliveries or services took place. In its first hearing of this case, a majority of the NLRB concluded that despite what was said on the signs, the picketing was really conducted for recognition purposes and was therefore not protected by the consumer picketing proviso (47 LRRM 1321). Subsequently, two new members were appointed to the Board, and upon reconsideration of the case the Kennedy Board held that the picketing was lawful because it was conducted merely to advise the public and caused no stoppages (49 LRRM 1648).

free, of course, to expand its jurisdiction at any time. The states have always had jurisdiction of labor disputes in intrastate commerce and cases involving violence, mass picketing, or other coercive conduct. This jurisdiction has now been broadened to include cases in interstate commerce which formerly fell in the "no-man's land" area.

Although the Landrum-Griffin Act appears to have eliminated the question of conflicting jurisdiction over cases of labor disputes, it does not necessarily follow that either management or labor will find that turning these problems back to the states is wholly satisfactory. At this writing, only 15 states and Puerto Rico have comprehensive codes regulating labor relations. In 35 states, parties excluded from protection of the Taft-Hartley Act by reason of the Board's jurisdictional standards do not have recourse to comprehensive labor laws governing labor-management relations. In such cases, these excluded parties will have to rely upon common-law doctrines or their own economic power. The small businessman and the weak union are thus still penalized by lack of size. This problem can be met only by enactment of labor relations laws in all of the states or by a major expansion of the personnel of the NLRB so as to enable that agency to enlarge its jurisdiction. Neither of these possibilities appears to be very likely at this time.

HOW UNIONS WERE AFFECTED

The Landrum-Griffin Act is based upon the premise that unions and officials of unions have in many instances disregarded the rights of individual employees and that individual union members have been powerless to protect themselves against such tactics. The act therefore contains numerous restrictions on unions and union officials while conferring new rights and privileges upon individual union members.

Restrictions on Internal Union Affairs

The Landrum-Griffin Act repeals those provisions of the Taft-Hartley Act that required the filing of information as to the union's constitution, bylaws, and financial reports and also the filing of non-Communist affidavits. It substitutes new provisions requiring more detailed reports concerning the internal operation and financial condition of the union. Most important is the change in approach relative to enforcement. Whereas the Taft-Hartley Act punished failure to file required reports with a denial of the right to use the procedures of the National Labor Relations Board, the Landrum-Griffin Act imposes direct and severe criminal penalties.

Every labor organization is required to adopt a constitution and bylaws and file a copy with the Secretary of Labor. Furthermore, to the extent that the constitution and bylaws do not cover these points, the union must file a detailed statement as to qualifications for, or restrictions on, membership; procedures with respect to such matters as levying of assessments; audit of the financial transactions of the organization; discipline or removal of officers and agents for breaches of trust; imposition of fines, suspensions, and expulsions of members; and numerous other details as to the internal administration of the union. Have these and other provisions in the act had much of an impact upon union constitutions? Based on a study of 43 labor union constitutions, both before and after the 1959 effective date of the act, Professors Philip Ross and Philip Taft conclude that there has been little substantive amendment of union constitutions in response to the provisions of the act. However, they also conclude that the provisions of the act and its attendant threat of Department of Labor intervention may, at least, foster habits of constitutional care and an extension of due process guarantees to organized minorities within a union.[14]

Unions must also file annual financial reports which, in addition to the usual balance sheet, must disclose loans aggregating more than $250 made to any officer, employee, or member; direct and indirect loans to any business enterprise; payments, including reimbursed expenses, to officers and employees who during the fiscal year received more than $10,000 union compensation; and "other disbursements including the purposes thereof."

The objective of Congress in requiring financial reports by unions to be filed with government was to improve financial practices of such organizations and to make significant financial transactions of the union open to the scrutiny of the union membership. Unfortunately, there is considerable evidence that reports are simply being filed and not used, and that little change has occurred in the internal financial practices of unions. According to one recent study:

. . . the law's reporting and disclosure provisions added nothing of substance to existing requirements . . . labor unions did not react with changes in either their written policies or actual practices in financial controls . . . the various reports filed with the federal government have been, as they were before the law, largely inaccurate and unused.[15]

It has been suggested that in order to improve union accounting practices, mandatory audits be required by qualified independent accountants for unions over a designated minimum size.[16]

---

[14] Philip Ross and Philip Taft, "The Effect of the LMRDA upon Union Constitutions," *New York University Law Review*, Vol. 43 (April 1968), pp. 305–33.

[15] Emery C. Turner, "What Has Landrum-Griffin Accomplished?" *Labor Law Journal*, Vol. 20 (July 1969), p. 391. For a critique of Turner's study, see Michael S. Gordon, "Title II of the Landrum-Griffin Act—Some Reflections on the Limits of Reporting and Disclosure," *Georgia Law Review*, Vol. 5 (Summer 1971), pp. 687–708.

[16] Turner, "What Has Landrum-Griffin Accomplished?" p. 402.

Restrictions on Union Officials

Under the provisions of many state laws, officers and directors of business corporations are held accountable to strict standards of fiduciary responsibility. The Landrum-Griffin Act applies this principle to officials of unions, stating that officers, agents, stewards, and other representatives of labor unions must conduct themselves in accordance with the rules of law generally applicable to the dealings of a trustee with other people's money. The act establishes a new federal crime—embezzlement or other unlawful conversion of a union's assets by an officer or employee of the union—punishable by a fine up to $10,000, imprisonment up to five years, or both. Drawing on the principle of minority stockholder suits in corporation law, the act provides that if an officer or other representative is accused of violating his fiduciary responsibilities and the union fails to take action against such officer or representative in a reasonable time after being requested to do so by a union member, the latter may, with the court's permission, bring his own suit in state or federal court for an accounting, and attorney's fees may be awarded out of any recovery. In addition, the act establishes detailed bonding requirements for officers, agents, shop stewards, or other representatives of employees of unions who handle funds or other property of the union.

A major objective of the 1959 legislation was to stamp out racketeering, crime, and corruption in labor unions. To this end the act contains provisions designed to bring to light possible conflicts of interest and similar shadowy transactions through which unscrupulous union officials and employers sacrifice the welfare of employees to personal advantage. Thus, the Landrum-Griffin Act requires officers and employees of labor unions (other than employees performing exclusively clerical or custodial duties) who have engaged in certain transactions enumerated in the act to file annual reports with the Secretary of Labor, covering not only themselves but their wives and minor children, and disclosing payments, stock, or other interests acquired in or from companies which the union represents or seeks to represent. The filing of false reports is made punishable by a fine of up to $10,000, a year in jail, or both. These reports, as well as the reports which employers and labor consultants must file, as discussed previously, are required to be available for public inspection.

Unions are also prohibited from making, "directly or indirectly," any loan or loans to officers or employees which result in a total indebtedness of such individual to the labor organization of more than $2,000. The phrase "directly or indirectly" is included in the act to bar deals such as those used by James R. Hoffa to camouflage his financial manipulations. Hoffa's own Local 299 in Detroit, according to McClellan Committee testimony, once loaned $25,000 to a man who immediately reloaned it to Hoffa!

Persons convicted of serious crimes are barred for a period of five years after conviction from holding any union position other than a clerical or custodial job. This provision was included in the act because the Senate's McClellan Committee had found that a number of unions were under the control of gangsters and hoodlums. Unfortunately, however, the mere fact that the government or individual union members can sue to remove from office an officer with a criminal record does not permit the NLRB to deny certification to such a union when it uses the processes of the Board in a representation procedure. As one NLRB trial examiner put it: "Any thug, gangster, or murderer who is at large can establish himself as a labor organization and, if designated as exclusive bargaining representative by a majority of employees . . . can obtain board certification."[17] Furthermore, the Landrum-Griffin Act lists certain crimes as a bar to holding office, but presumably a union leader convicted of a crime not on the prohibited list would not be barred from continuing to hold office.

The act imposes a similar prohibition against members of the Communist party and ex-Communists for a period of five years after they have quit the party. Violation of these provisions—with respect both to criminals and Communists—is punishable by a fine of not more than $10,000 or imprisonment for not more than one year, or both. Whether these severe penalties will prove more effective than the affidavit requirements formerly included in the Taft-Hartley Act in ridding unions of Communist officials is doubtful. Thus far no effective enforcement has occurred.

The Landrum-Griffin Act prohibits union representatives from requesting or receiving various types of payments from employers or their consultants. The use of force or threats of force against union members to interfere with the exercise of any of their rights under the act is made a federal offense. The act also requires every labor organization "to inform its members concerning the provisions of this Act"—a provision which has led many unions to reproduce the act verbatim in union newspapers.

Trusteeships

The constitutions of many international unions authorize the international officers to suspend the normal processes of government of local unions and other subordinate bodies to supervise their internal activity and to assume control of their property and funds. These so-called "trusteeships" have been widely used by responsible officials to prevent corruption, mismanagement of funds, and infiltration of Communists,

---

[17] *Business Week,* November 7, 1964.

and to preserve order and integrity within the union. However, the hearings before the McClellan Committee revealed that trusteeships have been used in some cases as a means of consolidating the power of corrupt union officials, of plundering and dissipating the resources of local unions, and of preventing the growth of competing political elements within the organization. For example, the McClellan Committee found that of the Teamsters' 892 locals, 113 were under "trusteeship"!

Title III of the Landrum-Griffin Act requires national or international unions to file reports with the Secretary of Labor concerning all trusteeships. The act expressly limits trusteeships so that they can be established only in accordance with the constitution and bylaws of the national or international union and can be imposed only for the purpose of "correcting corruption or financial malpractice, assuring the performance of collective bargaining agreements or other duties of a bargaining representative, restoring democratic procedures, or otherwise carrying out the legitimate objects of such labor organizations." In order to limit the duration of trusteeships without imposing a fixed term which would interfere with the legitimate activities of the union, the act merely provides that after a period of 18 months a trusteeship shall be "presumed invalid," and the court is directed to decree its discontinuance unless it is shown by clear and convincing proof that continuation is necessary for an allowable purpose. However, as was pointed out in Chapter 3, despite this provision, the United Mine Workers still maintained trusteeships imposed in the 1920s till 1972. The U.S. Department of Labor filed a suit in 1964 to bar these trusteeships, but the cases were allowed to languish for eight years. Finally in 1972, after the UMW had been exposed for numerous transgressions, two district courts issued orders disestablishing the trusteeships and ordering free elections in the affected districts.[18]

Although trusteeships affect less than 1% of all reporting labor organizations—in fiscal 1970 there were only 353 active trusteeships in effect[19]—nevertheless the Department of Labor has been criticized for its failure to proceed expeditiously to end dictatorial trusteeships. According to Robert P. Griffin, U.S. Senator from Michigan, whose name the Landrum-Griffin Act bears:

. . . the Department's unwillingness, or inability to proceed with dispatch has deprived over 170,000 of the 195,000 United Mine Workers members of the right to elect their own local officers. This egregious denial of democratic principle, growing out of the UMW's autocratic imposition and maintenance of trusteeships upon 19 of 23 union districts, has been allowed to languish unremedied for over 12 years—while the complainants, after more than 6 years

---

[18] *Monborne et al.* v. *United Mine Workers et al.*, Civil Action No. 71–690, U.S. Dis. Ct., W. Dis. Pa. (May 14, 1972); and *Hodgson* v. *United Mine Workers et al.*, Civil Action No. 3071–64, U.S. Dis. Ct., D.C. (May 24, 1971).

[19] U.S. Department of Labor, *Compliance, Enforcement, and Reporting*, p. 25.

of protests to the Secretary, were not even afforded a hearing on the merits until July 15, 1971.[20]

According to the senator, a far-reaching amendment to Title II, specifically addressed to the enforcement provision, is required to prevent the continuation or recurrence of this kind of denial of fundamental individual rights.

Restrictions on Union Organizing and Bargaining Tactics

As has already been pointed out, the Landrum-Griffin Act imposes prohibitions and limitations on the use of picketing and boycott tactics by unions. Union spokesmen believe that if the amendments to the Taft-Hartley Act had been brought in as a separate enactment in a different session of Congress, less restrictive provisions would have resulted. However, since the picketing and boycott sections were considered as part of an overall labor reform program aimed primarily at a few corrupt unions, the entire package was adopted into law.

Special Privileges for Unions in Construction Industry

The casual and occasional nature of the employment relationship between employer and employees in the construction industry caused many problems to develop in that industry because of the restrictive provisions of the Taft-Hartley Act. The Landrum-Griffin Act—in one of its few provisions intended to loosen restrictions on unions—recognizes these problems and amends the Taft-Hartley Act so as to make lawful so-called "prehire" agreements in the construction industry. Such agreements may now make union membership compulsory 7 days after employment (rather than 30 days, as is the case in other industries) in states where union shops are permitted. Union contracts also can require an employer to notify the union of job openings and give the union an opportunity to refer qualified applicants for such employment, and can specify minimum training or experience qualifications for employment.

HOW THE INDIVIDUAL WORKER WAS AFFECTED

A major objective of the Landrum-Griffin Act was to rid unions of gangster control and corrupt practices generally. The legislators believed that if they could provide union members with information about what was happening to union funds and other vital aspects of union activities, and if they could protect individual rights through a bill of rights and procedures insuring secret elections, union members would rid themselves of untrustworthy or corrupt officers.

---

[20] Robert P. Griffin, "The Landrum-Griffin Act: Twelve Years of Experience in Protecting Employee Rights," *Georgia Law Review*, Vol. 5 (Summer 1971), p. 635.

The Bill of Rights

Title I of the law purports to legislate into the internal laws and procedures of unions certain of the essential guarantees contained in the Bill of Rights of the Constitution of the United States. The act provides that every member of a union shall have equal rights to nominate candidates, to vote in elections or referendums of the union, to attend membership meetings, and to participate in the deliberations and voting upon the business of such meetings, subject to reasonable rules and regulations in the union's constitution and bylaws. Furthermore, every member is guaranteed the right to meet and assemble freely with other members; to express views, arguments, or opinions; and to express at meetings of the labor organization his views upon candidates in a union election or upon any other business before the meeting, subject to the organization's established and reasonable rules pertaining to the conduct of meetings.

Congress wanted to strengthen the hand of the individual member who sought to "buck the machine." Yet, at the same time, it recognized that it could not restrict the legitimate right of unions to carry on business at meetings in an orderly fashion. Therefore, the Landrum-Griffin Act subjected the exercise of individual union members' rights to "reasonable rules" and furthermore provided that nothing in this section of the act should be construed to "impair the right of a labor organization to adopt and enforce reasonable rules as to the responsibility of every member toward the organization as an institution and to his refraining from conduct that would interfere with its performance of its legal or contractual obligations."

The act seeks to limit the extent to which union dues and assessments can be raised without the will of the membership. The act also states that except for nonpayment of dues, no member of any union may be fined, suspended, expelled, or otherwise disciplined by such organization or by any officer thereof unless such member has been served with written specific charges, given a reasonable time to prepare his defense, and afforded a full and fair hearing.[21] Furthermore, unions are prohibited from limiting the right of any union member to sue in court, except that such member may be required to exhaust reasonable hearing procedures (not to exceed a four-month lapse of time) within the union before instituting legal or administrative proceedings against the union or its officers.

Many persons who favored adoption of other sections of the Landrum-Griffin Act opposed inclusion of the bill of rights in this enactment. They questioned whether or not unions should—or could—operate as model democratic institutions. Unions, they argued, are fighting organi-

---

[21] These procedural safeguards apply to union members as *members*. They do not relate to suspension or removal from union office. See *Congressional Record,* September 3, 1959, p. 17899.

zations; in many disputes with employers the very existence of the union may be in danger. In such cases, organizations typically require strong direction from the top. Furthermore, as unions mature, the role of professionals will become more and more important in determining policy, in much the same way that professional management of corporations has reduced the role of stockholders in decision making.

Claims have been made that the Landrum-Griffin Act, by encouraging dissent within the local union, has promoted some unrest and factionalism within unions which has tended to spill over into contract negotiation and grievance settlement, and caused contracts to be rejected by the rank and file at a greater rate than heretofore. Furthermore, some employers have expressed concern that union representatives who may now have to contend more strongly to maintain their jobs as union officials will be more inclined to make extreme demands and less likely to strike a bargain which might subject them to criticism by their rivals. A recent study, however, found no support for this contention and concluded that the existence of the act is cited as an excuse by unions and employers who have lost touch with the rank and file.[22]

Certain provisions of the act may hamper union government. For example, suppose the president of a union local believes that one member is an informer for the employer. Technically, he cannot suspend such member or even keep him from attending meetings, until the full statutory requirements have been complied with—written charges, time for defense, and full hearing. As a practical matter, however, in this and similar circumstances where the bill of rights impedes union action, the officers will probably go ahead and do what they think best, and then "see what happens." The act significantly omits any criminal penalties for violation of the bill-of-rights section, except where there is use of force or threat of violence. Civil remedies, such as an injunction, may not be very effective relief for a member, since there is no way a court can afford a member the right to attend or to speak at a meeting that has already been held. Therefore, although in theory the bill-of-rights section of the new law might be burdensome to unions, in practice this has not occurred nor is it likely to occur.

Fair Elections

Under both the Taft-Hartley Act and the Railway Labor Act, the union which is the bargaining agent has the power, in conjunction with the employer, to fix a man's wages, hours, and working conditions. The individual employee has no right to negotiate directly with the employer if he is dissatisfied with the contract made by his union representatives.

---

[22] Donald R. Burke and Lester Rubin, "Is Contract Rejection a Major Collective Bargaining Problem?" *Industrial and Labor Relations Review*, Vol. 26 (January 1973), pp. 820–33.

The federal government, which conferred these exclusive rights upon unions, has an obligation to insure that the officials of unions who wield this power are responsive to the desires of the membership they represent. The best assurance of this is free and periodic elections—a fact recognized by the AFL–CIO Ethical Practices Committee, which wrote into its code a requirement for frequent elections.

With these principles in mind, the legislators incorporated in the Landrum-Griffin Act detailed provisions relating to union elections. Every national or international union, except a federation of national or international unions, is required to elect its officers not less than once every five years[23] either by secret ballot among the members in good standing or at a convention of delegates chosen by secret ballot. Local unions are required to elect officers not less often than once every three years by secret ballot among the members in good standing. Officers of intermediate bodies between the internationals and the locals must be elected not less often than once every four years by secret ballot among the members in good standing or by labor organization officers representative of such members who have been elected by secret ballot.

The act provides that in any election required to be held by secret ballot, a reasonable opportunity shall be given for the nomination of candidates; and every member in good standing shall be eligible to be a candidate, subject to reasonable qualifications uniformly imposed (except for Communists and persons convicted of certain crimes, who are barred from holding office). Union members are guaranteed the right to vote for, or otherwise to support, the candidate of their own choice without being subject to penalty, discipline, improper interference, or reprisal. All candidates have to be treated equally, and every bona fide candidate is given the right, once within 30 days prior to the union election in which he is a candidate, to inspect the list of names and addresses of "all members of the labor organization who are subject to a collective bargaining agreement requiring membership therein as a condition of employment."[24] Unions are forbidden to spend dues money

---

[23] Although the intent of this provision was to insure that control of the presidency was periodically returned to the membership for a vote, there is evidence that the specification of the five-year maximum interval has probably lengthened rather than shortened the convention interval! See Marvin Snowbarger and Sam Pintz, *A Quantitative Appraisal of Presidential Turnover Rates before and after the Landrum-Griffin Act* (San Jose State College: Institute for Business and Economic Research, June 1970).

[24] In 19 states which have so-called "right-to-work" laws, union-shop contracts are unlawful. In these states, it would appear that the lists above referred to would not have to be maintained by the union or made available to candidates. While the language of this particular section raises questions as to both its applicability and its usefulness, another section of the act requires unions to "refrain from discrimination in favor of or against any candidate with respect to the use of lists of members." Therefore, if *any* list of members is available, even in the right-to-work states, it presumably must be made available on equal terms to all candidates.

in support of any candidate, and employers likewise are forbidden to spend money in support of candidates for union office. Detailed requirements are spelled out in the act as to the manner of sending election notices, counting votes, and other safeguards to insure a fair election. The act also establishes a procedure insuring that union officers guilty of serious misconduct may be removed by secret ballot elections.

The Secretary of Labor has ruled that unions may prescribe reasonable rules and regulations with respect to voting eligibility. They may "in appropriate circumstances defer eligibility to vote by requiring a reasonable period of prior membership, such as six months or a year, or by

TABLE 20–1

LMRDA Suits Filed by or against the Secretary of Labor, by Fiscal Year and Type*

Type of Suit	Fiscal Year										Cumulative Sept. 14, 1959–June 30,1970
	1961	1962	1963	1964	1965	1966	1967	1968	1969	1970	
Election	14	9	15	25	12	35	15	23	29	34	211
Subpena	3	4	8	3	8	5	2	1	0	3	37
Defensive	6	3	9	4	1	5	5	2	1	3	39
Reporting	2	1	4	6	0	4	4	6	3	5	35
Trusteeship	0	0	1	0	1	1	0	1	0	0	4
Agreements	0	0	0	0	1	0	0	0	0	0	1
Miscellaneous	0	0	0	0	0	0	0	1†	0	0	1†
Totals	25	17	37	38	23	50	26	34	33	45	328

* No suits were filed prior to fiscal year 1961.
† *United States* v. *Jalas.*
Source: U.S. Department of Labor, Labor-Management Services Administration, *Compliance, Enforcement, and Reporting in 1970 under the Labor-Management Reporting and Disclosure Act* (Washington, D.C.: U.S. Government Printing Office, 1971), p. 4.

requiring apprentice members to complete their apprenticeship training, as a condition of voting." The Secretary of Labor has expressly stated that such union rules may not be used to create special classes of nonvoting members.

As can be seen from Table 20–1, most of the litigation under the Landrum-Griffin Act involves election procedures. In the fiscal year ended June 30, 1970, 134 complaints were received by LMWP concerning election procedures (see Table 20–2). Of 42 civil actions brought during 1970 on behalf of the Secretary of Labor, 34 challenged union elections.[25] It is noteworthy that approximately 90% of all election complaints investigated to date by the Secretary of Labor relate to the election of *local* officers. Very few complaints—with a few notable exceptions—refer to election of intermediate or national officers. In one significant case, however, an investigation found that James B. Carey,

[25] U.S. Department of Labor, *Compliance, Enforcement, and Reporting*, p. 4.

long-time president of the International Union of Electrical, Radio and
Machine Workers, whose "reelection" had been announced, was in fact
defeated by 23,316 votes. Carey promptly "resigned."

More notorious was the disputed and much publicized 1969 election
of international officers of the United Mine Workers, after which
Joseph A. Yablonski, defeated opposition candidate for president and
two members of his family were murdered. Yablonski, hitherto a member of the entrenched "machine," had challenged W. A. "Tony" Boyle,
incumbent president, and after a vitriolic campaign—in which frequent
charges were made that the election was being "fixed"—succeeded in

TABLE 20–2

LMWP Union Election Activity, Fiscal 1970

Active election cases in fiscal 1970 154
    Based on formal election complaints received in fiscal 1970 134
    Based on formal election complaints received prior to fiscal 1970 . . 20
Election cases closed in fiscal 1970 127
    No violations found, complaint untimely, cases closed for other reasons . . . 48
    Insufficient evidence that violations may have affected outcome 24
    Voluntary compliance achieved 21
        Elections held under LMWP supervision 10
        Elections held without LMWP supervision 7
        Other corrective action taken 4
    Civil actions filed under section 402(b) 34
Election Cases Pending as of June 30, 1970 27
Elections supervised by LMWP under federal court order issued in title IV
    LMRDA actions 17
Civil actions pending in district or appellate courts as of June 30, 1970 71

    Source: U.S. Department of Labor, Labor-Management Services Administration, *Compliance,
Enforcement, and Reporting in 1970 under the Labor-Management Reporting and Disclosure Act*
(Washington, D.C.: U.S. Government Printing Office, 1971), p. 5.

winning 37% of the votes. Three weeks later came the murder. After the
election, the LMWP undertook the most intensive investigation in its
history and brought suit to set aside the election. In May 1972, a federal
judge ruled that a new election must be held[26] and the Justice Department has asked for a Labor Department monitorship over the financial
affairs of the United Mine Workers.[27]

The Labor Department has been sharply criticized for its failure to
institute an investigation of alleged irregularities which were brought to
its attention by a formal request on July 9, 1969, five months before the
election. However, George P. Shultz, who was then serving as Secretary
of Labor responded by stating:

Although the Secretary of Labor does have the power under Section 601(*a*)
of the Labor-Management Reporting and Disclosure Act of 1959 (LMRDA)

---

    [26] *Hodgson* v. *U.M.W.*, Civil Action No. 662–70 (U.S.D.C., District of Columbia),
Daily Labor Report 86 (May 2, 1972), pp. E–1 to E–8.
    [27] *Business Week*, May 13, 1972, p. 53.

to investigate election irregularities at any time, it is the Department of Labor's long-established policy not to undertake investigation of this kind without having a valid complaint under section 402(a) after an election has been completed.[28]

Perhaps a more active role by the Department of Labor would have established a climate in which the opposition forces would have had a fair chance in the election. As it was, in the words of the attorney for the Yablonski forces, "The Yablonski election was not lost on election day; it was lost, I believe, on the day that Secretary Shultz decided not to investigate the pre-election conduct of the UMWA. Boyle and his cohorts were free from that moment on to take action unhindered and unwatched."[29] In the second election held under strict Department of Labor monitorship, Boyle lost to insurgent Arnold Miller by 14,000 votes.

As a result of litigation and various court decisions relating to election procedures, guidelines are gradually emerging as to the kind of eligibility requirements which unions can impose as a condition of voting in an election. In general, the courts have held that such requirements violate the act if their effect in a particular case is to reduce those eligible to vote to a very small percentage of the membership. For example, in one case involving the Glass Bottle Blowers, the Supreme Court held unreasonable a union rule that only members who have attended 75% of monthly meetings over the last two years could be candidates for office or vote in union elections. It found that such a rule disqualified 490 out of the local union's 500 members! Similarly, the courts have ruled that qualifications in the National Maritime Union and in a local of the Hotel and Restaurant Workers' Union which bar a majority of membership from seeking office violate the Landrum-Griffin Act.[30] Undoubtedly the act has paved the way at least for challenging well-entrenched union officials and for ousting them when they obviously attempt to steal elections.

The perpetuation of what are, in effect, union dictatorships depends upon stifling democratic elections at the local level. The late Senator Robert A. Taft once said that "the employee has a good deal more of an opportunity to select his employer than he has to select his labor-union leader." Certain unions—particularly the Teamsters—have been able to keep the ruling clique in power by various devices which has disqualified opposition candidates or put them at a substantial disadvantage in obtain-

---

[28] Joseph L. Rauh, Jr., "LMRDA—Enforce It or Repeal It," *Georgia Law Review,* Vol. 5 (Summer 1971), pp. 645–6.

[29] *Ibid.,* p. 647.

[30] See *Wirtz* v. *Local 153, Glass Bottle Blowers Association,* 389 U.S. 463 (1967); *Wirtz* v. *National Maritime Union,* U.S. Dist. Ct., So. Dist., N.Y. (April 24, 1968), 68 LRRM 2349; and *Wirtz* v. *Hotel, Motel and Club Employees Union,* 88 S. Ct. 1743 (1968).

ing votes. The Landrum-Griffin Act strikes at these unfair methods and attempts to insure free and honest elections in unions. The safeguards contained in the law permit rank-and-file union members to express their wishes more freely than was possible in the past, and in some cases they have done so. In most unions, however, there is a general apathy among the membership with respect to union elections. On the other hand, there is among union leaders a strong desire for power and a repugnance to resuming status as an ordinary worker-member. The result is what one writer has called "the iron law of oligarchy."[31] It seems clear that legislation, without active interest on the part of union members, will not suffice to make unions democratic.

As we have noted at the beginning of this section, Congress apparently believed that if it could provide union members with information about the operation of their unions and could protect individual rights through requirement of democratic procedures, union members themselves would rid their unions of corruption. Congress thus assumed that a democratic union would be less inclined to corruption. However, experience suggests that this relationship does not always hold. The United Steelworkers, for example, would hardly be classed as a democratic union, yet it handles tremendous trust funds without a hint of corruption. On the other hand, some unions with substantial local autonomy have been infected with corruption. Corruption in a union may be more related to economic factors in the industry—such as severe competition and a highly mobile labor force—than to election procedures contained in the union constitution.

Voting by Strikers

Through an amendment of the Taft-Hartley Act, the Landrum-Griffin law eliminates the so-called "union-busting" provision contained in the Taft-Hartley Act. Section $9(c)(3)$ of that act provided that employees on strike who are not entitled to reinstatement shall not be eligible to vote. This provision had the effect of preventing any "economic striker" (an employee striking for higher wages, better conditions, or any reason other than his employer's unfair labor practices) who had been replaced by a new employee hired during the strike from voting in an NLRB election conducted during the strike. For example, in a case in the rubber industry the United Rubber Workers was certified as bargaining representative in an NLRB election. Following months of fruitless negotiations for a contract, the union struck, and the company replaced the strikers with new employees. Thereafter the employer filed for a new election and succeeded in throwing out the union, because the

---

[31] C. Peter MacGrath. "Democracy in Overalls: The Futile Quest for Union Democracy," *Industrial and Labor Relations Review*, Vol. 12 (July 1959), p. 508.

strikers were not permitted to vote. Under the amendment added by the Landrum-Griffin Act, such economic strikers retain their right to vote in any NLRB election conducted within 12 months of the start of the strike, subject to regulations established by the NLRB. In applying this statutory provision, the NLRB has ruled that it will presume that economic strikers have retained their interest in struck jobs, and that replacements were employed on a permanent basis, and that both therefore are eligible to vote. This means that the mere fact that a striking worker has taken a job elsewhere does not mean that he cannot vote in an election held in the company at which he and other union men are on strike. The NLRB places the burden of proof on the party challenging his vote to show that he is disqualified from voting.

HOW THE PUBLIC WAS AFFECTED BY THE ACT

Because the Landrum-Griffin Act deals primarily with the internal administration of unions, its impact upon the general public is somewhat limited. It was hoped, however, that the procedures it requires, by eliminating corrupt influences in unions, together with the provisions designed to tighten restrictions on picketing and boycotts, would reduce the area of industrial strife. There is little evidence one way or the other that this has occurred.

Beyond this is the strengthening of our democratic processes in the nation as a whole which comes from the practice of unionism under conditions where each union member is free to speak his mind and help to determine the overall policies of union government. Democracy is not something which can be carried out on rare occasions—like a treasured antique—and then put back in mothballs. It must be lived daily to survive. We cannot expect democracy in government to survive when employees in their daily lives see democratic forces subverted through intimidation and corruption.

APPRAISAL OF THE ACT

The Landrum-Griffin Act is a law with a very limited purpose. Its primary object is the reform of labor unions. It does not purport to be a law covering the broad aspects of collective bargaining, as did the Taft-Hartley Act. Nor is it intended to effect a broad revision of that act. The provisions which it includes amending the Taft-Hartley Act were added as an accident of its legislative history and for the most part bear some relation to the abuses which were the main object of the legislators' concern.

Interestingly enough, it is the amendments of the Taft-Hartley Act —particularly those which deal with restrictions on picketing and secondary boycotts—that have given rise to the most litigation and controversy. The main body of the Landrum-Griffin law has been incorporated in our industrial life with a minimum of court action. This does not mean that this act of Congress has reformed unionism or that many abuses still do not exist. The fact is, however, that the U.S. Department of Labor has been called upon to handle fewer complaints of violation of the act than many labor experts had anticipated.

Analysis of the legislative history of the Landrum-Griffin Act indicates that three basic principles motivated the legislators in drafting it:

1. There should be a minimum of interference by government in the internal affairs of any private organization; only essential standards of conduct should be established by legislation.
2. Given the maintenance of minimum democratic safeguards and availability of detailed essential information about the union, individual members are fully competent to regulate union affairs.
3. Remedies for abuses should be direct. Where the law prescribes standards, sanctions for the violation should also be direct.

There can be little argument with the first principle, although there will be considerable dispute as to whether or not the Landrum-Griffin Act goes far enough in implementing minimum standards. When the act was passed, union spokesmen contended that the provisions relative to disclosure would enable labor spies to obtain confidential information about the union's financial condition and to hamstring internal operation of the union. They further contended that the bill-of-rights provision would convert the union into a debating society and weaken it as a fighting organization. Neither of these contentions has been supported by subsequent experience under the act.

However, eight members of the House Labor Committee filed a minority report bitterly attacking the proposed labor reform bill for its omission of a guarantee of civil rights. In their words, "if there is to be a bill of rights in this legislation it must most assuredly include a guarantee of equal rights—the right of every workingman to join a union and not to be segregated within that union because of race, creed, color, or national origin." It was a fact of political life in 1959 that the Labor Reform bill probably could not have been passed if it had incorporated a civil rights provision. However, today the civil rights movement is much stronger, and federal and state laws passed in the intervening years have incorporated the view expressed by the minority report. We observed in the previous chapter how a federal court has broadened the purview of the unfair labor practices of the Taft-Hartley Act so as to encompass racial discrimination. The Civil Rights Act of 1964, has gone a long way toward accomplishing the broadening of the bill of rights of the Landrum-Griffin Act explicitly to guarantee such rights to members of labor organization.[32]

---

[32] For a discussion of civil rights and labor relations, see Chapter 23.

With respect to the second principle, some skeptics wonder whether the rank-and-file union member is really concerned about graft and corruption in his union any more than the average citizen really concerns himself about graft and corruption in government. Surveys have indicated, for example, that many Teamster members, despite the disclosure of corruption among their officers, still approve their leadership because they have "produced" for them in terms of high wages and excellent working conditions. Perhaps the conditions affecting the relationship of the average worker and his union are such that we should not expect democratic action to flourish in such an environment. As one writer puts it:

The conditions that currently characterize unions—the complexity of their organization, the increasing tendency to assume functions complementary to those of management, the status and salary gap existing between leaders and members, not to mention the psychological compulsion of the leaders to retain power, and the members' expectation that their union is primarily a service institution rather than a way of life—do not provide the soil in which the democratic process can operate.[33]

Nevertheless, maintenance of minimum democratic safeguards seems necessary to protect the rights of individuals and to insure that union action reflects the desire of the membership.

On the subject of the third principle, the Landrum-Griffin law takes a different approach from that of the Taft-Hartley Act. The latter penalized violation by unions of various provisions of the law by denying the union access to the procedures of the NLRB. This has the effect of punishing all the union members for the violations of their officials. The Landrum-Griffin Act, by contrast, imposes direct sanctions in the form of fines, imprisonment, and/or civil remedies through court action to insure compliance with the act. This is certainly a more mature and realistic approach.

The type of legislation embodied in the Landrum-Griffin Act was probably inevitable. Abuses in other aspects of business life—such as the securities market, banking, and drugs—have likewise brought forth detailed federal regulation. Unions thus far have been remarkably free from such internal regulation, despite the fact that they enjoy benefits and privileges under the income tax laws and the antitrust laws which are unique. No association or organization can long expect to enjoy such privileges without assuming major obligations.

Unions in our society are no longer mere private clubs or fraternal organizations whose internal affairs, admission, and fiscal policies are matters of concern to their membership only. On the contrary, they bear more resemblance to public utilities or government entities, subject to legal control of their internal affairs. When a union is certified as a collective bargaining agent, it has conferred upon it a government-

---

[33] MacGrath, "Democracy in Overalls," p. 524.

sanctioned monopoly and the unusual powers that flow from this privilege. It is incumbent upon government, which granted this power to unions, to insure that it is not abused. Even without special statutory regulation of their internal affairs, there is precedent for holding unions to rules of conduct requiring fair and equal treatment of employees represented by the union. For example, in *Steele* v. *Louisville & Nashville Railroad*,[34] the U.S. Supreme Court decided that a union certified under the Railway Labor Act could not lawfully make an agreement with an employer which would arbitrarily deprive nonmember Negro employees of their seniority rights. In so holding, the Court stated: "We think that the Railway Labor Act imposes upon the statutory representative of a craft at least as exacting a duty to protect equally the interests of the members of the craft as the Constitution imposes upon a legislature to give equal protection to the interests of those for whom it legislates.[35] Similarly, some state courts have enunciated the view that where a union is acting as a bargaining representative, it is acting as an agency created and functioning under provisions of federal law; therefore, exclusion of persons on the ground of race, for example, deprives such persons of rights guaranteed under the federal Constitution.[36]

Unions have an obligation to maintain democratic processes. They control the conditions under which their members spend most of their productive lives. More and more, they have a captive audience. A truck driver may move from one city to another, but he cannot long escape the far-flung power of the Teamsters' Union. The Landrum-Griffin Act takes a long step in the direction of attempting to insure democratic conditions in unions. Its success in achieving this objective will depend upon the support afforded this legislation by union leaders who profess to be interested in "clean" union government and, most important, upon the rank-and-file union membership who must want democratic government enough to use the tools which Congress has given them.

QUESTIONS FOR DISCUSSION

1. It has been said that a union is an organization that must always be ready for battle. Can such an organization function effectively on democratic basis? Do you consider the operation of most large corporations to be democratic? Why should unions be held to this standard? Discuss.

2. Discuss the so-called "bill of rights" incorporated in the Landrum-Griffin Act. In what way could these provisions handicap union action? Should

---

[34] 323 U.S. 192, 65 S. Ct. 226 (1944). See also *Miranda Fuel Company, Inc.*, 51 LRRM 1585.

[35] 323 U.S. 192, 202; 65 S. Ct. 226, 232.

[36] *Betts* v. *Easley*, 161 Kans. 459 (1946); *Thorman* v. *International Alliance of Theatrical & Stage Employees*, 49 Cal. (2d) 629 (1957).

the bill of rights have been broadened to include other rights, such as the right of free admission to a union? Discuss.

3. Assuming that there were abuses in the internal administration of unions, do you think that the power of the federal government should be invoked to cure such abuses? What other measures might have been taken to accomplish the same objective?

SUGGESTIONS FOR FURTHER READING

DERESHINSKY, RALPH M. *The NLRB and Secondary Boycotts*. Report No. 4, Labor Relations and Public Policy Series. Philadelphia: Industrial Research Unit, Wharton School of Finance and Commerce, University of Pennsylvania, 1972.

A concise monograph summarizing the law with respect to common-situs picketing, consumer boycotts, and hot-cargo agreements

ETELSON, JESSE I., and SMITH, FRANKLIN N., JR. "Union Discipline under the Landrum-Griffin Act," *Harvard Law Review*, Vol. 82 (February 1969), pp. 727–71.

An examination of 10 years of judicial experience under the Landrum-Griffin Act with particular reference to three major areas of controversy: scope of coverage, procedural safeguards, and remedies.

LANDRUM, PHIL M., *et al.* "Developments under the Landrum-Griffin Act: A Symposium," *Georgia Law Review*, Vol. 5 (Summer 1971), pp. 617–733.

A series of articles reviewing the accomplishments and shortcomings of the Landrum-Griffin Act.

TURNER, EMORY C. "What Has Landrum-Griffin Accomplished?" *Labor Law Journal*, Vol. 20 (July 1969), pp. 391–403.

A report on a study to evaluate the effectiveness of the reporting and disclosure provisions of the Landrum-Griffin Act.

U.S. DEPARTMENT OF LABOR, LABOR-MANAGEMENT SERVICES ADMINISTRATION. *Compliance, Enforcement, and Reporting Under the Labor-Management Reporting and Disclosure Act*. Annual Reports. Washington, D.C.: U.S. Government Printing Office

Annual reports which contain detailed statistical breakdowns of activities of the LMWP.

Chapter 21

THE GOVERNMENT IN LABOR DISPUTES—MEDIATION, EMERGENCY DISPUTES, AND STATE LEGISLATION

The previous chapters have been concerned with key federal legislation. These laws, however, are only part of the total role of the federal government in labor disputes. In this chapter, we shall discuss how the federal government attempts to settle labor disputes or to prevent them from erupting. In addition, we shall discuss how 50 states and some municipalities play a significant role in labor disputes in the private sector by means of "little Taft-Hartley acts," "little Landrum-Griffin laws," and other legislation.

MEDIATION OR CONCILIATION—THE FEDERAL SERVICE

The principal mediation agency in the United States is the Federal Mediation and Conciliation Service. (See Figure 21–1 for definitions.) It dates from the Act of 1913 which created the U.S. Department of Labor. This law contained a paragraph authorizing the Secretary of Labor to mediate labor disputes and to appoint "commissioners of conciliation" for that purpose. This phase of the U.S. Department of Labor's work quickly expanded until a special division was set up in the Department known as the United States Conciliation Service, with headquarters in Washington, D.C., and regional offices in the principal industrial centers of the nation. In 1947, the Conciliation Service, as a division of the Department of Labor, was abolished by the Taft-Hartley Act, and an independent agency, the Federal Mediation and Conciliation Service, whose functions remained basically the same, was substituted for it. This was done largely at the behest of employer groups who felt that if the Conciliation Service were to remain a division of the Department of Labor, conciliators themselves would inevitably reflect the prolabor bias of the Department.

In establishing a separate Mediation and Conciliation Service, the Taft-Hartley Act gave the Service the statutory base it previously lacked. In addition, Section 201 of the Taft-Hartley Act set forth the policy of the federal government as the peaceful settlement of labor disputes by collective bargaining. Section 203 directed the Service to minimize work stoppages by mediation and encouragement of voluntary arbitration; Section 204 admonished labor and industry to cooperate fully with the

FIGURE 21–1

DEFINITIONS

MEDIATION AND CONCILIATION are used interchangeably to mean an attempt by a third party, typically a government official, to bring disputants together by persuasion and compromise. The mediator or conciliator is not vested with power to force a settlement.

STRIKE NOTICE laws require the union and company to notify each other and certain public officials a specified number of days prior to striking or locking out.

STRIKE VOTE laws require an affirmative vote of either the union members or the employees in the bargaining unit before a strike may be called.

FACT FINDING involves investigation of a dispute by a panel, which issues a report setting forth the causes of a dispute. Usually, but not always, recommendations for settling the dispute are included in the report. Laws requiring fact finding usually provide that the parties maintain the status quo and refrain from strikes or lock outs until a stipulated period after the fact finders' report has been made. Once the procedure has been compiled with, however, the parties are free to strike and to lock out.

COMPULSORY ARBITRATION requires the submission of an unsettled labor dispute to a third party or board for determination. Strikes or lockouts are completely forbidden, and the arbitrator's decision is binding on the parties for a stated length of time.

SEIZURE involves temporary state control of a business which is or threatens to be shut down by a work stoppage. Strikes or lockouts are forbidden during the period of seizure, which lasts until the threat of work stoppage is abated.

efforts of the Service to settle strikes; and Section 205 established a labor-management advisory panel for the Service. Finally, Section 8(d) of the Taft-Hartley Act required labor and management to notify each other of intent to modify a collective agreement at least 60 days prior to the termination date of the agreement, and to notify the Service and any appropriate state agency 30 days later if no agreement had been reached.

The Mediation and Conciliation Service may be called into a dispute by either labor or management, or it may proffer its services. It has, however, no authority to force itself upon a recalcitrant employer or union. Of course, as a federal agency, it carries with it the prestige of the government, so that refusal to participate in a conference called by the Service is not usual.

Mediators often perform a valuable contribution in preventing strikes by bringing the parties together when bargaining has failed. A clever mediator can obtain concessions from the parties by adroit maneuvering, or otherwise find a basis for agreement when it is lacking, as, for example, when the bargaining adversaries are no longer able to communicate directly with one another, or fear to do so.

To accomplish their tasks despite a lack of authority, mediators must time their participation in a dispute correctly. If they enter the dispute too early or too often, the parties may prefer to save concessions for mediation instead of getting down to the business of seeking agreement. If mediators come in too late, the parties' positions may have become too hardened to permit concessions. Mediation is an art, and a valuable one. It cannot be squandered loosely if it is to be effective. The fact that the Mediation Service has been able to attract some excellent men during the last two decades has helped it to increase its ability to accomplish its important task.

State Mediation Agencies

Although almost all states have provisions in their laws for the adjustment of labor disputes, in only a few is it made a full-time job. Nor is this surprising, considering that in many states, there would not be enough work to keep even a single conciliator, let alone a board or commission, occupied. Other states prefer to leave adjustment work to the Federal Mediation and Conciliation Service, with such assistance from the state industrial commissioner, or the state department of labor, as can be rendered by such an agency. The states which, in contrast to the general rule, are most active in the adjustment of labor disputes are California, Connecticut, Massachusetts, Michigan, Minnesota, New Jersey, New York, Pennsylvania, and Wisconsin. In all these states a special agency devotes full time to the job.

The job of the state mediator is no different from that of his federal counterpart. He must be capable of bringing about an agreement by conciliation and persuasion, without authority or power to force compliance with his wishes. The fact that most states have not paid staff mediators anything in excess of a very modest income has made it difficult to find men willing to perform this valuable service. Nevertheless, both authors have encountered some able state mediators over the last several years who have been most helpful in critical disputes.

Municipal Adjustment Agencies

A number of municipalities have at one time or another established machinery for the adjustment of labor disputes. Most have depended upon the volunteer services of public-spirited citizens and have ceased to exist after these citizens retired. Their success has been varied. Experienced mediators have not been available to municipalities, and inexperienced ones have frequently done more harm than good. Strikes which occur on the outskirts of a city or in its suburbs may vitally affect a city, yet be outside the jurisdiction of its adjustment agency. And if state and federal agencies are already in operation, the intrusion of a municipal board may only complicate matters.

Louisville, Kentucky; Toledo, Ohio; and New York City have had the most active municipal mediation agencies. New York City maintains a special labor secretary to the mayor who attempts mediation; and if unsuccessful, he can refer the dispute for further mediation to a panel composed of one labor, one industry, and one public member.

Jurisdictional Hodgepodge in Mediation

Increasing concern has been expressed in recent years by many persons about the competition of mediators to obtain recognition in settling disputes. It is by no means uncommon to find both federal and state mediators, and occasionally, municipal ones also, competing for the job of settling the dispute. The Taft-Hartley Act specifically permits such dual mediation. In recent years, a "code of ethics" requires mediators to cooperate at least on a pro forma basis, but the urge "to get in on the glory" is strong. Moreover, the existence of mediators from different jurisdictions gives labor and management the opportunity to "shop around" in order to try and have the mediation work done by the one judged most sympathetic to the partisan viewpoint of one of the parties.

Mediation is certainly unlikely to be more effective because of the participation by more mediators in a single dispute. The authors have experienced both cooperation and lack of cooperation among state and federal mediators in various disputes. For the most part in our experience, the mediators have cooperated with each other as reasonable people working toward a common goal should. There continues to be, however, sufficient evidence of lack of cooperation to merit consideration both in Washington, D.C., and in the various state capitals of a plan to divide up mediation work so as to achieve optimum efficiency in helping to prevent industrial disputes.

ADJUSTMENT IN RAILWAY AND AIR TRANSPORT

Mediation in the railway and air transport industries is conducted by an agency especially set up for this purpose—the National Mediation Board. Moreover, under the procedure set forth in the Railway Labor Act which governs these two industries, mediation is combined with a strike notice and fact-finding procedure. This separate treatment has its historical roots in a series of laws dating back to 1888. Since then, railway labor problems have generally been governed by procedures different from those in other industries. An exception to this rule is the Labor-Management Reporting and Disclosure Act (Landrum-Griffin), which, unlike the basic provisions of the Taft-Hartley Act, applies to both railway and air transport.

The Railway Labor Act makes it the duty of labor and management to exert every reasonable effort to "make and maintain agreements concerning rates of pay and working conditions" and to attempt to adjust all differences by peaceful methods. A three-man, nonpartisan National Mediation Board then attempts mediation if the parties cannot agree among themselves. The Board is further instructed to urge voluntary arbitration if mediation proves unsuccessful. If arbitration is refused and the dispute is such as "substantially to interrupt interstate commerce," the Board is instructed to notify the President, who can create a special emergency board to investigate and publish findings. During the pendency of these various proceedings and until 30 days after the report of the emergency board, neither party may alter "the conditions out of which the dispute arose," except by mutual agreement. The parties, however, are under no legal obligation to accept the recommendations of the emergency board, and strikes or lockouts are permissible after the waiting period has expired.

A unique aspect of the Railway Labor Act is the requirement for compulsory arbitration of grievances and of other disputes arising out of the interpretation of agreements. The agency charged with this task (for the railroads only) is the National Railroad Adjustment Board. This Board is a bipartisan agency composed of 36 members, half of whom are paid and compensated by the carriers and half by the unions "national in scope." (Thus, smaller organizations of workers have no representation on the Adjustment Board.) The work of the Adjustment Board is divided into four divisions, each of which has jurisdiction over certain crafts. If a division deadlocks, referees are appointed by the National Mediation Board or by the division if it can agree on a selection.

The Railway Labor Act also provides elaborate safeguards for the free choice of employee representatives by setting forth a list of unfair labor practices similar to those contained in the National Labor Relations Act prior to the Taft-Hartley amendments. Enforcement is, however, different from that under the National Labor Relations Act, in that violations are punishable by criminal penalties and prosecution is under the jurisdiction of the U.S. Department of Justice. Because of the difficulties of proving willful intent to commit an unfair labor practice before a jury, there have never been any convictions and only one trial for unfair labor practices. However, railway unions have successfully brought a number of injunctive actions to force employers to cease and desist from alleged unfair labor practices.

Until 1951, the Railway Labor Act prohibited all types of union security and checkoff agreements. This prohibition was placed in the act in 1934 to prevent company unions from obtaining union security and automatic dues support from reluctant workers, and it had the support of the so-called "standard" unions. By 1951, the company unions had been ousted by defeats in representation elections, and the standard unions were able to persuade Congress to legalize union security and checkoff provisions. Unlike the Taft-Hartley Act, the Railway Labor Act provides no machinery for decertifying unions or for voting out union security provisions.

The Railway Labor Act also provides formal machinery for the selection of employee representatives. The National Mediation Board is required to make determinations in this regard and usually does so by representation elections. The bargaining unit under the Railway Labor Act is limited to a "craft or class," but the National Mediation Board has wide discretion in determining the definition of craft or class and in determining voting eligibility in representation elections.

Prior to World War II, the Railway Labor Act was hailed as a "model law," and frequent suggestions were made to enact similar legislation for industry generally. Since 1940, however, a number of strikes or near strikes, which were averted only by Presidential action or special legislation outside the procedures of the Railway Labor Act, have caused many former advocates of the "model law" concept to take a second and deeper look at the Railway Labor Act.

The effect of the elaborate procedure of the Railway Labor Act is to make collective bargaining completely perfunctory prior to the emergency board stage. Neither party tends to concede anything from its original position for fear of prejudicing its case before the emergency board. The procedure of the Railway Labor Act, which is supposed to supplement collective bargaining, has been used instead as a substitute for collective bargaining. Because they know that an important dispute is likely to end up before an emergency board, railway labor and management have just gone through the motions of bargaining until the emergency board hearings took place.

Such a development is probably inevitable. It is the easy way out for the parties to let someone else make the decision for them. In that way, they avoid the responsibility and, under the emergency board procedure, still remain free to act if the board's recommendation is unsatisfactory. In 1963, President John F. Kennedy and Congress refused to permit a strike over the fireman issue, and Congress enacted a special compulsory arbitration law to settle it. Other aspects of the same dispute were settled under the aegis of President Lyndon B. Johnson by mediation in 1964. Since then, Congress has passed special legislation several times to terminate strikes by railway employees. In these cases, the procedure of the Railway Labor Act failed to produce a settlement—as has been the case in almost every major dispute under the act's jurisdiction since 1940.

Experience under the state laws, which also have a fact-finding procedure, is similar to that under the Railway Labor Act.[1] Moreover, nowhere has the appointment of fact-finding or emergency boards been confined to emergencies by any realistic or even generous use of the term

[1] For an analysis of these state laws, see Herbert R. Northrup, *Compulsory Arbitration and Government Intervention in Labor Disputes* (Washington, D.C.: Labor Policy Association, 1966), pp. 263–94.

"emergency." In the case of the Railway Labor Act, for example, a dispute on the small railroads can apparently as easily cause the appointment of an emergency board as a dispute affecting most of the railroads in the nation. Once the appointment of an emergency or fact-finding board becomes commonplace, the public loses interest; and it is then exceedingly difficult, if not impossible, to rally public opinion behind the settlement in the manner which proponents of the fact-finding procedure claim could be effective. As noted later, proposals to amend the Railway Labor Act are now before Congress.

THE TAFT-HARTLEY ACT AND NATIONAL EMERGENCIES

The emergency disputes law which is applicable to industry not covered by the Railway Labor Act is found in provisions of the Taft-Hartley Act. Title I of this law requires that a 60-day notice be given by either union or management to the other party if a change in the collective agreement is contemplated and that such notices also be sent to appropriate federal and state mediation services. This procedure has become perfunctory, since unions generally automatically give notice in order to be free to strike if negotiations do not result in agreement. These notices have, of course, alerted the mediation agencies that a strike could occur, but it is possible that they may also have induced mediation where it was unnecessary.

Title II of the Taft-Hartley Act also requires that the President appoint a Board of Inquiry to investigate and report, without recommendations, on the issues of a dispute which "threatens" the national health or safety. The President can then direct the Attorney General to petition a federal district court for an injunction to prevent or terminate the strike or lockout. If the injunction is granted, the conditions of work and pay are frozen for the time being, and the parties are obliged to make every effort to settle their differences with the assistance of the Conciliation Service. If these efforts fail, at the end of 60 days the Board of Inquiry is required to make a public report on the status of the dispute, again without recommendations. The National Labor Relations Board is then required within 15 days to poll employees as to whether they will accept the last offer of the employer and to certify the result to the Attorney General within 5 days. The injunction then must be dissolved. By this time, 80 days will have elapsed since the first application for an injunction. If the majority of workers refuse the employer's last offer, then the President can submit the complete report to Congress, with or without recommendations for action.

As of July 1, 1972, boards of inquiry had been appointed under this section on 34 different occasions. In 16 cases a strike vote on the employer's last offer was taken; and in 8 cases, strikes occurred after the machinery of the act had been completely utilized.

The Taft-Hartley Act thus provides no ultimate sanctions against a national emergency strike after the fact-finding period has elapsed, other than the implied threat of possible congressional action and the force of public opinion. Experience under the Taft-Hartley Act emphasized what experience under the Railway Labor Act had already demonstrated— fact-finding reports have relatively little effect in mobilizing public sentiment so as to compel settlement of labor disputes unless there is really a grave national emergency affecting the entire country, or most of it.

The Last-Offer Vote

The last-offer vote has often been utilized to gain the unions more. They have simply told their memberships to vote no and they will obtain more, and this has happened in all cases in which a last-offer vote oc-

TABLE 21–1

Last-Offer Votes: Experience under Taft-Hartley and Pennsylvania Laws to July 1, 1972

Law	Number of Votes	Last Offer Accepted	Last Offer Rejected
Taft-Hartley Act	16	0*	15
Pennsylvania Utility Arbitration Act	9	1†	8

* In one case the employees rejected a subsequent and higher offer after the "last" offer had been rejected. In another case the union asked employees to boycott the vote; no one voted from this group.

† Vote conducted on January 24, 1951, just prior to 1951 Korean War wage freeze. Employees feared that to reject it would mean freezing existing wages.

Source: National Labor Relations Board and Pennsylvania State Labor Relations Board.

curred, more often without a strike than with one. It also happened in eight of the nine cases in which a vote was held under a similar procedure of the now defunct Pennsylvania Utility Arbitration Act (see Table 21–1). The only exception occurred the day before the Korean War wage stabilization program was scheduled to become effective in 1951. The workers voted to accept a settlement for fear of having their wages frozen at pre–last-offer levels. This is to be expected. An offer, once made, is rarely withdrawn, so why not vote no and probably get more?

Actually, there have been four cases in which the last-offer vote served the purpose of inducing agreement. Professor George W. Taylor has noted that the steel industry settled in 1960 partially because the "last" offer was about to be rejected, according to all forecasts.[2] In the 1962

[2] George W. Taylor, "The Adequacy of Taft-Hartley in Public Emergency Disputes," *The Annals*, Vol. 333 (January 1961), p. 79.

Lockheed case the union settled without the union shop because it feared that the employees would not support its insistence on this demand in the last-offer vote. Similarly, in the 1966 strikes of the United Automobile Workers at General Electric's jet engine plant in Evendale, Ohio, and of the Steelworkers at Union Carbide's defense work facility at Kokomo, Indiana, last minute withdrawal of demands and settlements were probably triggered by the belief of these unions that the employees might accept the companies' last offers.[3]

PROPOSALS FOR EMERGENCY STRIKE LAWS

The least success of the Taft-Hartley emergency procedure has occurred in the industry which has caused the most invocations of the procedure—stevedoring. Twelve of the 35 times that the machinery has been used have involved longshoremen or associated groups. In eight such cases, the strike resumed after the 80-day cooling-off period ended. In 1972, the West Coast longshoremen called off their strike only after Congress passed special legislation which would have ordered the men back to work and set up a special compulsory arbitration board unless the parties settled by a given date—which they did.

The breakdown of the procedures of the Railway Labor Act and the failure of Taft-Hartley Act's emergency procedures to resolve longshore labor crises has induced many, including the Nixon administration, to advocate special legislation for all major transportation industries. President Nixon's proposal would abolish the Railway Labor Act and incorporate the Taft-Hartley 80-day injunction provision in a law covering railway, airline, maritime (including longshoring), and trucking. If the strike threat were not abated after 80 days, the President would have three alternatives: extend the injunction for 30 days; require partial operation for a period as long as six months; or appoint arbitrators who would have to choose as a binding settlement the final position of one of the parties in the exact form in which it was presented.

This proposal is one of many which have attempted to grapple with the difficult problem of providing a procedure which brings a settlement to labor disputes that are injuring an important segment of the public and, at the same time, avoiding destroying the capacity of unions and management to settle disputes through collective bargaining. The problem arises because of the role of the strike, paradoxically, in inducing settlement, and the impact on bargaining of withdrawing the right to strike. In

---

[3] Another form of strike vote legislation requires an affirmative vote of employees before they strike. The War Labor Disputes (Smith-Connally) Act of World War II and several state laws incorporated this idea, but unions made it a vote of confidence, and thus assured an overwhelming strike vote as a vote of confidence of employees for their negotiators. See Northrup, *Compulsory Arbitration*, pp. 295–99, for a description of these laws.

Chapter 7, we noted that if a strike hurts only one of the parties, as when the other is subsidized by welfare, the strike does not serve its purpose of motivating agreement—it no longer acts, as Professor George W. Taylor put it, "as the motive power which induces a modification of extreme positions and then a meeting of minds. The acceptability of certain terms of employment is determined in relation to the losses of a work stoppage that can be avoided by an agreement. In collective bargaining, economic power provides the final arbitrament."[4]

Dr. Taylor then described what occurs when third-party determination or intervention is substituted for the collective bargaining system:

When the rights to strike and to lockout are withdrawn, as during a war or under compulsory arbitration, a most important inducement to agree is removed. The penalties for failing to agree—stoppage of production and employment—are waived. Even more devastating consequences result. Each party is reluctant to make any "concessions" around the bargaining table. That might "prejudice" its case before whatever Board is set up to deal with labor disputes. In addition, the number of issues is kept large and formidable. Demands that customarily "wash out" in negotiations are carefully preserved for submission to the Board. Why not? There is everything to gain and nothing to lose by trying to get one's unusual demands approved without cost.[5]

There are, however, situations when the strike does not serve its purpose. This can occur if a strike exerts greater pressure upon the public or the government than it does on the parties. "The parties can hold out longer than the public or the government. In consequence, a strike which creates a public emergency exerts primary pressure upon the government to intervene and also to specify the terms upon which production is to be resumed."[6] Such situations are typified by railroad strikes or shutdowns of other key transportation services, for example, New York City subways, or utility or government services upon which a significant sector of the public depends for the orderly working of their daily livelihood.

The American system basically depends upon restraint of the parties to avoid confrontations in areas where strikes are considered intolerable—that is where they impact more on the public than on the parties themselves. The question today, after the breakdown of the Railway Labor Act, and the failures of the Taft-Hartley emergency procedures in longshore labor crises, as well as in the face of long strikes in other key industries, is whether that dependence is misplaced.

In an endeavor to protect the public and at the same time to encourage, rather than to discourage, settlement by the parties themselves, the various states and many foreign democratic countries and their political

---

[4] George W. Taylor, "Is Compulsory Arbitration Inevitable?" *Proceedings of the First Annual Meeting, Industrial Relations Research Association, 1948*, p. 64.

[5] *Ibid.* See also Northrup, *Compulsory Arbitration*, p. 183.

[6] Taylor, "Is Compulsory Arbitration Inevitable?" p. 65.

subdivisions have enacted various ingeniously drawn laws incorporating fact finding, seizure, compulsory arbitration and various combinations of these procedures.[7] (See Figure 21–1 for definitions.) None has been found to have succeeded both in preventing strikes *and* in encouraging the parties to settle their disputes without regular intervention. Fact finding, such as occurs under the Railway Labor Act, is the least successful because it inhibits the collective bargaining process without providing alternative means of settlement. Hence, when the procedure has been completed, the strike can still legally occur. Seizure holds the strike in abeyance, but does not resolve anything. Moreover, an employer finds it very difficult to understand when government seizes a facility temporarily and negotiates a costly agreement which the employer must then agree to in order to repossess his property.

Compulsory arbitration is, of course, designed as a substitute for strikes. It has been used for most of this century as such in Australia and New Zealand. There collective bargaining as we know it occurs but little. Instead, disputes are submitted to arbitration courts for determination. Yet even here strikes are not only common, but actually occur much more frequently than in the United States. They are usually short and are designed to pressure employers to grant more than was won at the arbitration court. Although such strikes are illegal, penalties are relatively rarely assessed. Politicians do not like to fine powerful unions or masses of employees. As a result, there is now sentiment both in New Zealand and Australia to narrow the scope of compulsory arbitration and to rely more on collective bargaining—as we in the United States are considering the opposite course.[8]

There is thus no easy answer. If the right to strike is curtailed, and other procedures substituted for strikes, the collective bargaining method of settlement will probably inevitably be inhibited, and thus the procedure adopted to prevent strikes will be regularly utilized. Its effectiveness in preventing strikes will probably then decline. Nevertheless, in an age of technological and industrial interdependence, this could be the lesser of two evils. Moreover, if wage and price stabilization continues, collective bargaining is already restrained, and strikes to breach government wage order or ceilings are illegal. Under such circumstances, we may be moving closer to a new era in which government determination of

---

[7] For an analysis of this experience, see Northrup, *Compulsory Arbitration*, especially pp. 215–441.

[8] For excellent analyses of the situation in Australia and New Zealand, see Kingsley Laffer, "Does Compulsory Arbitration Prevent Strikes? The Australian Experience," in Richard L. Rowan (ed.), *Collective Bargaining: Survival in the 70's?* (Labor Relations and Public Policy Series, Report No. 5 [Philadelphia: Industrial Research Unit, Wharton School of Finance and Commerce, University of Pennsylvania, 1972]), pp. 154–78; and Noel S. Woods, "The Industrial Relations Situation in New Zealand," *Journal of Industrial Relations*, Vol. 12 (November 1970), pp. 360–65.

the conditions of employment could be more significant than our present system of collective bargaining.

STATE LABOR RELATIONS ACTS

In 1937, the year in which the Supreme Court sanctioned the Wagner Act, Massachusetts, New York, Pennsylvania, Utah, and Wisconsin adopted legislation patterned on the Wagner Act.

In 1939, however, the Pennsylvania and Wisconsin laws were amended to incorporate restrictions on employers and unions, as well as on employees, thus foreshadowing the Taft-Hartley Act. Laws modeled on the Taft-Hartley Act are now in effect in 12 states[9] and the Territory of Guam; those that resemble the Wagner Act are found in four states[10] and Puerto Rico. A number of states have also enacted limited purpose legislation, some of the Landrum-Griffin type.

Jurisdiction

Coverage of the state labor relations acts is limited by (1) the extent of federal preemption and (2) restrictions imposed in the state laws. Between the passage of the Taft-Hartley Act in 1947 and the enactment of the Landrum-Griffin Act of 1959, the jurisdiction of state laws was severely limited to intrastate commerce business not within the purview of the Taft-Hartley law. Amendments contained in the Landrum-Griffin Act specifically gave the states jurisdiction over cases which might fall within the Taft-Hartley Act's jurisdiction, but which the National Labor Relations Board declined to accept under its jurisdictional standards of August 1, 1959. More recently, the jurisdictions of many state laws, as will be discussed in the following chapter, have been expanded to encompass public employees and/or employees of hospitals and other nonprofit groups. In the private sector, however, state activity has tended to stagnate despite the passage of a few new laws in the last decade.[11] State agencies handle annually only about 10% as many as the 35,000 cases which come before the National Labor Relations Board, and one half of these are New York State labor relations cases. Moreover, the typical state case involves a small shop with few employees.

---

[9] Colorado, Hawaii, Kansas, Michigan, Minnesota, North Dakota, Oregon, Pennsylvania, Utah, Vermont, West Virginia, and Wisconsin.

[10] Connecticut, Massachusetts, New York, and Rhode Island. (Massachusetts regulates union entrance requirements and union security provisions but remains basically a Wagner type without union unfair labor practices.)

[11] See Harold A. Katz and Bruce S. Feldacker, "The Decline and Fall of State Regulation of Labor Relations," *Labor Law Journal*, Vol. 20 (June 1968), pp. 327–45.

Unfair Labor Practices

Both the "little Wagner acts" and the "little Taft-Hartley acts" follow the unfair labor practice provisions of the federal act insofar as employer unfair labor practice provisions are concerned. Some also include in their proscriptions specific prohibitions against the blacklist, employer espionage, and other matters which were included within the Taft-Hartley Act's general restrictions on restraint of employees for union activity. The unfair labor practices in the "little Taft-Hartley laws" which are directed against employees and unions may be divided into four categories:

1. Prohibitions of violence and similar activities which were almost universally unlawful before the passage of the labor relations acts—for example, sit-down strikes, sabotage, and mass picketing.
2. Restrictions on peaceful tactics such as picketing and organizing campaigns, especially where coercion is alleged.
3. Limitations on union objectives which make illegal all efforts to achieve a forbidden objective, such as a make-work rule.
4. Regulation of the internal affairs of unions, such as financial matters, election procedure, and eligibility for union office.

Many of these laws thus contain provisions which are similar to those in both the Taft-Hartley and the Landrum-Griffin acts, including the provision in the latter law designed to safeguard the finances and the rights of workers in their relationship with unions. Most provisions controlling union and employee conduct are, however, designed to limit strikes, picketing, or boycotts, or to preclude union interference with the peaceful designation of a bargaining agent.

Representation Disputes

The representation procedure is, in general, similar in most states to that provided under the Taft-Hartley Act. Decertification procedure is not, however, always provided for, although Pennsylvania and Wisconsin, for example, do have something similar.

Administration

Administration of the state labor relations acts is vested in several different types of administrative establishments. In some, typified by the state labor relations boards of New York and Pennsylvania, a single-purpose agency modeled on the National Labor Relations Board was created to handle only unfair labor practice and representation matters arising under the labor relations acts of the states. A second type of administrative agency, such as that in Colorado, Wisconsin, or North Dakota, is multipurpose. It administers the labor relations act in addition to several other functions—such as mediation of labor disputes, or even functions like workmen's compensation, safety, minimum wages, and other protective legislation. As in the case of the National Labor Relations Board, state labor relations agencies cannot enforce their own orders, but must apply to the courts for enforcement.

Specific Laws Regulating Weapons of Conflict

Besides these comprehensive state laws which have been discussed, many states have enacted legislation outlawing or controlling the weapons of conflict in labor-management relations. Thus, 11 states bar picketing of homes;[12] two, of courts;[13] 18 prohibit mass picketing, or blocking plant entrances;[14] and 6 forbid picketing by a union representing only a minority of employees, or by a group that is ineligible to raise a representative election question before the appropriate state agency.[15] Many of these laws are designed to protect individuals or small businesses from coercive union activity.

The constitutionality of many of these provisions remains in doubt, especially in cases in which the Taft-Hartley Act has jurisdiction. As was noted in Chapter 8, governmental regulation of the weapons of conflict involves the difficult question of coercion and free speech, as well as a conflict of state and federal jurisdiction. Hence it is not surprising that the law is unsettled in these areas of social policy.

On the other side have been the several new laws which prohibit or discourage the recruiting of replacements for strikers. Twelve states now have such laws,[16] as have several cities. The purpose of such laws is, of course, to strengthen union bargaining power by making it more difficult to replace strikers. Organized labor has now secured the passage of laws in 11 states[17] making it illegal to require the submission to lie-detector tests as a condition of employment, and in three other states,[18] requiring the licensing of lie-detector machine operators. There is considerable controversy in industry concerning the reliability of such tests and machines. Finally, in this specific law area, we should note again the

---

[12] Alabama, Arkansas, Colorado, Connecticut, Florida, Hawaii, Illinois, Kansas, Michigan, North Dakota, and South Dakota.

[13] Louisiana and Massachusetts.

[14] Arkansas, Colorado, Florida, Georgia, Hawaii, Kansas, Maine, Michigan, Mississippi, Nebraska, New Mexico, North Dakota, South Carolina, South Dakota, Texas, Utah, Virginia, and Wisconsin.

[15] California, Massachusetts, Michigan, New Mexico, Oregon, and Texas.

[16] Delaware, Hawaii, Iowa, Louisiana, Maine, Maryland, Massachusetts, Michigan, New Jersey, Pennsylvania, Rhode Island, and Washington.

[17] Alaska, California, Connecticut, Delaware, Hawaii, Maryland, Massachusetts, New Jersey, Oregon, Rhode Island and Washington.

[18] Arkansas, Florida and Nevada.

existence of 19 state "right-to-work" laws,[19] which were examined in Chapter 6 and which outlaw compulsory unionism.

"Little Norris–La Guardia Acts"

Laws similar to the Norris–La Guardia Act have been enacted by 25 states[20] and Puerto Rico. As on the national scene, these laws have caused the number of injunctions issued in labor disputes to decline sharply. There is, however, tremendous variation in these anti-injunction laws, partially because many have been amended over the years to permit curbs on boycotts, picketing, and other weapons of conflict, and also because some state courts have tended to interpret the laws very narrowly, while others have interpreted them very broadly.

Although there are some exceptions—notably in Massachusetts and Pennsylvania—the trend seems to be a tendency on the part of state legislatures to reduce the immunities in state anti-injunction acts and a tendency on the part of state courts to interpret laws so as to grant relief when they feel it is warranted. In view of the size and strength of labor unions today as compared with the 1930s and 1940s, when most of these anti-injunction laws were adopted, it is not surprising that both legislatures and courts perceive a greater need to restrain strikes, boycotts, and picketing than was the case 25 years ago.

"Little Landrum-Griffin Laws"—Reporting, Disclosure, and Democracy

State labor relations acts in a number of jurisdictions provide for safeguards of union finances and members' rights. Reporting and disclosure laws involving union finances are also in effect in other states;[21] but in nearly all cases, enforcement mechanisms are lacking.

In addition, five states—California, Massachusetts, New York, Washington, and Wisconsin—have enacted legislation requiring disclosure about the activities of health and welfare funds set up by labor-management agreements. These laws require full disclosure of the income, disbursements, and operations of the covered funds, but they all lack

---

[19] Alabama, Arizona, Arkansas, Florida, Georgia, Iowa, Kansas, Mississippi, Nebraska, Nevada, North Carolina, North Dakota, South Carolina, South Dakota, Tennessee, Texas, Utah, Virginia, and Wyoming.

[20] Arizona, Colorado, Connecticut, Hawaii, Idaho, Illinois, Indiana, Kansas, Louisiana, Maine, Maryland, Massachusetts, Minnesota, Montana, New Jersey, New Mexico, New York, North Dakota, Oregon, Pennsylvania, Rhode Island, Utah, Washington, Wisconsin, and Wyoming.

[21] Alabama, Connecticut, Florida, Hawaii, Kansas, Massachusetts, Minnesota, New York, Oregon, South Dakota, Texas, Utah, and Wisconsin. The reporting requirements of the laws of Hawaii, Kansas, Massachusetts, Utah, and Wisconsin are not separate laws but are included in the "little Taft-Hartley laws" of these states.

effective enforcement mechanisms. Connecticut, which once had such a law, repealed it in 1967. As noted in Chapter 3, even the federal law, .enacted in 1962, appears inadequate to police effectively the burgeoning welfare funds amassed by unions, and more stringent national legislation is likely to be passed. The states do not appear either to have the will or the means to police union government, so that it has become and will continue to be a federal task except in special cases.

An unusual law is that enacted in 1952 by both New Jersey and New York to regulate waterfront conditions in the port of New York. It established a bistate Authority to control crime on the waterfront by barring those convicted of felonies from serving as waterfront union officials and by regulating waterfront hiring practices. Although considerable success has been achieved by this Authority, particularly in bringing stability and fairness in the hiring of longshoremen, the Authority's own reports emphasize that crime on the waterfront, in New York as in many other ports, still flourishes. Pilfering, loan sharking, and "kickbacks" remain problems difficult to eliminate in a labor market where more men want jobs than there are jobs available and where the opportunity for preying on the job seeker, the customer, and the public is great. The rise of similar organized thievery at New York airports has resulted in a move to place these areas under control of the Waterfront Commission.

The two most comprehensive state laws aimed at furthering union democracy are the Minnesota Labor Union Democracy Act of 1943 and the New York Labor and Management Improper Practices Act of 1959. The Minnesota law regulates the details of union elections, providing that they must be held at least once every four years by secret ballot. The state can disqualify the union as a bargaining agent in case of violation. The law also gives the state the right to appoint a temporary labor referee to take charge of the union and to conduct a fair election. Although widely heralded when enacted, this law has never been invoked nor utilized.

The New York law is very similar to the financial reporting sections of the Landrum-Griffin Act. It requires financial reporting by both employers and unions, imposes a fiduciary obligation on union officers and agents, and forbids conflict-of-interest transactions. The law also applies to employers and to labor relations consultants in a similar manner as the Landrum-Griffin Act by requiring annual reports on expenditures related to interference, restraint, or other attempts to sway employees away from their rights to choose unions as bargaining agents.

The passage of the Landrum-Griffin Act immediately after New York enacted its legislation has tended to overshadow the New York law. Because of the broad coverage of its provisions, few unions are outside the purview of the Landrum-Griffin Act. Congress decided, however, not to bar concurrent state legislation, for it provided in Section 603(a) of the Landrum-Griffin Act that "except as explicitly provided to the contrary, nothing in this statute shall reduce or limit the responsibilities of any labor organization . . . or take away any right or bar any remedy to which members of a labor organization are entitled under any other federal law or law of any state." What role a concurrent law like New York's Labor and Management Improper Practices Act can and will play, in view of the far-reaching character of the Landrum-Griffin Act, still remains to be determined. Since Congress decided to exercise the full scope of federal jurisdiction in regulating internal union affairs, the states have not found it desirable to legislate further in this field.

Limits on Union Political Expenditures

A final group of laws aimed at controlling union finances are those which limit a union's right to utilize regular union income from membership dues, fees, etc., for political purposes. Four states—Pennsylvania, Texas, Indiana, and Wisconsin—limit union political contributions. The first two are rather narrow, the latter two rather broad in their restrictions. Like the proscription in the Taft-Hartley Act, however, their aim is to force unions to raise money for political purposes voluntarily and directly, instead of utilizing dues money, which may be contributed by employees who oppose the aims or people for which the contribution is given. In general, these laws have been ineffective.

THE DECLINE OF STATE LABOR LEGISLATION

Despite their variety, state labor laws are today relatively insignificant, and indeed, often dormant. Federal preemption and the desire of unions and companies for uniform regulations have insured this result. Although many state laws have been poorly designed and unwisely administered, the takeover by the federal government is not without its adverse consequences. By permitting states wider latitude, Congress and the courts could have utilized states as experimental laboratories for various forms of labor legislation and regulation. The diversity of interests in the various states insure a wide variety of approaches to problems. Excessive federal preemption rules out experimentation, new solutions, and experience, all of which might well contribute to improved labor relations nationally.

QUESTIONS FOR DISCUSSION

1. Is mediation a difficult job to perform? Explain your answer.
2. Do you think that legislation can be devised which would both protect the country against strikes in emergency situations and maintain normal collective bargaining relationships? What type of legislation would be most advantageous to accomplish these two objectives? Explain your answer.

3. Does state labor legislation now on the books provide a comprehensive body of labor law for intrastate business? Do you think it should? Explain your answer.

SUGGESTIONS FOR FURTHER READING

KATZ, HAROLD A., and FELDACKER, BRUCE S. "The Decline and Fall of State Regulation of Labor Relations," *Labor Law Journal,* Vol. 20 (June 1969), pp. 327–45.

An excellent summary of the various state laws regulating labor relations and the reasons for their declining significance.

ROWAN, RICHARD L. (ed.). *Collective Bargaining: Survival in the 70's?* pp. 129–306. Labor Relations and Public Policy Series, Report No. 5. Philadelphia: Industrial Research Unit, Wharton School of Finance and Commerce, University of Pennsylvania, 1972.

A series of articles by several government, business, union, and academic authorities on mediation, emergency strikes, the Australian compulsory arbitration experience, and transportation labor problems.

SIMKIN, WILLIAM E. *Mediation and the Dynamics of Collective Bargaining.* Washington: Bureau of National Affairs, Inc., 1971.

The former head of the Federal Mediation and Conciliation Service discusses the role of mediation and its nature and the problems of the mediator under different and varying circumstances.

Chapter

22

PUBLIC POLICY AND THE
PUBLIC EMPLOYER

A feature of the 1960s was the rapid increase in government employee unionism and the rising incidence of strikes among government employees. Initially, labor relations scholars tended to regard such activities as growing pains associated with the development of private sector—like collective bargaining, in the public sector. That public sector bargaining involves some fundamental differences with its counterpart in the private sector is now becoming increasingly clear. This chapter reviews collective bargaining developments in government employment and analyzes the differences between the public and private sectors.

GOVERNMENT EMPLOYMENT

Since 1950, government employment has grown more rapidly than the total labor force, increasing at an average annual rate of 3.3%.[1] In 1971, as was pointed out in Chapter 1, the federal government employed 2.7 million civilians and 2.8 million were in the Armed Forces, whereas 10.2 million persons worked for local and state governments. Excluding Armed Forces personnel and those who work for private industry but supply goods and services purchased by government, we are concerned with a civilian public labor force of near 13 million—more than 15% of the civilian labor force.

For the next 20 years, the public labor force is not projected to increase at such a rapid rate as it did in the previous two decades. Public education employment, now 23.8% of all government employment, increased most rapidly between 1950 and 1970 but will advance much more slowly; federal civilian employment will increase only slightly; and the armed forces in the absence of international crises, will stabilize. On the other hand, noneducational state and local government employment is expected to advance at a rapid rate. Figure 22–1 illustrates current and projected government employment by sector.

---

[1] *The U.S. Economy in 1990*, prepared by The Conference Board for the White House Conference on "The Industrial World Ahead: A Look at Business in 1990" (1972), p. 18.

FIGURE 22–1

Government Employment, 1950–70, and Projected to 1990

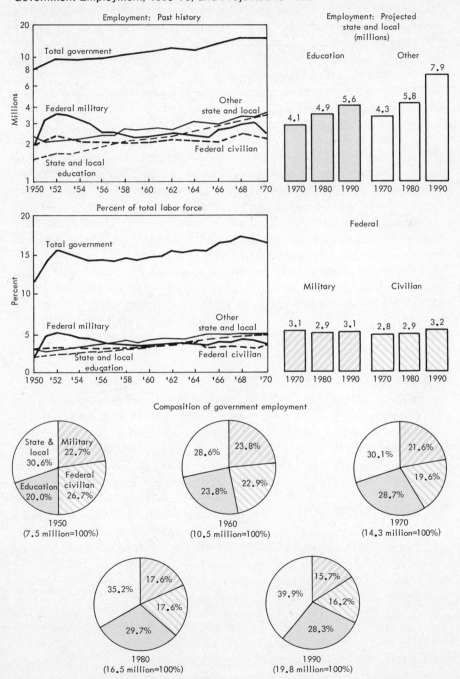

Sources: Department of Commerce; The Conference Board.

In 1990, therefore, the federal government will still be the largest employer, but at the same time will employ a smaller percentage of all government employees. In 1950, 26.7% of all government employees were federal civilian workers; by 1970, only 19.6% were in this category; by 1990, the figure is expected to decline to 16%. The reason is that, although the federal government's budget now includes a host of expensive items not considered a federal function in past years (education, medical assistance, pollution control, mass transit, etc.), increasingly the programs are administered by the states and municipalities. This decentralization will be advanced if President Nixon's revenue sharing proposals are enacted, but in any case it will continue because of the greater efficiency of the federal government in raising money through taxes and the greater capacity of the state and local governments to administer with flexibility and to tailor programs to varying needs and constituencies. The expectation that this decentralized approach will continue accounts for the projected rise of state and local public employment. The fact that the bulk of government employment is at the state and local level, and will remain so in larger proportions, considerably enhances the view that public policies toward such employment, except insofar as federal employees are concerned, should emanate from those government levels. As we shall discuss later, this is now the case in general, but there is a strong movement to propel the federal government into this arena, particularly on the part of organized labor.

UNIONS AND STRIKES IN GOVERNMENT

Public employee unionism is not new, but its growth in recent years has been phenomenal. In the 12 years between 1956 and 1968, the percentage of all union members, who were employed by the government, increased from 5% to 11%. Since the mid-1950s, the public sector unions have been the only ones in the labor movement who have increased their membership at a rate faster than the increase in the labor force. Between 1960 and 1970, the American Federation of State, County, and Municipal Employees (AFSCME) saw its membership increase from 185,000 to 400,000; the American Federation of Government Employees (AFGE), the largest union of federal employees, from 70,000 to 325,000; and the American Federation of Teachers (AFT) from 56,000 to 205,000.[2] By 1971, various unions in the postal service claimed to represent virtually all eligible workers under their jurisdiction. Symbolic of the changing role of government employee unions was the election of the presidents of both AFSCME and AFGE to the AFL–CIO Executive Council.

In addition to these, which might be termed "regular unions," other

---

[2] Joseph P. Goldberg, "Public Employee Developments in 1971," *Monthly Labor Review*, Vol. 95 (January 1972), pp. 56–57.

organizations have been acting as bargaining agents for government employees and growing rapidly. Thus, chapters of the Policemen's Benevolent Association serve policemen in this regard, and the National Education Association, claiming 1 million members, once only the professional organization of public school teachers, now represents in collective bargaining (or "professional negotiations" as NEA spokesmen euphemistically term the process) many thousands more teachers than does its union rival, the American Federation of Teachers. Moreover, NEA chapters have conducted strikes, manned picket lines, and otherwise acted as militantly as have AFT locals. In fact, the employees in the public sector are today represented by a multitude of unions, quasiunions and associations, which added together make the public sector more highly organized than its private counterpart. Such diversity of organizations also adds to the negotiations problems and contribute to the difficulties of peaceful settlement. Moreover, the militancy of employee organizations in the public service has frequently "manifested itself in a determination to achieve union goals regardless of the law."[3] As stated by two very perceptive students of the subject:

The result has been conflict: between public employee unions and political leaders and between unions and those groups seeking enhanced control over governmental decisions affecting them. Some disputes have been settled, but only under the threat of a disruption of governmental services. Others—more

TABLE 22–1(a)

Work Stoppages by Level of Government, 1960, 1969, and 1970*

Year	Total			State government			Local government		
	Number of Stoppages	*Total Workers Involved*	*Man-Days Idle during Year*	*Number of Stoppages*	*Total Workers Involved*	*Man-Days Idle during Year*	*Number of Stoppages*	*Total Workers Involved*	*Man-Days Idle during Year*
1960.....	36	28,600	58,400	3	970	1,170	33	27,600	57,200
1969.....	†411	160,000	745,700	37	20,500	152,400	372	139,000	592,200
1970.....	‡412	333,500	2,023,200	23	8,800	44,600	386	168,900	1,330,500

° Includes stoppages lasting a full day or shift or longer and involving 6 workers or more.
† Includes 2 stoppages of federal employees, affecting 600 workers and resulting in 1,100 man-days of idleness.
‡ Includes 3 stoppages of federal employees, affecting 155,800 workers and resulting in 648,300 man-days of idleness.
Note: Data on stoppages and workers involved refer to all stoppages beginning in the year; man-days idle refer to all stoppages in effect during the year. Because of rounding, sums of individual items may not equal totals.
Source: U.S. Bureau of Labor Statistics.

[3] Harry H. Wellington and Ralph K. Winter, Jr., *The Unions and the Cities* (Studies of Unionism in Government [Washington, D.C.: Brookings Institution, 1971]), p. 35.

TABLE 22–1(b)

Workers Involved as a Percent of Total Employment, 1960, 1969, and 1970

Year	All Work Stoppages	Government Work Stoppages		
		Total	State	Local
1960.............	2.4	0.340	0.060	0.600
1969.............	3.5	1.311	.807	2.013
1970.............	4.7	2.661	.329	2.359

Note: Data on stoppages and workers involved refer to all stoppages beginning in the year; man-days idle refer to all stoppages in effect during the year.

TABLE 22–1(c)

Average Number of Workers Involved per Stoppage, 1960, 1969, and 1970

Year	All Work Stoppages	Government Work Stoppages		
		Total	State	Local
1960.............	396	794	323	836
1969.............	435	*389	554	374
1970.............	578	†810	383	438

* Includes 2 stoppages of federal employees, with an average of 300 workers involved.
† Includes 3 stoppages of federal employees, with an average of 51,900 workers involved.
Note: Data on stoppages and workers involved refer to all stoppages beginning in the year; man-days idle refer to all stoppages in effect during the year.

TABLE 22–1(d)

Man-days of Idleness per Worker, 1960, 1969, and 1970

Year	All Work Stoppages	Government Work Stoppages		
		Total	State	Local
1960............	14.5	2.0	1.2	2.1
1969............	17.3	*4.7	7.4	4.3
1970............	20.1	†6.1	5.1	7.9

* Includes 2 stoppages of federal employees which resulted in an average of 1.8 man-days of idleness per worker involved.
† Includes 3 stoppages of federal employees, with an average of 4.2 man-days of idleness per worker involved.
Note: Data on stoppages and workers involved refer to all stoppages beginning in the year; man-days idle refer to all stoppages in effect during the year.
Source: U.S. Bureau of Labor Statistics.

than a few—have been settled only after an illegal strike that creates the atmosphere of a crisis if not the fact itself. And those disputes involving highly charged political issues, such as a police civilian review board or school decentralization plan, or touching society's most sensitive nerves by pitting a union of one race against a citizenry of another, have frequently left an ugly residue of racial and ethnic tension. The effect of such labor disputes on the social and political fabric of New York City—and of the events of Memphis on the nation—surely demonstrates their deadly potential.[4]

The rising militancy of public workers, as indicated by their propensity to strike, is illustrated by the data in Table 22–1. In 1960, there were 36 stoppages of government employees involving 28,600 employees and 58,400 man-days idle; in 1970, the figures were 412 stoppages, 333,500 employees, and 2,023,200 man-days. The bulk of the stoppages have been in local government, with teachers and librarians having the highest strike incidence, but policemen, firemen, sanitation workers, doctors and nurses, and various clerical and manual workers have all been involved. Federal employees have rarely been involved, although well-advertised stoppages of airport traffic controllers and postal workers did disrupt air travel and postal service in recent years.

Compensation

Historically, the public sector has paid lower wages than the private one, but it often has provided more liberal benefits. The 1960s saw the wage relationship change, undoubtedly a result of the rising power of public employee organizations. The Federal Pay Comparability Act of 1970 now requires the President to see that federal employee pay rates are comparable with private enterprise pay rates for the same levels of work. Successive salary increases voted by Congress at the urging of the strong federal employee unions' lobby, plus "catch-up" increases to conform to the Pay Comparability Act, have resulted in substantial annual gains—6.2% per year since 1965.[5]

Urban classroom teachers saw their salaries rise even more dramatically, increasing 14.1% between 1967 and 1969 alone.[6] At the same time, firemen and policemen topped this with their salaries rising 17.3% in the same biennium.[7] As noted in Chapter 5, benefits of government employees have also continued to rise, sometimes to such an extent, as in the case of pensions, that the fiscal integrity of local government bodies are in

---

[4] *Ibid.*

[5] "Government Employees' Salary Trends," *Current Wage Developments* (U.S. Bureau of Labor Statistics, No. 284 [September 1971]), pp. 36–37.

[6] *Ibid.*, p. 47.

[7] *Ibid.*, p. 57.

doubt.[8] There can be no doubt that public employee unions have produced for their members.

The question left unanswered by this record of conflict and union success is whether and to what extent collective bargaining is the appropriate labor policy for the public sector. An examination of the differences between the public and private environments and of the existing regulations and legislation will aid in shedding light on this question.

Public Sector Bargaining: The Traditional Arguments

In the private sector, collective bargaining, theoretically, is a means of achieving labor peace, of increasing participation by workers in determining the terms and conditions under which they labor, of giving employers a force through which to work in political arenas, and of equalizing or increasing employee bargaining power viz-à-vis the employer.[9] Anyone who has read the previous chapters will, of course, understand that private sector bargaining works imperfectly—indeed, so imperfectly that once again, the federal government in 1971 was forced to intervene to avoid runaway inflation. Nevertheless, there remains a strong presumption that collective bargaining may still be preferred to other methods of industrial relations, for example, compulsory arbitration, primarily because it permits the parties themselves to determine their own industrial fate. The cost to the public of permitting such price/wage distortions as may result from excessive union power in some sectors of the private economy has been, over long periods at least, inherently limited by the economic constraints of the market.

Sovereignty and Strikes

The argument for transferring the private sector bargaining system to the public sector is formidable and has wide support. Moreover, it has overcome many decades of traditional opposition based on the theory of sovereignty. For many years the assumption was that since the government represents the sovereign power, it alone could set the terms and conditions for the employment of its employees. Critics quickly pointed out that sovereign authorities can delegate and share authority. As early as 1912, with the passage of the Lloyd–La Follette Act, the federal government conceded to its employees the right to petition, to confer, or to request changes in their conditions of employment without interference, and this was generally interpreted to mean approval of federal employee

---

[8] For details of New York City's pension debacle, see A. H. Raskin, "Politics Upends the Bargaining Table," in Sam Zagoria (ed.), *Public Workers and Public Unions* (Englewood Cliffs, N.J.: Prentice-Hall, Inc., for the American Assembly, 1972), pp. 139–42.

[9] See Wellington and Winter, *Unions and the Cities,* pp. 8–9.

unionism. Nevertheless, many states and municipalities questioned the
right of public employees to unionize or declined to bargain, or even to
confer, with representatives of employees. Often, government leaders
that did bargain refused to sign contracts, limiting arguments to verbal
understandings or else posting the results of "agreements" on bulletin
boards as managerial decisions.[10]

A second traditional argument advanced against permitting collective
bargaining for government employees is that strikes would inevitably
result (as they have) and that strikes against government are both of an
insurrectionary nature and intolerable because vital services would be
interrupted. In the post–World War II period, several states passed laws
forbidding strikes and providing for severe penalties for strikers. The
tone of such legislation was similar to that of the Taft-Hartley Act of
1947 which states:

It shall be unlawful for any individual employed by the United States or any
agency thereof including wholly-owned government corporations to participate in any strike. Any individual employed by the United States or by any
such agency, who strikes, shall be discharged immediately from his employment, and shall forfeit his civil service status, if any, and shall not be eligible
for reemployment for three years by the United States or any such agency.

Opponents of the traditional ban against public employee strikes quite
correctly have noted that strikes are not insurrections, that many public
workers provide less essential services than do private ones, and that the
status of employees should not change because private interests sell their
companies to public agencies or vice versa. Certainly, there is much truth
in these assertions. Strikes for higher wages are obviously not insurrections; a massive withdrawal of minor government clerks is not only no
inconvenience to the public but it might even aid the public by illus-
trating the nonessential character of much government work. On the
other hand, a strike of privately operated railroads could cause tremendous inconvenience, or even a national emergency. Finally, as many
transit systems are sold to public bodies, should their employees lose the
right to strike? When private companies purchase public power plants, as
they have on many occasions, do the employees then obtain the right to
strike? In each case, a strike causes the same impact on the public, whether
the striking employees are from the public or private sector.

Arguments on these narrow grounds have set the tone of public policy
since the late 1950s. The federal government by Executive Order, and a
majority of the states by legislation, have encouraged collective bargaining on the private sector model. Although the federal government and

---

[10] Court decisions of recent years would appear to invalidate state laws or local
ordinances which deny public employees the right to join unions. On the other
hand, absent specific legislation to the contrary, no public body is required to bargain
with a union of its employees. For details see, *ibid.,* pp. 69–82.

most state laws do not legalize strikes of government employees, three states[11] do permit such strikes under certain conditions, and government leaders, whatever the legislation, generally do not enforce penalties when such strikes occur. After a review of the existing public policy, we shall examine whether in fact collective bargaining in the public sector or the private model can be expected to work in the public interest.

FEDERAL EMPLOYEE REGULATION

Although a few state laws encouraging public employee bargaining antedated modern federal action, it was Executive Order 10988, issued by the late President John F. Kennedy, January 17, 1962, that set the tone for current policy. Even though the Lloyd–La Follette Act of 1912, as already noted, gave federal employees the right to join unions, prior to the Kennedy order the federal government did not have a consistent program of union recognition and collective bargaining for its employees. Some agencies, such as the Tennessee Valley Authority, recognized unions and dealt with them as exclusive bargaining agents, even signing contracts with them. Others, which have less discretion in determining conditions of employment, dealt with unions in much the same manner but did not sign contracts. In such cases, notices were sometimes posted on bulletin boards over the signature of the agency or department manager embodying the substance of what had been agreed to with the government employees' union. Many agencies, however, neither recognized nor dealt with unions.

Outside of the Post Office Department, where union organization in 1961 covered 84% of the employees, government-owned shipyards and arsenals, and special "independent" agencies such as the TVA, the extent of organization in the federal government service was not large prior to the Kennedy order. It has mushroomed dramatically since then. The order provided for three separate forms of recognition—exclusive, formal, and informal—depending on the extent to which employees designated unions to represent them. Bargaining is necessarily restricted as to scope because Congress establishes wages and benefits, and compulsory union membership is not permitted.

On October 29, 1969, President Nixon modified federal policy by Executive Order 11491. It provides for exclusive representation only, based on majority rule. The Nixon order sets forth unfair labor practices and standards of union conduct on the Taft-Hartley and Landrum-Griffin model, and designates the Assistant Secretary of Labor for Labor-Management Relations to administer charges pursuant to these sections and

---

[11] Hawaii, Pennsylvania, and Vermont. See below for a discussion of these and similar laws.

also to make bargaining unit determinations. Bargaining scope continues to be limited and compulsory union membership banned.[12]

Federal government employee unions have historically lobbied for higher wages and benefits through legislative action. The smaller scope of bargaining, particularly in view of their oft-demonstrated influence with Congress, is therefore not necessarily a disadvantage. The Postal Reorganization Act of 1970 may, however, presage a change of method toward greater bargaining and less legislation.

Subchapter II of the 1970 Postal law, which abolished the Post Office Department and set up an independent government corporation to handle the mails, puts postal employees under the Taft-Hartley Act instead of under Executive Order 11491, insofar as representation and unfair labor practices are concerned. The postal law, however, prohibits strikes, outlaws all union security arrangements except the voluntary checkoff, and provides for fact finding and, if required, compulsory arbitration, to resolve impasses. Of major significance right now is that Subchapter II provides that wages, hours, and working conditions are to be negotiated by postal unions which have exclusive bargaining rights. Moreover, whereas both Executive Orders 10988 and 11491 contain strong management rights clauses, Subchapter II instead appears to make union proposals restricting technological changes or limiting subcontracting matters of mandatory bargaining.[13]

The Federal Pay Comparability Act of 1970 also increases the scope of bargaining for federal employees. The law transfers to the President the establishment of salaries of classified federal employees but retains a veto for Congress. Unions are given a very substantial role in the steps which precede the President's determination:

A Federal Employee Pay Council is established, with five members of employee organizations. Their views are to be sought and given "thorough consideration" by the President's agents (the Office of Management and Budget and the Civil Service Commission) on such matters as the coverage of the annual BLS survey (which serves as the basis for comparison with private enterprise levels for the same levels of work), the process of comparing statutory pay rates with these levels, and the actual adjustments proposed to achieve comparability. The report to the President by his agents is to include the views thus presented. An independent Advisory Committee on Federal Pay is also established. For presidential appointment of the three members, persons are to be recommended by the Director of the Federal Mediation and

---

[12] For good summaries of the federal public employee bargaining arrangements, see Lee C. Shaw, "The Development of Federal and State Laws," in Zagoria, *Public Workers and Public Unions*, pp. 24–26; and Harriet E. Berger, "The Old Order Giveth Away to the New: A Comparison of Executive Order 10988 with Executive Order 11491," *Labor Law Journal*, Vol. 21 (February 1970), pp. 79–87.

[13] Shaw, "Development of Federal and State Laws," p. 25.

Conciliation Service who are "generally recognized for their impartiality, knowledge, and experience in the field of labor relations and pay policy." The advisory committee is to review the annual report of the President's agents, consider further views presented in writing by employee organizations, the President's agents, and other government officials, and report its findings and recommendations to the President.[14]

The procedure leaves open to the unions their effective lobbying privileges in case they do not like the President's determination. This two bites at the apple procedure—bargaining and political maneuvering—is one of the factors that distinguishes the public sector situation from the private. Although the above procedure purports to further bargaining and to decrease lobbying, it would appear to do that only if the unions are satisfied with the results.[15]

STATE AND MUNICIPAL REGULATION

Wisconsin in 1959 adopted the first state public employee bargaining law; and by 1972, 20 states had followed suit.[16] In addition, 15 states have enacted separate statutes covering teachers,[17] ten special acts for firemen and policemen,[18] and others have enacted laws providing for collective bargaining arrangements governing public urban transit districts,[19] port authorities, or other public bodies which take over and operate formerly private facilities. Private hospitals and other such nonprofit organizations are sometimes covered by public employee laws, sometimes by legislation affecting private employees, and sometimes by neither. States may have laws covering most or all employees in addition to legislation separately covering special groups. In Pennsylvania, publicly owned transit appears to be covered by two somewhat contradictory laws, and police and firemen are subject to a third law.

The general public employee legislation is of two kinds: the most common provides for required collective bargaining on the Taft-Hartley Act model; a minority, however, only compel the public bodies "to meet and confer" with representatives of employees. The trend is definitely for

---

[14] Goldberg, "Public Employee Developments," p. 62.

[15] *Ibid.*

[16] California, Connecticut, Delaware, Hawaii, Kansas, Maine, Massachusetts, Michigan, Minnesota, Nebraska, Nevada, New Hampshire, New Jersey, New York, Oregon, Pennsylvania, Rhode Island, South Dakota, Vermont, Washington, and Wisconsin.

[17] Alaska, California, Connecticut, Delaware, Idaho, Kansas, Maryland, Minnesota, Montana, Nebraska, North Dakota, Oregon, Rhode Island, Vermont, and Washington.

[18] Firemen only: Alabama, Florida, Georgia, Idaho, Wyoming and Vermont. Firemen and Policemen: Oklahoma, Pennsylvania, Rhode Island, and South Dakota.

[19] For transit, see Darold T. Barnum, "From Public to Private: Labor Relations in Urban Transit," *Industrial and Labor Relations Review*, Vol. 25 (October 1971), pp. 95–115.

the latter to be supplanted by the former. Some state agencies establish separate agencies to administer the legislation; others provide that existing administrative bodies assume these duties, which include bargaining unit determination, unfair labor practice enforcement, and, in many cases, impasse resolution techniques.

Bargaining Unit Problems

The inexperience of state and local administrators has led to a large number of fragmented bargaining units and a host of concomitant problems familiar to students of labor relations in the construction, railroad, printing, maritime, air transport, and amusement industries, which are organized on a craft union basis. Except in a few cities, such as Philadelphia, recognition has usually been given to unions on an extent-of-organization basis regardless of administrative efficiency or employee affinity of interest. Then as other employees unionize, new units are recognized. The result has been exacerbated union rivalries and consequent attempts of one union to gain increases in excess of another and, in many cases, almost continual turmoil. New York City is an extreme example of this problem.[20]

Inexperienced public officials have also failed to give heed to private sector experience in other ways. Professional and clerical employees have sometimes been submerged into units dominated by blue-collar workers, causing unrest, dissatisfaction, and recruitment difficulties. Confidential employees (for example, secretaries to administrators), supervisory employees, and even middle-management personnel have been placed in bargaining units with the result that their value to management has been dissipated. In other situations, governmental units have negotiated increases with unions and not provided increases for supervisory and managerial personnel, causing the latter to unionize in order to seek redress, as they have in Pennsylvania. And as in the 1930s in the private sector, collective bargaining in the public sector has sometimes so enhanced union power and deflated that of supervisors and lower management that the latter have sought unions of their own, quit their jobs, or ceased to attempt to work effectively.

The Scope of Bargaining

Of major importance in the public sector has been the scope of bargaining. This is now primarily a state and local problem, for the executive orders have limited the scope of bargaining in the federal service.[21]

---

[20] See Raskin, "Politics Upends the Bargaining Table," pp. 139–42.

[21] There are rumbles, however, particularly in the Department of Health Education and Welfare, where employees have attempted to overrule policies of the Nixon Administration. This is part of the policy–union–civil service conflict discussed below.

Teachers negotiate about classroom size, curricula and student discipline; professors demand the right to elect department chairmen; social workers have struck against more stringent welfare regulations and demand restrictions be placed on case loads; policemen, firemen, nurses, and others negotiate terms affecting the scope of their work and the extent and degree of protection afforded the public. As a result, the public employee unions assume considerable power over and above other interest groups to determine the extent and quality of public service. In the words of Wellington and Winter: "When this occurs, the scope of bargaining in the public sector must be regulated in a manner that will adequately limit the role of unions in the political decision-making process."[22]

Civil Service Conflicts

Collective bargaining in most government sectors is imposed on existing civil service regulations. These regulations often set forth rules for promotion, pay increases, and job protection. Sometimes this results in restrictions over what may be bargained, conflicts in the locus of authority, or bargaining for improvements over and above what is provided automatically by law. Thus, if the promotion process is set forth in law, it cannot be altered by bargaining, absent further enabling legislation. On the other hand, employees who have processed grievances through the collective bargaining grievance machinery have, if not satisfied, started the process all over again via civil service procedures. Contrary and conflicting rulings have resulted. In Pennsylvania, where teachers receive automatic wage increases of $300 each year, the teachers' unions bargain for how much *above* these increases they should receive. It remains to be seen, in view of these conflicts, whether collective bargaining and civil services rules and procedures can co-exist and, if so, in what form.[23]

Impasse Resolution

The authors were able to state accurately in previous editions of this book that "no government body in the United States concedes the right of its employees to strike." This is no longer true. Three states—Hawaii, Pennsylvania, and Vermont—legalize public employee strikes where no emergency or major inconveniences are involved, and the Supreme Court of Michigan has apparently afforded this right to public employees without explicit legislative sanction.[24] As already noted, the Taft-Hartley Act

---

[22] *Unions and the Cities*, p. 142.

[23] For a further analysis of the problems associated with the imposition of collective bargaining on existing civil service, see U.S. Department of Labor, Labor-Management Services Administration, *Collective Bargaining in Public Employment and the Merit System* (Washington, D.C.: U.S. Government Printing Office, 1972).

[24] Shaw, "Development of Federal and State Laws," p. 23.

contains an explicit prohibition against strikes of federal employees, and in all other states, whether or not specific legislation exists, the courts probably will enjoin public employee strikes as illegal.

Where states have public employee legislation, the most common type of impasse resolution procedure is mediation followed by fact finding. Since this does not supply a final resolution unless accepted by both parties, and since strikes have increasingly occurred, many jurisdictions are moving toward compulsory arbitration. Policemen and firemen favor this approach, undoubtedly because their pleas seem certain to fall upon sympathetic arbitral ears.

The principal reason why compulsory arbitration has not gained more adherents is that it removes final fiscal authority from the electorate to a third party who is not responsible to that electorate. Thus, in Pennsylvania generous arbitration awards for policemen or firemen have compelled elected officials to alter town budgets and curtail some services in order to provide the policemen and firemen compensation ordered by arbitrators pursuant to the state law. Perhaps the solution is to devise comprehensive regulations limiting the scope of arbitral authority, but this is difficult to accomplish.

A number of states, including New York, provide penalties for strikers, or unions officials, and/or unions which engage in strikes. Such penalties include checkoff revocations, fines, and jail terms. They have not deterred strikes. It may be that they are not sufficiently harsh. More often, however, politicians decline to invoke penalties, and this is likely always to be the case. The reason is clear: politics, not economics, is supreme in public employee collective bargaining—a major reason why strikes in the public service cannot serve the purpose of motivating agreement.

Strike Policy in Public Employment

In the private sector, as we have noted in previous chapters, collective bargaining is theoretically constrained by economic realities and the fact that the strike induces settlement by hurting both parties. Of course, this system works haltingly and better in some periods and in some industries than others. Moreover, government policy, by such actions as intervention in disputes, enhancing the power of one of the parties too greatly, or by paying welfare to strikers, often inhibits the effectiveness of the system.

Nevertheless, the constraints are real. The construction unions seemed to be able to gain increases in the late 1960s beyond any limits; yet in 1972, their leaders were attempting to hold local unions in line because of their widespread loss of work to nonunion competitors. Periodically, unions have negotiated wage decreases, fought for tariffs to exclude foreign competitors, or otherwise demonstrated their concern for eco-

FIGURE 22-2

Philadelphia Public Workers' Earnings Caught Up Quickly with Those in Other Major Cities

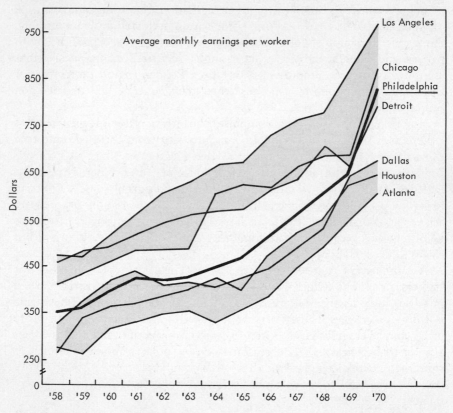

Source: Data, *City Employment in 1958 . . . 1970*, GE-No. 1, U.S. Department of Commerce, Bureau of the Census; chart, reproduced from *Federal Reserve Bank of Philadelphia Business Review*, March 1972, p. 8.

nomic constraints. These same constraints have forced employers to endure long strikes in order to maintain economic viability.

The demand for labor in the private sector is thus elastic in varying degrees. To the extent that unions push up wages, they risk a trade-off for unemployment. Some, like the United Mine Workers, have done this almost with impunity; yet in nearly all cases, the elasticity of demand for labor reduces union wage push.

In the public sector, however, the service demand is usually inelastic. Indeed, the service is likely to be performed by government because it is a natural monopoly. Union wage pushes in such instances are likely to be resisted only slightly because of this inelasticity. And when a strike occurs, the clamor for resumption of service is likely to be overwhelming: the strike hurts the public before it hurts the union. *Politically*, the union cannot be resisted.

It is the political factor which gives the unions such power in the public service. Opposing the union in a tense situation is likely to give the politician few new friends and many enemies. The public wants the service; that it will get that service at the expense of deterioration in others is not usually immediately discernible. To an ambitious politician who desires to remain in office or to go on toward better things, there is often really no choice.

This is particularly true where the impact of concessions show up later, such as in the case of pensions. Concessions can sometimes be made at little present cost, but at phenomenal costs later, when perhaps a new incumbent must wrestle with resultant revenue problems. The immense pension liabilities of Philadelphia and New York are cases in point. In the former city, for example, one negotiation—1971—probably added a $33\frac{1}{3}\%$ increase to pension costs which were already high!

Political alliances between public employees and incumbent politicians are not new. With the former in strong unions, however, they take on new meaning. Through both economic and political pressure, the public employees exert powerful influences to enhance their economic well-being. In Philadelphia, for example, after becoming a principal supporter of former Mayor James H. J. Tate for reelection, the union secured dramatic raises in public employee wages (see Figure 22–2). Very large wage increases have been likewise occurring in all governmental areas as Figure 22–3 shows:

Government workers at all levels achieved average monthly earnings gains well in excess of the cost of living. During the period 1965–1970 they also made gains relative to workers in other industries. The average gain in monthly earnings in the private sector was 4.7 percent per year—well below all gains in the public sector. While some industries such as contract construction posted gains comparable to those in the public sector, earnings changes in industries with occupational structures similar to those of governments did not increase as much. For instance, annual increases in earnings in finance, insurance, and real estate—an industrial class with a work force similar to many governmental units—averaged 5.1 percent over the last five years. This is a full percent below the average for any level of government.

This rise in earnings gains means that priority for government service allocation may well be passing from a variety of interest groups to unions. As one study noted:

When a firm's costs rise and internal economizing is unsuccessful, it must receive higher prices from consumers or accept lower profits. Since large city governments don't make profits, they must receive higher "prices" to continue operating at the same level. Governments "raise prices" by increasing taxes— the price of public services to citizens. This solution has fallen on hard times,

FIGURE 22-3

Government Workers at All Levels Have Achieved Real Gains

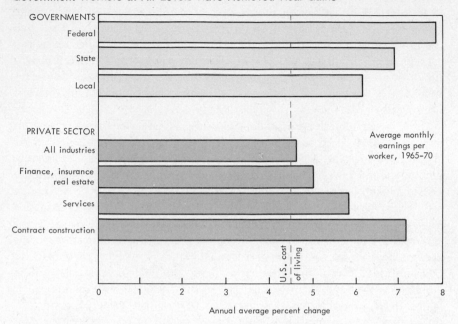

Source: Reproduced from *Federal Reserve Bank of Philadelphia Business Review*, March 1972, p. 16. The estimates of earnings changes for the private sector are based on data on average weekly earnings, Table C-5, *Employment and Earnings*, U.S. Department of Labor, Bureau of Labor Statistics. Comparisons here are tempered because growth in workers' earnings in the private sector are affected more by changes in hours worked per week than those of government workers. Thus, average *hourly earnings* of government workers probably did not exceed those of private sector workers as much as did monthly earnings over this period.

however. Taxpayers across the land are "revolting" against increased levies. . . .

If no other source of funds can be tapped, the only alternative for a government is to slash expenditures and services. If the price of theater tickets or dinners goes up, people generally go out less often. In sum, the taxpayers of large cities face a Hobson's choice. If wage changes raise the cost of police protection and city taxpayers refuse to fork over higher taxes, "somebody else"—the state house or even the White House—must foot the bill or there will be less protection. The same goes for schools, streets, and social welfare. The laws of economics apply just as clearly to governments as to firms. Public employees can not be paid more unless greater sacrifices are made.[25]

Another reason for believing that strikes should not play a part in public employee bargaining is the extent to which race can exacerbate such situations. Teachers' strikes in New York, garbage collectors' strikes

[25] James L. Freund, "Wage Pressures on City Hall: Philadelphia Experience in Perspective," *Federal Reserve Bank of Philadelphia Business Review*, March 1972, p. 17.

in Memphis and Atlanta, and public hospital employees' strikes in Charleston, South Carolina, have been just a few such strikes with strong racial overtones. The extent of blacks in municipal work and whites in municipal authority indicate a potential for public employee strikes to become racial conflicts. On that ground alone, with the emotional content and the possibility of deep changes resulting, it would seem better not to consider strikes for impasse resolution.

Given this combination of political and economic power, and the explosive environment, it seems unrealistic to suppose that public employee strikes can serve a constructive purpose for the public good. It must be recognized that some will occur. It must also be recognized that other forms of settlement, for example, compulsory arbitration, are imperfect instruments often yielding unsatisfactory results. Certainly, we need new social experimentation and engineering to provide us with new tools to resolve public employee problems. But to transfer the collective bargaining mechanism as developed in the private sector to the public sector ignores the fundamental institutional differences between the two. As concluded by Wellington and Winter:

We believe that in the cities, counties and states [as well as in the federal government] there are other claimants with needs at least as pressing as those of the public employees. Such claimants can never have the power the unions will win if we mindlessly import into the public sector all the collective bargaining practices developed in the private sector. Make no mistake about it, government is not "just another industry."[26]

QUESTIONS FOR DISCUSSION

1. What are the features of public employment which distinguish it from private employment? How should these features influence public policy determination?
2. Why has most union activity and strikes in the public sector occurred in the cities? Have municipal unions been successful and, if so, by what criteria?
3. How will the Federal Pay Comparability Act affect salary determination and collective bargaining in the public service?

SUGGESTIONS FOR FURTHER READING

Moskow, Michael H. *Teachers and Unions: The Applicability of Collective Bargaining to Public Education.* Philadelphia: University of Pennsylvania Press, 1966.

Shils, Edward B., and Whittier, C. Taylor. *Teachers, Administrators, and Collective Bargaining.* New York: Thomas Y. Crowell Co., 1968.

---

[26] *Unions and the Cities,* p. 202.

Perry, Charles R., and Widman, Wesley A. *The Impact of Negotiations in Public Education*. Worthington, Ohio: Charles A. Jones Publishing Co., 1970.

Three studies of unionism and collective bargaining in public education.

Moskow, Michael H.; Loewenberg, J. Joseph; and Koziara, Edward C. *Collective Bargaining in Public Employment*. New York: Random House, Inc., 1970.

An analysis of collective bargaining in all levels of government.

Stanley, David T. *Managing Local Government Under Pressure*. Washington, D.C.: Brookings Institution, 1971.

Wellington, Harry H., and Winter, Ralph K., Jr. *The Unions and the Cities*. Washington, D.C.: Brookings Institution, 1971.

Two excellent studies of the theory and practice of collective bargaining and its impact on city government.

Zagoria, Sam (ed.). *Public Workers and Public Unions*. Englewood Cliffs, N.J.: Prentice-Hall, Inc., 1972.

A series of well-written articles on various aspects of public employee collective bargaining.

Chapter
23

CIVIL RIGHTS AND EQUAL
PAY LEGISLATION

The Civil Rights Act of 1964, as amended in 1972, makes it unlawful for a company, union, employment agency or joint labor-management apprentices committee to discriminate because of religion, race, sex, or national origin. Similar legislation exists in nearly all states outside of the South. In addition, federal and state laws proscribe discrimination on the basis of age and require that equal pay be paid for equal work regardless of sex. Obviously, such legislation profoundly affects the employment process and the collective bargaining relationship.

TITLE VII OF THE CIVIL RIGHTS ACT OF 1964, AS AMENDED

In previous chapters we have pointed out that, despite great gains, black citizens and other minorities, are disproportionately concentrated in the lower income positions, are disproportionately among the unemployed, and suffer numerous educational and income disadvantages. This remains true despite a decade of great gains for minorities in which they progressed more rapidly than the population as a whole. One reason for the progress was the sustained high prosperity of the 1960s with its concomitant labor shortages and therefore employment opportunities for virtually all members of the work force. Another reason was the concentration of private and public efforts on civil rights, including especially nondiscriminatory employment. The key legislation was Title VII of the Civil Rights Act of 1964, the Equal Employment Opportunity Title. In 1972, this title was amended to expand its coverage and to enhance the powers of its administrative agency.

Legislative and Administrative Background

Since World War II, the federal government through Presidential Executive Orders and the states via legislation have attempted to deal with the problem of employment discrimination and unequal opportunity. On June 25, 1941, President Franklin D. Roosevelt issued Executive Order 8802, the first of several of this type. It established the

President's Committee on Fair Employment Practice which operated throughout the war period. Although the Committee held hearings, dramatized the issue of Negro employment, and undoubtedly contributed to the increase in the utilization of Negro manpower, its lack of statutory authority prevented it from securing compliance with its orders when discriminating employers or unions balked. Thus, it failed to make an appreciable change in the employment practices of the railroad or West Coast shipbuilding industries, where employers' discrimination was buttressed by active union support, if not leadership.

The President's Committee on Fair Employment Practice ended its life in 1945, after being denied funds by Congress. It was followed by a succession of committees whose jurisdiction was limited to establishments doing business under contracts with the federal government. These committees were first set up by President Harry S Truman, and then reorganized by each succeeding President. Initially, they relied on persuasion and publicity. Moreover, they lacked jurisdiction over unions, who are not party to government controls, but who, particularly in the construction industry, are often, as the suppliers of labor under closed-shop contracts, the focal point of discrimination.

Executive Order 10925, issued by the late President Kennedy on March 6, 1961, and the subsequent Order 11246 of President Johnson, which President Nixon has allowed to remain in effect, introduced a new concept, "affirmative action," which requires employers doing business with the government, actively to seek out minorities. This concept has had a profound impact on employer hiring and promoting policies; it will be discussed later after reviewing the basic law, Title VII of the Civil Rights Act of 1964, as amended.

New York State, the first to take state action in this field, enacting its nondiscrimination law in 1945. As of July 1972, some 35 states, nearly all of those outside of the South, had enacted similar laws. Such legislation operates similarly to that on the federal level, which is described later. Like state labor relations activities, and in spite of the fact that federal law, relating to civil rights specifically reserves a place for state laws, state equal opportunity legislation appears to have declined in significance during recent years. The same is true for the municipal ordinances which several large cities have enacted to deal with equal opportunity. Where a federal law exists, it apparently takes over despite congressional attempts to safeguard state action.

TITLE VII—COVERAGE AND CONTENT

Title VII, as amended, applies to interstate employers of 15 or more persons, to unions which have 15 or more members, and to employment agencies. States and local governments are covered by Title VII, except for employees directly chosen by elected officials as advisors, cabinet

FIGURE 23–1

Unlawful Employment Practices under Title VII, Civil Rights Act of 1964, as Amended

---

DISCRIMINATION BECAUSE OF RACE, COLOR, RELIGION, OR NATIONAL ORIGIN

Sec. 703. (a) It shall be an unlawful employment practice for an employer—

(1) to fail or refuse to hire or to discharge any individual, or otherwise to discriminate against any individual with respect to his compensation, terms, conditions, or privileges of employment, because of such individual's race, color, religion, sex, or national origin; or

(2) to limit, segregate, or classify his employees in any way which would deprive or tend to deprive any individual of employment opportunities or otherwise adversely affect his status as an employee, because of such individual's race, color, religion, sex, or national origin.

(b) It shall be an unlawful employment practice for an employment agency to fail or refuse to refer for employment, or otherwise to discriminate against, any individual because of his race, color, religion, sex, or national origin, or to classify or refer for employment any individual on the basis of his race, color, religion, sex, or national origin.

(c) It shall be an unlawful employment practice for a labor organization—

(1) to exclude or to expel from its membership, or otherwise to discriminate against, any individual because of his race, color, religion, sex, or national origin;

(2) to limit, segregate, or classify its membership, or in any way to classify or fail or refuse to refer for employment any individual, in any way which would deprive or tend to deprive any individual of employment opportunities, or would limit such employment opportunities or otherwise adversely affect his status as an employee or as an applicant for employment, because of such individual's race, color, religion, sex, or national origin; or

(3) to cause or attempt to cause an employer to discriminate against an individual in violation of this section.

(d) It shall be an unlawful employment practice for any employer, labor organization, or joint labor-management committee controlling apprenticeship or other training or retraining, including on-the-job training programs to discriminate against any individual because of his race, color, religion, sex, or national origin in admission to, or employment in any program established to provide apprenticeship or other training.

OTHER UNLAWFUL EMPLOYMENT PRACTICES

Sec. 704. (a) It shall be an unlawful employment practice for an employer to discriminate against any of his employees or applicants for employment, for an employment agency or joint labor-management committee controlling apprenticeship or other training or retraining, including on-the-job training programs, to discriminate against any individual, or for a labor organization to discriminate against any member thereof or applicant for membership, because he has opposed any practice made an unlawful employment practice by this title, or because he has made a charge, testified, assisted, or participated in any manner in an investigation, proceeding, or hearing under this title.

(b) It shall be an unlawful employment practice for an employer, labor organization, or employment agency or joint labor-management committee controlling apprenticeship or other training or retraining, including on-the-job training programs, to print or publish or cause to be printed or published any notice or advertisement relating to employment by such an employer or membership in or any classification or referral for employment by such a labor organization, or relating to any classification or referral for employment by such an employment agency, indicating any preference, limitation, specification, or discrimination, based on race, color, religion, sex, or national origin, except that such a notice or advertisement may indicate a preference, limitation, specification, or discrimination based on religion, sex, or national origin when religion, sex, or national origin is a bona fide occupational qualification for employment.

members, or personal staff members. The U.S. Civil Service Commission is directed by Title VII to enforce an equal employment policy consistent with Title VII for federal agencies and employees. Title VII's general coverage is further enhanced by reference to the Landrum-Griffin's definition of employers who are designated in interstate commerce which, as noted in Chapter 20, contains the most comprehensive such definition to be found in major labor legislation. Finally, the 1972 amendments specifically brought private and public nonreligious educational institutions within Title VII's purview.

The basic proscriptions of the law are set forth in Figure 23–1. The coverage of the law extends to joint labor-management committees or other organizations controlling apprenticeship—thus closing a loophole found in many state fair employment laws. It permits religion, sex, or national origin to be utilized where valid occupational classification calls for such a distinction (for example, a model, a Kosher butcher, or a teacher in a girls' school or in a religious seminary), but the 1972 amendments define "religion" to include all aspects of religious observance, practice, and belief so as to require employers to make reasonable accommodations for employees whose "religion" may include observances, practices, and beliefs which differ from standard employment schedules. This could well involve difficulties in continuous operation industries where employees decline to work on their sabbath (not necessarily Sunday) despite the need to man the operations on that day.

Administration

The act established an Equal Employment Opportunity Commission, a five-man independent agency appointed by the President with the consent of the Senate. Like other federal agencies, this Commission is empowered to establish regional offices and to appoint staff pursuant to civil service regulations, to subpoena records, and to prescribe rules and regulations for carrying out its duties. The 1972 amendments also provided for the appointment of an independent EEOC General Counsel on the NLRB model, who is responsible for litigation, and with the concurrence of the EEOC Chairman, for the appointment of regional attorneys.

Charges must be filed with the EEOC by, or on behalf of, an aggrieved individual within 180 days of the occurrence of the alleged unlawful practice. Where there is a state law or municipal ordinance proscribing discrimination or providing for a means of relief, no action may be taken by the EEOC until it has notified and given the state or local agency 60 days to act or, if the state or local agency is in its first year of existence, 120 days to act. The law specifically permits state laws to exist concurrently, provided such laws do not require or permit the doing of any act which would be an unlawful employment practice. Moreover, the Commission is urged to enter into agreements with state agencies for the utilization of the latter's services to carry out the functions of the federal law. Records are required to be kept by employers, unions, and employment agencies so as to provide information of compliance with the act.

Where there is no state or municipal agency, or where the latter has not acted to the satisfaction of the EEOC, the Commission attempts to settle the matter by conciliation. The records and proceedings of conciliation activities are confidential and cannot be made part of later proceedings except by consent of the parties. If the EEOC feels conciliation is unsuccessful, it may bring a civil action in a U.S. District Court for redress of the alleged violation. If the respondent is, however, a state or local government body, the conduct of any court action becomes a function of the U.S. Attorney General rather than of the EEOC's General Counsel. The court may order redress, elimination of the violation, "such affirmative action as may be appropriate," damages, back pay, etc. Even though no action in court is brought by the EEOC or the Attorney General, an individual who feels aggrieved may initiate his own case in court. In that case, the EEOC or the Attorney General may participate as intervenors if "the case is of general public importance." Federal government employees can file charge in court if they are dissatisfied with actions taken by the U.S. Civil Service Commission in regard to alleged discrimination.

An additional section (707) permits the Attorney General to bring a civil action where he believes that any person or group of persons is engaged in a pattern or practice of resistance to the full enjoyment of any of the rights guaranteed by Title VII, requesting relief, including an injunction, to overcome such resistance. The Attorney General may request the appointment of a three-judge court to hear such a case—in which event, appeal is directly to the Supreme Court, thus bypassing the courts of appeal. The 1972 amendments provide that this power will be transferred to the EEOC in 1974 unless the President submits a reorganization plan to the contrary which is not overridden by Congress.

Before proceeding to court, the Commission may hold a public hearing, examine witnesses, and make findings. Individuals subpoenaed or otherwise objecting to an investigation may appeal to the courts within 20 days after being served.

Relation to Other Laws

As we have noted, the Civil Rights law drafters were very careful to consider the effect of the new law on similar state and local enactments. But there is no mention of Taft-Hartley, Landrum-Griffin, or other federal statutes. For example, a union may be charged with an unlawful employment practice by the Equal Employment Opportunity Commission for discriminating against Negroes at the same time that it is being certified as the bargaining agent for these same discriminated-against employees by the National Labor Relations Board. The Equal Opportunity title also sheds no light on whether picketing or boycotts by racial groups are "labor disputes" within the meaning of the Norris–La Guardia Act, a decision which judges will have to make before deciding whether such demonstrations can be enjoined.

Nor is the EEOC the sole federal authority to combat discrimination. Persons who feel aggrieved may file a case under the arbitration clause of a union contract, under Title VII of the EEOC, with state or municipal laws, with the Office of Federal Contract Compliance pursuant to Executive Order 112461, or in all these forums. If they lose in one, they can try another. In 1972, the House of Representatives proposed making EEOC the sole federal authority to combat discrimination, but this provision was eliminated in the final bill. Hence it is possible to keep a case alive almost indefinitely.

EEOC Impact

Prior to 1972, the EEOC had no authority to bring court cases on its own, although the Attorney General did have, and used extensively, the authority to bring "pattern and practice" of discrimination cases. From its inception until then, the charge was uncritically made that the EEOC was inadequate and should have powers similar to those of the National Labor Relations Board. The 1972 amendments were a compromise between those who would vest EEOC with the vast administrative authority of the NLRB and those who believed no change was appropriate.

As a matter of fact, EEOC made up for its lack of authority to initiate court proceedings by filing friend of court or *amicus* briefs, to which the courts have obviously given very careful attention. In addition, cases brought by the Attorney General have had a profound impact. Of course, the great changes in employment patterns wrought since 1965 must be attributed in part to the average citizen's desire to comport with the law. Moreover, the fact that employers and unions must file sex and race employment data with the EEOC increases their consciousness of their obligations under the law. Fortuitously, the law became effective at the height of the greatest boom in our industrial history, and the combination of the two contributed to the great change; but the policy of the law certainly played a major role.

In court enforcement matters, the most significant are probably the pattern cases, but individual cases have achieved key decisional victories. For example, the "rightful place" doctrine, preventing the impact of past discrimination from continuing unabated, was won in an individually brought case,[1] supported by EEOC, as was the testing decision involving

---

[1] *Quarles* v. *Philip Morris, Inc.*, 279 F. Supp. 505 (E.D.Va., 1968).

Duke Power Company.[2] The former doctrine was enhanced and expanded in a pattern of discrimination case.[3] The pattern cases have also been used with effectiveness in several building trades cases[4] and successfully to upset the discriminatory seniority system in a major trucking situation—the first break in such union-management policies found in the key over-the-road trucking industry.[5] Numerous other key cases and litigations could be cited to illustrate the significance of EEOC litigation.

Because equality of opportunity remains an elusive goal, the charge has frequently been made that EEOC's alleged inadequate powers were a key factor in preventing redress of that inequality. This was, for example, the principal hypothesis of a 1970 study by another government agency, the U.S. Civil Rights Commission.[6] Yet the reasoning behind this and similar studies is fundamentally simplistic. They assume that if any inequality exists, it is because employment discrimination exists and peoples' rights are not properly enforced.

Of course, effective government support and enforcement of equal employment opportunity are absolute necessities if we are to achieve equal employment. This has been documented innumerable times. Equally well documented, however, is that such government action is insufficient in itself to achieve equality. It cannot overcome inadequate training and education; its effectiveness is limited when employment is declining; it cannot immediately offset a history of discrimination; it cannot move people from one location to jobs in another; and it cannot reorder the job structure of an industry to a marked degree, although it can, and has, recast discriminatory upgrading policies and seniority systems.

The situation in the aerospace industry is a case in point. In 1966, 21 of the largest companies in this industry employed 788,022 persons in 127 establishments, or about two thirds of the industry's total.[7] Of these

---

[2] *Griggs* v. *Duke Power Co.*, U.S. Sup. Ct. (March 8, 1971).

[3] *U.S.* v. *Local 189, United Papermakers et al.*, 282 F. Supp. 39 (E.D. La., 1968); affirmed 416 F. 2d 980 (5th Cir., 1969); Cert. denied, 397 U.S. 919 (1970).

[4] Two significant cases are *Local 53* v. *Vogler*, 407 F. 2d 1047 (CA 5), 1969; and *Dobbins* v. *Local 212*, IBEW, 292 F. Supp. 413 (S.D. Ohio, 1968). For numerous other EEOC and state commission cases, see *Race Relations Law Survey*, various issues.

[5] *U.S.* v. *Roadway Express, Inc.*, Civil Action No. C–68–321, U.S.D.C. (E.D. Ohio, September 1, 1970); see also *Jones et al.* v. *Lee Way Motor Freight, Inc.*, 431 F. 2d 245 (CA–10), 1970.

[6] *Federal Civil Rights Enforcement Effort* (Washington, D.C.: U.S. Government Printing Office, 1970).

[7] Herbert R. Northrup et al., *Negro Employment in Basic Industry* (Studies of Negro Employment, Vol. I [Philadelphia: Industrial Research Unit, Wharton School of Finance and Commerce, University of Pennsylvania, 1970]), Part III, pp. 165–66, 172–73; Part VIII, pp. 726–28.

employees, 179,436 were classified as professionals in 1966, of whom only 0.8%, or 1,435, were black. This looks like a highly discriminatory pattern of employment. Moreover, in 1968, these same companies had, if conventional ratings are utilized, improved little. Their total professional employment declined a bit to 179,041, their black professional complement increased slightly to 1,598, but the black percentage was still only 0.9%.

But if one looks at the total picture, a different situation emerges. In 1966, when 21 companies in the aerospace industry had a professional black ratio of only 0.8%, they employed approximately 40% of all black professionals in manufacturing industry reporting to the EEOC. Moreover, Professor Robert Kiehl of the Newark College of Engineering, who has been keeping a careful record of the demand and supply of Negro engineering talent since the mid 1950's, found in October 1970 that:

1. Only about 2 percent of engineering students are black, but that percentage is not increasing, and did not increase between 1962 and 1970.
2. Government fair employment practice legislation has greatly aided black engineers in finding jobs, but apparently has not increased the supply.
3. There seems to be no question but that there are widespread education and employment opportunities for blacks in engineering. . . .
4. The relative lack of information on engineering coupled with employment discrimination of the past seem to be the chief reasons for the apparent lack of interest of blacks in the profession today.[8]

Studies of other professions yield similar results: opportunities available, but going begging, and slow accretion at best at the supply level. Certainly, it would not appear that EEOC's new powers will solve this problem.

Likewise, where the need is for trained personnel,[9] where employment is declining,[10] or turnover low,[11] or location (for nonracial reasons) has altered from cities which are heavily black to areas where few minori-

---

[8] Robert Kiehl, *Opportunities for Blacks in the Profession of Engineering*, a study prepared for the Manpower Administration, U.S. Department of Labor (Newark: Foundation for the Advancement of Graduate Study in Engineering, 1970), pp. 13–14.

[9] See Theodore V. Purcell and Daniel P. Mulvey, *The Negro in the Electrical Manufacturing Industry* (Racial Policies of American Industry, Report No. 27 [Philadelphia: Industrial Research Unit, Wharton School of Finance and Commerce, University of Pennsylvania, 1971]); and Herbert R. Northrup et al., *The Negro in the Air Transport Industry* (Racial Policies of American Industry, Report No. 23 [Philadelphia: Industrial Research Unit, Wharton School of Finance and Commerce, University of Pennsylvania, 1971]).

[10] Northrup, *Negro Employment in Basic Industry*, Part V (Rubber Tires); Herbert R. Northrup and Richard L. Rowan et al., *Negro Employment in Southern Industry* (Studies of Negro Employment, Vol. IV [Philadelphia: Industrial Research Unit, Wharton School of Finance and Commerce, University of Pennsylvania, 1970]), Part III (Tobacco).

[11] Northrup, Rowan, *Negro Employment in Southern Industry*, Part I (Paper).

ties dwell,[12] greater EEOC powers are not likely to enhance minority employment.

Perhaps the real problem in assessing the extent of success which the EEOC has experienced is the fact that different people, differently placed, view the matter by quite different standards. This "gap in understanding" that Professor Bernard E. Anderson noted between the management in public utilities and the EEOC is equally applicable in all industries:

The commission, being an enforcement agency, looks to the statistical record for evidence that equal employment, in fact, exists in business firms. Corporate managers, however, often emphasize company progress in changing the focus, direction, and energy devoted to equal employment issues. Such changes within the business firm may not result in significant numerical gains in the number of black workers employed or promoted during a one- or two-year period. The modification of traditional employment practices is no less real to corporate managers even though the results may not meet EEOC measurement criteria. To management, changes in the employment process that might result in long-term gains for black workers are often considered more important than short-term gains in numbers employed. The difference of opinion between EEOC and industry representatives regarding the meaning and relative importance of affirmative action programs and affirmative action results is one of the most difficult issues in the equal employment area today.[13]

The OFCC and Affirmative Action

Perhaps more significant in terms of achieving equal employment than the work of the EEOC are the rules and regulations adopted pursuant to Executive Order No. 11246, particularly General Order No. 4 of the Office of Federal Contract Compliance. The OFCC, which administers the Executive Order, has set standards above and beyond Title VII which must be adhered to by government contractors. General Order No. 4, issued on November 20, 1969, sets forth in great detail what affirmative action requires of companies. This includes: (1) an analysis of all major job classifications and an explanation of why minorities may be underutilized; (2) the establishment of goals, targets, and affirmative action commitments designed to relieve any shortcoming identified; and (3) the development and supply of data to government organizations,

---

[12] Walter A. Fogel, *The Negro in the Meat Industry* (Racial Policies of American Industry, Report No. 12 [Philadelphia: Industrial Research Unit, Wharton School of Finance and Commerce, University of Pennsylvania, 1970]). See also Robert Ozanne, *The Negro in the Farm Equipment and Construction Machinery Industry* (Racial Policies of American Industry, Report No. 26 [Philadelphia: Industrial Research Unit, Wharton School of Finance and Commerce, University of Pennsylvania, 1972]).

[13] Bernard E. Anderson, *Negro Employment in Public Utilities* (Studies of Negro Employment, Vol. III [Philadelphia: Industrial Research Unit, Wharton School of Finance and Commerce, University of Pennsylvania, 1970]), p. 207.

including not only racial-occupational figures in great detail but also progression charts, seniority rosters, and an analysis of applicants by race for the various jobs.

Most concerns, and certainly those of any significant size are federal contractors. As a result, they are under constant pressure to increase and to upgrade their minority employment and to engage in other types of affirmative action. The latter would include recruiting visits to secondary schools with high black enrollment and to Negro colleges in order to obtain recruits for white-collar jobs, advertising for employees in Negro community newspapers, and ending of recruitment restricted either to walk-ins or to referrals by families of previously employed employees. Affirmative action might instigate special training courses for the transfer and upgrading of black employees into certain all-white departments in the plant. It can involve special programs for the hard core as described above. It might carry out special recruitment to increase the proportion of black foremen. It usually also involves companies appointing an executive called an "Equal Employment Opportunity Coordinator." By making this either a full-time position or one in which the executive has major responsibility, the government hopes to prevent the normal production, sales, or other executive duties from crowding out attention to equal employment.

In the construction industry, the OFCC has set specific goals by craft in many cities pursuant to its "Philadelphia Plan" concept. This marks the first in-depth attack on the invidious union-management discrimination which has been so pervasive in construction and which has denied blacks a reasonable share of much skilled construction work.

THE NEED FOR EDUCATION AND TRAINING

Regardless of the powers vested in EEOC, OFCC, or various state agencies, equality on the job will not be possible as long as a disproportionate number of blacks and other minorities continue to be uneducated, unskilled, and untrained. Until this inequality has been remedied, black workers will continue to be overrepresented in the unemployed, the underemployed, and the unskilled. Today, as Professor Charles C. Killingsworth has noted, despite the heritage of slavery and years of discrimination "and despite the continuing necessity for efforts to eliminate racial discrimination, there appears to be a reasonable basis for doubting that this factor is the principal *present* source of economic disadvantage for the Negro. If it is not, then continuing insistence that it is may well divert attention and effort from other more important sources and remedial measures."[14]

---

[14] Charles C. Killingsworth, *Jobs and Income for Negroes* (Washington, D.C.: National Manpower Policy Task Force and University of Michigan, 1968), pp. 31–32.

DISCRIMINATION BECAUSE OF SEX AND AGE

The year 1964 was a banner one for the feminists. In June the "equal pay for equal work" law, enacted in 1963, became effective. And then, just a few weeks later, Congress passed the Equal Opportunity law, which forbade discrimination by sex as well as by race, color, creed, or national origin. This law, as noted, became effective in mid-1965. In addition, sex discrimination is outlawed by most state antidiscrimination legislation.[15]

Equal Pay for Equal Work

The equal pay law was enacted as an amendment to the Fair Labor Standards Act. Therefore, its coverage is identical with that of the federal minimum wage law (see Table 16–1, pp. 496–97). It is administered and enforced by the Wage and Hour and Public Contracts Division of the U.S. Department of Labor.

The equal pay law, in brief, provides that it is illegal to pay women less than men (or conversely, men less than women) for doing the same work, and it is unlawful for a union or its agents to cause or attempt to cause an employer to discriminate in wages on the basis of sex. Furthermore, elimination of existing differentials by a wage reduction is prohibited. The act contains a general exception for differentials based on any other factor than sex. In addition, three specific exemptions—wage differentials based on merit, seniority, and piece rates or incentives—are specifically permitted.

It may take years of litigation to determine what is or is not equal pay. For example, if the employment of women requires additional material handling personnel in order to move heavy parts, obviously women are not doing the same work as men who could move the material as well as do the work being done by the women. But there are many gray areas which are not so obvious. The best protection for both employers and unions is to have a well-thought-out, formalized wage structure based on job evaluation, so that rates are as objectively established as possible. The application of such a program can eliminate any vestiges of wage differentials and, perhaps more importantly, preclude charges that they exist.

Title VII of the Civil Rights Act is now beginning to have a profound effect on women's rights. Moreover, the Office of Federal Contract Compliance has begun to enforce the no-discrimination regulations regarding sex and to require affirmative action programs of government

---

[15] Any vestiges of sex discrimination which may exist in American society appears doomed if the amendment to the Constitution passed by Congress in 1972, which outlaws such discrimination, is ratified by the necessary number of states.

contractors designed to increase the number of women in the better jobs particularly. Already women are obtaining positions in management and the professions hitherto closed to them. The tempo of such advancement is likely to increase with the 1970s, perhaps about to be as significant for female employment as the 1960s were for black employment.

Age Discrimination

One more type of discrimination is forbidden by law—age discrimination. In 1967, Congress enacted the Age Discrimination in Employment Act, which became effective six months later. This law is administered under the Secretary of Labor by the Wage and Hour and Public Contracts Division, the same agency which enforces the Fair Labor Standards and Equal Pay Acts. The law applies to companies and unions employing, or having a membership of 25 persons or more, and to employment agencies. General coverage is otherwise similar to that of the Fair Labor Standards Act.

In addition to the federal law, 35 states have enacted such laws over the years. In general, these laws do not interfere with the operation of a bona fide seniority system, or with compulsory retirement programs. There is, however, a fine line between compulsory early retirement to make way for a younger and more vigorous person, and age discrimination; and between insisting on younger persons for physically strenuous jobs, and age discrimination. It may be many years before legal definitions of where those lines are, can be made. So far, however, the impact of the act has not been great.

QUESTIONS FOR DISCUSSION

1. How has the Equal Opportunity law altered racial patterns in the South? In northern cities? Explain your answer.
2. Assume that you are a construction employer and that you hire through unions. Two of them have never referred a Negro to you. What is your status under the Equal Opportunity law, and what can you do to avoid being charged with an unlawful employment practice without encouraging union antagonism?
3. Which act is more likely to affect employment opportunities for women: the Equal Pay Act or the Equal Opportunity law?

SUGGESTIONS FOR FURTHER READING

Age Discrimination in Employment Act of 1967.   U.S. Department of Labor, Employment Standards Division, 1972.
    A report discussing the act, the problems, and the current status of enforcement.

The Negro Employment Situation. Report 391. U.S. Department of Labor. Bureau of Labor Statistics, 1971.

   A succinct survey of the black employment situation.

THE RACIAL POLICIES OF AMERICAN INDUSTRY. Philadelphia: Industrial Research Unit, Wharton School of Finance and Commerce, University of Pennsylvania, Philadelphia, 1968.

   A series of monographs (27 in print by July 1972) analyzing the extent of black employment, each one concerned with a particular industry. Select one and examine why black employment varies between the industry of your selection and others and why different firms in one industry have varying degrees of black employment.

PART VII

Concluding Observations

Chapter

24

SOME LABOR PROBLEMS

OF THE FUTURE

Throughout this book, we have stressed the new trends and developments which have modified the context and environment of labor economics during recent years and which promise to affect conditions much more substantially during the balance of this decade. By way of a summary and conclusion, attention is directed to some of these factors once more.

UNEMPLOYMENT—AND INFLATION

From the end of the Korean War in the early 1950s until almost the mid-1960s, the United States was plagued with unemployment which regularly exceeded 5% of the labor force and rose to over 7% in times of recession. Then, under the impetus of government fiscal policy, including a tax decrease, and a business boom, unemployment fell below 4% in 1965 and remained below that figure for several years. But the unemployment and poverty in our large cities and among minority groups continued to remain high, and to complicate the problem, prices moved steadily upward. It was apparent that increased demand wiped out much of the basic unemployment in society. Yet, the unemployment which remained, proved hard core and difficult to overcome; and further increases in demand not only did not reach the remaining unemployed but in addition accentuated the inflationary aspects of a high-level economy.

By the time that the Nixon administration took office in 1969, inflation was the most serious problem. Policy then shifted to "cooling" the economy. Unemployment rose again to around 6%, but prices continued to increase as powerful unions secured their largest wage increases despite a falling off of demand. Finally came the wage-price freeze of 1971 and the stabilization program. Obviously, we have not succeeded to developing an acceptable compromise between the twin monsters of unemployment and inflation.

Both the private and the public sectors of our economy have recognized the problem and have attempted to alleviate the structural defects which aggravate inflation and impede employment. That only the surface has been scratched is obvious; and that much more needs to be learned as to how to make the hard-core unemployed become self-reliant members of our society is equally clear. The fact that blacks, our largest minority racial group, makes up so disproportionate a number of the disadvantaged unemployed, both complicates the problem and makes its solution more urgent. The race issue is the most serious internal social problem of our age. Finding jobs for blacks and making them productive, job-filling members of our society is undoubtedly the key to the solution of this problem.

Most persons agree that a key element in any program to rehabilitate the hard-core unemployed is a major revision of the nation's welfare programs and an improvement of the schools, particularly in the inner cities. Welfare reform has been a key aspect of the Nixon administration program, but it is not clear whether the massive payout contemplated under this reform measure will accomplish its purpose. The school situation, which is responsible for so many programs of remedial education —that is, to teach adults what they should have been taught in school, particularly reading and arithmetic skill—is, despite massive expenditures, still far from solution. Studies fail to demonstrate, for example, that adults who are functionally illiterate, can be made into useful members of the labor force by existing methods of instruction or curriculum. It is likely, therefore, that despite massive federal spending and private action, the difficult-to-employ will continue to be a major problem for industry, unions, and government throughout the 1970s.

Although great strides have been made in training in recent years, much more needs to be done. The great tragedy revealed by the Civil Rights Act and similar state laws is, now that jobs are open to blacks, so many are unable to make use of opportunities. We need not only emphasis on training the unemployed but also on training for upgrading. People with limited education and background who were hired as laborers and expected to be laborers all their lives may be beyond training for better jobs, but we must be sure. Government policies are needed to stimulate new methods of such training without the dampening effect of red tape and frustration.

Such problems also pose major challenges for unions. Seniority programs devised in another era need change and flexibility if they are to survive. Moreover, unions have generally not been oriented toward helping the hard-core unemployed; they have been more concerned with obtaining maximum benefits for their members who are already employed. Can union leaders continue to maintain this attitude in view of the nature of the unemployment problem? Can employed union members simply shut their eyes to the fact that union wage policies may restrict employment opportunities? What positive programs for stimulating employment can union leaders logically espouse?

Minimum Wages and Shorter Hours

In the area of governmental policy a new look has yet to be taken at the impact of minimum wage laws. All available data point to a major problem of structural unemployment concentrated among the poorly educated, the least skilled, and the minority group members of the labor force. When we raise minimum wage rates, as we seem to do at regular intervals, these workers are the first to lose their jobs. Are these men and women better off when employed at what society concedes to be substandard rates of pay; or should they be either unemployed on temporary grants under our unemployment compensation system or consigned to relief? Or should they be paid a government subsidy and kept at work? In a similar vein, is not the regular advocacy of a substantially shorter workweek without pay reduction ill-conceived by reason of its costly burden on employers and its resultant probable impact on employment?

Security and Costs

How much "security" do we crave, and what will it cost? If government-sponsored prepaid medical care is adopted, what will the resultant increased taxes do to the prospects for expansion in our economy and hence to the prospects for a decrease in the rate of unemployment? If, as seems likely, ever larger fringe benefits induce a preference among employers for overtime rather than new hires, is our security system building more security for the majority and continued insecurity for those unemployed?

Year after year, in prosperity as well as in depression, the welfare costs of our major cities have risen, and the number of people on relief have increased. Why cannot welfare recipients be made self-supporting members of society? Are welfare and minimum wage legislation related? How about welfare policies and the impact thereon of union wage policies?

To alleviate poverty, some would make cash handouts in the form of a "negative income tax." This would perhaps simplify record keeping and administration of welfare, but it would not provide either the dignity or the self-reliance of an income-producing job. Moreover, more cash handouts would seem to be inflationary in an economy already concerned about inflation. Would further inflation mean an ever higher negative income tax, and thus would the costs, as in welfare, keep rising?

Collective Bargaining and Unionism

What about collective bargaining in an economy where unemployment, job security, retraining, civil rights, and manpower utilization become the key issues? Can management and unions really deal with these problems as they have dealt with wage issues? If they cannot, what are the alternatives? What has the government to offer as a solution? These very problems are most serious and are certainly not solved in the one industry—railroads—where the government has intervened longest and most consistently.

Can the labor movement contribute to the solution of the basic problems of which unemployment is the central issue? Many observers doubt it. They note that unions have already accomplished their big job: attaining recognition of the dignity of labor. The fact that unions have essentially done the job they set out to do is the very fact that may now bring about their eventual downfall. The late Sumner H. Slichter made this point many times in urging labor to take a broader view of its role in the American economy.

For two decades, unions had a major appeal to workers because union leadership was attuned to the current needs of the labor force. Unions were growing, and their very growth was a dynamic factor of appeal. But after the mid-1950s, unions first lost ground both in terms of total members and proportion of the labor force unionized; then, despite the prosperity which has greatly increased union membership in the mid-1960s, union membership gains failed to keep pace with the growth of the labor force. This leaves the union movement heavily dependent in the private sector upon the business cycle for growth, membership, and income.

The failure of unions to grow may be blamed on many things. Some AFL–CIO adherents blame it on managerial opposition to unions, although this does not explain why unions grew despite the same opposition in earlier years. The late Walter Reuther claimed that the "stand-pat" leadership of George Meany was at the root of the problem, but his attempt to create "a new labor movement" was very unsuccessful.

Actually, unions may well be suffering from the same inability to please that has harassed many once-popular public figures. Old appeals do not always bring the same results in the entertainment field, the advertising field, the political field, or the union field. Unions have been strangely unable to appeal to many of the new recruits of the labor force. Throughout the 1960s, the labor force will continue to see more additions from the quite young, the older worker, the part-time worker, the previously rural worker, the more highly educated worker, the relatively affluent worker, and the "middle-class-minded" worker. The old appeals that brought workers into unity in unionism in the 1930s are not appropriate to the new workers of the 1970s, even where these workers are occupying jobs of one-time union adherents. Yet, unions have been strangely unable to adapt themselves to the appeals that would be meaningful to the prospective member of the 1970s. When the new workers are in the unions, often as a result of compulsory unionism, the degree of rejection of contracts testifies to the communication gap between leaders and the rank and file.

Beyond the union-centered inability to meet the new prospect on his own terms, there is an added dimension that we noted in our description of trends in the labor force. This is the fact that the mix of work has changed as well. Even if there had been no change in the ideas and attitudes of the production worker to whom the union had the greatest appeal in the last generation, a significant shift in ratio toward the predominance of white-collar work has been taking place for at least the last 20 years, and this shift is accelerating daily. This shift is well recognized by union mentors, but not so well seen is what to do about it. At one union convention after another the subject of the organization of white-collar workers is discussed. By now, it is generally conceded that new appeals—and, indeed, new appealers—must be found if the white-collar people are to be organized. Large sums of money have been appropriated for organizing campaigns, and studies have been undertaken to determine the type of appeal which will interest white-collar workers, without evident success.

But if the big unions ever do seriously tackle the organization of white-collar workers in the private sector, they face a risk far greater than the declining membership rolls that now plague them. The risk is that the unions will have to undergo a change in their own philosophies to become consonant with the contemplated changes in appeals. It is as though a producer were seeking some new advertising technique to reach a new sales market. He sometimes finds—as the unions may, too—that it takes more than just a new appeal; often, it really requires a new product before the sale is won. If this might be the case in the unions' quest for members in the white-collar ranks, then we could expect the most revolutionary changes in the trends of union thinking.

What would happen, on the other hand, if the union official who is trying desperately to attract white-collar employees to membership should start talking like a conservative in politics after all the years of enunciating a party line in political matters that was so clearly liberal? Would this cause a loss in present membership, or would it bring out a new interest and approval from present members? Nobody knows. The problem is that in many crucial matters of wages and hours and working conditions, there is a broad disparity between what white-collar workers believe and what unions have for many years proclaimed as the belief of their membership. In order to maintain an appeal to both groups, the union would, in effect, have to espouse two philosophies and finally accept a split personality that might be disastrous in its appeal either to blue-collar workers or to white-collar workers.

On the other hand, it is equally difficult for today's union leadership to appeal to the poverty-stricken or for the union rank and file to concern itself with the problems of the poor. With union members having middle-class income, their concerns are less and less those of the slum population and more and more those of the typical suburbanite. A labor movement that has successfully carried its members so fast and so far up the income ladder finds it more and more difficult to represent, or even to communicate with, the downtrodden.

The race issue portends a severe problem for union leadership. They (like most other white people) failed to sense the Negro mood and impending crises which has turned once prounion black leaders into sharp critics of unionism. The AFL–CIO has adopted a liberal program. But it has had difficulty selling this program to many of its constituent unions and to the rank and file. Racial antagonism among unionized workers remains strong in many places, and several key unions, particularly in the building trades have obstructed, rather than furthered, employment opportunities for blacks. The paucity of blacks among the top echelon and key leadership of American unions is further illustrative of the gap between organized labor and the black community.

Government Employee Unionism

The one area where unions have made remarkable advances is in the public sector. Were it not for these gains, union membership would have fallen back considerably farther in relation to the expansion of the labor force. Public employee unionism has been considered—by unions, government officials, and many academicians—as merely an extension of collective bargaining in the private sector. The analysis in Chapter 22 points up the questionable nature of this conception. The economic constraints and the political pressures are too different in the public sector for the private analogy to be valid. Yet public employee union pressures continue to be exerted in the same manner as in the private sector, and these unions lobby hard and successfully for legislation which, seemingly uncritically, insures that private sector tactics and strategy will be employed in public bargaining. Will this impact on the labor movement generally? Suppose, which it is not difficult to believe, that the public, weary of strikes and interruptions in public services, and angered by the inflationary wage increases brought by unionism to public employees, moves to end the freedom to strike in the private as well as the public sectors? Or as the extraordinarily liberal pensions now extant in the public sector (retirement after 20 years service at age 50 at half the last years' salary, including overtime) become common knowledge, will these matters continue to be left to private deals in the public *or* private sectors? In short, will the excesses of public employee bargaining lead to a drastic curtailment of all collective bargaining?

Unionism and the Service Economy

Over the years, unionism and collective bargaining have survived and prospered primarily in manufacturing industry. Tremendous union gains in wages and benefits have been matched by increases in productivity, so that the public did not pay the total costs. Union strikes inconvenienced the public, but not so severely, because manufactured goods could be stockpiled ahead of the strike or made up after its cessation.

Now the economy is a service one, with unionism spreading particularly into the governmental and quasi-governmental sectors, such as hospitals. Strikes and substantial wage increases engendered by union power have a direct and profound impact on the public. When essential services are impaired, the public is both immediately affected and profoundly disturbed. Sharply rising wage increases have not been offset by productivity increases in the service sectors. Rather they have been followed by sharp increases in taxes and/or sharp curtailment of services. Strikes followed by higher school taxes, less frequent garbage collection, or $100 per day rent for semiprivate hospital rooms, do not endear the collective bargaining mechanism to the public. It may well be, as these trends continue, that we are observing the demise of the American industrial relations system as we have known it, and that even before the end of this decade, it will be a far different one.

Lack of Flexibility

Of all the trends within labor that might have serious portent both as to the future of unions and as to the future of labor-management relations, the most significant seems to be the inability to adjust to changing circumstances. Union leadership appears to be less flexible, less able to reject the old ways and embrace the new ways, than business management. Such, however, may be the fate of a movement as contrasted with an enterprise. The labor movement, perhaps because it is or was a movement—a cause—cannot turn lightly about simply to meet some present and perhaps short-term need. Based as it has been in the conflicts of the old Industrial Revolution, it has difficulty in responding now to the fact that the old Industrial Revolution is over. In the words of A. H. Raskin of *The New York Times,* an astute and sympathetic commentator on the labor scene: "American labor is suffering from an advanced case of hardening of the arteries. It is standing still in membership and organizational vigor at a time when radical changes in technology are revolutionizing industry in ways that may prove as dramatic as the more publicized developments in space travel and nuclear weapons."

Need for New Concepts

The need for new concepts is not confined to the labor movement but is required on all fronts, in view of the changing direction of the use of the labor force. For example, trends point to an ever larger percentage of the labor force being occupied in producing "public goods" instead of private products. All one has to do is to look about his city, town, or state to see an increasing share of our productive forces going into such channels as construction of roads, schools, universities, and hospitals. Today, education boasts the biggest payroll in the country; hospitals employ over 2 million persons—more than twice the number of the basic steel industry. The trend of employment in these fields is increasing; that of manufacturing is declining.

We have already noted the importance of this shift for collective bargaining and for the labor movement. But what relevance does this have for historical measurements of productivity? Will the concept really be useful for comparable purposes over time when the product of today is ever more one of governmental or quasi-public services? Will this trend accentuate the possibility of inflation because, as otherwise unemployed labor is used in this kind of project, more dollars are put into the income stream as part of payment of wages, but no product emerges that is immediately usable to offset the increased purchasing power? Inefficiency in the private sector leads to fewer sales, smaller profits, and even company disappearance. Managements that fail to produce profits in the private sector lose their jobs. What constraints occur in the public and nonprofit sectors under similar circumstances and what are the implications for government labor policy and collective bargaining?

GOVERNMENTAL INTERVENTION

The same questions may be asked of our governmental labor policies. Are our laws attuned to the economy of the 1970s or to that of the 1930s? The labor policy of the United States has developed slowly and haltingly. No one court decision or legislative act can be singled out as representing the beginning of governmental labor policy. Much of our present policy, it is true, stems from the Great Depression and the period of the Roosevelt administration, during which great strides were made toward formulating present labor policies. Nevertheless, each period of history has made some contribution to the present status of labor legislation and governmental action. For example, even the most revolutionary of all labor laws—the National Labor Relations Act—had its roots in state and railway labor legislation of the 1890s.

At various stages of American labor history, different aspects of labor policy have been stressed by legislators and labor leaders. For example, encouragement of collective bargaining by protecting the right of labor to organize was of prime importance in our labor policy in the period from the birth of the National Recovery Administration to enactment of the National Labor Relations Act. Restraints on activities of unions were especially emphasized in the post–World War II era, representing, in part, a reaction to certain excesses of unions during the period of unrestricted union organization. Protection of minority group rights was the dominant theme of the 1960s. Women's rights and public employee bargaining could be the key collective bargaining issues of the 1970s. Labor policy is thus continually evolving. Laws are passed which at the time may represent majority thinking. But majority thinking is not static, and as views alter, labor legislation reflects the changing trend in public opinion.

It is natural to assume, therefore, that labor policy will continue to evolve in the future. While many future developments cannot be predicted, certain trends are already evident. Thus, for example, a developing labor policy will undoubtedly continue to grapple with the amount and coverage of minimum wages and social security, the extent of the workweek, the issue of emergency strikes, the rights of public employees, and the rights of union members of minority groups and women—all issues which have been before the public for several decades.

Actually, the United States has no labor policy but rather a patchwork of policies, comprehensive but not consistent. There is, for example, no uniformity of treatment among the states. State labor relations, workmen's compensation, unemployment insurance, and minimum wage laws differ widely. The accident of location determines the extent of employee protection. Although the Landrum-Griffin Act did define some areas of delegation between federal and state laws, great inconsistencies occur in such areas as picketing, boycotts, mediation, and strike control legislation. A nonferrous industry strike saw intervention by several governors and at least three senators; a decision by the Johnson administration that the Taft-Hartley Act, which has been utilized in far less significant disputes, did not apply to this case; the appointment of an extralegal fact-finding board; and mediation by three cabinet officers. Not only legislation, but also government action needs to be clear and consistent.

The inconsistency of federal legislation, as noted in previous chapters, is very real. For example, the Norris–La Guardia Act conflicts with the Taft-Hartley Act, and the latter law with the Landrum-Griffin Act. There have been cases in which persons have been sentenced to jail for actions which violated the Landrum-Griffin Act and yet have been recognized as legitimate union officials by the Taft-Hartley Act. This means that management has been required to deal with law violators and racketeers or itself violate a law.

Welfare legislation adds a further inconsistency. Thus, even though a strike may be contrary to public policy or even illegal, the strikers may be aided by being given food stamps, welfare payments, or in two states and on the railroads, unemployment compensation. Whether collective bargaining can survive if strikers are subsidized by the public purse, or in any case, whether the welfare system should be diverted to care for otherwise well-paid workers who exercise their right to strike, are questions that have not received full consideration by Congress and by the various state legislators.

Although the Civil Rights law was made consistent with state legislation of the same type, its relation to the Taft-Hartley Act was not given serious consideration. Other inconsistencies exist in the coverage of various laws. Railway and airline employers and employees who come under the Railway Labor Act have rights and duties different from those of their fellow employees and employers who come under the National Labor Relations Act. Likewise, the railway industry has a separate social security system, while airline pilots have a special (and extraordinary) minimum wage law.

There is also inconsistency of purpose between the two current goals of labor policy: promoting collective bargaining and regulating certain union activities. It remains doubtful that the government at both the federal and state levels can continue to maintain both a spur to union growth and a strong deterrent to certain activities which can affect union growth.

Inconsistency a Part of the Democratic Process

The fact that there are basic conflicts in the national labor policy should not be surprising. Indeed, all things considered, perhaps it is surprising that there are not more inconsistencies in existing legislation. Labor legislation is enacted in response to pressure of public opinion and influences exerted by various interest groups. In some states, labor's political position is strong; in others, it is weak. State labor laws reflect this fact.

Moreover, neither labor nor industry alone can command sufficient votes to sway Congress. When in disagreement over legislation, both must appeal for support to that huge, vague group known as the "middle class," which holds the balance of power in our society, insofar as such a balance exists. As the electorate shifts first one way and then another, the complexion of Congress and state legislatures changes. Legislation in the highly controversial field of labor relations reflects these changes.

There nevertheless is a real need for a general overhauling of our disjointed system of conflicting and overlapping labor laws. Even if agreement could not be reached as to the basis on which such laws should be improved, it might at least be possible to achieve a greater degree of uniformity than now exists among the various laws. Unfortunately, however, achievement of even such limited agreement is not too likely in view of the basic conflicts of interest, not only between labor and industry but also within both labor and industry groups. The present system of "push and pull" of pressure groups to secure labor legislation favorable to themselves is likely to remain with us for some time to come.

The 1972 amendments of Title VII of the 1964 Civil Rights Act may mark an important departure from past labor relations administration and a move toward integration of our labor legislation. Liberal and labor groups urged that the powers and activities of the Equal Employment Opportunity Commission be modeled upon those of the National Labor Relations Board. Instead Congress gave EEOC no power of its own to issue orders, but instead the authority to appeal directly to the courts for action against alleged violators of the act. Some observers believe that a similar process should be adopted for all labor agencies in order to avoid the inconsistencies described above and also to assure greater continuity and consistency in the decisional process, instead of the wide swings of law interpretations which have featured the history of the National Labor Relations Board after each set of new appointees.

Need for Defining Role of Unions and Management

In Chapter 4, we considered the problem of defining the scope of managerial prerogatives. We need not repeat the considerations there discussed. Suffice it to say that the problem of preserving entrepreneurial freedom to manage business while affording union membership security will be telescoped in importance in coming years by the ever-growing extent of union demands. Although union leaders, by and large, believe in maintenance of the American system of free enterprise, their continuing search for means to afford security to their membership must inevitably produce a narrowing of the area of business initiative. Layoffs, technological change, and production policies are likely to be moved more and more into the orbit of union consultation and control. Union attempts to prove management's ability to pay higher wages and other benefits will lead to increasing interest by unions in company accounting systems and managerial policies.

No one can say where the ever-widening scope of union demands will end. It is safe to hazard a guess, however, that labor and management in the United States will ultimately work out a *modus vivendi* which will differ from that reached in other countries and which will reflect the peculiar character of American democracy and the American industrial environment. Such a compromise must recognize the basic need of the worker to feel secure in his job and to participate fully in the industrial process. At the same time, it is important that management be left free to plan, to invent, and to improve production methods so that not only labor but also the public at large may benefit from the efficiency of the capitalistic system.

The decades ahead will continue to witness a step-up in the tempo of the economic struggle between the United States and the Soviet Union. Soviet spokesmen have clearly stated their objective of surpassing the United States in economic production. Their success in space and their demonstrated capacity to produce sophisticated war materiel are proof that their aims cannot be taken lightly. More immediately, the competition of the European Common Market countries and of Japan insures that the United States risks a high-cost position in world markets, with resultant loss of business and unemployment, unless our costs are brought into line and inflation controlled.

This very real threat raises the question of whether or not the American economy can any longer afford the make-work rules, the restrictions imposed on new laborsaving devices, the slowdowns and walkouts which have become an accepted part of the labor-management scene in recent years. What is needed is a "new look" for labor, a new *rapprochement* between labor and management, a new recognition by both labor and management that preservation of our way of life requires not only a willingness to fight but also a willingness to produce.

The need for increased efficiency in production is accentuated by the rapid rise of overseas competition. We cannot meet this threat by raising tariffs. The only sound answer is an accelerated rate of increase in output per man-hour in this country through application of the most advanced technology. Can labor leaders rise to this challenge—and if so, can they convince their membership of the necessity for abandoning traditional policies in sharp conflict with the present needs of the nation? Never before in our history has there been such a need for forceful, farseeing labor leadership!

Need for Defining Role of Industry and Government

The problem of demarcating the respective scopes of unions and management has its counterpart in the larger social question of the proper balance between individual initiative and government control. This basic issue is met not only in debates over the merits of government control or stabilization of wages, but also in the development of labor policy. It seems clear that in coming years, union organizations will attempt to saddle industry with new and heavy obligations growing out of the worker's need for security. Unions have seized upon the idea that industry should provide for depreciation of the human machine in the same way that it provides for depreciation of capital equipment. This idea has been given concrete form in demands for liberalized pensions, health insurance, life insurance, free dental care, and other benefits. The basic question is whether such benefits, assuming that they are justified, should be provided by industry or government—and in either case, how much of our national income should be devoted to security.

The notion that industry, on its own initiative, should amortize its human costs in the same manner as it has customarily amortized its mechanical costs is an attractive one; yet, it must be recognized that there are definite shortcomings to this view. The primary difficulty in having pensions, supplementary unemployment benefits, or other plans financed and administered by individual firms without any overall supervision or integration by government is that such plans are bound to differ from one company to another. As a consequence, they are likely to be haphazard and incomplete in their coverage, unequal in the amount of their benefits, and unduly favorable to workers who have the good fortune either to be members of strong unions or to work for prosperous concerns. Strong unions have already demonstrated their ability to require employers to make enormous contributions to employee welfare funds, but their very success has often brought damaging unemployment and less security to many members of the work force. The history of industrial relations in the bituminous coal industry is an extreme case in point.

A further element of unfairness in leaving the settlement of pensions and other aspects of a welfare program to the processes of collective bargaining is that the costs of such programs must ultimately be borne by all consumers in the form of lower real income, since—to the extent that companies bear the cost of pension plans—costs and prices of their products will tend to rise. This means that the public generally must pay for the disproportionate benefits which may be obtained by strong unions in particular industries. Moreover, as long as welfare plans remain a matter for collective bargaining, there will be constant rivalry among unions in various industries to increase the benefits obtained for their membership, in order to outdo other unions. The consequences of such rivarly upon industrial costs, profits, and employment could be serious.

The alternative to individual company welfare plans is government benefits under an expanded and liberalized social security program. This approach has the advantage of enabling workers to share equally in benefits, regardless of whether they are organized or unorganized, members of strong unions or of weak unions. Moreover, the principle has already been established under the Social Security Act that workers should contribute to support of the cost of the program—a principle which seems to commend itself for its fairness. But an expanded government-administered welfare program for employees also has its drawbacks. It means rising taxes, increasing bureaucracy, and growing intervention by labor in politics so as to make its influence and demands felt in the determination of the extent and disposition of benefits. Pensions are, of course, only the beginning. The politics of union organization require that union leaders, in order to retain the allegiance of their membership, must constantly obtain new benefits for employees. If government, rather than employers, becomes the fount from which new benefits are to be sought, labor may use its political influence to obtain for American workers a "cradle-to-grave" welfare program similar to that obtained by British labor from its labor government. By encouraging fringe expansion through wage control, government encourages expansion of all benefit programs.

Employee demands for protection against insecurity thus present industry with a challenge and a dilemma. Either industry must accept its responsibilities and take the initiative in developing a broad program designed to protect workers from the risks and hazards of industrial life—with unforeseen consequences upon costs, profits, and employment —or labor may take the other road, which leads to increasing government regulation and taxation of industry, and to increasing dependence by workers upon the government to solve their problems. The decisions made with respect to this aspect of labor policy may thus have profound repercussions upon the pattern of American economic life and may influence the nature of the balance which is ultimately struck between government regulation and individual enterprise in our economy.

Labor Policy in a Democracy

A cornerstone of our democratic form of government has been the use of national policy to control great aggrandizements of power. As a nation, we have long recognized that when particular groups become so powerful that their actions can seriously interfere with market processes and endanger the public interest, government regulation may be required. Thus, the Sherman Antitrust Act recognized the evils inherent in combinations of corporations designed to restrain trade or monopolize an industry. Likewise, our graduated income tax and heavy estate tax were intended, in part, to restrict the concentration of economic and political power which would flow from the amassing of great fortunes passed on from generation to generation without tax.

With this history of the role of governmental regulation in our democratic society, it seems almost inevitable that the extent of regulation of unions will expand as they grow in strength and economic power. To date, the function of government has been primarily to provide the basis for equality of bargaining power between management and labor. The Wagner Act sought to prevent large, strongly entrenched corporations from using their power to throttle unions in their infancy by resort to discriminatory practices. Then, as unions grew in membership and strength, the need for such one-sided intervention in the labor market lessened; and Congress enacted the Taft-Hartley Act in an effort to pare down some of the rights given unions and to equalize bargaining power in the labor market, and the Landrum-Griffin Act to protect members from arbitrary union power. The Civil Rights law, like Landrum-Griffin, is primarily designed to protect individual employees—here members of minority groups.

It might be thought that with the development of strong union organization and the achievement of relative equality in bargaining power between industry and labor, government could now withdraw to the sidelines and let the parties fight it out. Unfortunately, however, the very equality of power between the parties in mass-production industries where strong unions confront large corporations, each with extensive financial resources, increases the possibility of prolonged work stoppages, with their attendant inconvenience to the public. Although, as has been pointed out in the earlier discussion in this text, few such stoppages actually create national emergencies, nevertheless, the stoppages are serious enough to give rise to a hue and cry that something should be done to prevent such interference with the orderly flow of production, or in the case of public employees, with the orderly operation of government.

There are, of course, some persons who believe that the only way to deal with this problem of the battle of the giants is to restore the working of a free market by breaking up unions and large corporations—by "atomizing" competition, as it is called—so that the unions and corporations which are left to deal with each other will be too small seriously to affect the market or the public by reason of their occasional disputes. This possibility, whether or not desirable in theory, is plainly impractical. Our industrial system, as now constituted, is too dependent upon our large, integrated corporations to warrant such a change; and as long as corporate units remain large, union organizations must also be large, in order to bargain effectively for their membership.

The struggle between strong unions and large corporations will continue to lead to a demand by the public for further government regulation of union activities. The pressure for such action is growing as inflation plagues us; for many people have come to believe—either rightly or wrongly—that union demands for wage increases, backed up by the threat of the strike, have been a major cause of the upward trend in prices since World War II. The result may be further restriction of certain rights—such as the right to strike—which unions believe are fundamental to our democracy.

There are few absolute rights in our society. Rights are implicit with obligations. We cherish freedom of speech, but a man cannot yell "fire" without cause in a crowded theater. A democratic society can afford to give rights and privileges to groups only if those rights and privileges will not be abused and the rights of the public will be respected. Congress has prevented railway and longshore strikes since the middle 1960s by a variety of stopgap laws. The more powerful an organization becomes, the greater is the damage it can inflict upon society by abuse of its rights, and therefore the more circumspect must society be to see that such organizations respect their obligations to the community. Today the existence of nonunion and foreign competition is a powerful brake on possible abuses of union bargaining power in many industries, just as the existence of strong competition is a brake on the abuses of corporate power. If unions gradually eliminate such nonunion competition, the chance for abuse of power will be accentuated, and a real test will be presented for enlightened labor leadership. Unless union leaders exercise real self-restraint in the exercise of their powers, they may find that government will prescribe the restraints as it now restrains wages.

Labor policy in a democracy must also recognize that government regulation is not a panacea. Every walkout which inconveniences the public should not be met with a demand that "there ought to be a law." Free unionism and free collective bargaining are institutions which are worth preserving. By contrast, the growth of government bureaucracy and the intervention of government in the labor market are tendencies which should not lightly be encouraged. In labor policy, as in other national policies, we must follow the middle road. As a general rule, labor and industry should be given every opportunity to work out their problems without government regulation, except in situations where injury to the public is apparent and substantial, and justification from the point of view of legitimate union conduct is lacking.

The obligations of unions in a free society have yet to be clearly defined. The Landrum-Griffin Act is a step in this direction. The Civil Rights law is another. Future delineation of the obligations of unions and of the rights of union members would help to clarify, in part, the role of government and of industry as well. Especially needed is a clear policy involving public employee unionism and bargaining. Whatever the ultimate role which government, industry, and unions will play in our society, we may be sure that it will follow a pattern reflecting the needs of our highly integrated industrial economy and the traditional concepts of our democratic society.

QUESTIONS FOR DISCUSSION

1. Write a short statement of what you think the national labor policy should encompass. How does actual policy differ from this?
2. What is the major labor problem today, and why do you think it is so significant?

SUGGESTIONS FOR FURTHER READING

Bok, Derek C., and Dunlop, John T. *Labor in the American Community*, pp. 456–487. New York: Simon & Shuster, Inc., 1970.

An examination of how the American labor movement might look in the future.

Rowan, Richard L., (ed.). *Readings in Labor Economics and Labor Relations*, Part VI, "Public Policy and Labor Relations," pp. 541–624.

A series of articles and excerpts from pertinent legislation dealing with the public policy of the United States.

INDEX OF AUTHORS CITED

INDEX OF SUBJECTS

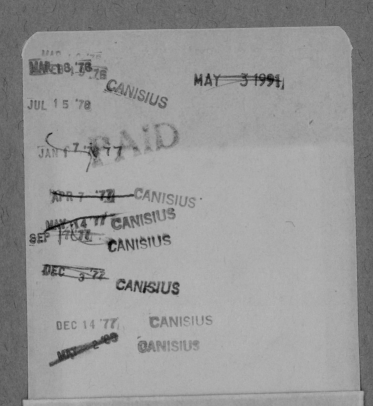